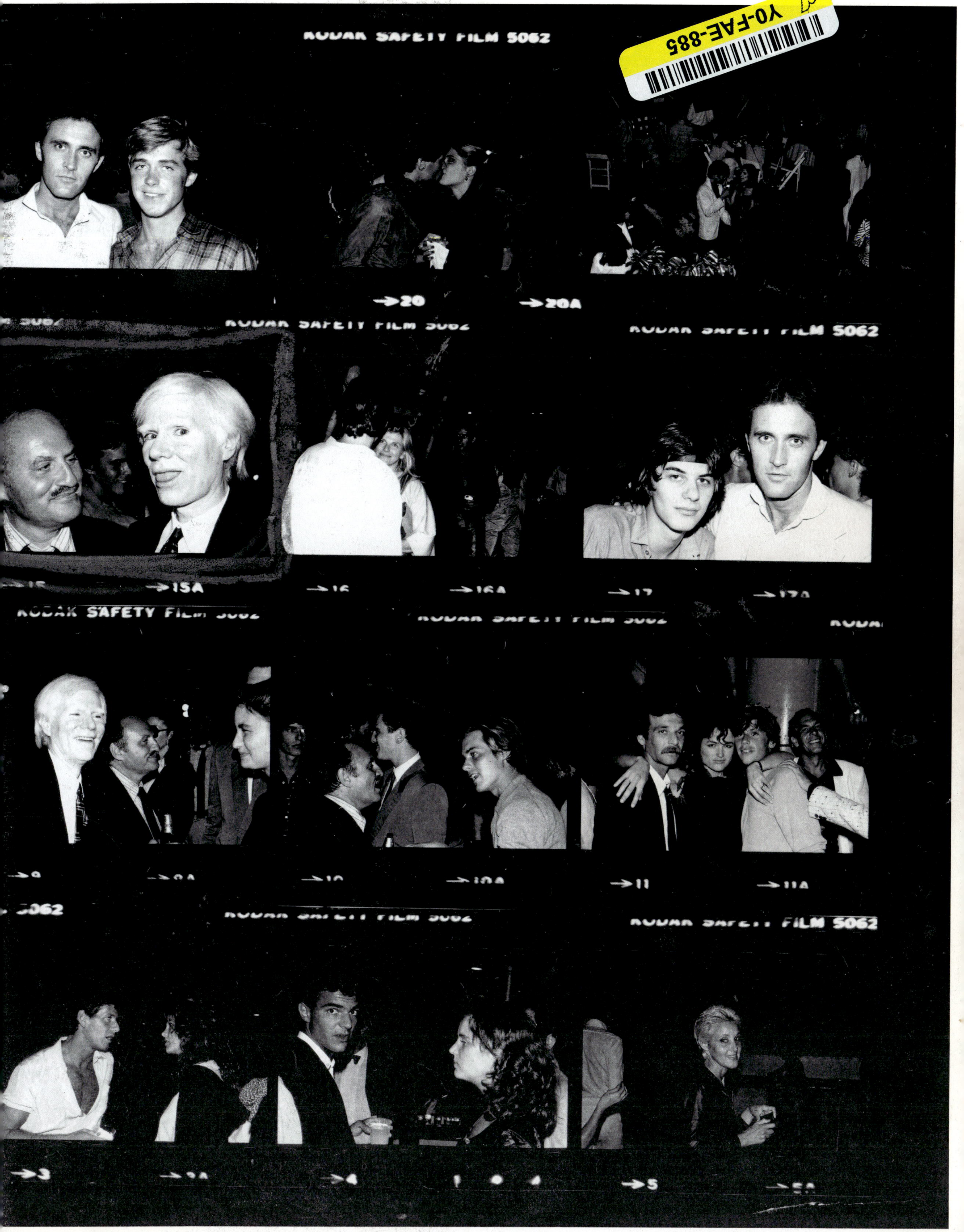
KODAK SAFETY FILM 5062
→20
→20A
KODAK SAFETY FILM 5062
→15A
→17
KODAK SAFETY FILM
→11
→11A
5062
KODAK SAFETY FILM 5062
→3
→4
→5

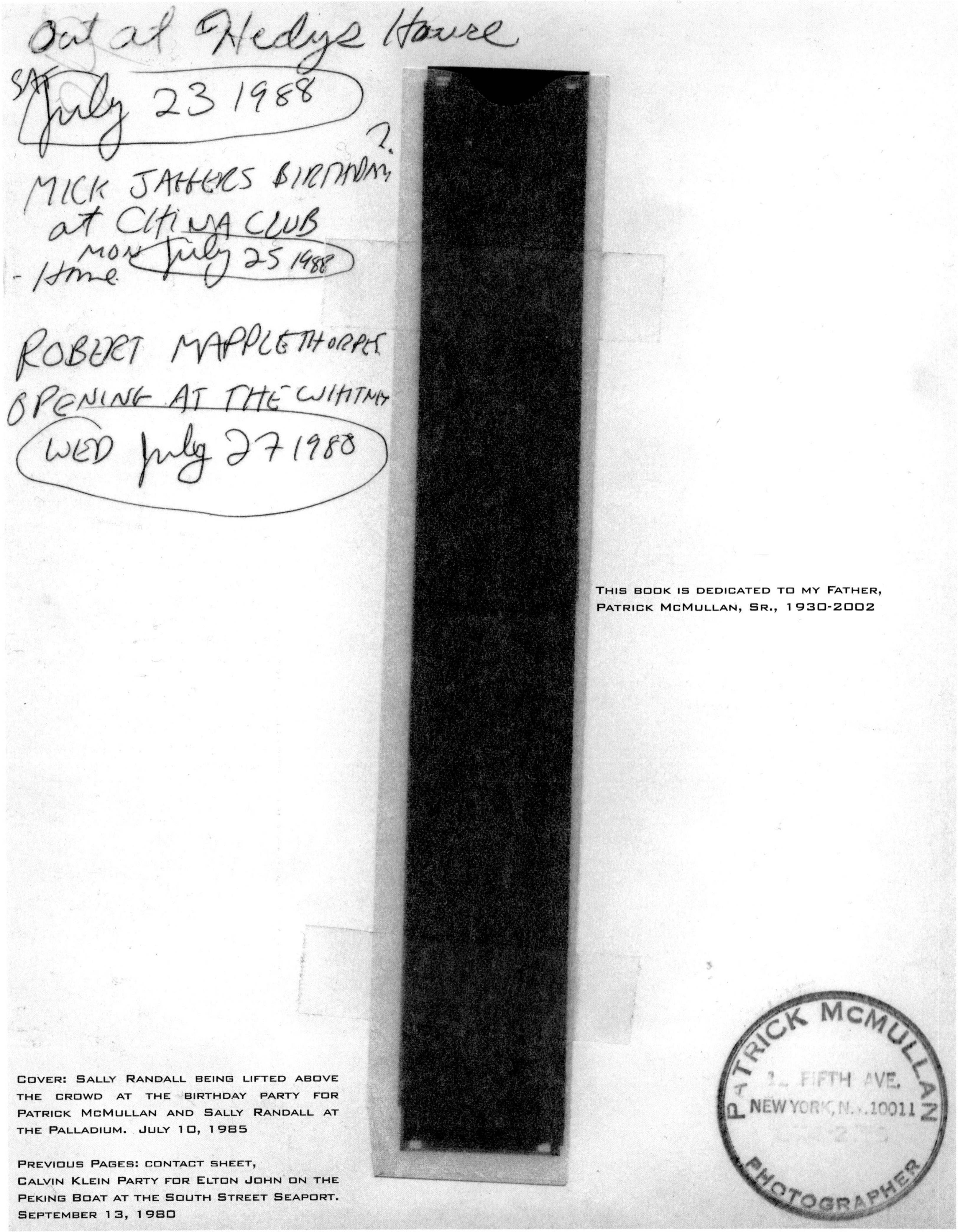

This book is dedicated to my Father,
Patrick McMullan, Sr., 1930-2002

Cover: Sally Randall being lifted above the crowd at the birthday party for Patrick McMullan and Sally Randall at the Palladium. July 10, 1985

Previous Pages: contact sheet,
Calvin Klein Party for Elton John on the Peking Boat at the South Street Seaport.
September 13, 1980

PATRICK McMULLAN

so80s

A PHOTOGRAPHIC DIARY OF A DECADE

INTRODUCTION
BY JAY McINERNEY

Foreword: Michael Musto
Afterword: Tama Janowitz
With Commentary By: Bob Colacello
Tom Ford
Glenn O'Brien
Paige Powell
Jeffrey Slonim
Richard Turley

With an Essay by
Cookie Mueller*, first
published in November 1988.

*Published with the permission of the Estate of Cookie Mueller, and its executor, Richard Turley.

POWERHOUSE BOOKS

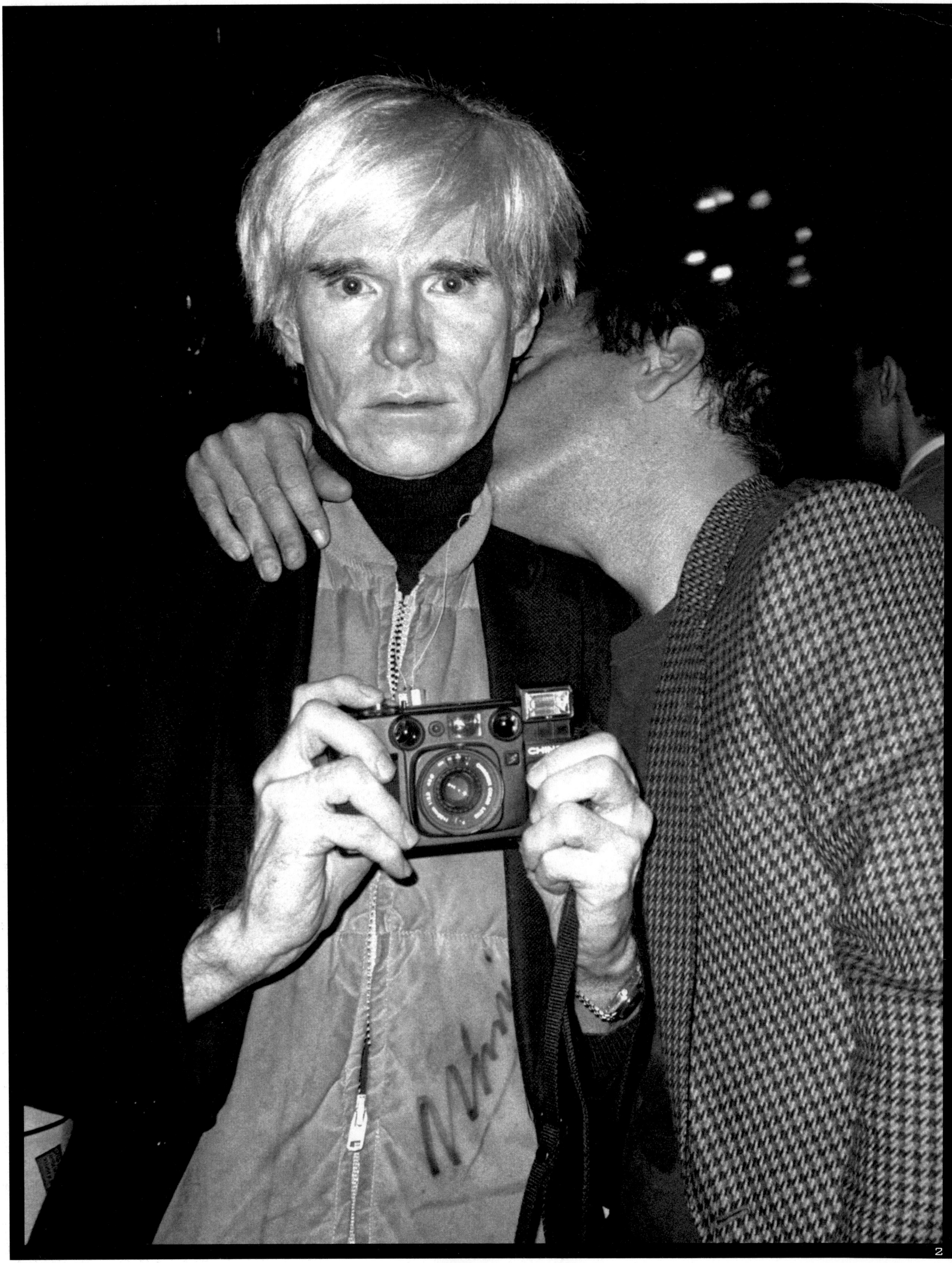

PATRICK McMULLAN

so80s

A PHOTOGRAPHIC DIARY OF A DECADE

ADDITIONAL COMMENTARY

SUSAN AINSWORTH, TOM AUSTIN, KEVIN BACON, MARC BALET, DAVID BARTON, SUSANNE BARTSCH, KARON BIHARI, PHILLIP BLOCH, SUSAN BLOND, SAM BOLTON, MARY BOONE, DIANNE BRILL, LADY BUNNY, RONNIE CUTRONE, KEVIN DOWNS, JOHNNY DYNELL, LISA EDELSTEIN, PATRICIA FIELD, DANNY FIELDS, SHELLY DUNN FREMONT, VINCENT FREMONT, BRAD GOOCH, ERIC GOODE, CORNELIA GUEST, PAT HACKETT, ANGELA JANKLOW HARRINGTON, DEBBIE HARRY, NIKKI HASKELL, R. COURI HAY, CAROLINA HERRERA, JANE HOLZER, BEAUREGARD HOUSTON-MONTGOMERY, IMAN, BETSEY JOHNSON, NAN KEMPNER, HEDY KLINEMAN, JULIE LANKE, LARISSA, FRAN LEBOWITZ, PERRI LISTER, BENJAMIN LIU, ROXANNE LOWIT, ROBERT LUND, CHRISTOPHER MAKOS, ANN MAGNUSON, SYLVIA MILES, ISAAC MIZRAHI, CLAIRE O'CONNOR, SALLY RANDALL, JOHN B. REINHOLD, ALAN RISH, JOAN RIVERS, STEPHEN SABAN, ELIZABETH SALTZMAN, JANIS SAVITT, ARNOLD SCASSI, KENNY SCHARF, IAN SCHRAGER, TONY SHAFRAZI, LIZ SMITH, STEPHEN SPROUSE, IVANA TRUMP, CHI CHI VALENTI, DIANE VON FURSTENBERG, RON WANLESS, GEORGE WAYNE, BOBBY ZAREM

DESIGNED BY MARIE HAVENS

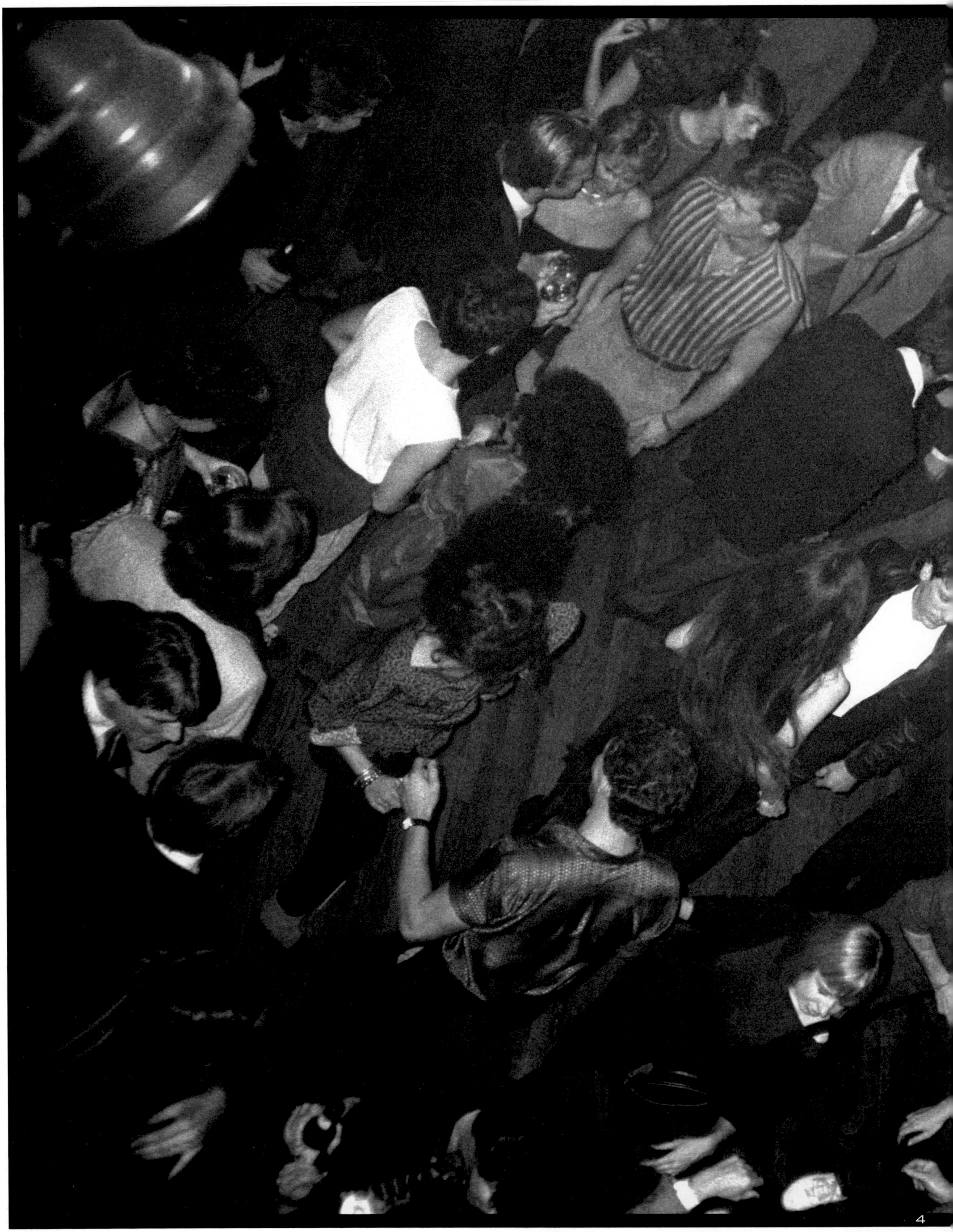

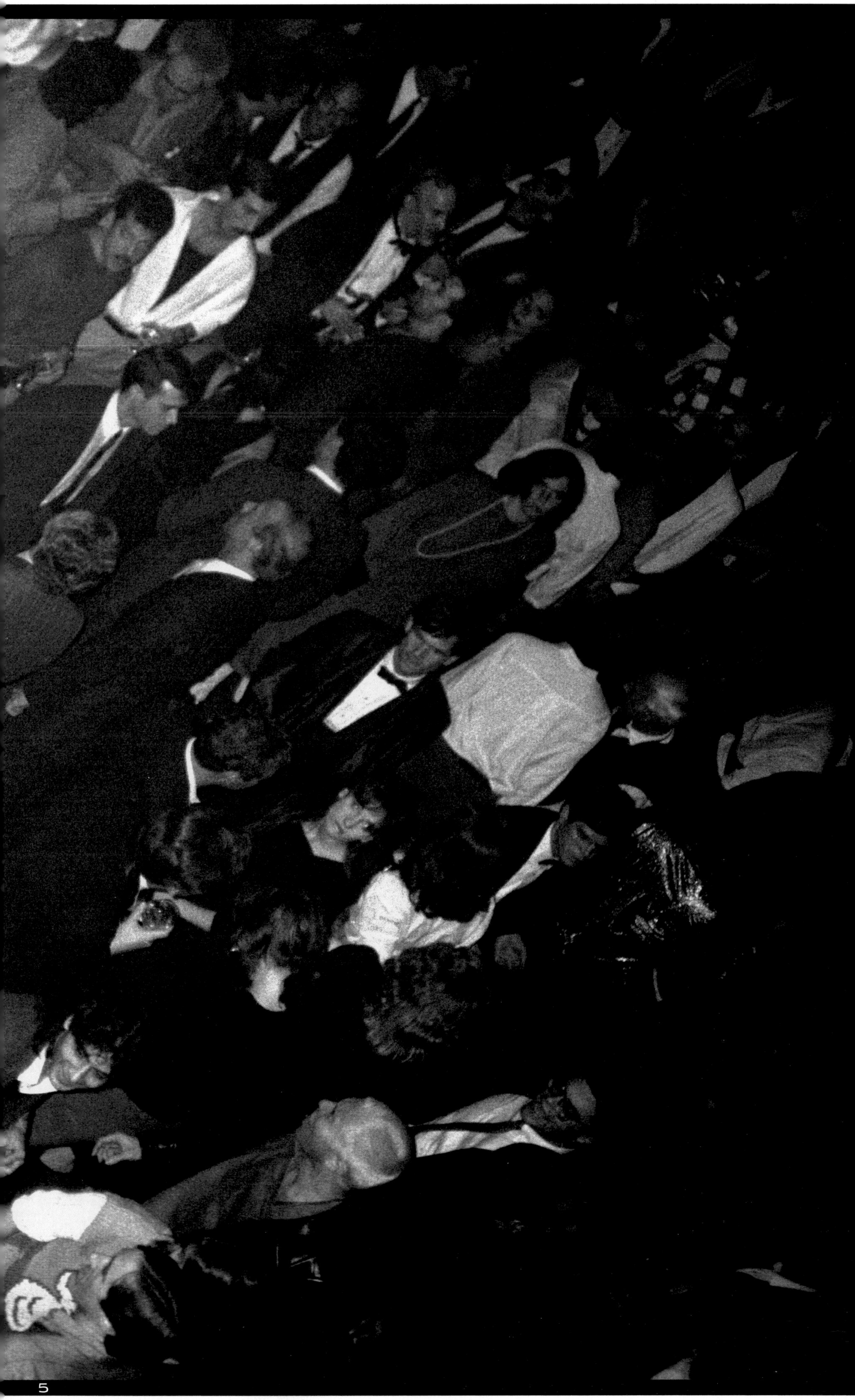

PAGE 2:
ANDY WARHOL AND
STEVE RUBELL AT DIANNE
BRILL'S BIRTHDAY PARTY
AT DANCETERIA.
APRIL 5, 1984

THIS PAGE:
CROWD AT THE INTERVIEW
MAGAZINE PARTY AT
LIMELIGHT.
NOVEMBER 9, 1983

Patrick McMullan's images of the New York nightlife of the 80s vibrate with a curious tension between theatricality and intimacy, between staginess and spontaneity. Perhaps never in the history of the nocturnal pursuit of fabulousness has a group so self-consciously performed as did the denizens of the Mudd Club and Area and the Palladium. And yet, particularly at the beginning, the stage was an intimate one--the idea of the nightlife as performance art was still new and fresh, the principal players were a relatively small and self-selected band of sisters and brothers, most of whom knew each other--and McMullan's snapshot aesthetic reflects this sense of intimate conspiracy.

For all the elitist exclusivism practiced by this tribe, a curious form of democracy prevailed beyond the velvet ropes and the scary doormen; those famous in the mundane daytime world beyond Tribeca required validation from the scene, which was created and maintained by club kids, drag queens, drug dealers, and performers without portfolios; a scene in which night creatures Sally Randall, James St. James, and Dianne Brill were at least as fabulous as Cher and Matt Dillon. Andy, who had predicted it all, was first among equals. Perhaps this was only true for a moment--at the beginning. Viewed chronologically, McMullan's deceptively artful snapshots document the appropriation and reification of the idea over the course of the decade... ah yes, here comes Sly Stallone and Morgan Fairchild.

McMullan was there from the beginning--a goofy kid from Long Island with an Instamatic, secretly shaping the scene as he documented it. He had unknowingly apprenticed for this curious career with long nights at Studio 54 in the 70s, but his party going was interrupted when he was diagnosed with cancer in 1981. After almost a year of chemotherapy, he was invited by his friend Ian Falconer to recuperate at the Los Angeles home of David Hockney. More than just by the climate, Patrick was invigorated by the photo albums he discovered in the house, which recorded Hockney's life in elaborate detail, and inspired Patrick to document his own life and times, in his own immaculate way. Not long after he returned to Manhattan Patrick began taking pictures, and in one of those strokes of serendipity which seem to inform his life, met Annie Flanders at a party. Flanders had just started Details magazine, which was becoming the official organ of the downtown nightlife.

He started following writer Stephen Saban around to the clubs, carrying his little Instamatic and snapping shots of the artists and the debs, the rockers and the drag queens, the pretty boys and girls of the night. It's hard to believe now, but this was pretty much a new idea at the time. The downtown club scene was an underground subculture, which passed well under the radar of the mass media at the time. And given the nature of much of the activity at these places, a camera might not have necessarily been welcome. But the word disarming was invented to describe Patrick. People didn't mind posing for him. Eventually they were desperate to pose for him. Eventually his camera, and his images, became a defining aspect of the scene, his portraits an increasingly artful record of an inherently ephemeral world.

In retrospect, it's hard to miss the dark undercurrents between the frivolity and artful posturing. This was the decade when sex turned deadly, as did the drugs that fueled the revelry. An inordinate number of these young night crawlers are no longer among us. Some of them left behind significant bodies of work in the arts, music, and fashion while others survive mainly in these images.

Jay McInerney
NYC, 2003

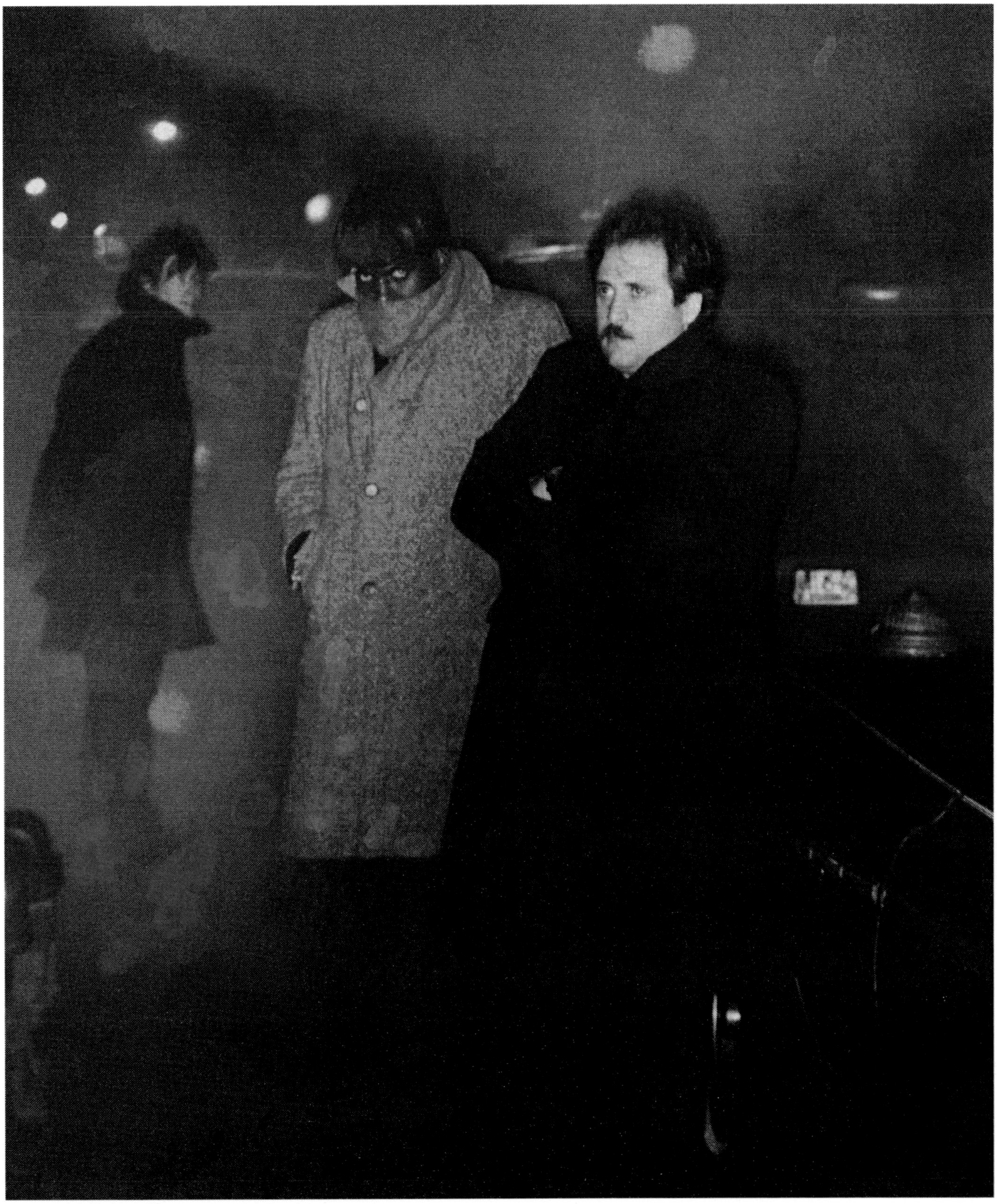

Russell Buckingham, Mojo, and Vito Bruno after hours.
1985

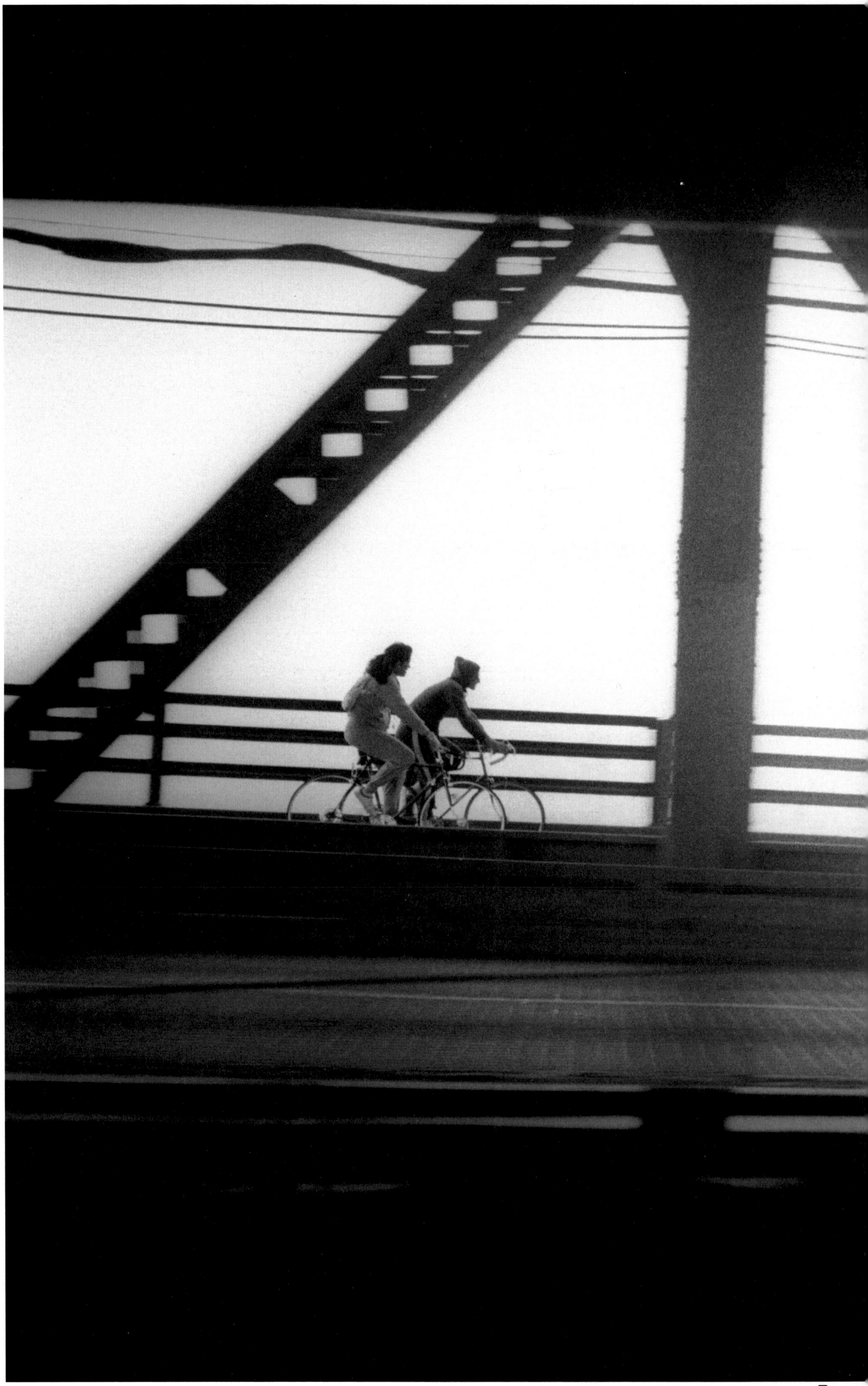

Williamsburg Bridge
Early 1980

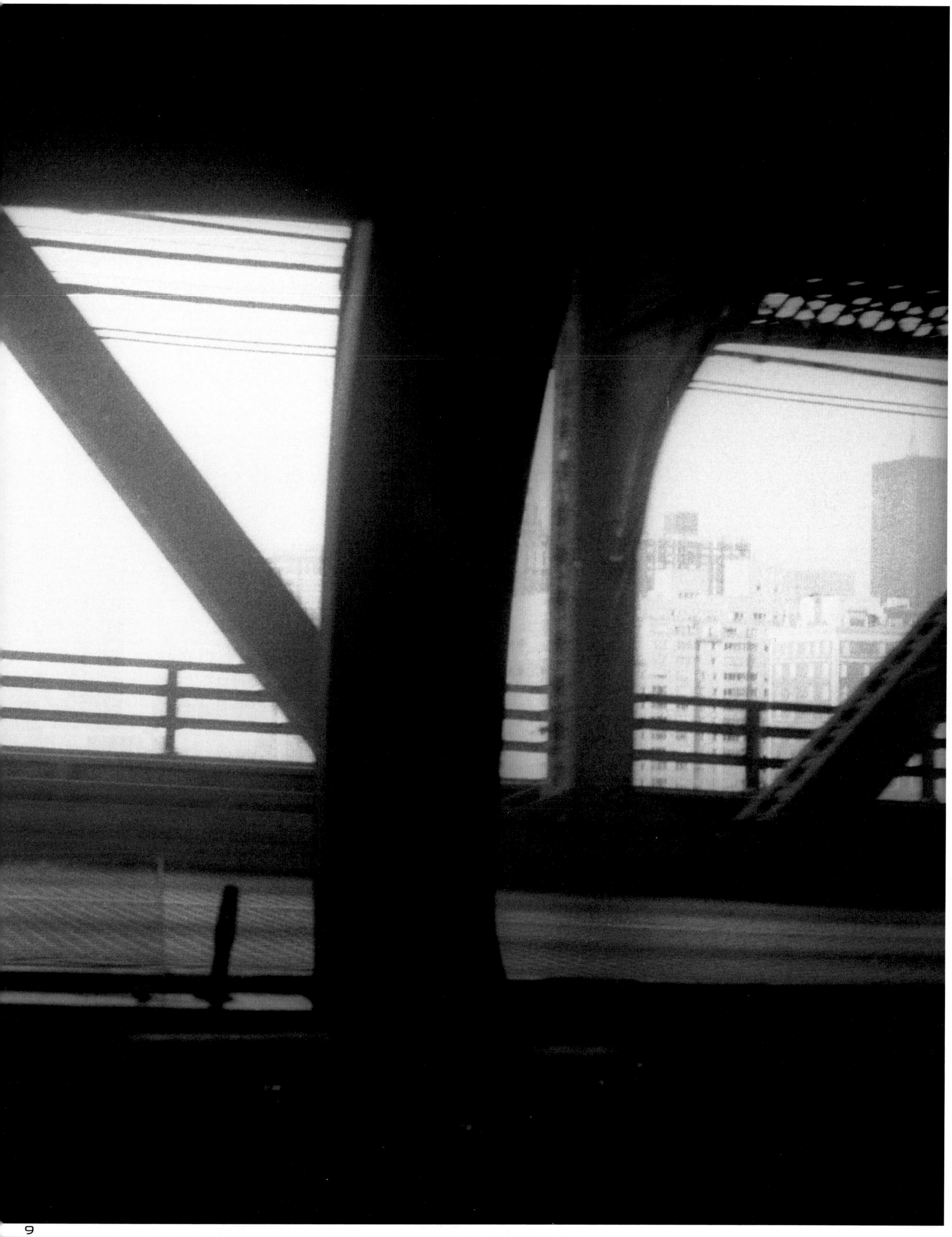

New York nightlife in the 80s felt like that game where you dream up the ultimate dinner-party guest list--the one where you'd invite JFK Junior, Jean-Michel Basquiat, Andy Warhol, and Debbie Harry, if you could. Every night felt like a glamorous combination of strange bedfellows, all of whom possessed iconic personal styles, seemed to know each other, and were always having the time of their lives. To a large extent, that was the case. Wall Street, SoHo, and the dance scene all exploded at once and collided together, and the early part of the decade felt like a lavish and eccentric, member's only club. For a while, extreme creativity was as valued as extreme wealth, and the nightlife reflected both ends of the spectrum.

Of course, there was a certain amount of mythmaking going on, and Patrick McMullan helped to create those myths with his pictures. He was good at it, because he was an insider; so when he took pictures of the rich and famous or the wanna-be famous they weren't annoyed. Unlike the camera guys who lurked outside, Patrick had credentials: he actually had an invitation. He got the shot because he was a member of the family. I've known Patrick for more than twenty years and I still think he learned his best tricks back then. He'd approach people with a drink in his hand, talk to them as if they were old friends, and then take their picture.

Celebrity media took off in the 80s. The photographs of the beautiful, the powerful, and the plain outrageous hanging out together during that time have an almost manic energy because everybody had something to promote--even if it was just their own notoriety. There was a rush that came from being at the biggest party at the center of the world. It felt like anyone could be famous just for being original. 1980s fashion made that process a lot more exciting than it is today. It wasn't exclusively about wearing labels or looking like a model. There was more cachet to breaking the rules. If you looked unique, if your hair was extreme enough and your outfit provocative enough, you too could make it into the picture. Providing you'd been invited to the party, of course.

Tom Ford
March 2003

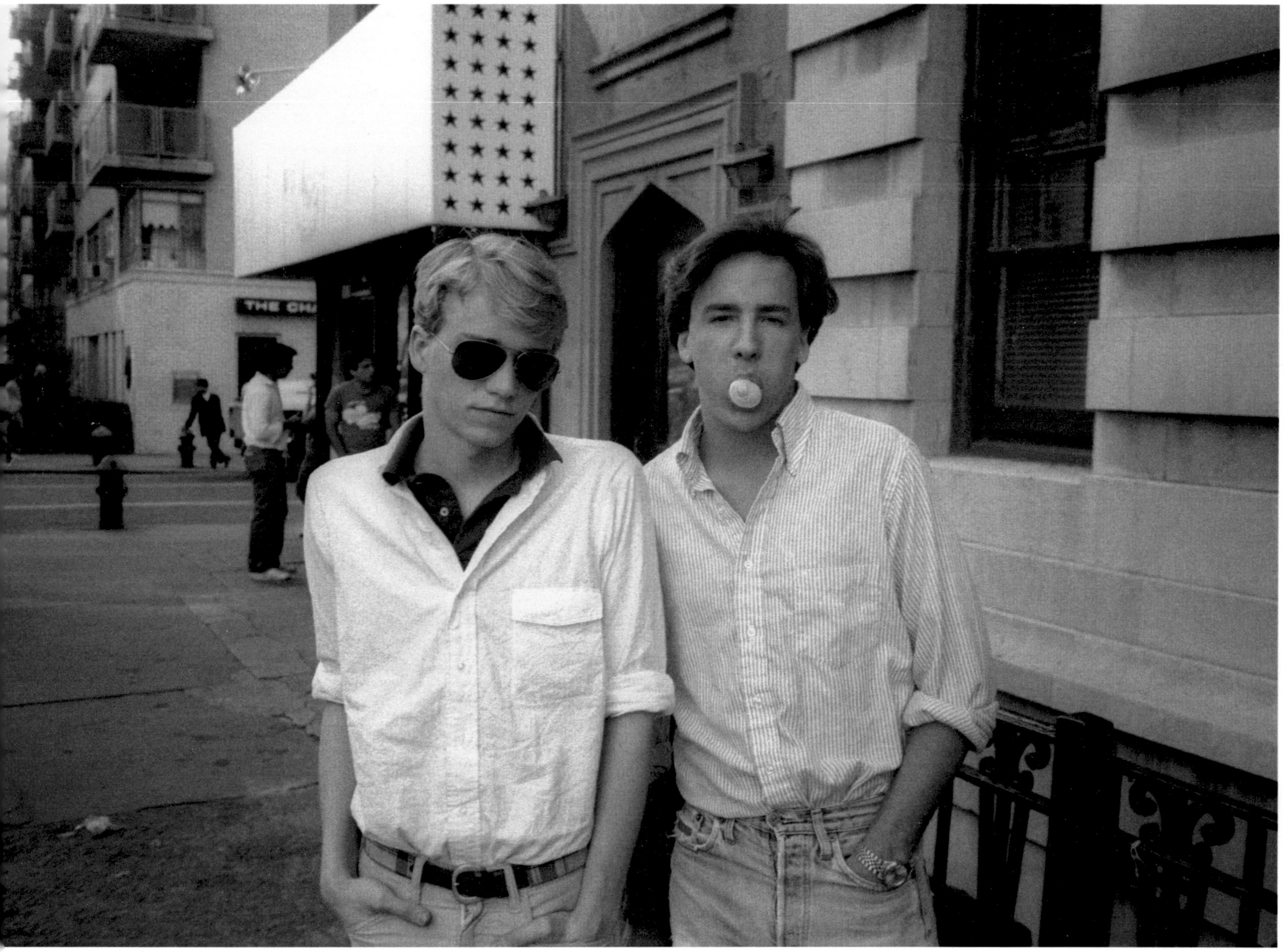

IAN FALCONER AND TOM FORD
ON 5TH AVENUE, OUTSIDE OF PATRICK'S APARTMENT.
EARLY 1980

"THE 80s--THAT WAS WHEN I DIED AND WAS REBORN." DEBBIE HARRY

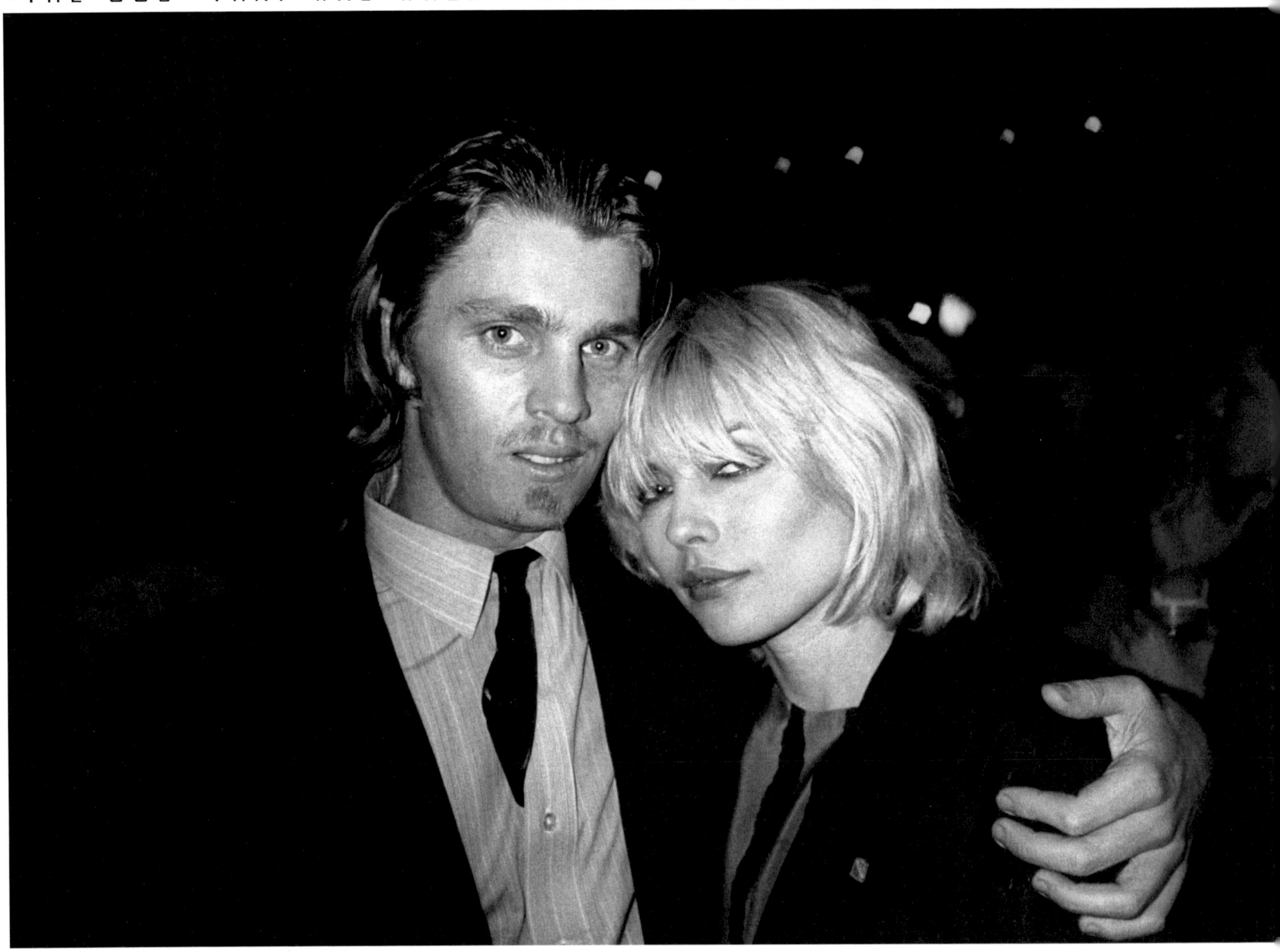

CHRISTOPHER MAKOS AND DEBBIE HARRY
AT STUDIO 54 FOR THE INTERVIEW MAGAZINE PARTY.
1980

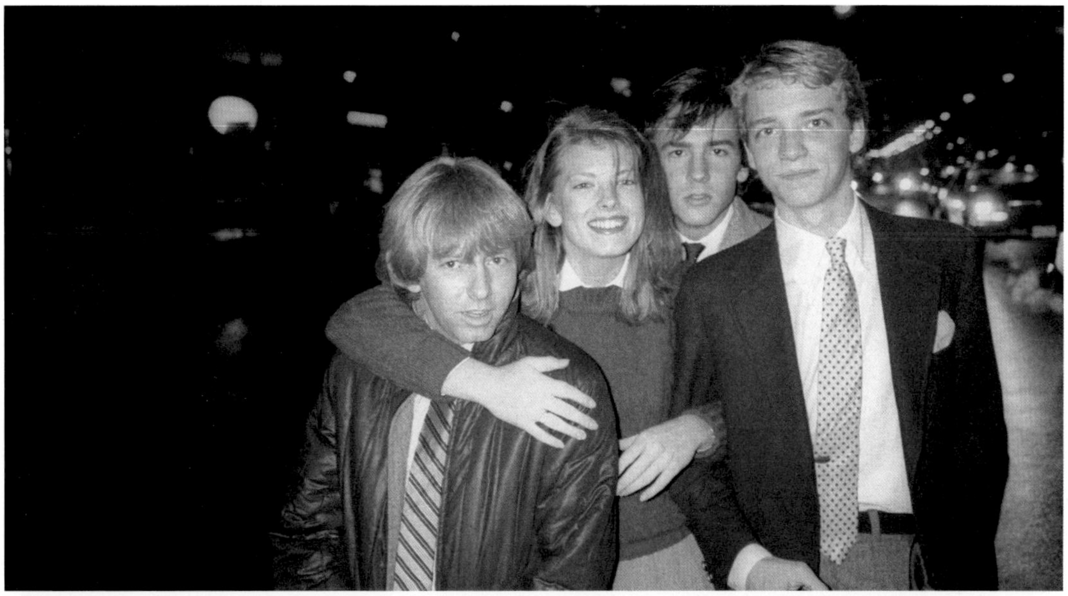

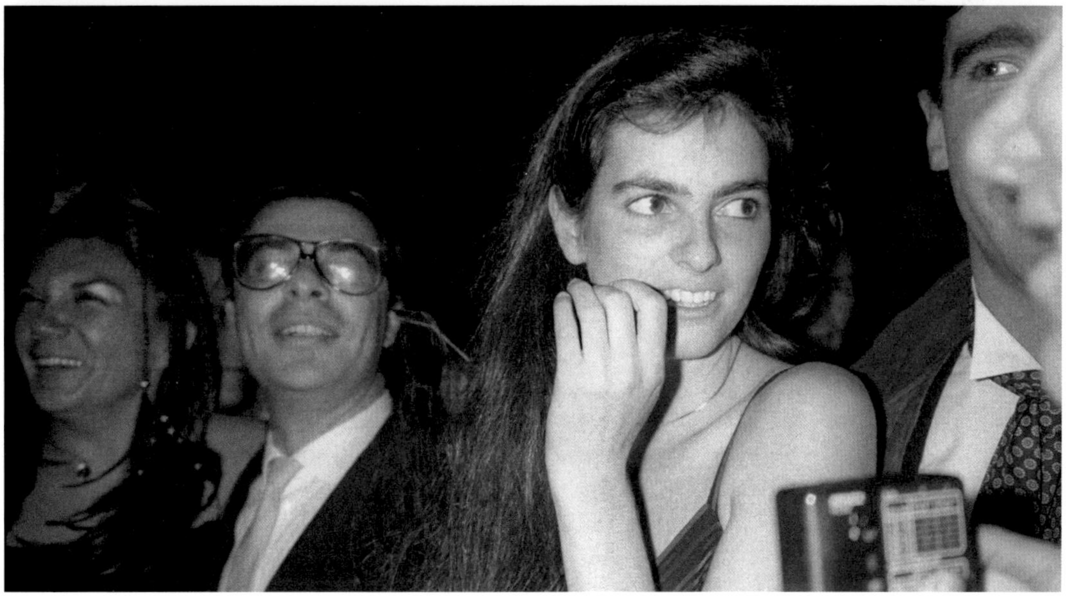

Top: Rupert Smith, Cindy, Tom Ford, and Ian Falconer
going to Studio 54. 1980
Bottom: Carmen D'Alessio, Bob Colacello, Mary Richardson,
Name Unknown, and Andy Warhol shooting next to Patrick
at Studio 54. 1980

"The early 80s in New York were even better than the 60s in London."
John B. Reinhold

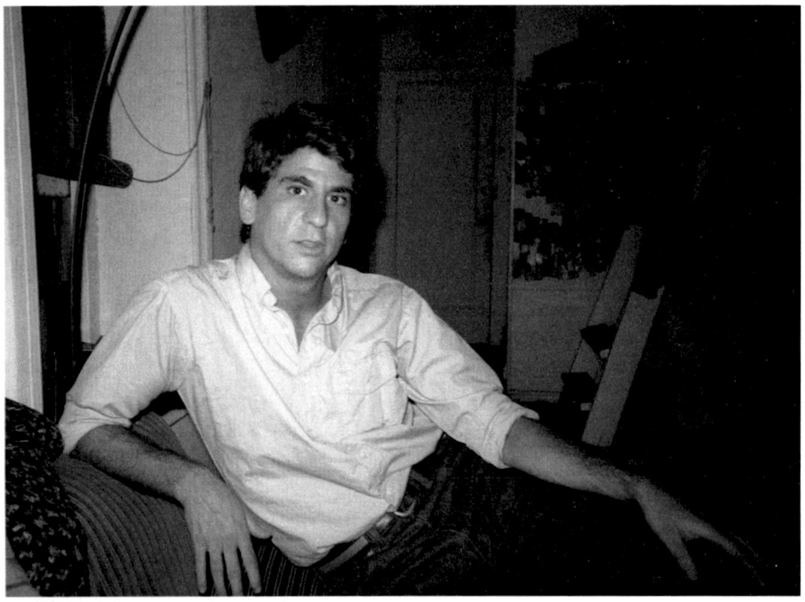

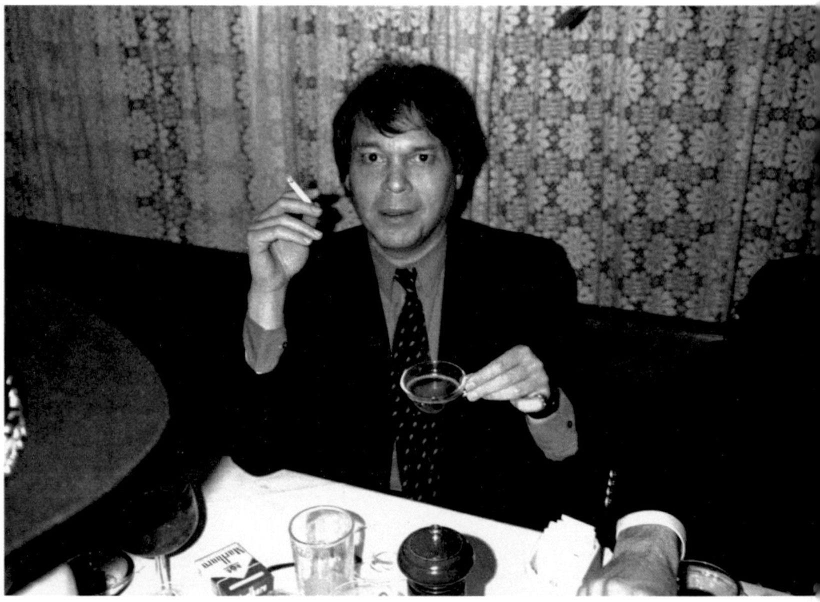

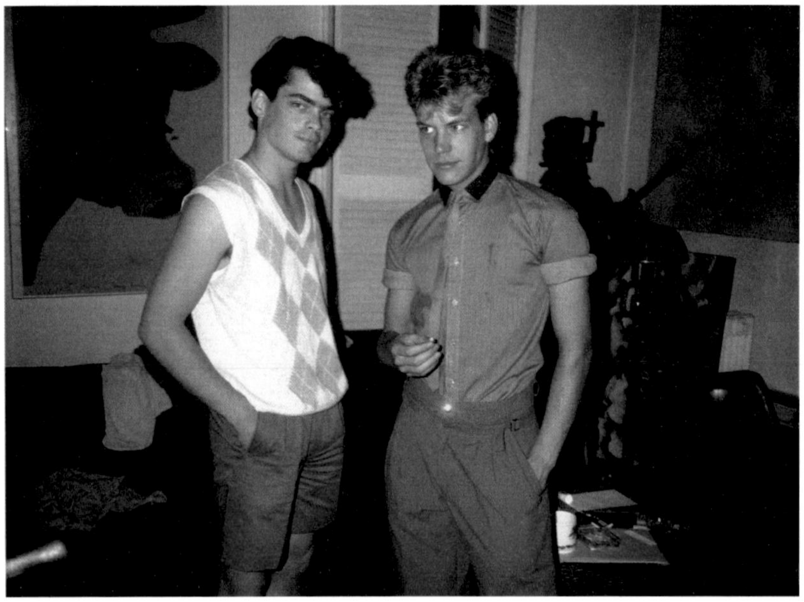

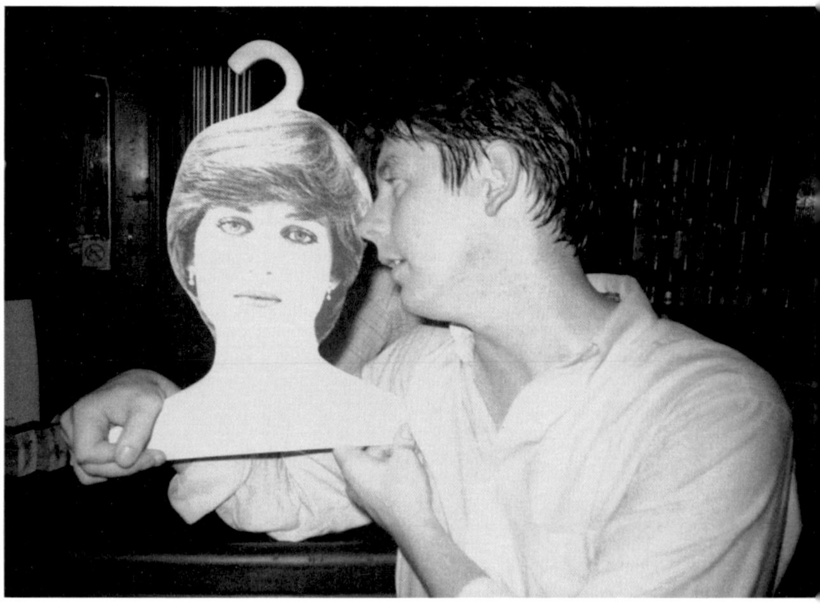

Top Left: David Rockwell at Patrick's 5th Avenue apartment. Summer 1981
Top Right: John B. Reinhold at 65 Irving Place. February 21, 1981
Bottom Left: Kevin Downs and Garren at Patrick's 5th Avenue apartment. July 1983
Bottom Right: Guy in bar with Princess Diana hanger. Summer 1981

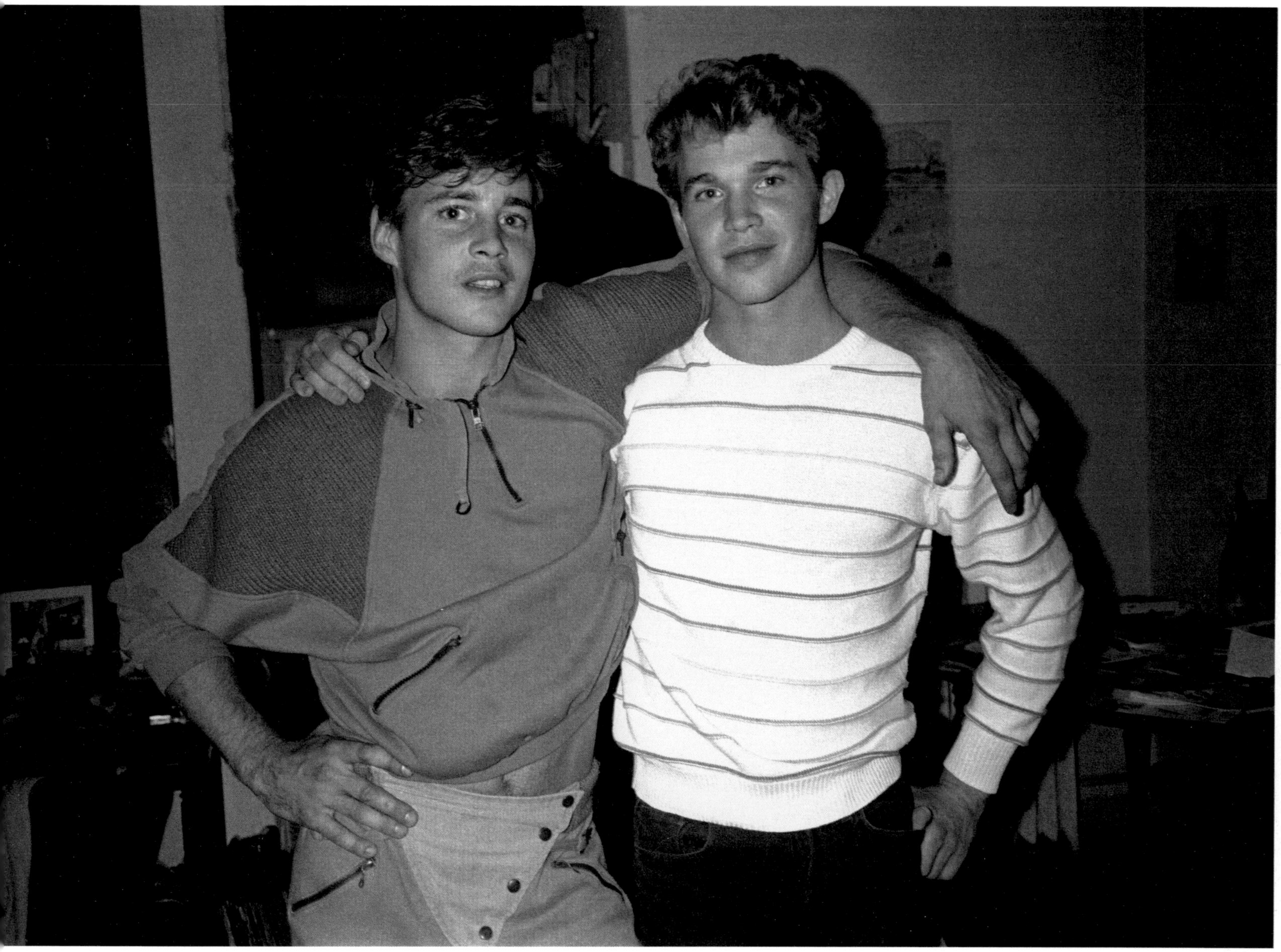

Patrick Taylor and Eric Ewell
at Patrick's 5th Avenue apartment.
1983

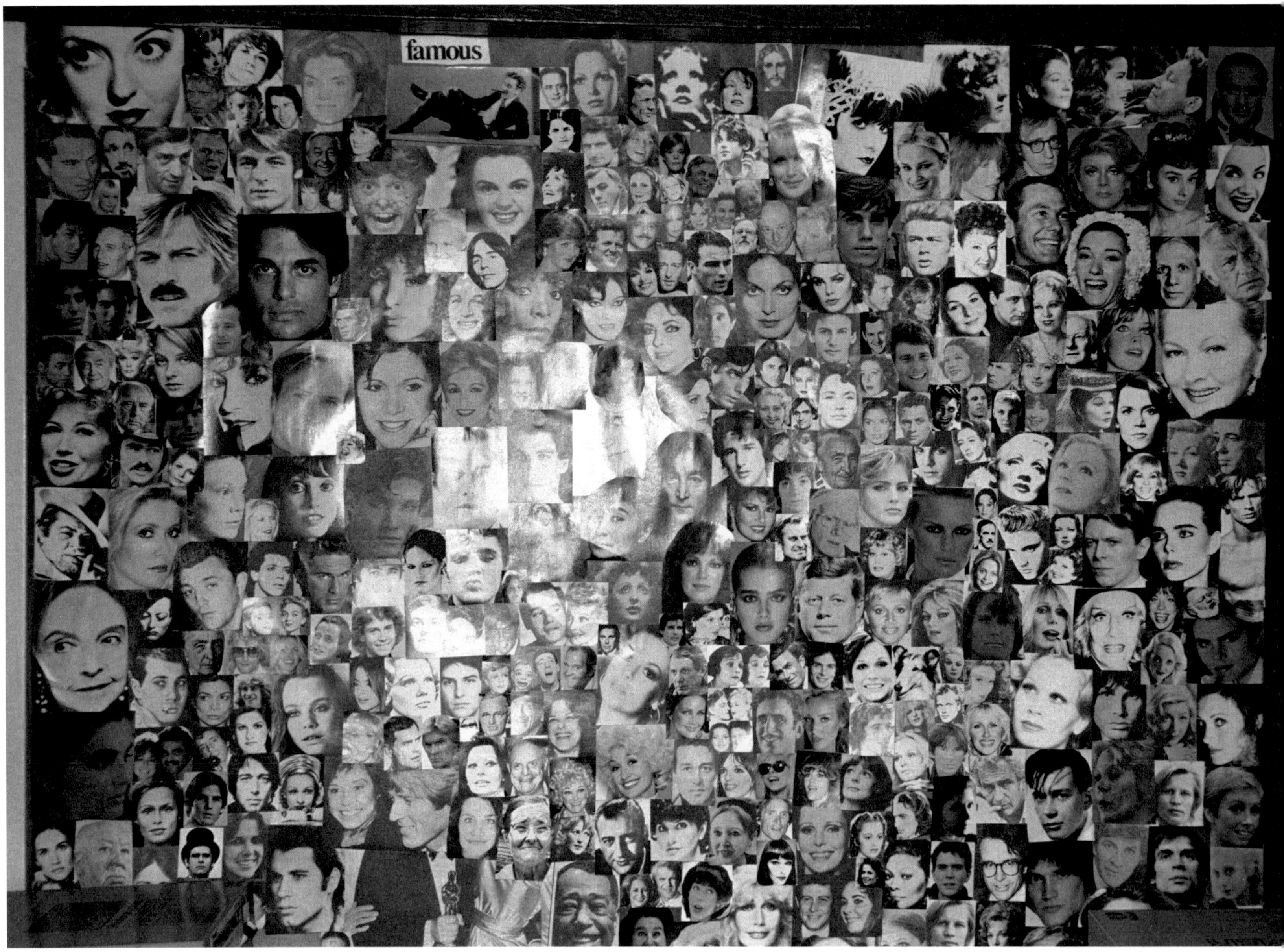

PATRICK MCMULLAN'S "COLLAGE OF FAMOUS FACES"
AT HIS 5TH AVENUE APARTMENT.
FALL 1983

Henry Geldzahler
at Patrick's 5th Avenue apartment.
August 1981

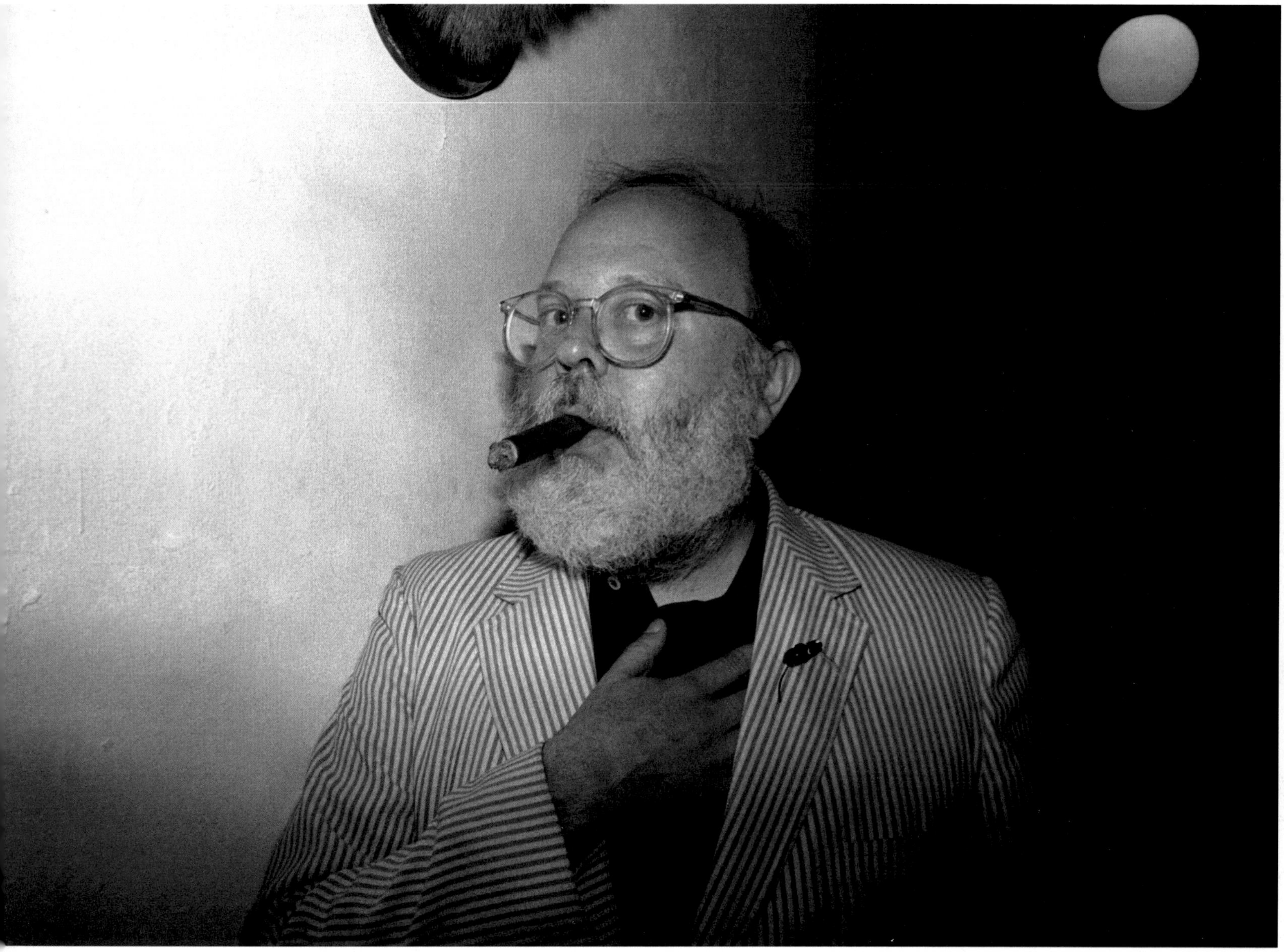

Henry Geldzahler
at Patrick's 5th Avenue apartment.
August 1981

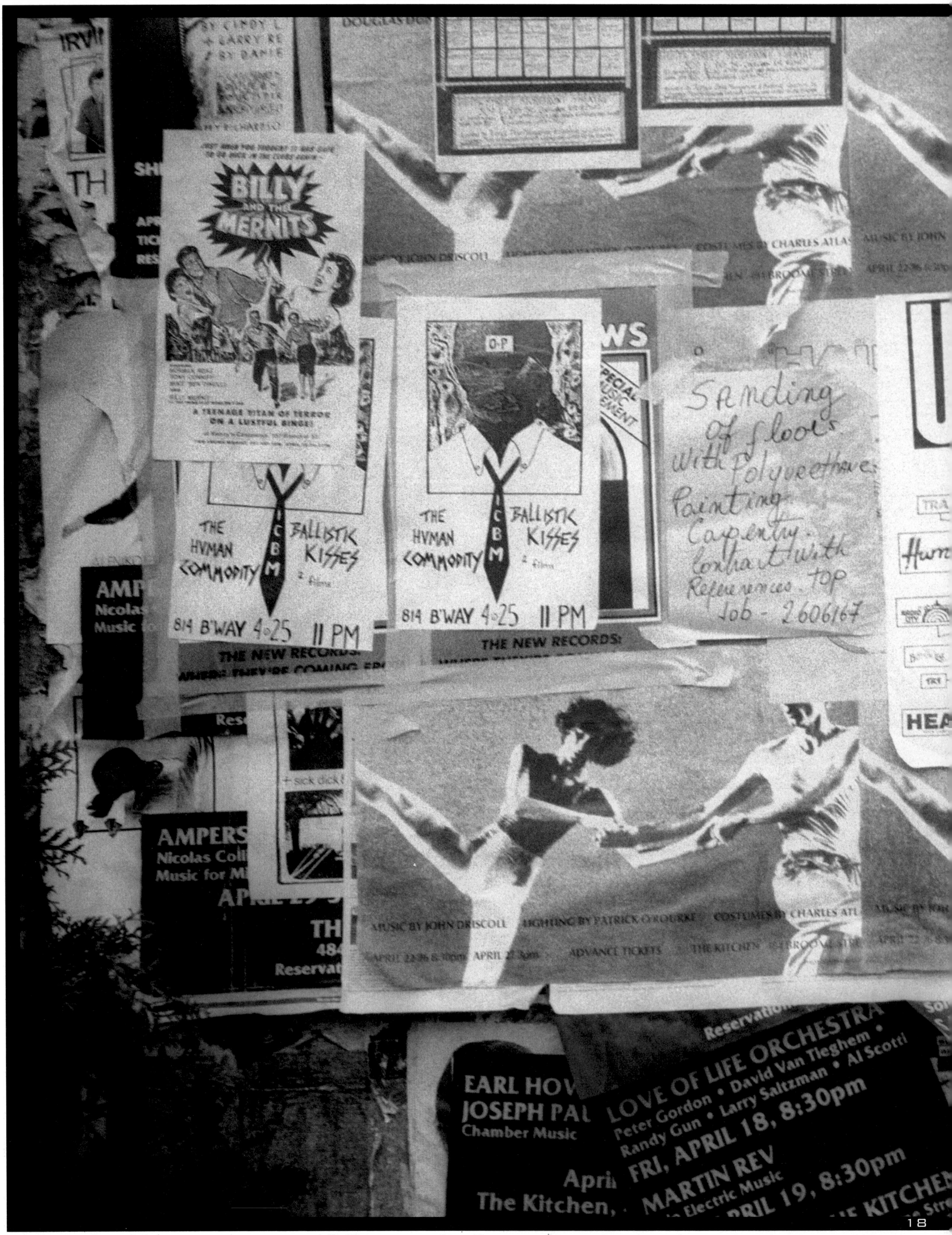

BILLY AND THE MERNITS
A TEENAGE TITAN OF TERROR ON A LUSTFUL BINGE!
THE HVMAN COMMODITY
ICBM
BALLISTIC KISSES
814 B'WAY 4-25 11 PM
THE NEW RECORDS:
Sanding of floors with Polyurethane Painting Carpentry. Contact With References. TOP Job - 2606167
AMPERS
Nicolas Coll
Music for Mi
MUSIC BY JOHN DRISCOLL
COSTUMES BY CHARLES ATLAS
ADVANCE TICKETS
THE KITCHEN
EARL HOW
JOSEPH PAU
Chamber Music
The Kitchen,
LOVE OF LIFE ORCHESTRA
Peter Gordon • David Van Tieghem •
Randy Gun • Larry Saltzman • Al Scott
FRI, APRIL 18, 8:30pm
MARTIN REV
Electric Music
APRIL 19, 8:30pm

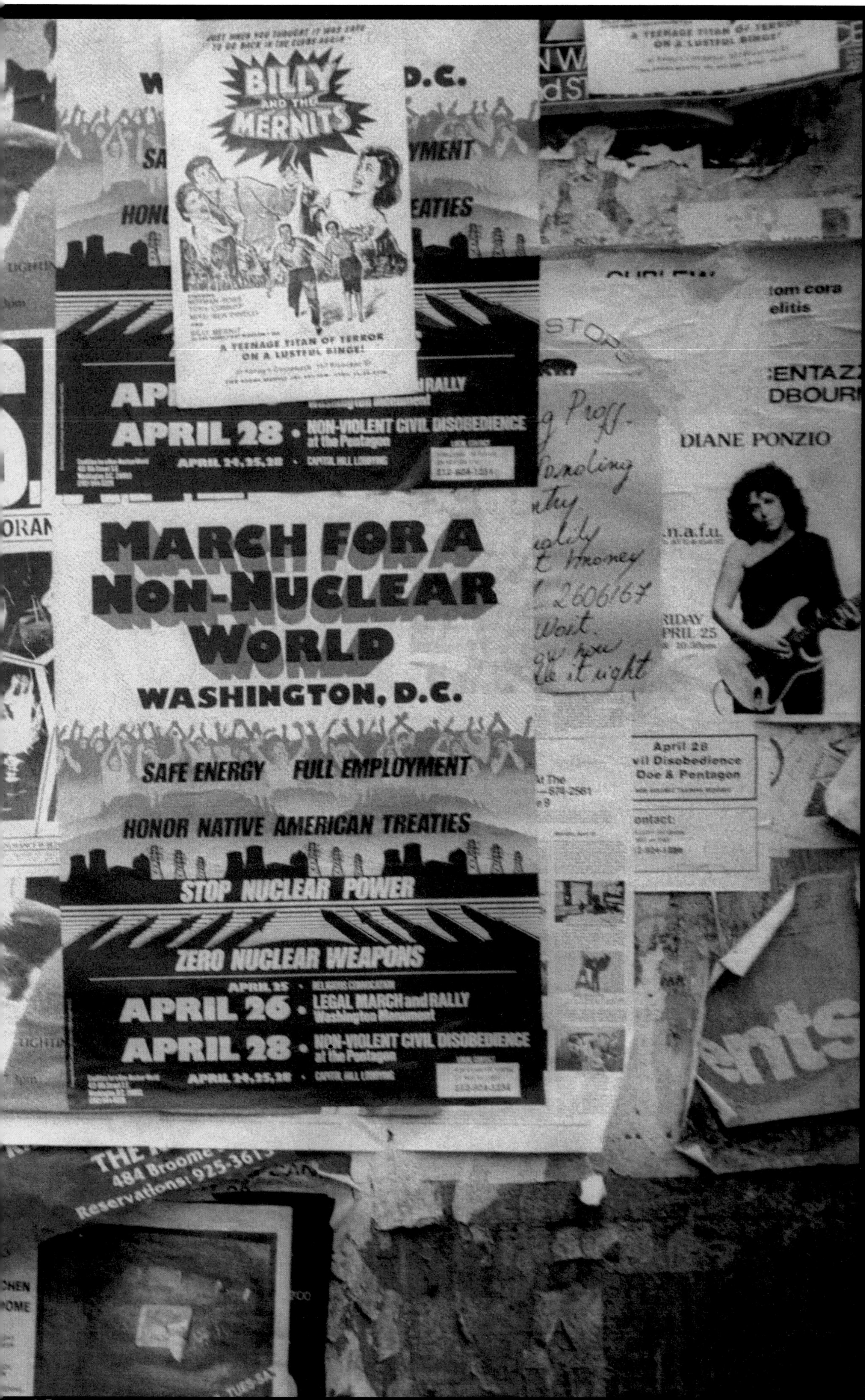

Wall of torn flyers in Lower Manhattan. Early 1980

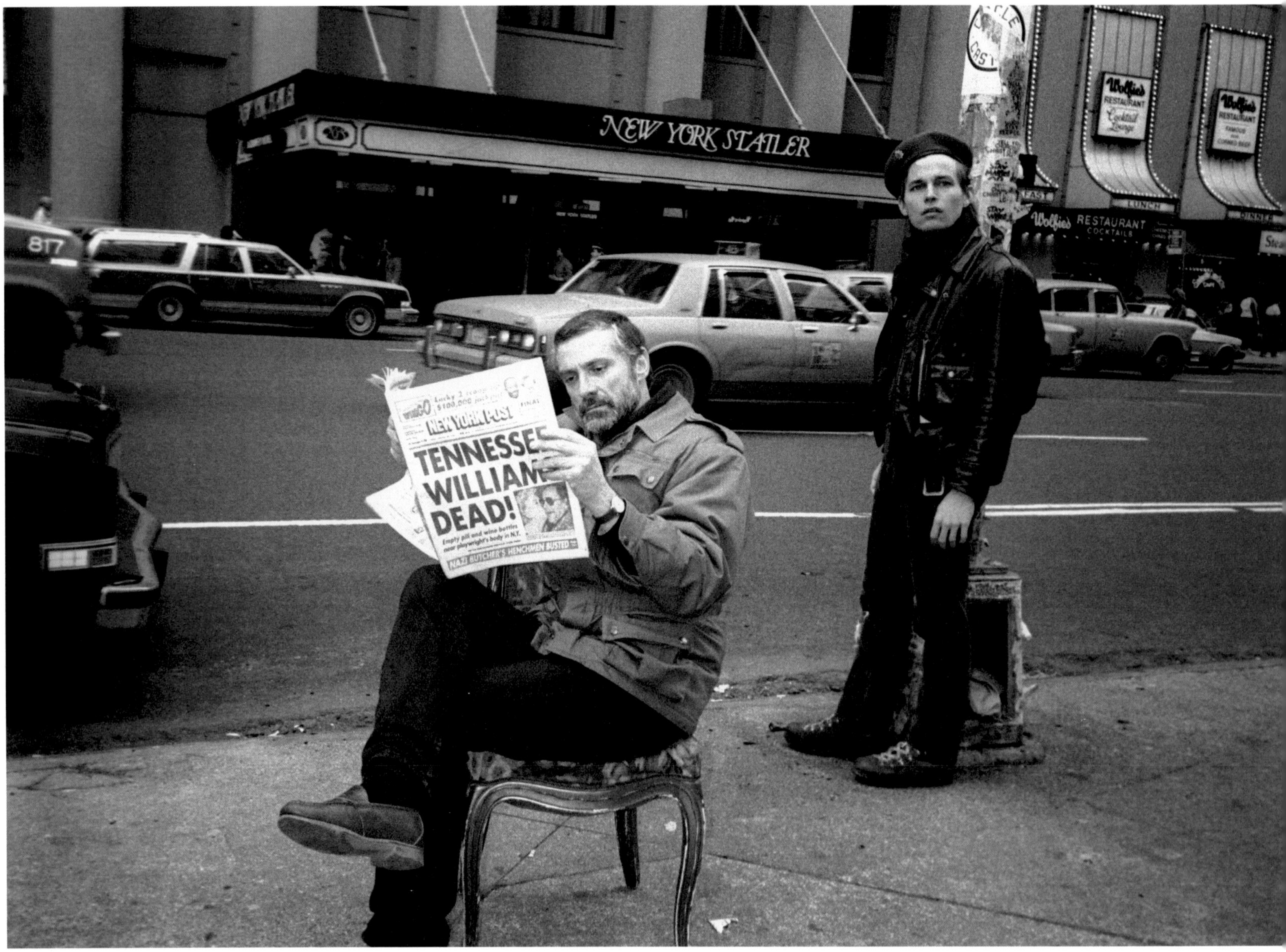

TERRY STEVENSON AND TOM COTE
ON 7TH AVENUE.
FEBRUARY 24, 1983

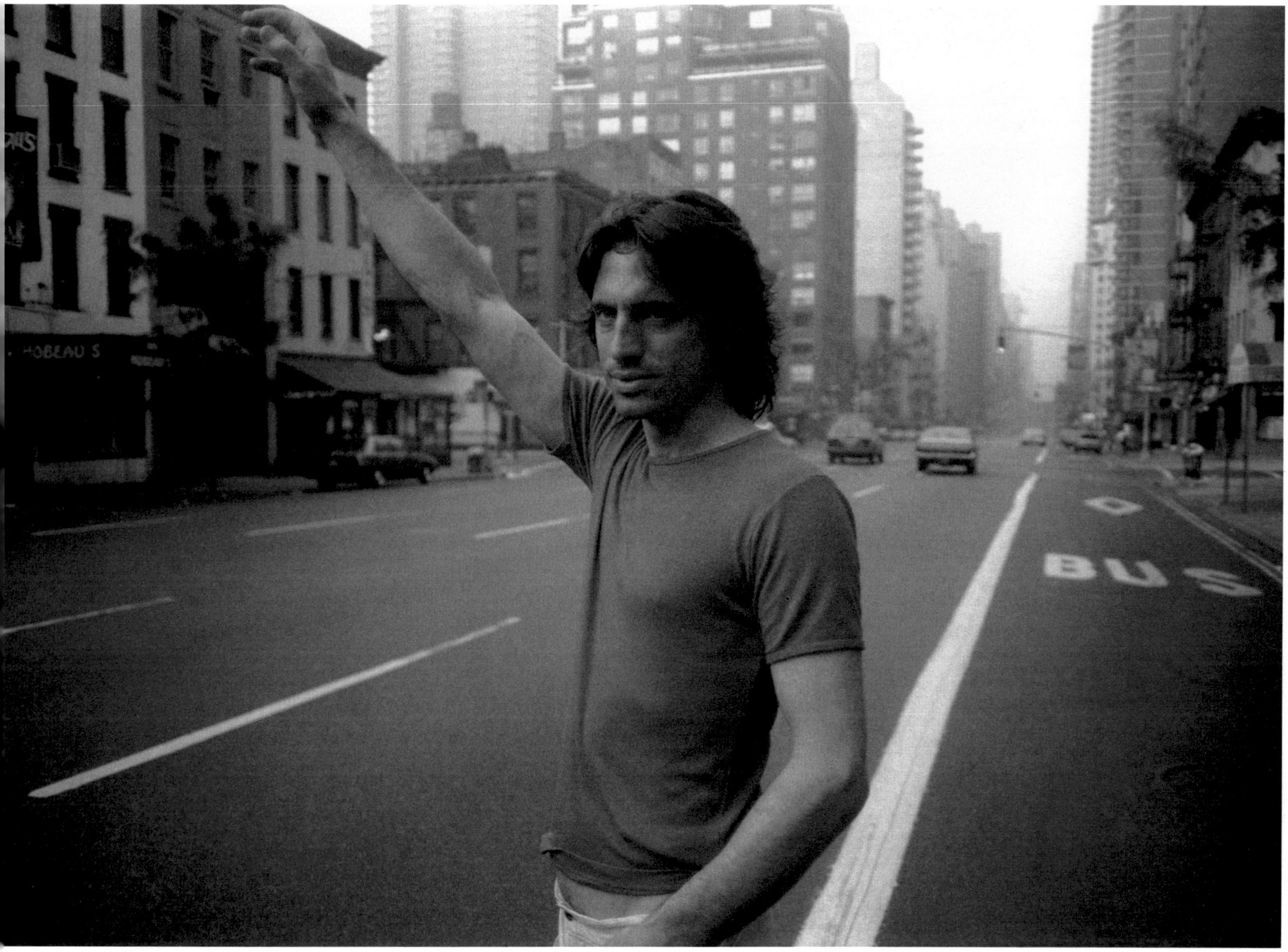

MICHAEL AFTER HOURS, HAILING A CAB.
JUNE 2, 1986

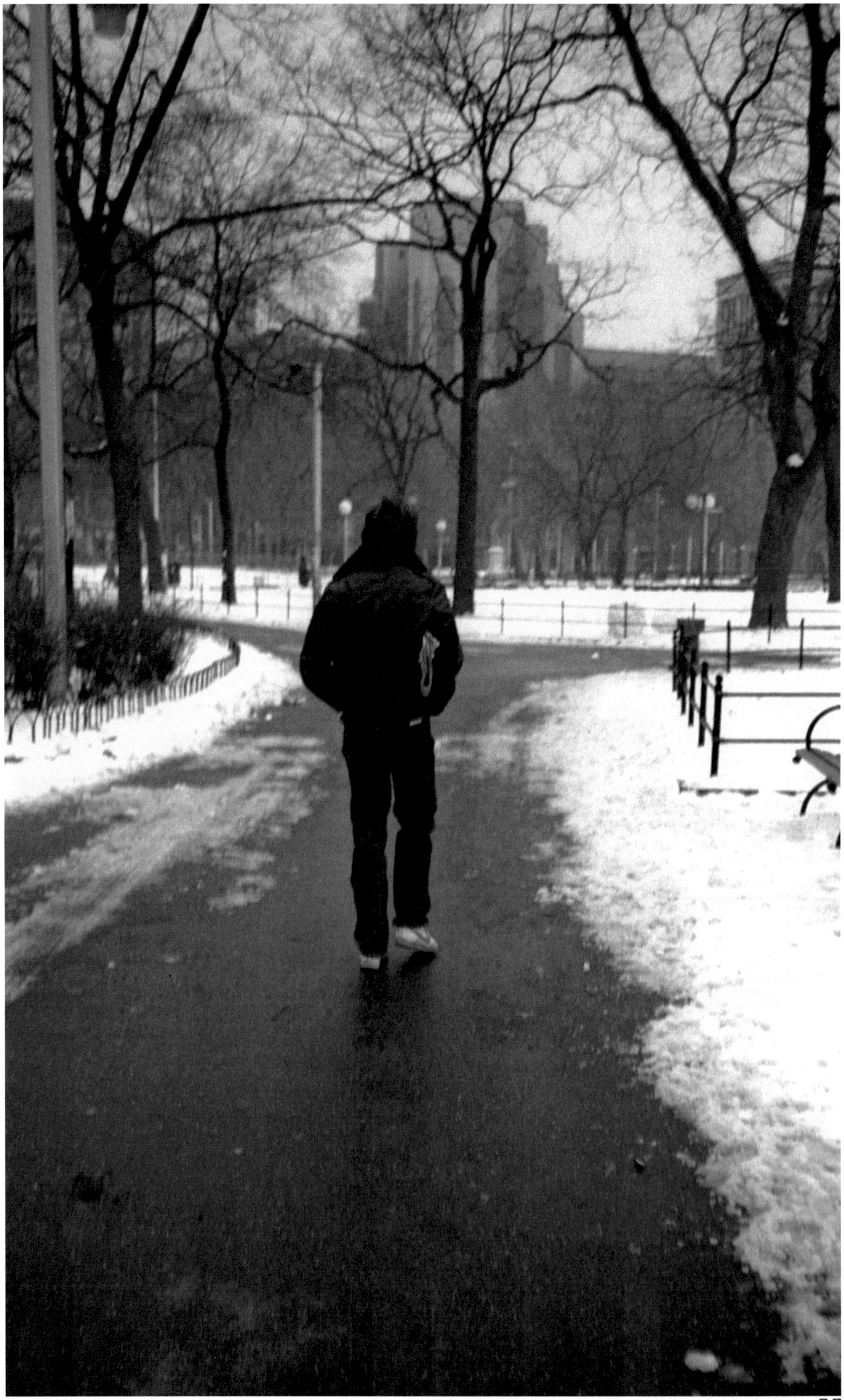

Chris in Washington
Square Park.
December 1983

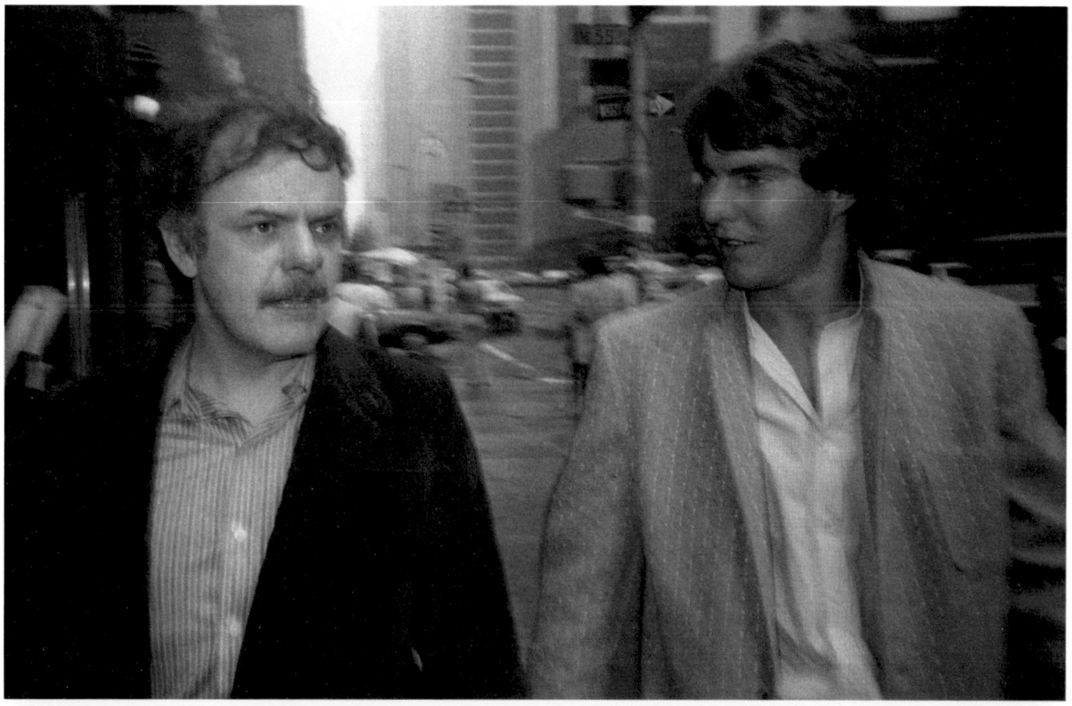

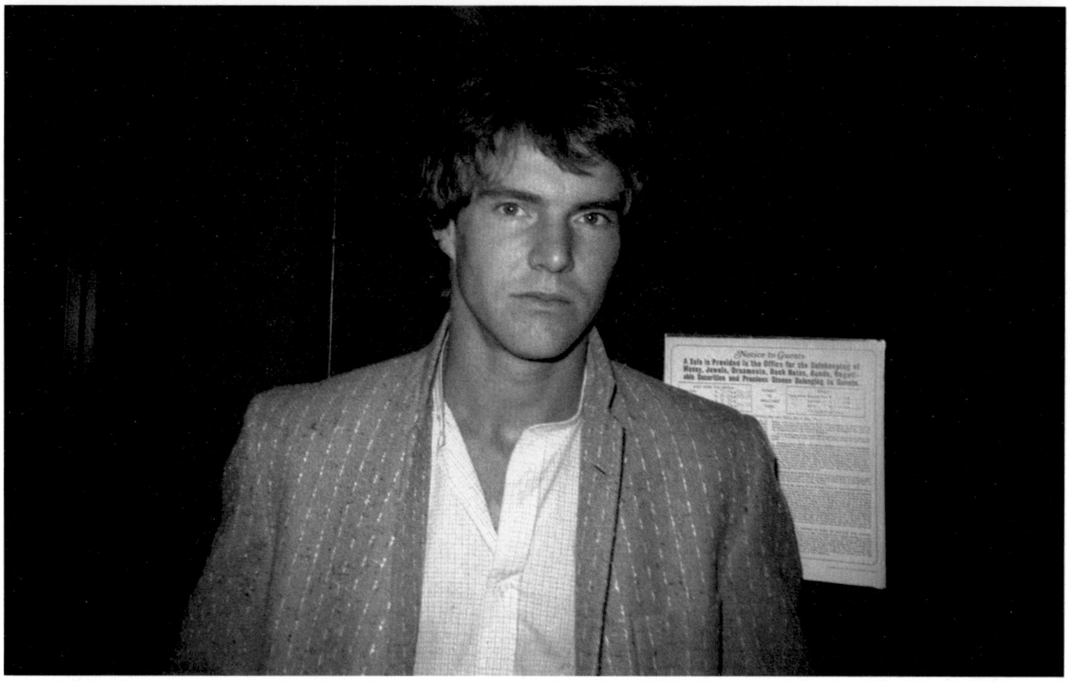

TOP: DONALD LYONS AND DENNIS QUAID
IN MIDTOWN MANHATTAN.
BOTTOM: DENNIS QUAID IN THE HALLWAY OF A NYC HOTEL.
SUMMER 1981

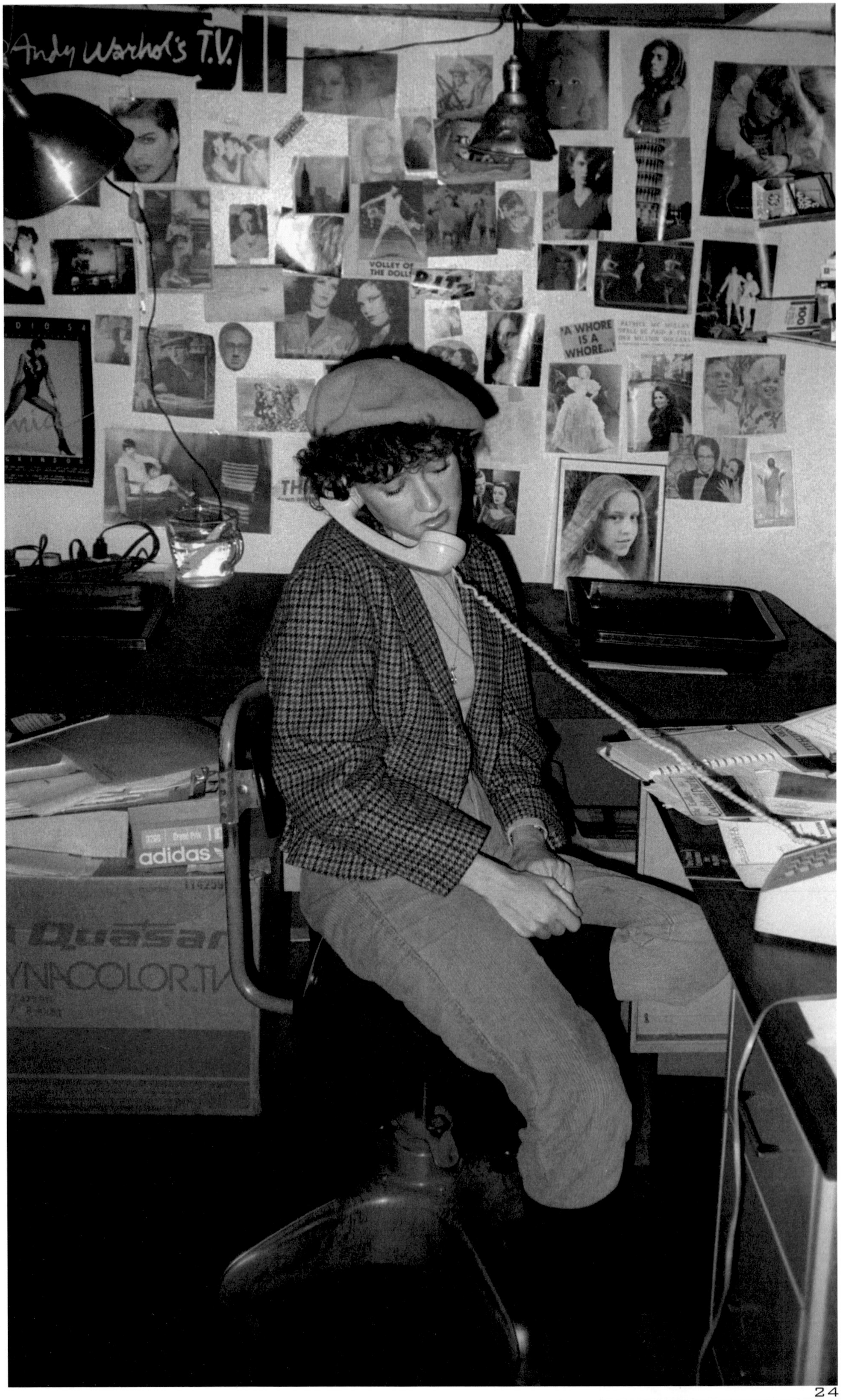

Margie Beck
at Patrick's 5th
Avenue apartment.
November 9, 1983

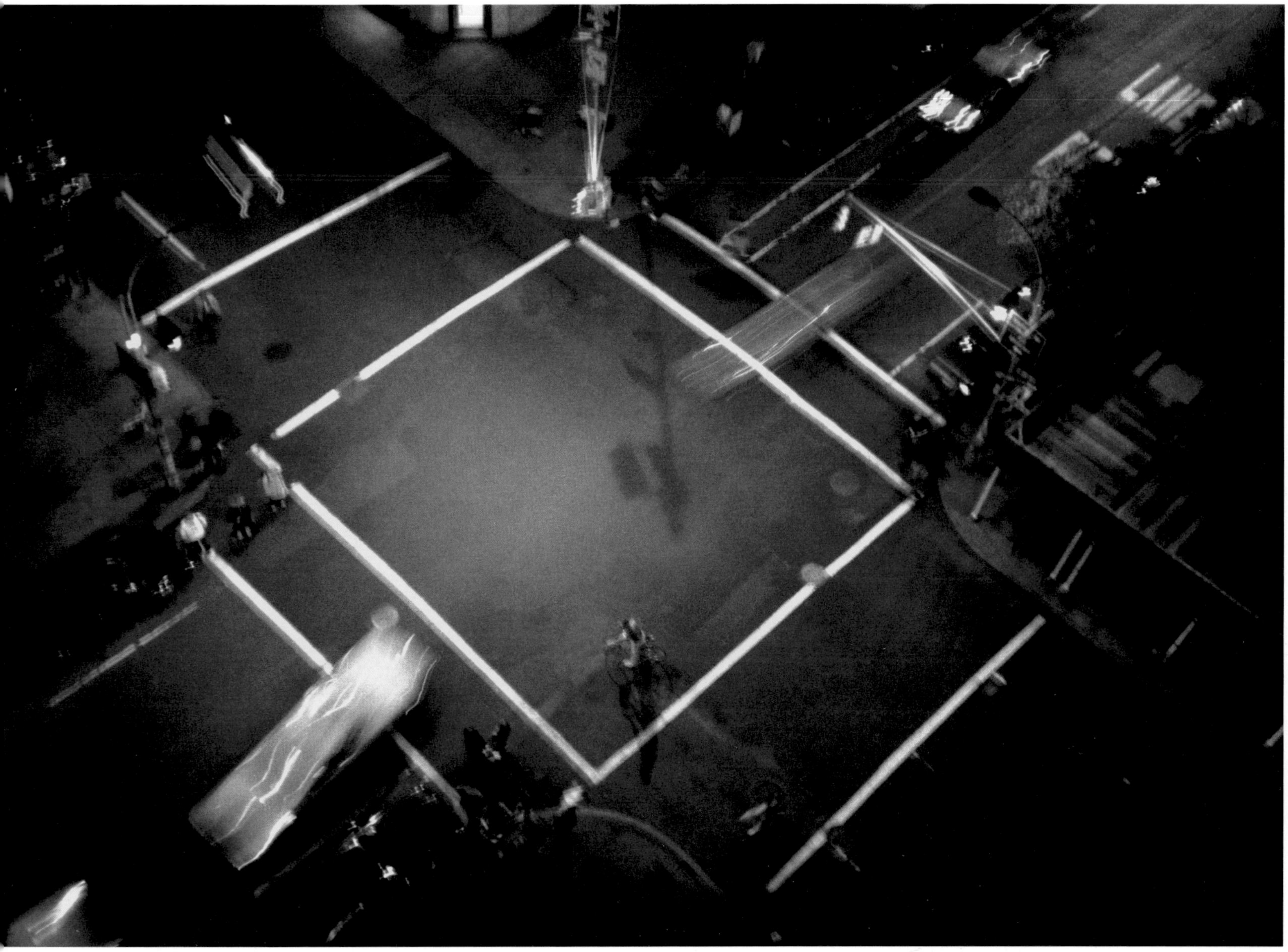

Aerial view of 5th Avenue and 8th Street.
Early 1980s

World Trade Towers
1980

1

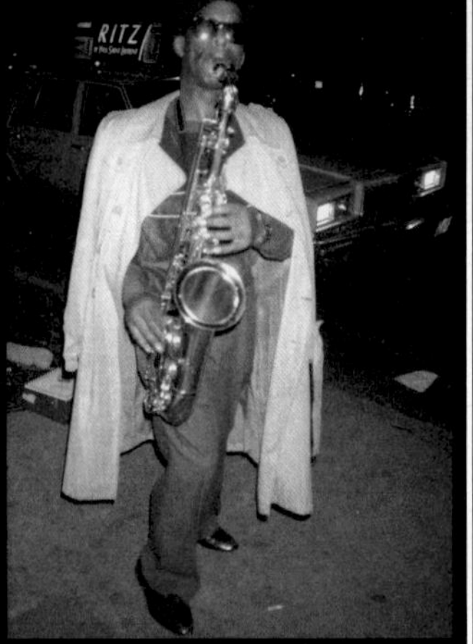

2

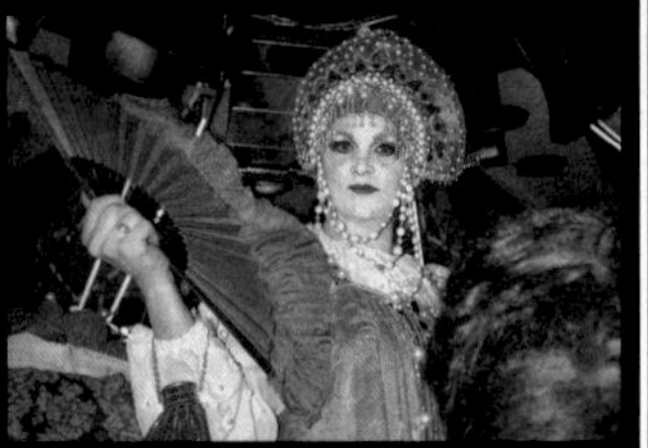

1: Saxophone player in Times Square. Saturday, September 27, 1986
2: Performer at the Copacabana. November 30, 1989

3: Neil Barry and Zach Galligan at the Out of Bounds Party at Revolution. July 23, 1987
4: Michael Musto at the Moroccan Party at Limelight. Thursday, July 23,1987

3

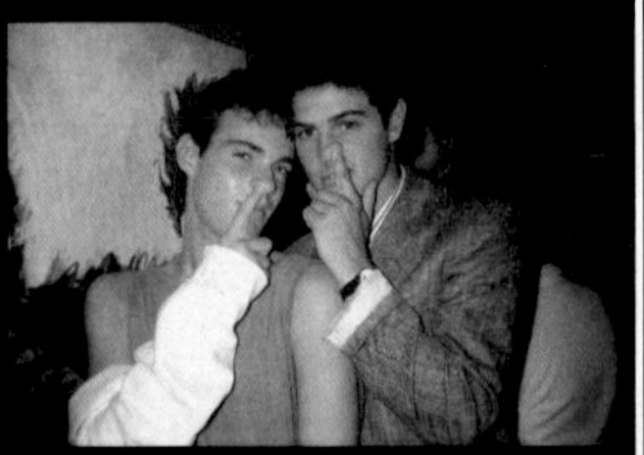

4

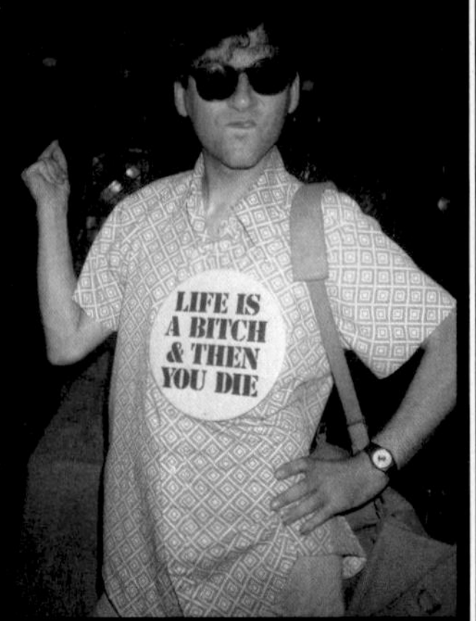

Right: Times Square, June 1984

Erase all recent images of New York--the nightly club raids and Disney stores of the Giuliani era and the "quality of living" concerns and imposed good behavior after that. Back in the 80s, nightclubs were places where you were allowed--and even encouraged--to misbehave, as long as you did so with some flair, creativity, and even money. With dough practically falling from the sky (at least until the town's bottom fell out), glamour and conspicuous consumption were our gods, and we worshipped them in the style of born-again believers, going mad for the excesses of realty wife Ivana Trump, TV diva Joan Collins, gilded-set Lily Cornelia Guest, and downtown it girl Dianne Brill. These women were extravagant, lusty, busty, and--in a perfect reflection of that era--had attached themselves to tons of marvy moolah.

And it was there to burn and play with. The downtown clubs spent a fortune providing a Felliniesque backdrop for us to perform a nightly movie against, and we were free to choose our characters, costars, and dialogue at whim. The invitations alone were three-act plays, ranging from elaborate color foldouts to a capsule that separated in water, spewing out the party info as if by pharmaceutical magic. That last pill came courtesy of Area, the sprawling Tribeca club which drummed up a new theme every month, the in-house drag icon Bernard Zette morphing from Anne Frank to a mermaid to a framed work of surreal art, never breaking character until it was time to get paid and go home. Meanwhile, Limelight's stained glass decor became the (sac-) religious setting for downtown musical revues, transsexual birthday parties, and other debauches that wouldn't have been allowed when the same space was a church or a drug treatment center. And the same nonconformist spirit popped up in less lavish hangouts like Danceteria and the Pyramid, which popped up to serve performance with an attitude that made you feel like you were in on the world's most fabulous joke.

The prevailing club crowd consisted of "celebutantes"--seemingly contradictory amalgams who were both bohemian and driven (preferably by limo). These creatures of the night--like the lunchbox-wielding James St. James (now the author of the acclaimed book Disco Bloodbath)--acted wacky to a fault, but hoped to become extremely rich and famous while doing so. Most lived off trust funds, allowing them to spend every night in the clubs, chasing after publicity, free drink tickets, and the next evening's invites. Meanwhile, their uptown counterparts, also sponsored by the folks, spent all their time being photographed at boutiques, benefits, and the burgeoning Hamptons. They were the Cathys to the downtown Pattys--different, but oh so the same--so it's no wonder that attempts at cross-pollination clicked. Clubbies would head uptown for fashion galas and Tama Janowitz dinners, while Blaine Trump and Joan Rivers slummed their way down to Limelight and Area, and the culture clash was so loud it was thrilling.

Whether up, down, or midtown, we were all scrambling for our 15 minutes, and it wasn't that much of a challenge; you could find yourself a bold-faced celebrity simply because you worked the door at a hot club (like the enormous, art-driven Palladium) or even just went to one. Empty fame was encouraged, and I remember being torn between celebrating this kooky trend and partaking of it, wearing over-the-top outfits partly because they guaranteed a mention in the Daily News, while making sure to notice the other people in sequined pajamas to write up in my own column!

The downtown dress code demanded humor and ingenuity, even if you could only afford to live in the kind of cheapo East Village hovel that's probably an overpriced Belgian restaurant now.

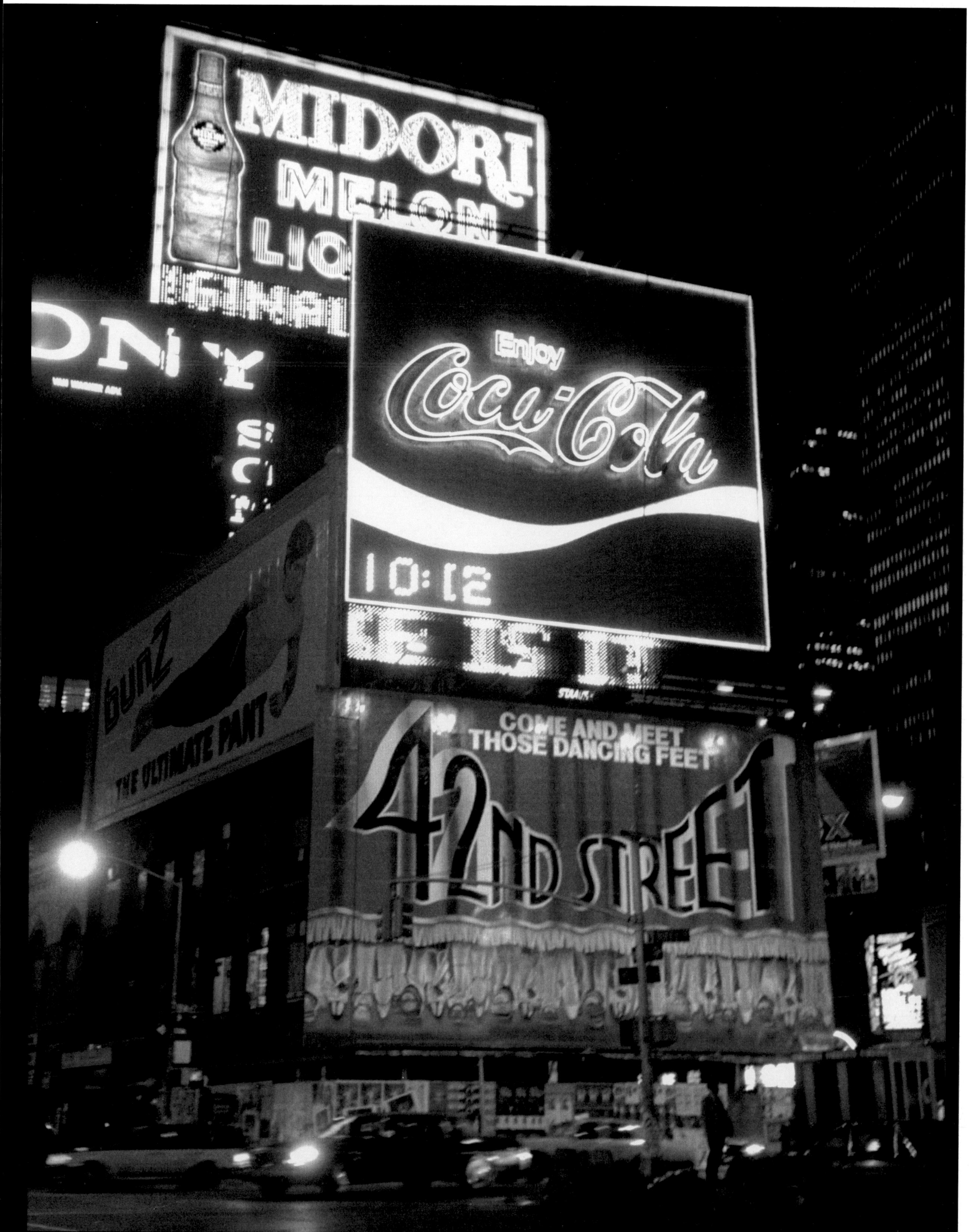
MIDORI
MELON
Enjoy
Coca-Cola
10:12
bunz
THE ULTIMATE PANT
COME AND MEET
THOSE DANCING FEET
42ND STREET

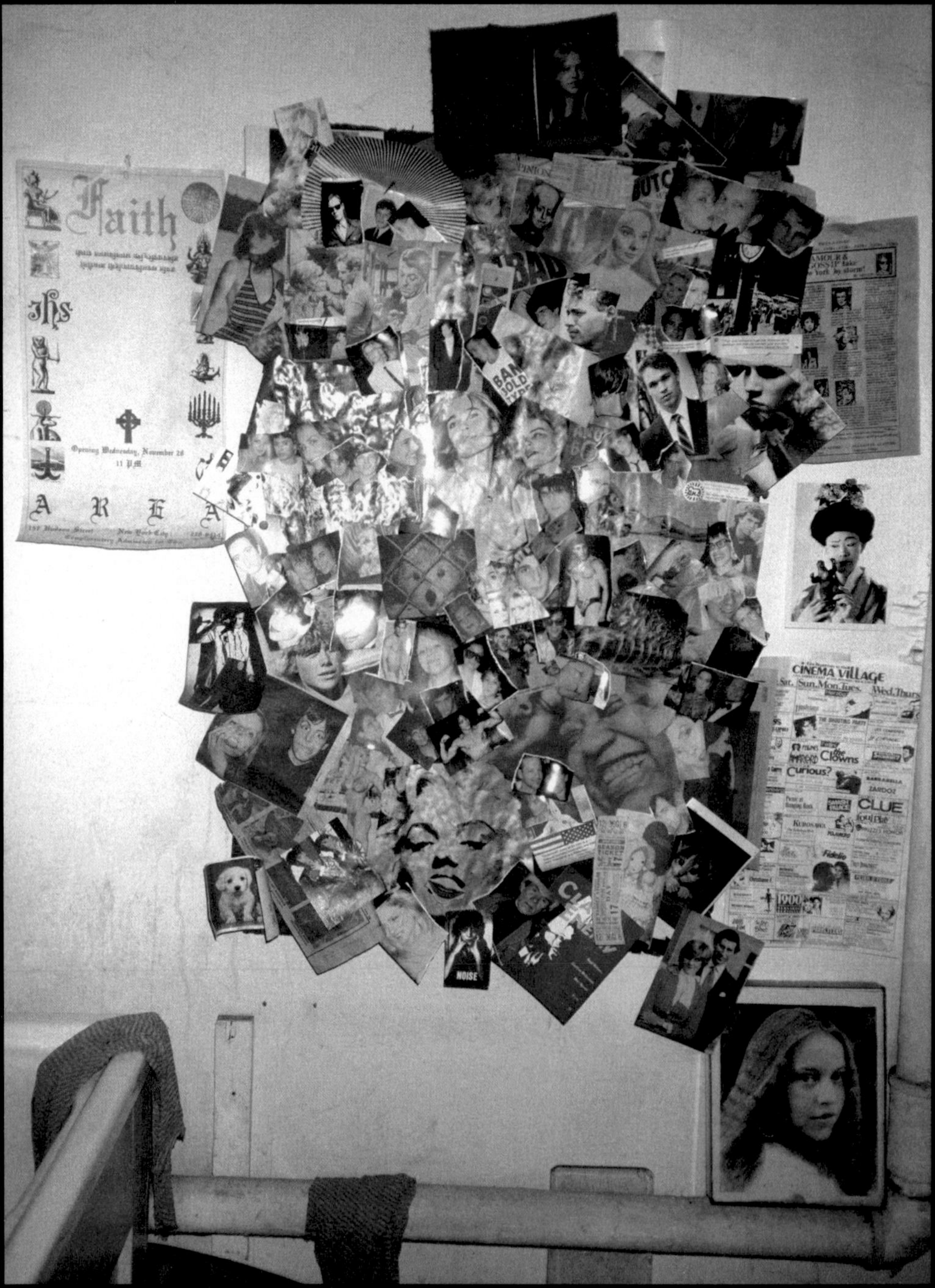

PATRICK'S PHOTO COLLAGE ON THE KITCHEN WALL
OF HIS 5TH AVENUE APARTMENT.
MONDAY, OCTOBER 13, 1986

Some rough-and-ready drag queens--like Hapi Phace and Tabboo!--were rising up the ranks, and this was way before cross-dressers had talk shows and cosmetics company contracts. These "gals" had a subversive edge that might never be recaptured in the Jerry Springer era, when cross-dressers became de riguer mass entertainment, court jesters for Nielsen families. Add to the club mix some wealthy Europeans, pop star drop-ins (Boy George, Duran Duran, and the rising Madonna), and a bevy of drug dealers, hangers on, wanna-bes, and crashers, and you've got the 86 crowd--all of whom were angling for a mention in Stephen Saban's Details magazine column and sometimes even in my own Village Voice one. Ironically, it was when they relaxed for a second and acted like themselves that they were at their most quotable.

Everyone was carrying on with no limit, the cartoony spectacle of those famous for being famous providing the central attraction of the pleasure dome. The more comfortably eye-catching the better, and the sight of Ms. Brill (a Jayne Mansfield-type who accessorized club major-domo Rudolf) or Dean Johnson (a 6'6" bald rock 'n ranter in a dress who spit out a little ditty called "Fuck You!") could lift you out of the doldrums brought on by the hideously conventional real world. And if the lord king muse Warhol was there too, the event was truly validated, providing some kind of tacit encouragement to the artistic and marketing dreams of the yearning throngs.

Andy's death in 87 dealt the scene a major blow, leaving a hole that was never cosmetically filled. At the same time, the devastation of AIDS had made an increasing impact, though the club and society crowds generally just parties harder in order to avoid confronting it. When the gay community mobilized to demand action from President Reagan in response to the epidemic, a few clubbies donned combat boots and leaped into the fray, but most tightened their cha-cha heels and opted for a world where the biggest crisis was how to sneak your three guests into the VIP room.

By this point, the hype, the phonies, and the conflicting aspirations were wreaking havoc on any integrity that used to be at the heart of the party. The celebutante crowd had paved the way for club kids--wilder, more impressionable brats with even higher shock thresholds--and the uptown crowd would rather have died than ever have to meet them, so both camps existed in self-imposed exile. By then, the New York scene simply had to implode and reinvent itself, but fortunately the era of glitz and effusion had all been recorded by Patrick McMullan's loving, penetrating gaze.

Michael Musto
NYC, 2003

5
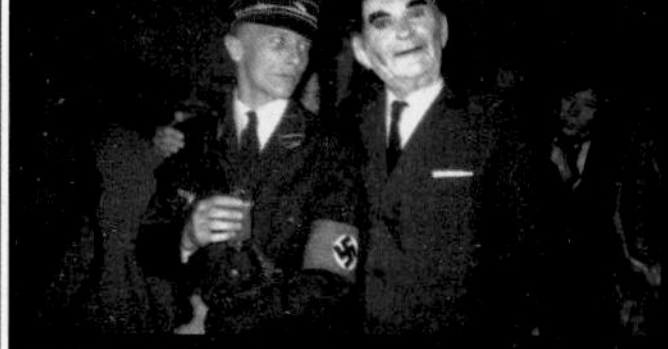

6
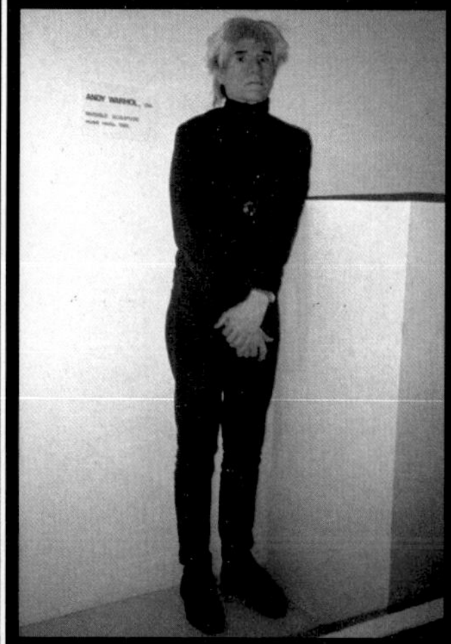

7
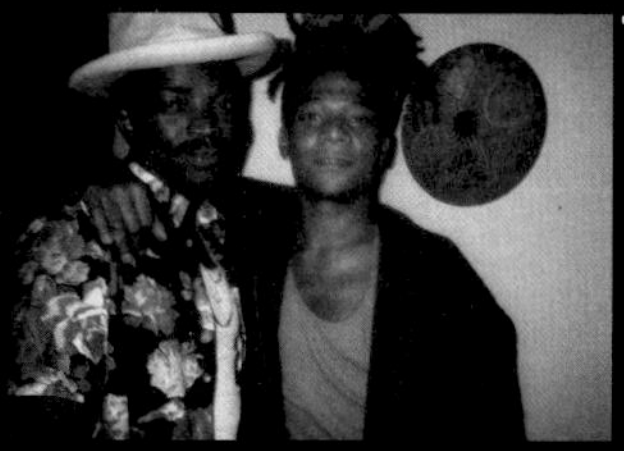

5: Nazi and Reagan costumes at the War Party at Area. October 1984

6: Andy Warhol as the "Invisible Sculpture" at Area. March 1985

7: Fred Brathwaite (Fab 5 Freddy) and Jean-Michel Basquiat at Anita Sarko's Voodoo Party at the Palladium. Friday, June 13, 1986

8
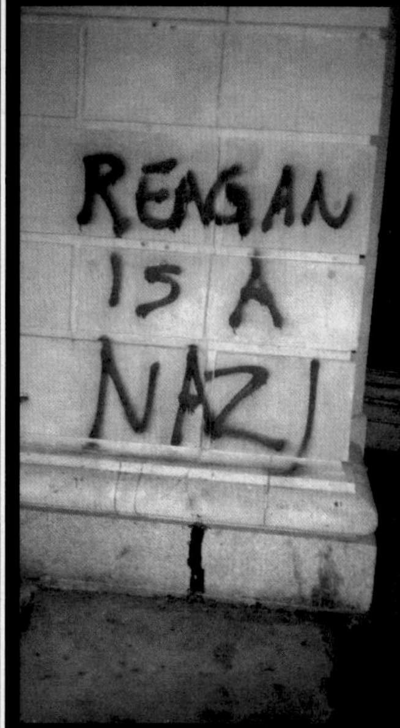

8: "Reagan is a Nazi" Graffiti on New Year's. January 1, 1986

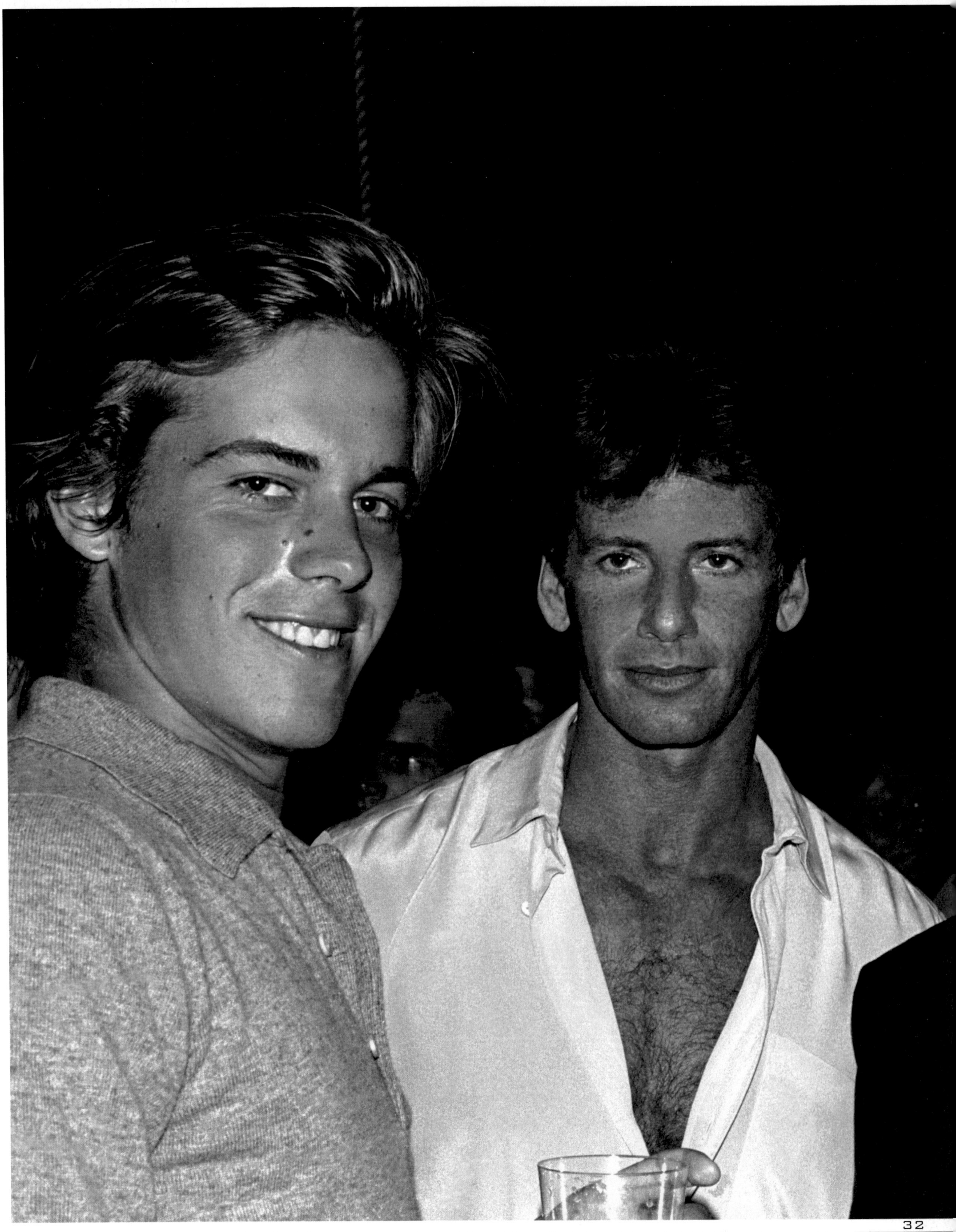

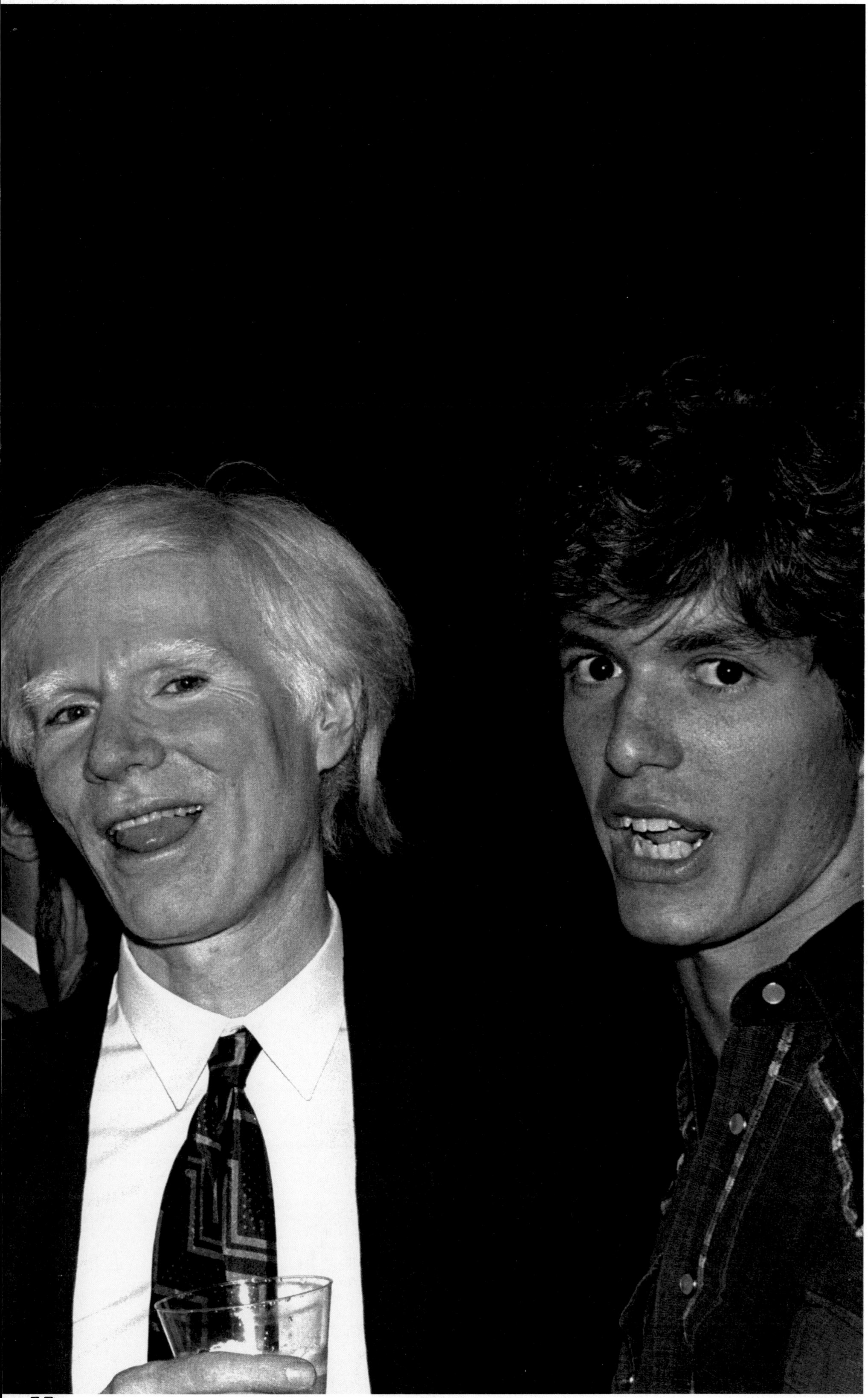

John Samuels (Stockwell), Calvin Klein, Andy Warhol, and Tom Styron at the Calvin Klein Party for Elton John on the Peking Boat at the South Street Seaport. September 13, 1980

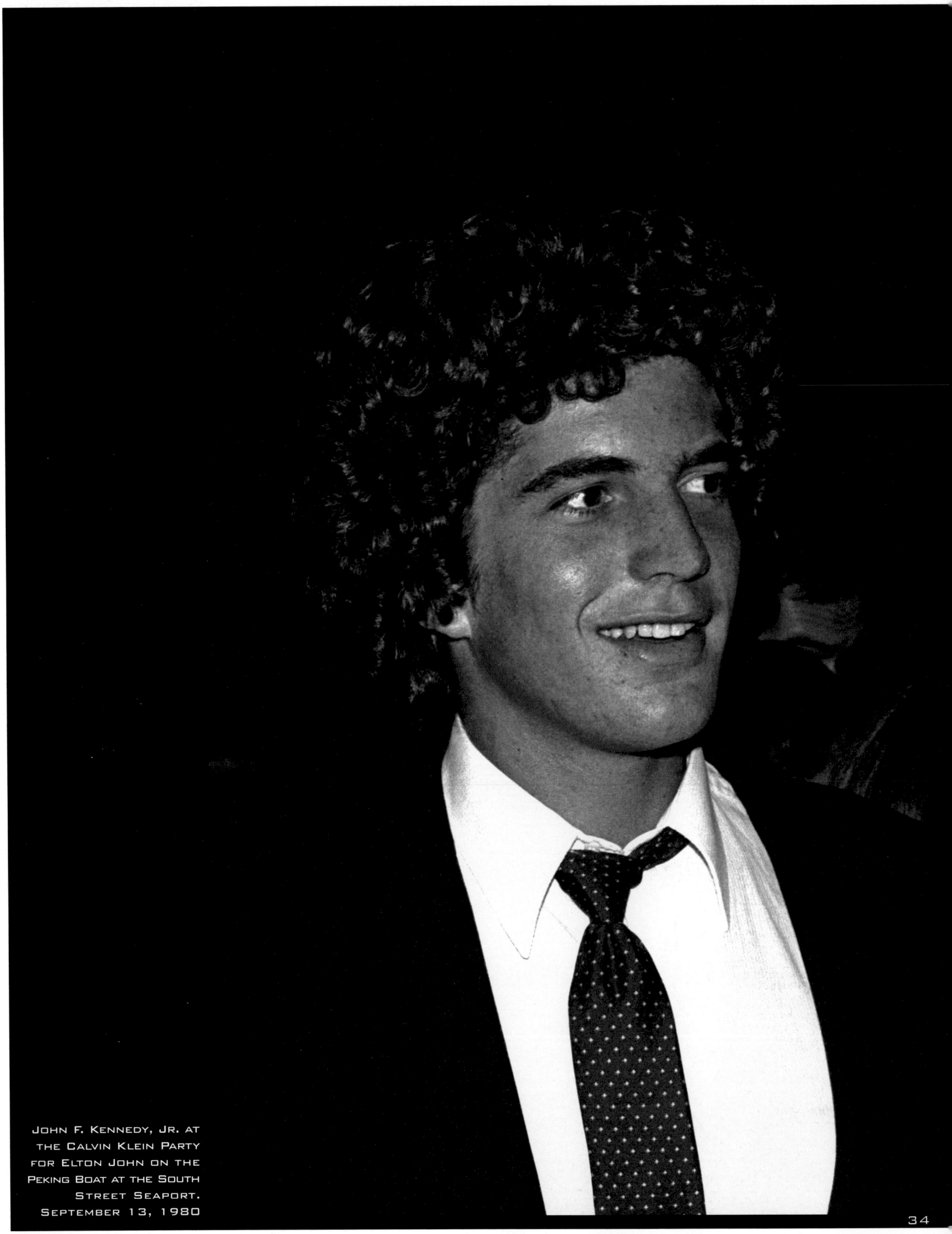

John F. Kennedy, Jr. at the Calvin Klein Party for Elton John on the Peking Boat at the South Street Seaport. September 13, 1980

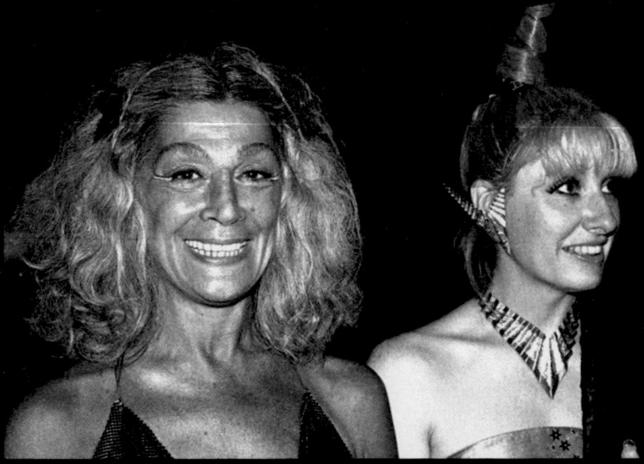
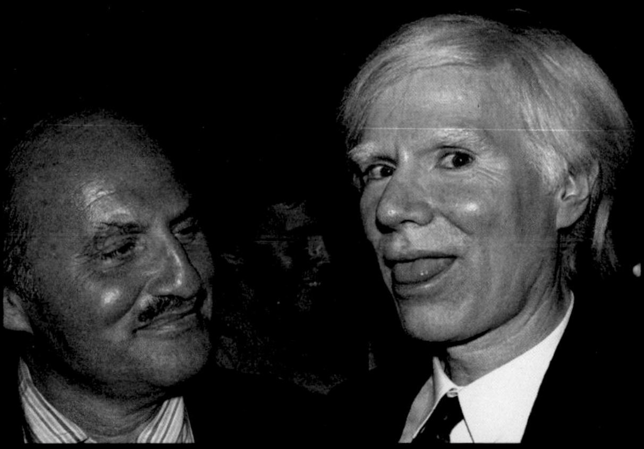
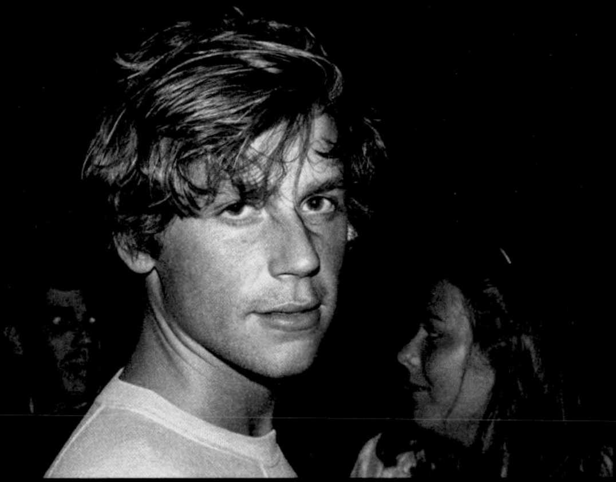
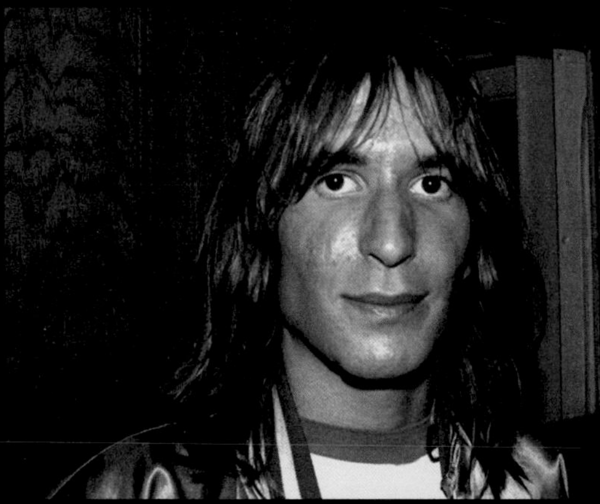
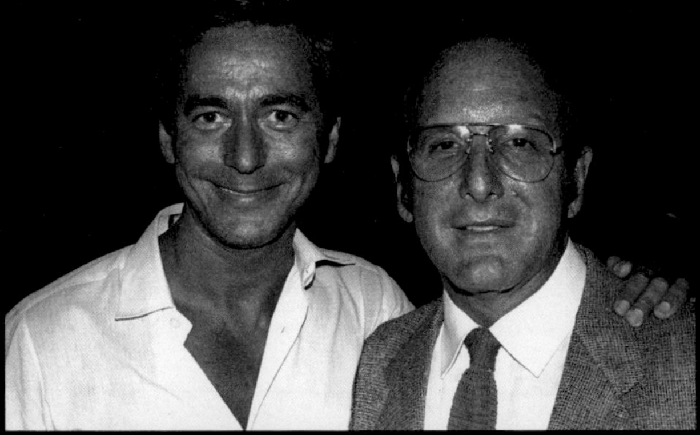
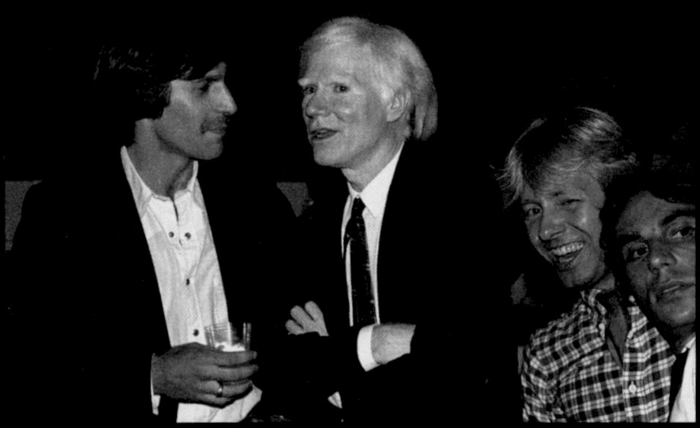

Top Left: Sylvia Miles and Zandra Rhodes
Top Right: Lester Persky and Andy Warhol
Middle Left: Kevin Haley
Middle Right: Larry Dvoskin
Bottom Left: Bob Feiden and Clive Davis
Bottom Right: Name Unknown, Andy Warhol, Rupert Smith, and Pierre
at the Calvin Klein Party for Elton John on the Peking Boat
at the South Street Seaport.
September 13, 1980

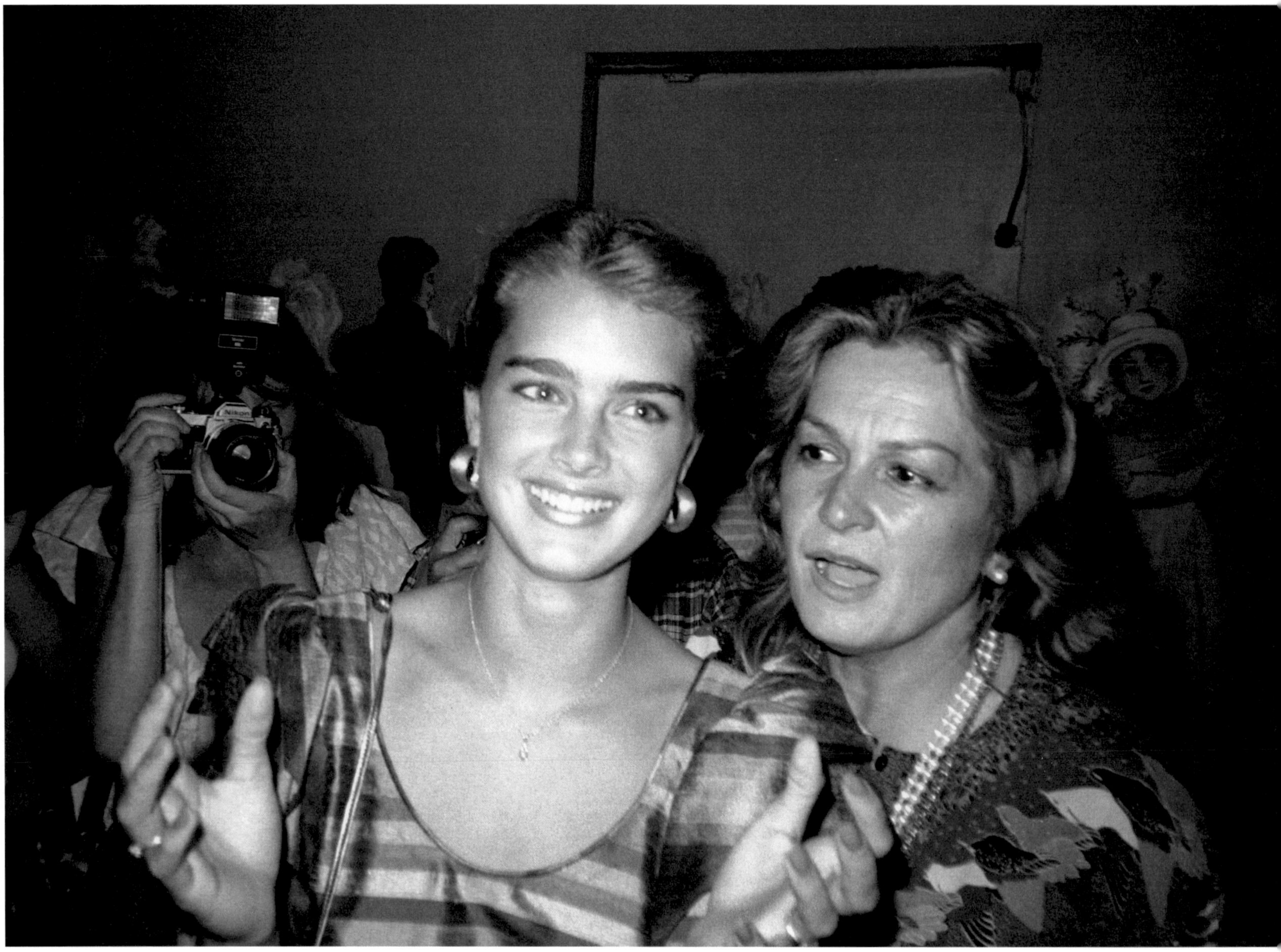

"IN THE 80s WE NEEDED MUCH LESS RETOUCHING." MARC BALET

BROOKE SHIELDS AND HER MOTHER, TERI SHIELDS
AT THE ENDLESS LOVE PARTY.
JULY 1981

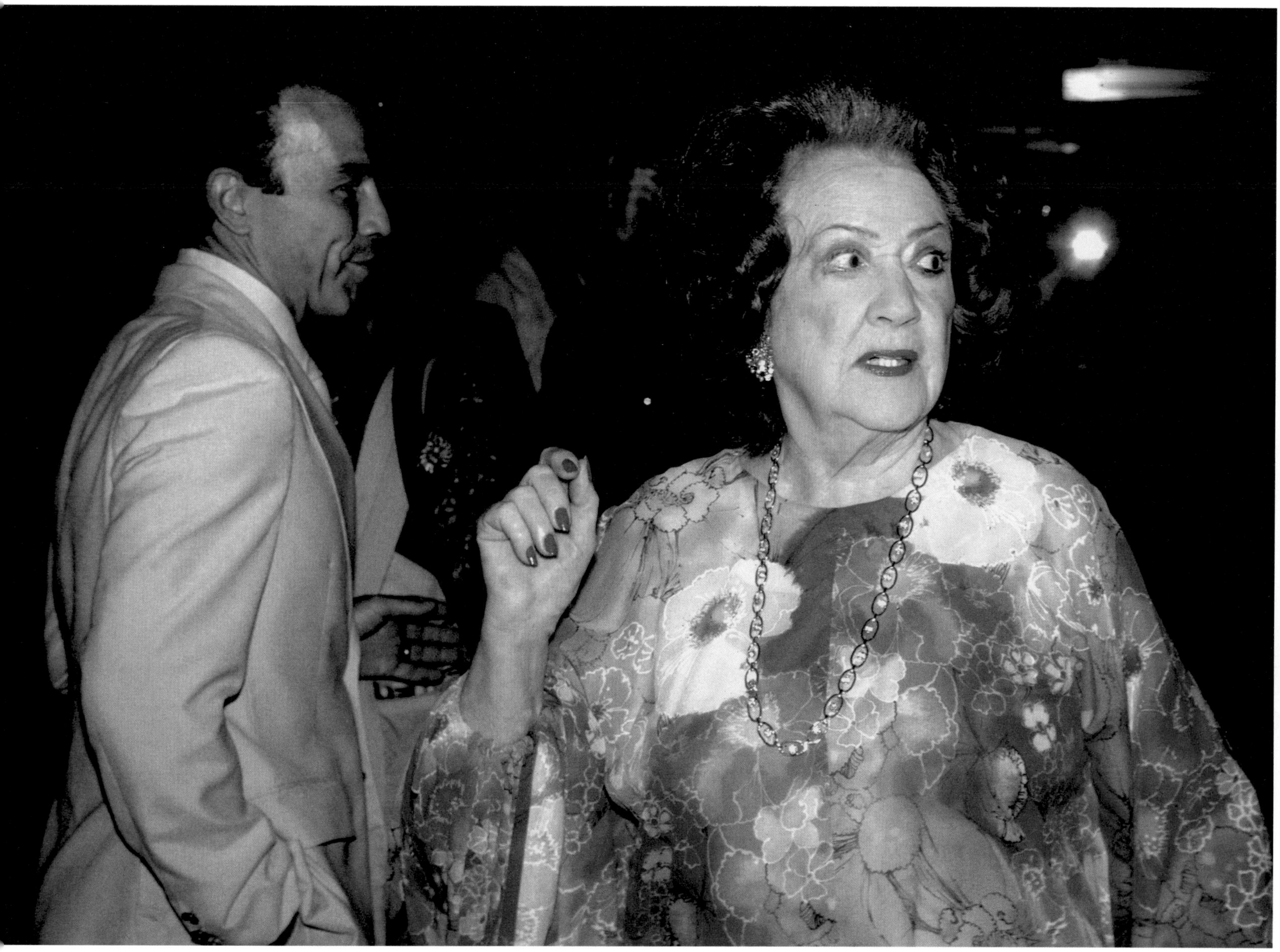

Ethel Merman
at the Endless Love party.
July 1981

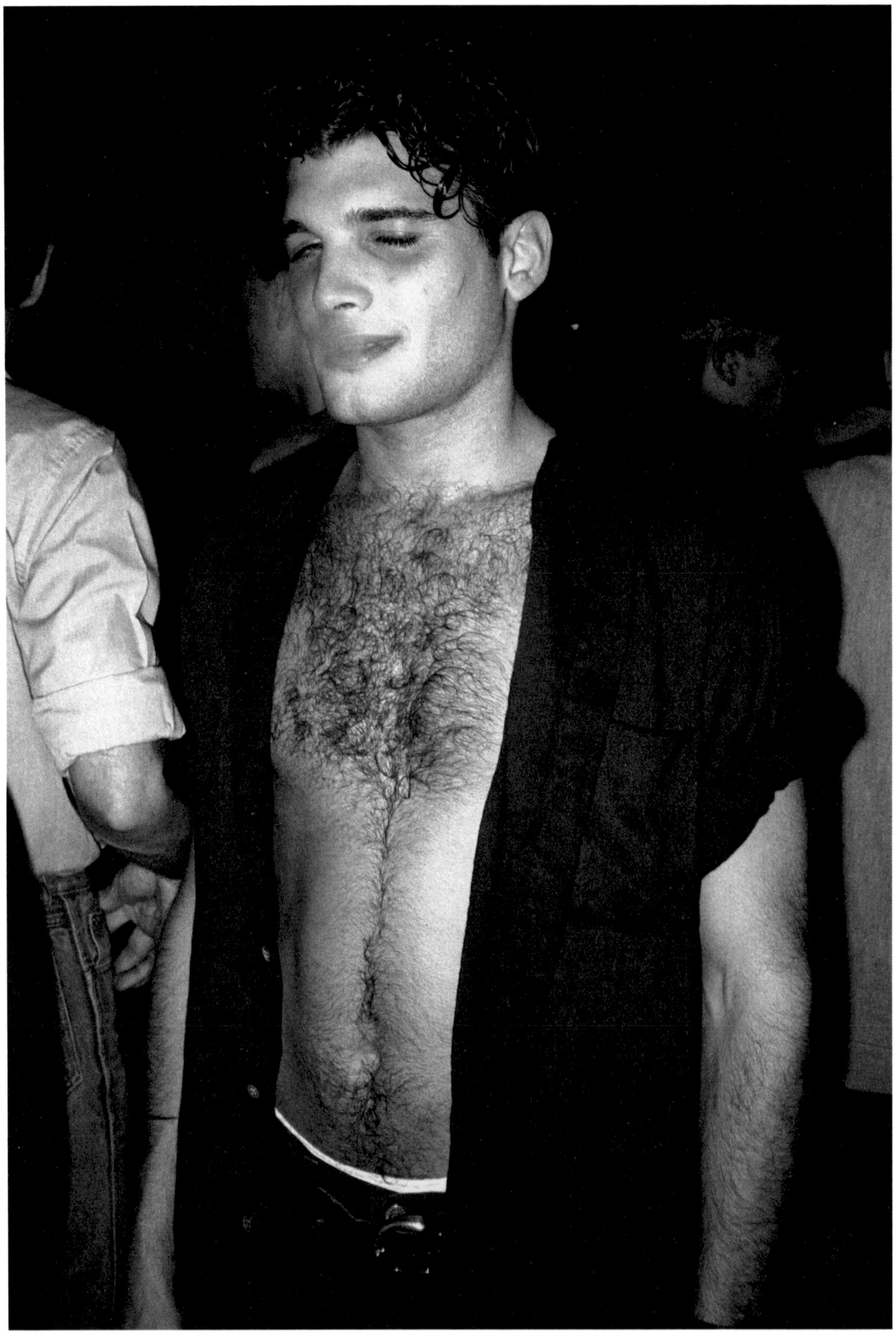

"I was a baby as a bus boy living the glam life, the parties and the decorations at Studio 54 were like make believe voyages into another consciousness.... I can't even remember most of what I did or saw due to excessive mental stimulation."
Phillip Bloch

Phillip Bloch
at Studio 54.
1982

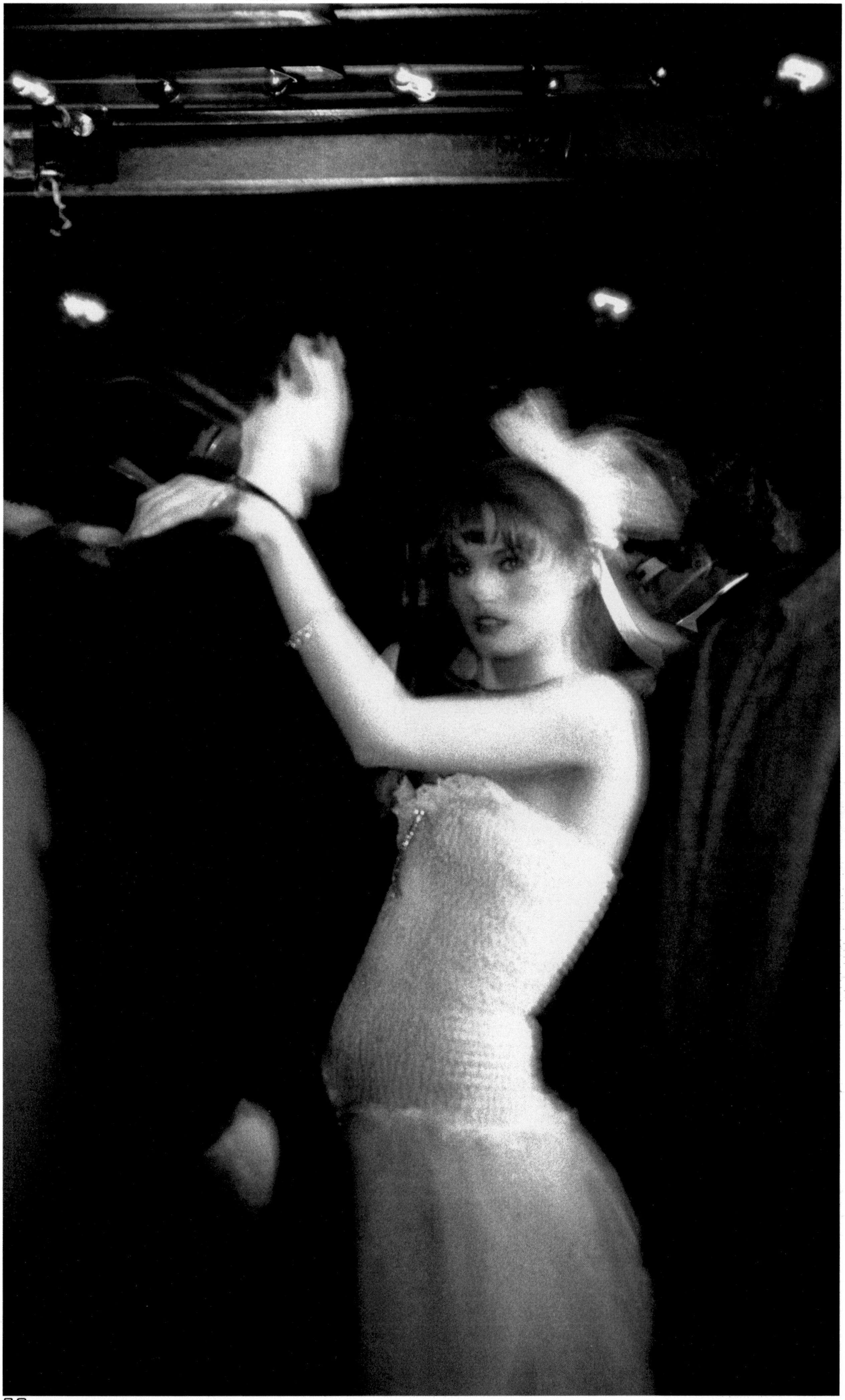

"The 80s were all about excess--excessive drugs, excessive sex, Studio 54, and Andy Warhol. If you were lucky, and Andy anointed you, you were a superstar and all doors were open to you.

What the 80s weren't about was yoga, Buddhism, and behaving yourself. I wish I could turn back the clock; trust me, I lived it to the hilt and sadly, it will never be that good again."
R. Couri Hay

Studio 54
Early 1980

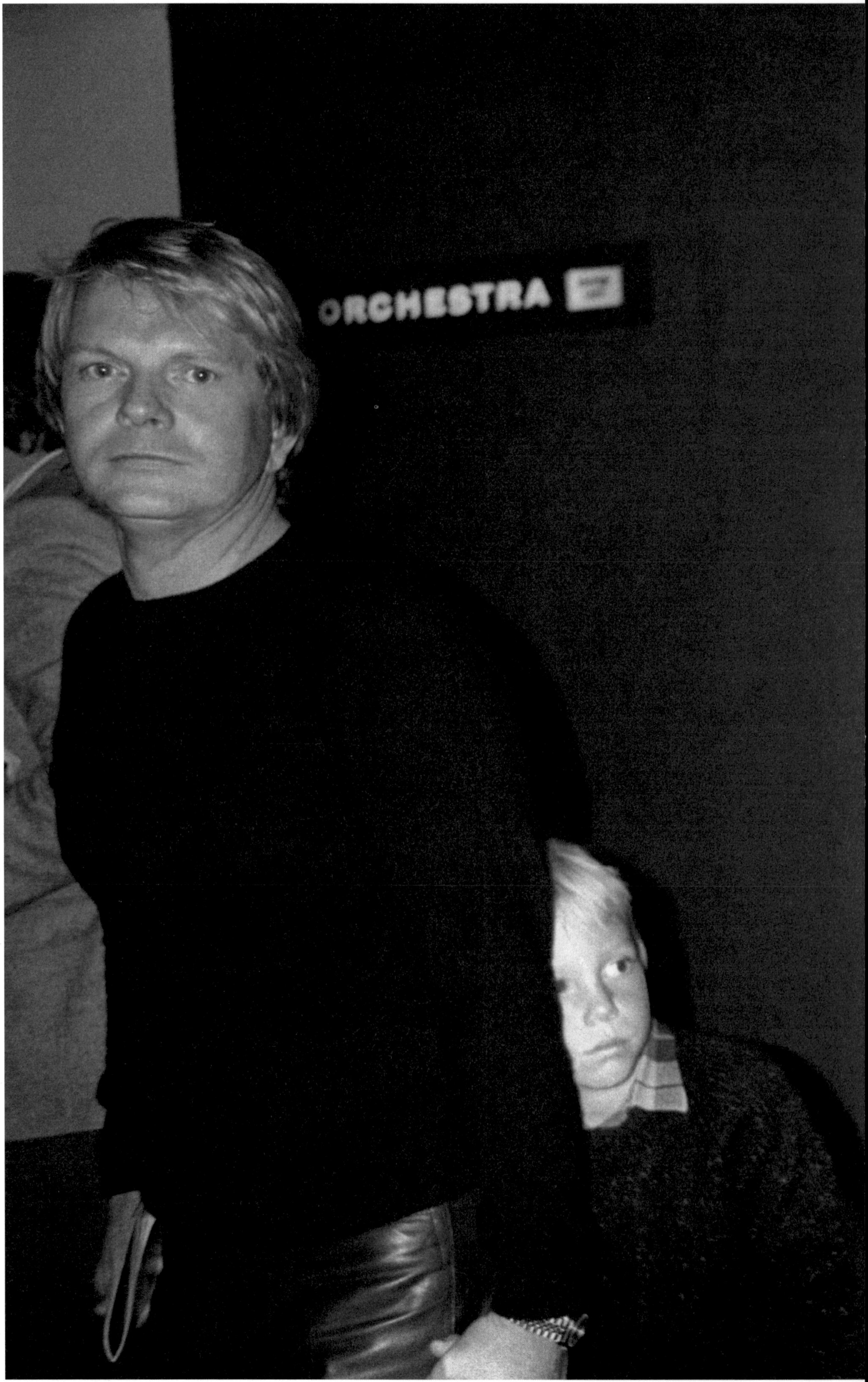

CHER WITH HER SON ELIJAH BLUE ALLMAN AT THE MINSKOFF THEATRE TO SEE THE "MARILYN" MUSICAL. DECEMBER 1983

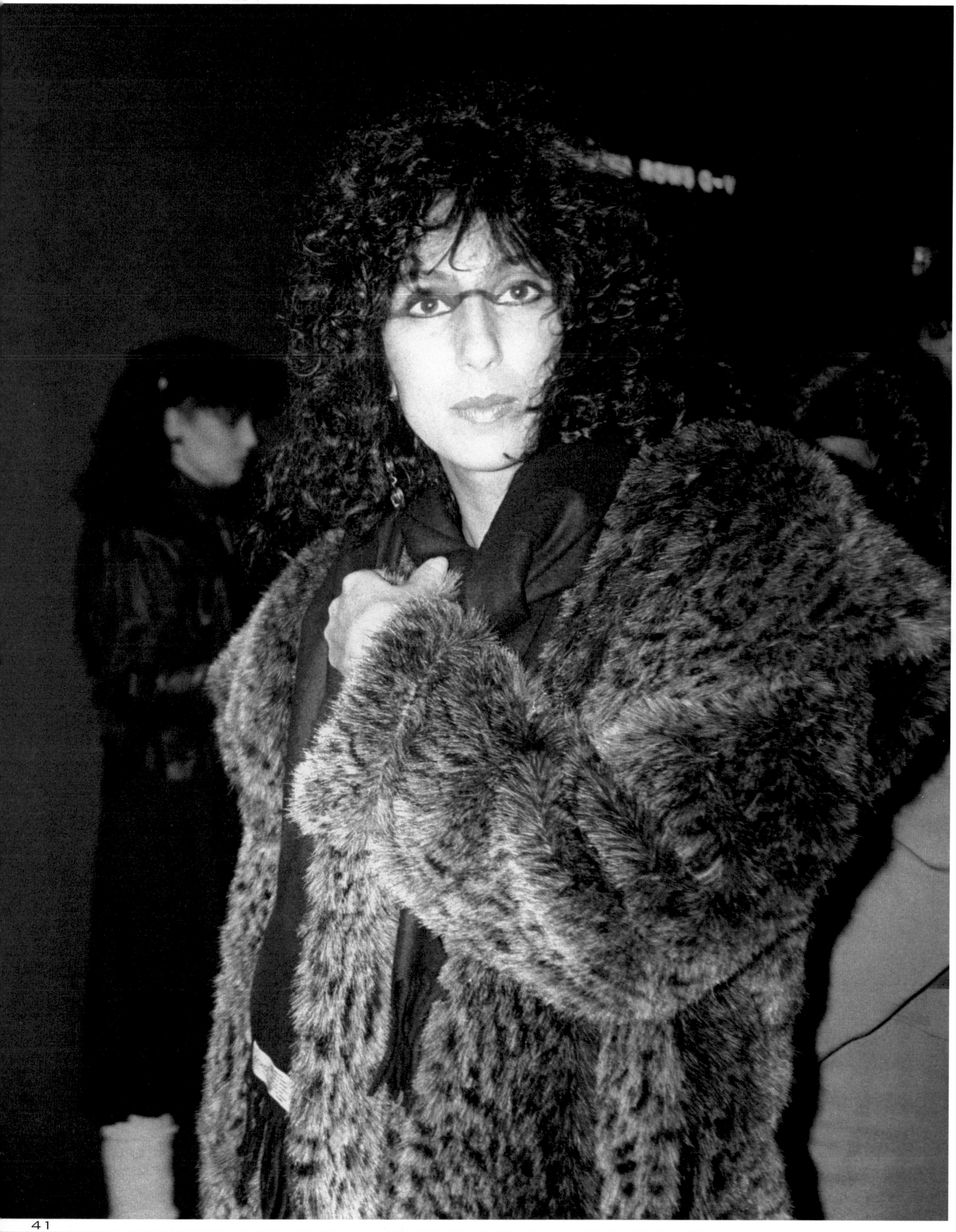

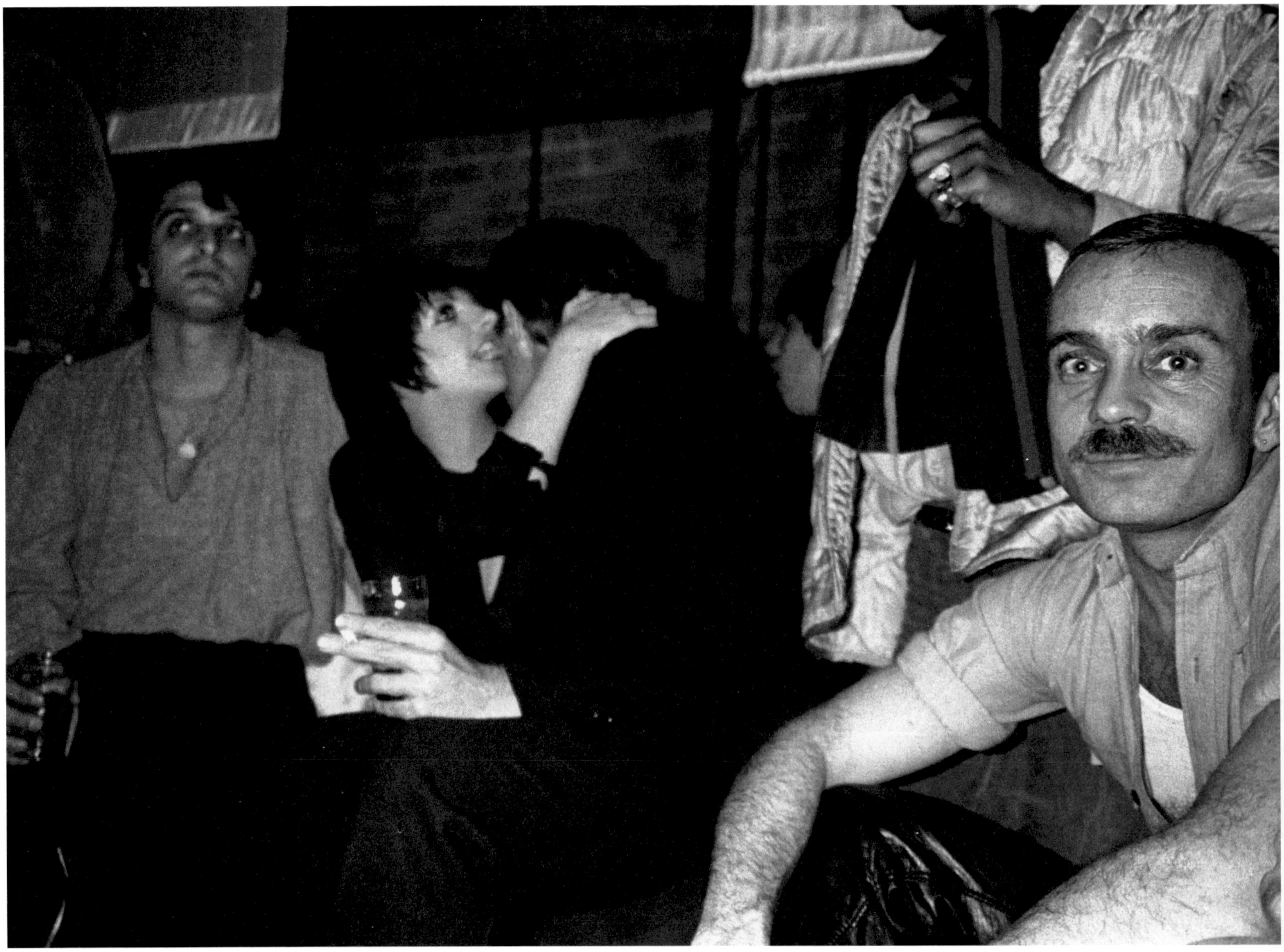

"By the early 80s many people in the party and club circuit in New York City were mimicking Andy Warhol's habit of taking a camera everywhere. It seemed everyone had a small auto focus camera. Patrick was different; he always seemed to be on a mission to document the denizens of New York nightlife, with his camera. Patrick had the charm, energy, enthusiasm, and the timing to have the famous and not so famous allow themselves to be engulfed in the white light of his flash.
Vincent Fremont

Mark Gero, Liza Minnelli, and Halston
at Studio 54.
1981

Carly Simon at Limelight.

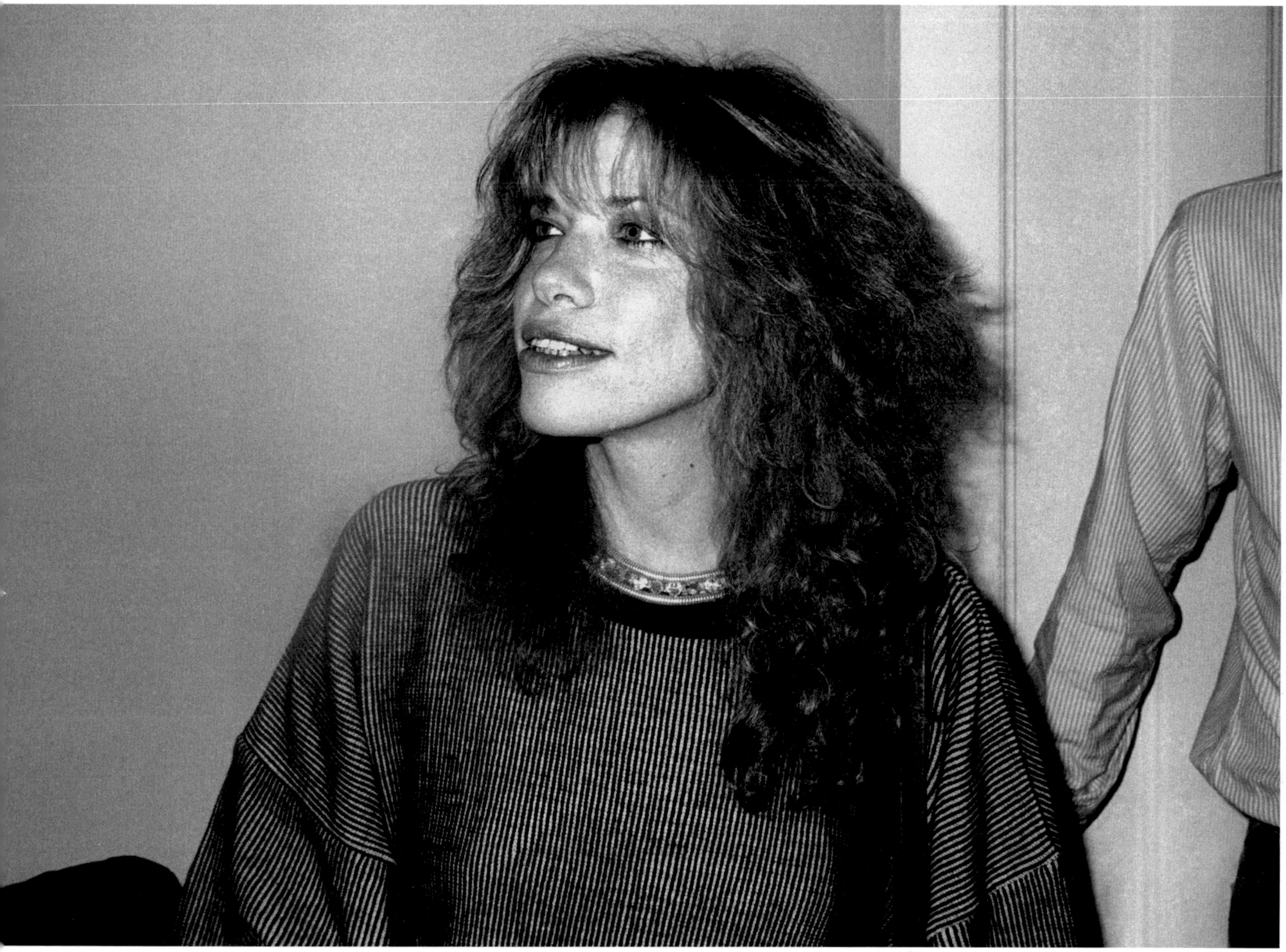

Carly Simon
at Limelight.
November 23, 1983

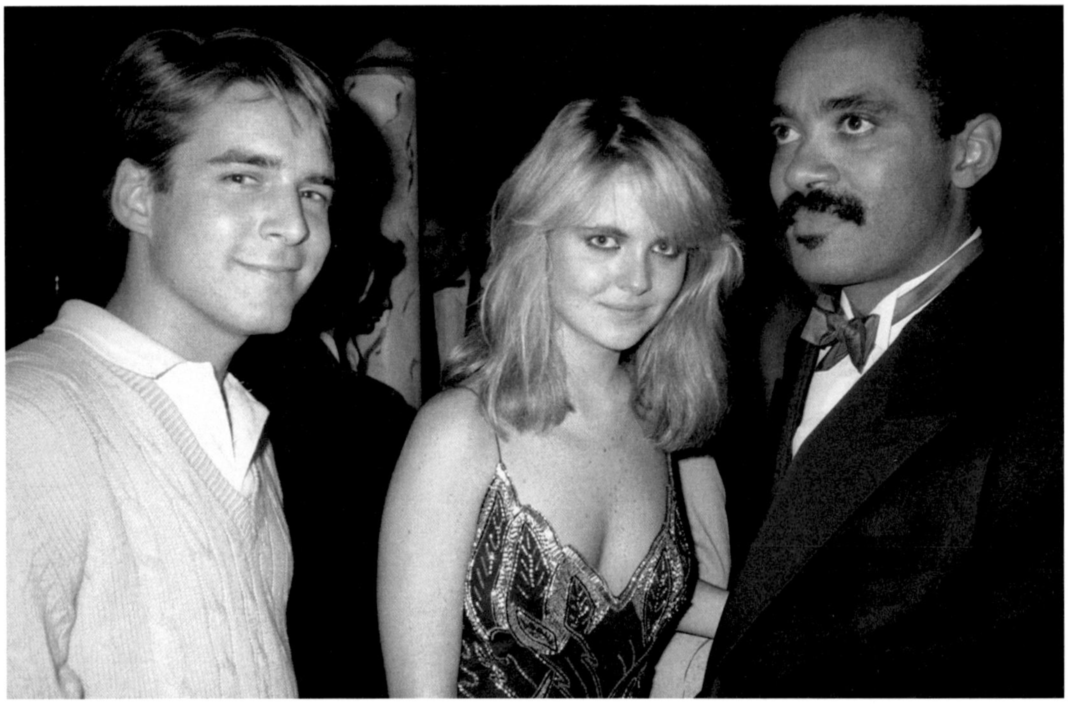

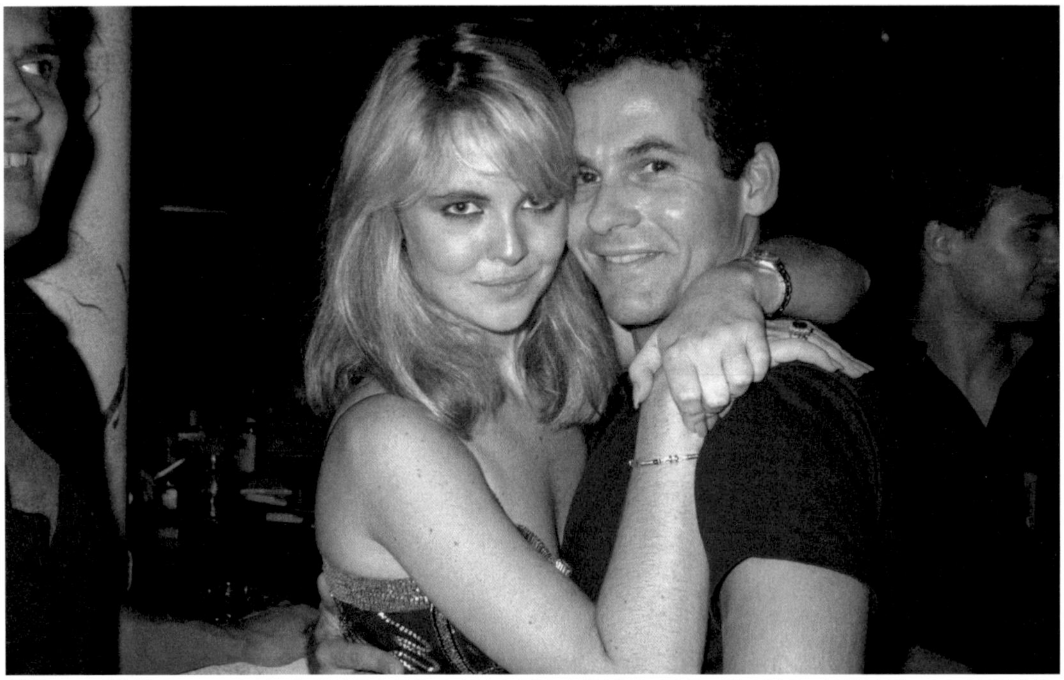

"The 80s... an extraordinary time to have been alive!"
Cornelia Guest

top: Rob Robinson, Cornelia Guest, and Fabrice
Bottom: Cornelia Guest and R. Couri Hay
at the 212 magazine party at Studio 54.
December 1983

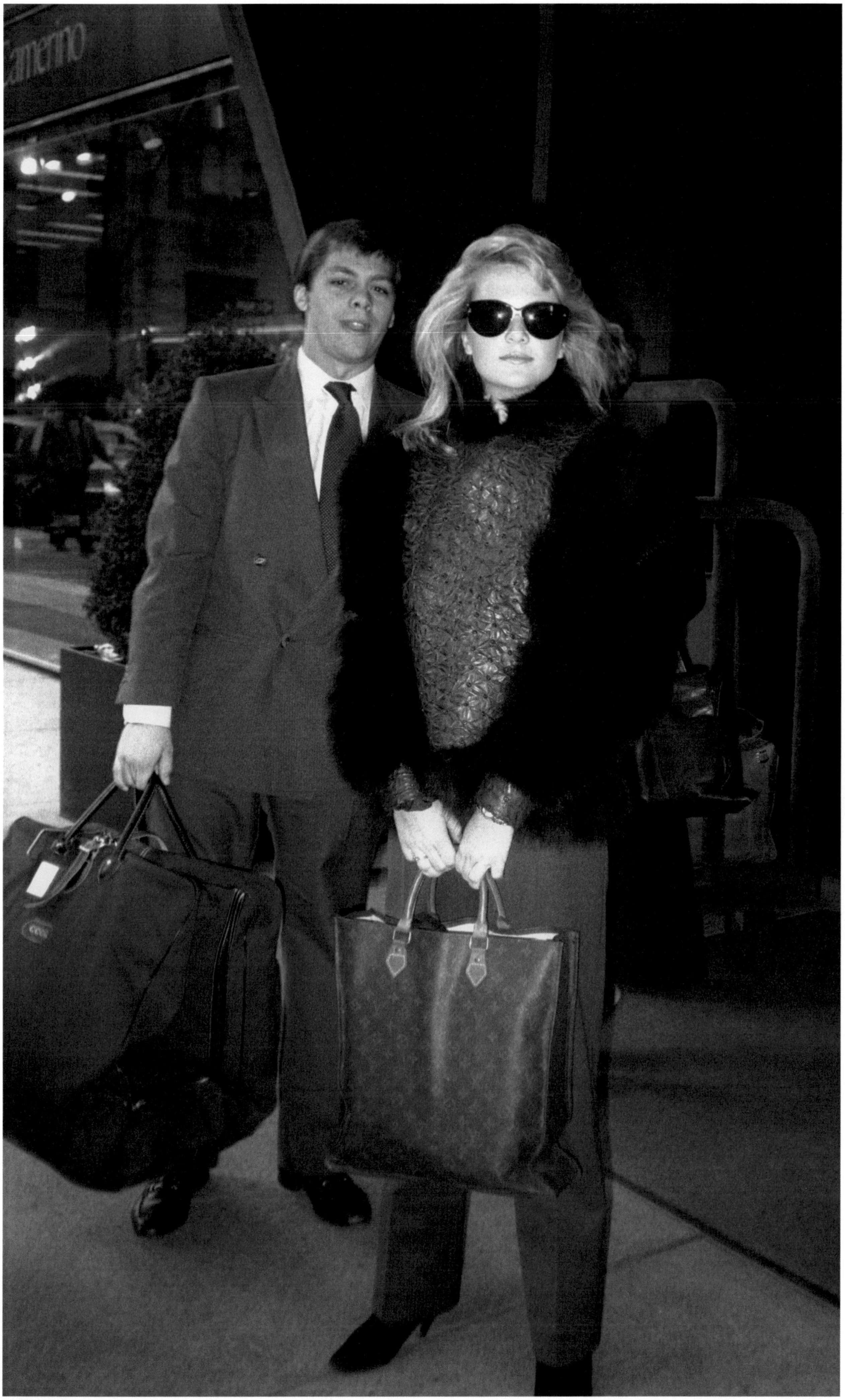

CORNELIA GUEST
LEAVING HER APARTMENT
IN THE OLYMPIC TOWERS.
NOVEMBER 18, 1983

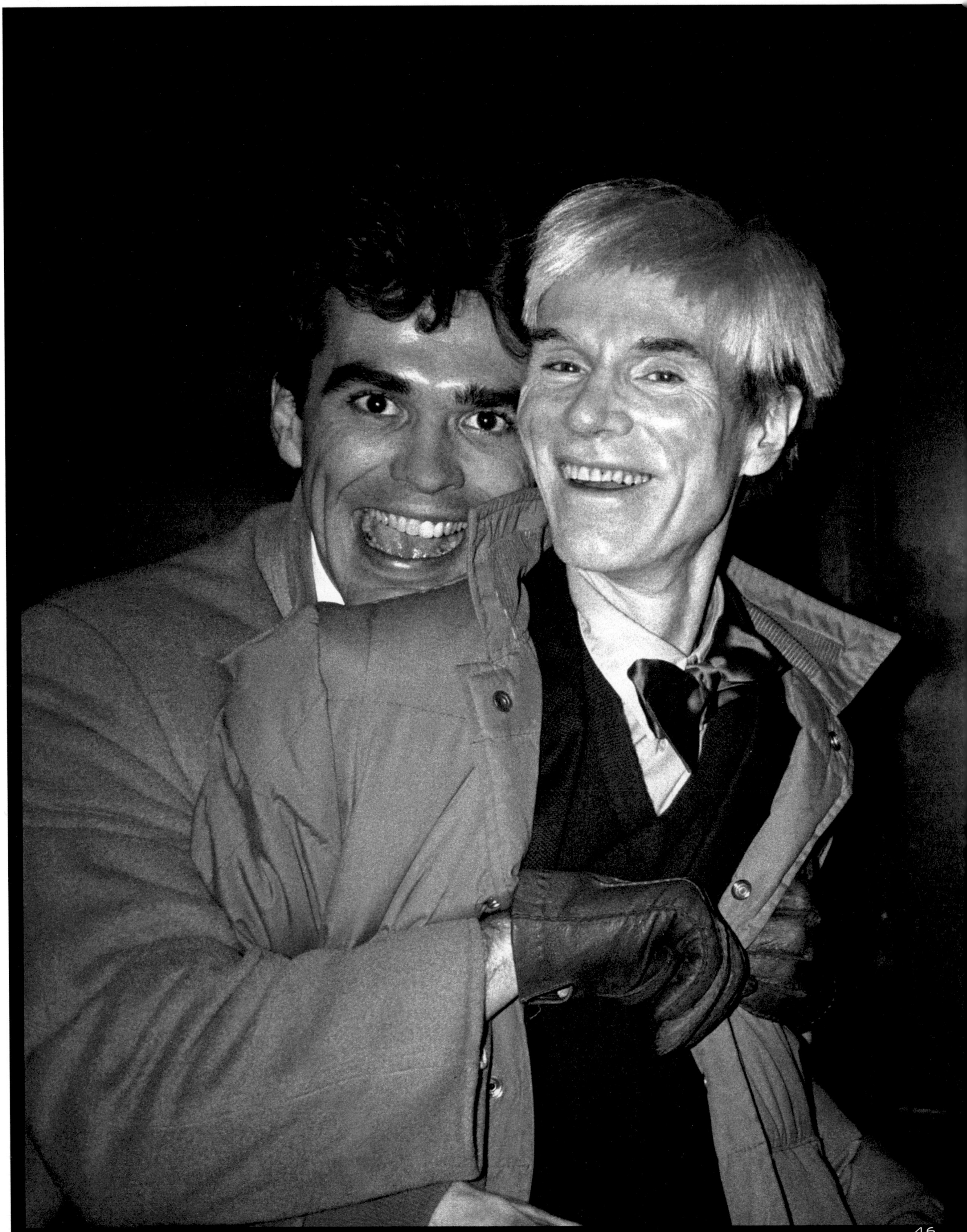

"The 80s were extraordinary times. There was an explosion of art and creativity, and an abundance of fun and freedom. They make the 60s feel like the 50s."
Tony Shafrazi

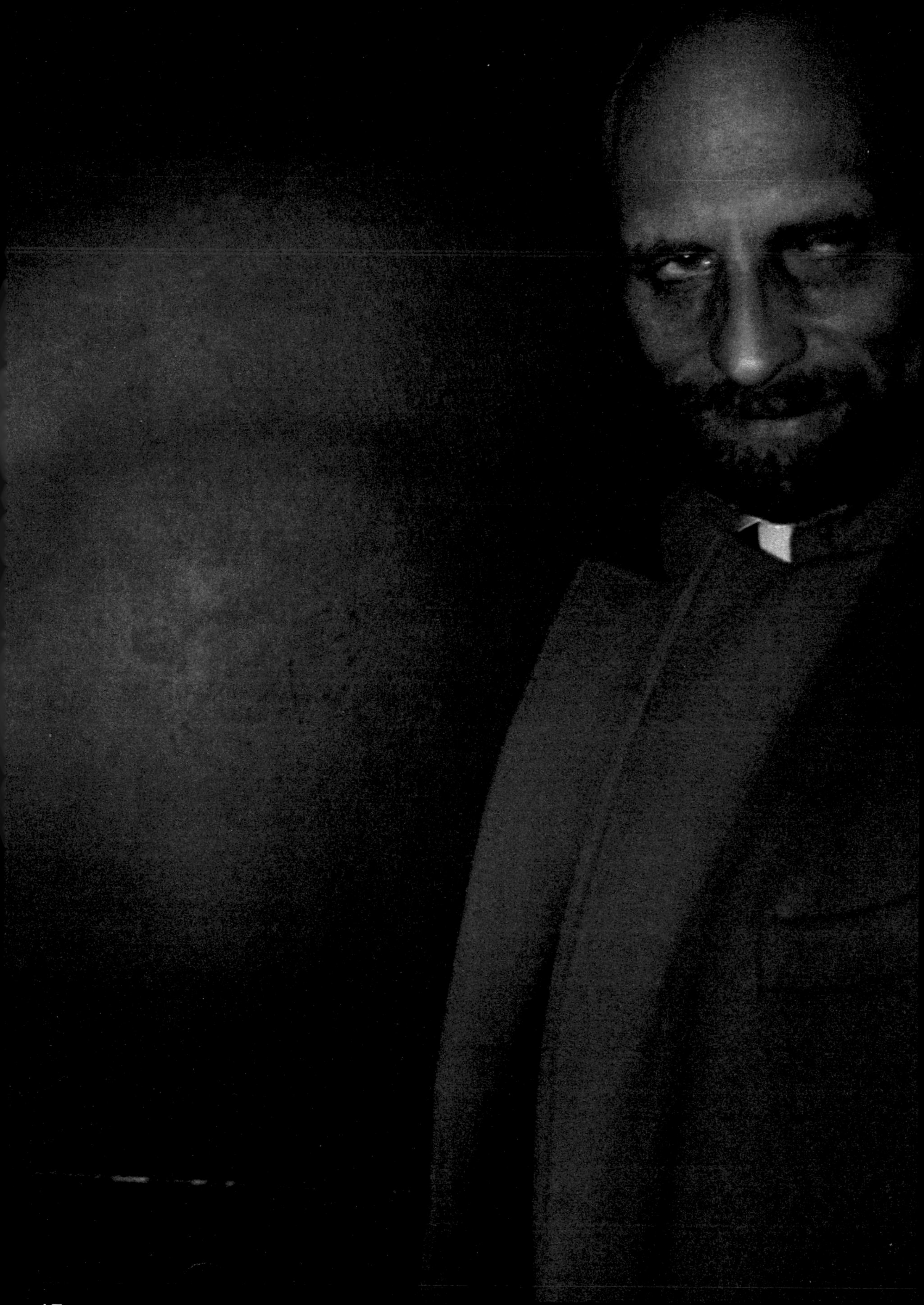

Name Unknown hugging Andy Warhol, and Michael Maslansky. February 1981

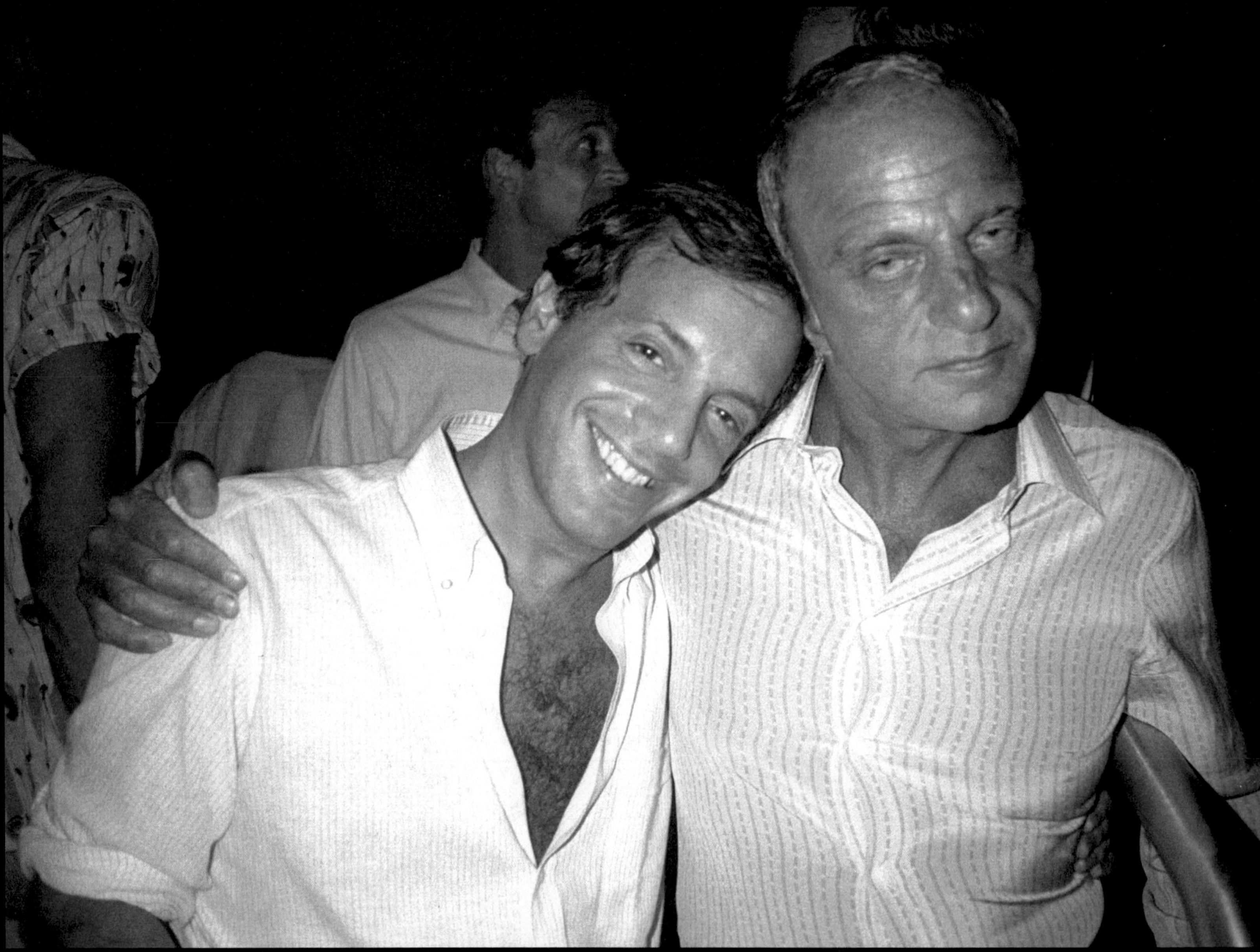

Steve Rubell and Roy Cohn
at Roxy.
Summer 1982

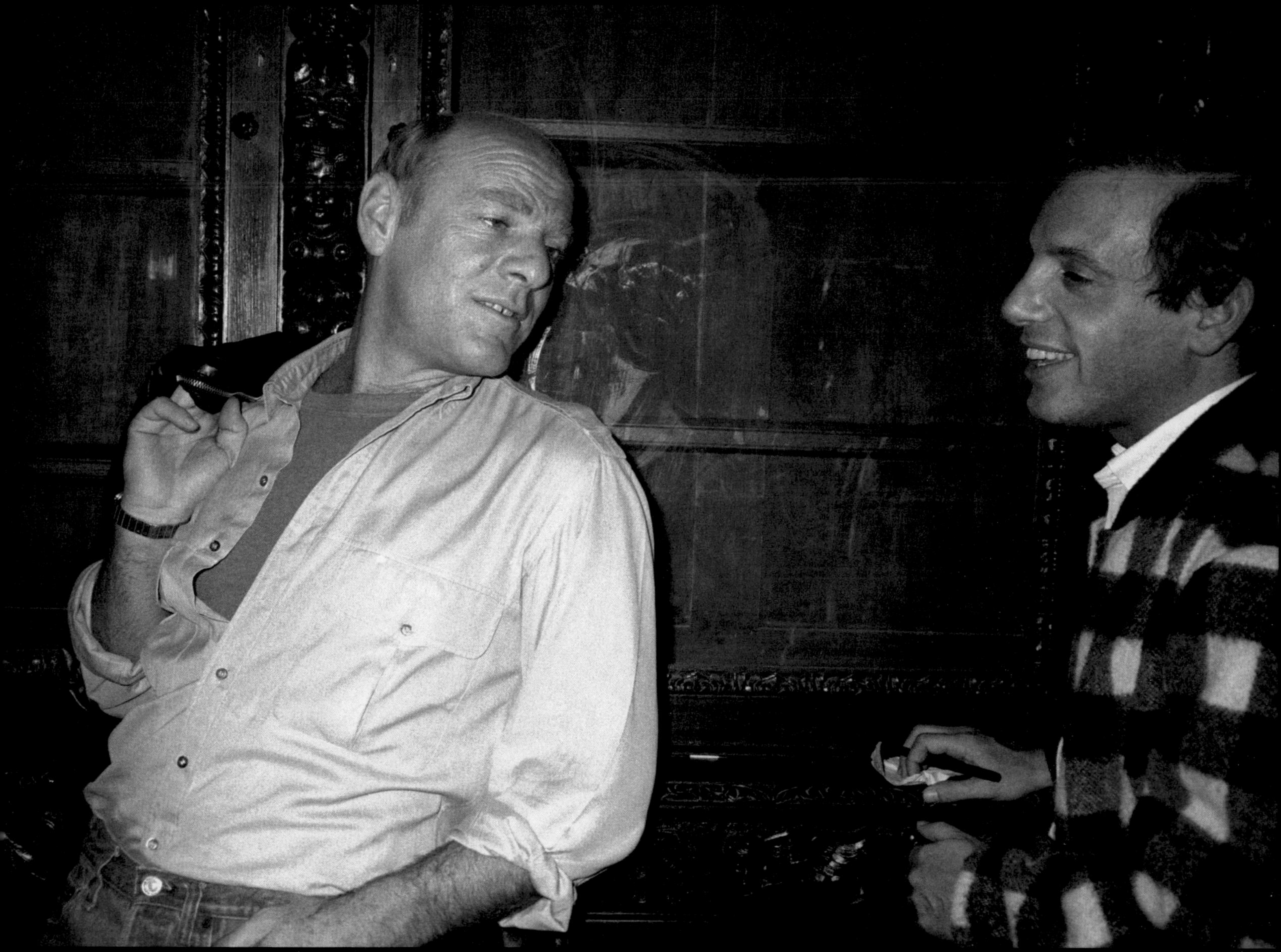

Barry Diller and Steve Rubell
at the Interview magazine party at Limelight.
November 9, 1983

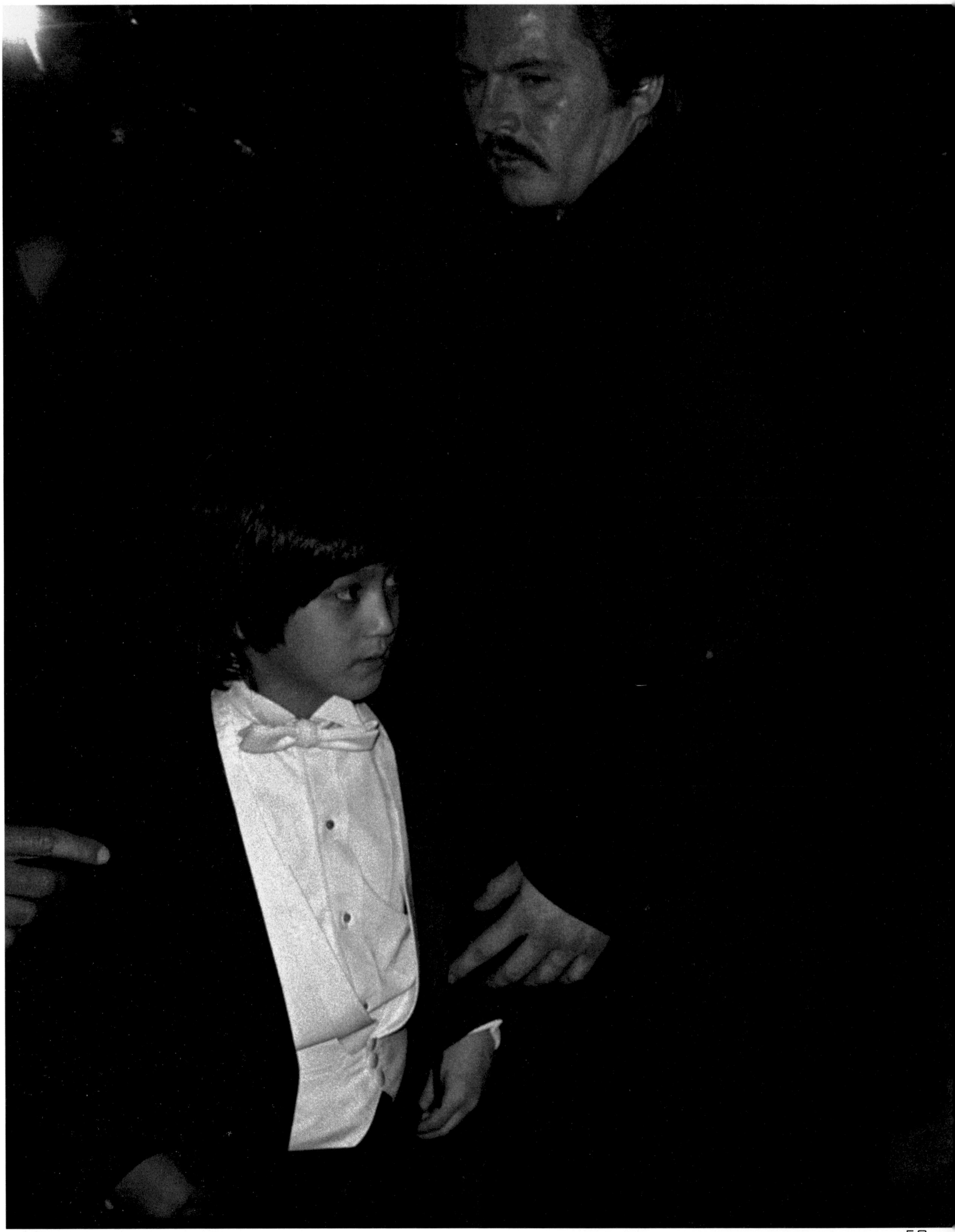

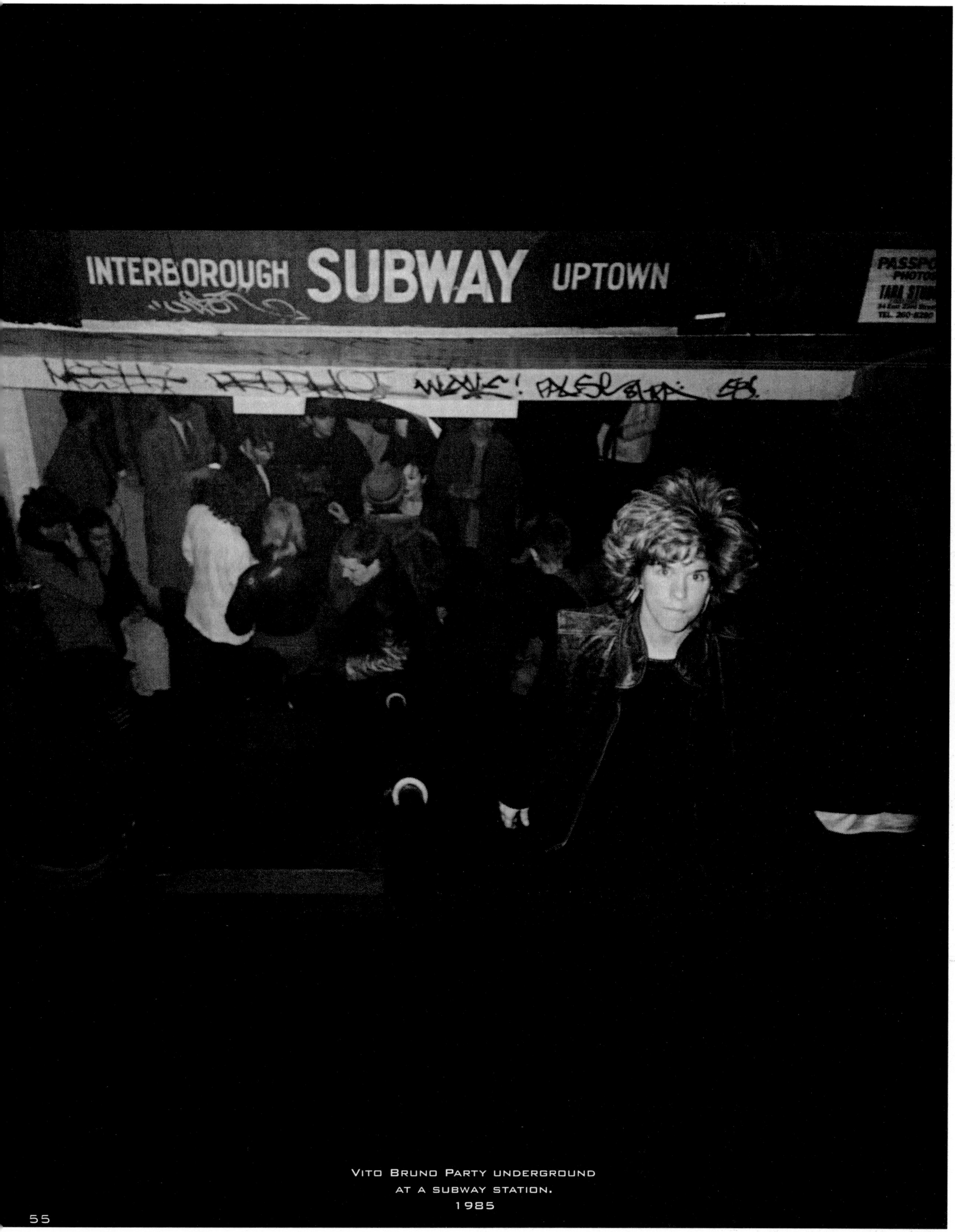

Vito Bruno Party underground
at a subway station.
1985

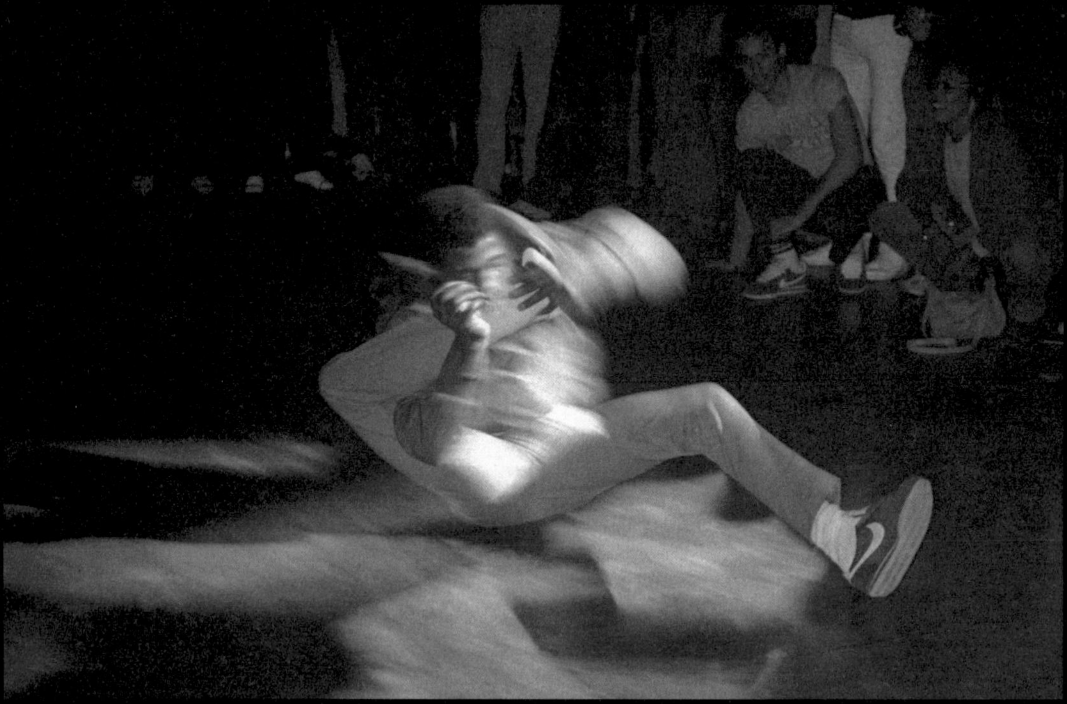

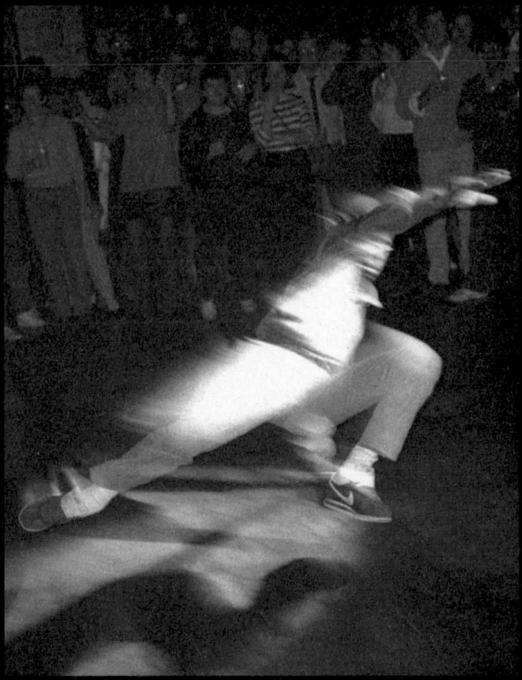

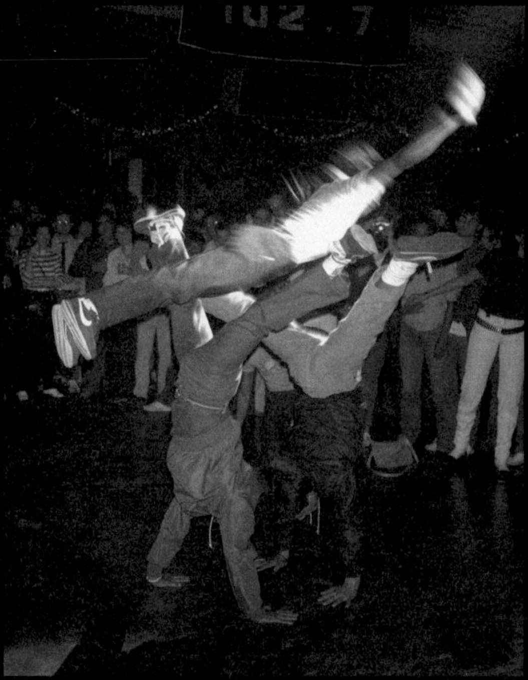

Breakdancers at The Ritz.
December 1983

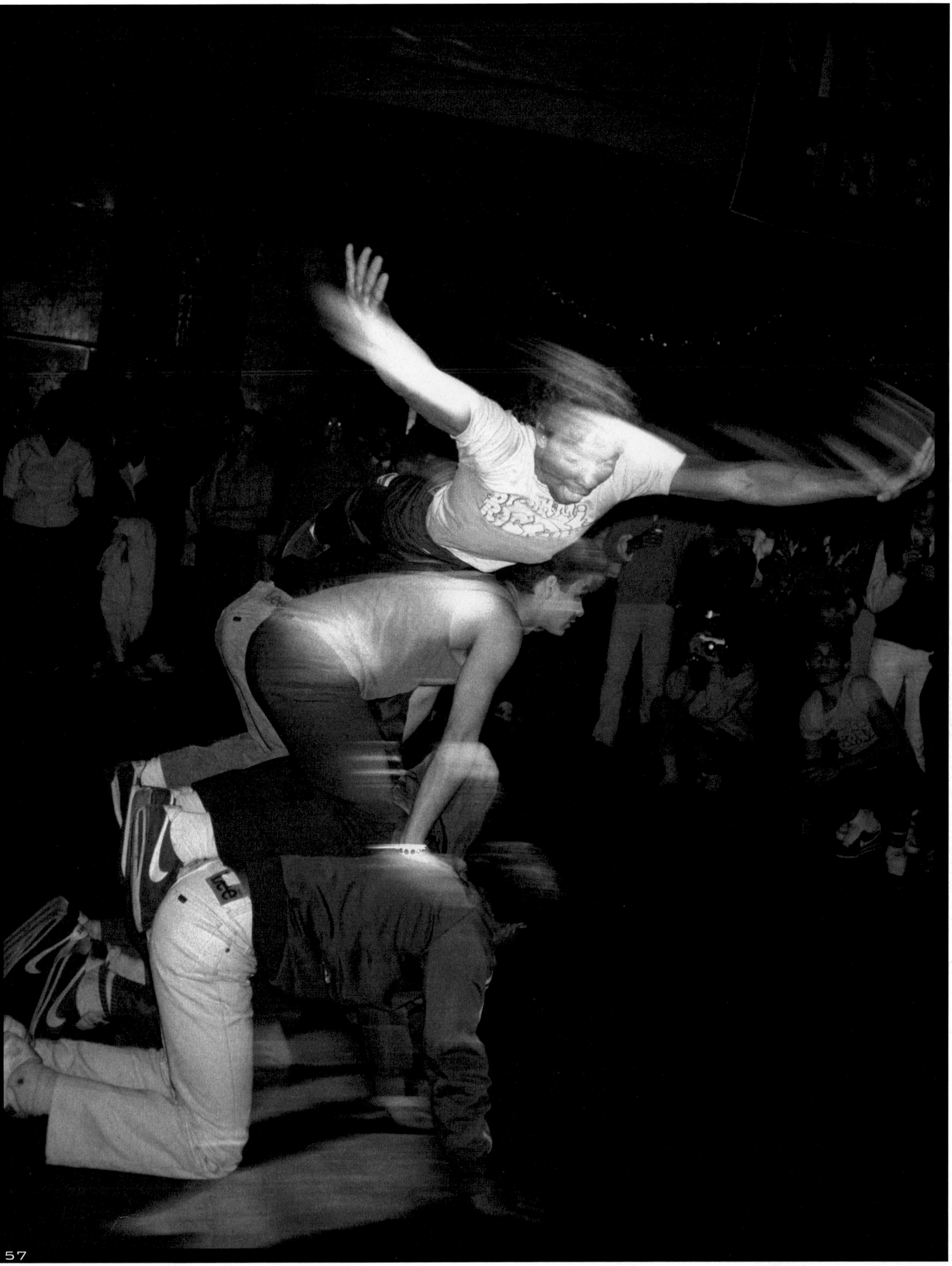

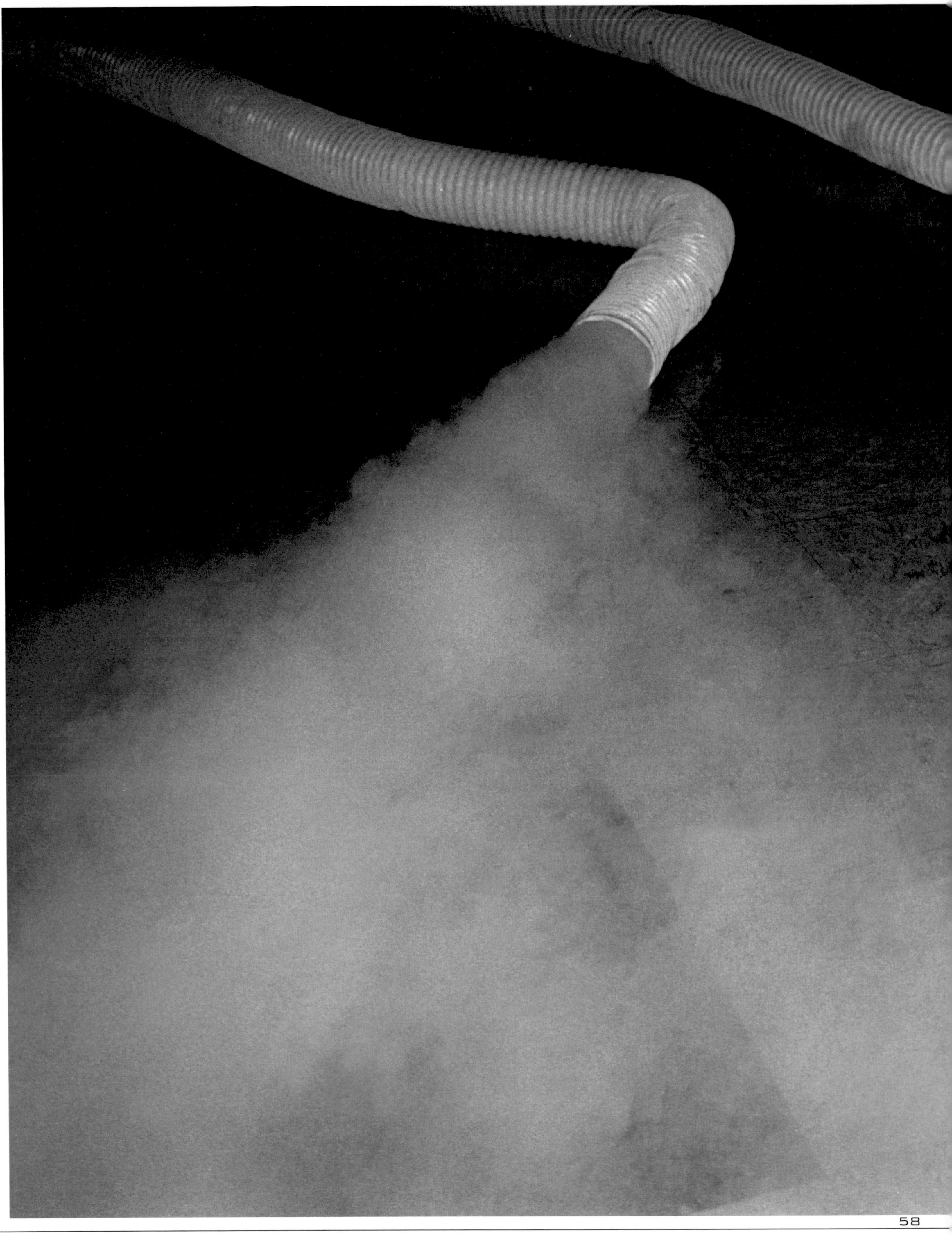

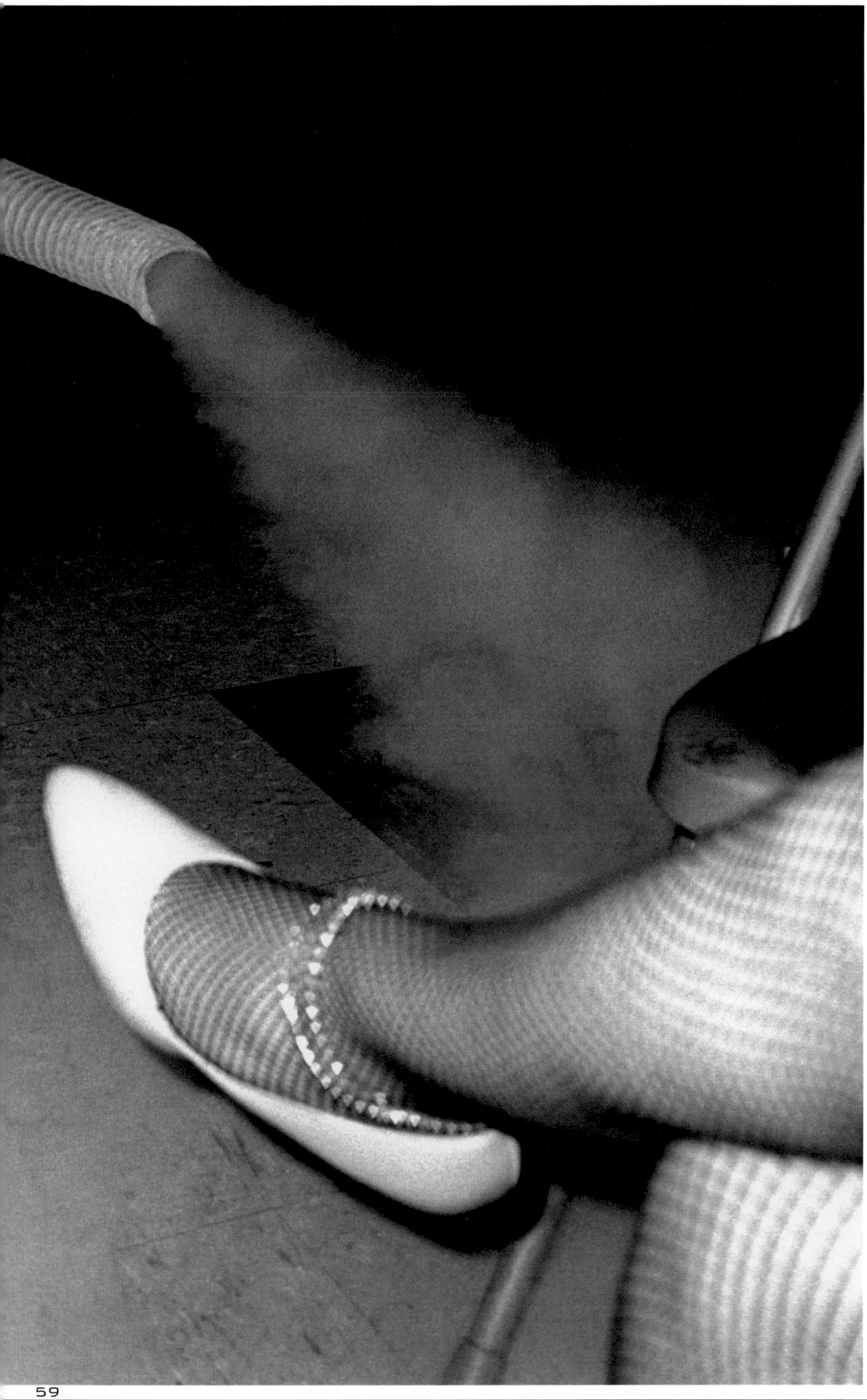

I remember the 80s... As a journalist who covered New York nightlife in depth and at great length from 1978 to 1990, I probably had a drink and a line in the VIP room of every club that ever was, from the Mudd Club, the granddad of postmodern nightlife, to the World, its funny uncle. During the whole of that time, that purple-and-black, fluffy-haired, dancing-with-myself decade, all anyone I met ever wanted to know, other than who had the blow, was the secret to getting past the doorman. I always told them to be yourself and accessorize. But the actual secret was to have the blow.
Stephen Saban

Smoke Tubes
at Danceteria.
December 1983

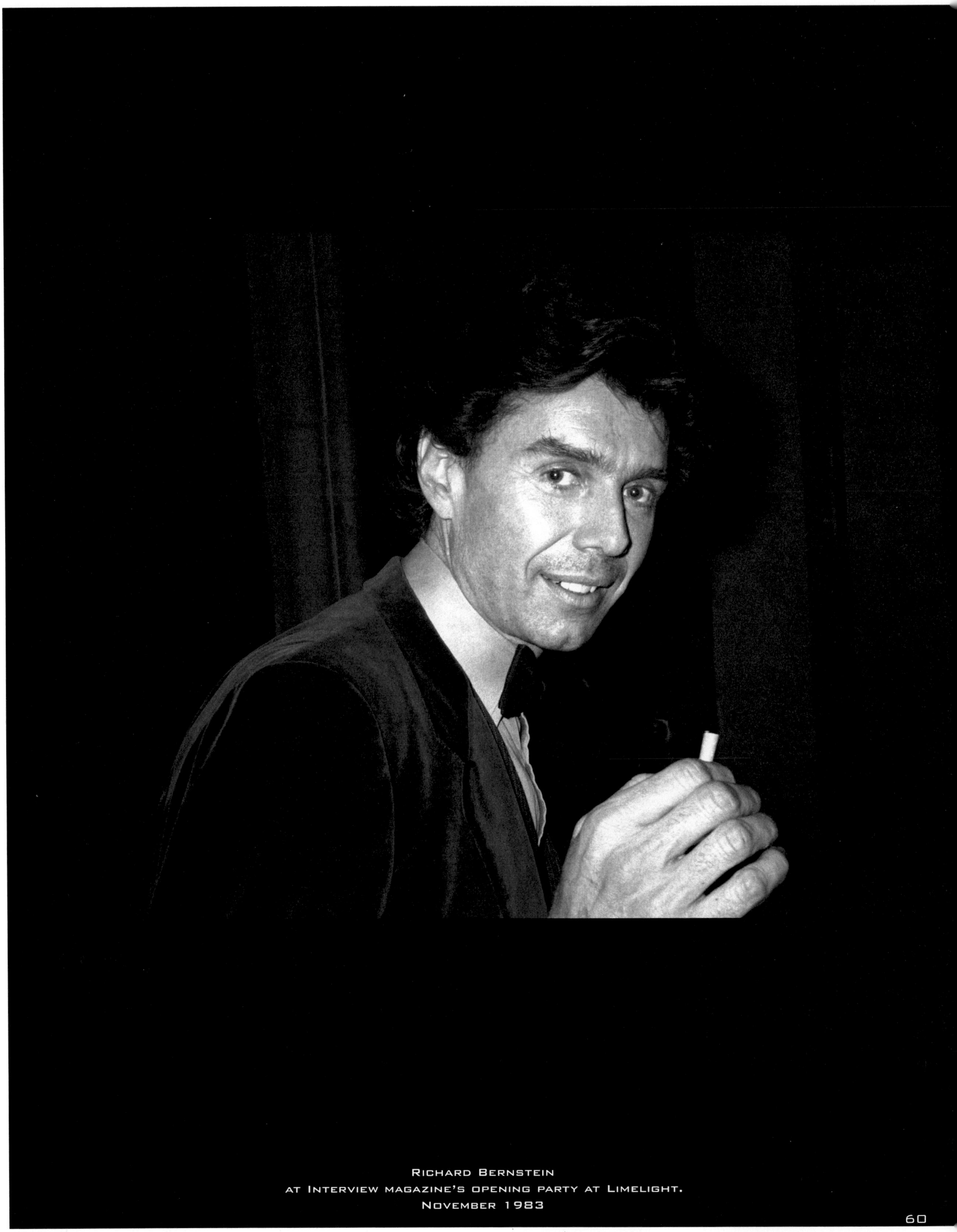

Richard Bernstein
at Interview magazine's opening party at Limelight.
November 1983

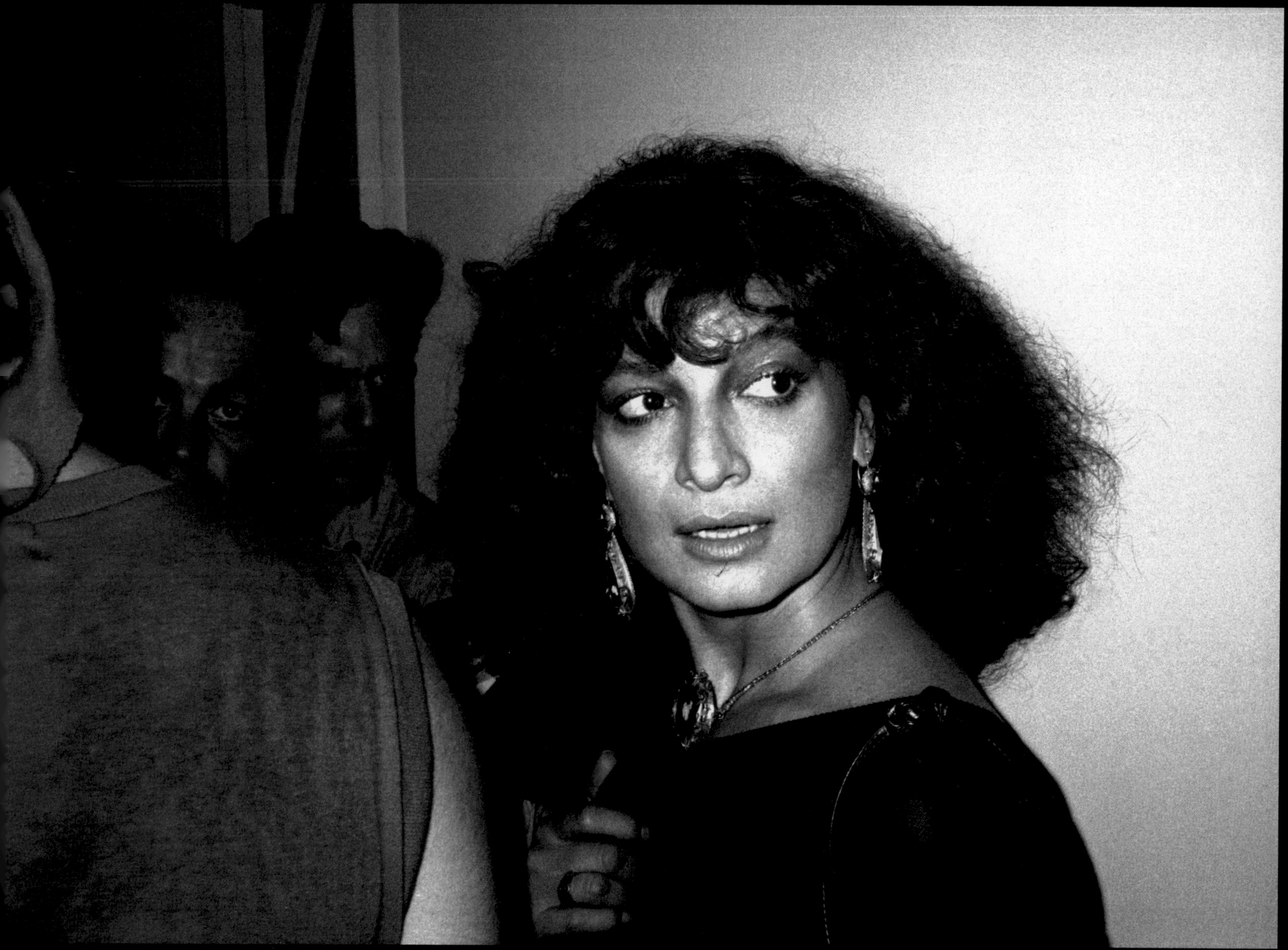

Daniela Morera
at Interview magazine's opening party at Limelight.
November 1983

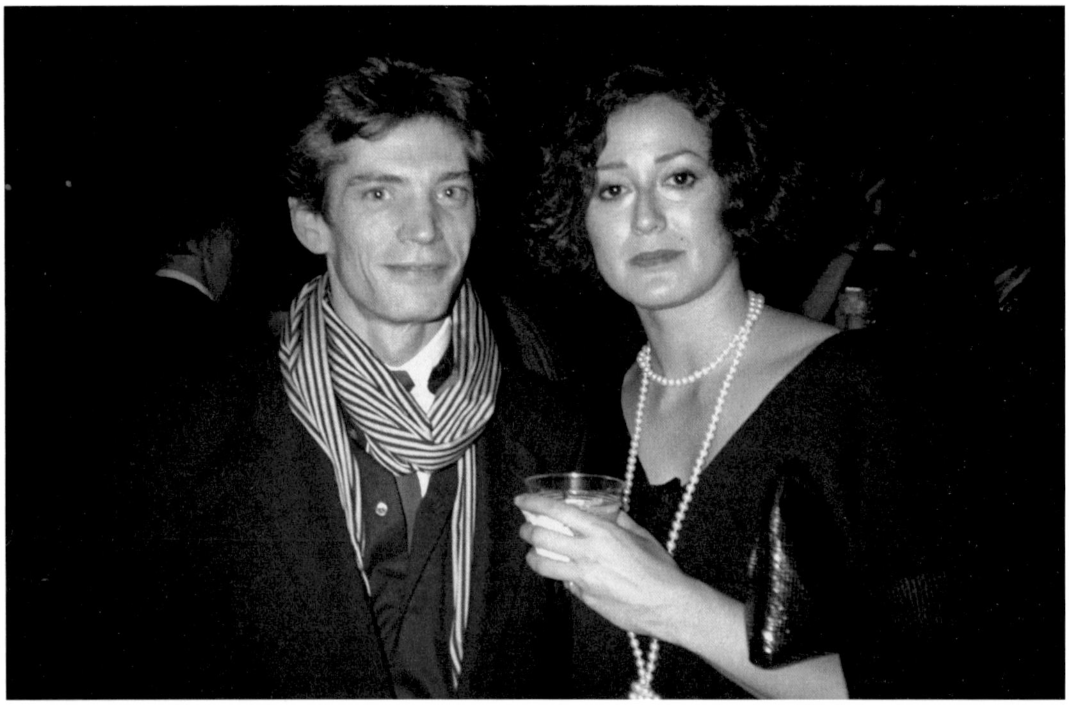

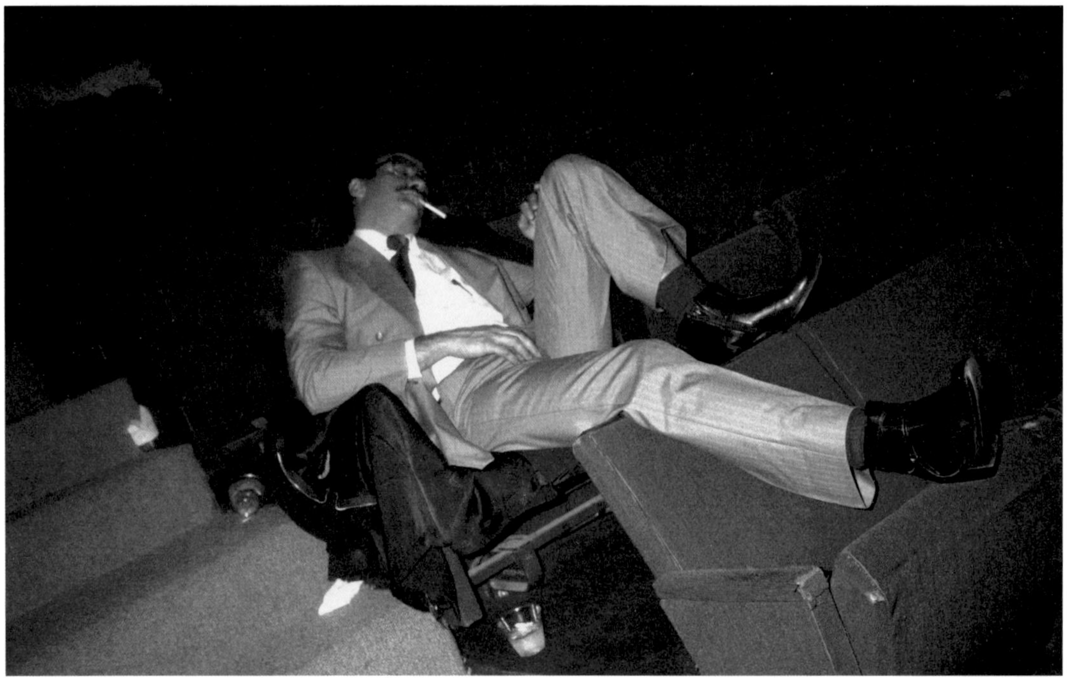

Top: Robert Mapplethorpe and Catherine Olim
Bottom: Man asleep in the theater
at the NY Film Festival. 1983

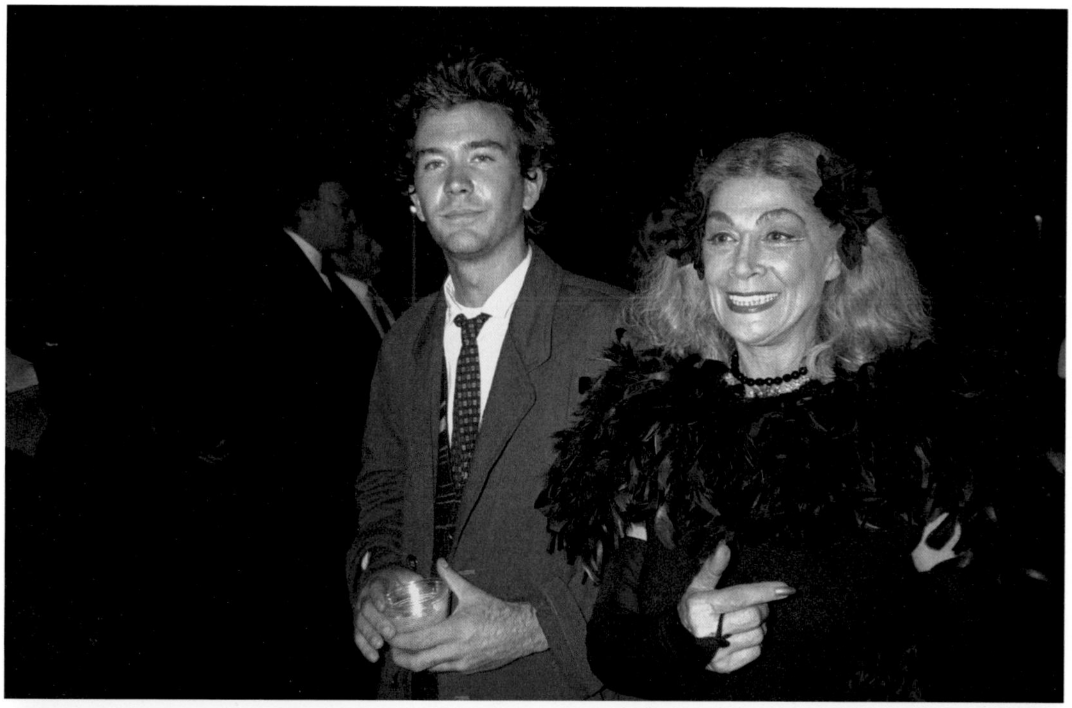

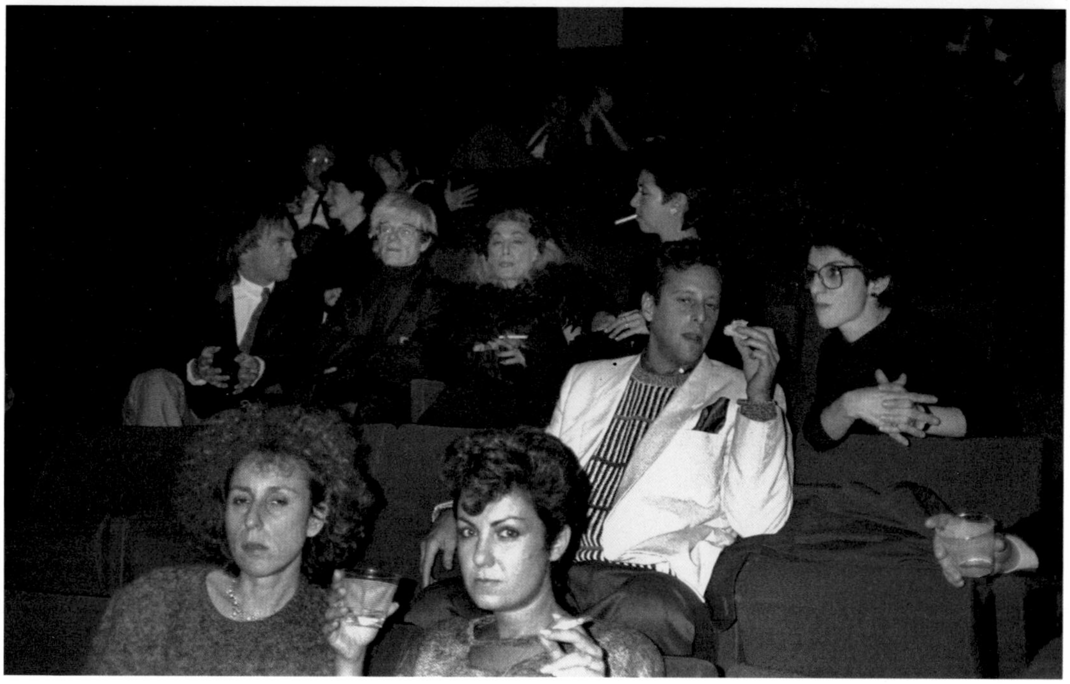

TOP: TIMOTHY HUTTON AND SYLVIA MILES
BOTTOM: JON GOULD, ANDY WARHOL, AND SYLVIA MILES
AT THE NY FILM FESTIVAL. 1983

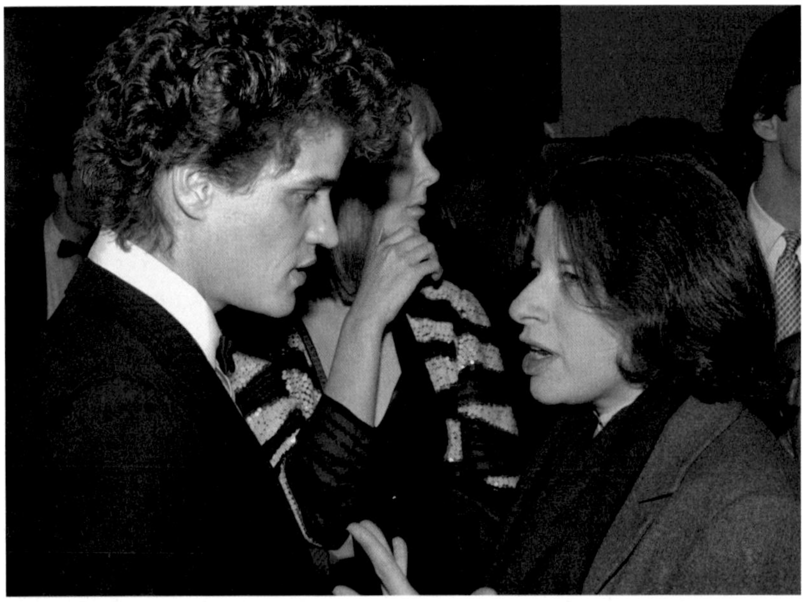

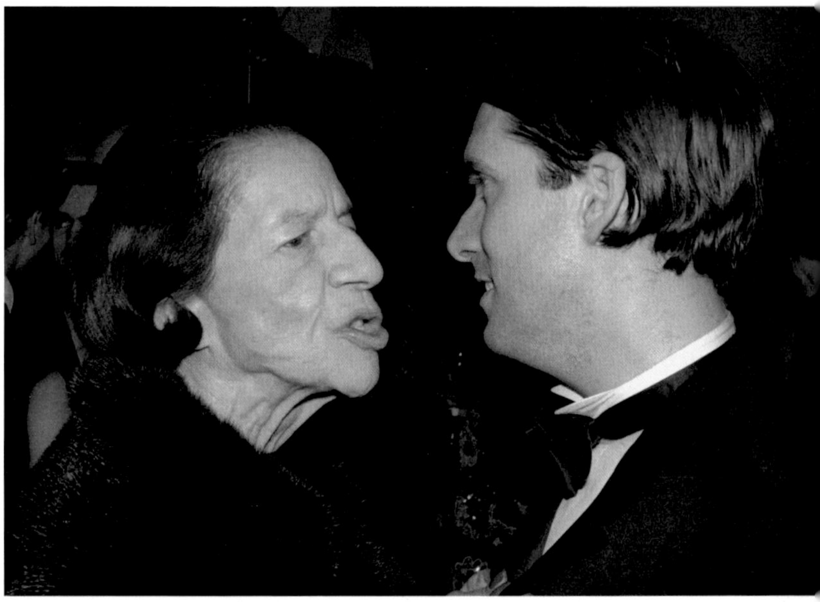

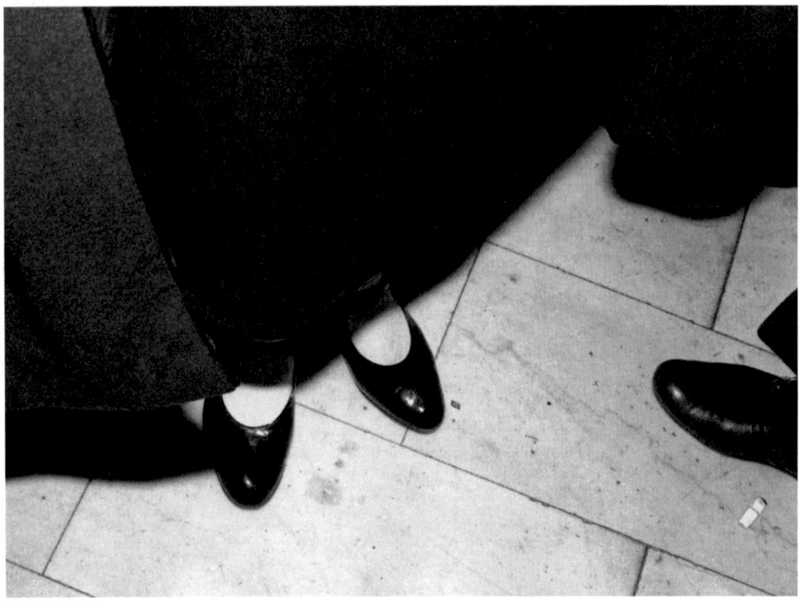

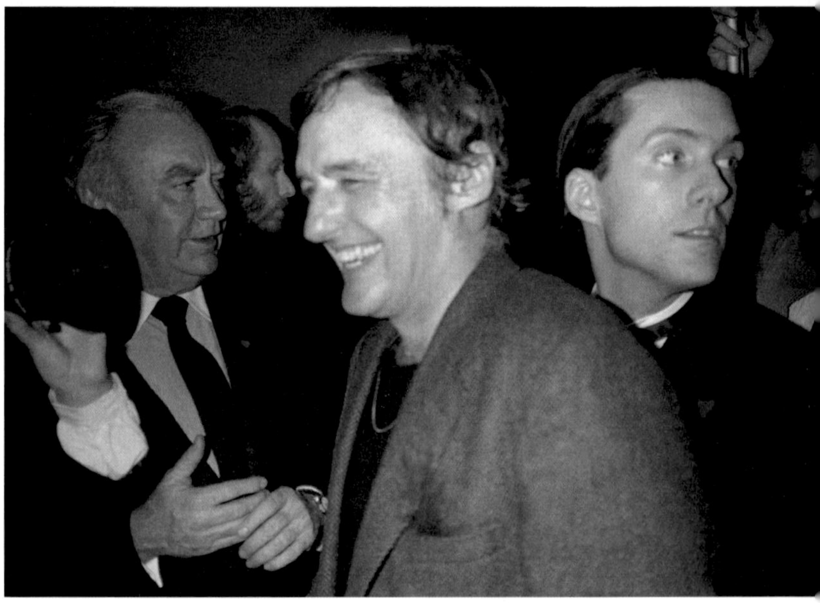

Top Left: Jay Johnson and Fran Lebowitz
Top Right: Diana Vreeland and Edmund Gaultney
Bottom Left: Gina Metcalfe's shoe portrait
Bottom Right: Hugh Carey, Dennis Hopper, and Edmund Gaultney
at the Edmund Gaultney Gallery opening for Cossey.
February 14, 1981

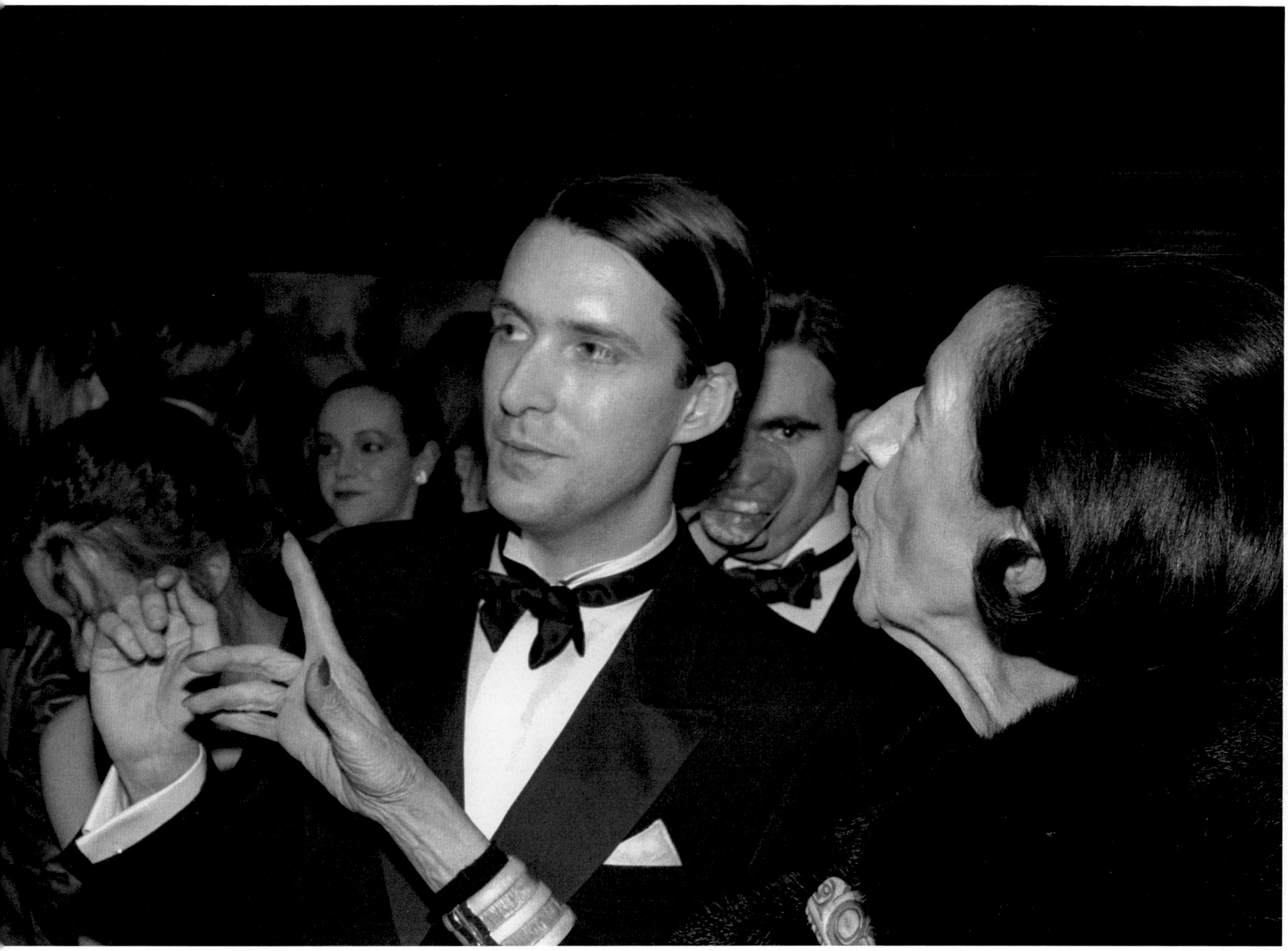

Edmund Gaultney and Diana Vreeland
at the Edmund Gaultney Gallery opening for Cossey.
February 14, 1981

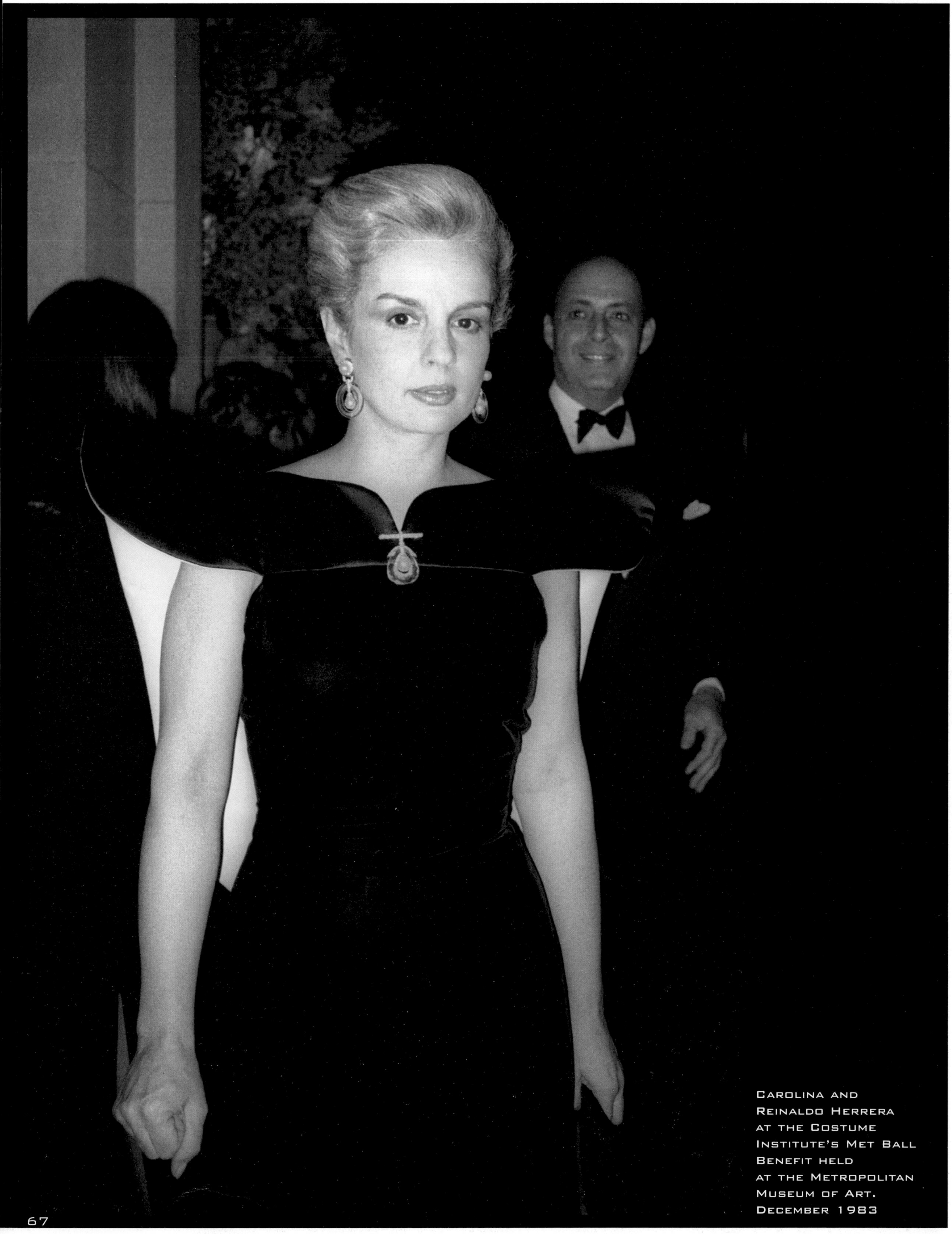

Carolina and Reinaldo Herrera at the Costume Institute's Met Ball Benefit held at the Metropolitan Museum of Art. December 1983

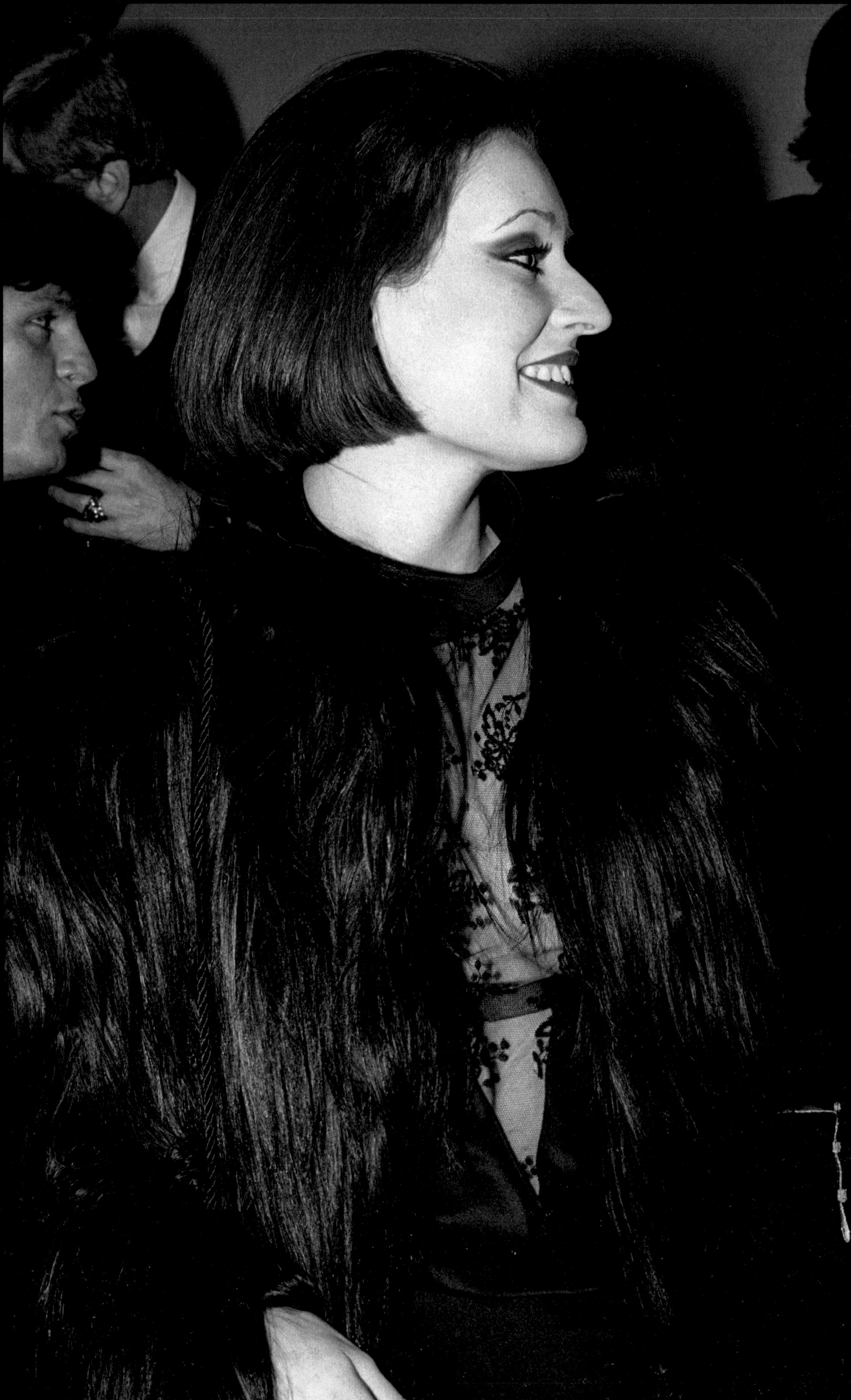

Antonia de Portago
at the Edmund Gaultney
Gallery opening.
February 14, 1981

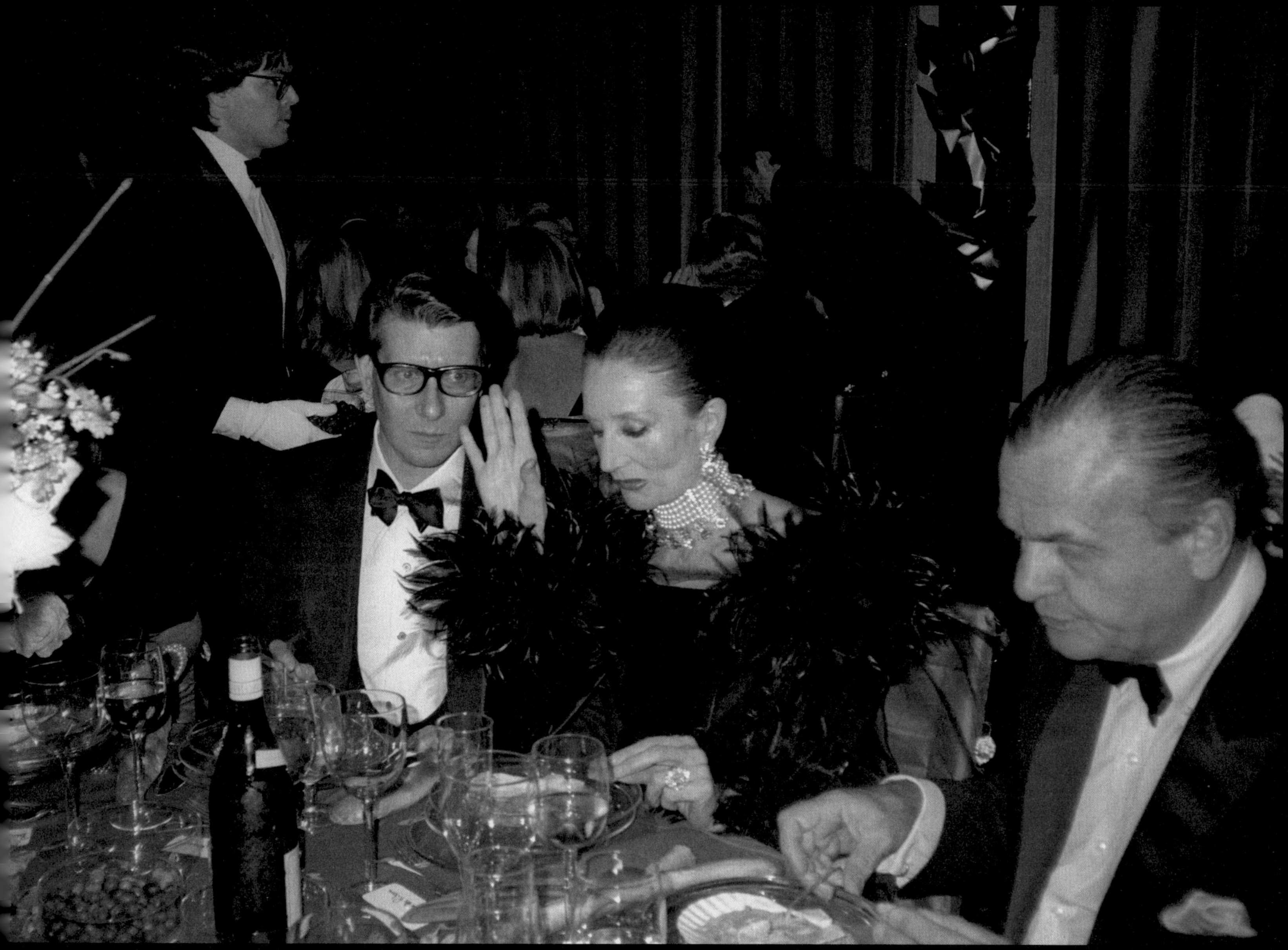

Yves Saint-Laurent, Countess Jacqueline de Ribes, and Bill Blass
at the Costume Institute's Met Ball Benefit held
at the Metropolitan Museum of Art.
December 1983

"God love the 80s! We were twenty years younger full of pep, energy, and ideas, oh the fun and the extravagance...every day was a costume party and every night was new year's eve."
Nan Kempner

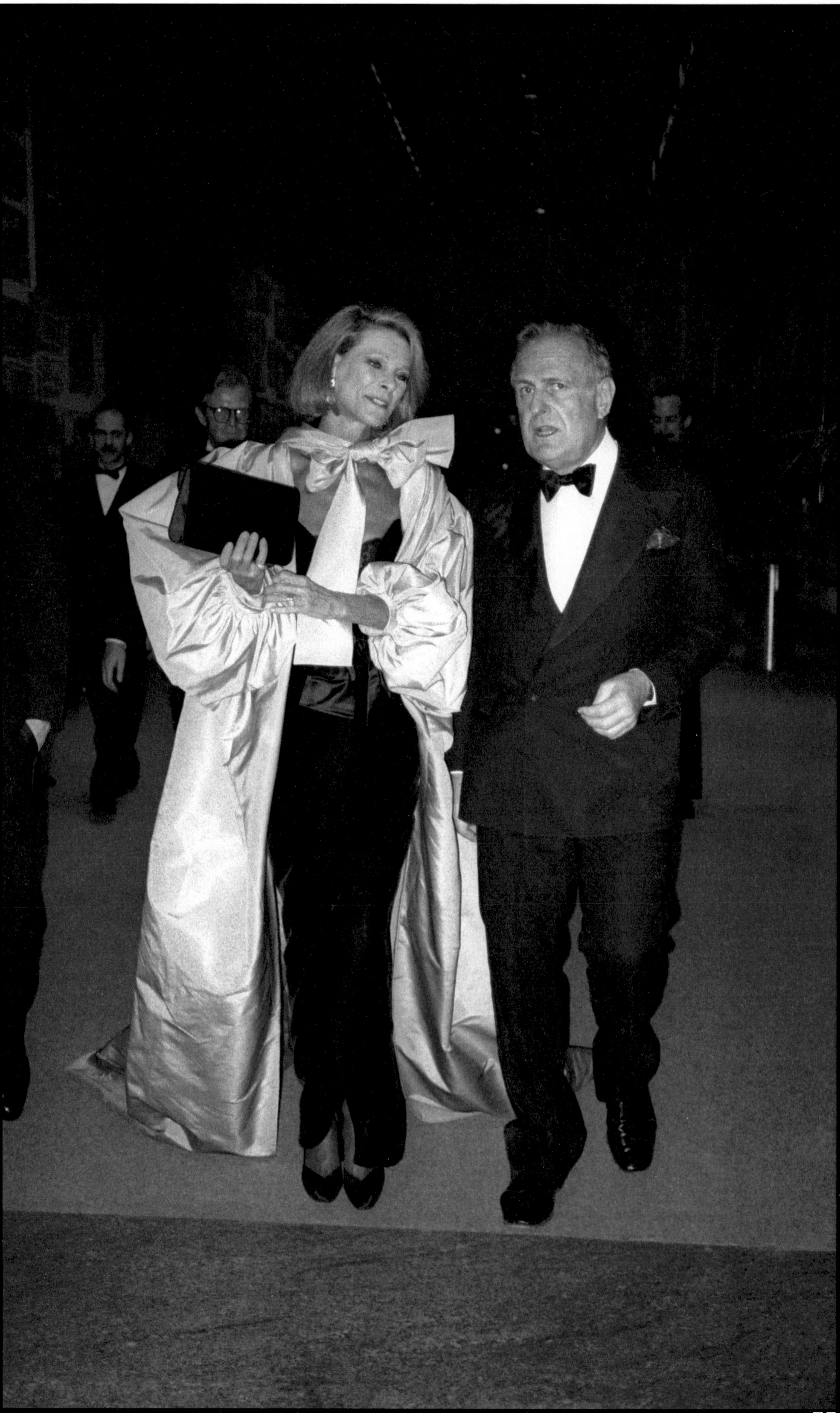

Nan Kempner and John Richardson at the Costume Institute's Met Ball Benefit held at the Metropolitan Museum of Art. December 1983

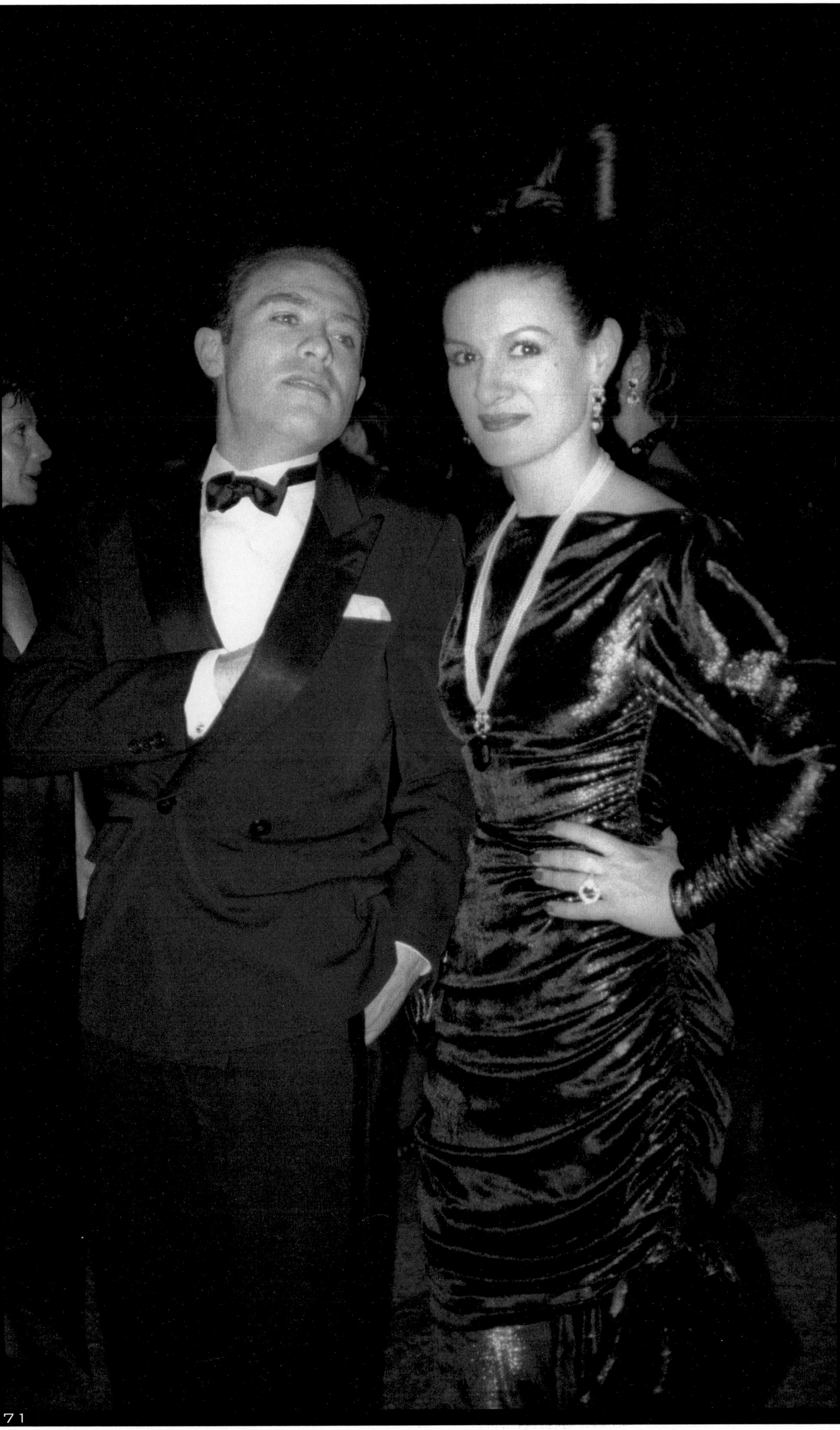

Raphael-Lopez Sanchez and Paloma Picasso at the Costume Institute's Met Ball Benefit held at the Metropolitan Museum of Art. December 1983

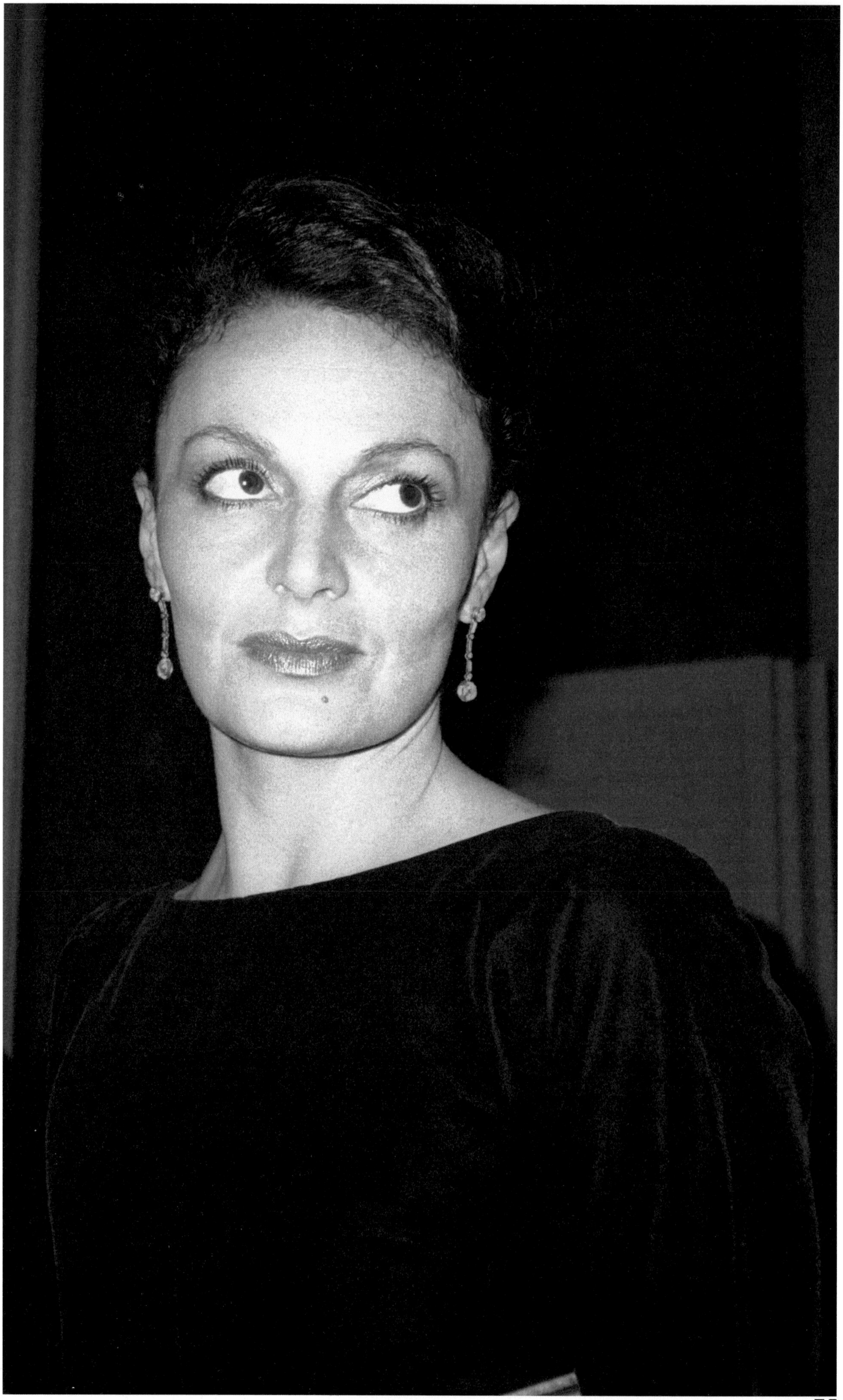

Diane von Furstenberg at the Costume Institute's Met Ball Benefit held at the Metropolitan Museum of Art. December 1983

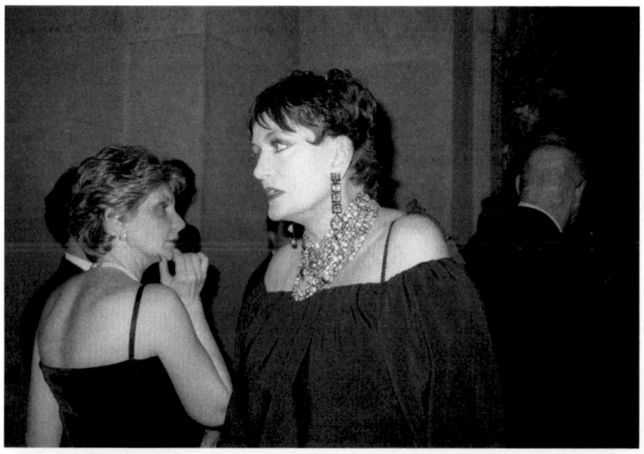
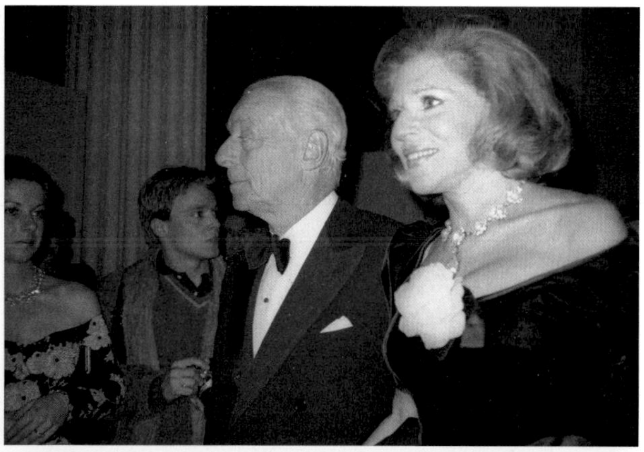
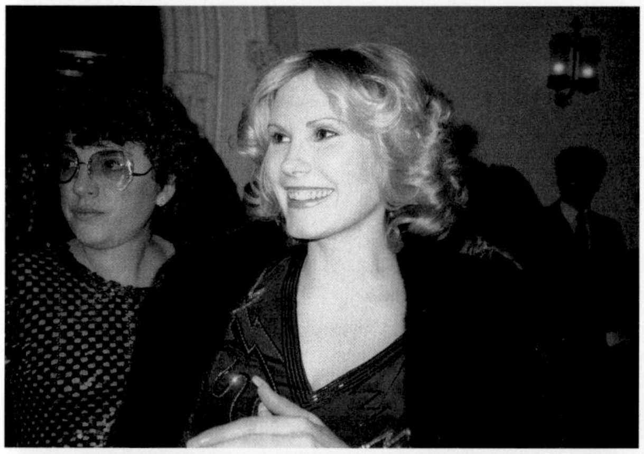
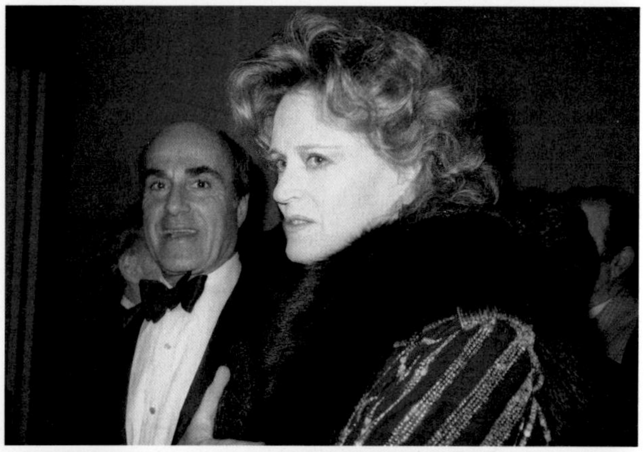
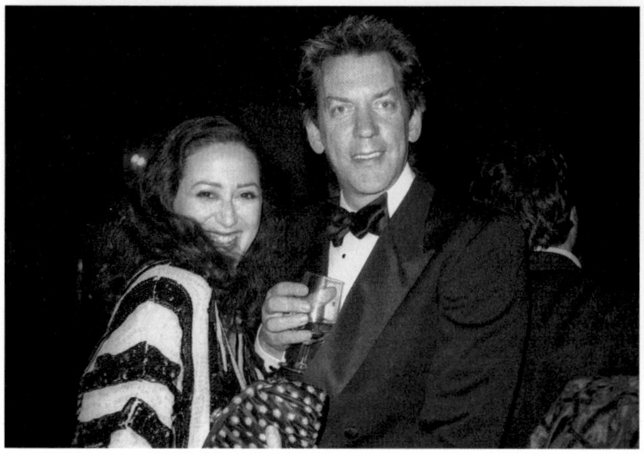
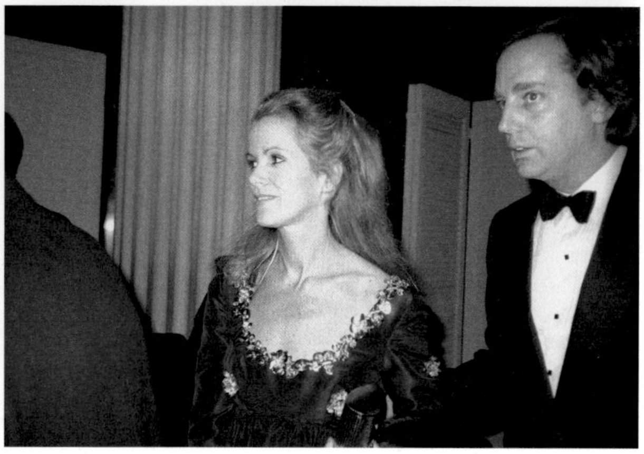

TOP LEFT: MAXINE DE LA FALAISE MCKENDRY
TOP RIGHT: GUY AND MARIE-HELENE DE ROTHSCHILD
AT THE COSTUME INSTITUTE'S MET BALL BENEFIT. DECEMBER 1983
MIDDLE LEFT: RITA JENRETTE AT THE NIGHT OF 100 TREES AT LIMELIGHT. DECEMBER 1983
MIDDLE RIGHT: ALEXIS SMITH AND GUEST AT THE COSTUME INSTITUTE'S MET BALL BENEFIT.
DECEMBER 1983
BOTTOM LEFT: CATHERINE OLIM AND DONALD SUTHERLAND
AT THE METROPOLITAN CLUB PARTY FOR THE BEST. DECEMBER 1983
BOTTOM RIGHT: BLAINE AND ROBERT TRUMP AT THE COSTUME INSTITUTE'S MET BALL BENEFIT.
DECEMBER 1983

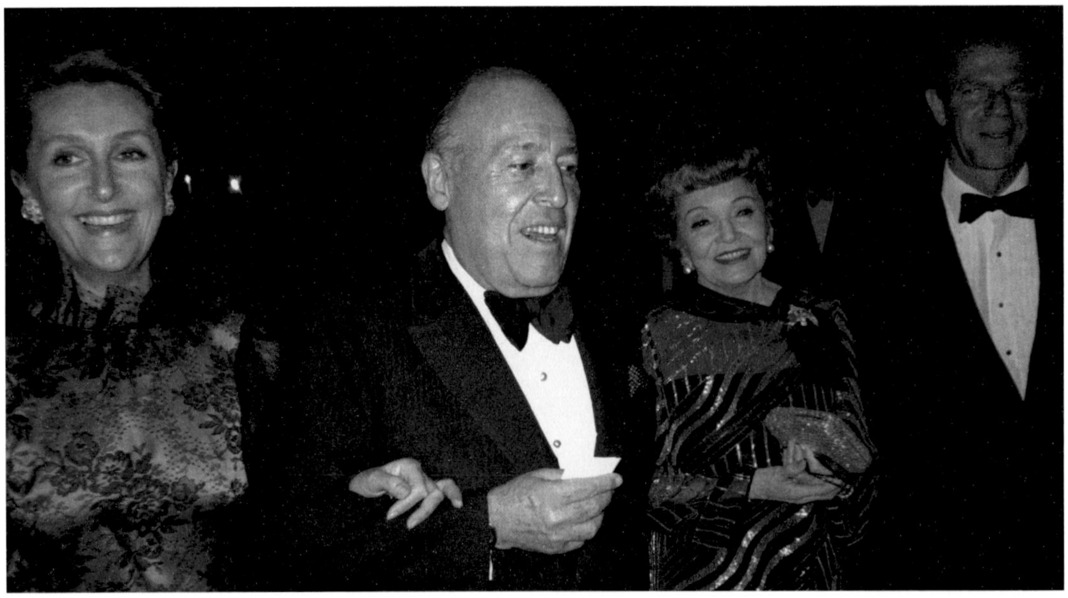

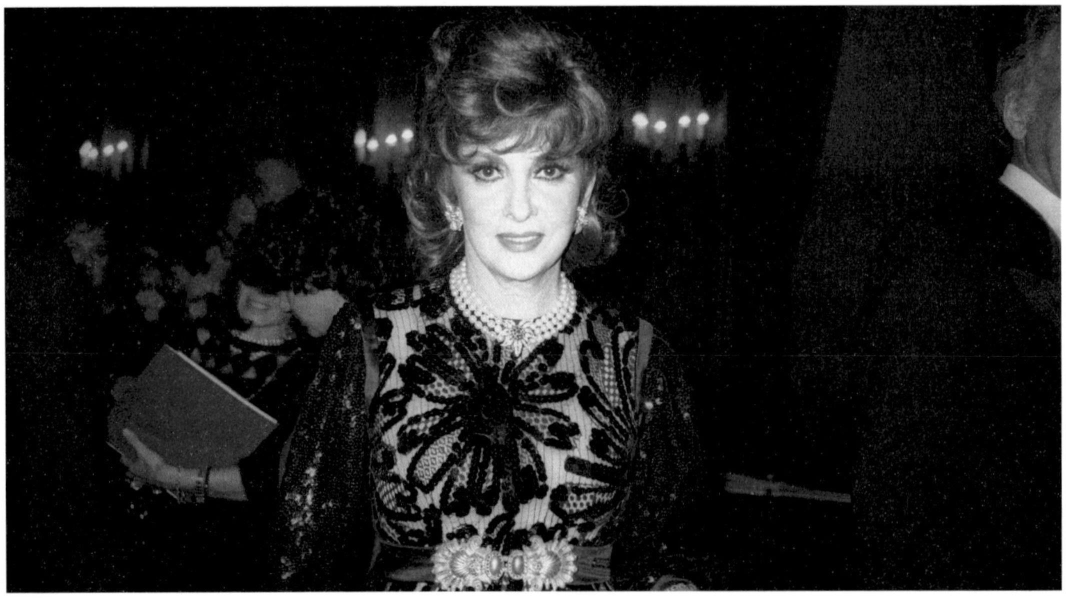

Top: Jerry Zipkin and guest, and Claudette Colbert and Peter Rogers
at the Costume Institute's Met Ball Benefit held
at the Metropolitan Museum of Art. December 1983
Bottom: Gina Lollobrigida
at the Metropolitan Club Party for The Best. December 1983

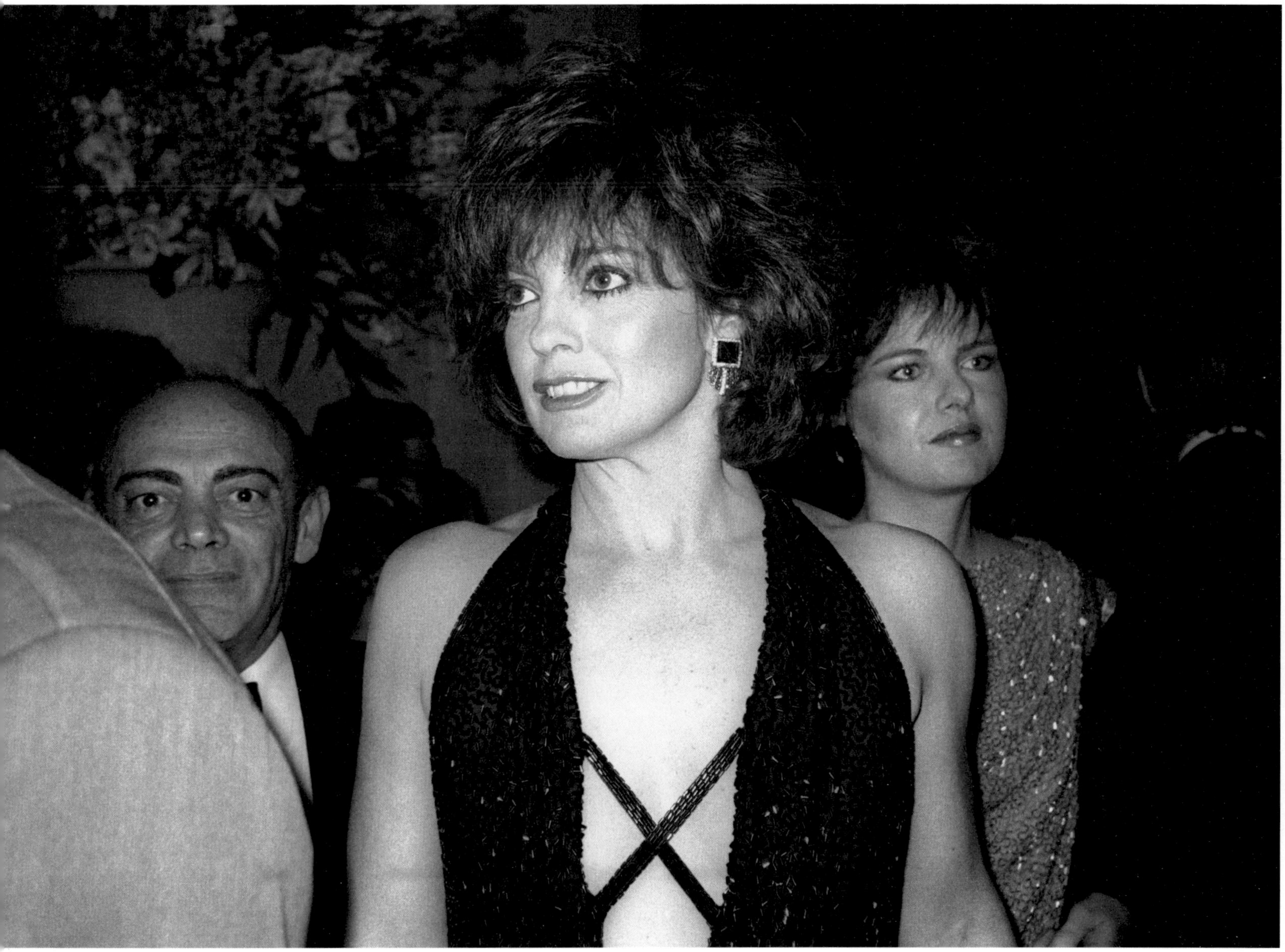

Linda Gray
at the Costume Institute's Met Ball Benefit held
at the Metropolitan Museum of Art.
December 1983

The 80s was a fabulous time for me. There were hundreds of gala events and I attended almost all the major ones. There were more Scaasi evening dresses and ball gowns worn during the decade then from any other designer. (Fifty-seven seen in one night at the Metropolitan Museum Gala alone!)

I was out dancing with my clients almost every night and having a ball! Also in 1989 Barbara Bush wore her Scaasi 'Barbara Blue' inaugural gown to great acclaim, and her picture was flashed across the world making Scaasi a household name. It was my decade and I loved it!

Arnold Scaasi

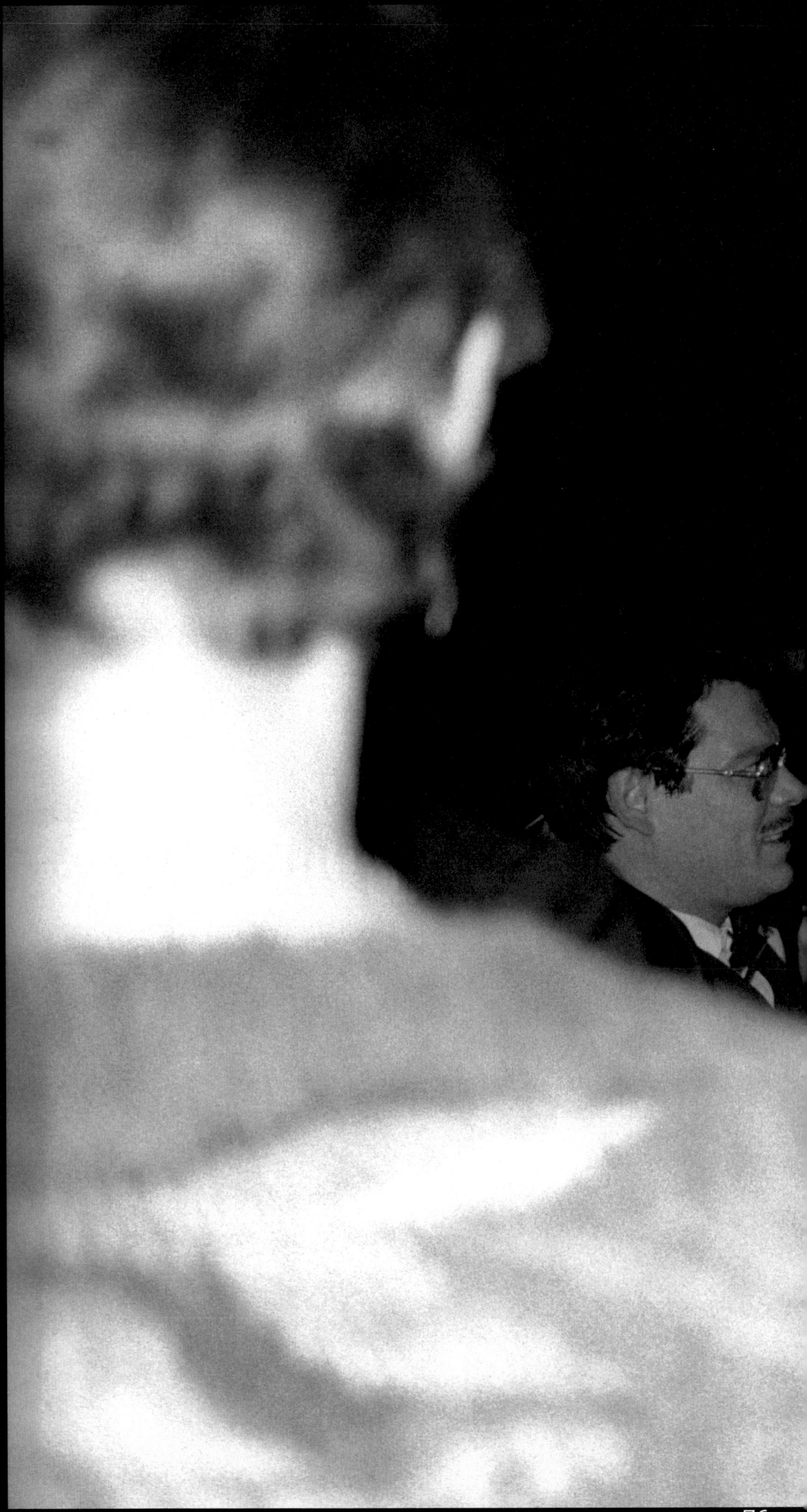

Tom Gates (left) and Catherine Deneuve at the Costume Institute's Met Ball Benefit held at the Metropolitan Museum of Art. December 1983

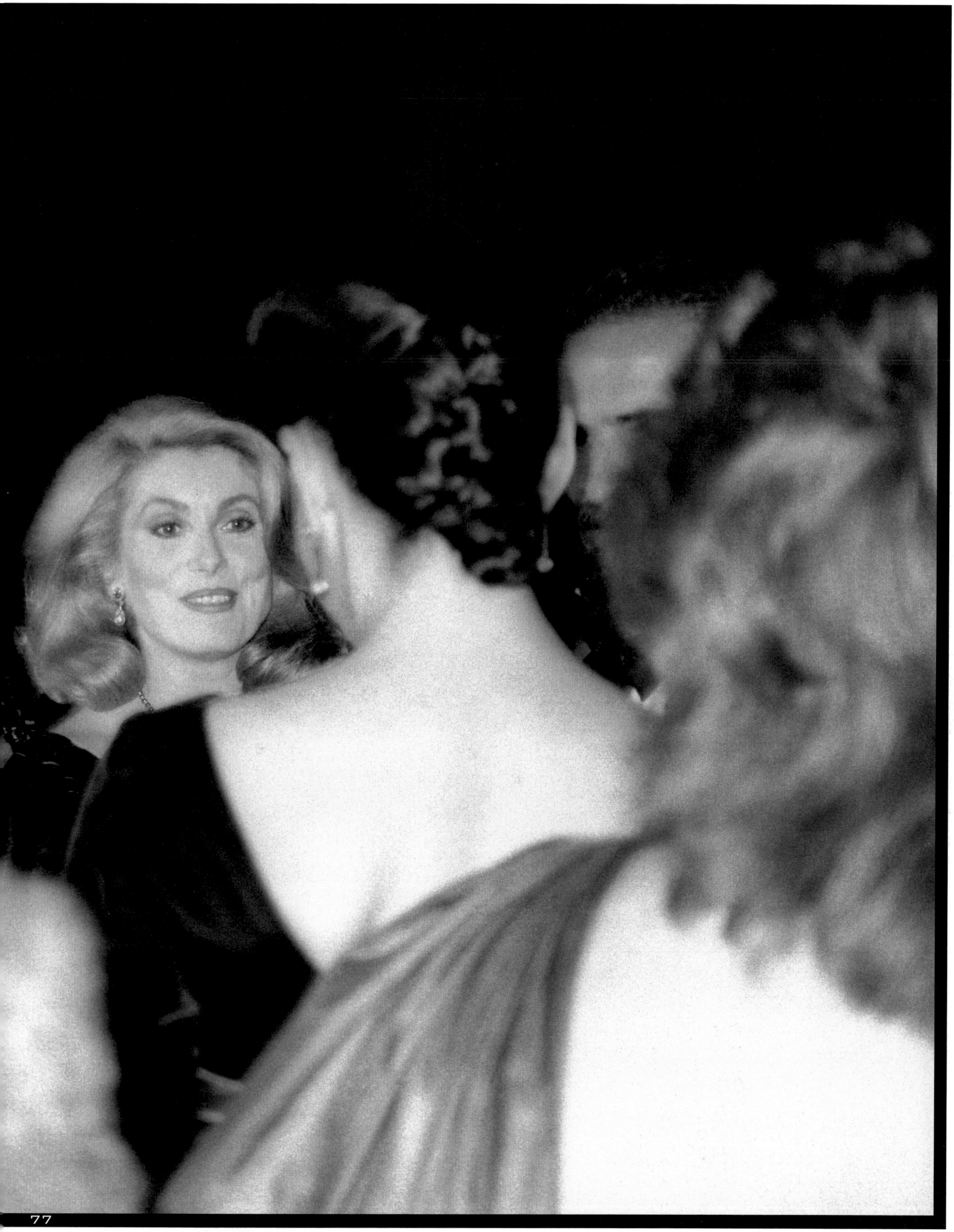

"The 80s were the last great burst of madness of the twentieth century. The world and New York in particular went wild. Patrick McMullan, young and without malice, was there with his camera to record the fun, the frenzy, and the decadence of all that madness."
Carolina Herrera

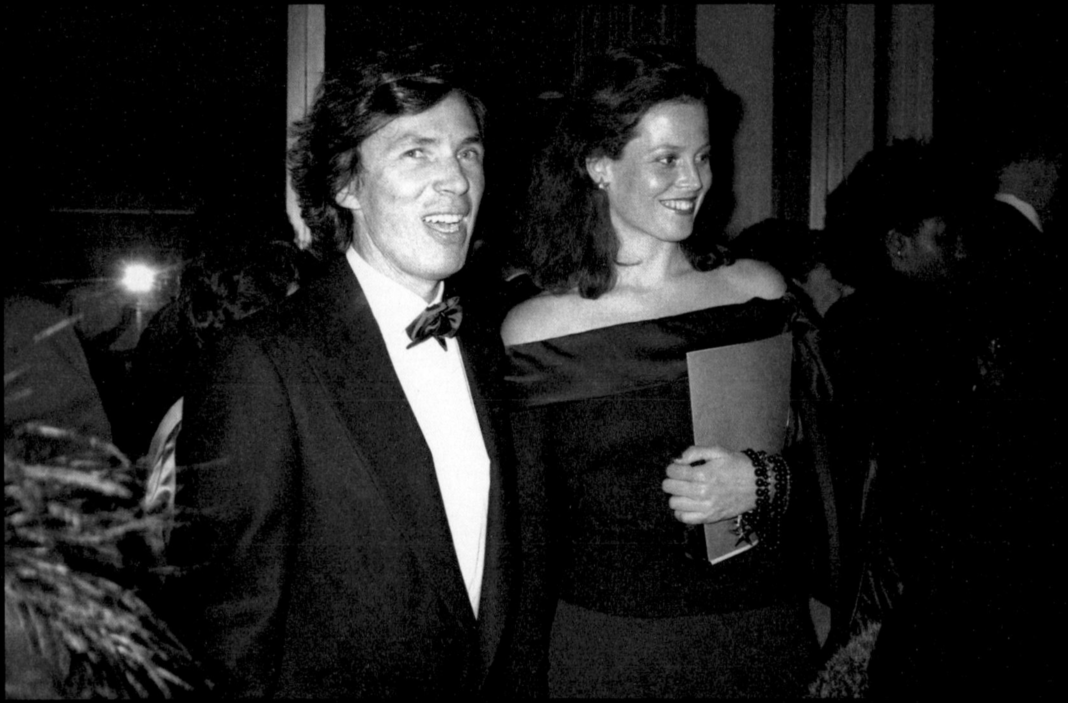

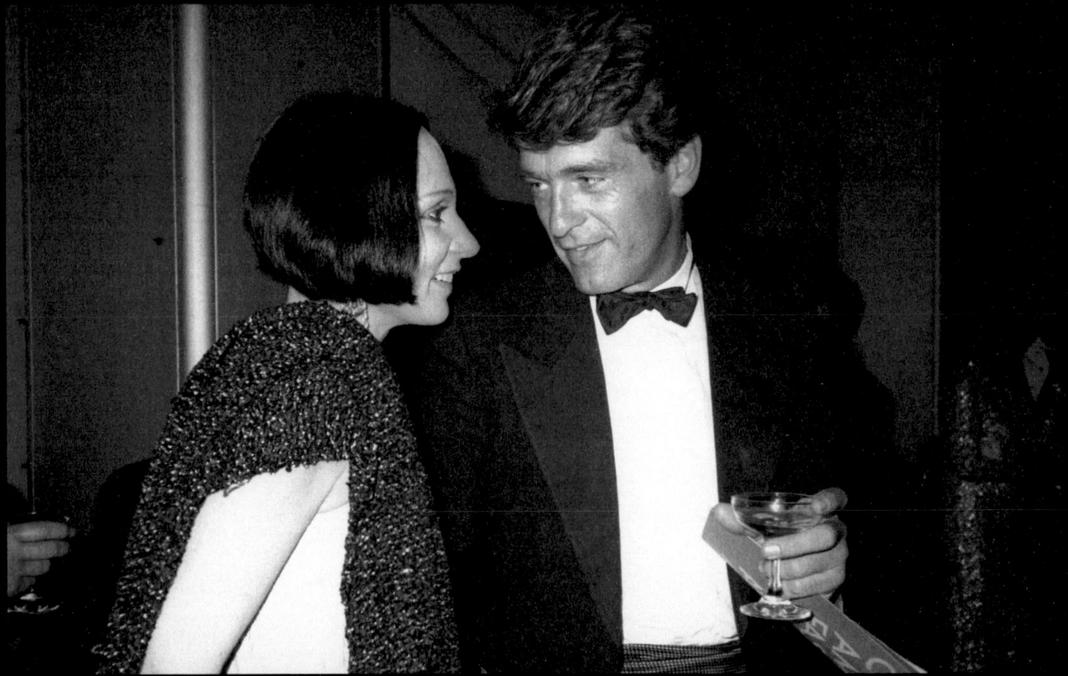

Top: Perry Ellis and Sigourney Weaver
Bottom: Mary McFadden and Ingo Thouret
at the COTY Awards.
September 1983

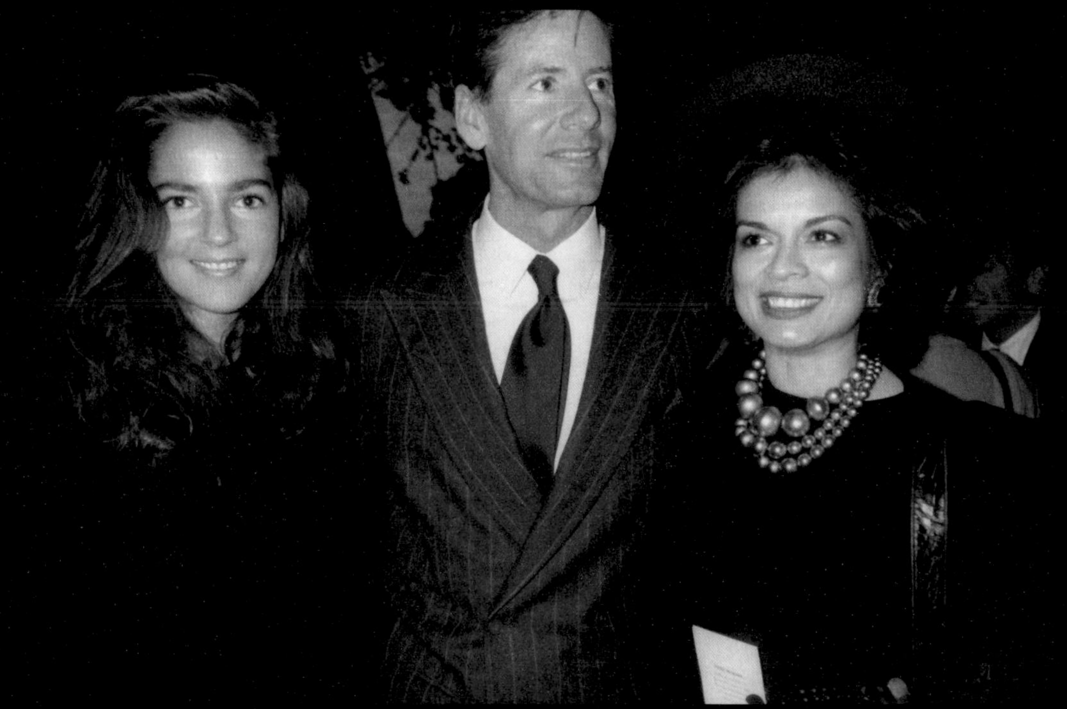

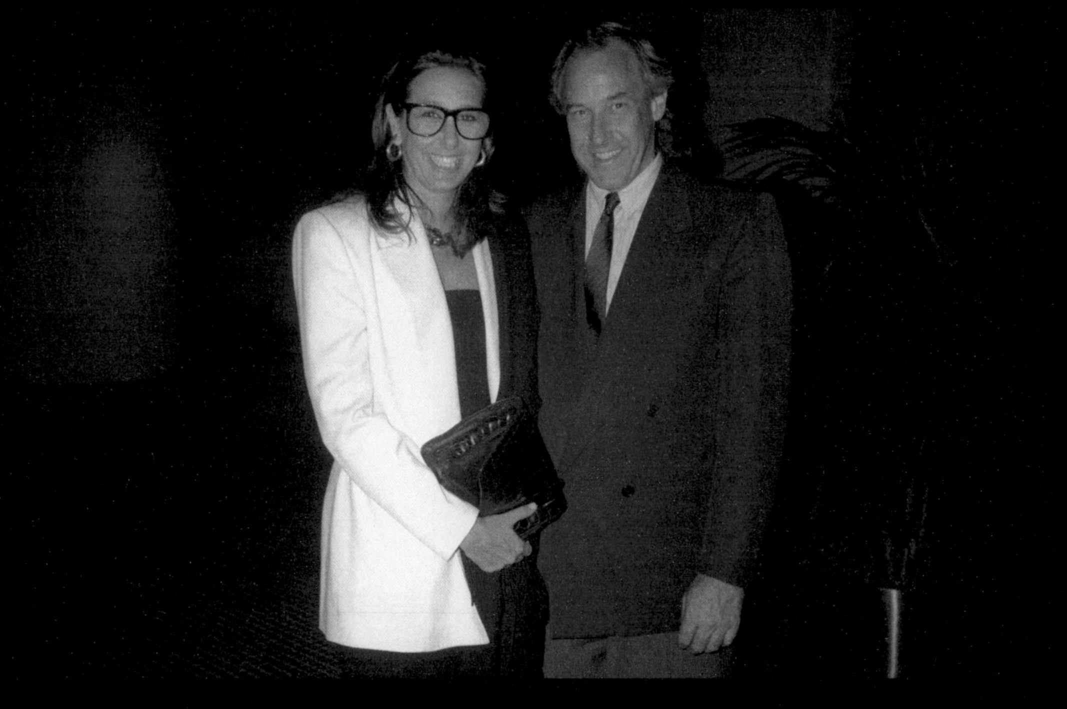

Top: Kelly Klein, Calvin Klein, and Bianca Jagger
at the Andy Warhol Memorial Tribute held at the Diamond Horseshoe.
April 1, 1987
Bottom: Donna Karan and Stephen Weiss
at the Liza Minnelli opening night party.
May 28, 1987

"Patrick McMullan performs a most valuable municipal service--he goes out so you don't have to."
Fran Lebowitz

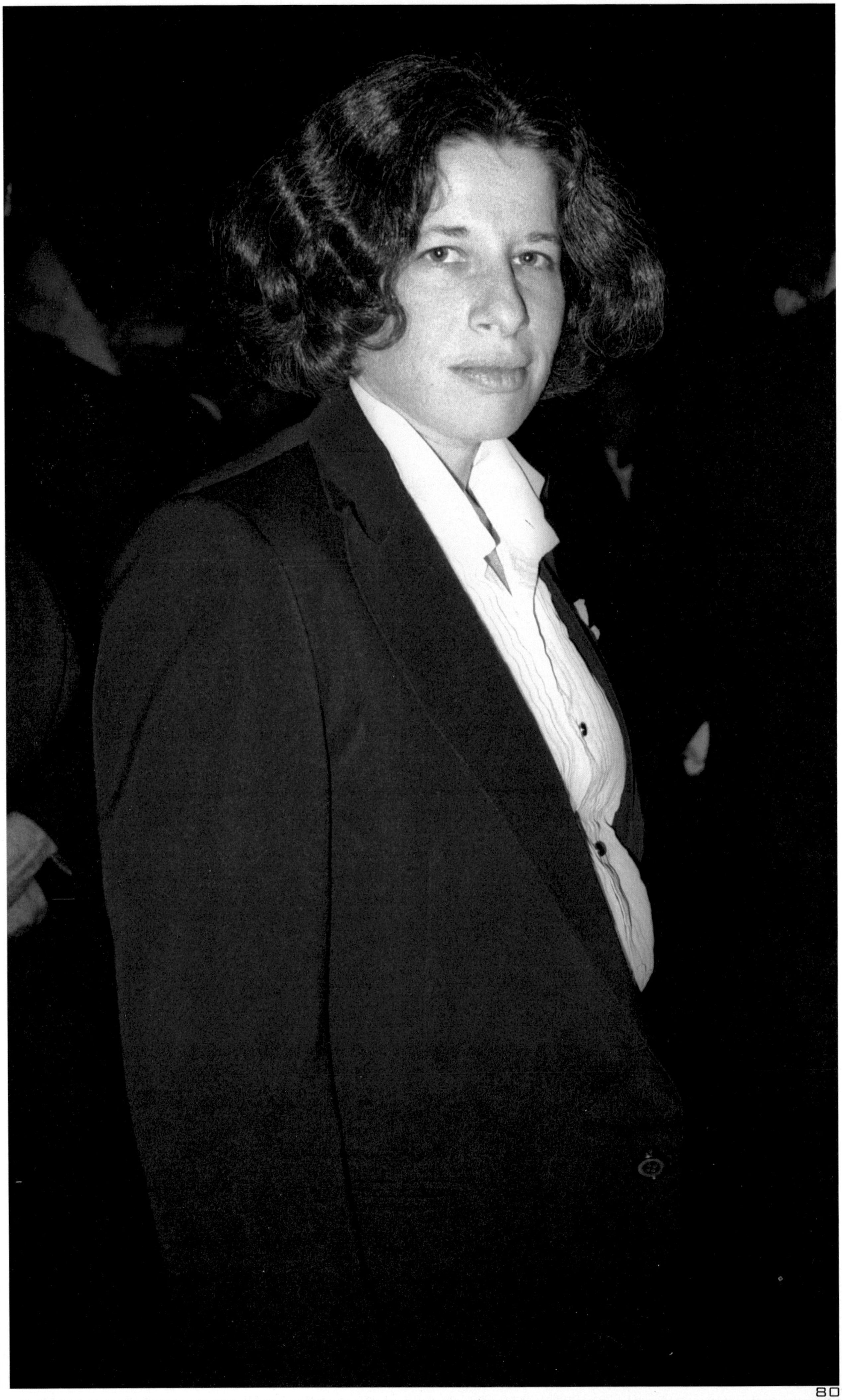

Fran Lebowitz at the Costume Institute's Met Ball Benefit held at the Metropolitan Museum of Art. December 1983

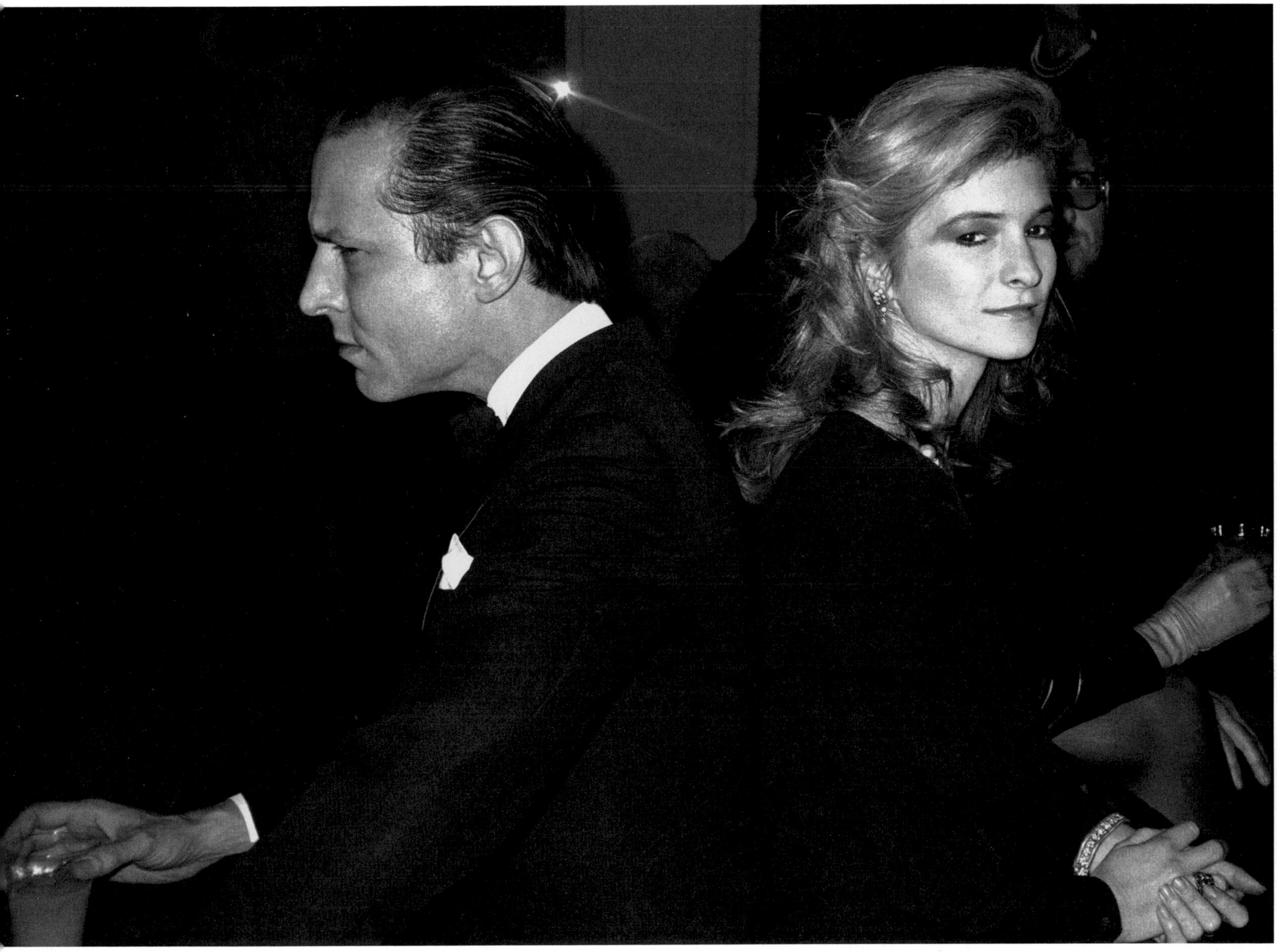

Fred Hughes and English friend Natascha
at the Michael Jackson Party held at the American Museum of Natural History.
September 13, 1983

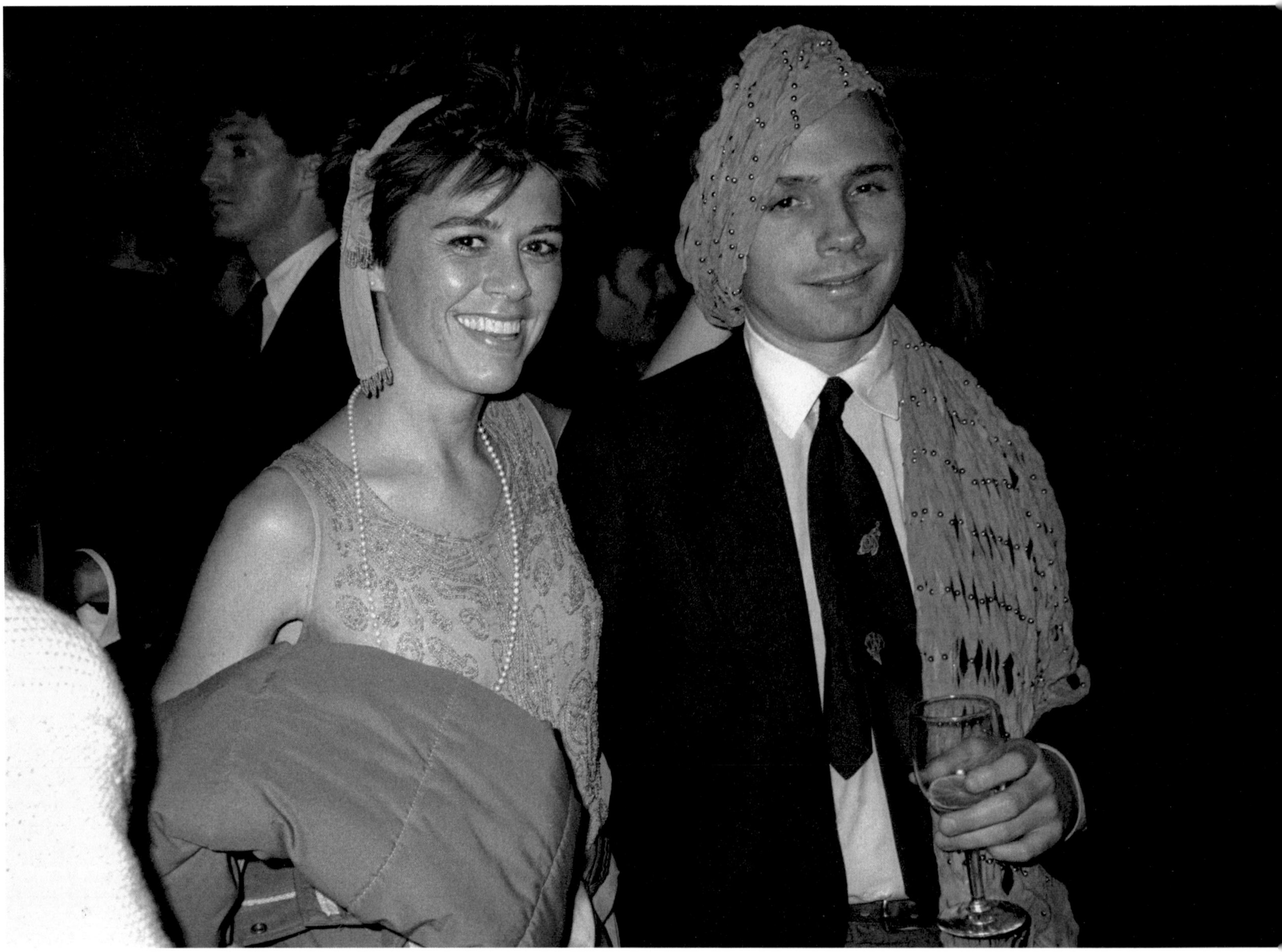

PAIGE POWELL AND ROBERT HAYES
AT THE TOWER GALLERY OPENING.
FALL 1983

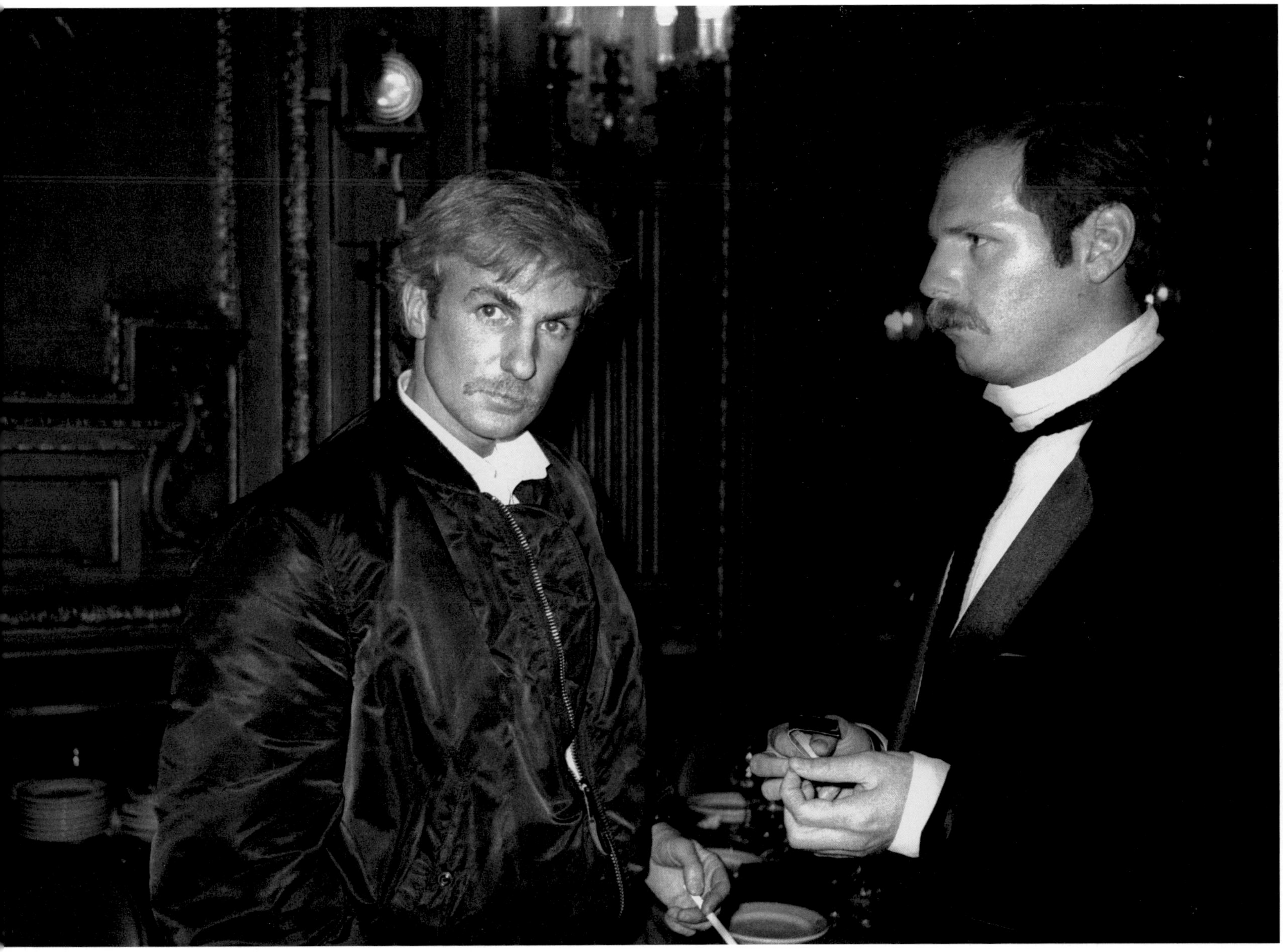

CLAUDE MONTANA AND BUTZ
AT THE METROPOLITAN CLUB PARTY FOR THE BEST.
DECEMBER 1983

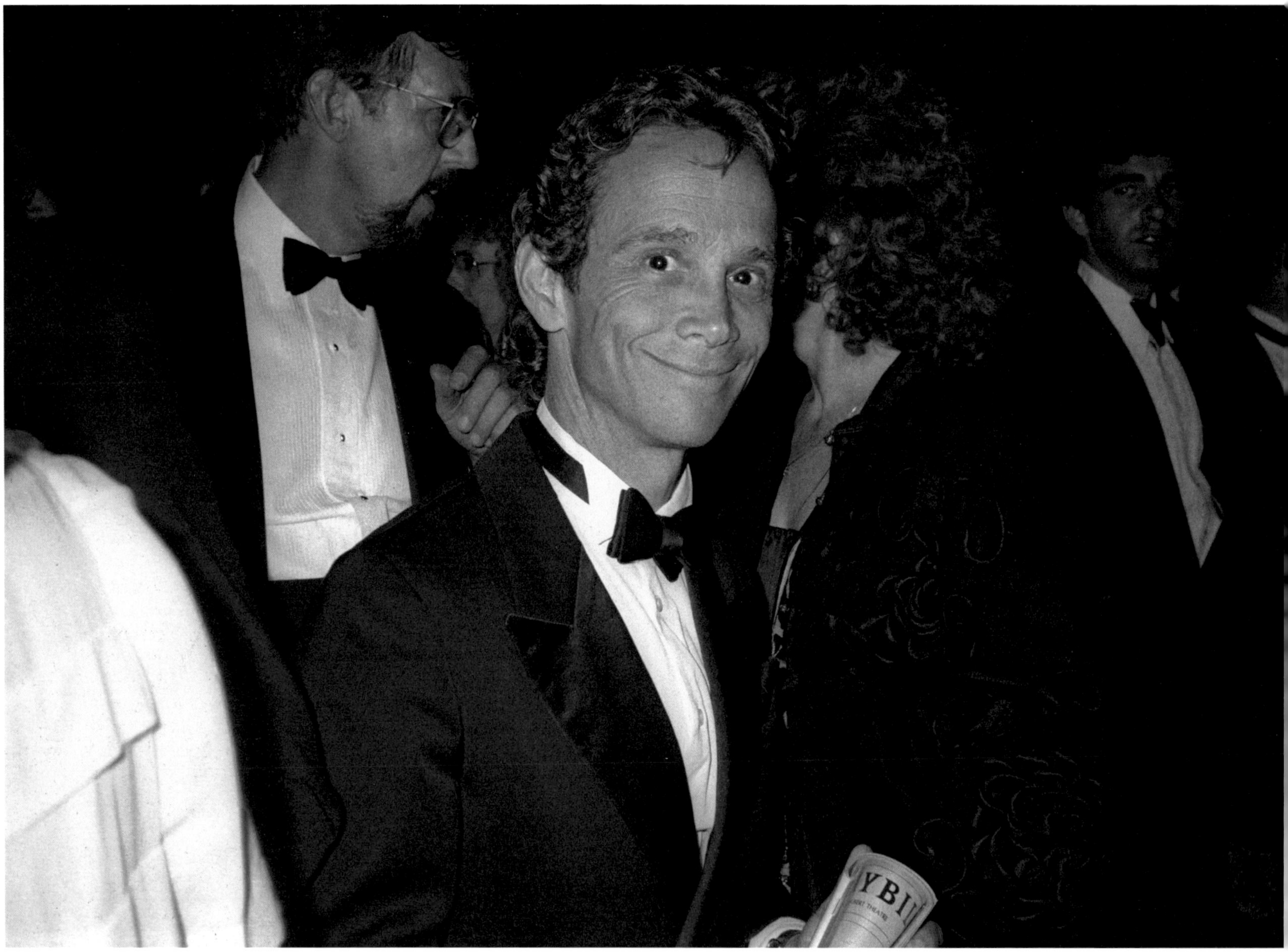

Joel Grey
at the Chorus Line party.
1983

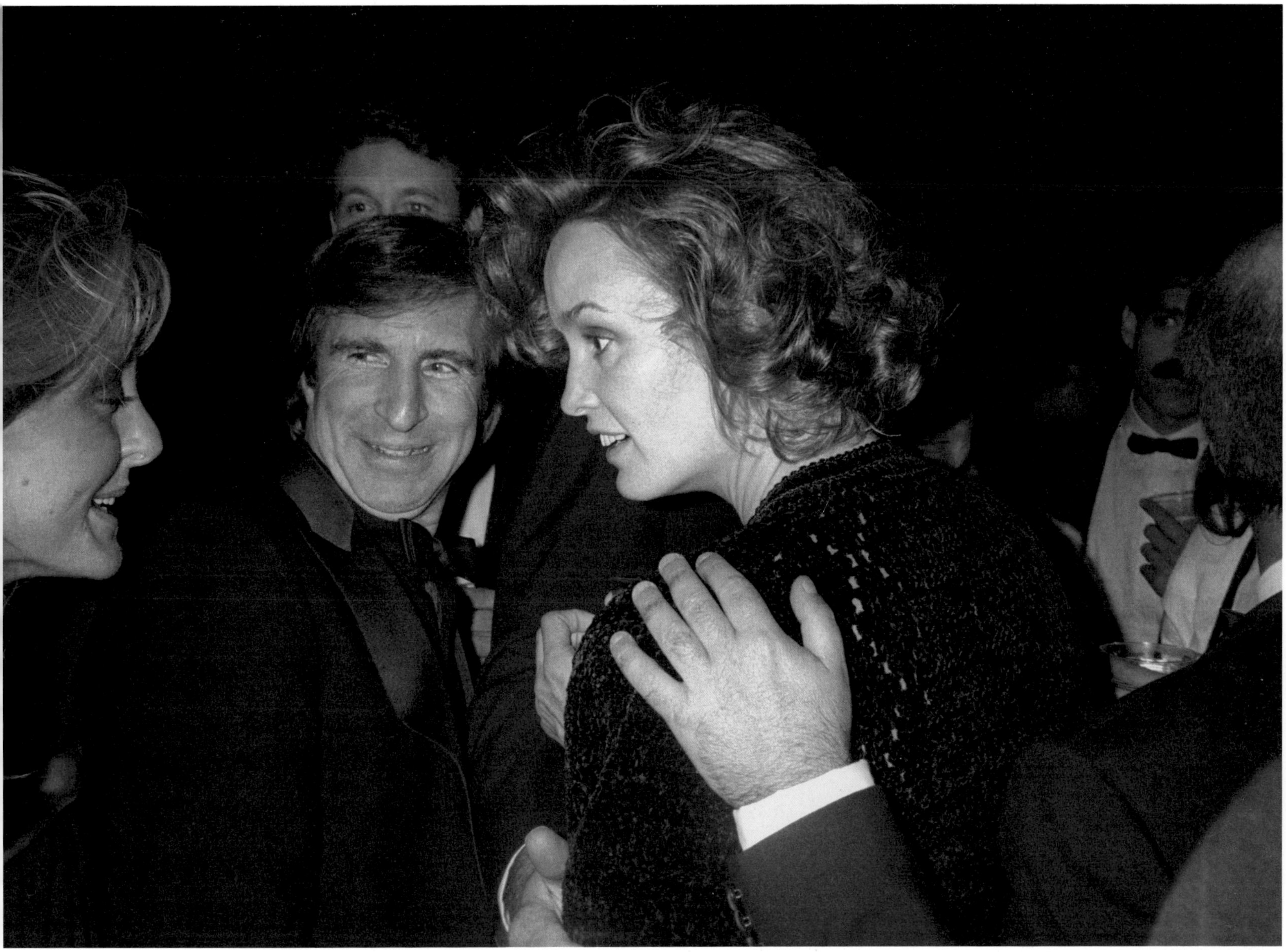

Jessica Lange
at the NY Film Festival.
1983

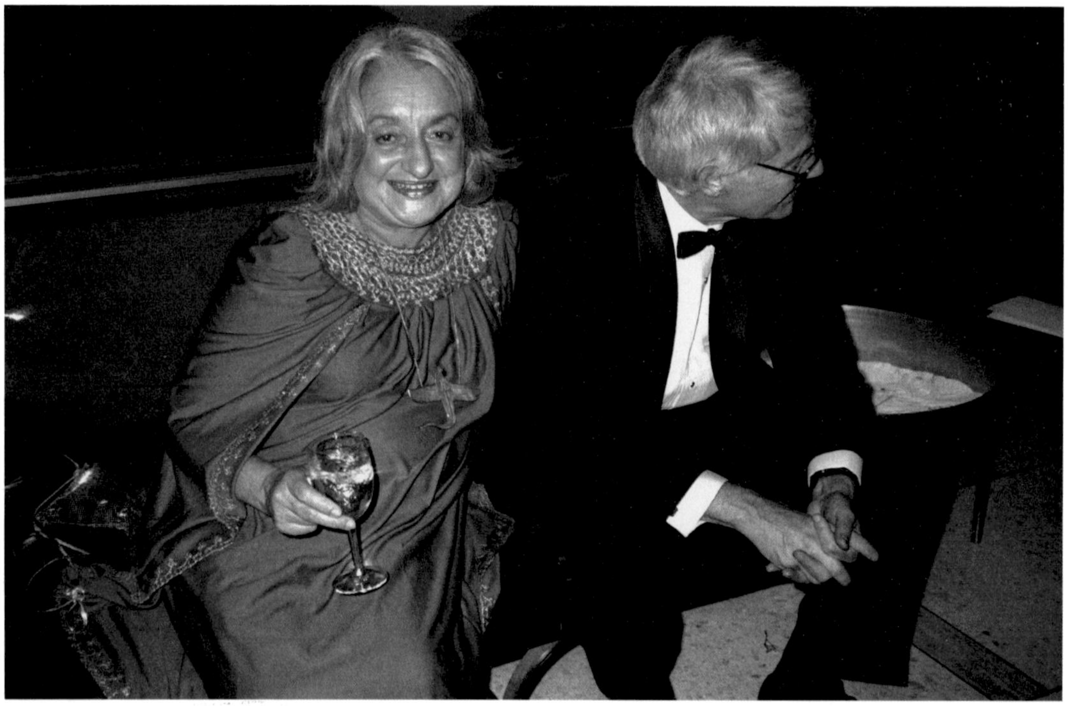

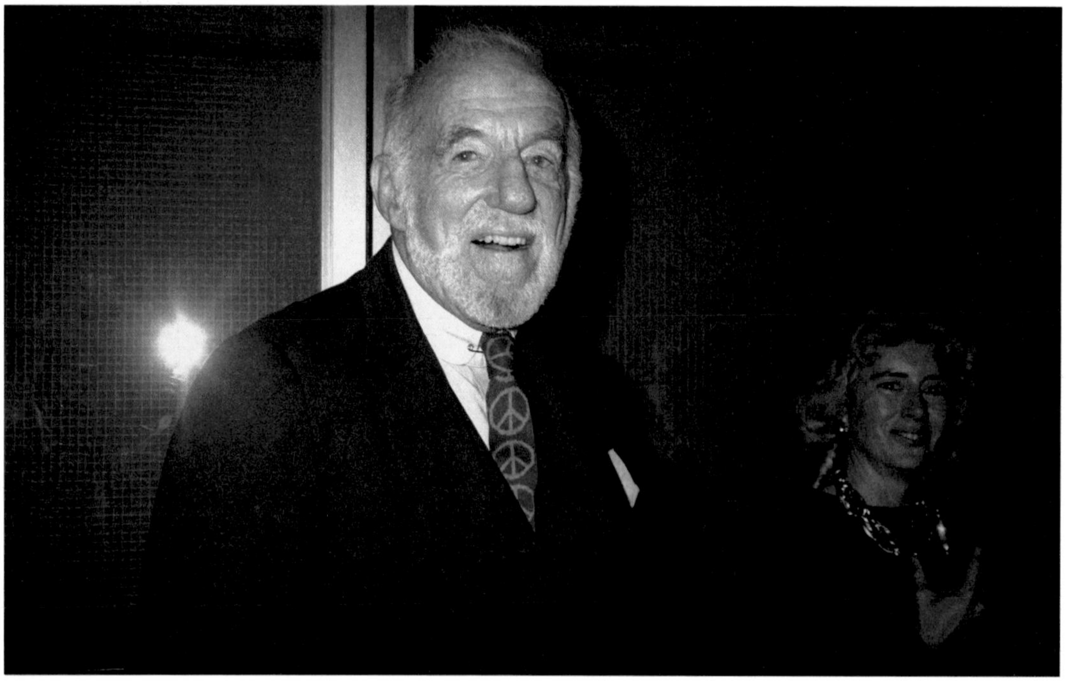

Top: Betty Friedan and Name Unknown
Bottom: Dr. Benjamin Spock
at Esquire magazine's 50th anniversary party at Avery Fisher Hall.
November 7, 1983

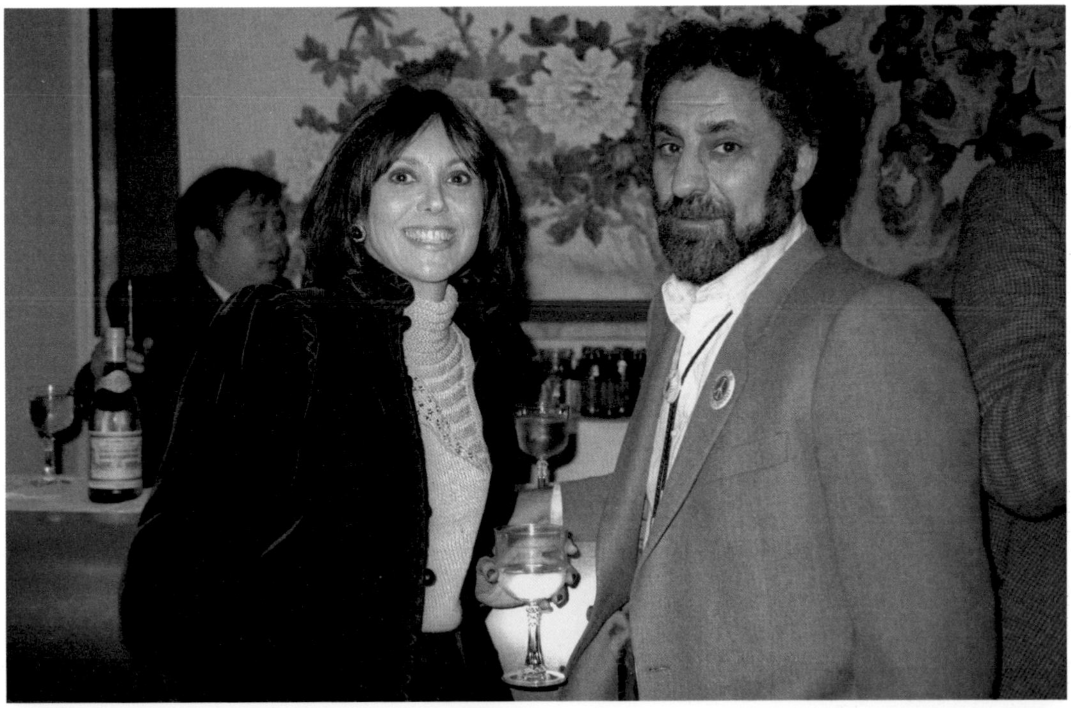

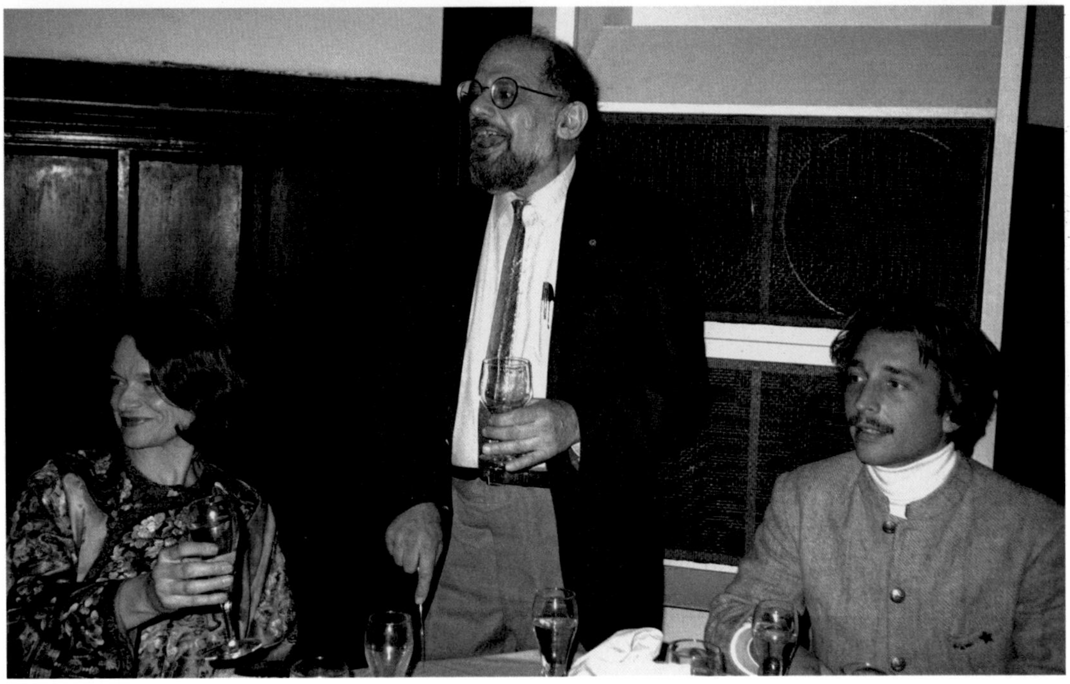

Top: Marlo Thomas and Abby Hoffman
at Karen Black's premiere for the film She Can Bake A Cherry Pie.
December 1983
Bottom: Allen Ginsberg
speaking at the dinner party for William Burroughs at Limelight.
February 1984

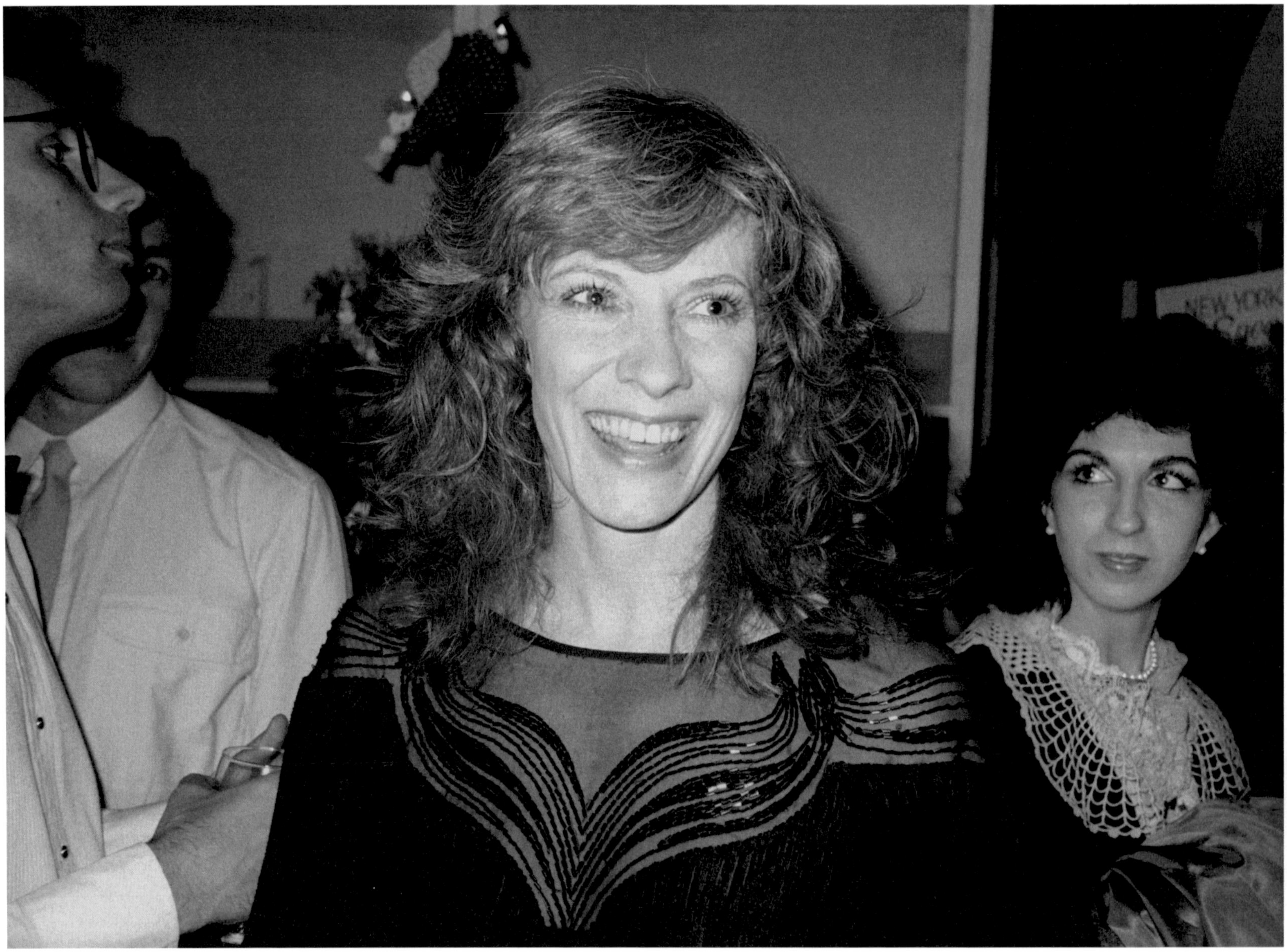

BETTY BUCKLEY AND PATTI KOSTER
AT THE NIGHT OF 100 TREES AT LIMELIGHT.
DECEMBER 1983

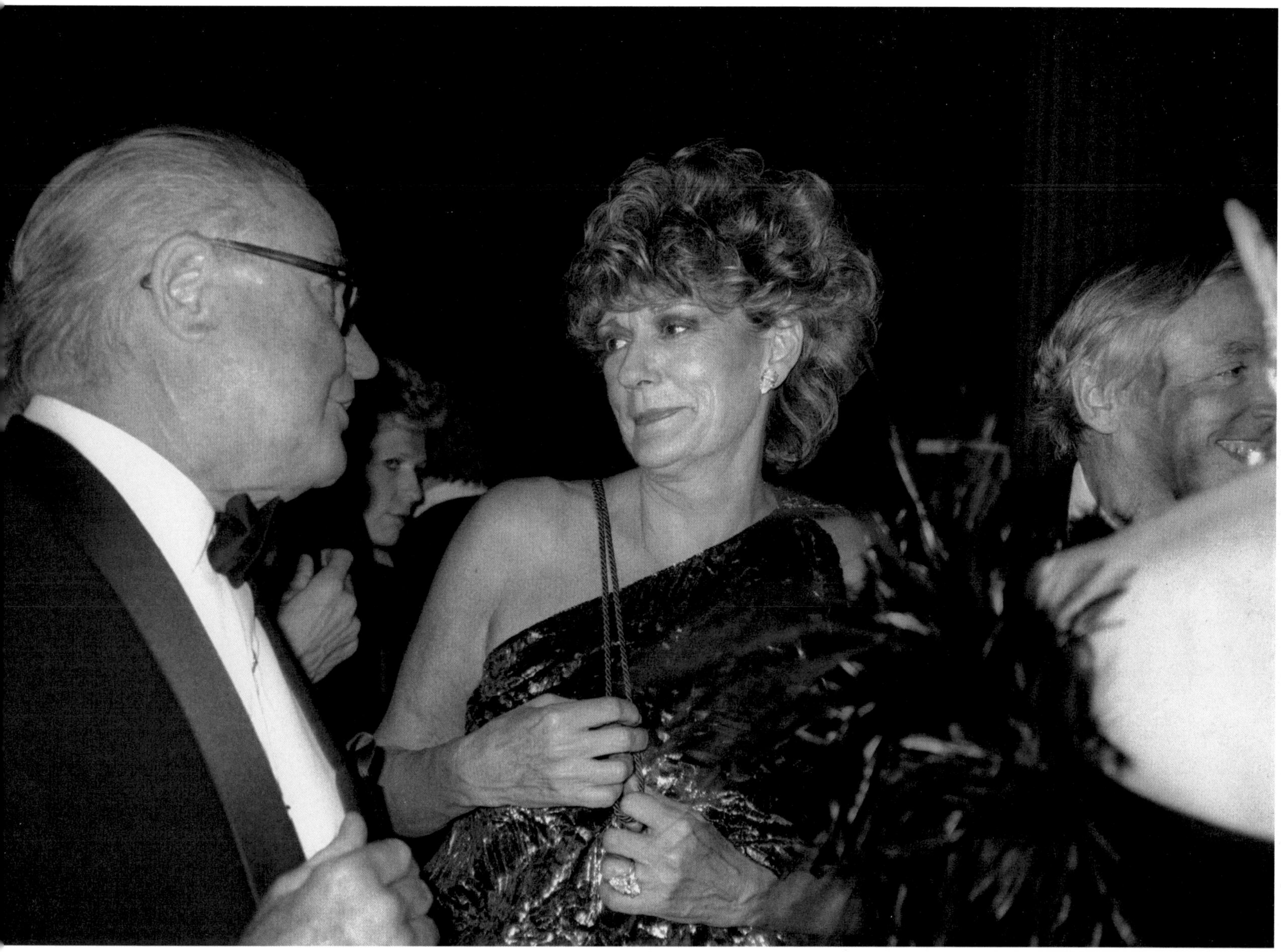

Name Unknown, Pat Buckley, and William F. Buckley
at the Costume Institute's Met Ball Benefit held
at the Metropolitan Museum of Art.
December 1983

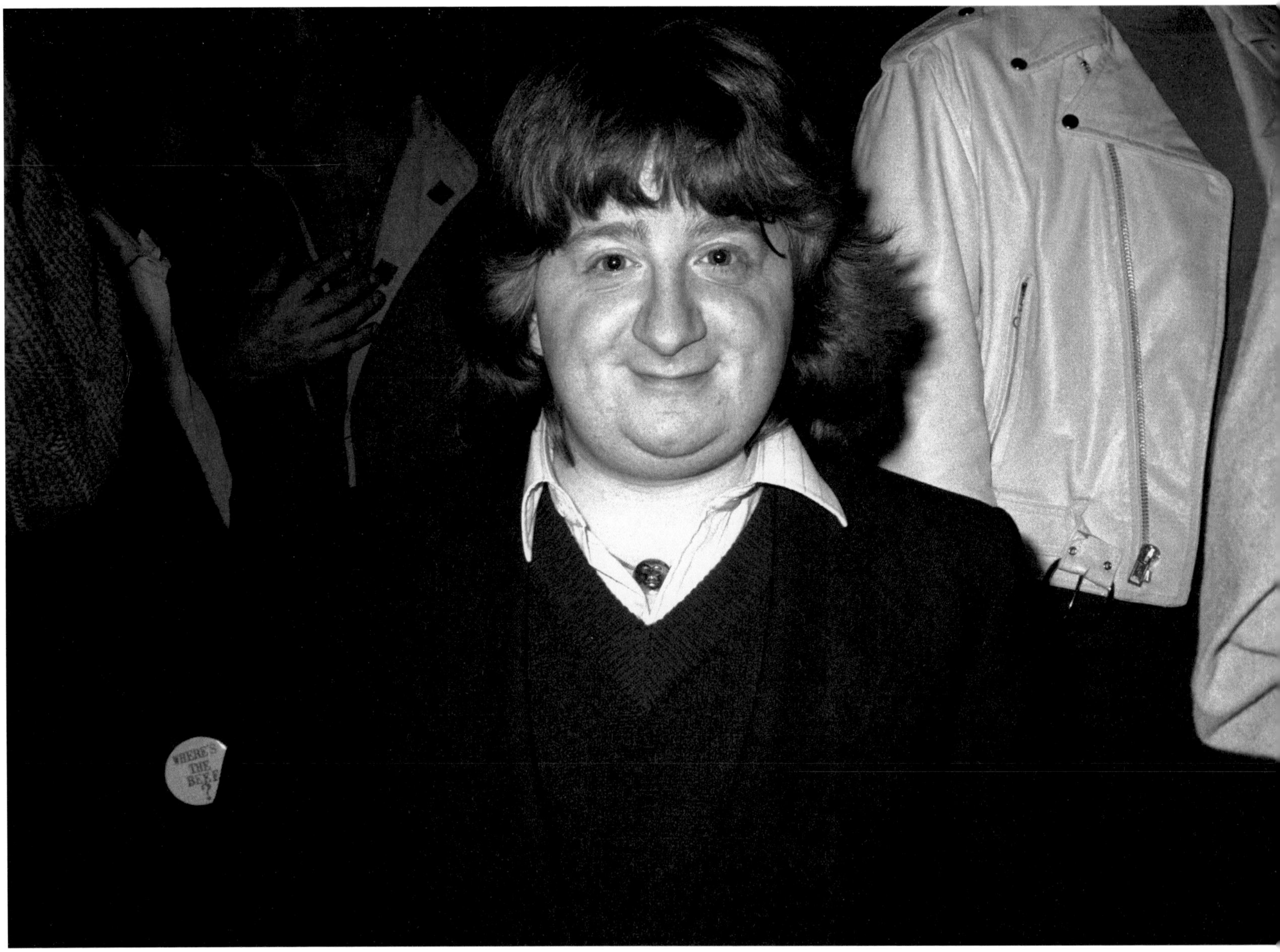

MASON REESE
AT LIMELIGHT FOR THE BRITISH INVASION FASHION SHOW
HOSTED BY SUSANNE BARTSCH.
APRIL 1983

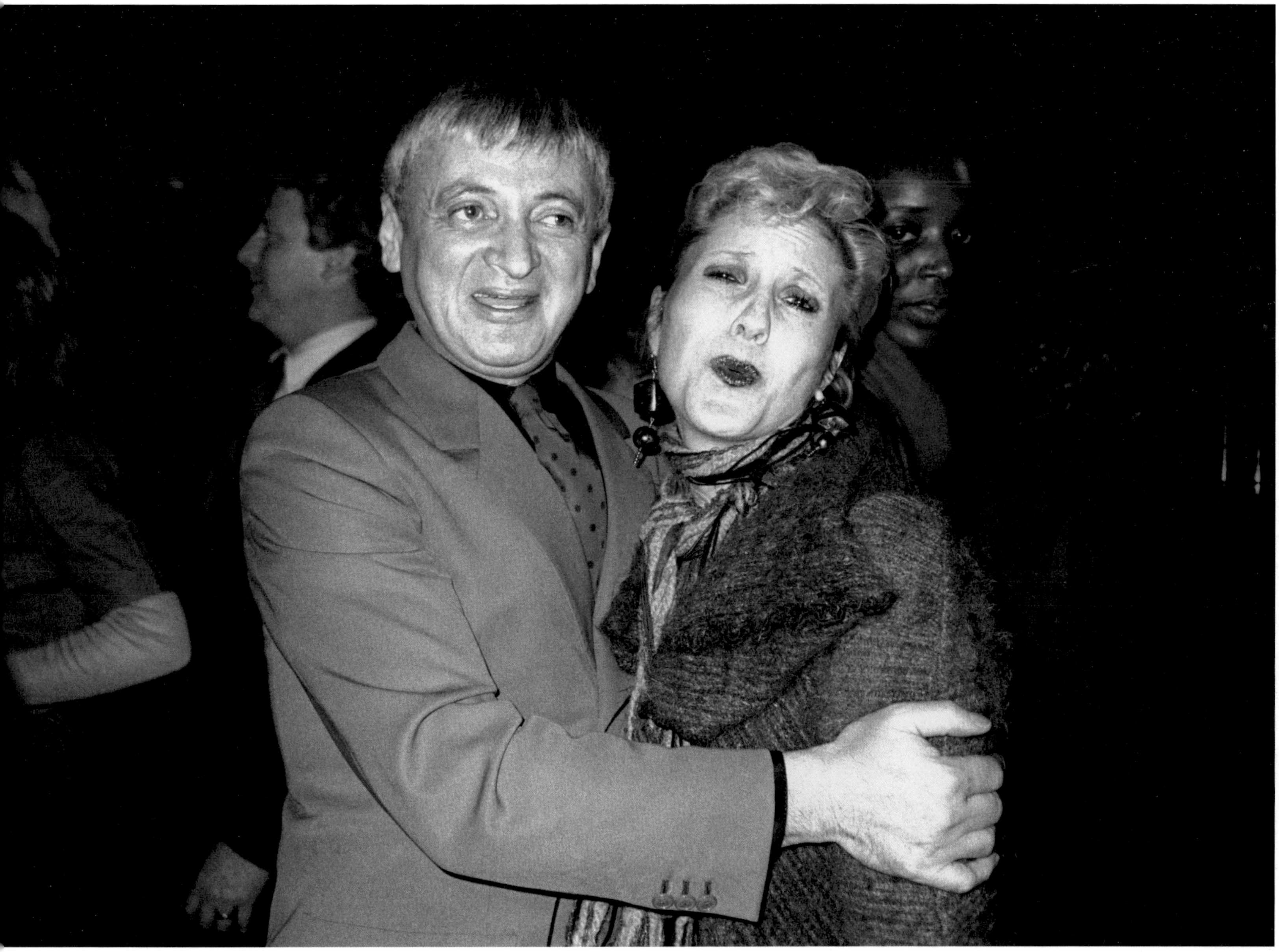

Jacques Bellini and Tinkerbelle
at the Red Parrot.
December 1983

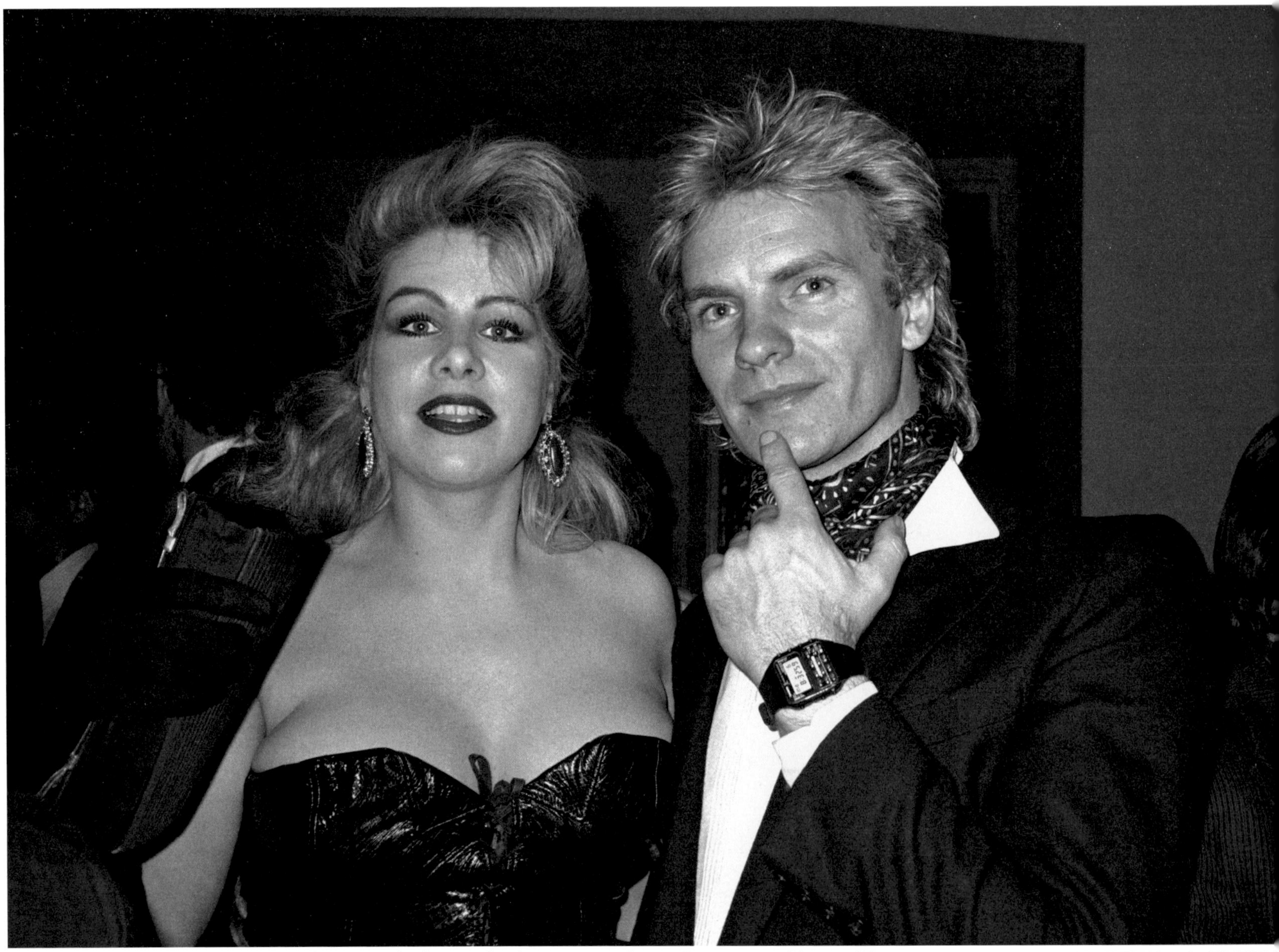

"Now we say 'it girl'--she's our 'in'--she's 'our girl,' she's over. Next. Then we said she is royal, a queen even, 'Queen of the Night.' A few of us worked the title through the 80s with a commitment of an elected position a 'so 80s' approach. Self promotion as a way of life. Please, what could be more fabulous!"
Dianne Brill

Dianne Brill and Sting
at William Burroughs event held at Limelight.
February 1984

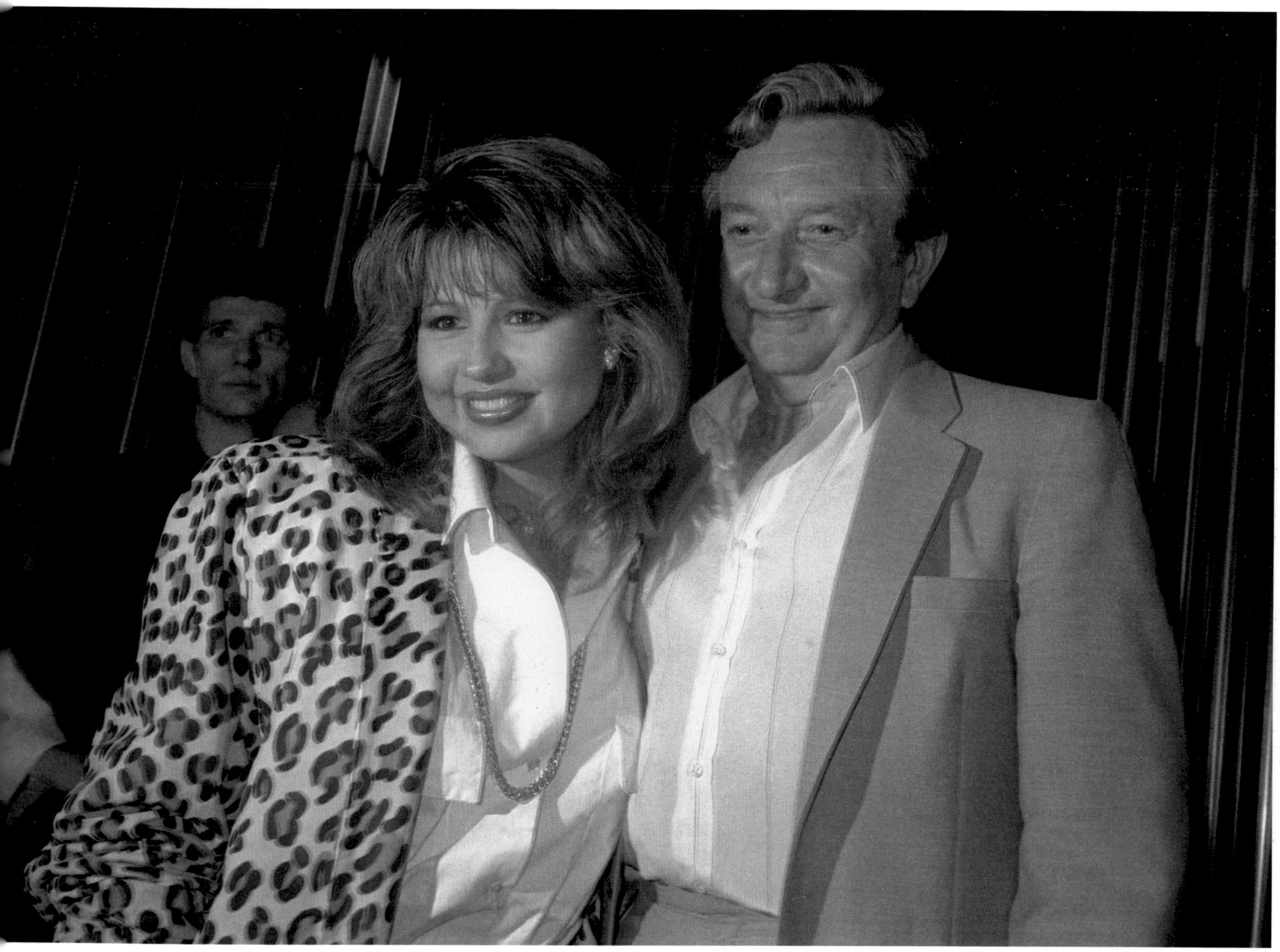

John Carmen (in background), Pia Zadora, and Meshulam Riklis
at the Jackson Family Party at Limelight.
Sunday, August 5, 1984

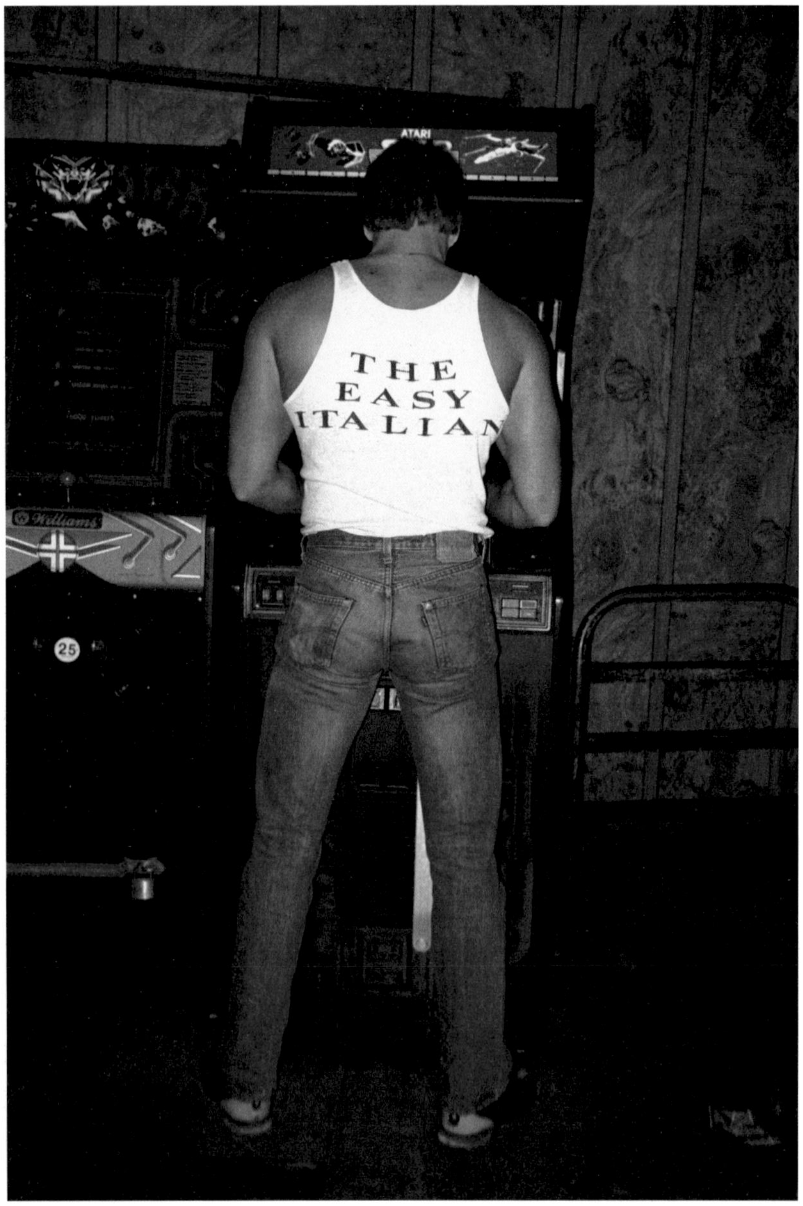

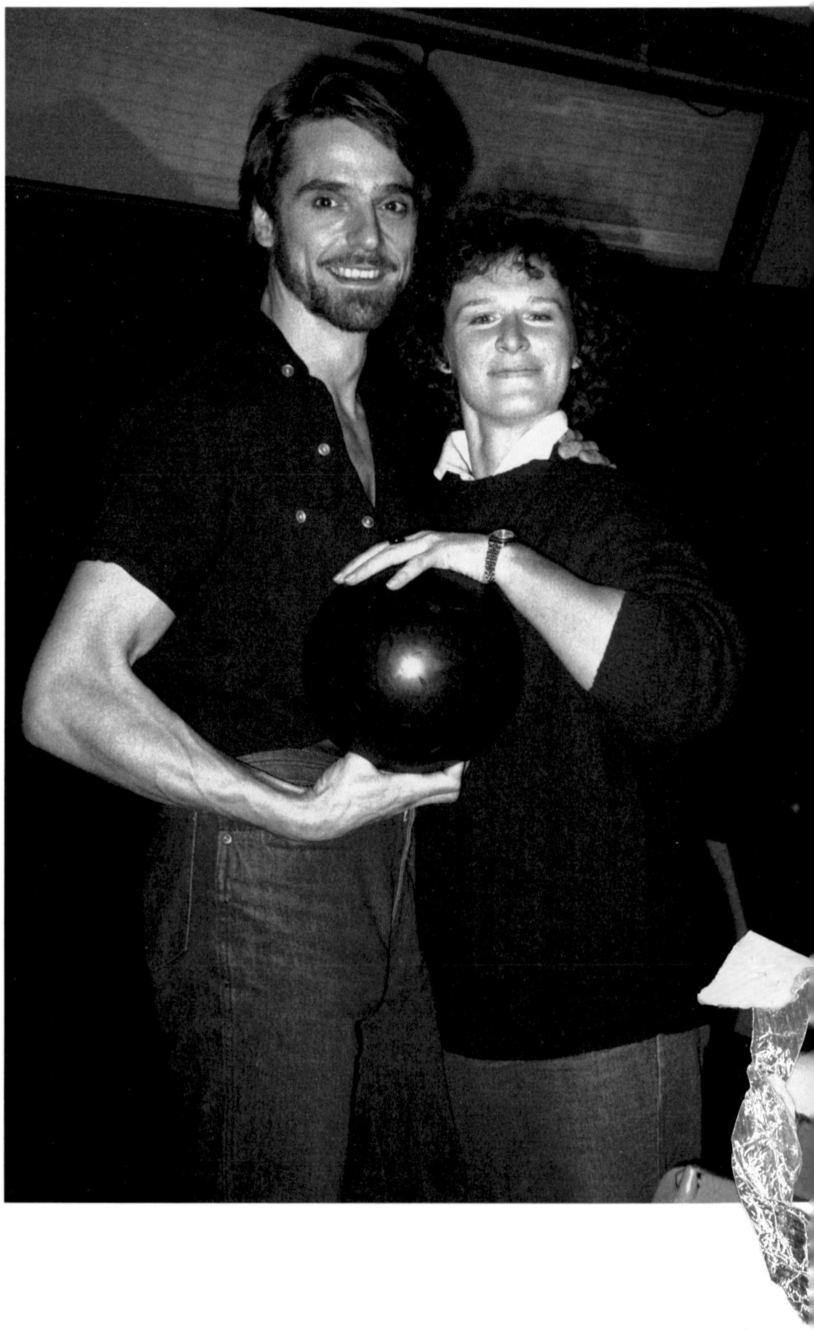

Top Left: The "Easy Italian"
Top Right: Jeremy Irons and Glenn Close
at the Bowling Club, Bowlmor Lanes.
December 1983

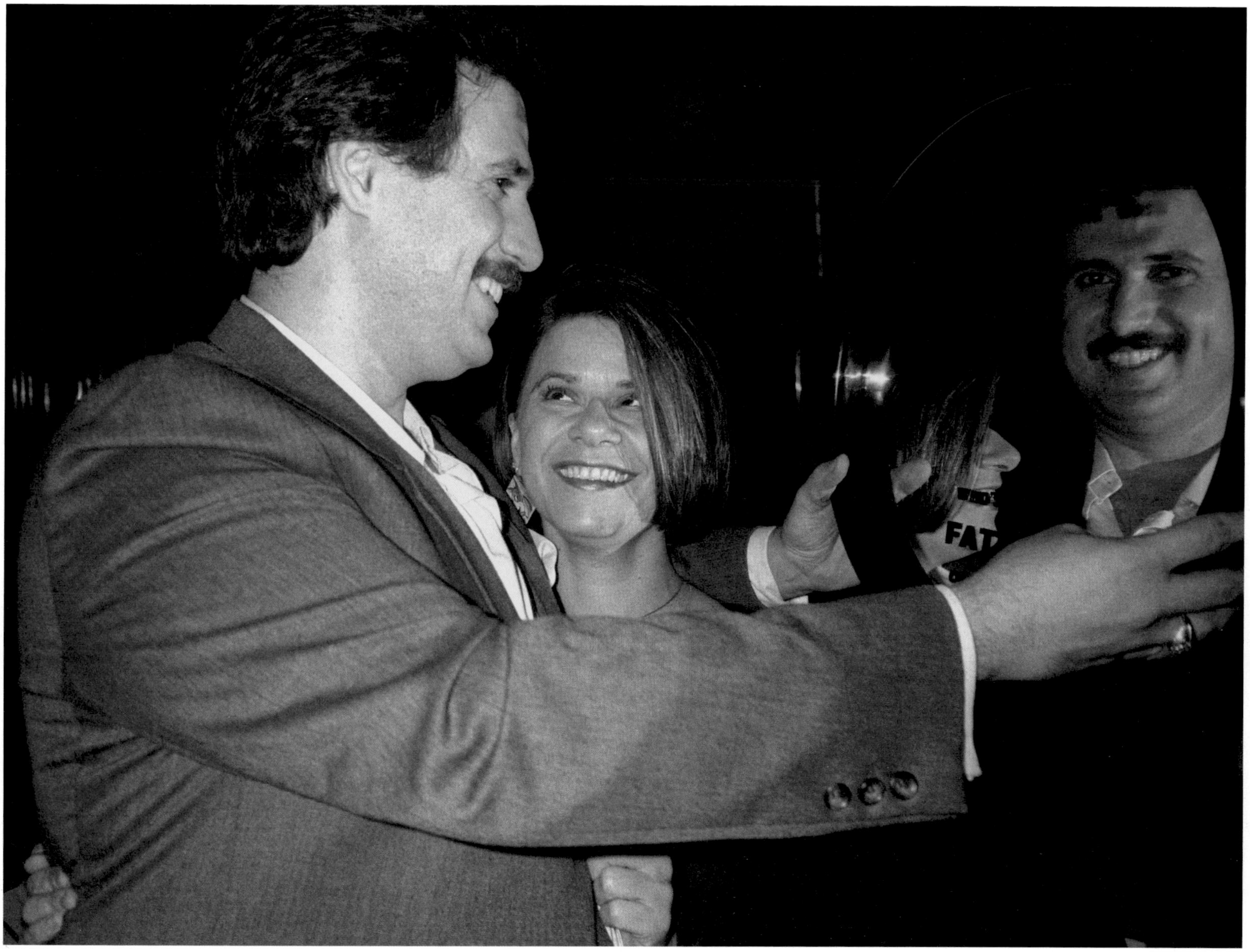

Vito Bruno and Janet Paist
at Vito Bruno's birthday party at Area.
Wednesday, October 3, 1984

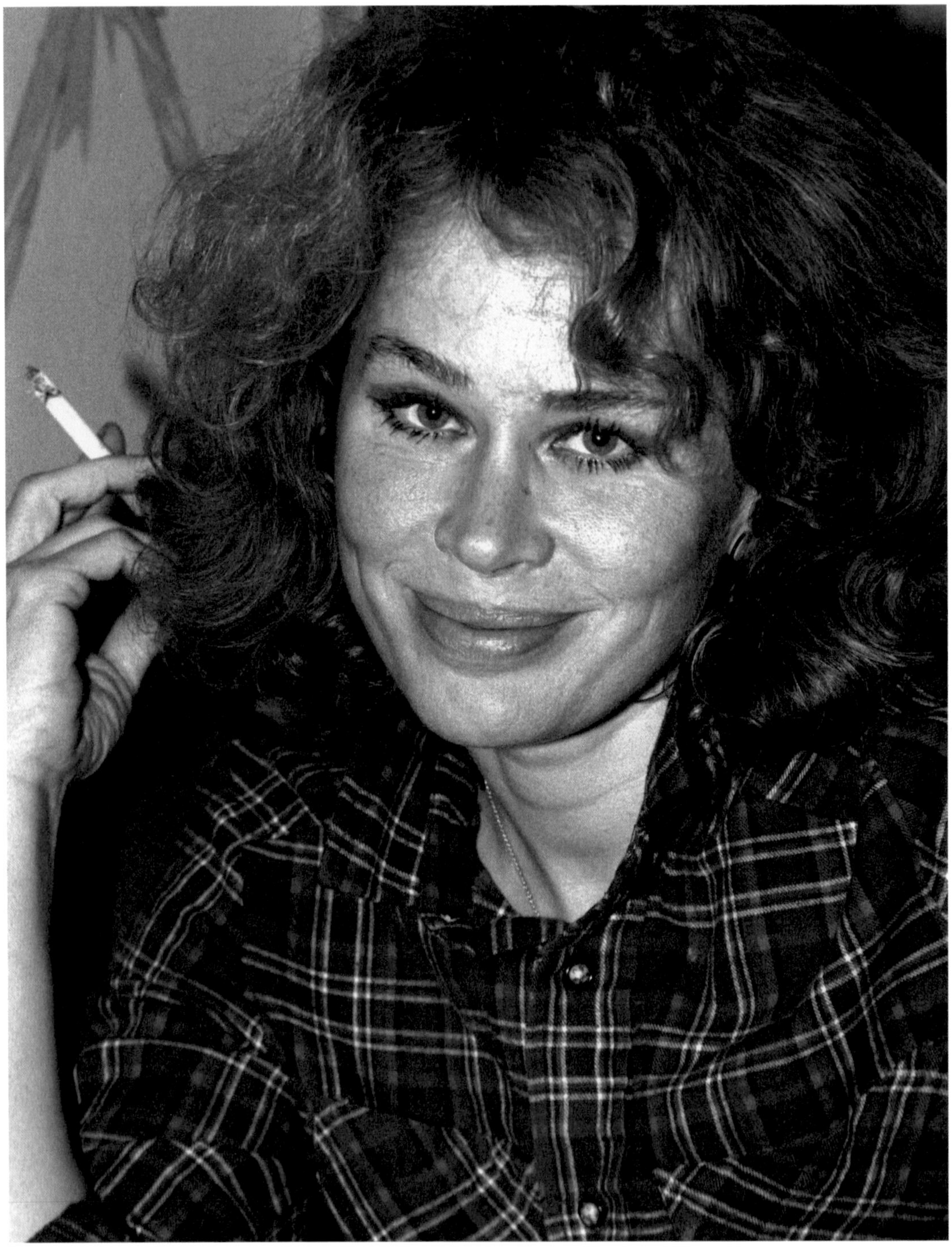

Karen Black
Portrait Series for 212 magazine.
December 1983

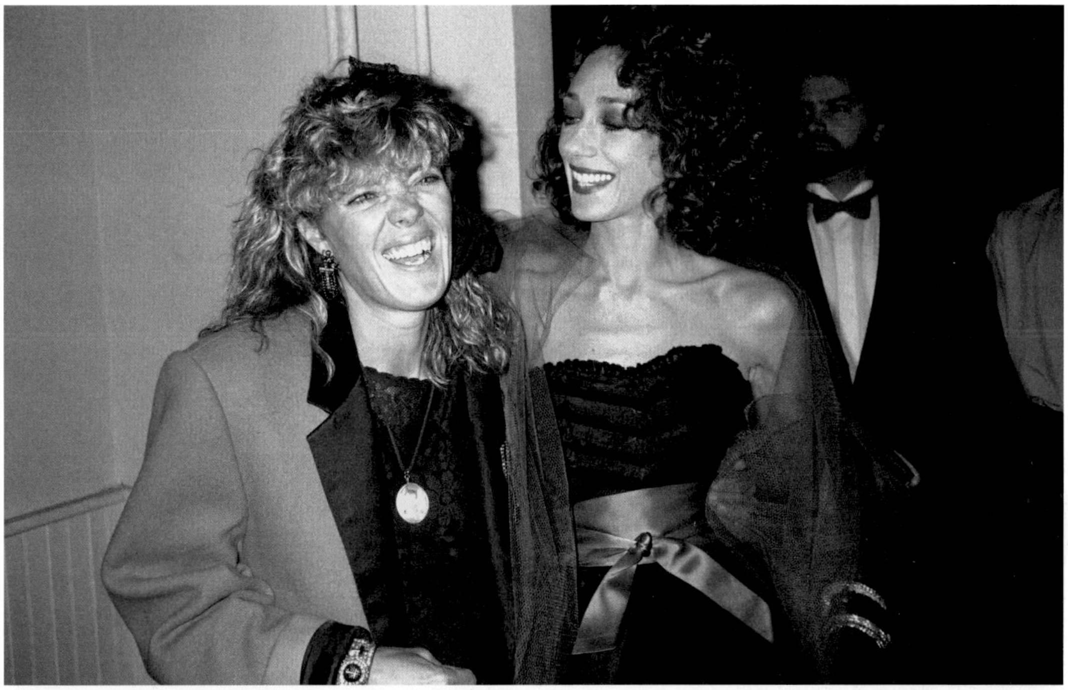

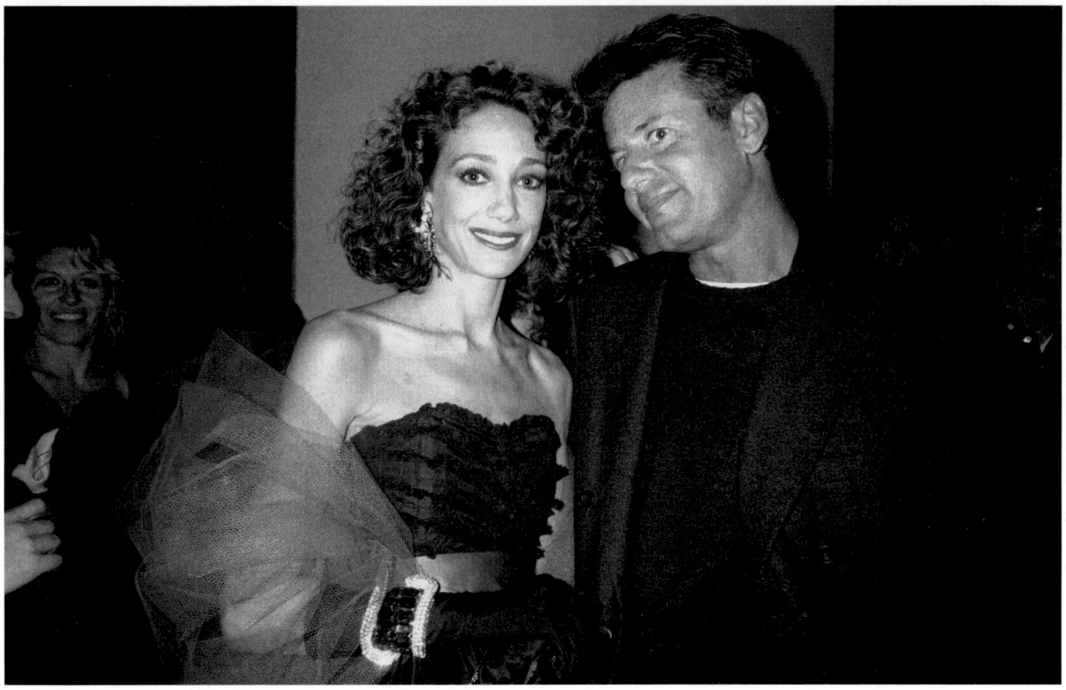

Top: Berry and Marisa Berenson
Bottom: Marisa Berenson and Calvin Klein
at Marisa Berenson's Dressing Up book party held at Limelight.

"Once upon a time there was a Golden Age with no cell phones, Internet lounges, political correctness or Starbucks. There was, however, original art, great music, fun fashion, sensational nightlife, cheap coffee, raw sex and social interaction. Ah, the 80s... I remember them well."
Ronnie Cutrone

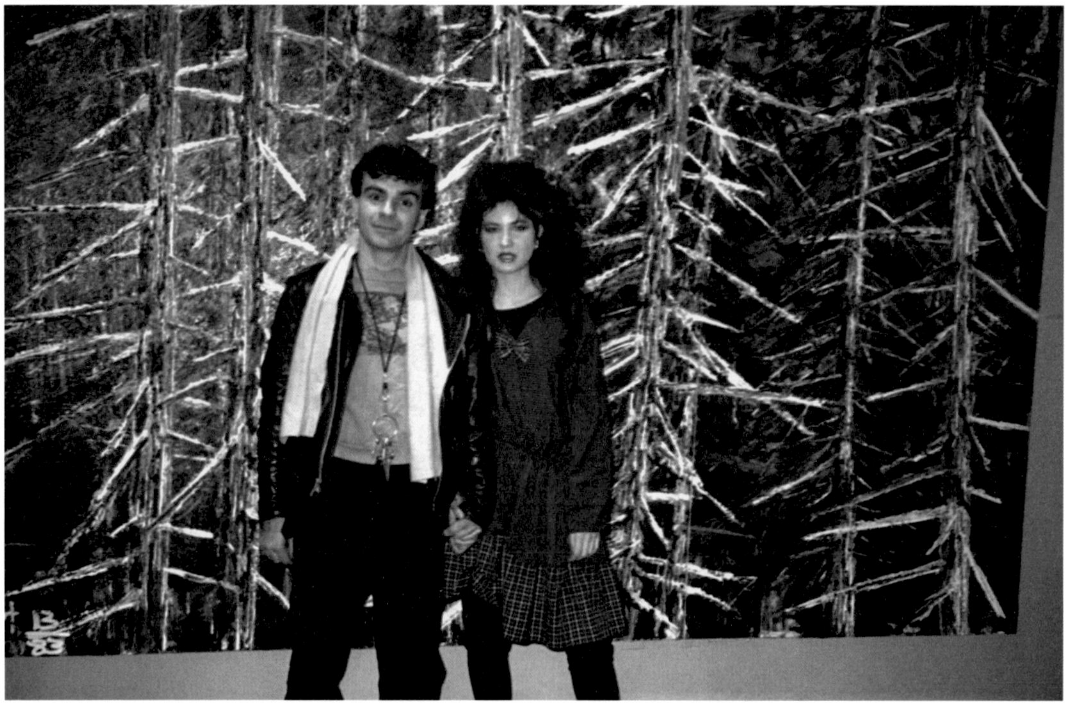

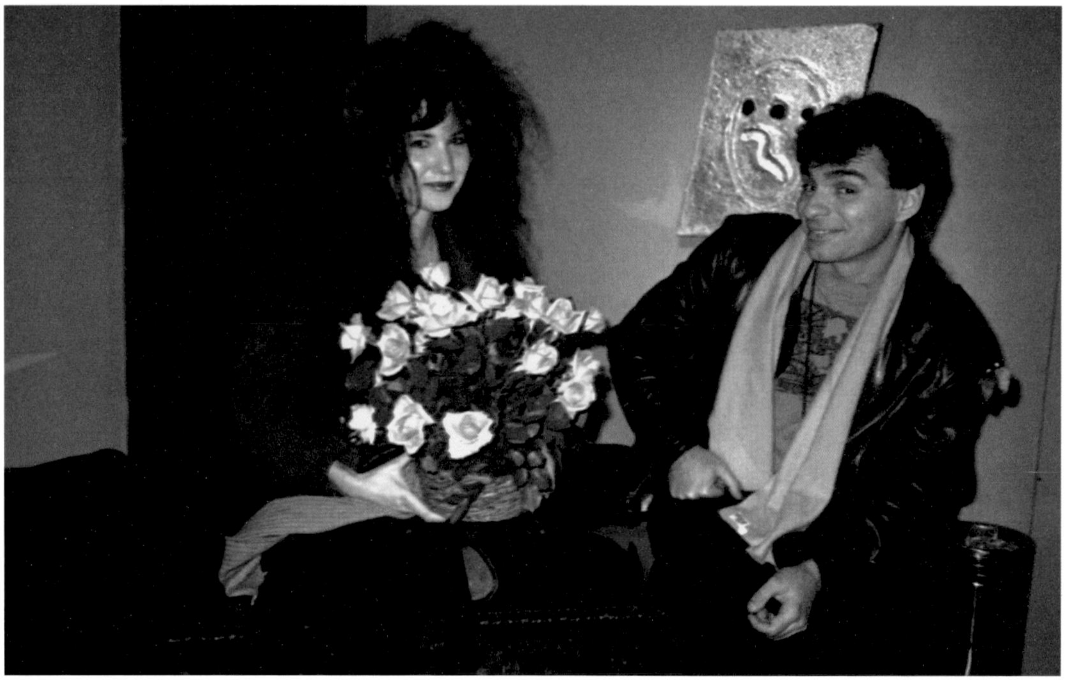

Top: Ronnie Cutrone and Tama Janowitz
Bottom: Tama Janowitz and Ronnie Cutrone
at the Charles Cowles Gallery. December 1983
Right: Keith Haring at the 611 Broadway studio.
August 14, 1984

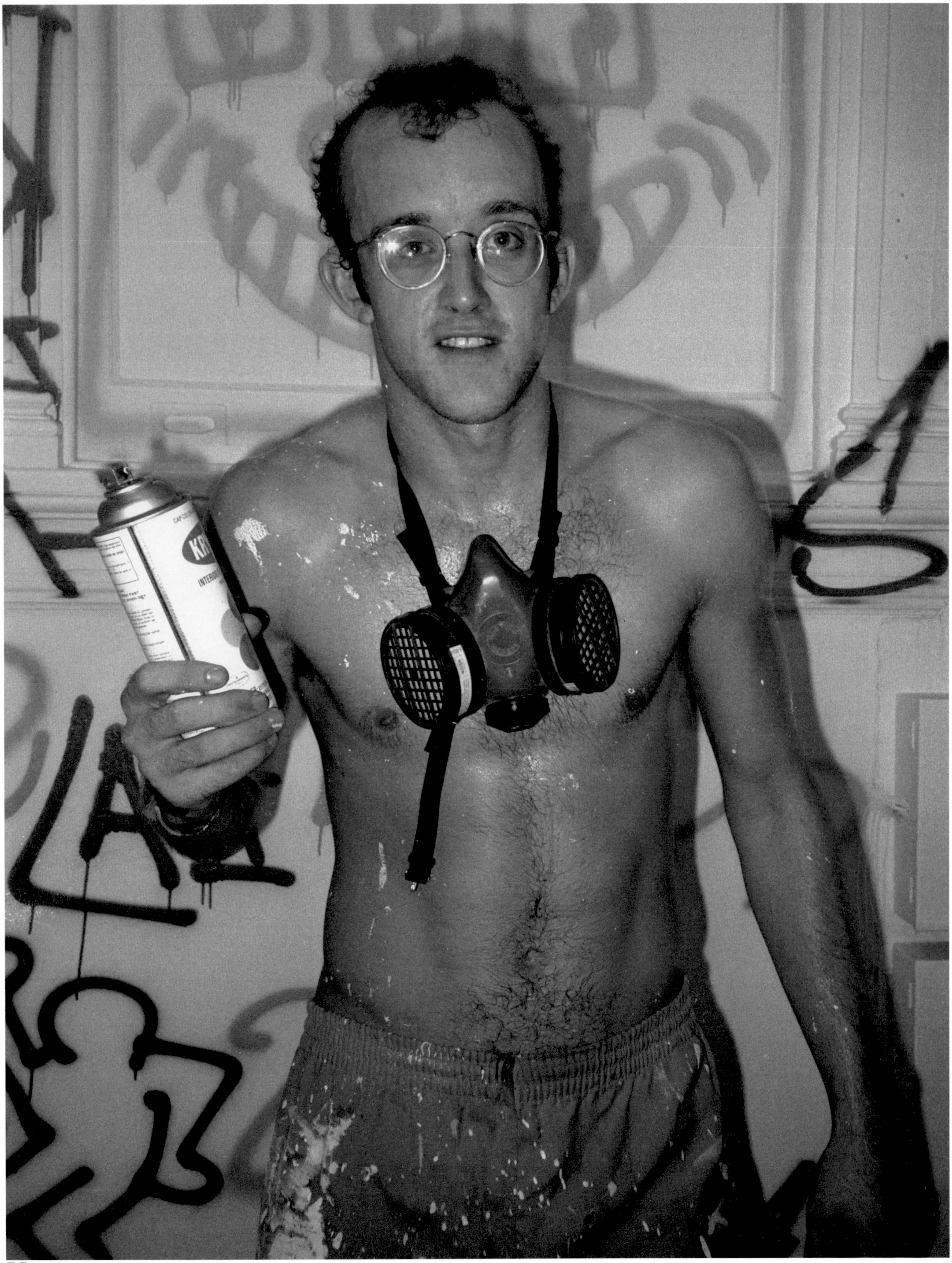

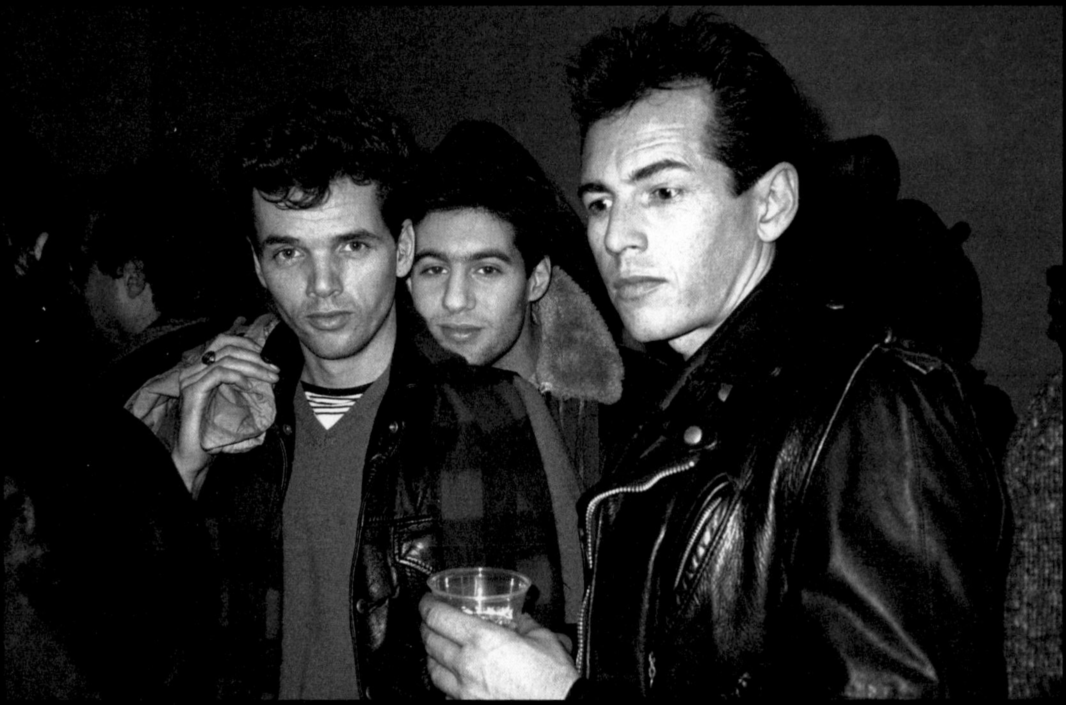

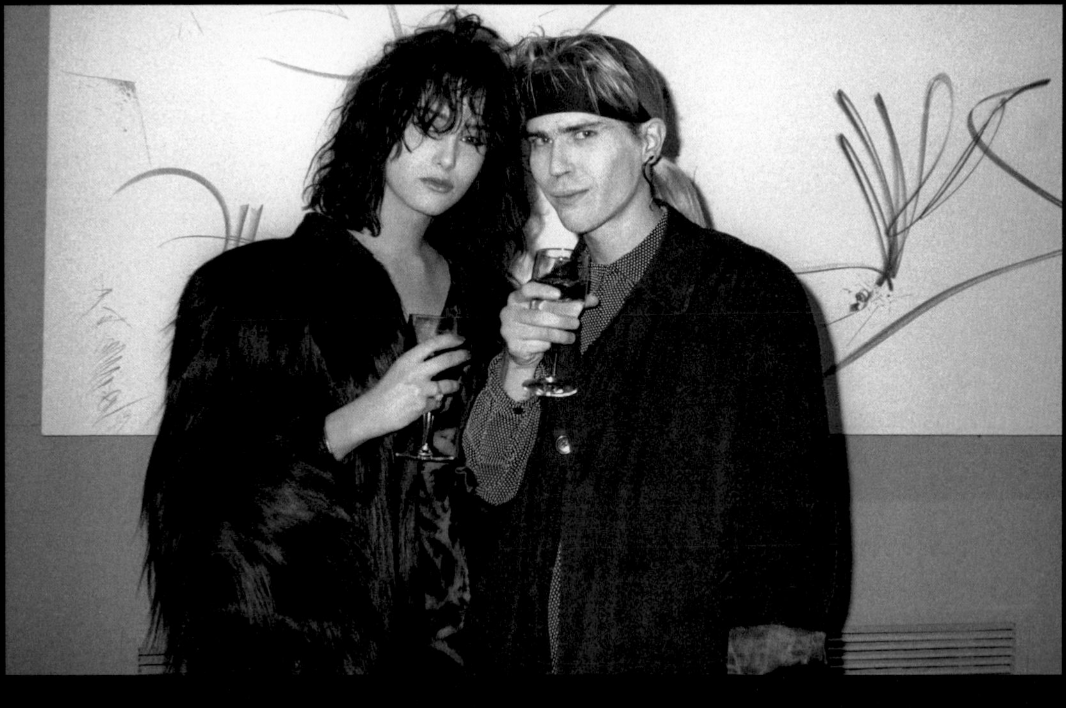

Top: Marcus Leatherdale, John Dugdale, and James Ford
at the Bette Stoler Gallery. December 1983
Bottom: Leza Cruz and Jim Breese
at the Tower Gallery opening. Fall 1983

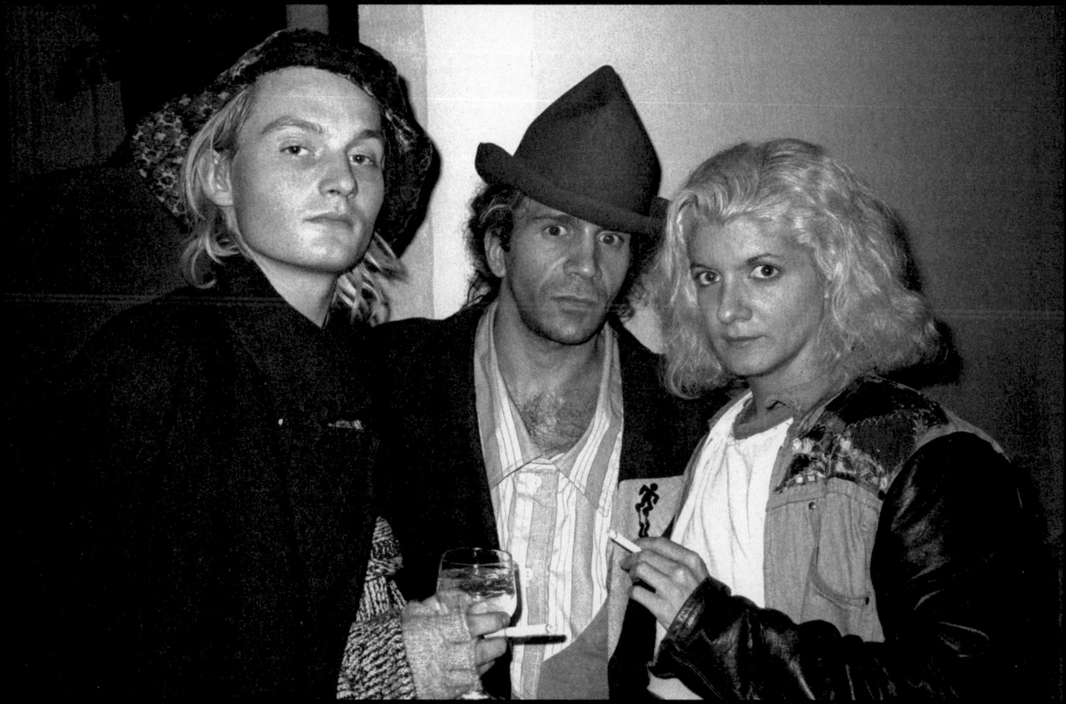

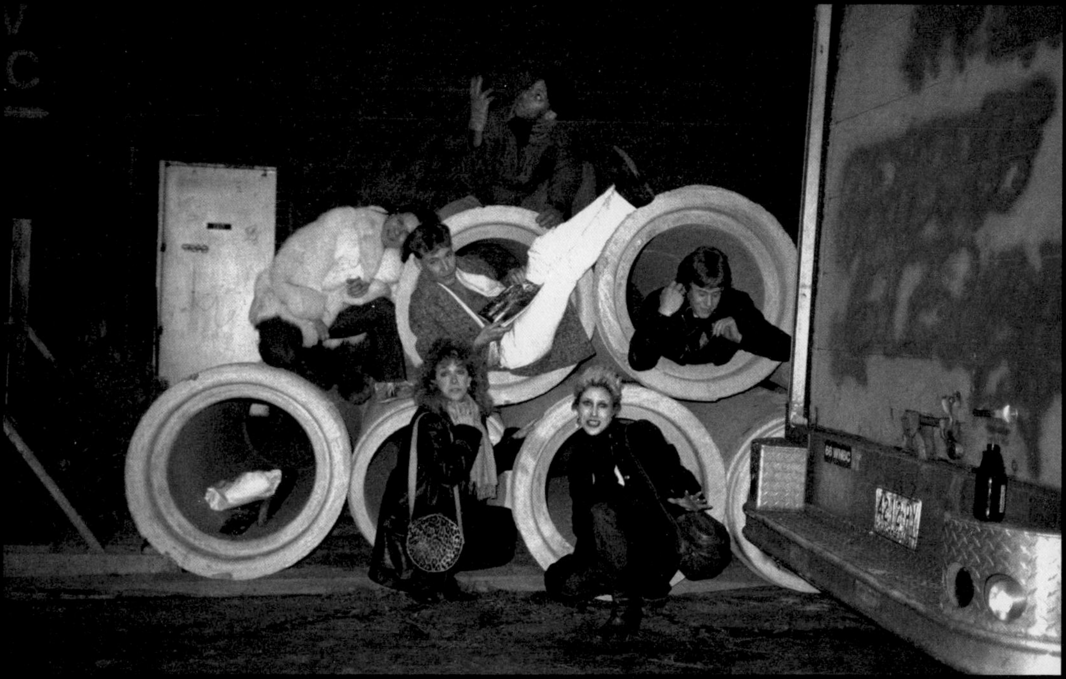

Top: Fetish, Genaro Palermo, and Chi Chi Valenti
at Danceteria. December 1983
Bottom: (top to Bottom) Name Unknown, Janet Paist, Burt, Chris,
Karon Bihari, and Tinkerbelle on the street, after Kamikaze.
December 1983

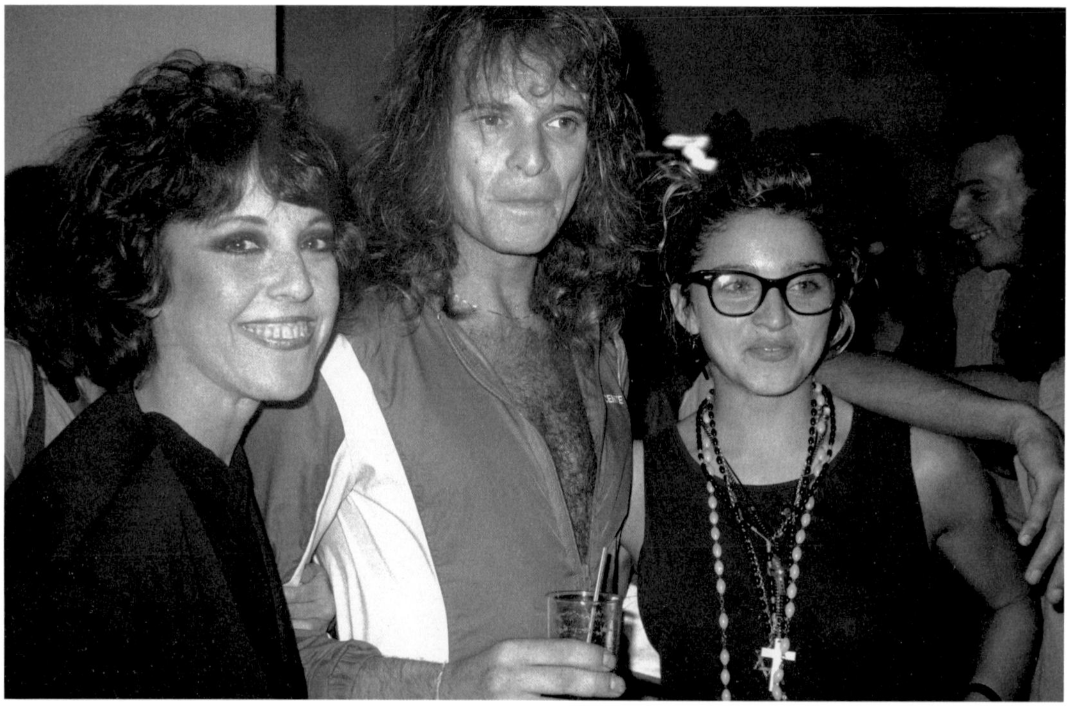

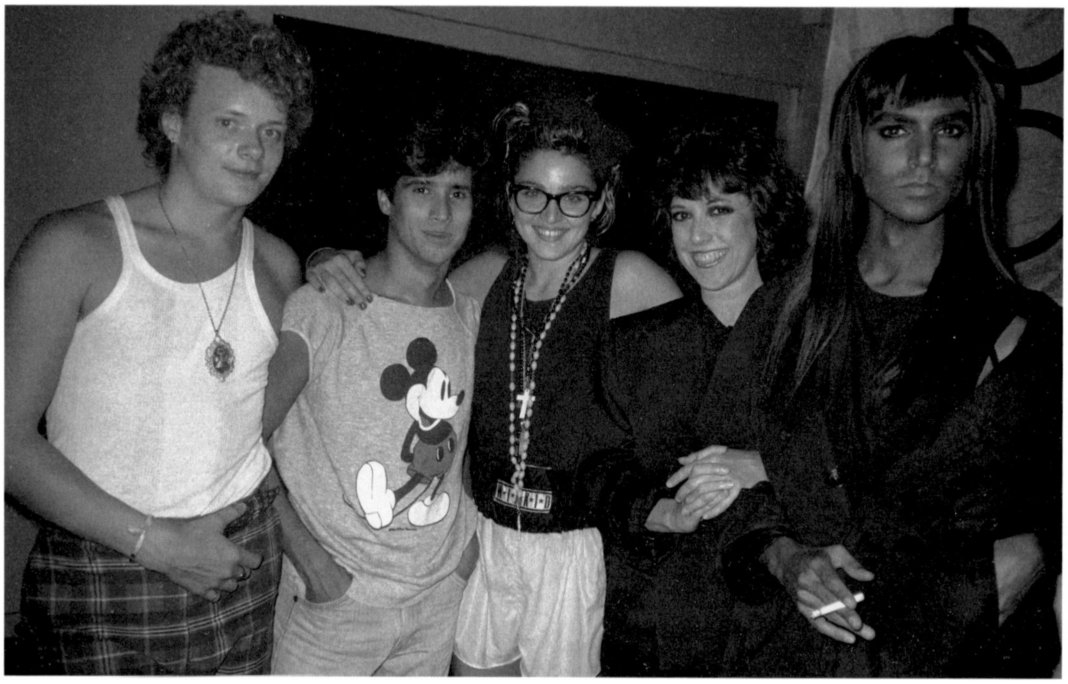

Top: Lisa Robinson, David Lee Roth, and Madonna
Bottom: Martin Burgoyne, John "Jellybean" Benitez, Madonna, Lisa Robinson, and Steven Meisel
at David Lee Roth's birthday party held at Area. 1984

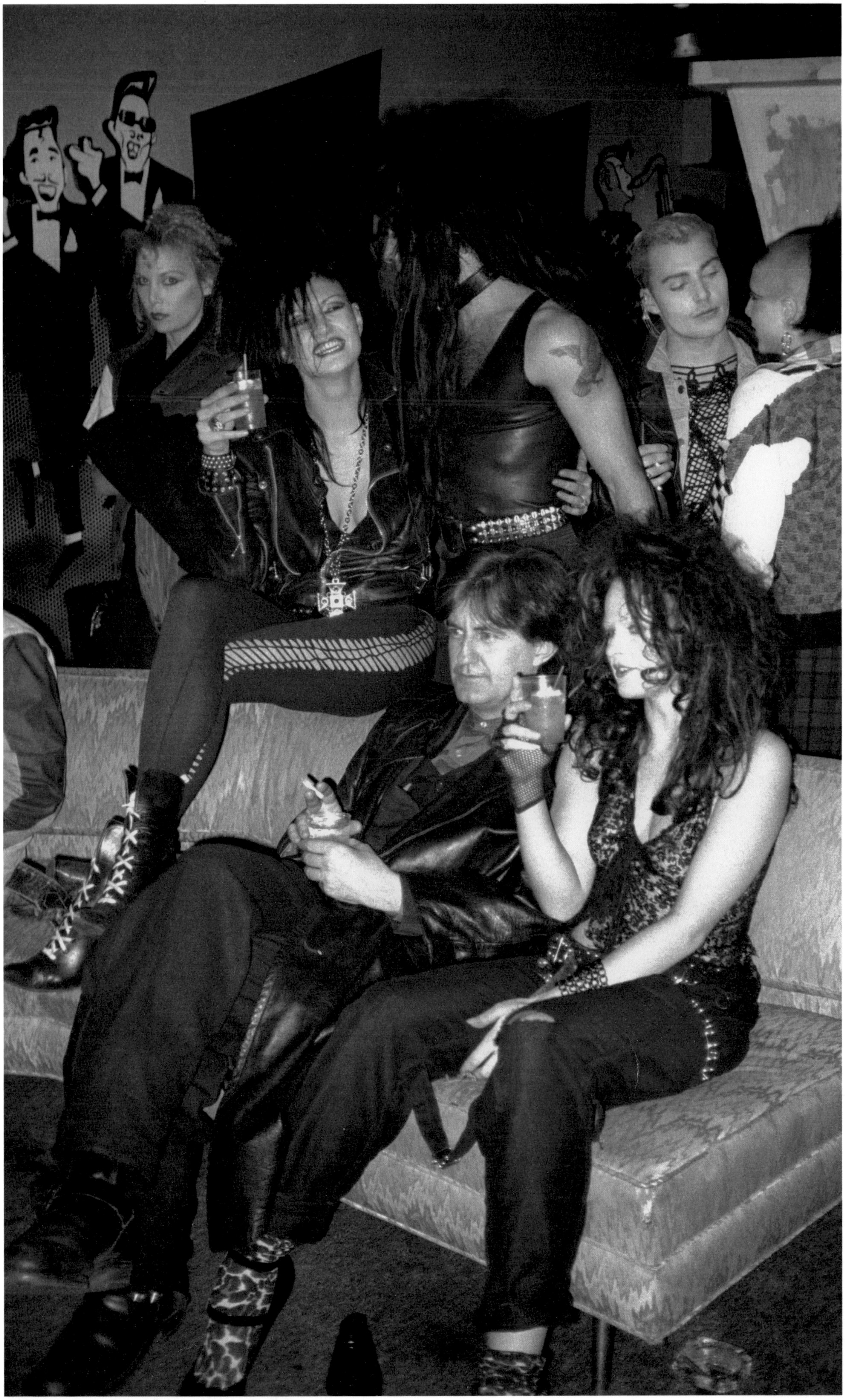

"Patrick's photos are a window onto the lost New York of the 80s--exuberant, vulgar, experimental and ultimately innocent.

Downtown was adventure and sex, with Stephen Saban chronicling the freaks and the angels; Uptown was tradition and gloss, pouf skirts meticulously documented in W. Separated by the 14th Street DMV, both soaked in aspiration and ambition."
Susan Ainsworth

Stephen Saban and friends at Danceteria. December 1983

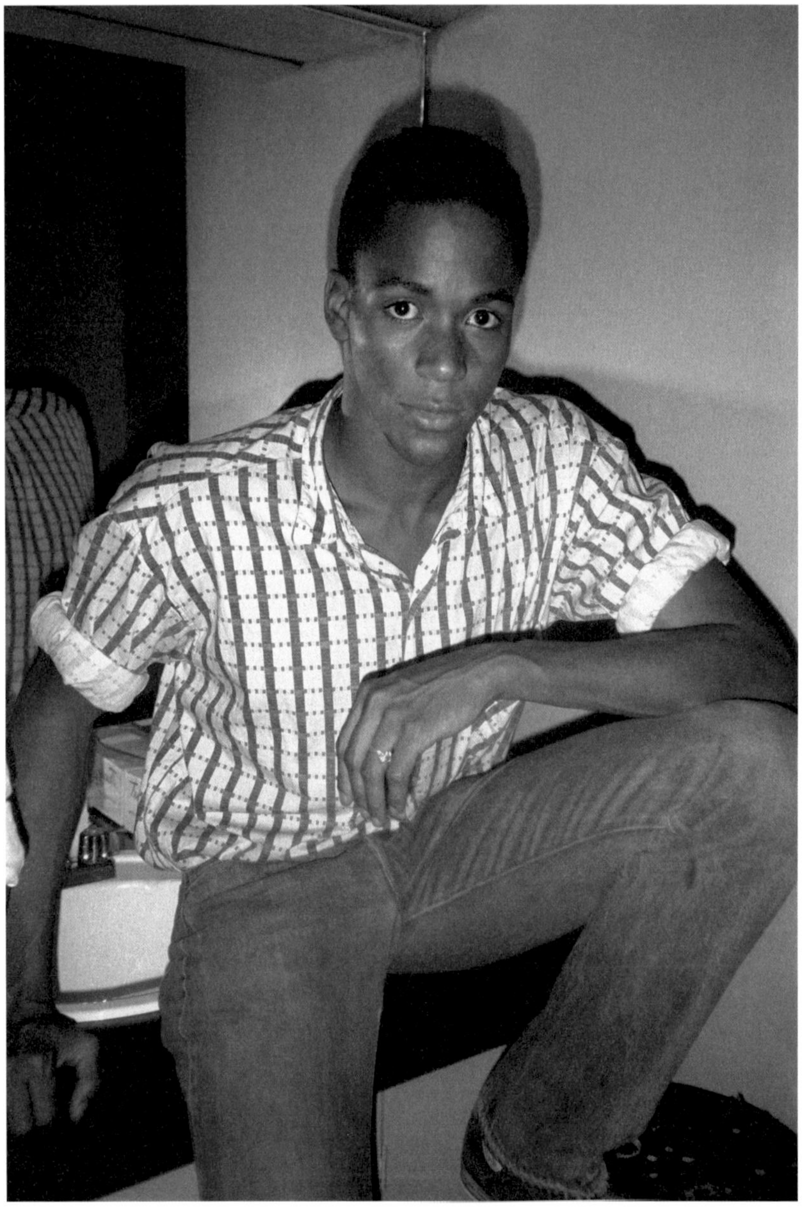 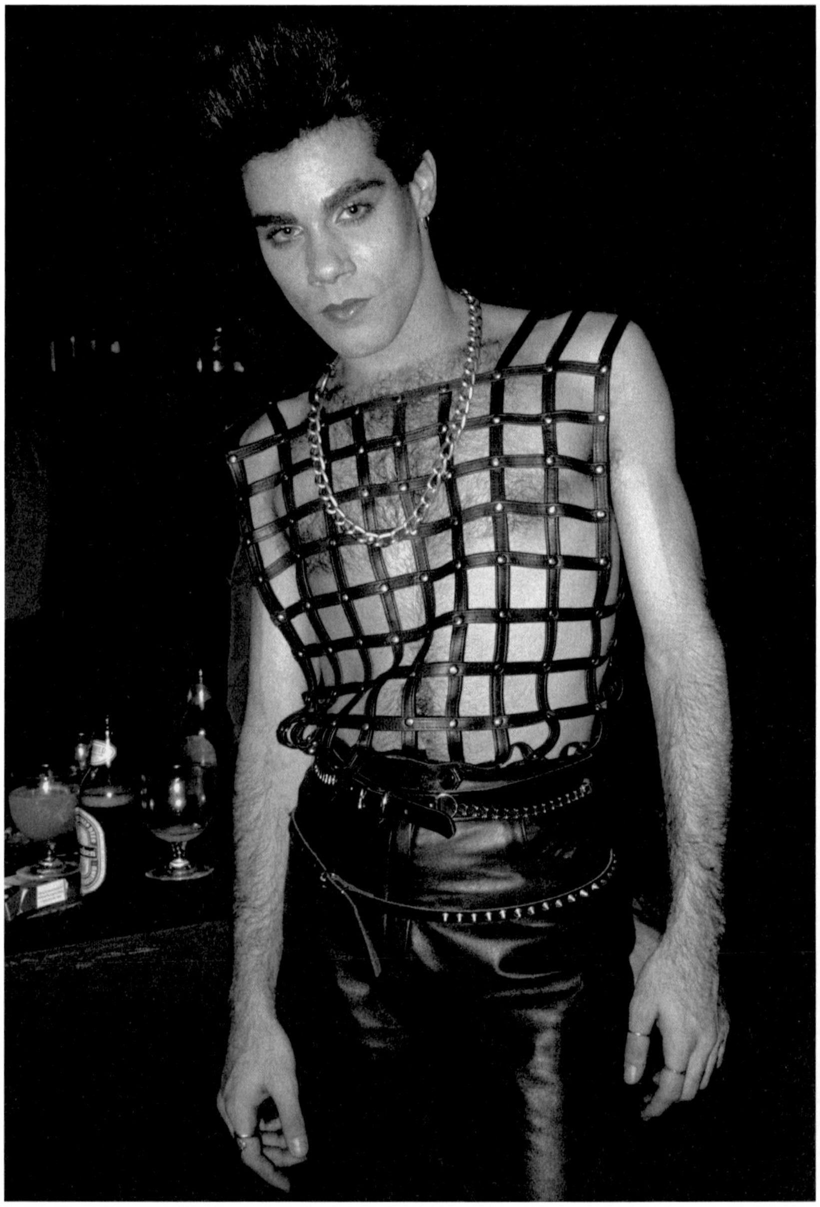

Top Left: Desmond Cadagan at Area.
Saturday, October 3, 1984
Top Right: Guest at Perri Lister's birthday party at the Cat Club.
April 10, 1984

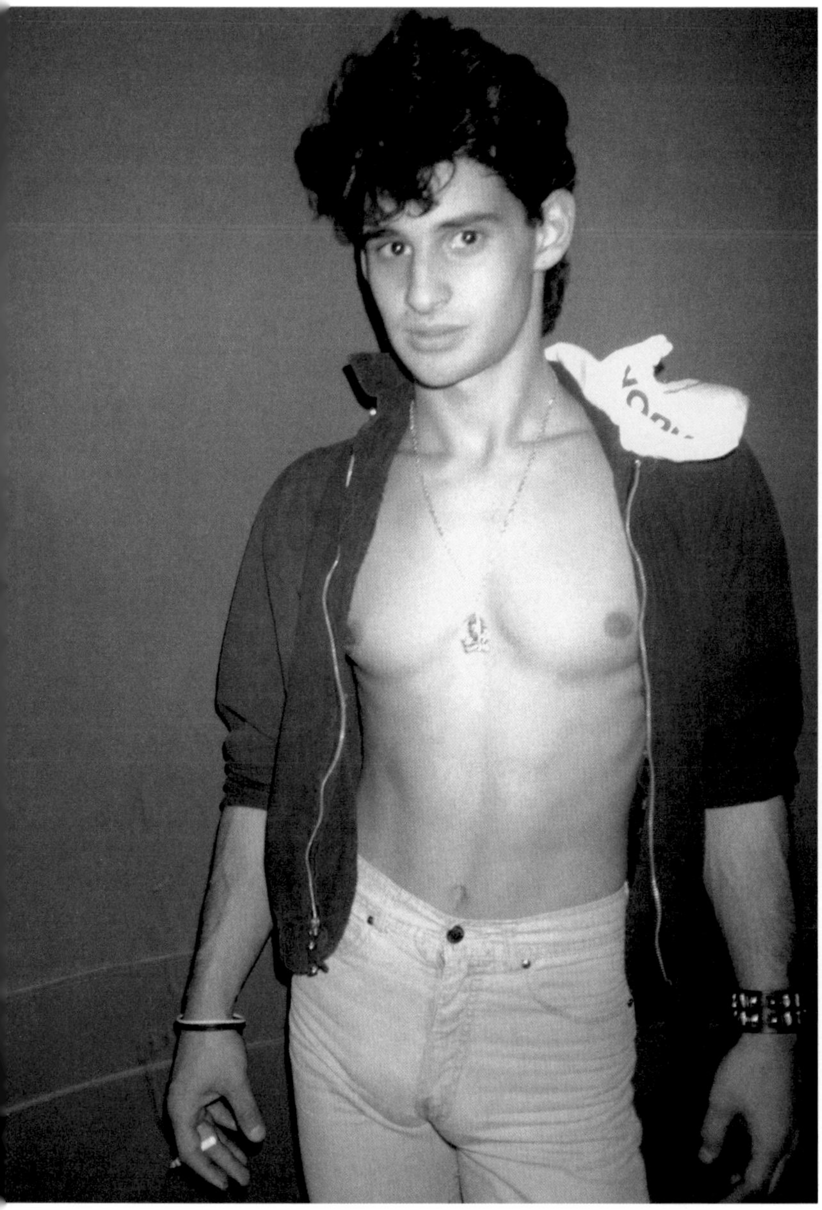

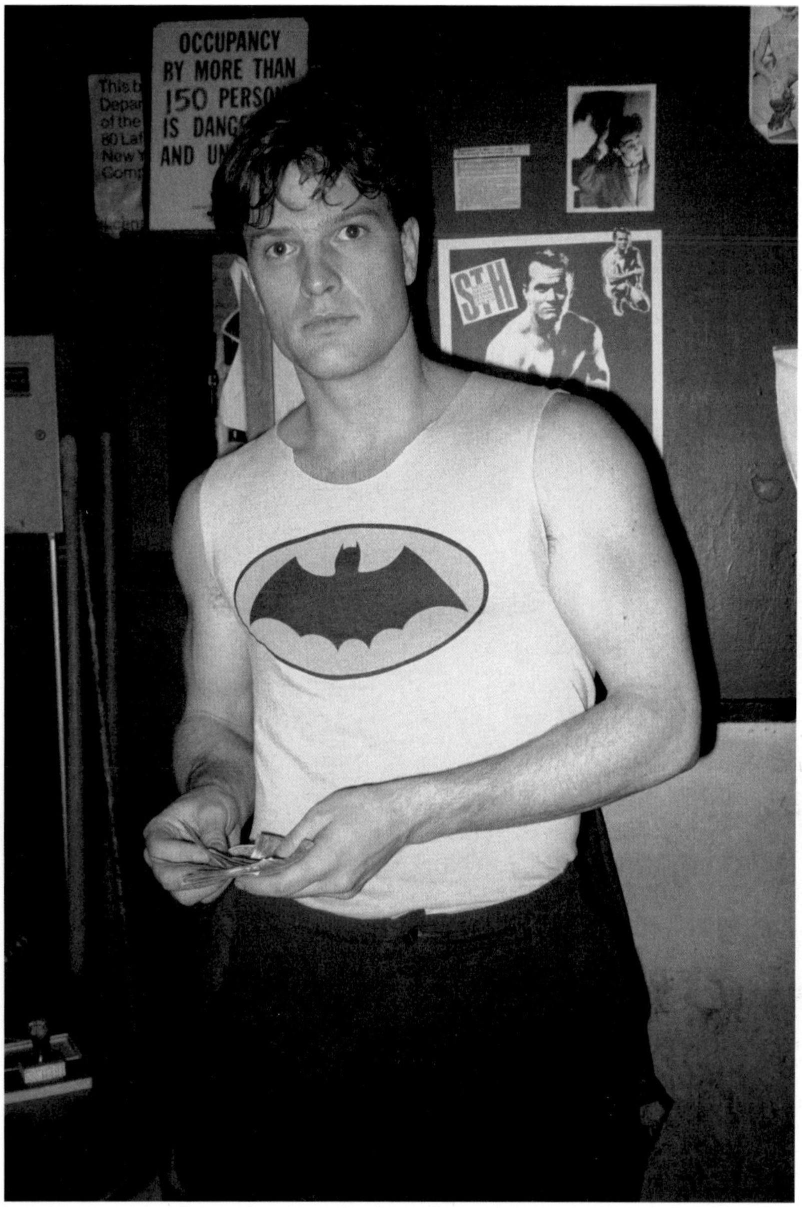

Top Left: Club boy at the Palladium. 1985
Top Right: "Bat Boy" at the Pyramid Club.
Sunday, May 20,1984

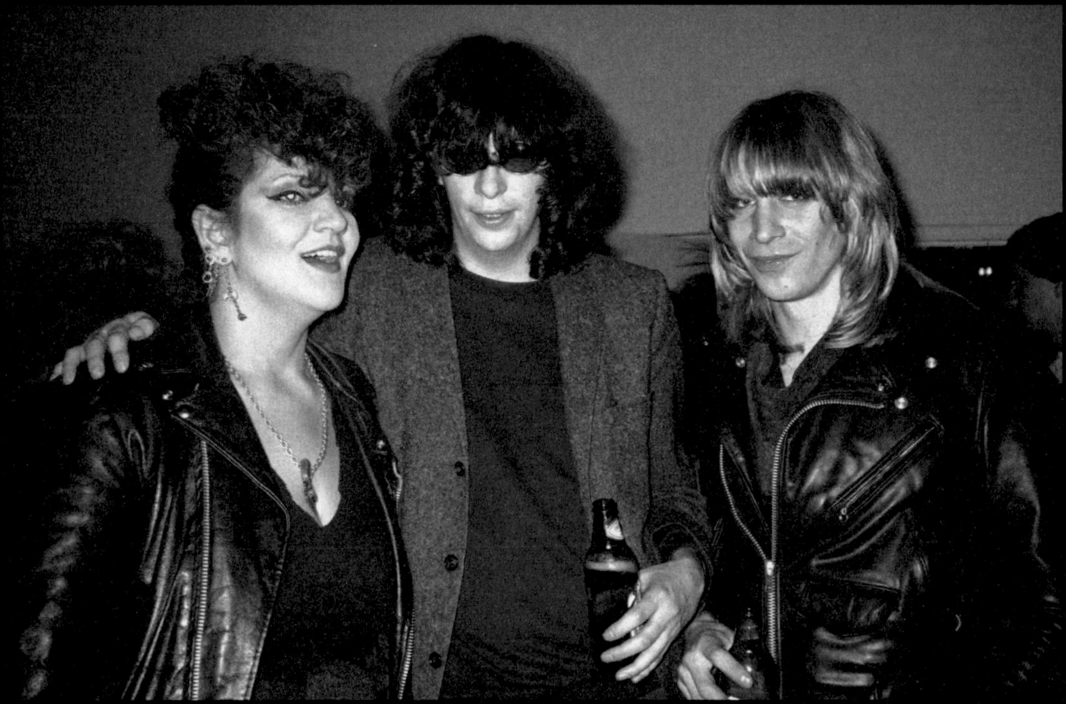

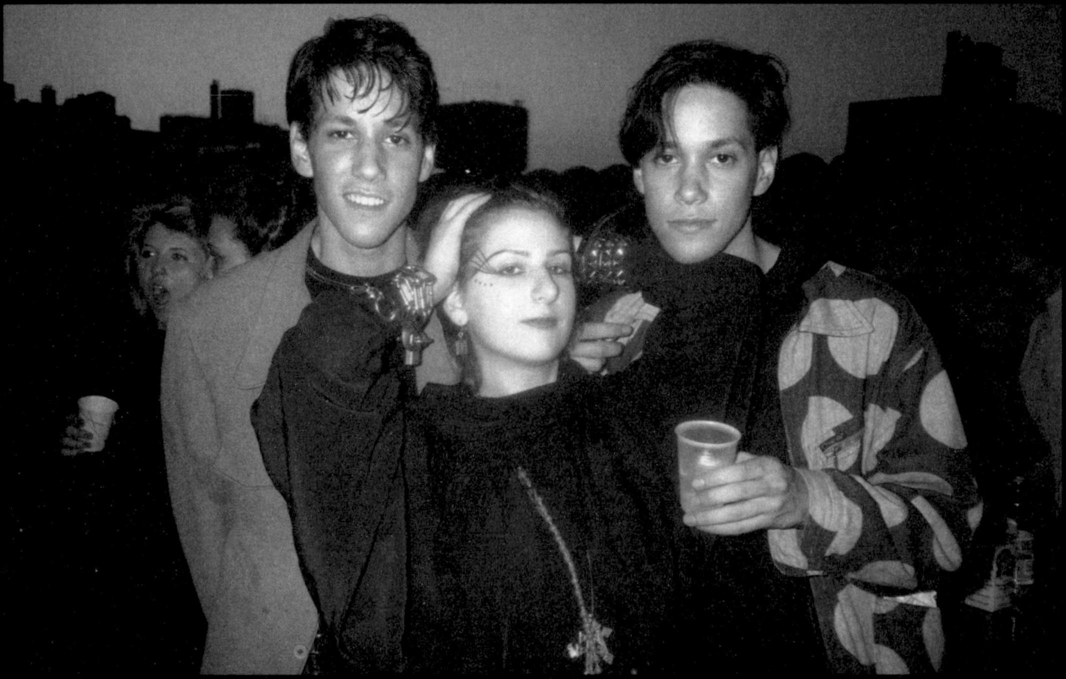

Top: Robin Cradle, Joey Ramone, and Randy Rockets
at the Gary Glitter party and concert at Limelight. May 15, 1984
Bottom: Charles and Allen Rosenberg and Miriam Bendahan
at the "Roof Top" party on 2nd Avenue.
Friday, June 13, 1986

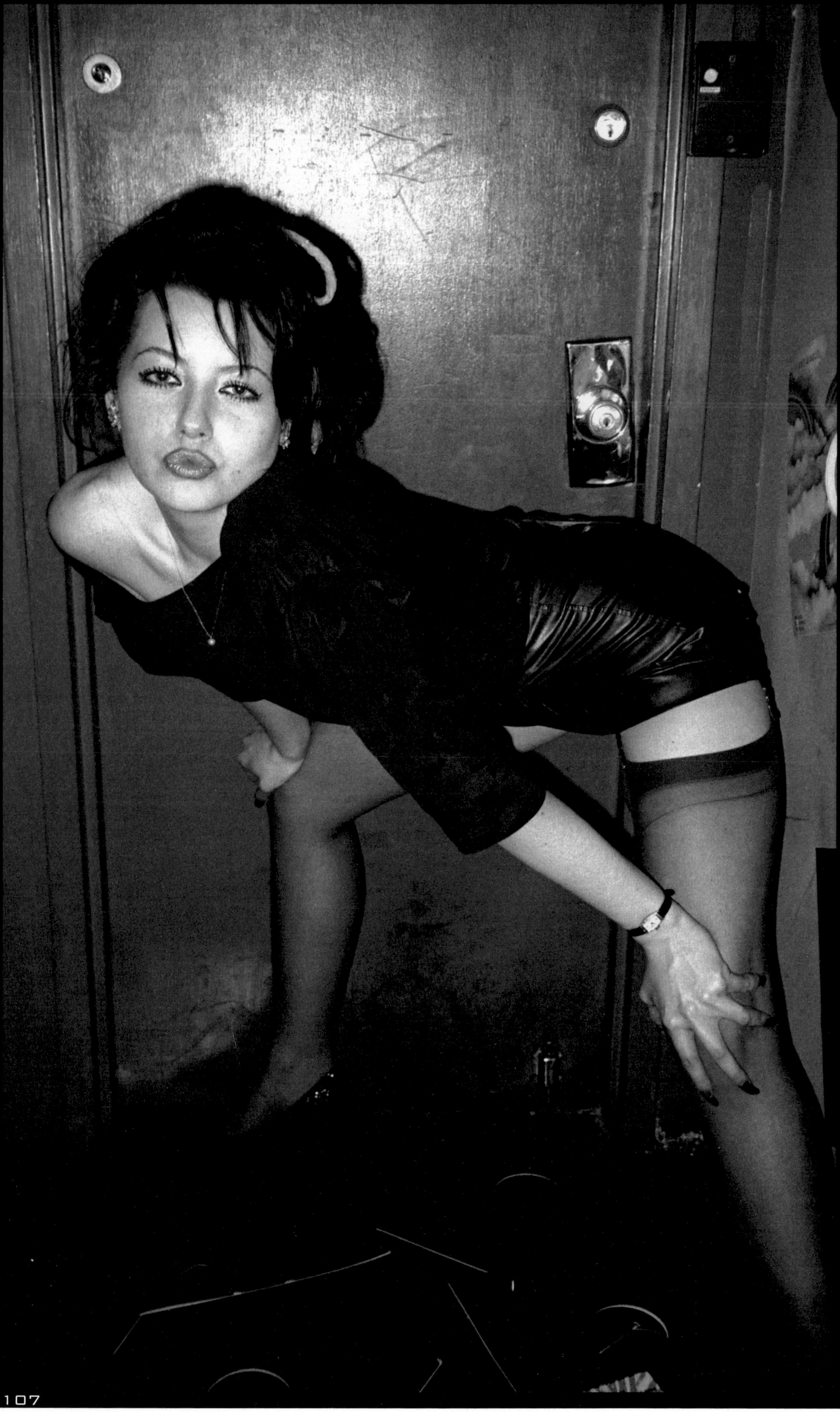

...THE 80S IN NEW YORK WERE A TIME LONG AGO AND FAR AWAY--BEFORE STARBUCKS, AND THE GAP--WHEN THERE WAS AN UPTOWN FOR FANCIES AND PREPPIES, A DOWNTOWN FOR DARK CLUBS AND FREAKS AND PUNKS, A WEST VILLAGE FOR KINKY SEXY LATE NIGHTS, AN EAST VILLAGE FOR DRUGS AND ART, AND TIMES SQUARE.

YOU COULD TELL WHERE PEOPLE WERE FROM (OR WHERE THEY WANTED YOU TO THINK THEY WERE FROM) BY THE WAY THEY DRESSED, THEIR HAIR, AND THEIR ATTITUDE.

NOW EVERYBODY LOOKS LIKE THEY SHOP AT DIESEL OR THE GAP AND EVERYBODY MEETS AT STARBUCKS. THIS IS FINE, BUT NOT AS MUCH FUN.

ALAN RISH

CHRISTINE AT DANCETERIA.
FEBRUARY 1984

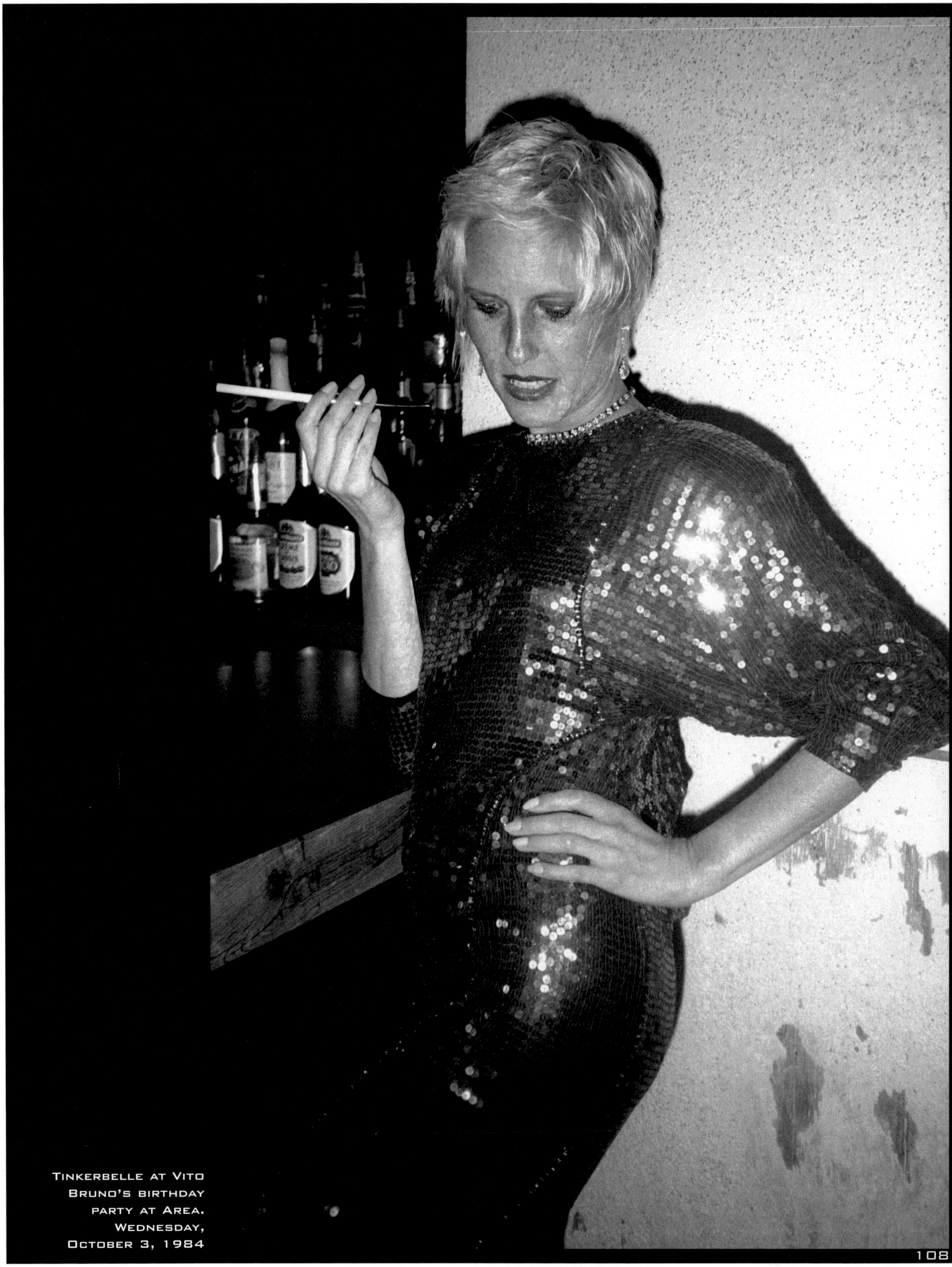

Tinkerbelle at Vito Bruno's birthday party at Area. Wednesday, October 3, 1984

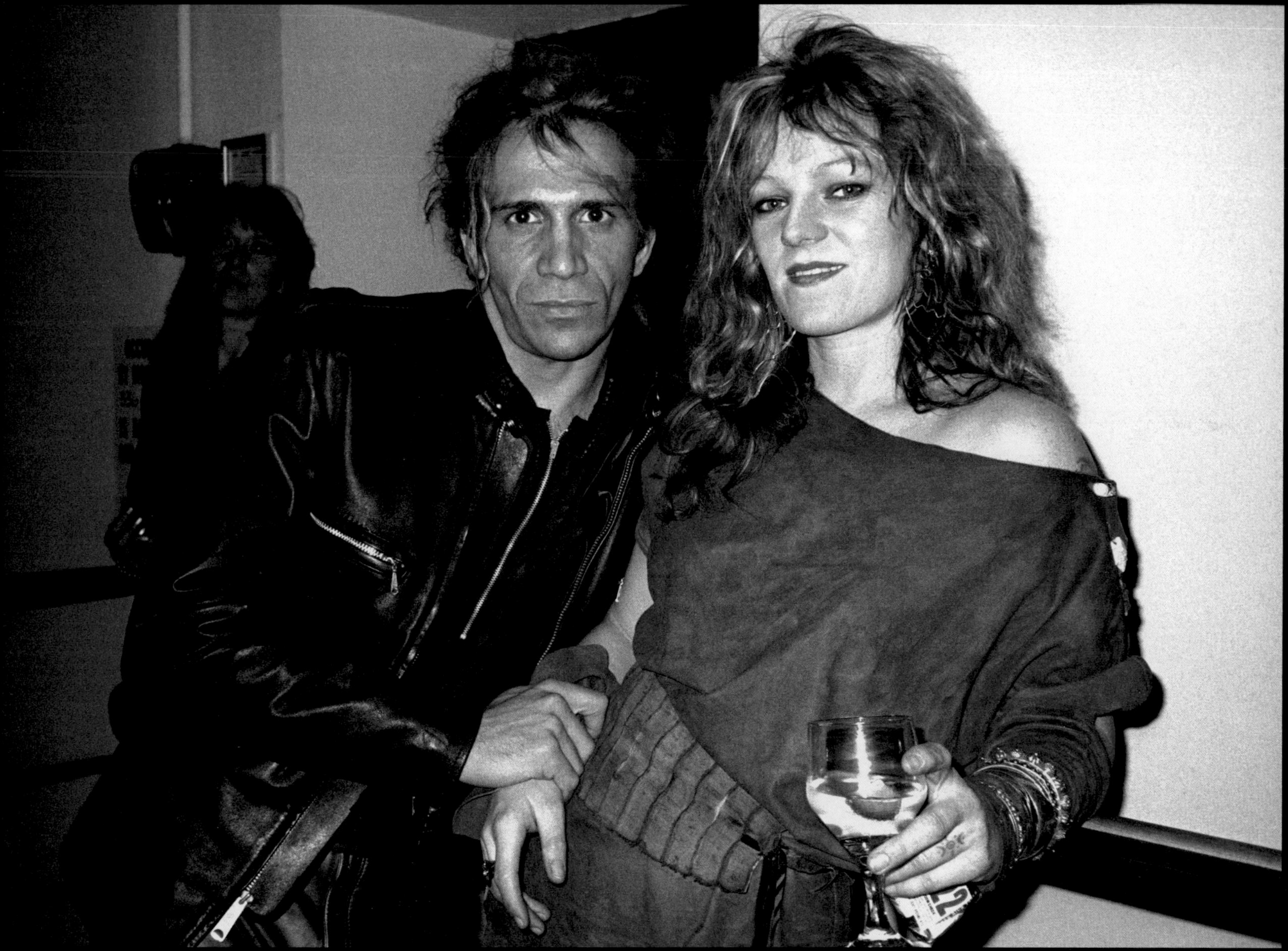

GENARO PALERMO AND COOKIE MUELLER
AT ALAN RISH'S MONDAY NIGHT PARTY AT LIMELIGHT.
JANUARY 1984

"I was down at Area one night sitting with Andy and our mutual friend Ed Walsh, and with Kevin Jarre who had written the Stallone movie Rambo. Ed had met Andy in Chicago in 1965 when Ed was still in high school and the Velvet Underground had gone there to play.

Andy looked around at the art installation that night--I think it was the two girl roommates watching TV in their living room--and at all the 80s kids with the looks and the energy jumping around and he said, 'God, it's so much fun--it's just like the 60s again.' Ed said, 'Yeah, but with better hair-care products."

Pat Hackett
Warhol confidante and
Editor of The Andy Warhol Diaries

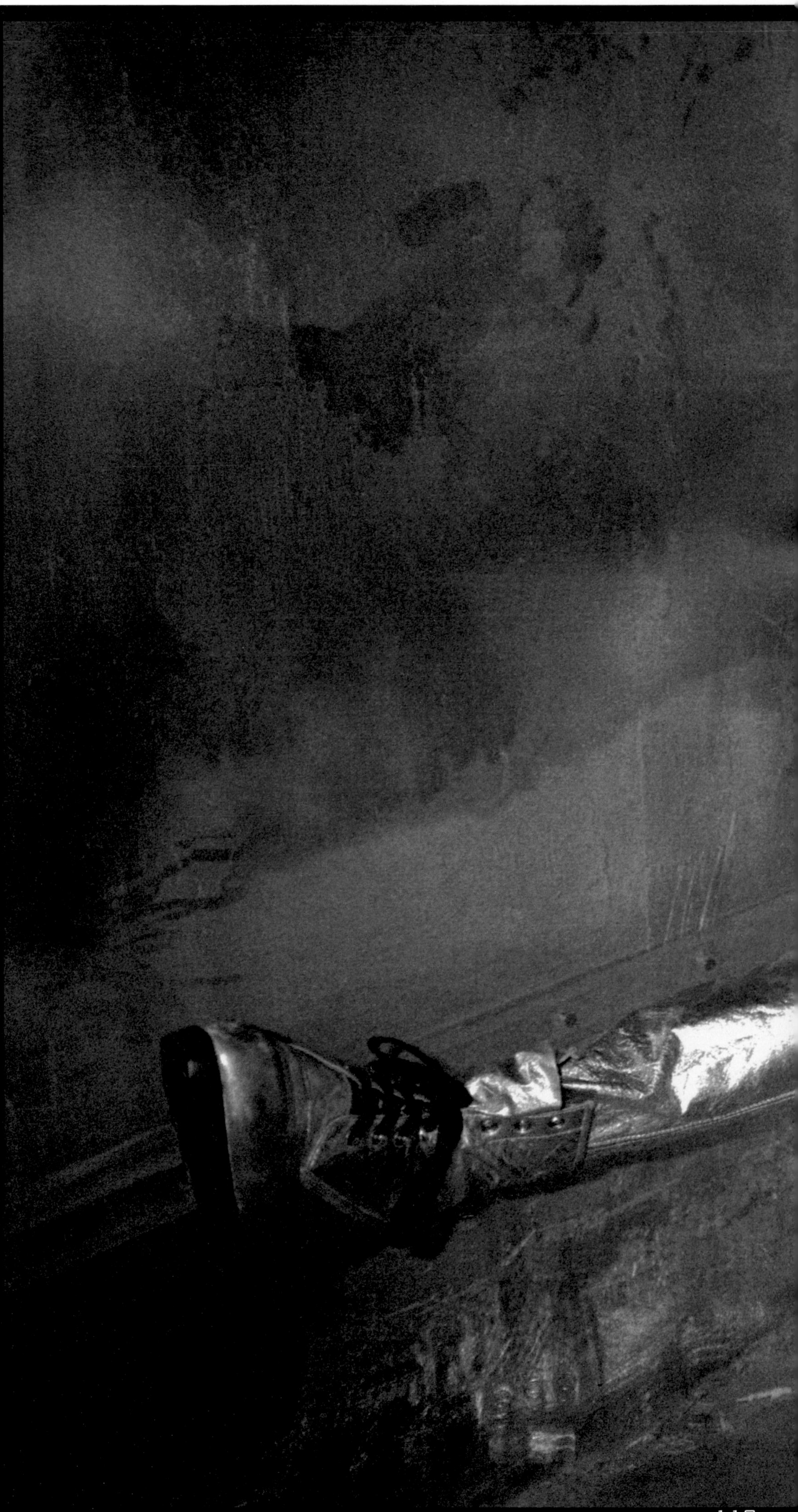

Display at Area.
November 4, 1984

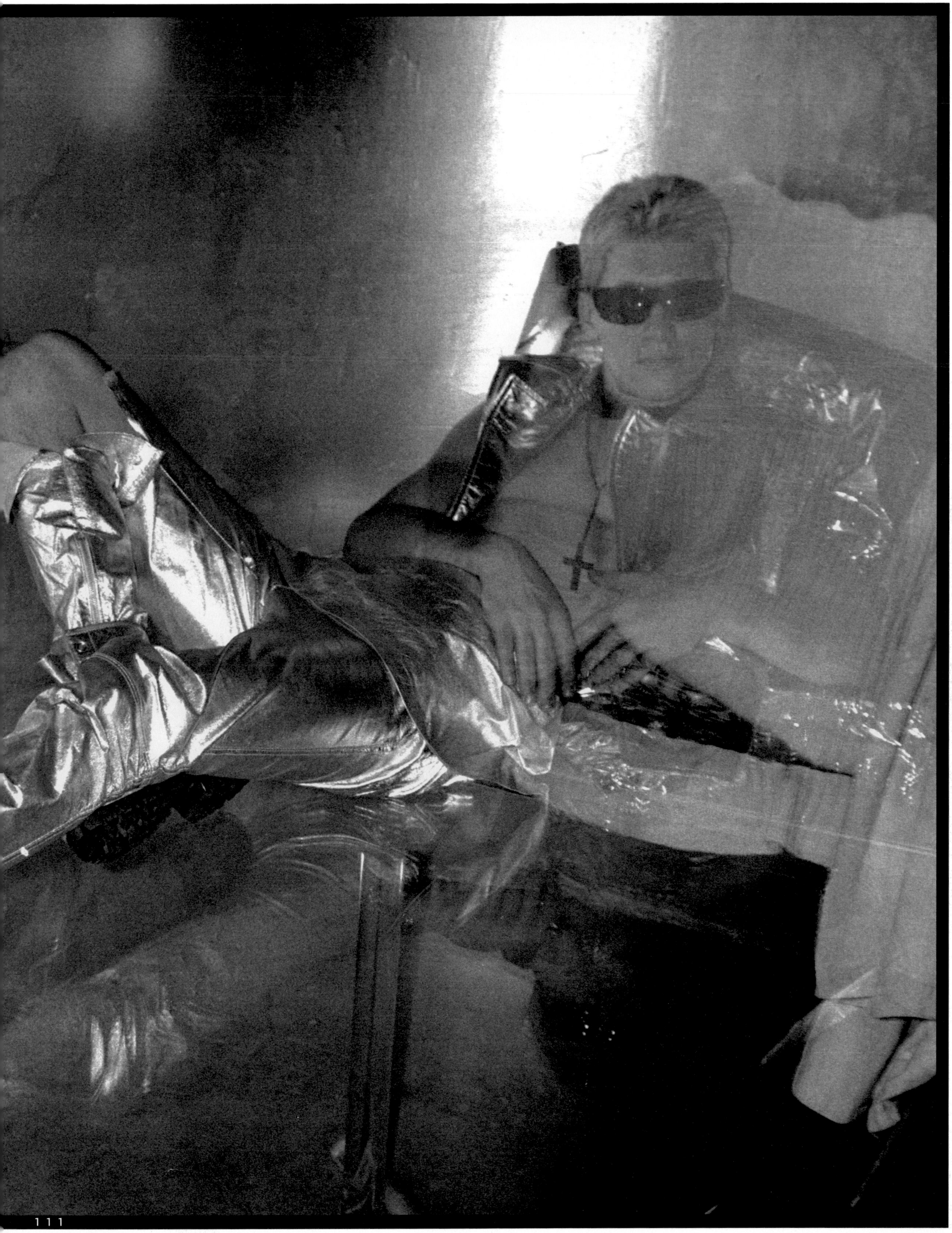

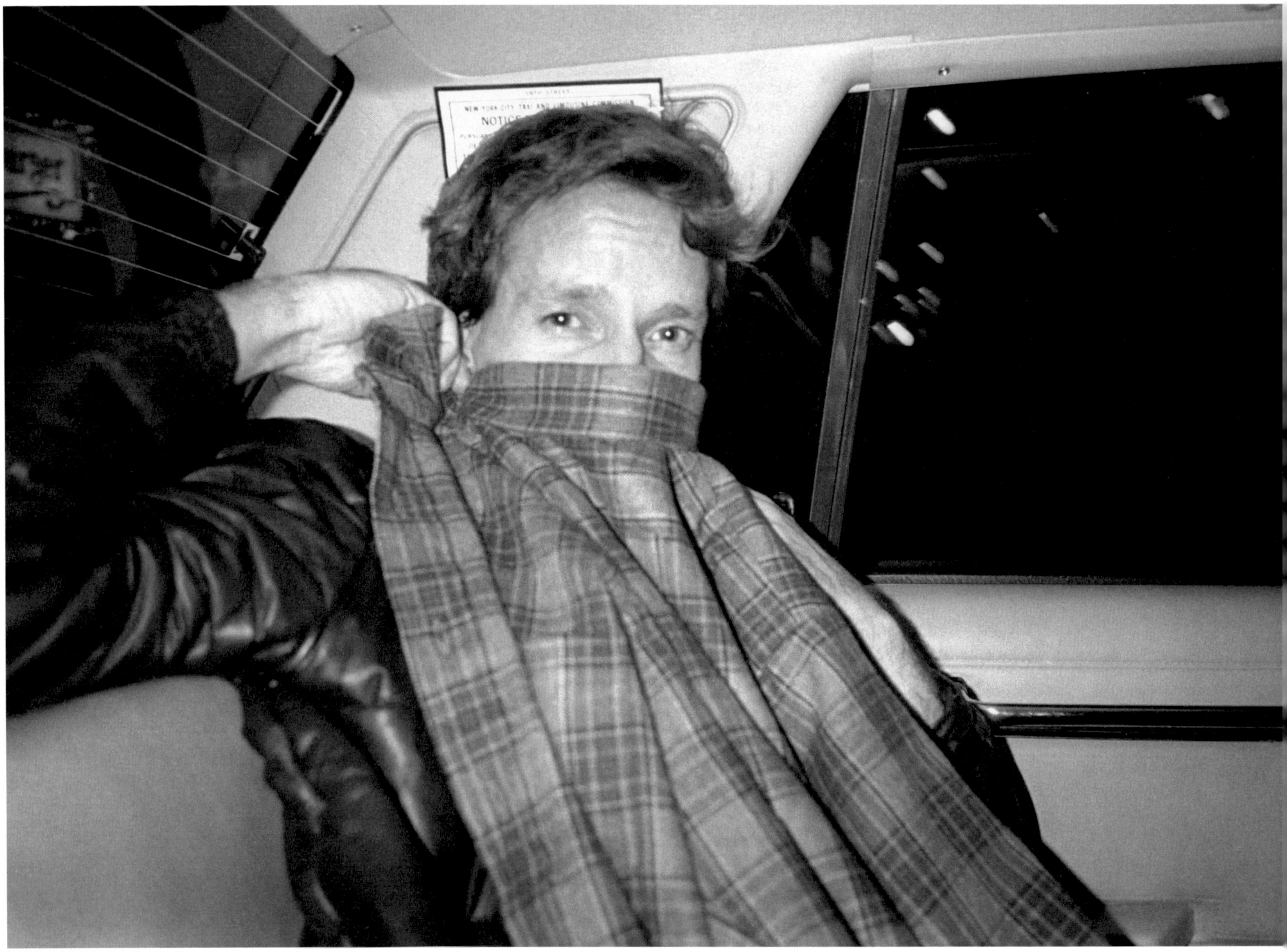

Don Munroe
1983

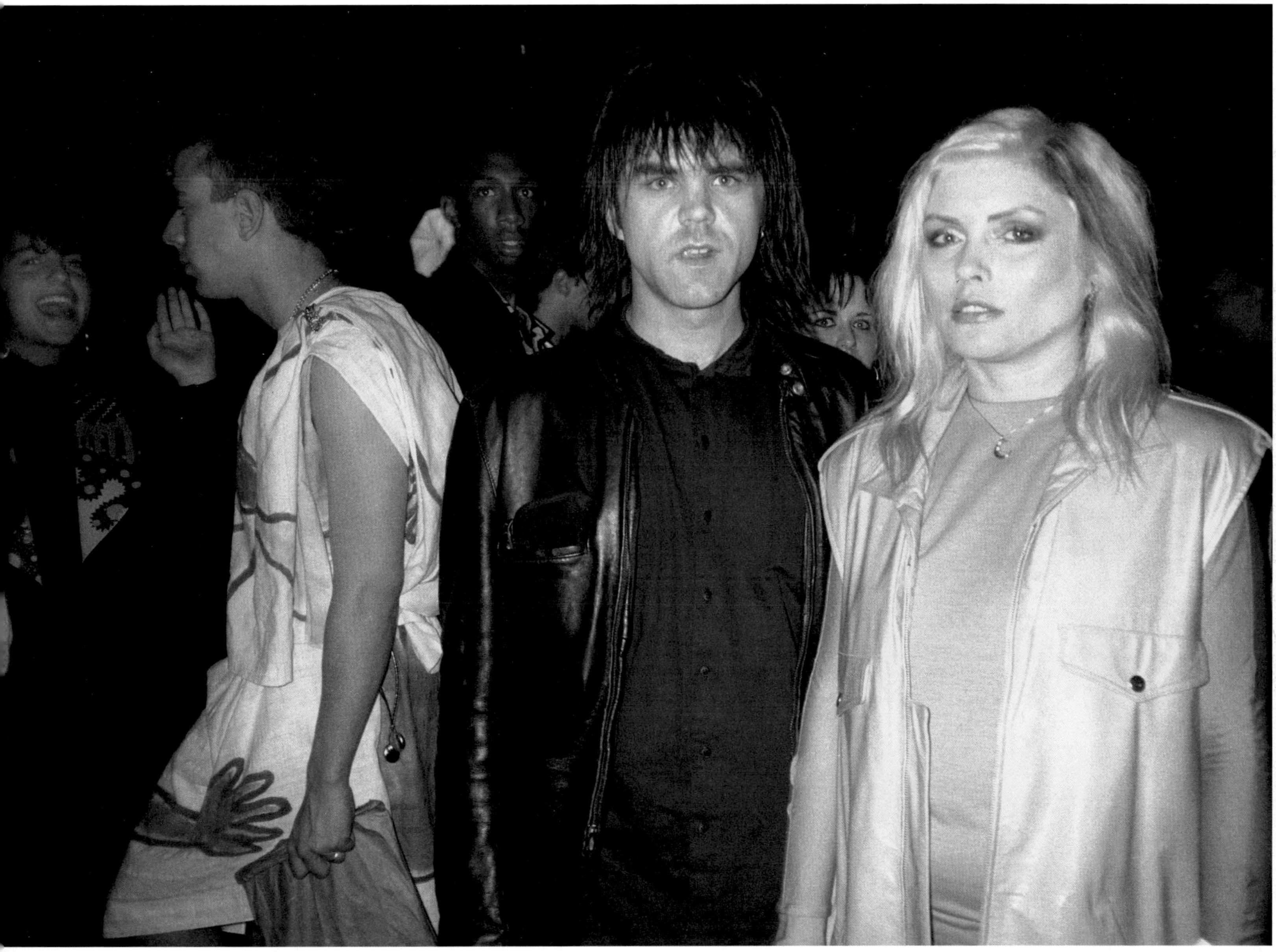

Stephen Sprouse and Debbie Harry
at Keith Haring's Party of Life at the Palladium.
May 21, 1986

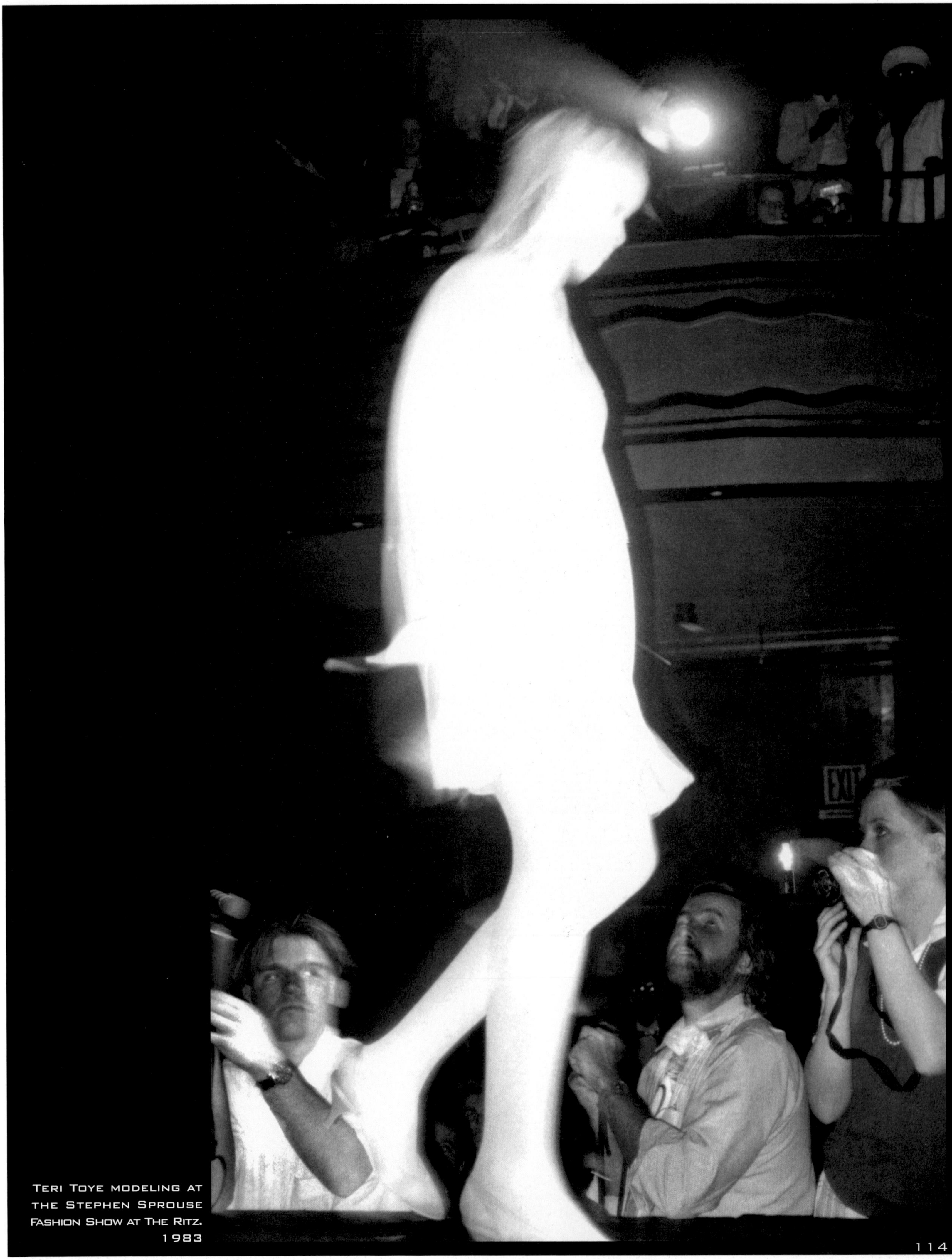

Teri Toye modeling at the Stephen Sprouse Fashion Show at The Ritz. 1983

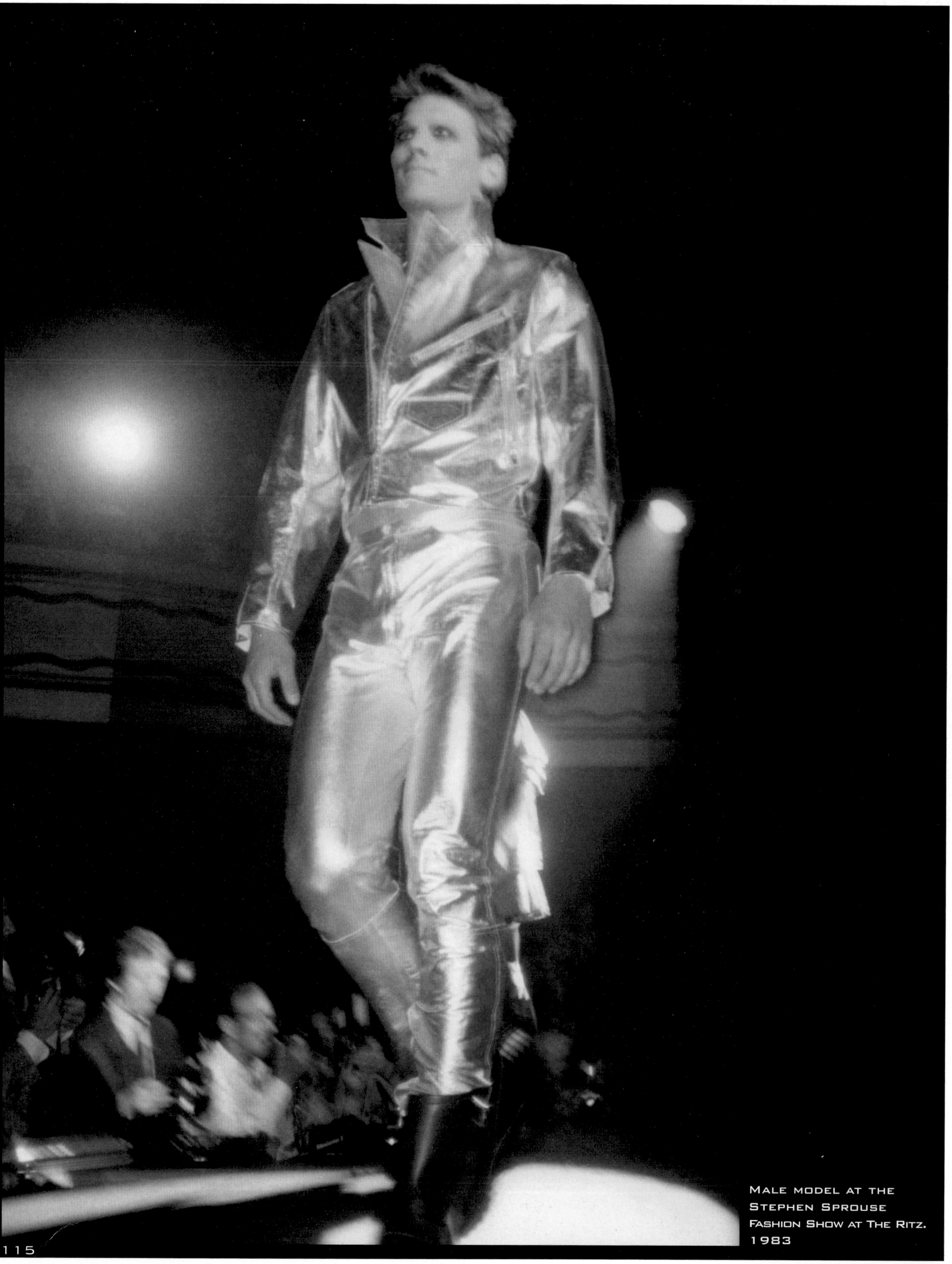

MALE MODEL AT THE STEPHEN SPROUSE FASHION SHOW AT THE RITZ. 1983

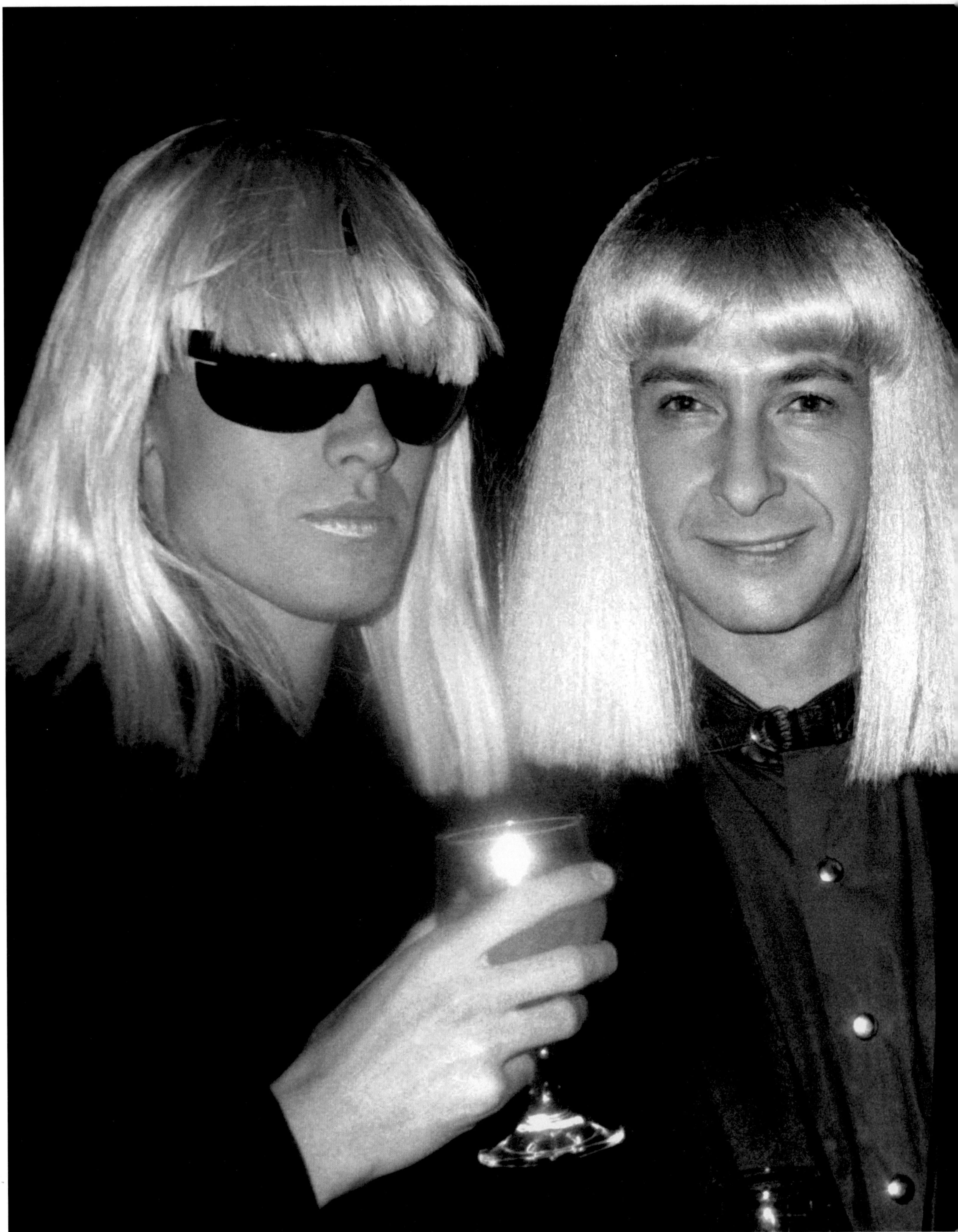

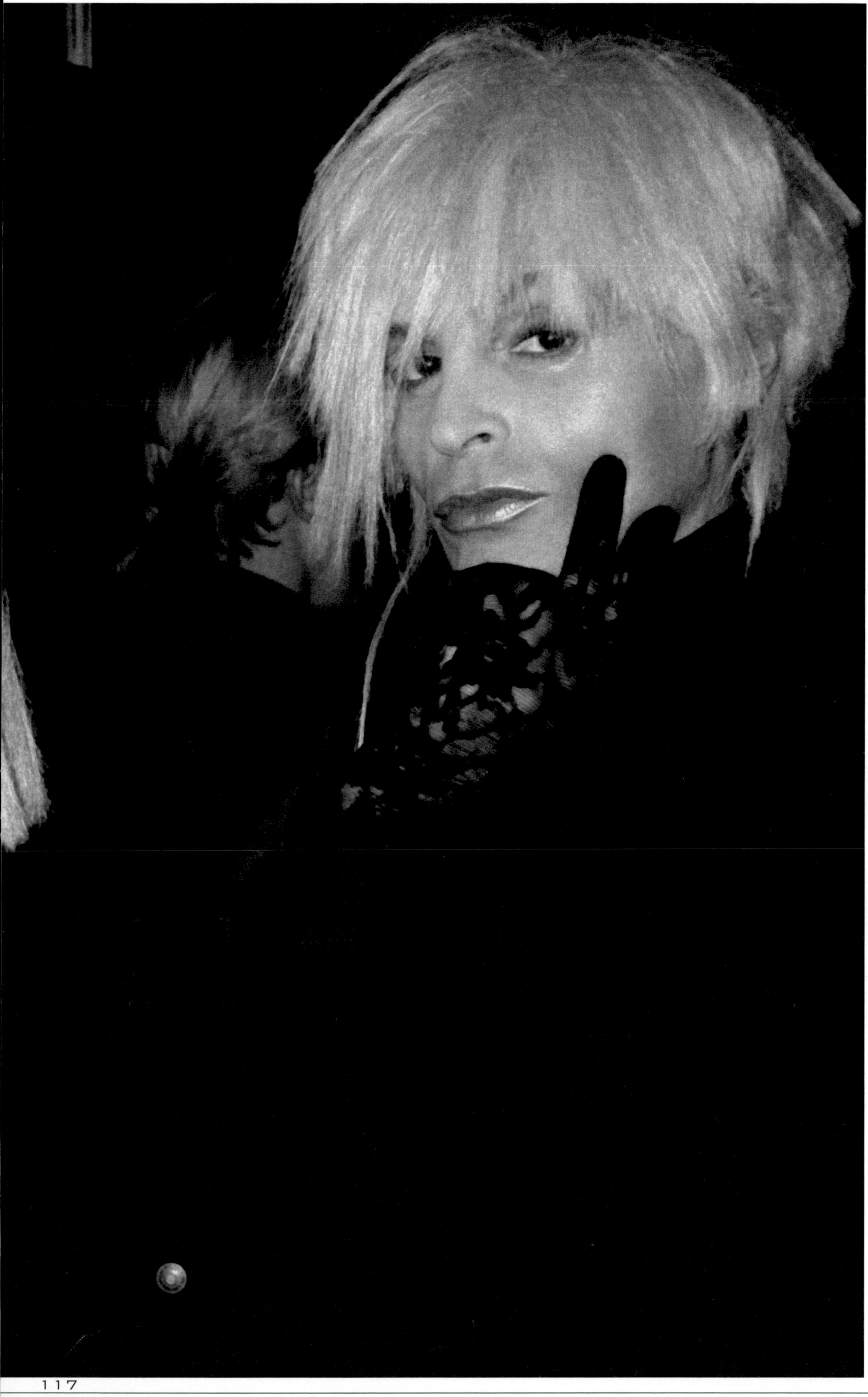

Nikki Paige, David King, and Way Bandy at Limelight for the Wig Party.
1983/84

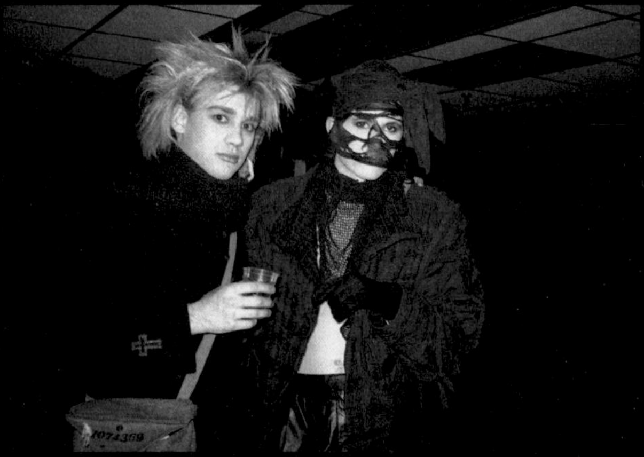

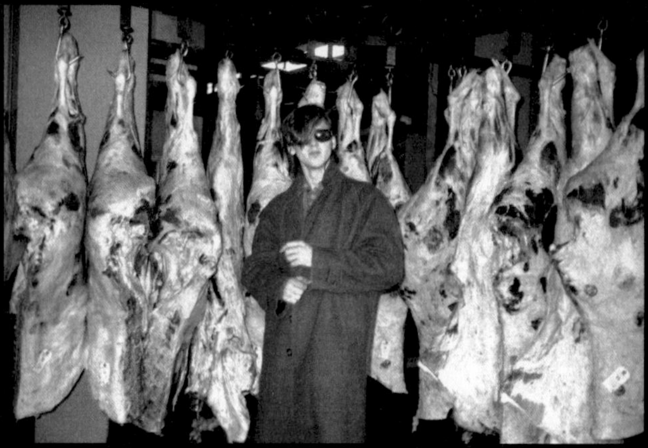

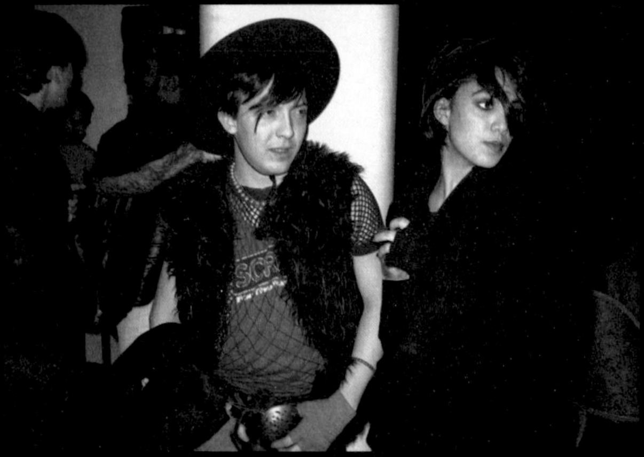

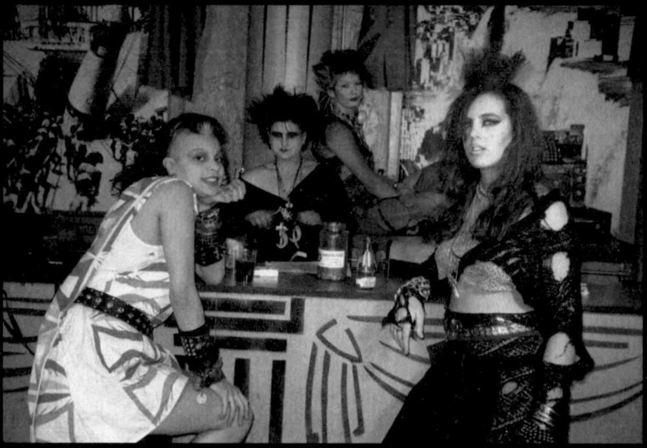

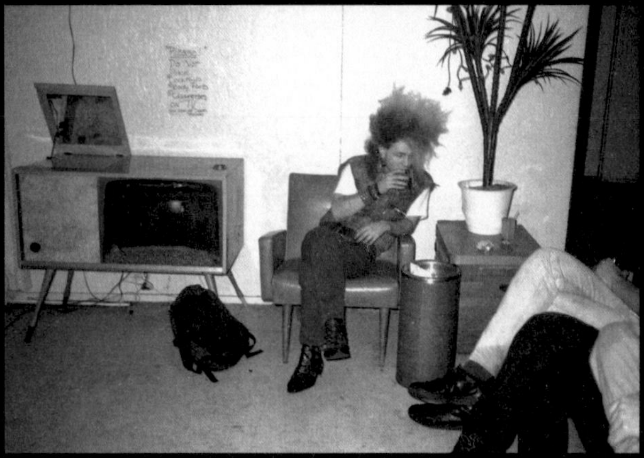

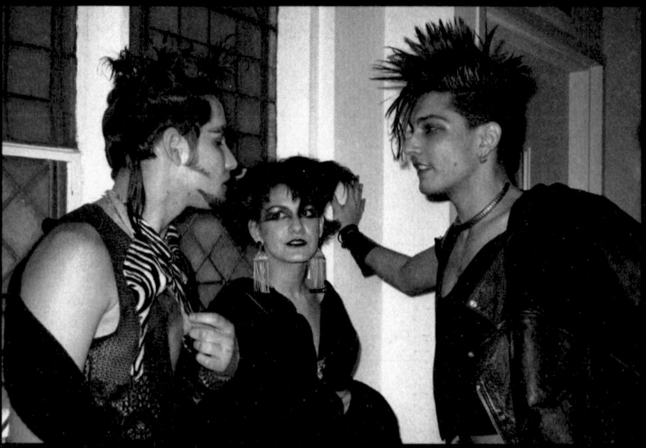

Top Left: Name Unknown and Michael Schmidt at Danceteria. December 1983
Top Right: Name Unknown in the Meat Packing District after hours. April 3, 1984
Middle Left: Mars Williams of the Psychedelic Furs and friend at Danceteria. December 1983
Middle Right: The Bat Girls at Danceteria. March 1984
Bottom Left: Name Unknown at the Pyramid Club. December 1983
Bottom Right: Punk kids at Mackenzie Phillips' party at Limelight. February 1984
Right: Alley "War" graffiti. December 1983

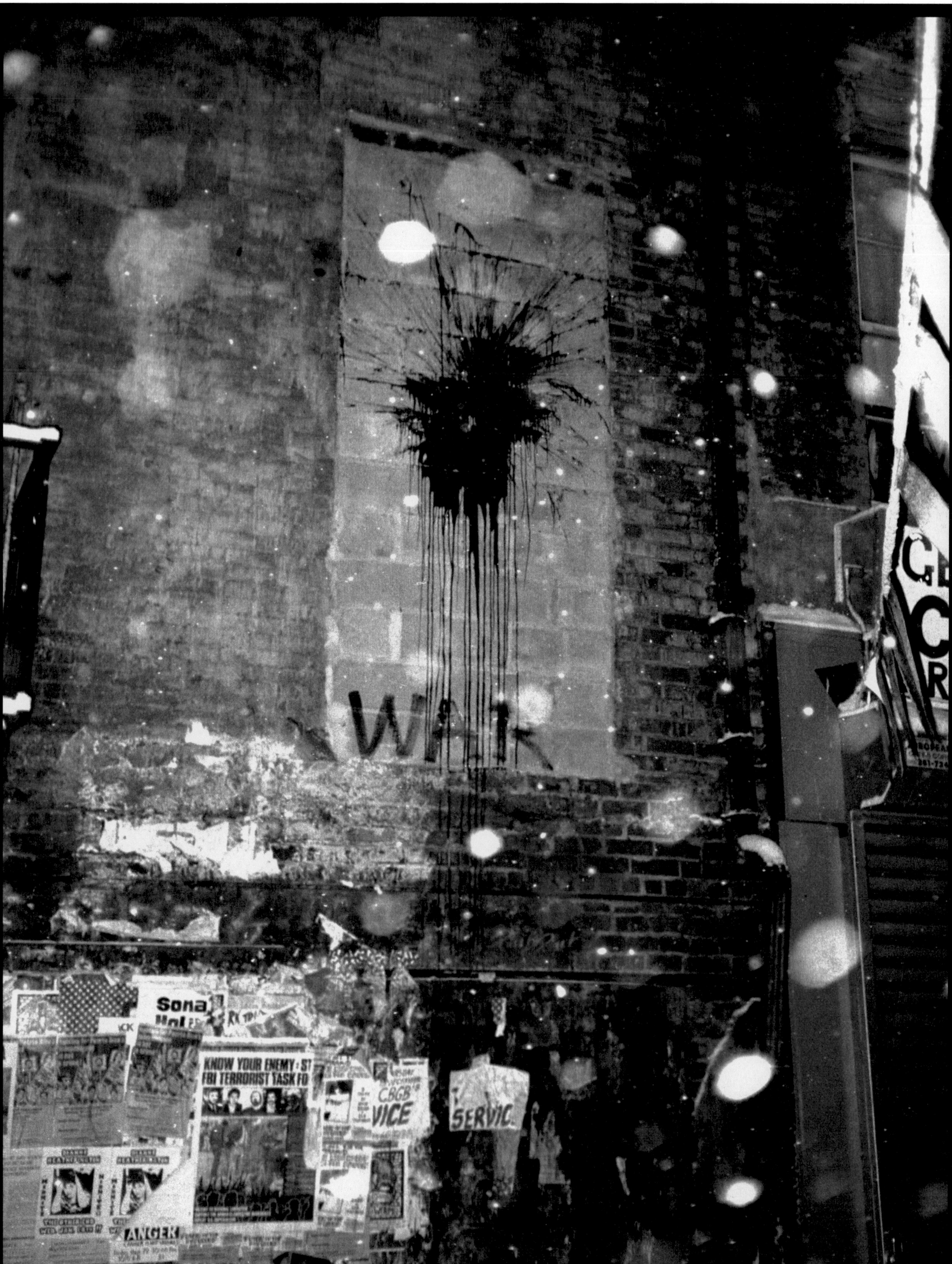
WAR
KNOW YOUR ENEMY : ST
FBI TERRORIST TASK FO
CBGB
VICE
SERVIC
ANGER

In the 80s, unlike now, people weren't always exactly what they seemed, and New York was an adventure of money.

At the insane zenith of the contemporary art world, my ex-wife bought tons of art for a company in Florida. The ass-kissing from gallery owners was spectacular and shameless: one evening, we were nauseatingly grateful to be invited to some chic dinner and the opening of the club Heartbreak Café, but as it turned out, my wife was the only valid client. The place went out of business a week later.

On another evening spent downtown--we actually walked up to a trendy couple on the street and asked if they knew a good place to hear jazz. The woman turned to us and sneered, "Jazz? Why don't you just go to Bloomingdale's?"

But they took pity and actually brought us to the Mudd Club, then at it's height. They got in for free, we paid double, and that's still the best club memory ever. For rube Miamians in their twenties, it was heady stuff, nightlife nirvana.

Tom Austin

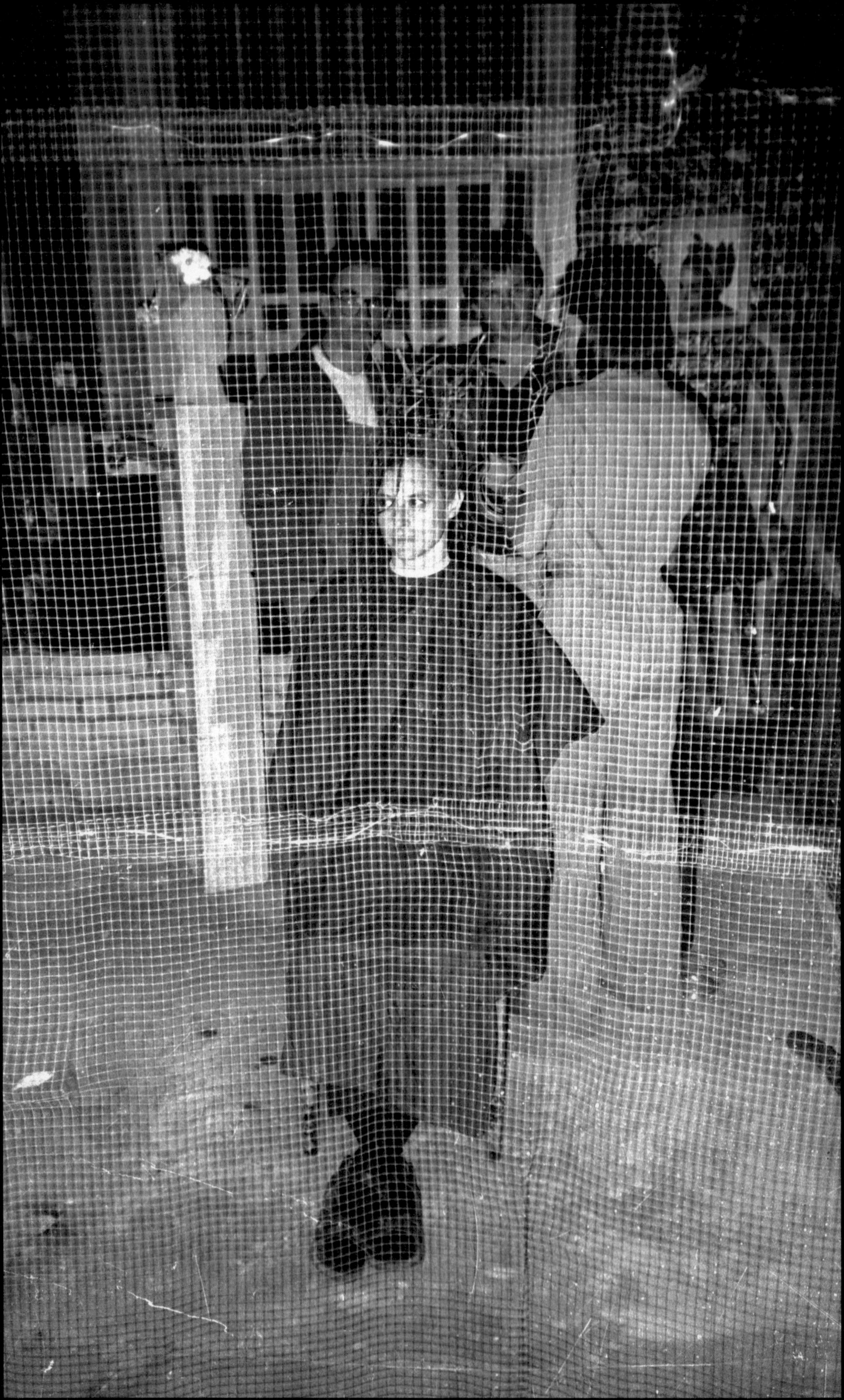

Installation at a downtown gallery opening. Thursday, October 11, 1984

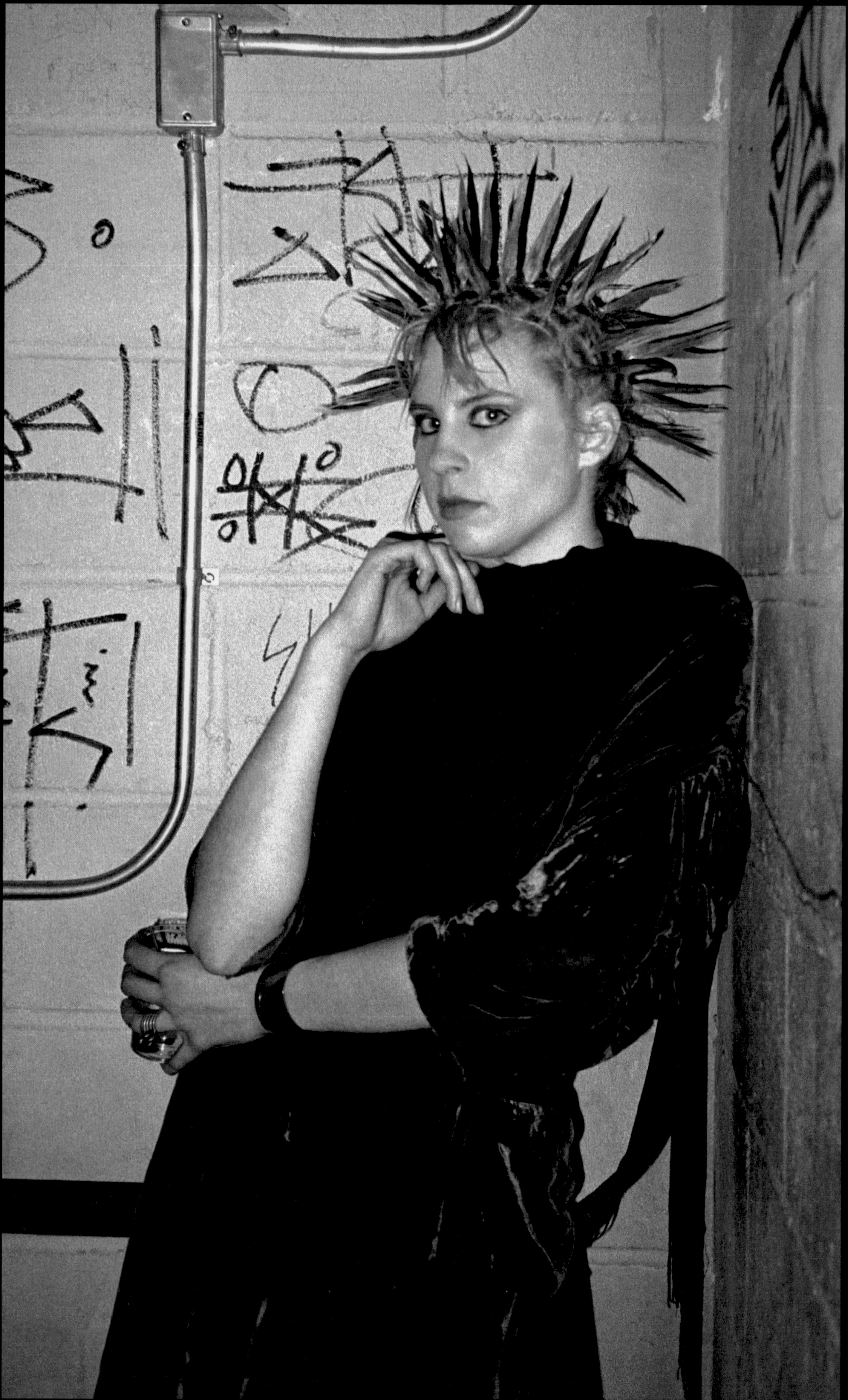

"THE 80s--ALIVE, PUN
ROLL, CRAZY FAST, UP ALL NIGHT, WORK ALL DAY, MEGA CREATIVE, EXTREME--A COOL PARALLEL OF THE 60s."
BETSEY JOHNSON

CHARLOTTE HARLOT
AT DANCETERIA.
DECEMBER 1983

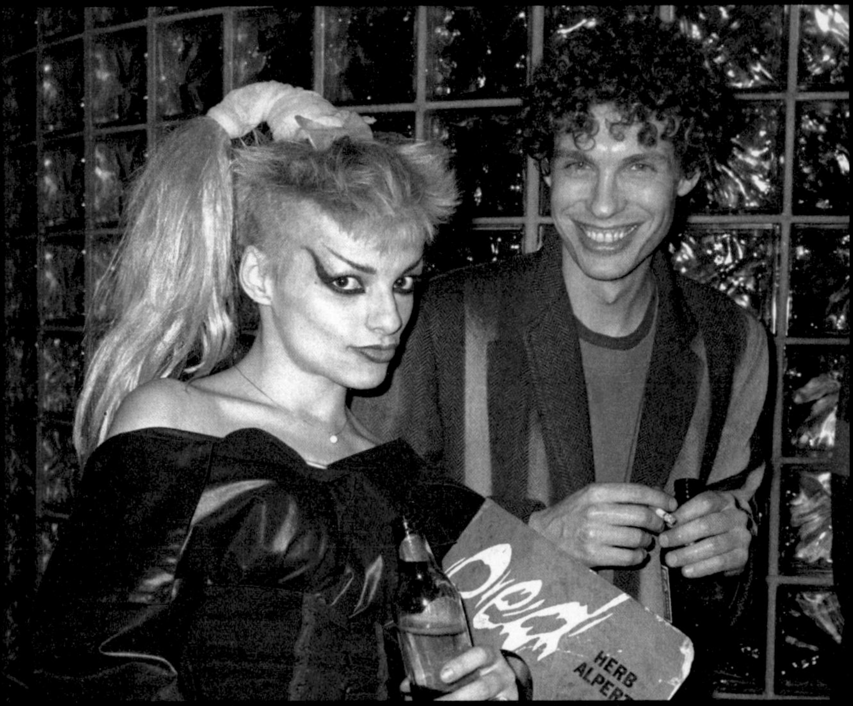

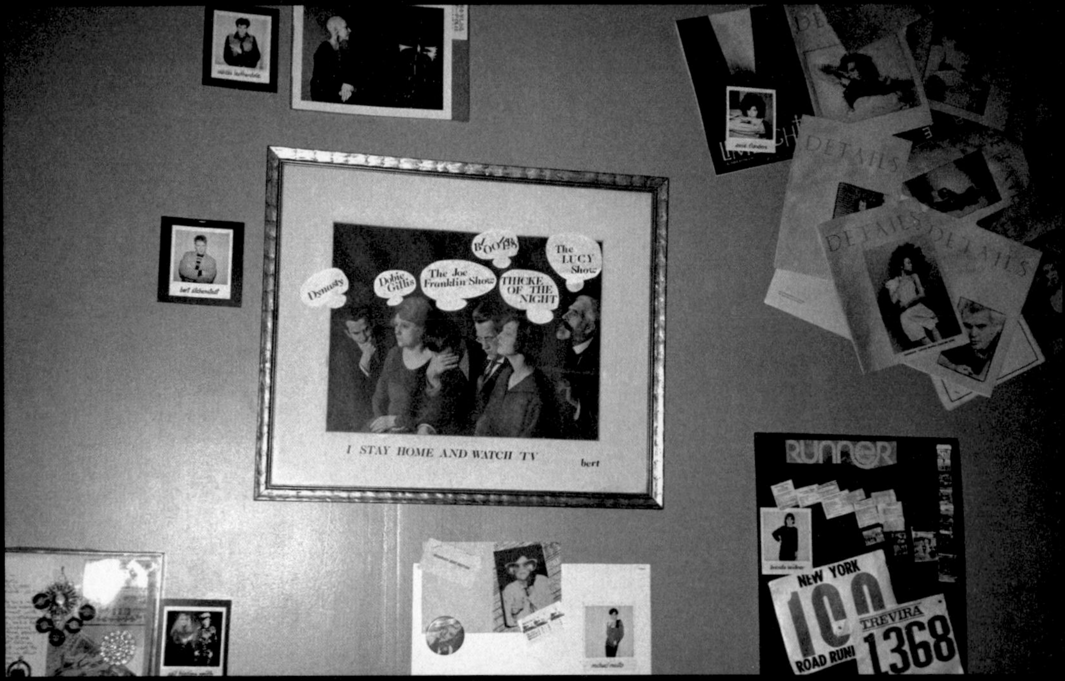

Top: Nina Hagen and Richard Sohl at Danceteria.
February 1984
Bottom: Wall at Danceteria
at the "I don't go out much anymore" party.
March 1984

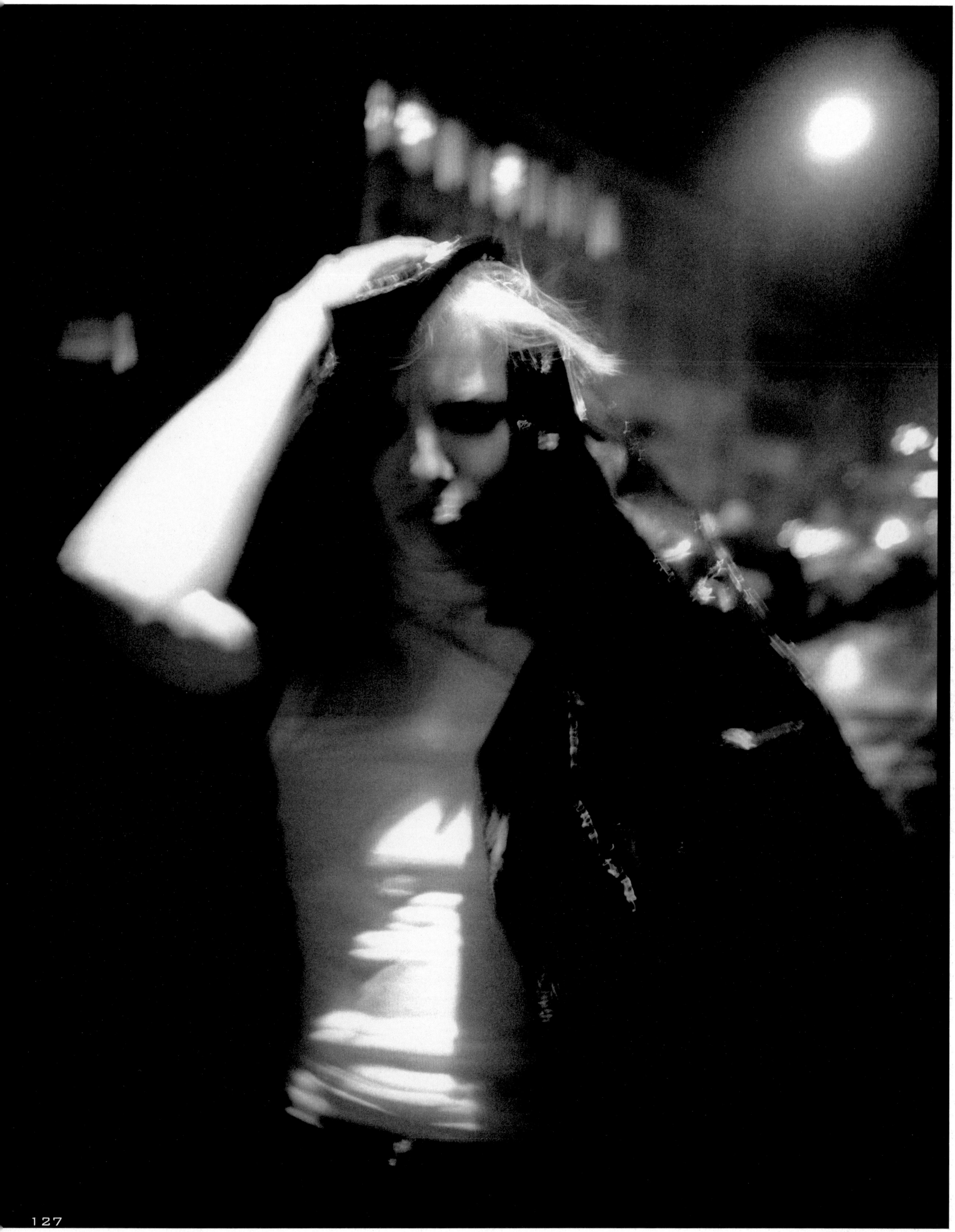

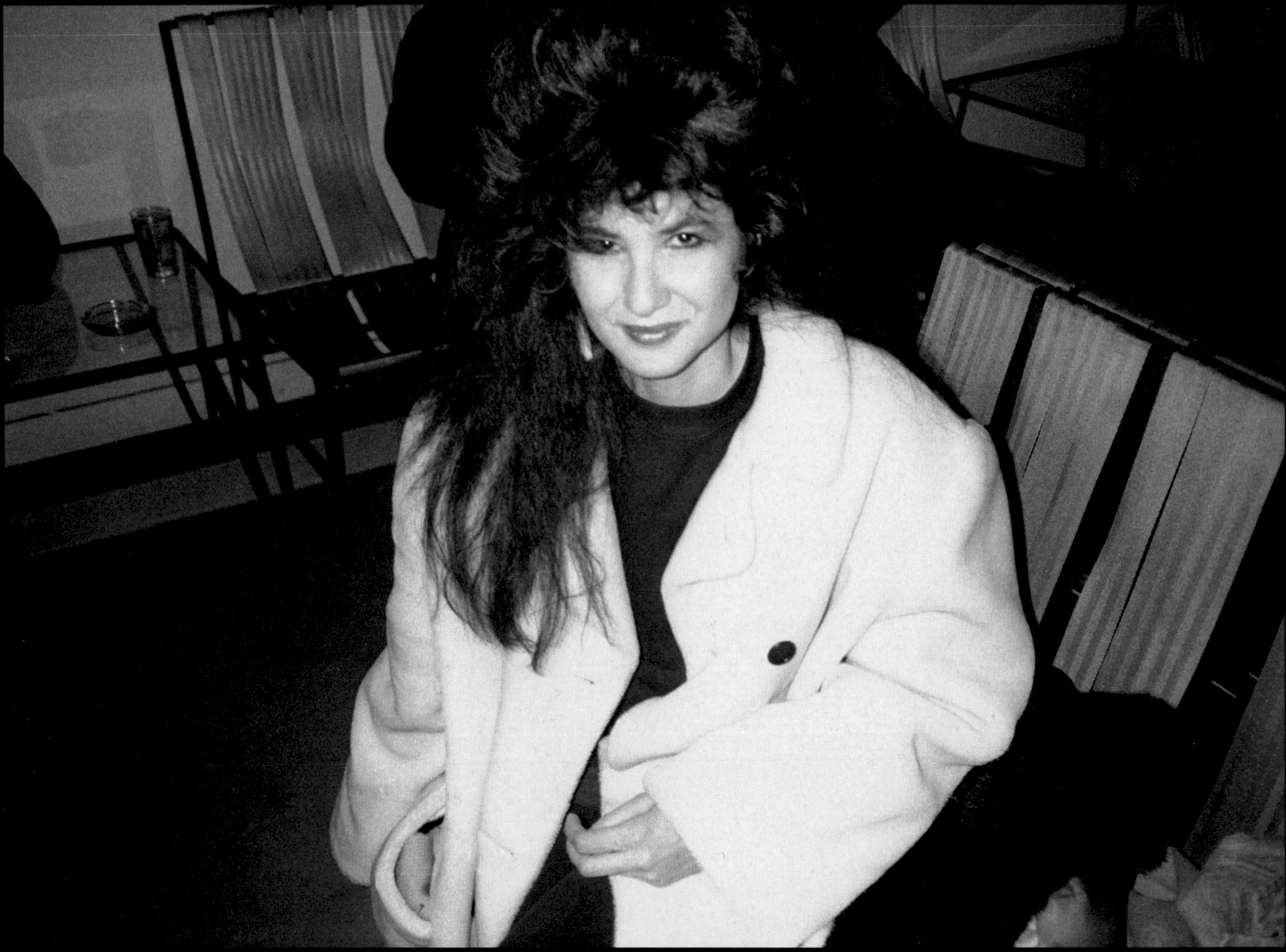

Tama Janowitz
at Cookie Mueller's party at Area.
December 6, 1984

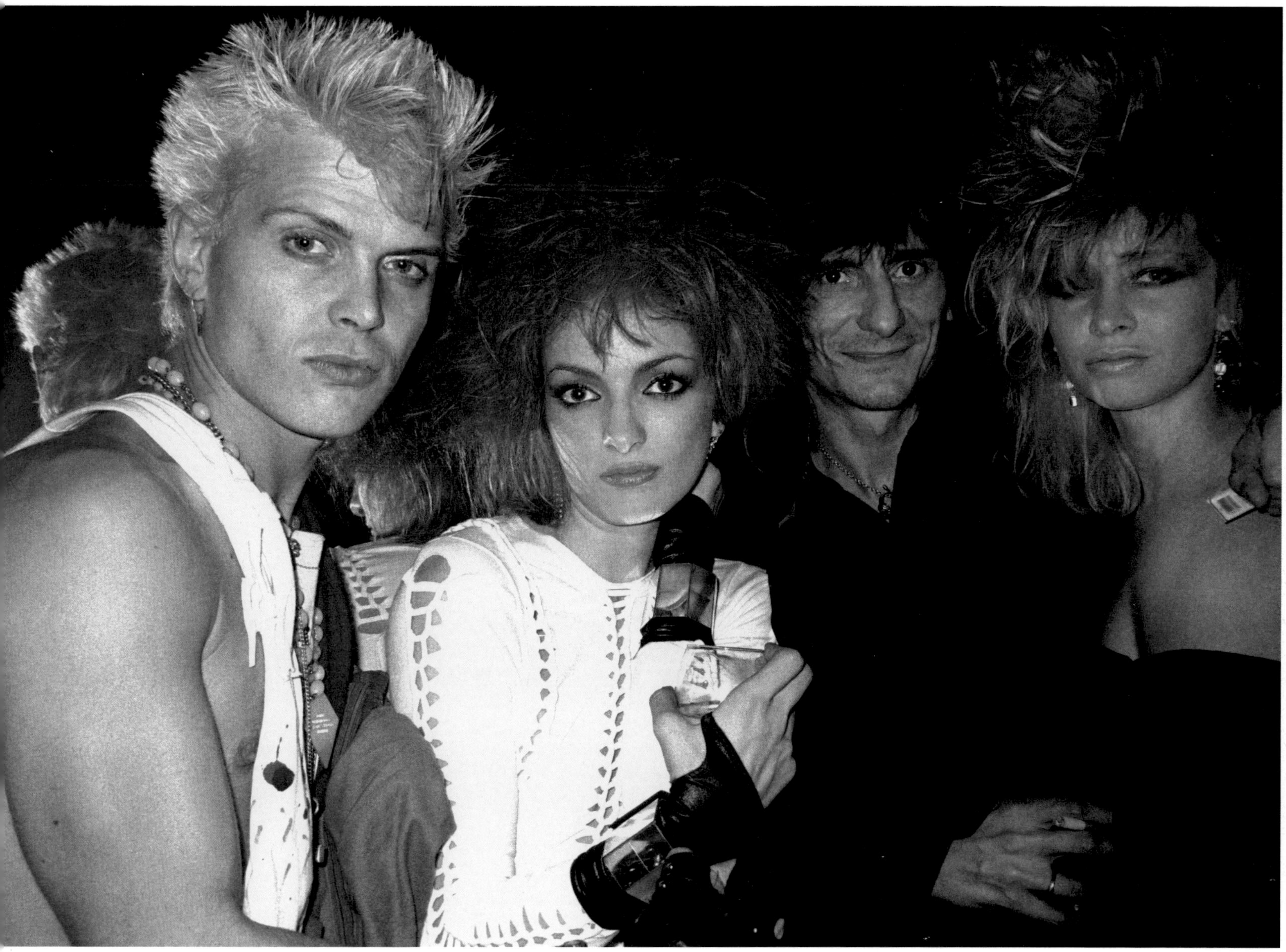

Billy Idol, Perri Lister, and Ron and Jo Wood
at Perri Lister's birthday party at the Cat Club.
April 10, 1984

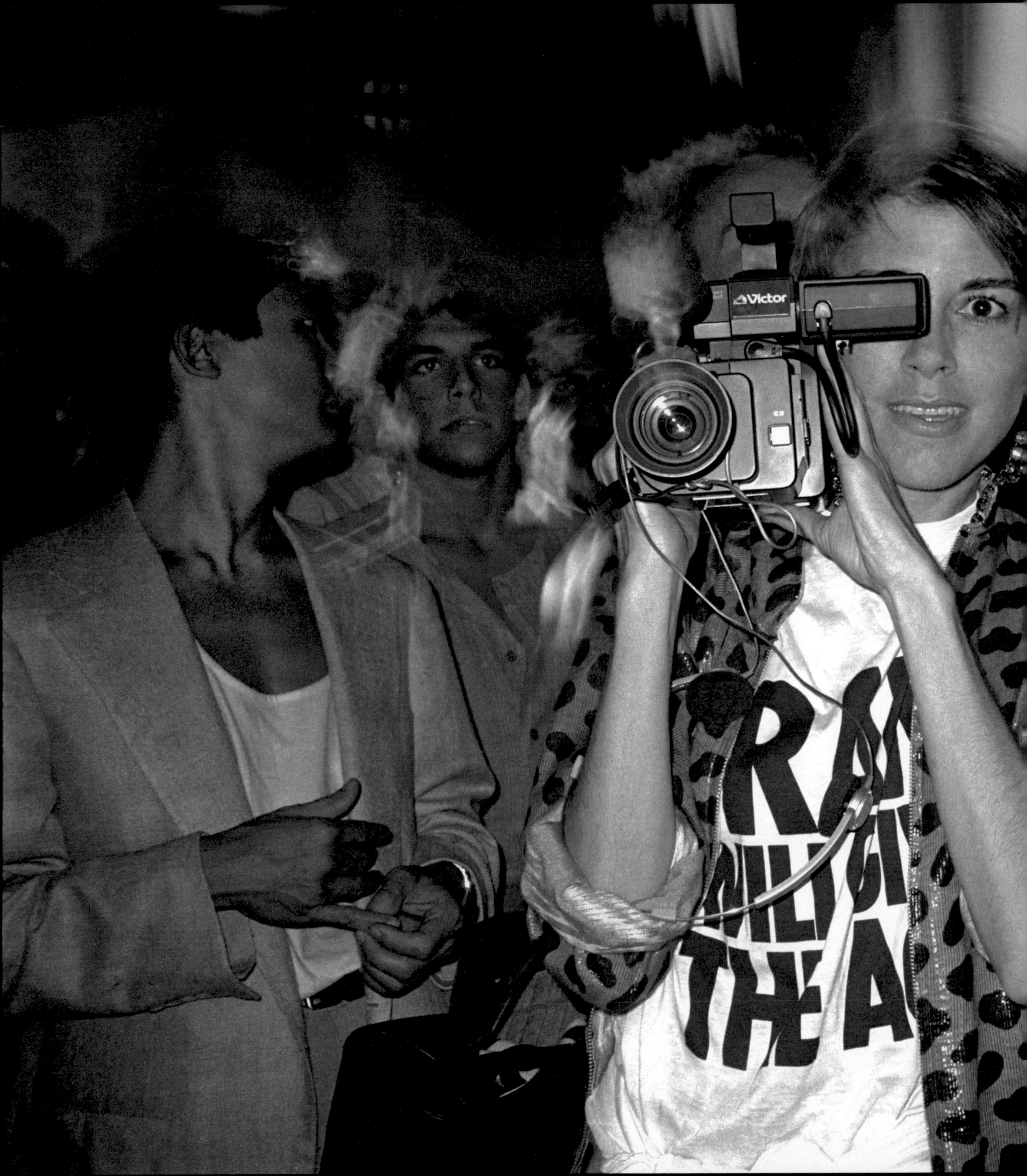

Top: Paige Powell with video camera at the Jackson Party at Limelight. Sunday, August 5, 1984
Top Right: A screen shot of Billy Idol
Middle Right: A screen shot of Nick Rhodes and Simon Le Bon
Bottom Right: A screen shot of Simon Le Bon and Cyndi Lauper at Rick Blume's MTV Awards Party. Friday, September 14, 1984

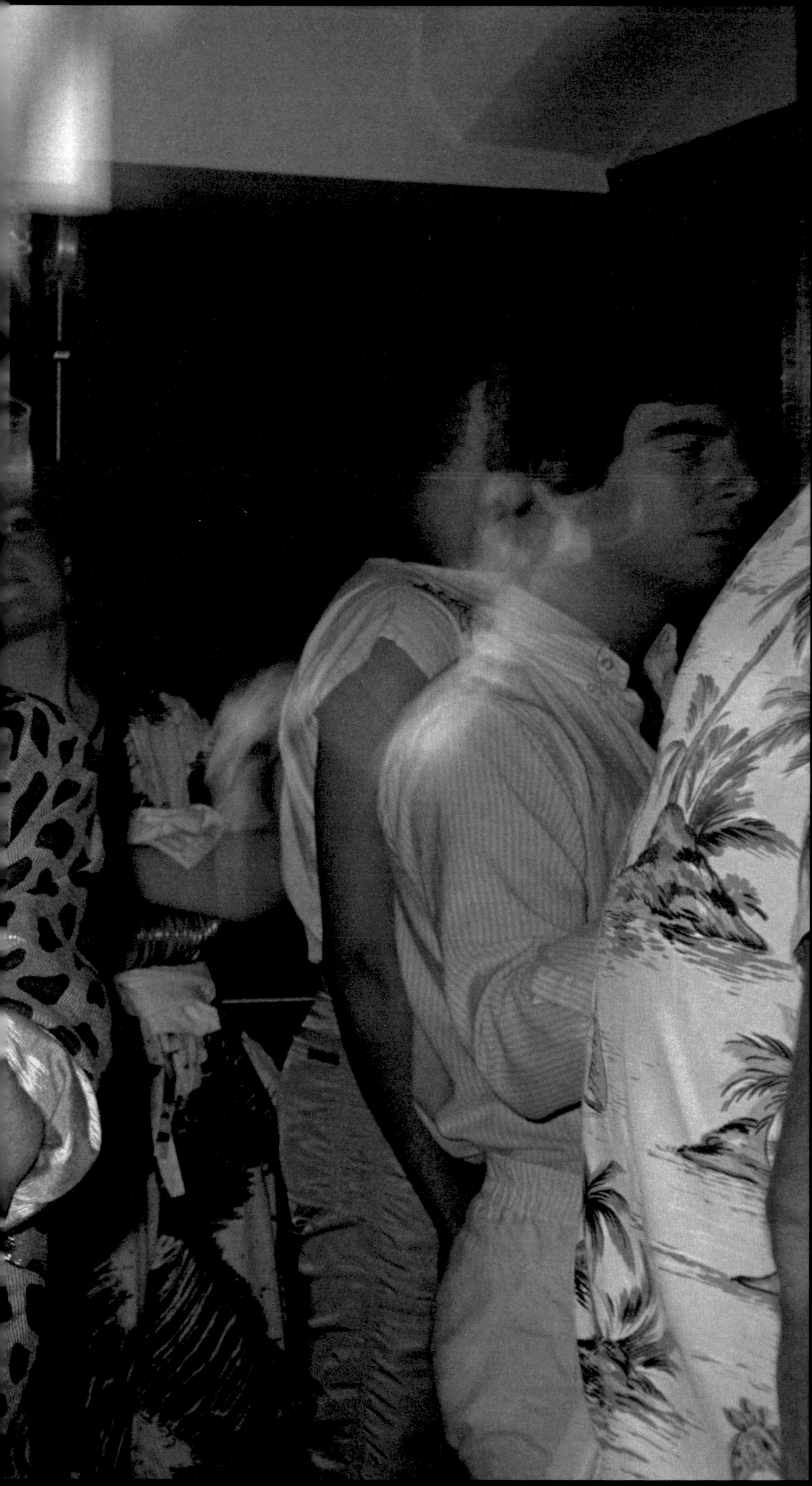

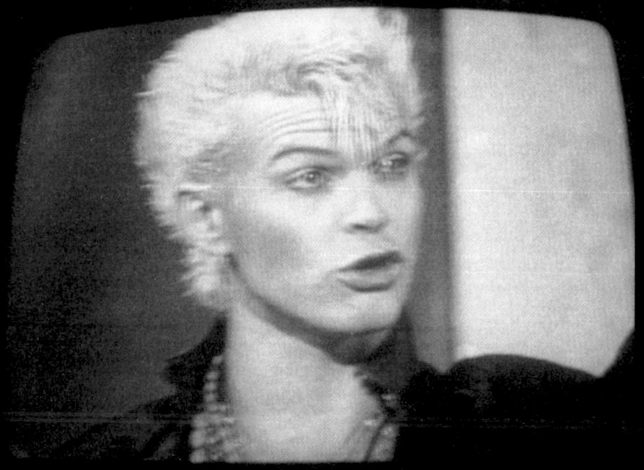

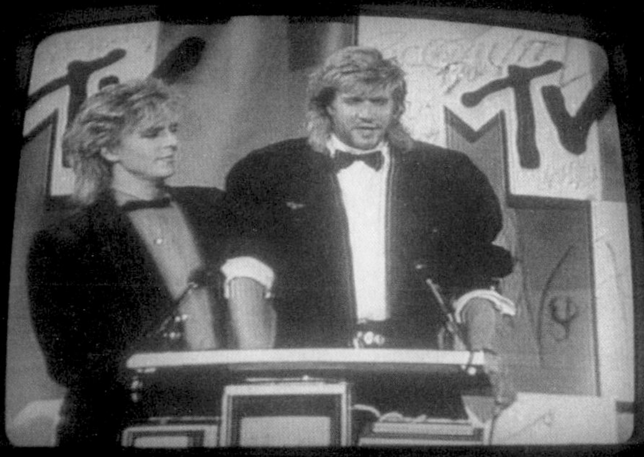

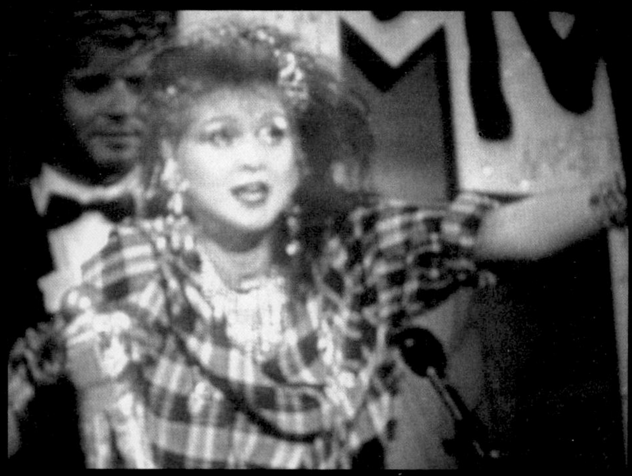

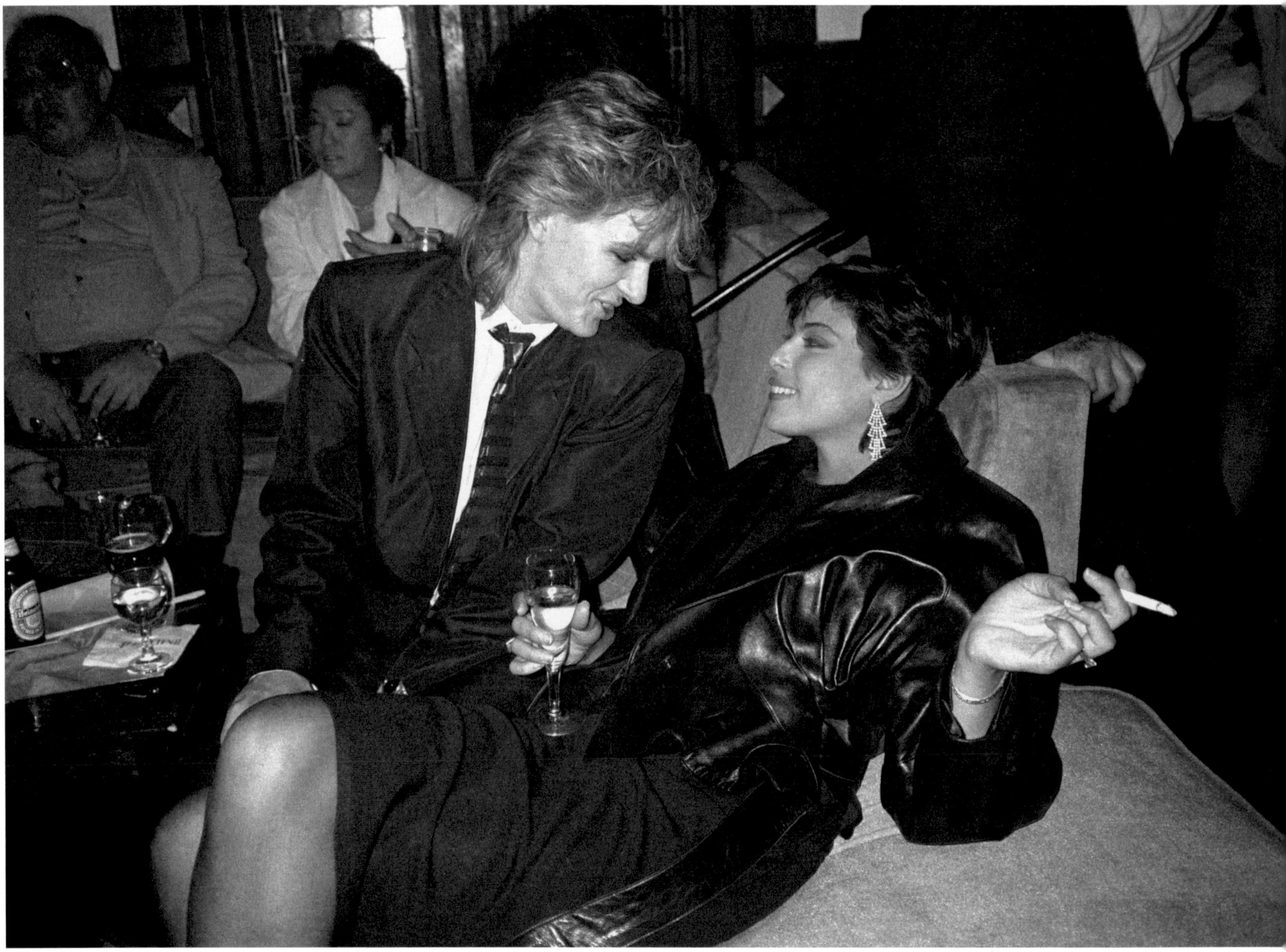

Nick and Julianne Rhodes
at Nile Rodger's birthday party at Limelight.
September 19, 1984

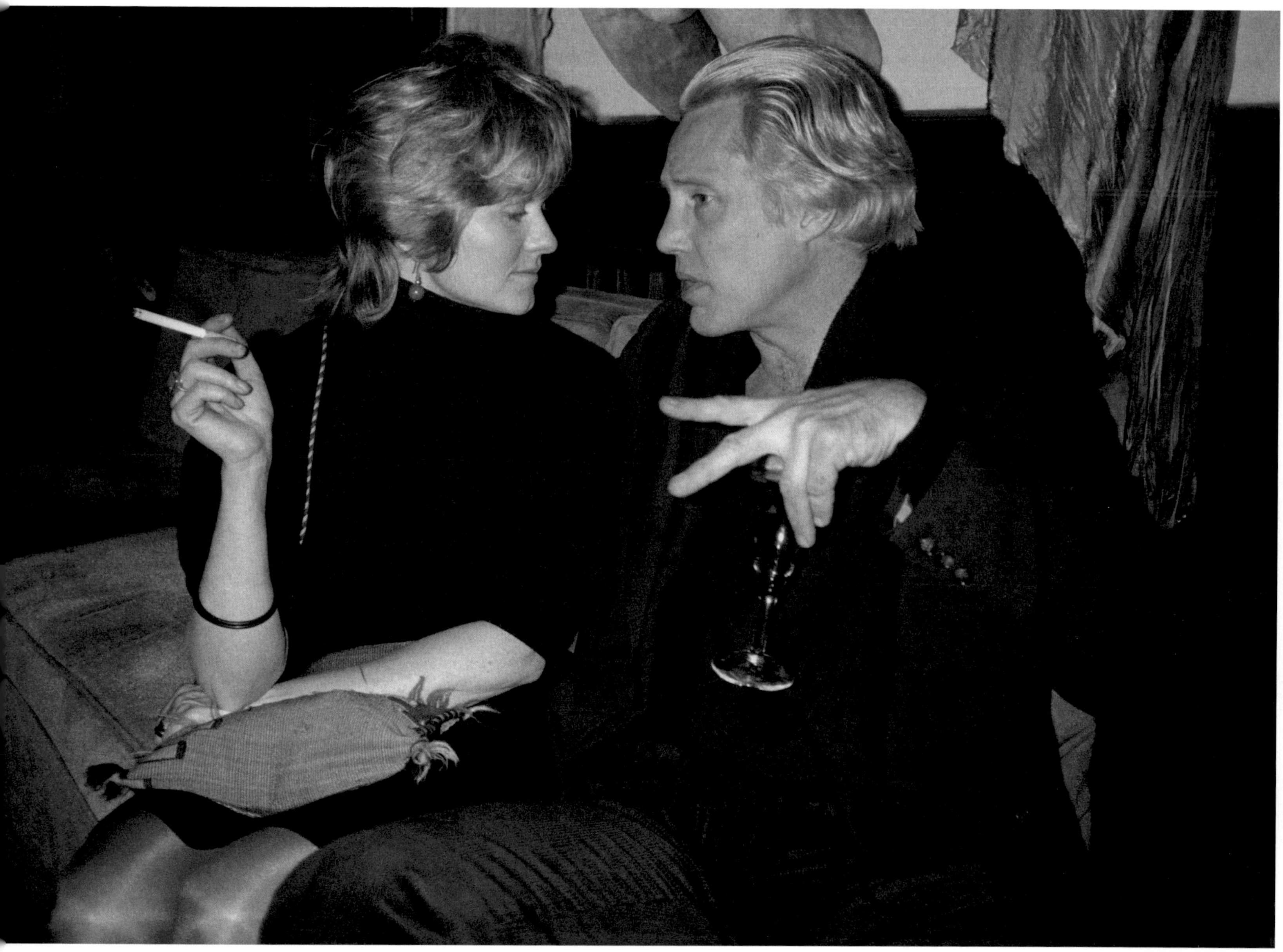

Christopher Walken and his wife Georgianne
at Limelight.
December 20, 1984

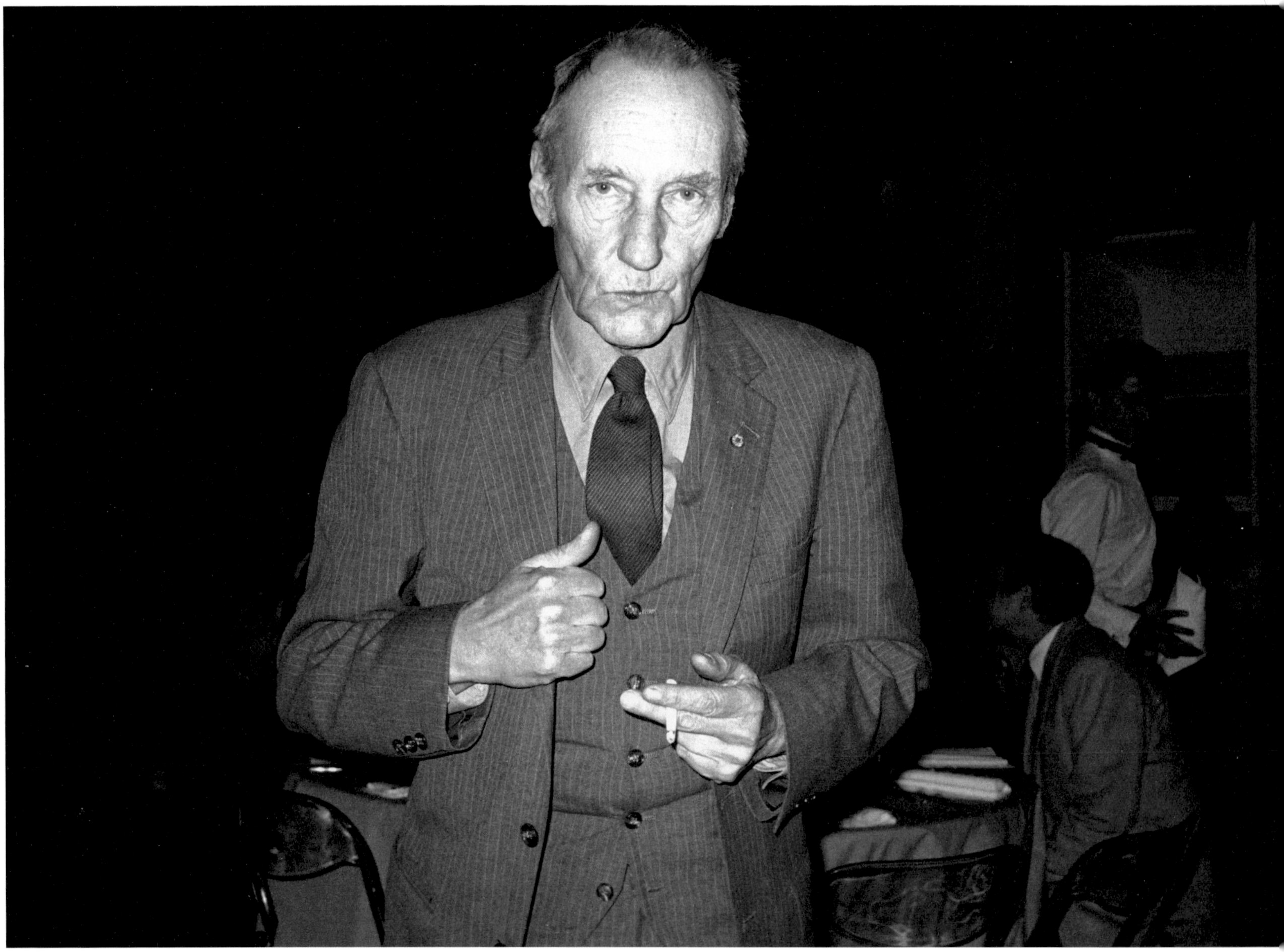

William Burroughs
at the dinner party thrown in his honor at Limelight.
February 1984

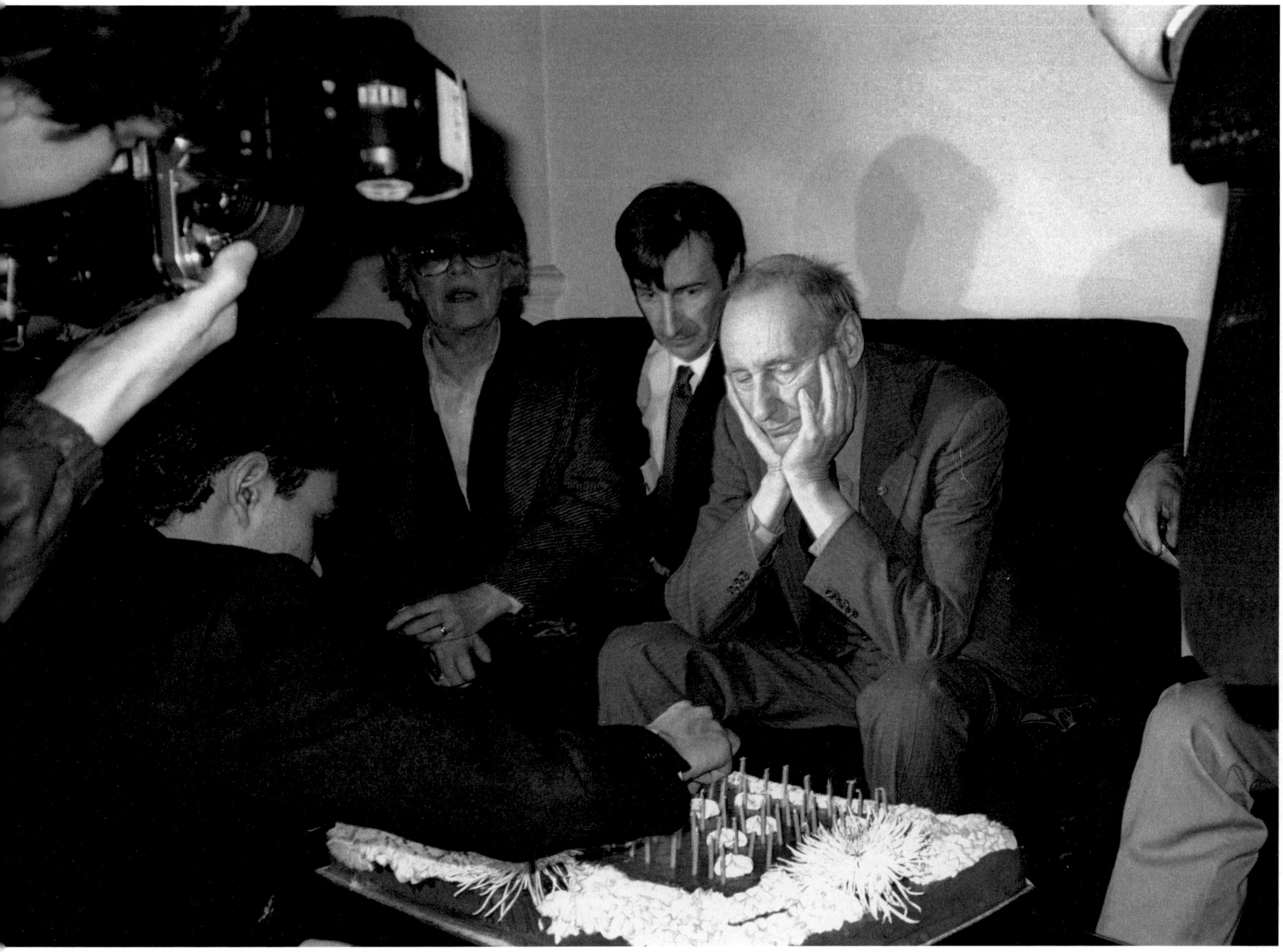

VICTOR BOCKRIS AND WILLIAM BURROUGHS
AT THE DINNER PARTY THROWN IN HIS HONOR AT LIMELIGHT.
FEBRUARY 1984

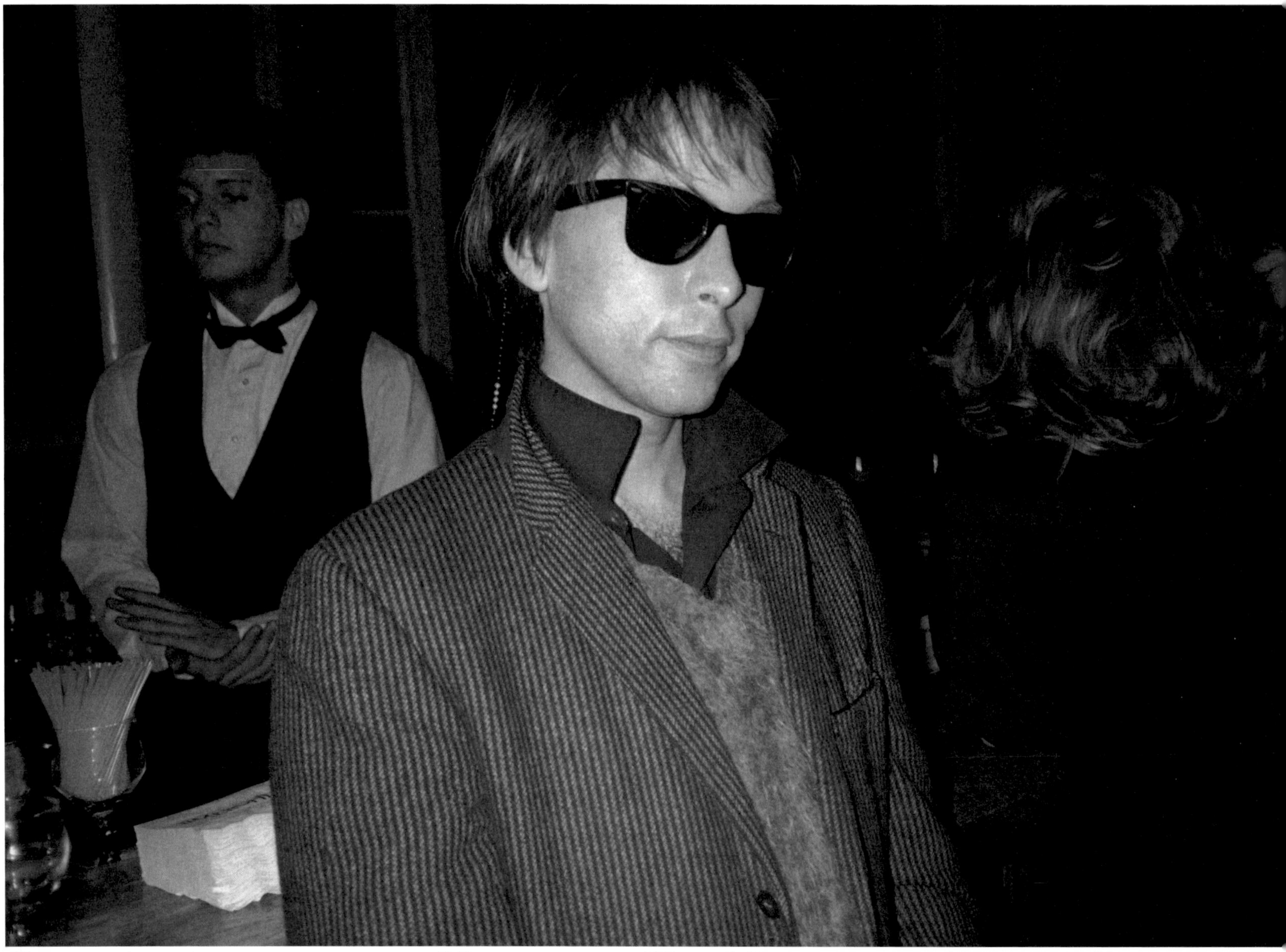

"I HAVEN'T THOUGHT ABOUT THE 80s SINCE THE 70s..." BEAUREGARD HOUSTON-MONTGOMERY

Beauregard Houston-Montgomery
at the Night of 100 Trees Party at Limelight.
December 18, 1984

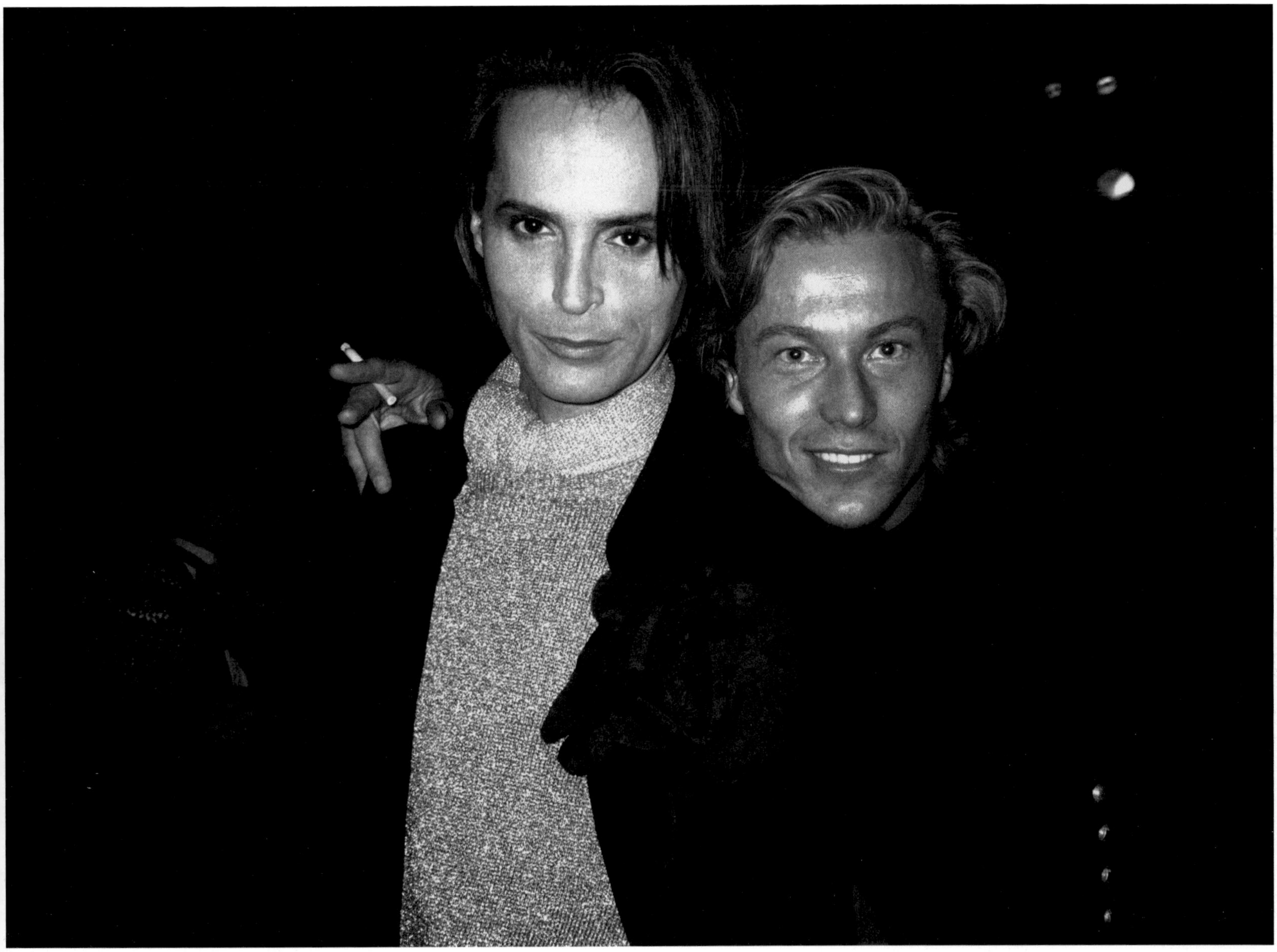

Way Bandy and Eigel Vesti
at Alan Rish's birthday party at Danceteria.
May 17, 1984

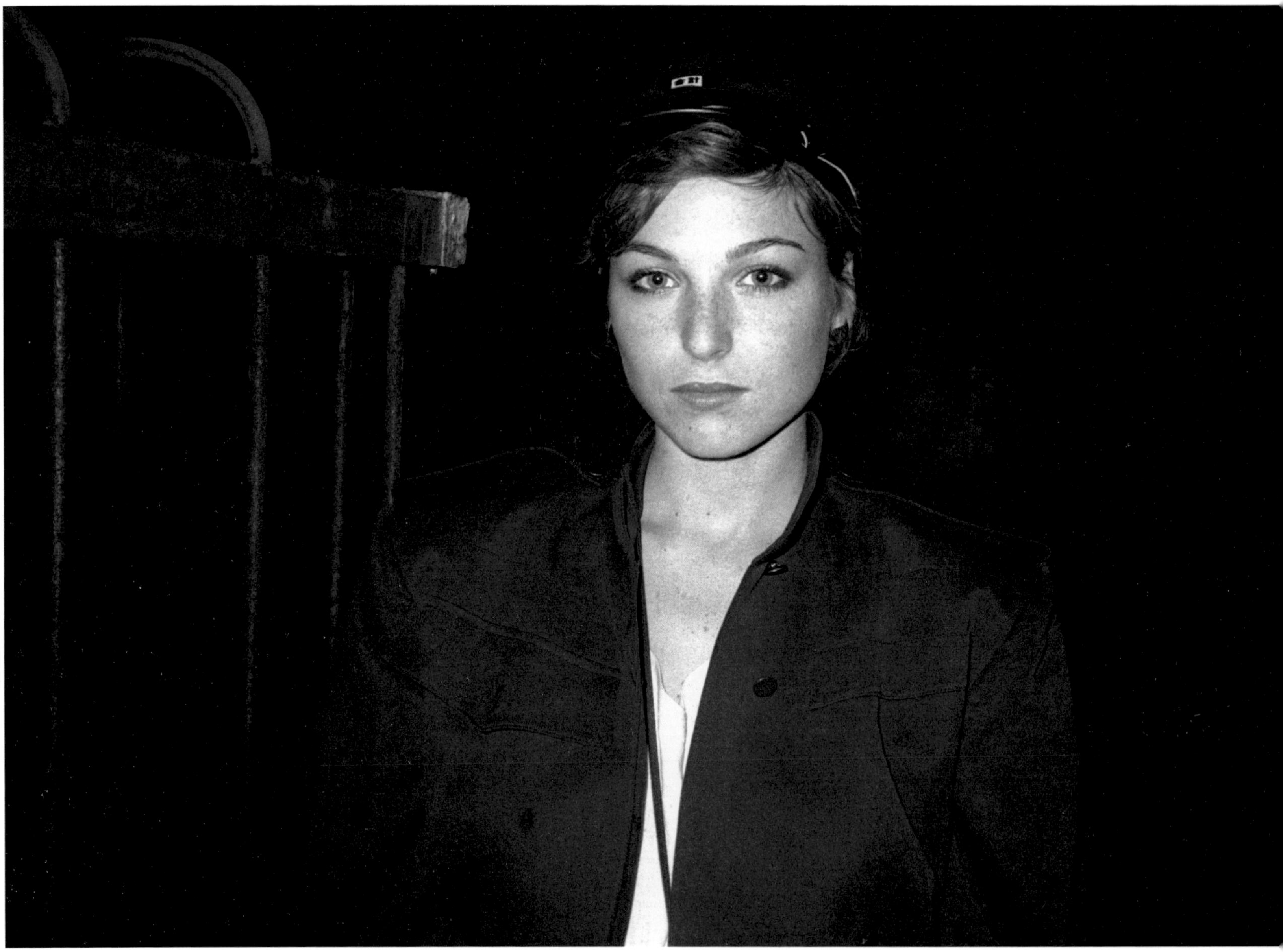

TATUM O'NEAL
AT THE BOY CRAZY BOOK PARTY AT AREA.
MAY 11, 1984

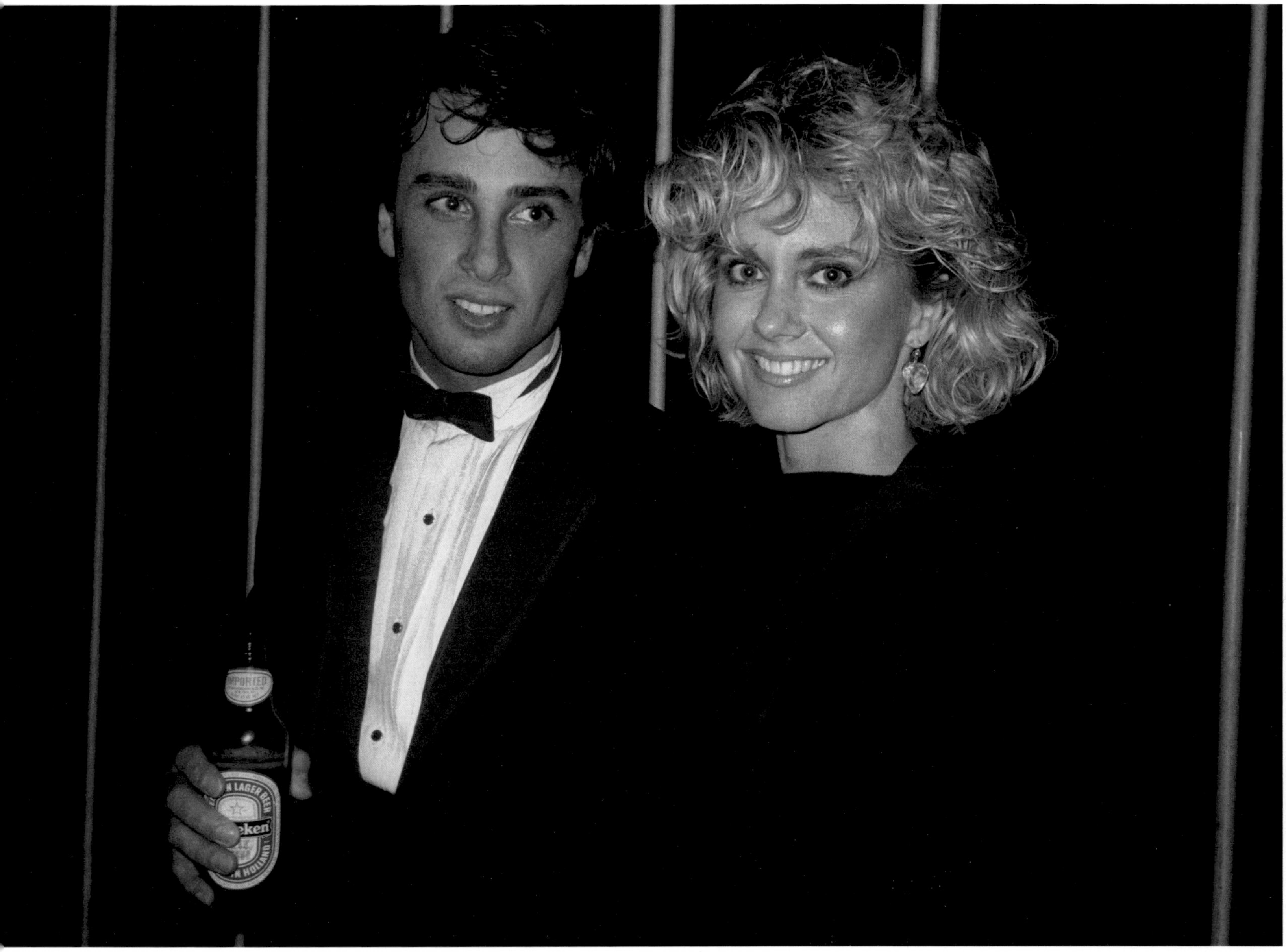

MATT LATTANZI AND OLIVIA NEWTON-JOHN
AT THE BOY CRAZY BOOK PARTY AT AREA.
MAY 11, 1984

THE 80S BEGAN AS ONE ENDLESS NIGHT, LIVED OUT IN CLUB BATHROOMS AND ON 3 A.M. STAGES--A TRAVELING PARTY THAT MOVED AND MUTATED LARGELY BY WORD OF MOUTH. FROM THE MUDD CLUB AND CLUB 57 TO PYRAMID, DANCETERIA, AND AREA, CREATIVITY WAS KING, AND CLUBS BIRTHED ARTISTS, HOMEMADE STARS, AND CULTURAL MOVEMENTS AT A DIZZYING PACE. THE NIGHT THE PALLADIUM OPENED, WITH ITS GIGANTIC SCALE AND MANUFACTURED CELEBRITIES, THIS FERTILE CITY OF NIGHT BEGAN A DOWNWARD SPIRAL THAT IT HAS NEVER REALLY RECOVERED FROM. ONE CANNOT SPEAK OF THE 80S WITHOUT REMEMBERING THOSE CLUBS, THAT MAGIC, AND AN ERA WHEN NIGHTLIFE COULD INSPIRE AND UPLIFT. AT THE TIME, WE DIDN'T KNOW WHAT A RARE GIFT THAT WAS.
CHI CHI VALENTI

ANDREA BOURGEOIS WITH A NYC FIREMAN AFTER HOURS ON THE STREET.
SATURDAY, SEPTEMBER 29, 1984

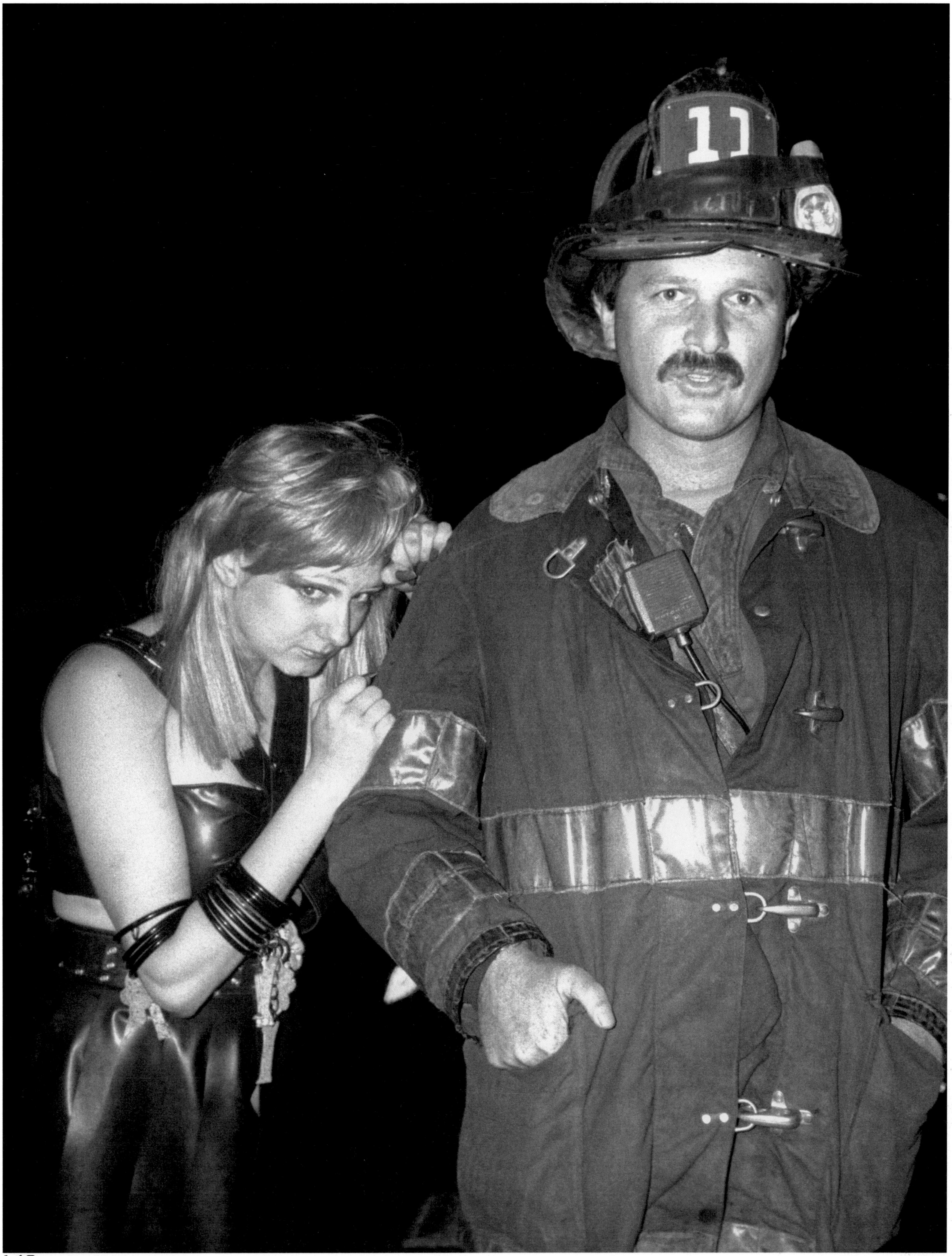
11

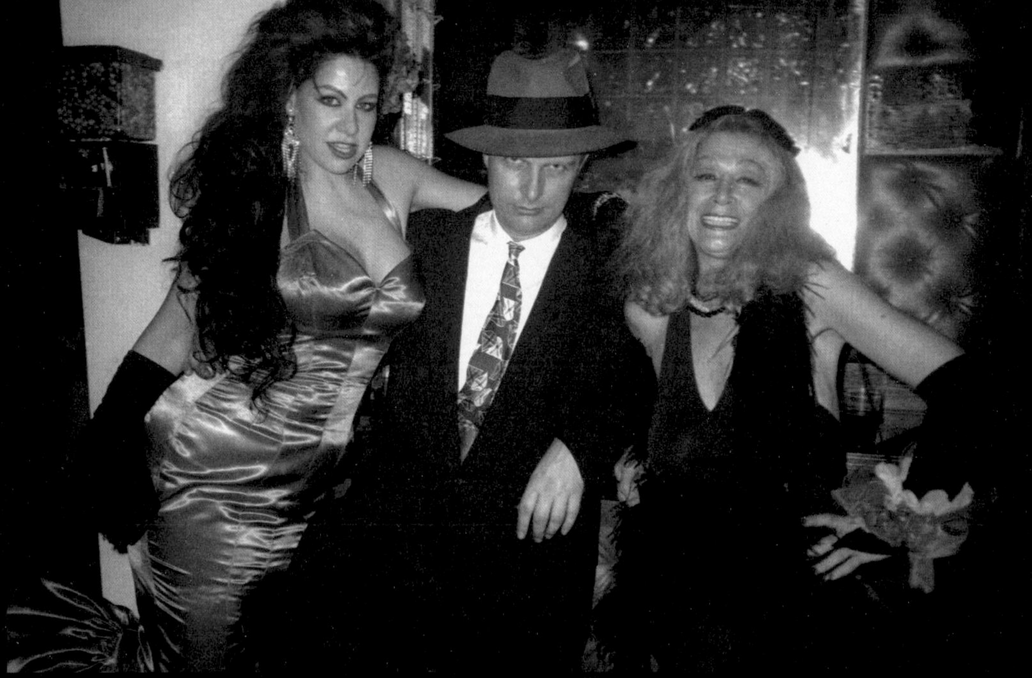

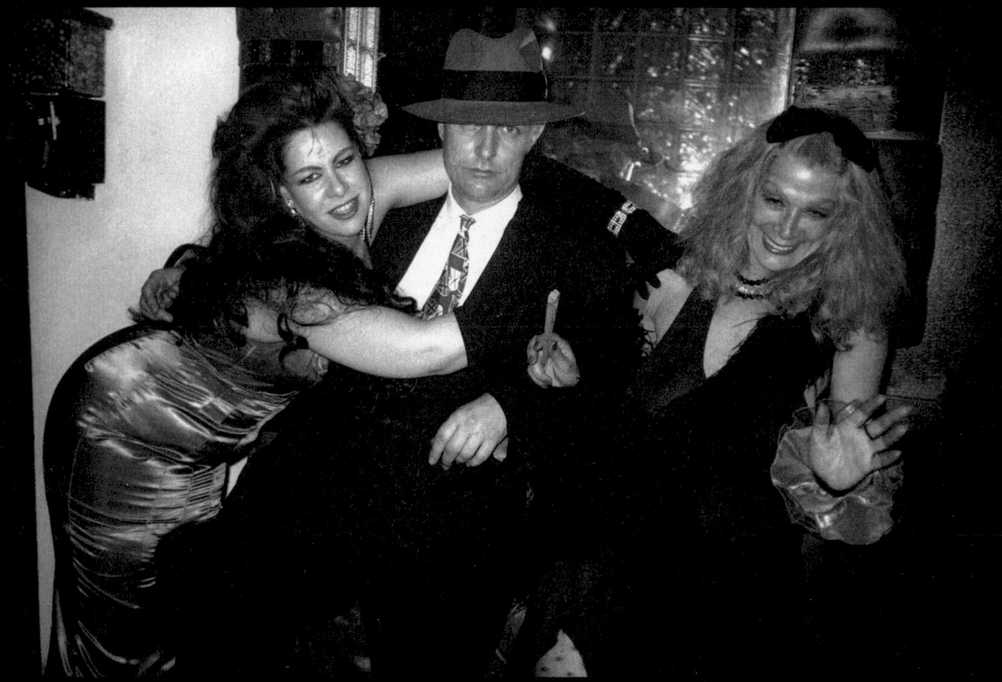

DIANNE BRILL, RUDOLF, AND SYLVIA MILES
AT MARCUS LEATHERDALE'S TANGO PARTY AT DANCETERIA.
WEDNESDAY, JUNE 13, 1984

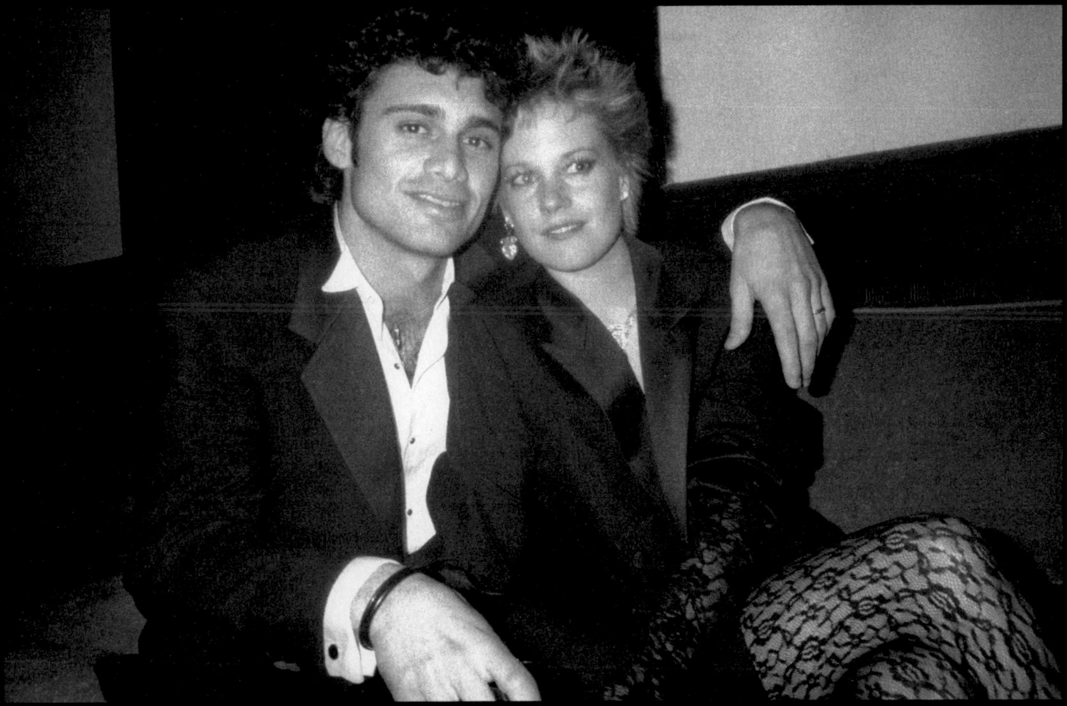

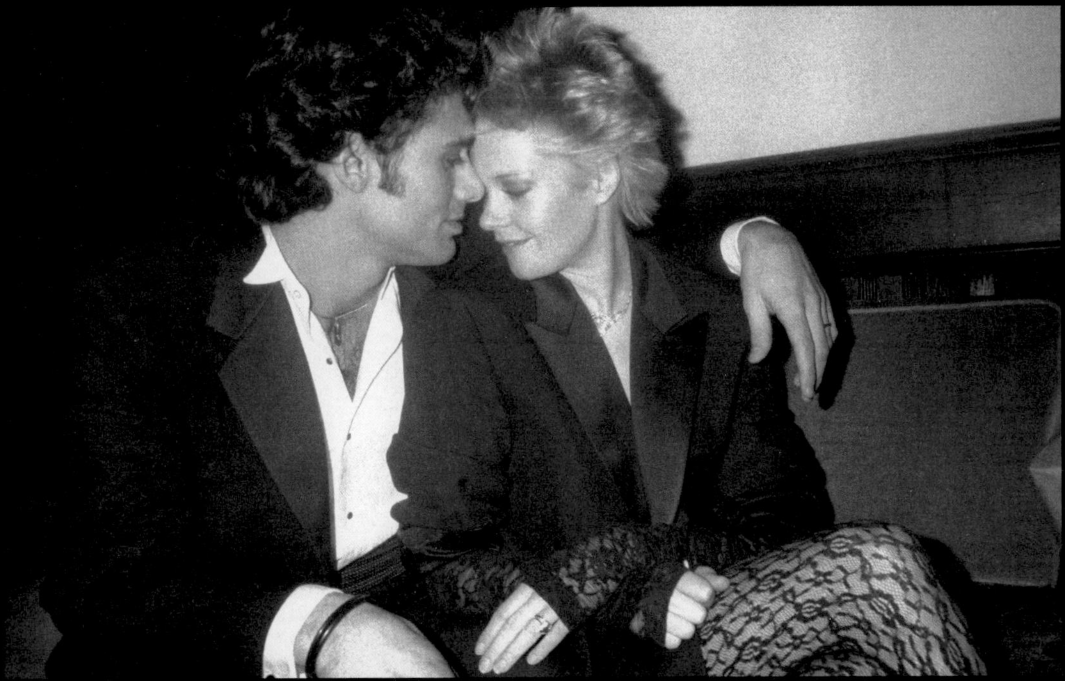

Steven Bauer and Melanie Griffith
at Limelight's anniversary party.
November 27, 1984

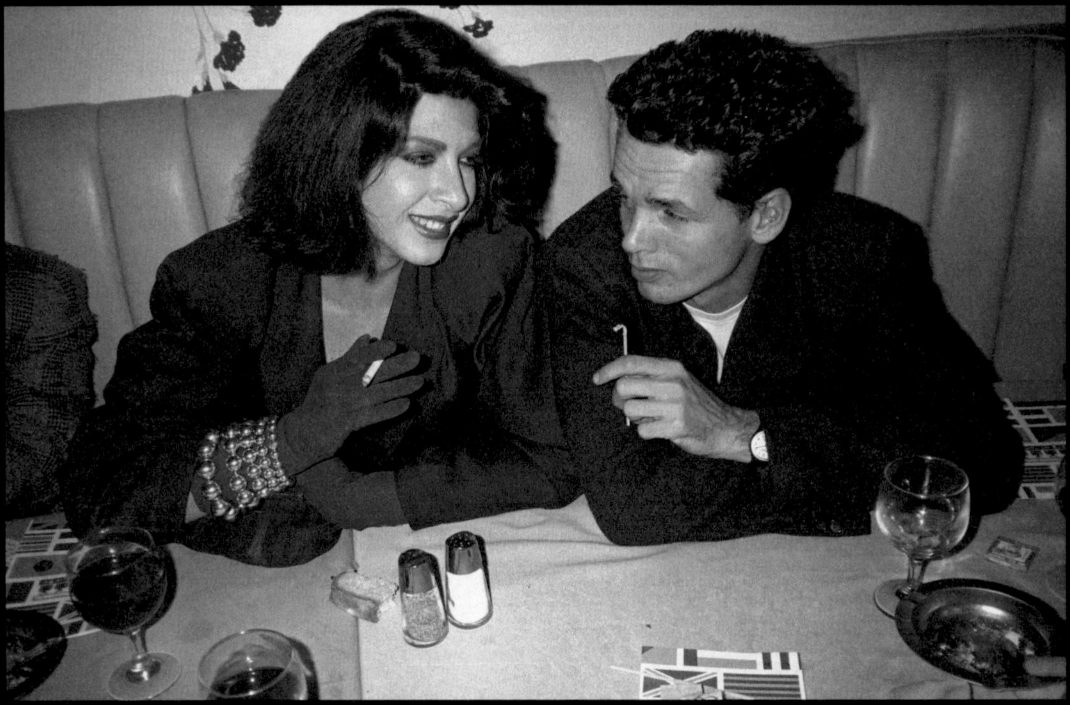

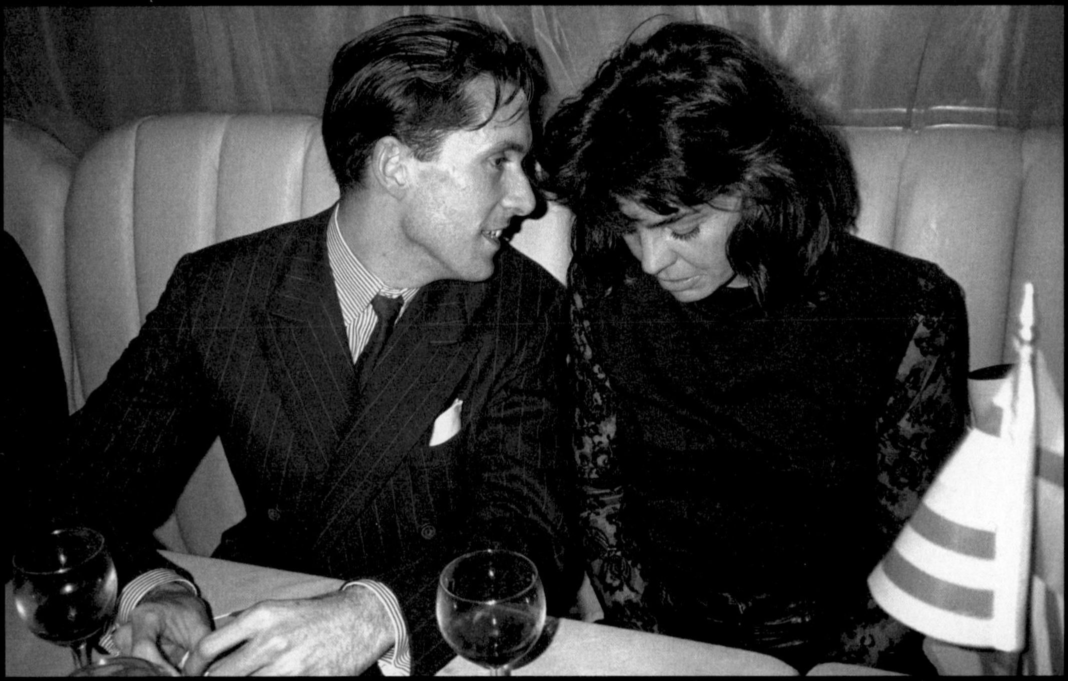

Top: Janis Savitt and Marcus Leatherdale
Bottom: Edmund Gaultney and Sylvia Martins
at the dinner for Hedy Klineman at El International.
November 3, 1984

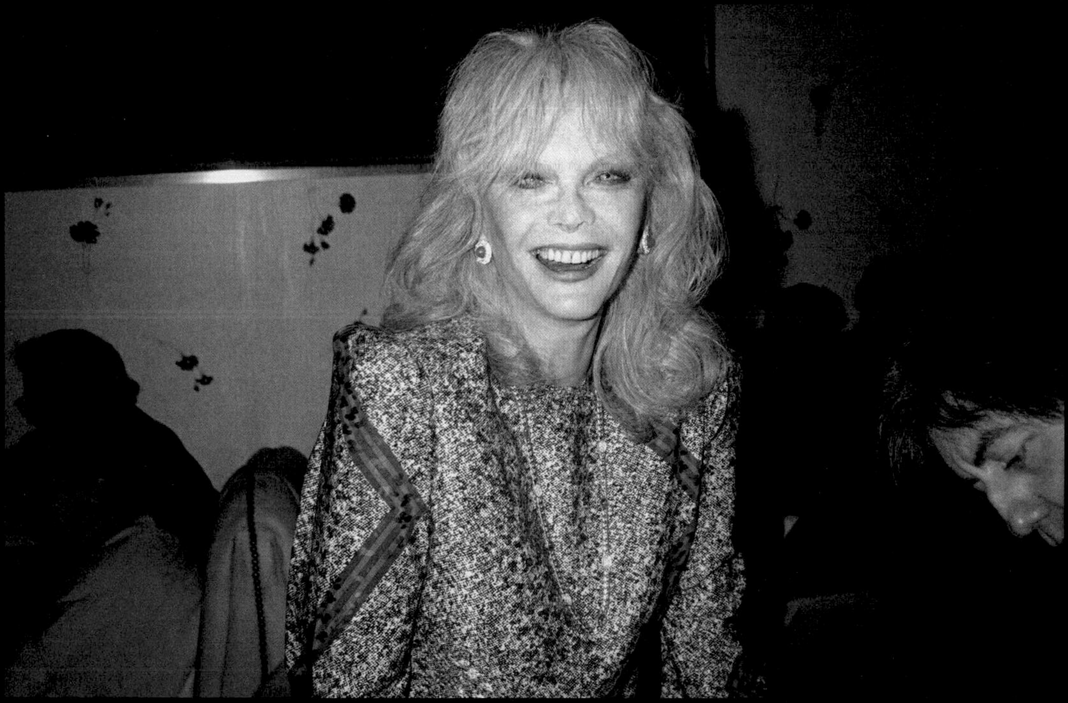

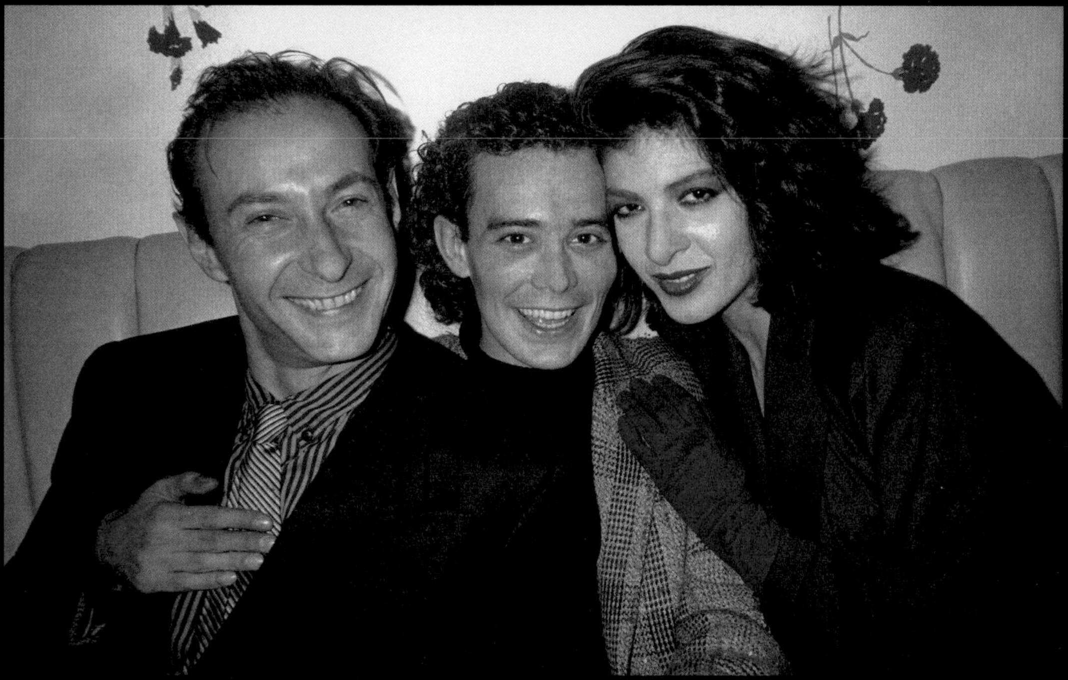

Top: Monique Van Vooren and Stephen Saban
Bottom: David King, Alan Rish, and Janis Savitt
at the dinner for Hedy Klineman at El International.
November 3, 1984

During the 80s, someone invented the concept of parties with open bars and free food. Patrick and I referred to these functions as "rubber" (short for "rubber chicken") and those who attended them as "special people" (from a book on abnormal, mutated freaks entitled Very Special People).

I made 2,342 close personal friends in the Limelight VIP room. 797 of them have since died of various 80s-associated ailments (AIDS, drugs, rock 'n roll) but the other 1,545 are still "very special" to me.

Claire O'Connor

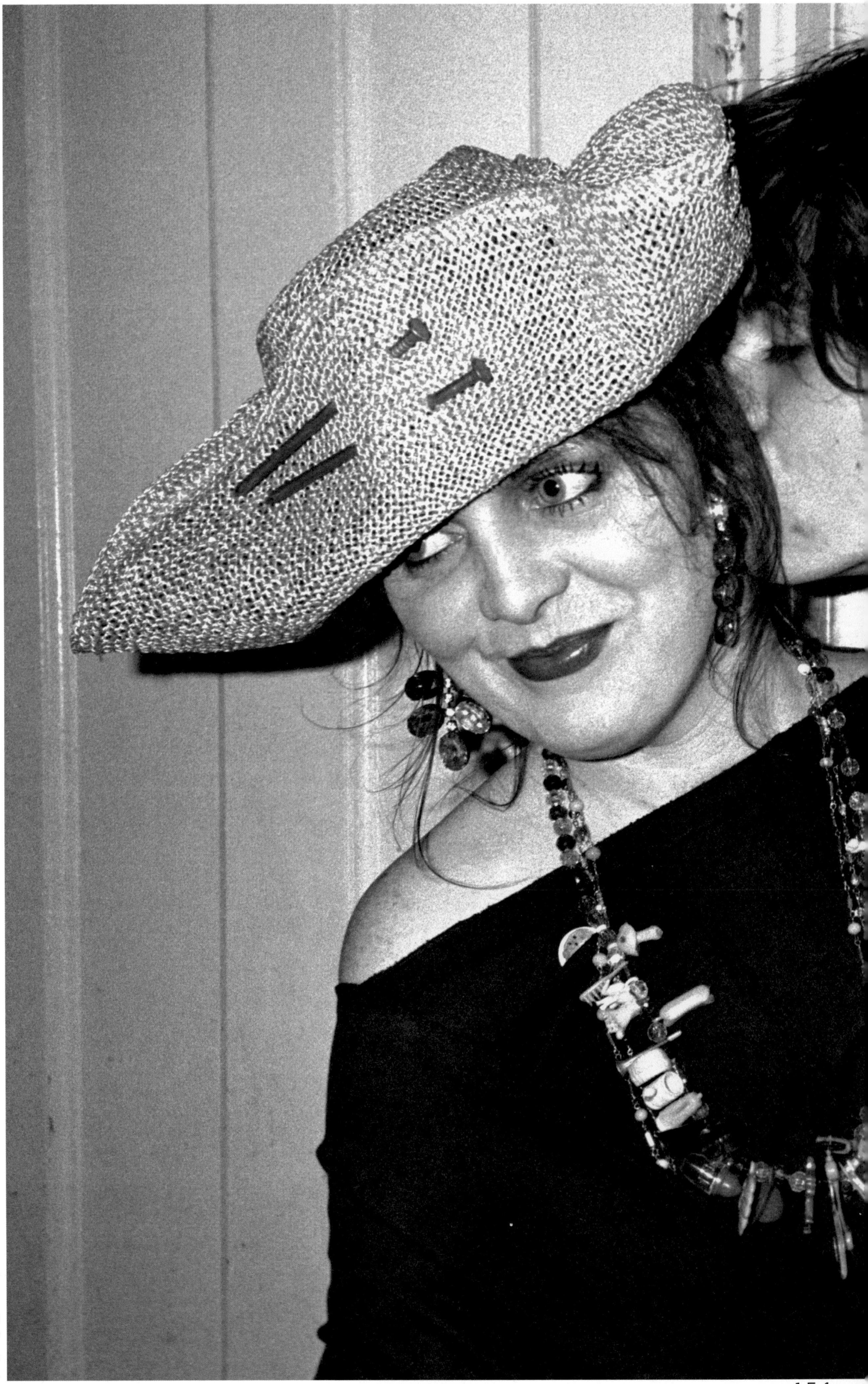

Claire O'Connor and Adam Bomb at Nile Rodgers' birthday party at Limelight. September 19, 1984

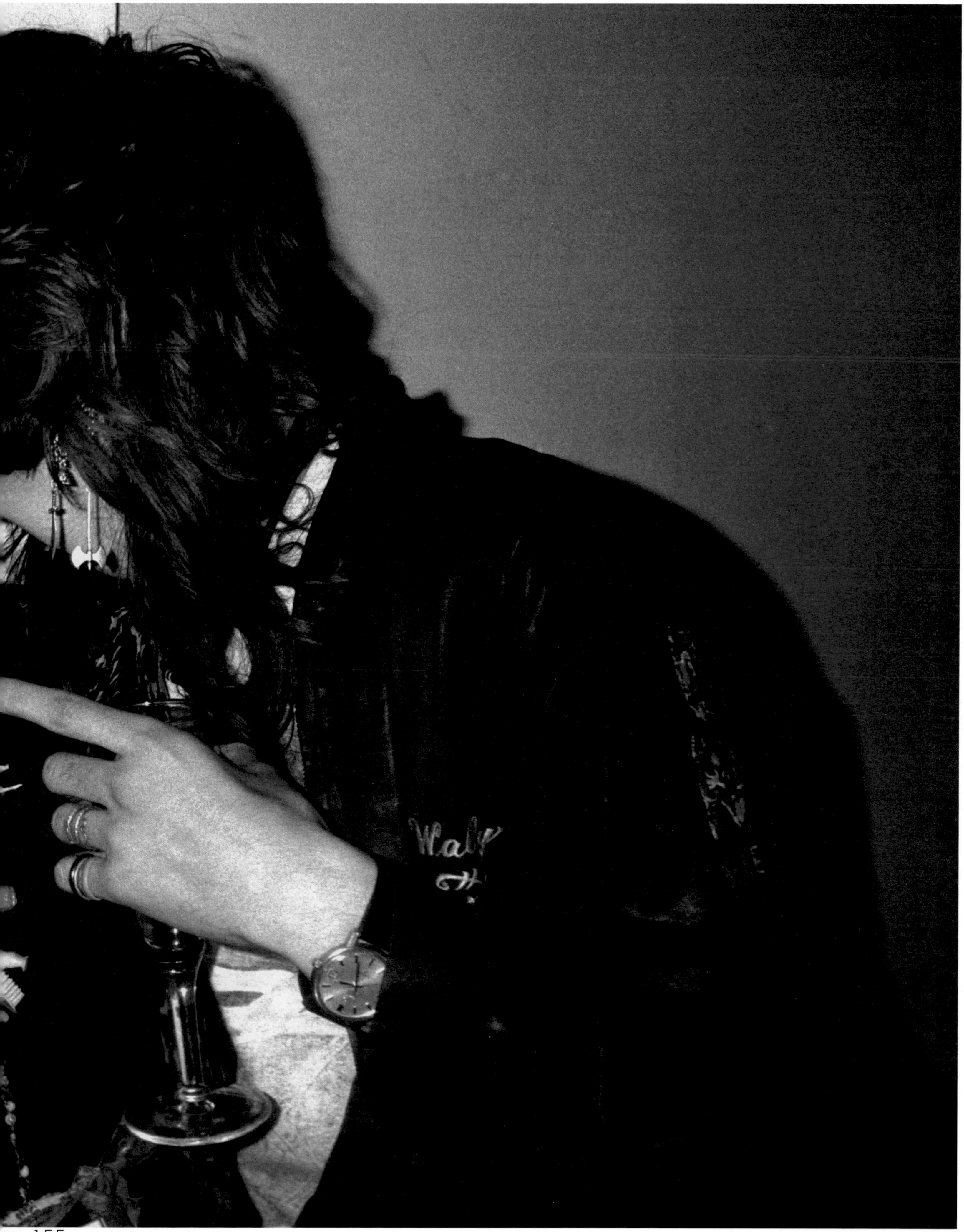

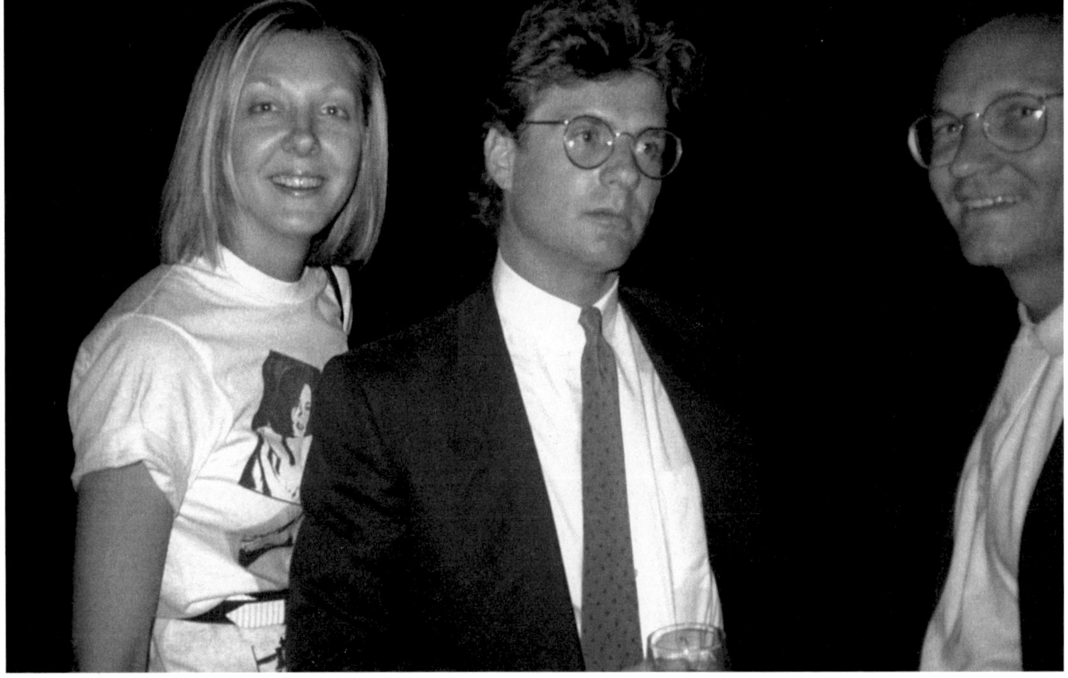

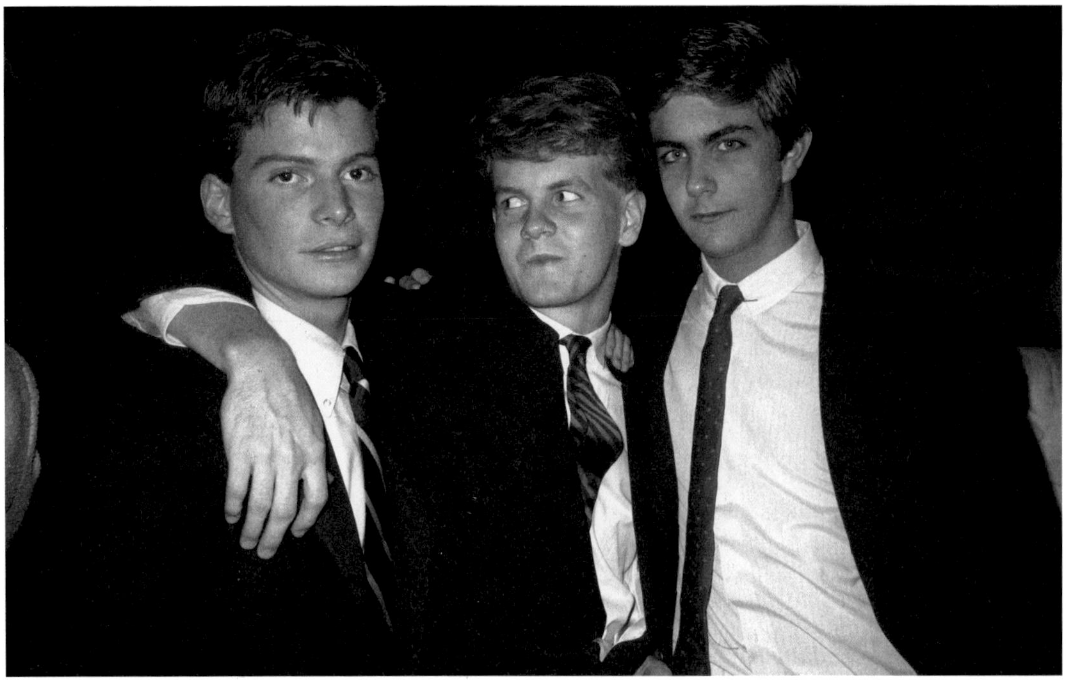

Top: Shelly Dunn Fremont and Vincent Fremont
at Limelight. July 1984
Bottom: Nick Beavers, John Flanigan, and Ted Owen
at Alan Rish's birthday party at Danceteria.
May 17, 1984

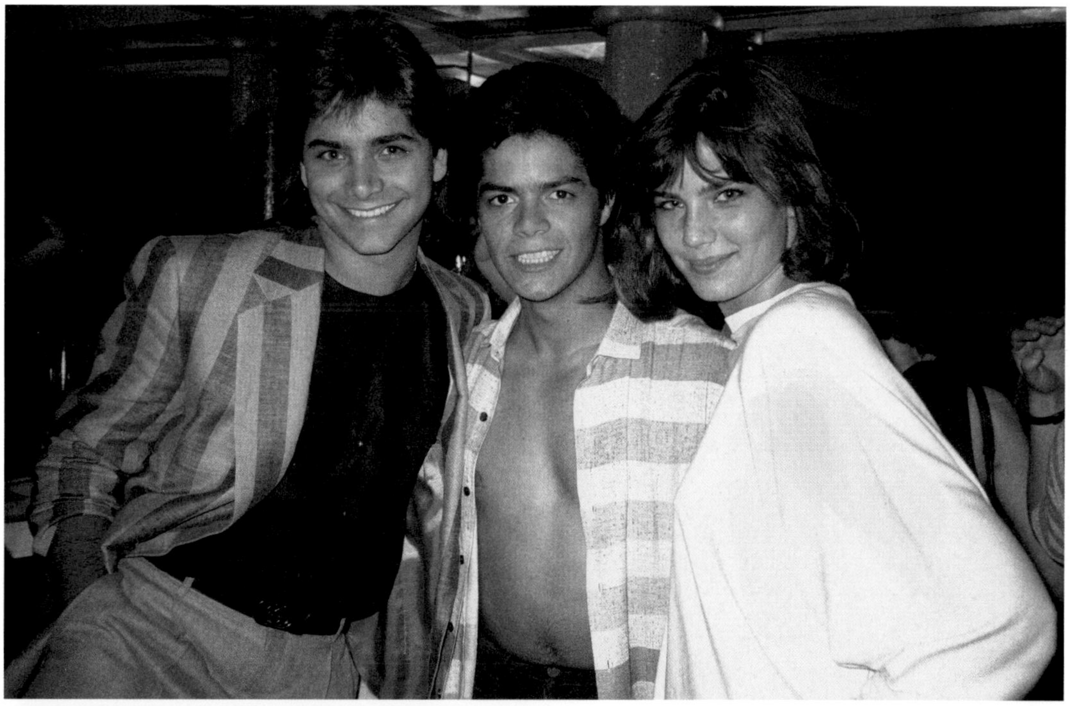

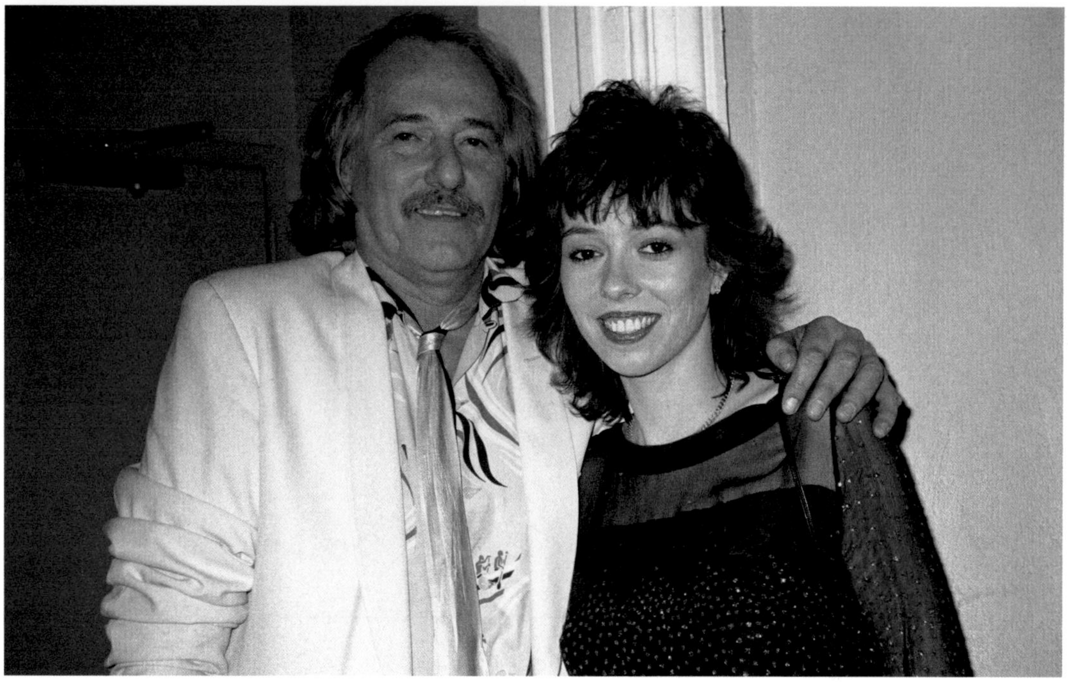

Top: John Stamos, Esai Morales, and Elizabeth McGovern
at the Boy Crazy book party at Area. May 11, 1984
Bottom: John and Mackenzie Phillips
at the Mackenzie Phillips party at Limelight. February 1984

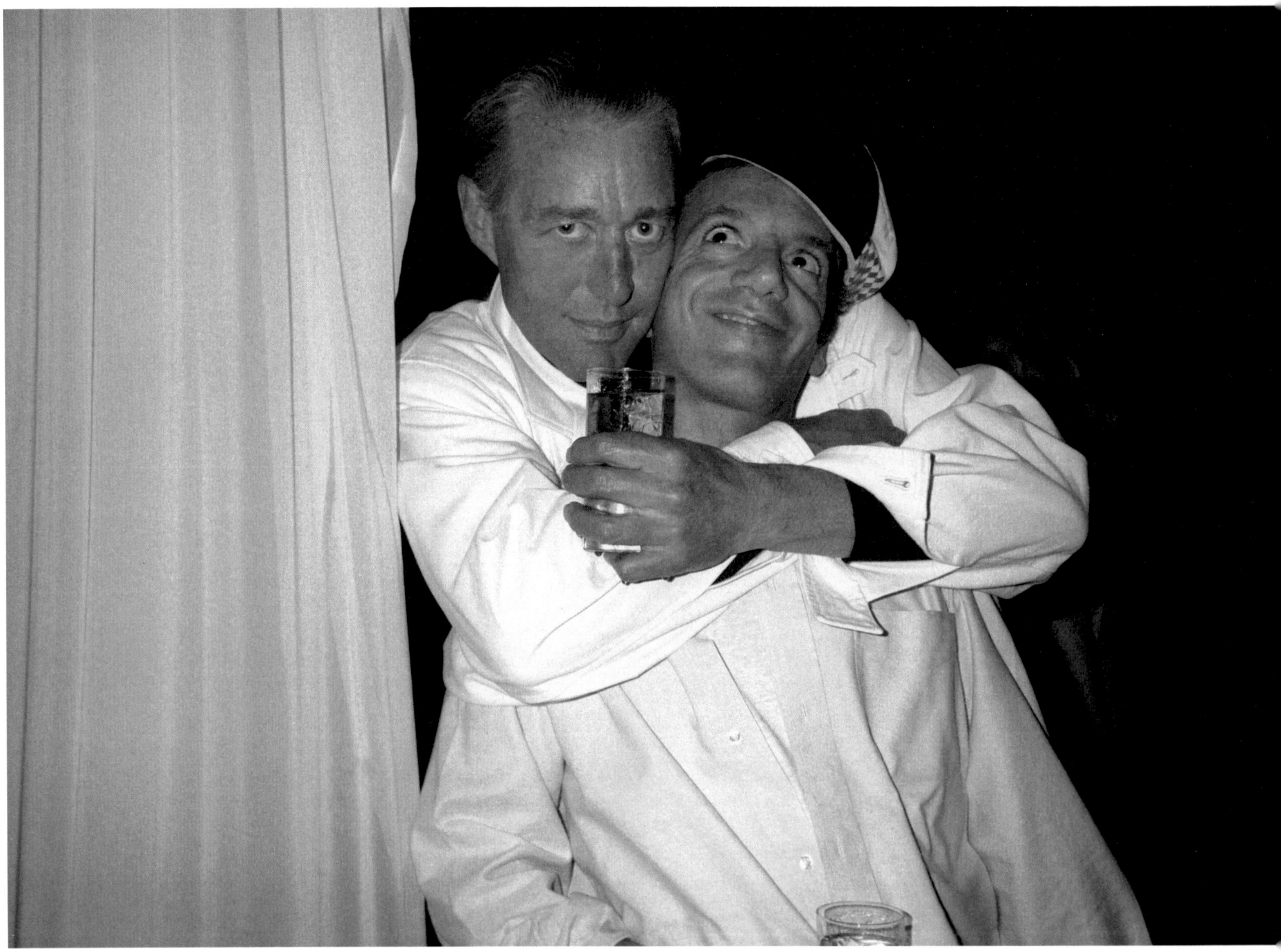

HALSTON AND STEVE RUBELL
AT THE PALLADIUM.
JUNE 20, 1985

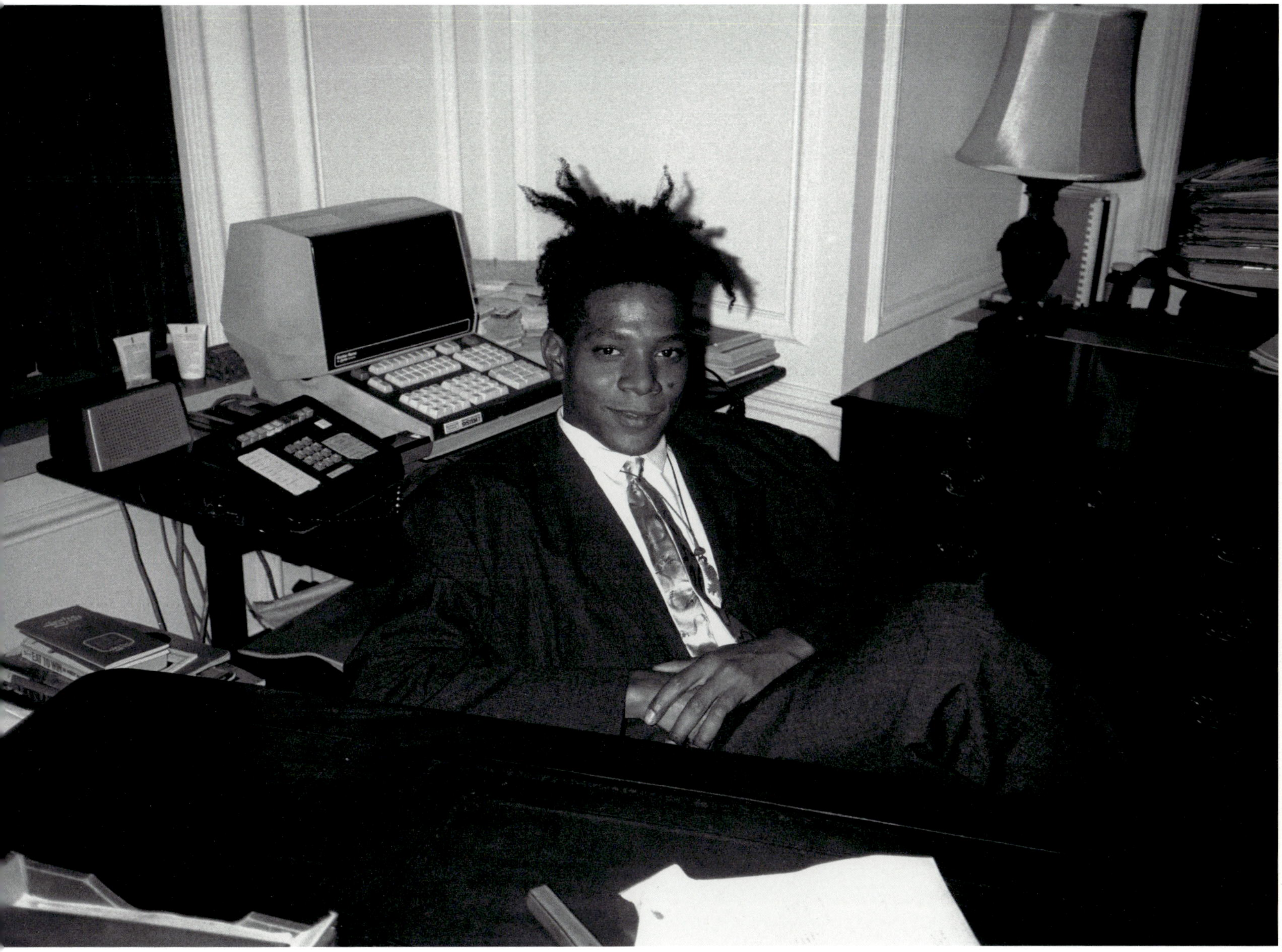

JEAN-MICHEL BASQUIAT
AT THE SURPRISE BIRTHDAY PARTY FOR SUSANNE BARTSCH AT THE RAINBOW ROOF,
AT STEVEN GREENBERG'S OFFICE, 30 ROCKEFELLER PLAZA.
THURSDAY, SEPTEMBER 19, 1985

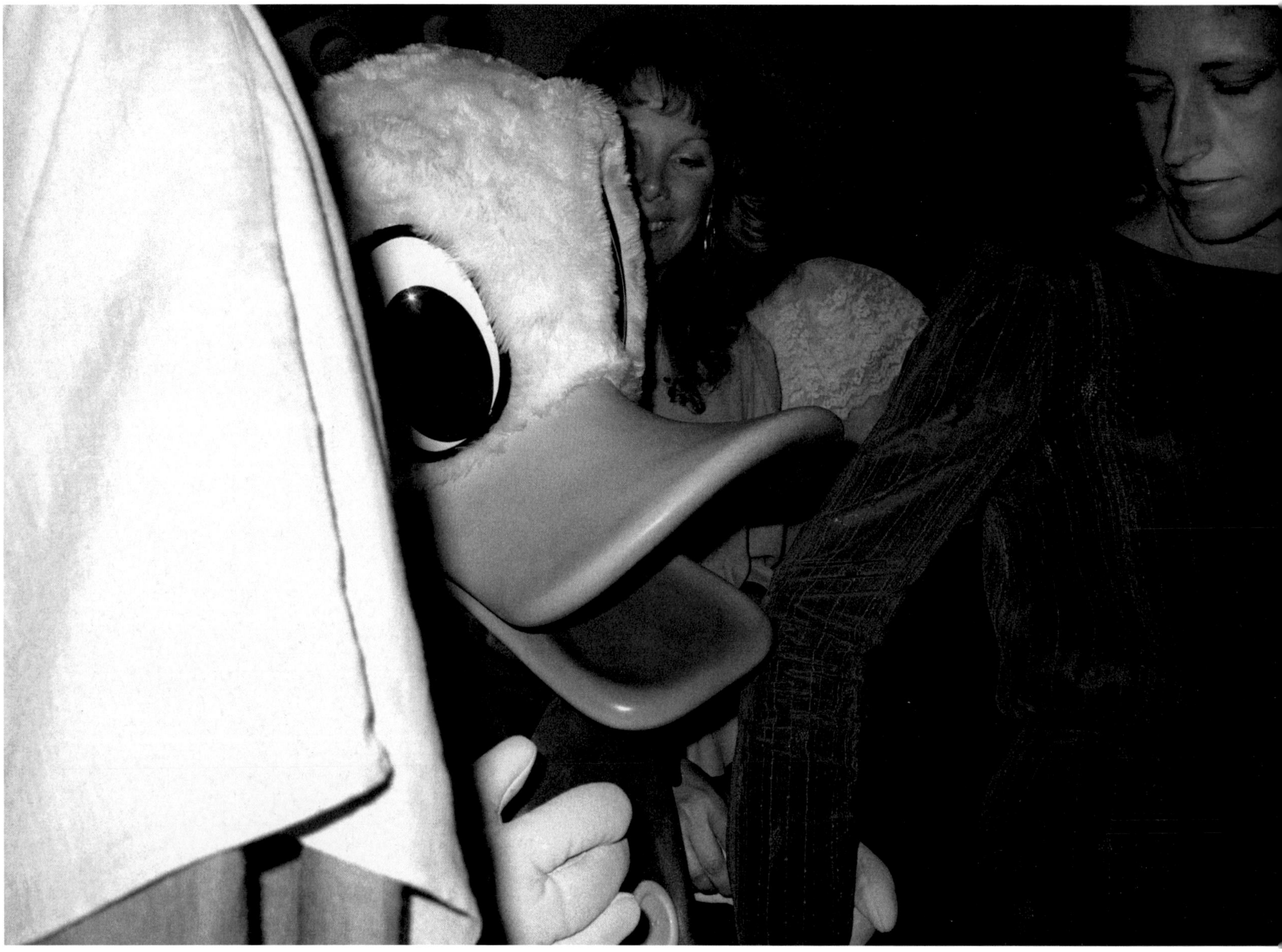

Duck in the crowd
at Shirley MacLaine's birthday party at Limelight.
April 23, 1984

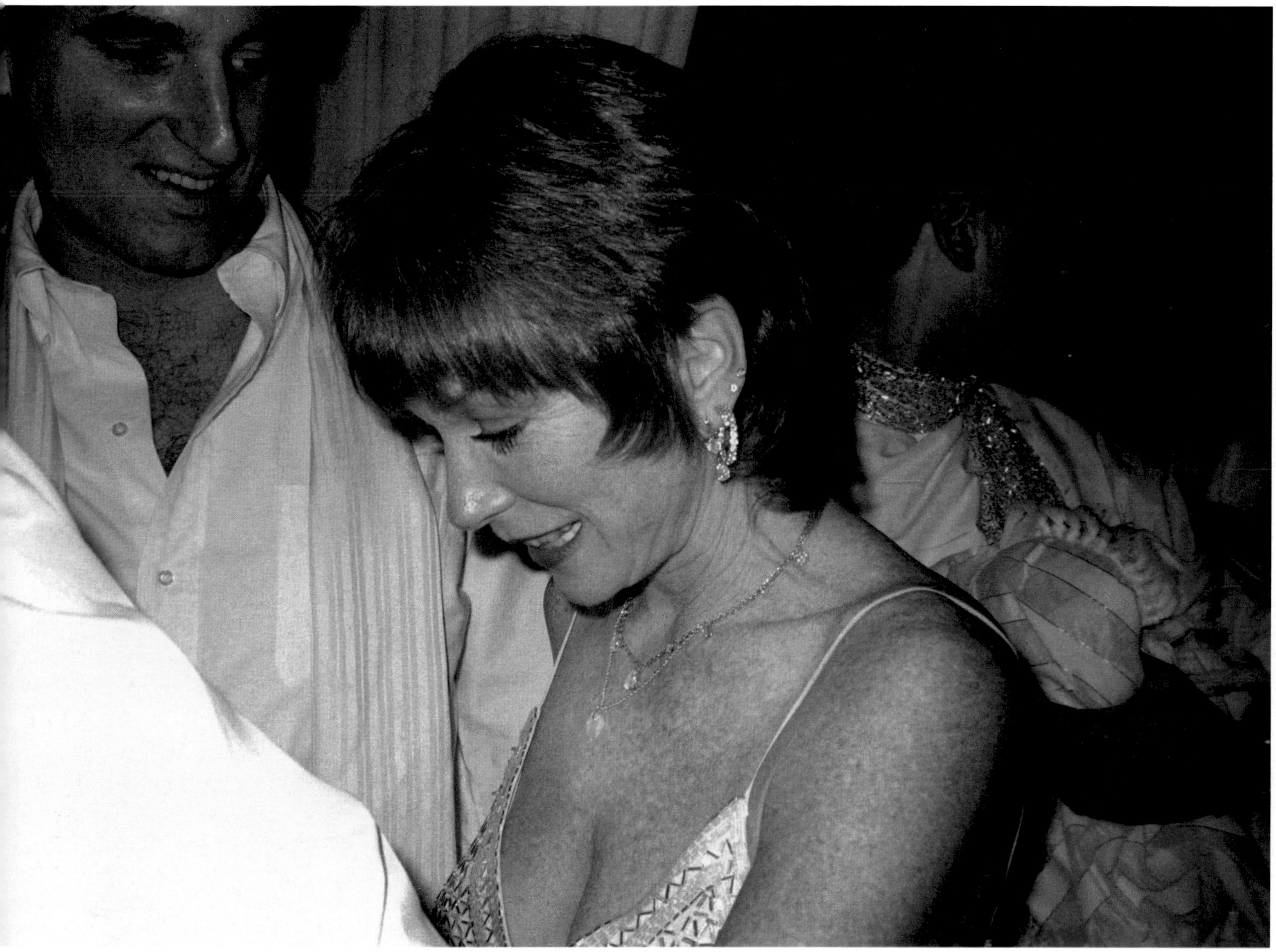

Shirley MacLaine
at her birthday party at Limelight.
April 23, 1984

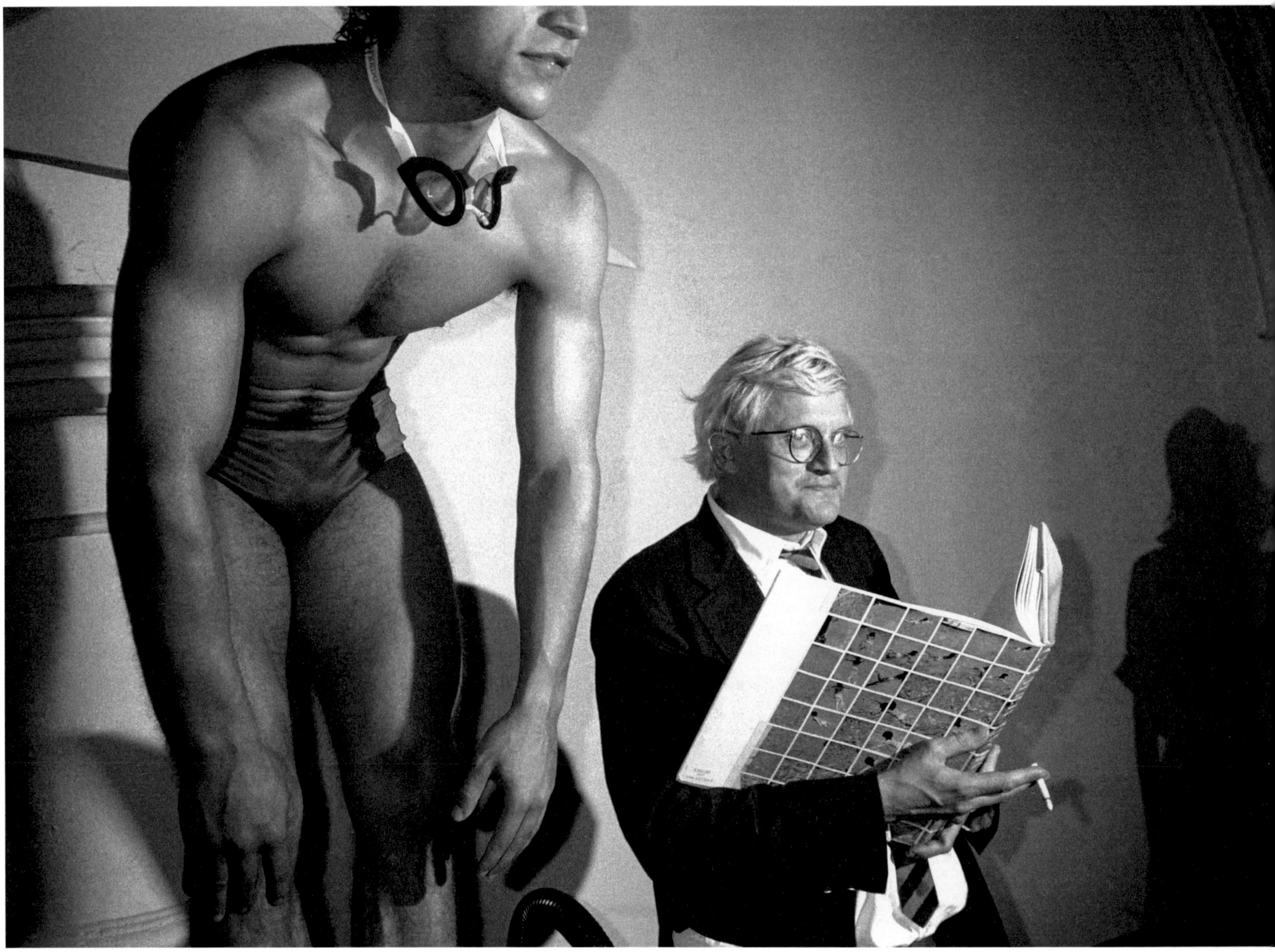

David Hockney
at his book release party at Limelight.
October 15, 1984

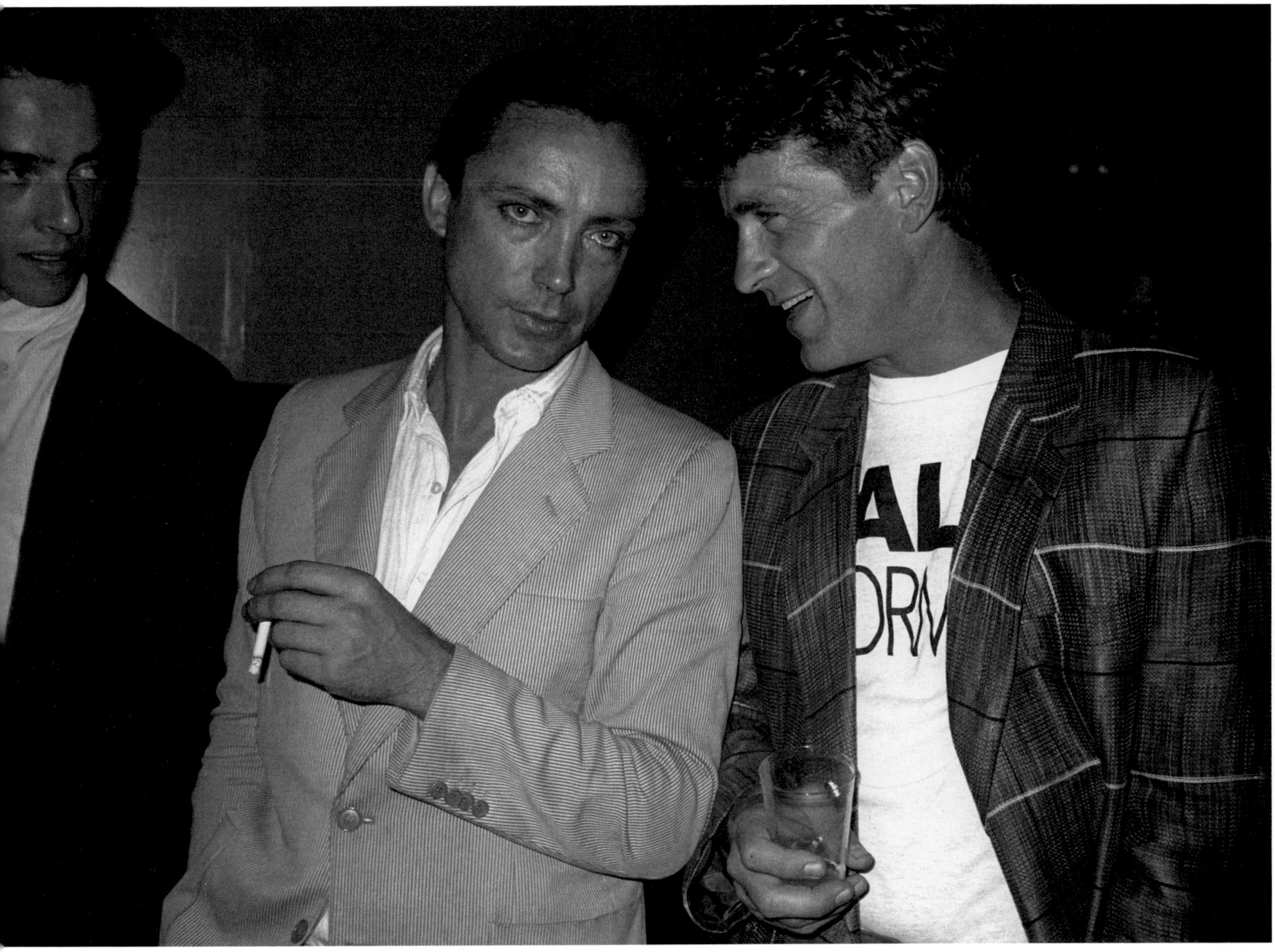

Udo Kier and Ingo Thouret
at Marcus Leatherdale's party at Danceteria.
June 13, 1984

"ALONG WITH THE 80S CAME MY TEENS.... SO MANY MISTAKES TO BE MADE, I THINK I MADE THEM ALL...FROM PLASTIC DRESSES, RUBBER DRESSES AND ALL-TOO-SEE-THROUGH DRESSES...TO BATHING SUITS ON TRAMPOLINES.... BLACK HAIR, BLOND HAIR, PINK HAIR...CANDY NECKLACES, RUBBER BRACELETS...MEN'S PAJAMAS WORN AS DAY-WEAR...HOT PANTS AND MOTORCYCLE JACKETS.... HOW DID I GET THIS JOB ANYWAY???"

ELIZABETH SALTZMAN

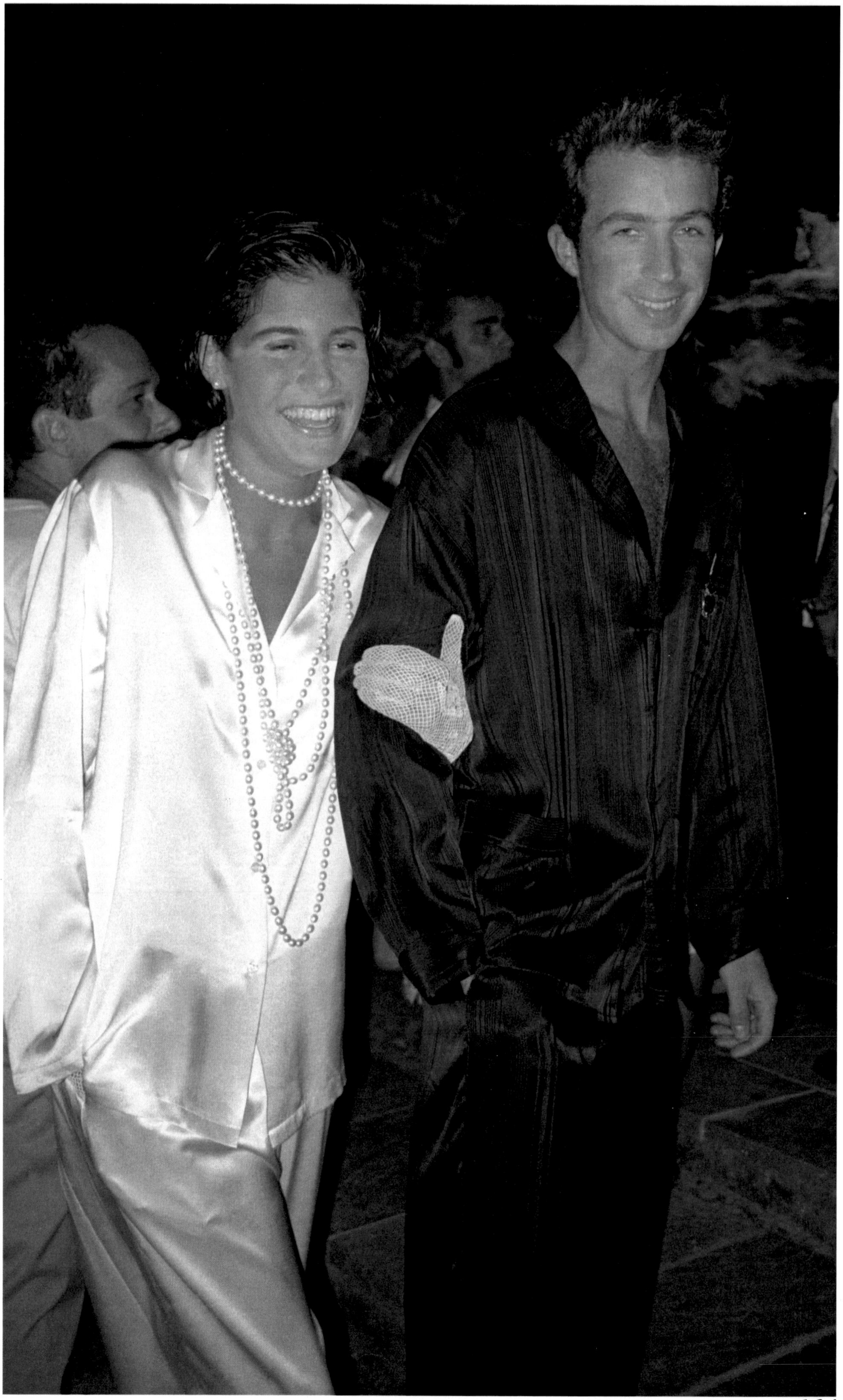

ELIZABETH SALTZMAN AND ERIC GOODE AT THE CHRISTOPHER MAKOS SHIRT PARTY. JULY 1984

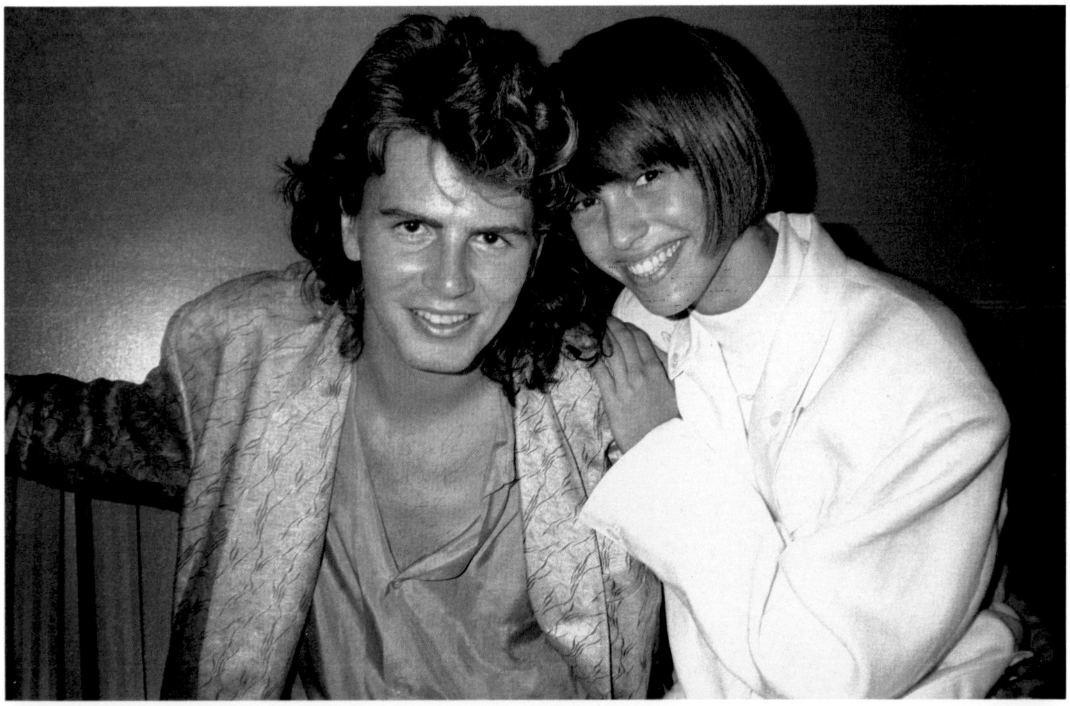

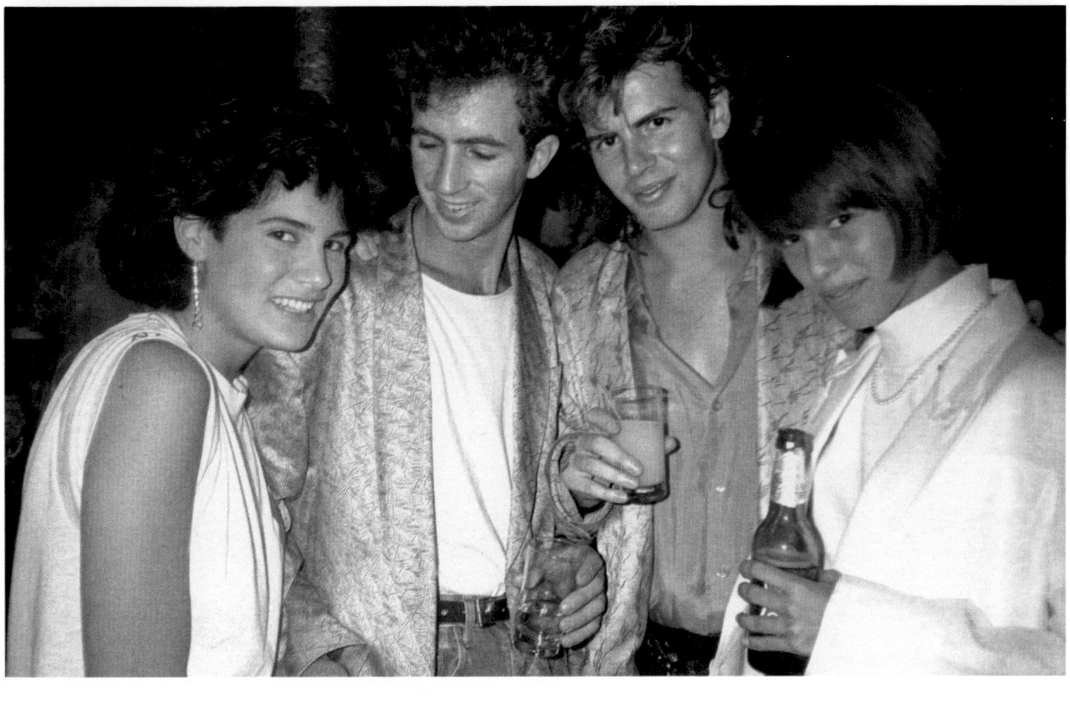

TOP: JOHN TAYLOR AND SAMANTHA PHILLIPS
BOTTOM: ELIZABETH SALTZMAN, ERIC GOODE, JOHN TAYLOR, AND SAMANTHA PHILLIPS AT AREA. SATURDAY, OCTOBER 3, 1984

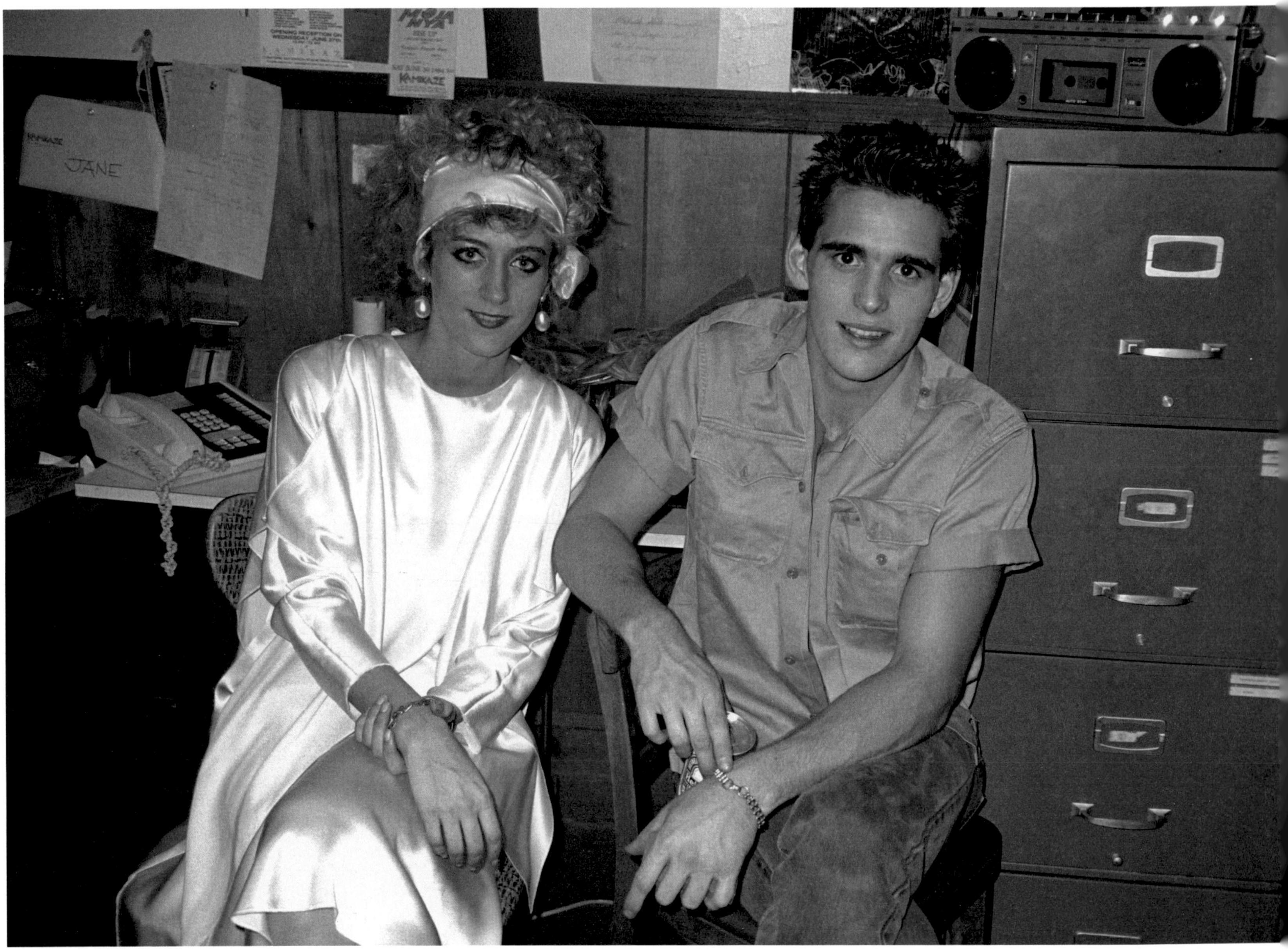

Stacy Teele and Matt Dillon
at the Kamikaze office
during the celebrity art show. 1984

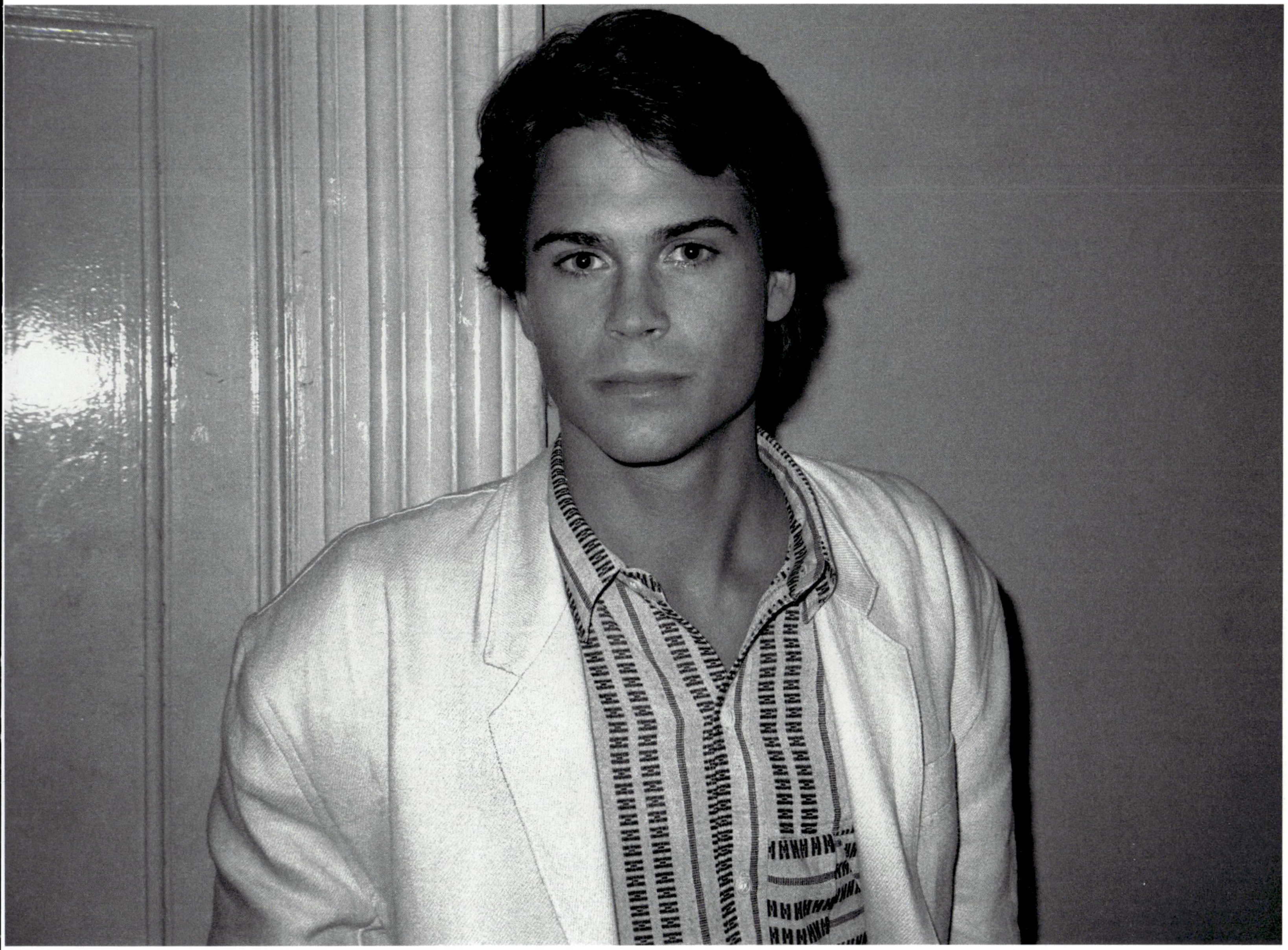

Rob Lowe
at Limelight.
1984

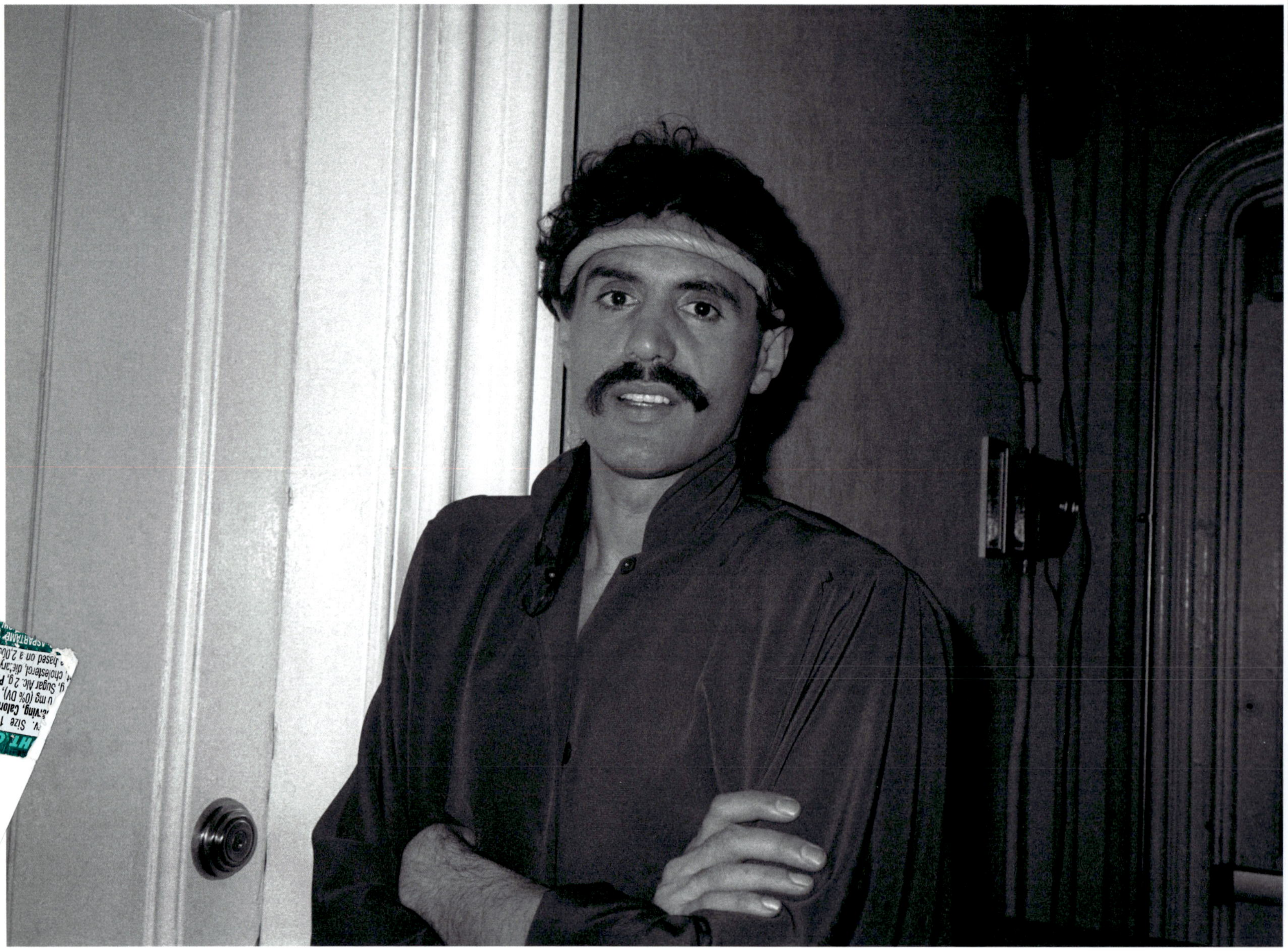

Antonio Lopez
March 1984

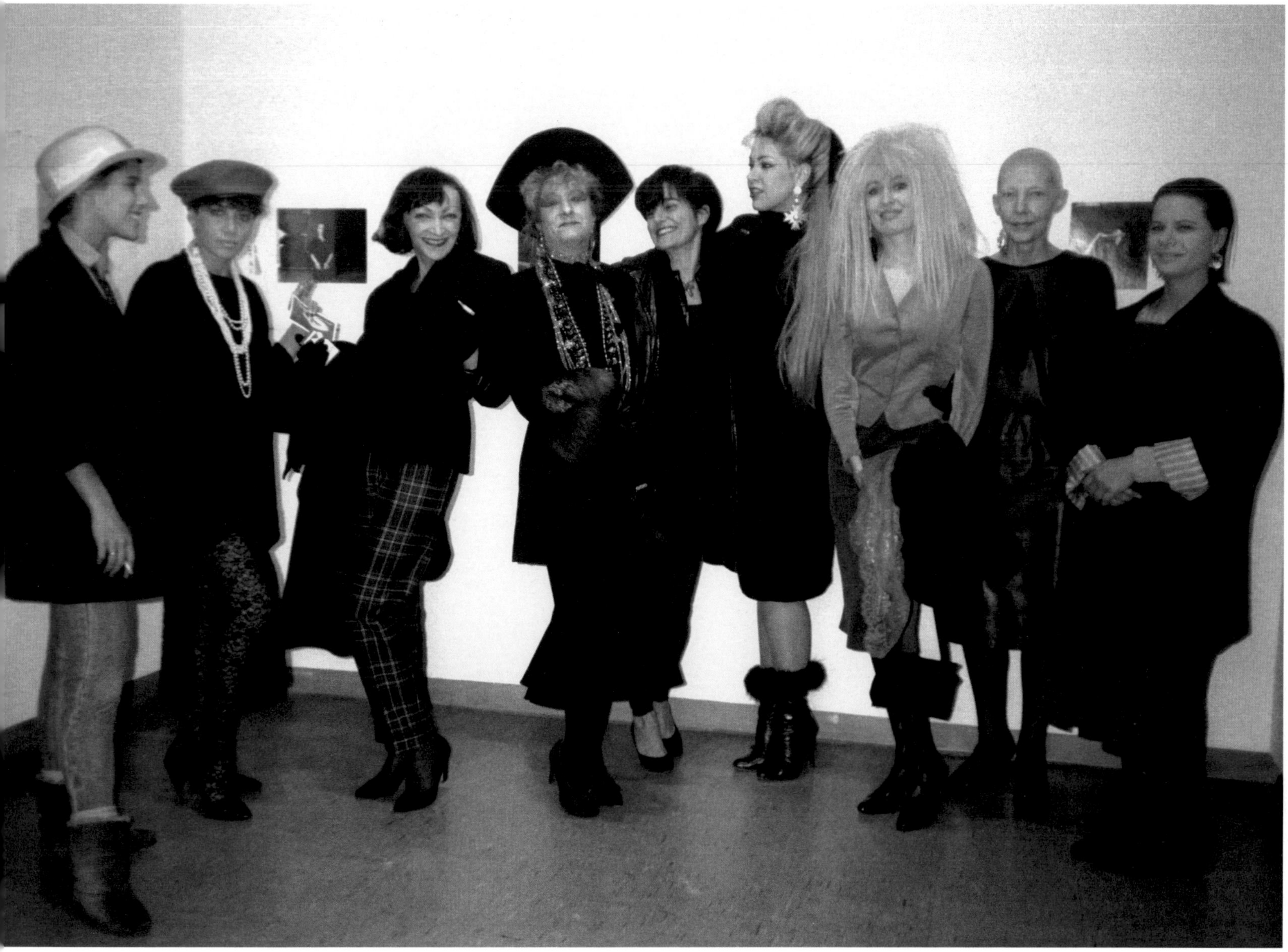

Tina Rathbone, Debora Waknin, Larissa, Anita Sarko, Patricia Field, Dianne Brill, Antonia de Portago, May Alexander, and Janet Paist at the Marcus Leatherdale opening at the Grey Arts Gallery. November 1984

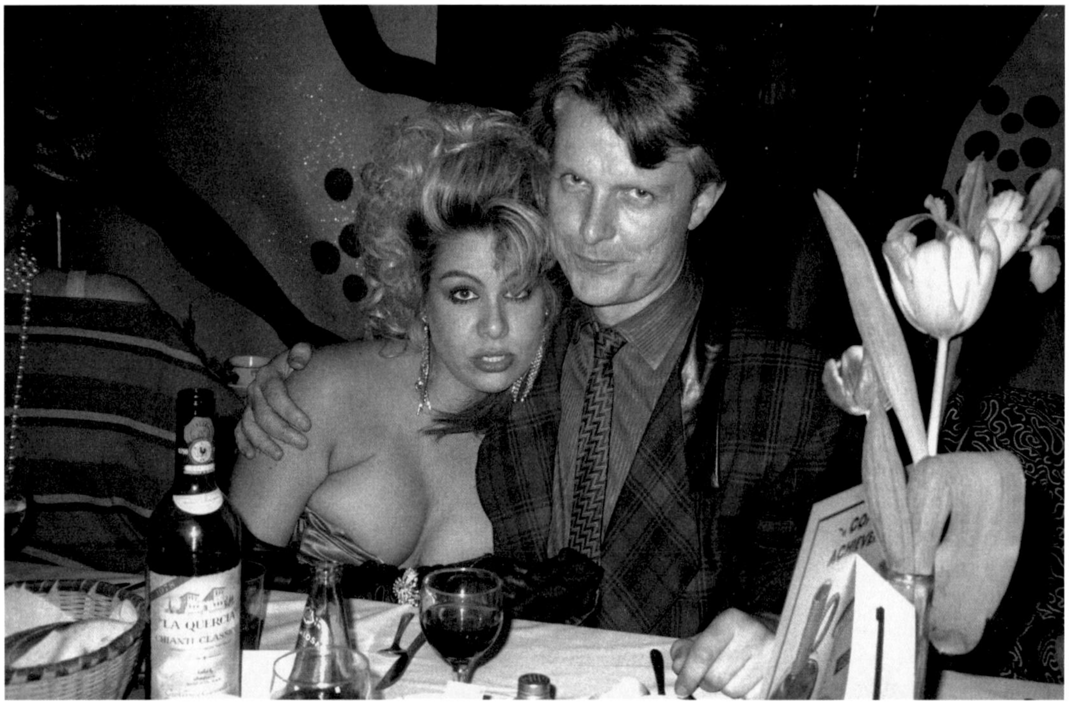

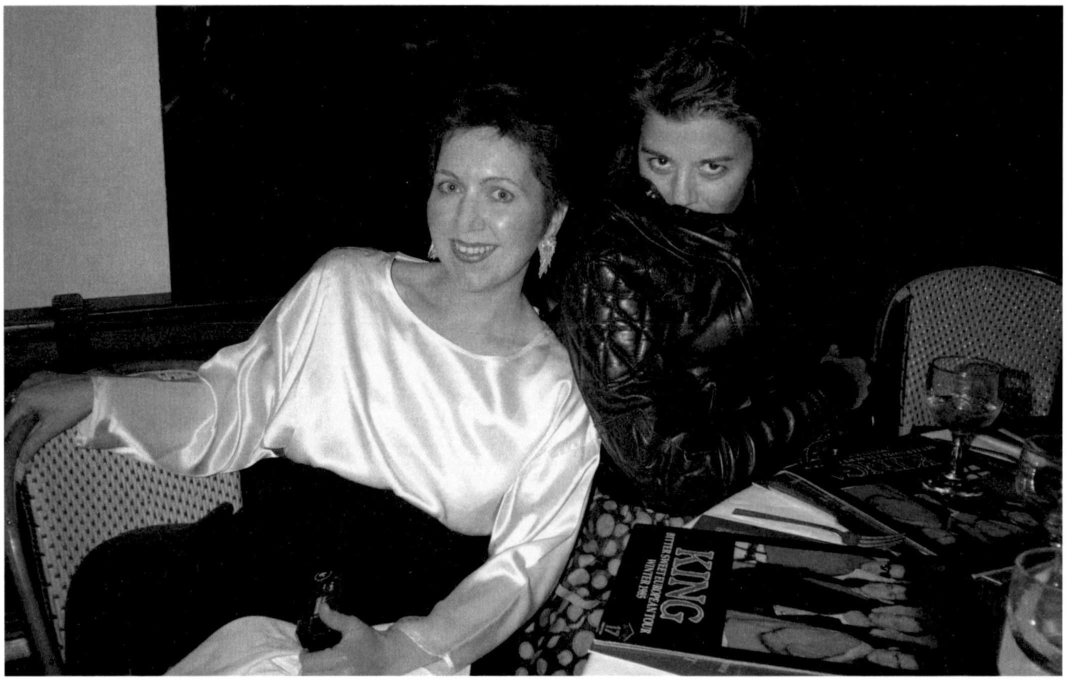

TOP: DIANNE BRILL AND RUDOLF
AT DIANNE BRILL'S BIRTHDAY PARTY AT DANCETERIA. APRIL 5, 1984
BOTTOM: PAT HACKETT AND PAIGE POWELL
AT THE DINNER PARTY FOR PAUL KING AT THE WATER CLUB.
FRIDAY, APRIL 11, 1986

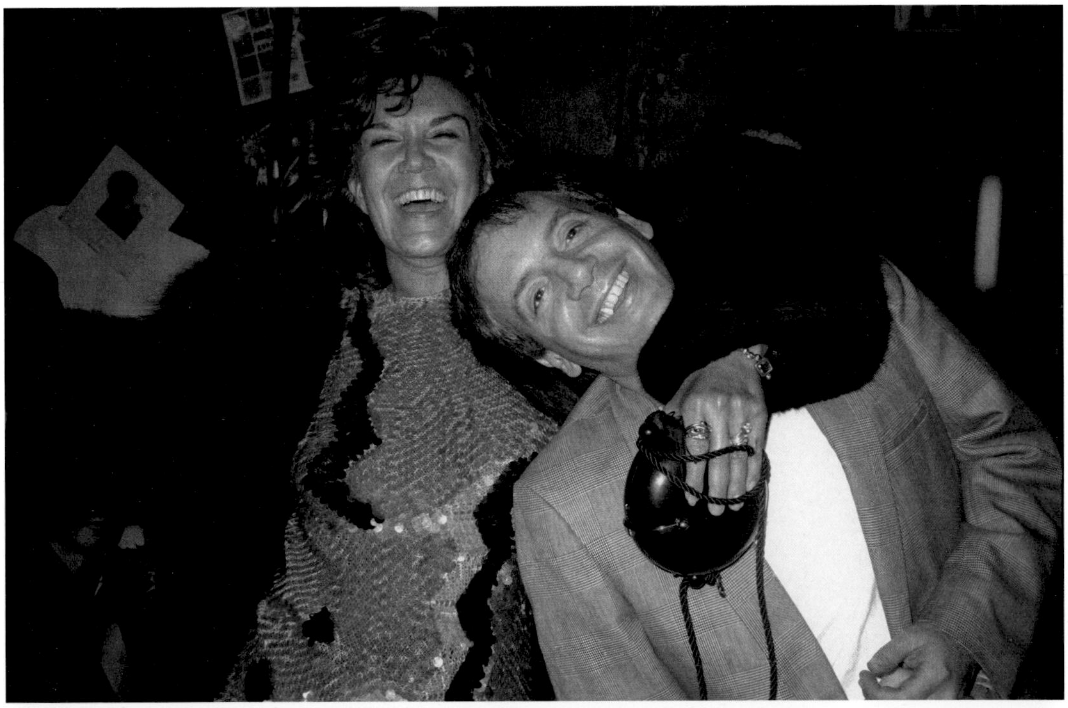

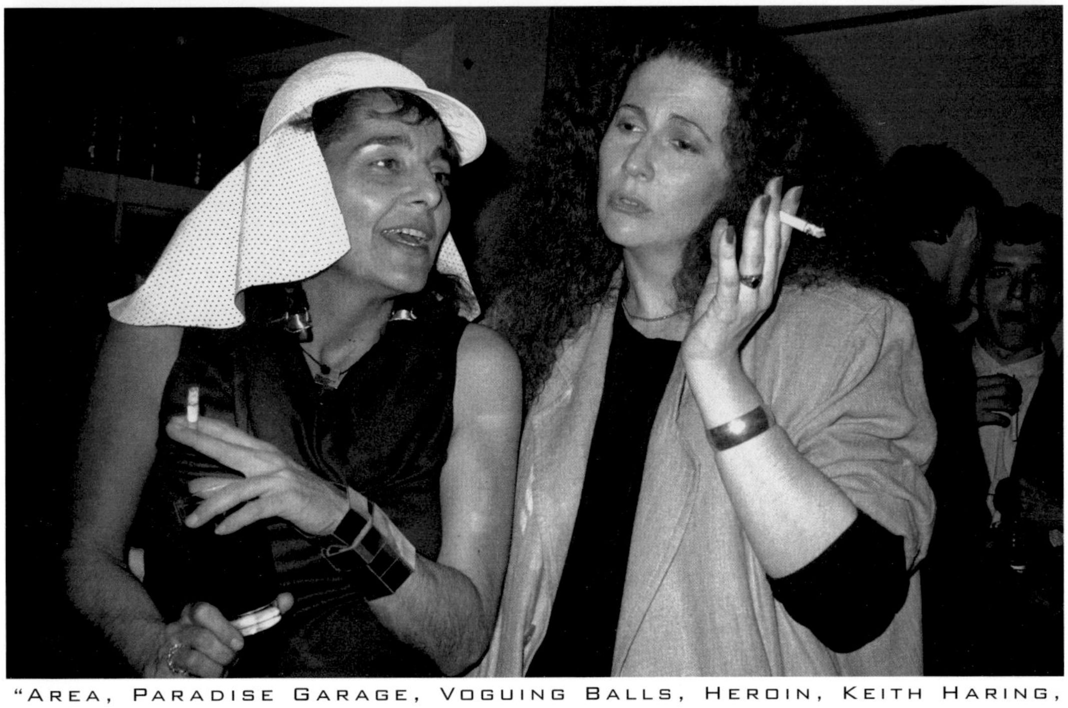

"AREA, PARADISE GARAGE, VOGUING BALLS, HEROIN, KEITH HARING, JEAN-MICHEL BASQUIAT. THE LAST TIME NEW YORK CITY WAS GREAT."
PATRICIA FIELD

TOP: CARMEN D'ALESSIO AND STEVE RUBELL
AT DANCETERIA. FEBRUARY 1984
BOTTOM: PATRICIA FIELD AND ANDIE MILLER
AT AREA. FRIDAY, MAY 18, 1984

The 80s began in early 1978 and ended in October 1987. It was shorter than most decades because it was open all night. It was a very interesting time because rich people still spoke to poor people (some of whom had homes in Manhattan) and there was still an oral tradition of fame. New York was plagued by crime, but was much safer than it is today. People had a lot of sex but they didn't talk about it as much as they do now. Artists were respected members of the community and being in fashion required little more effort than a flip through one or two magazines under the hair dryer. I have requested that when I die my ashes be scattered in the 80s.
Glenn O'Brien

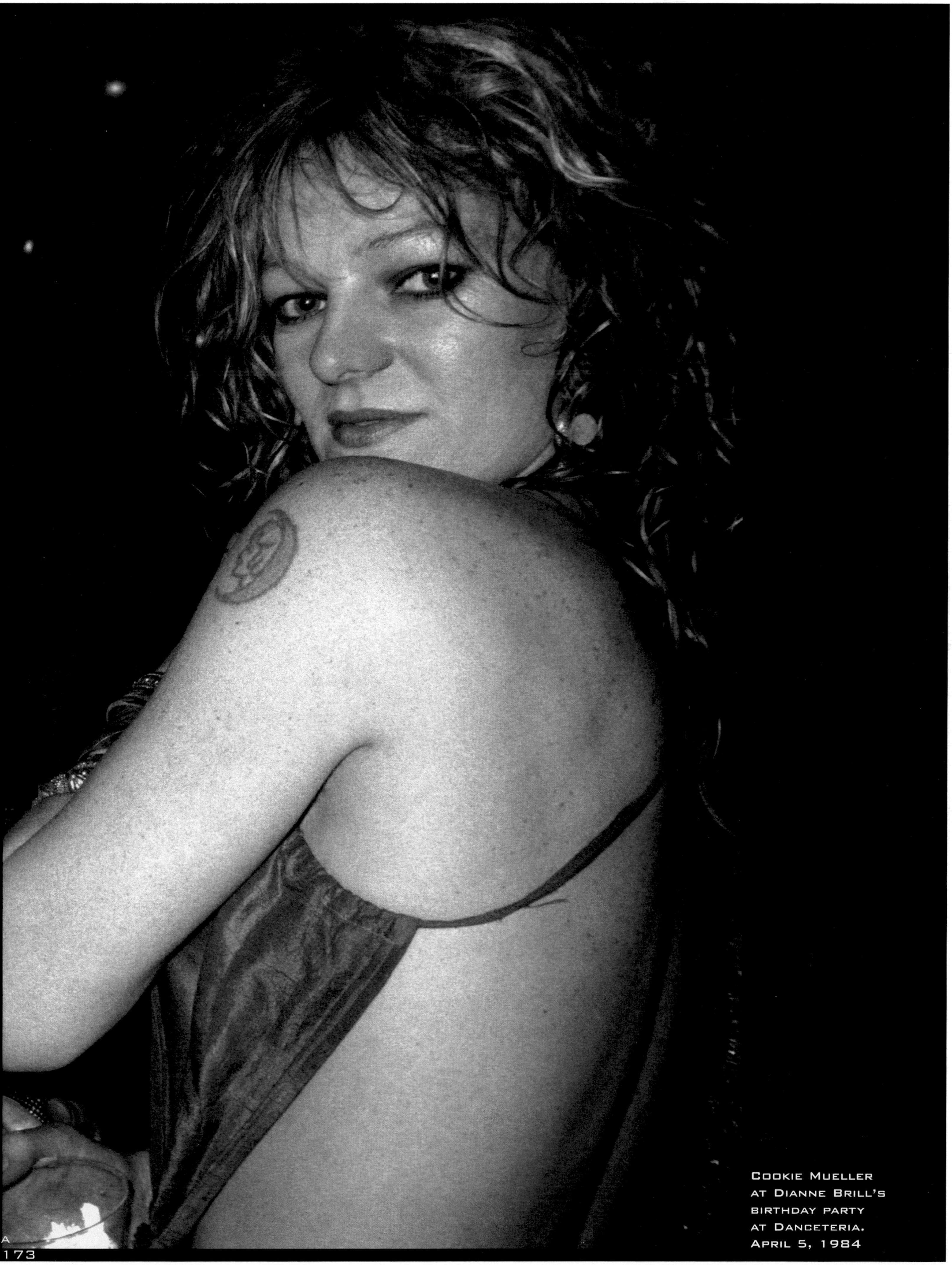

Cookie Mueller
at Dianne Brill's
birthday party
at Danceteria.
April 5, 1984

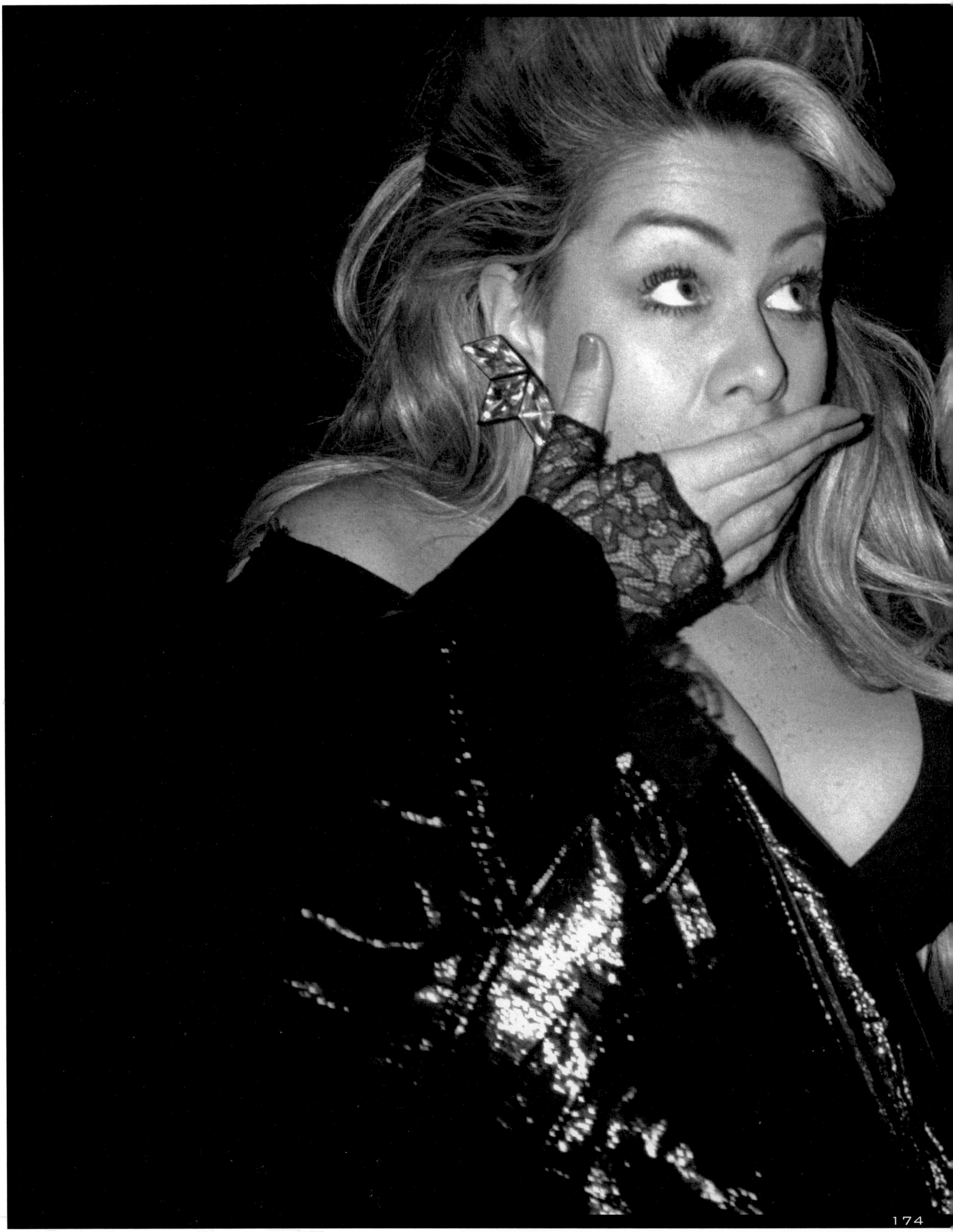

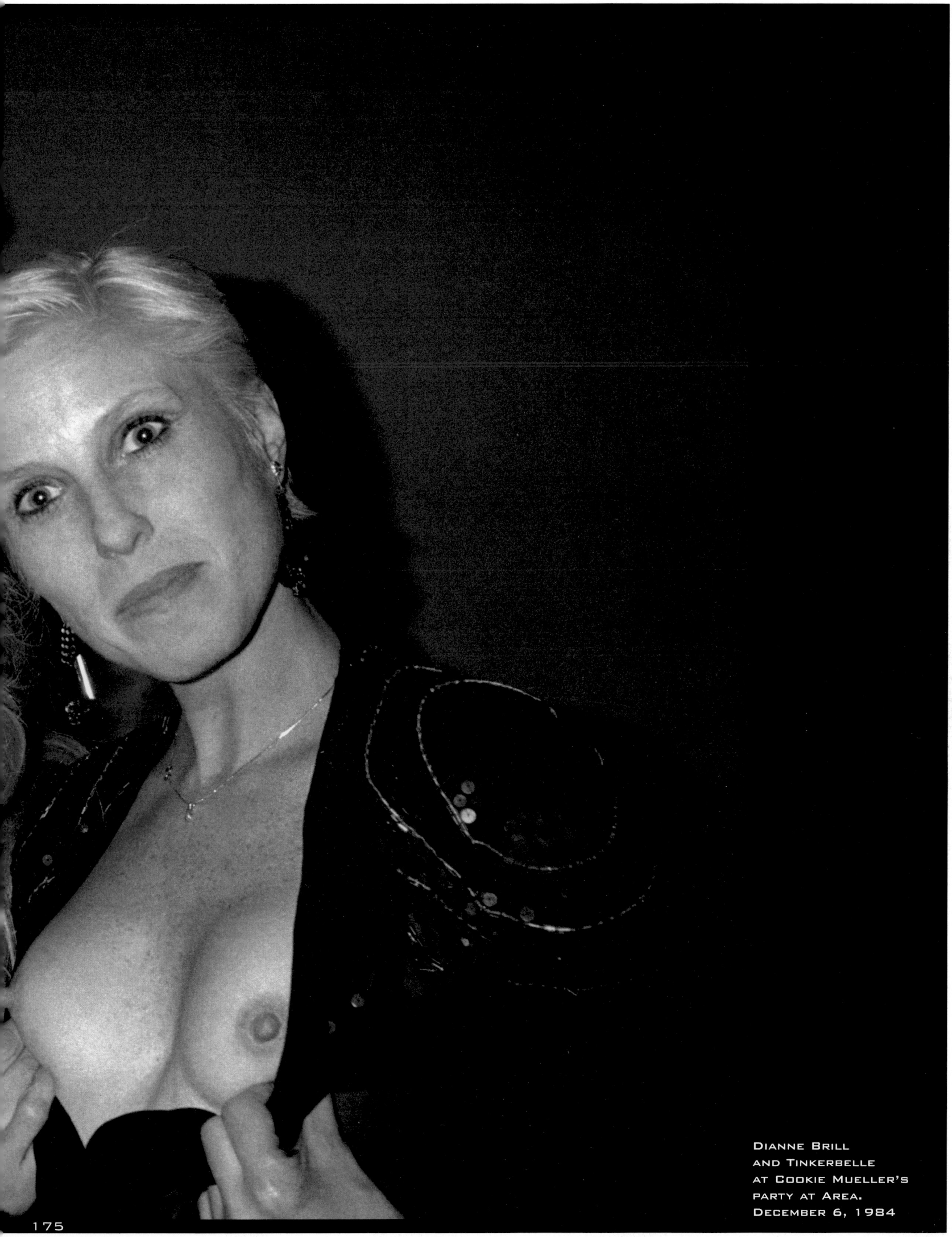

Dianne Brill
and Tinkerbelle
at Cookie Mueller's
party at Area.
December 6, 1984

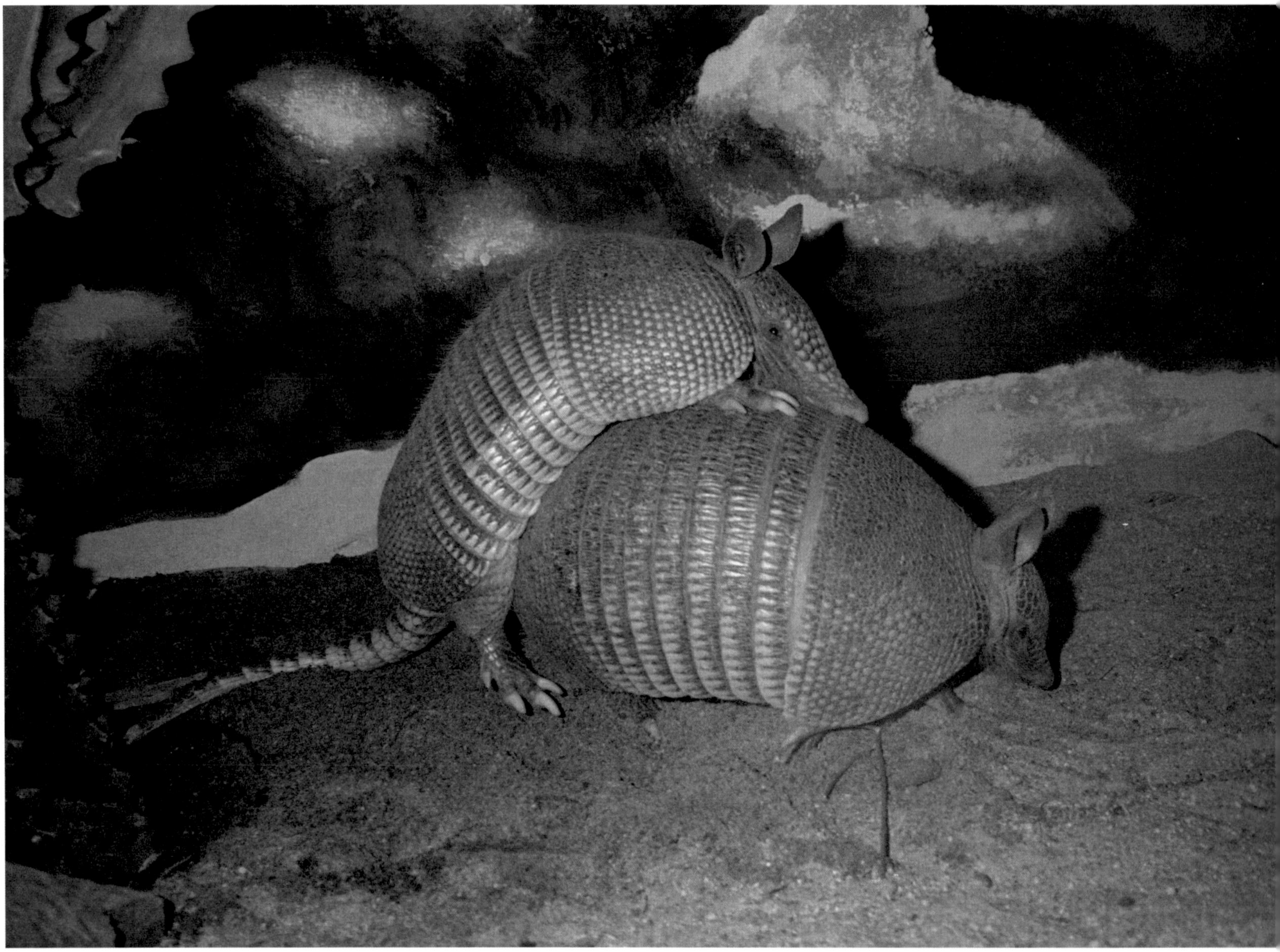

"AREA HAD NO RULES, NO CRITICS, NO CURATORS; AND LIKE THE PEOPLE WHO WENT THERE...NO PERMANENCE. IT WAS CREATED TO COME AND GO; IT WAS NEVER MEANT TO LAST. AREA WAS ABOUT FLUX AND ABOUT CHANGE. AND WHEN CHANGE BECAME PREDICTABLE, WE CLOSED."
ERIC GOODE

"THOSE FUCKIN' ARMADILLOS"
AT THE REOPENING OF AREA.
SEPTEMBER 5, 1984

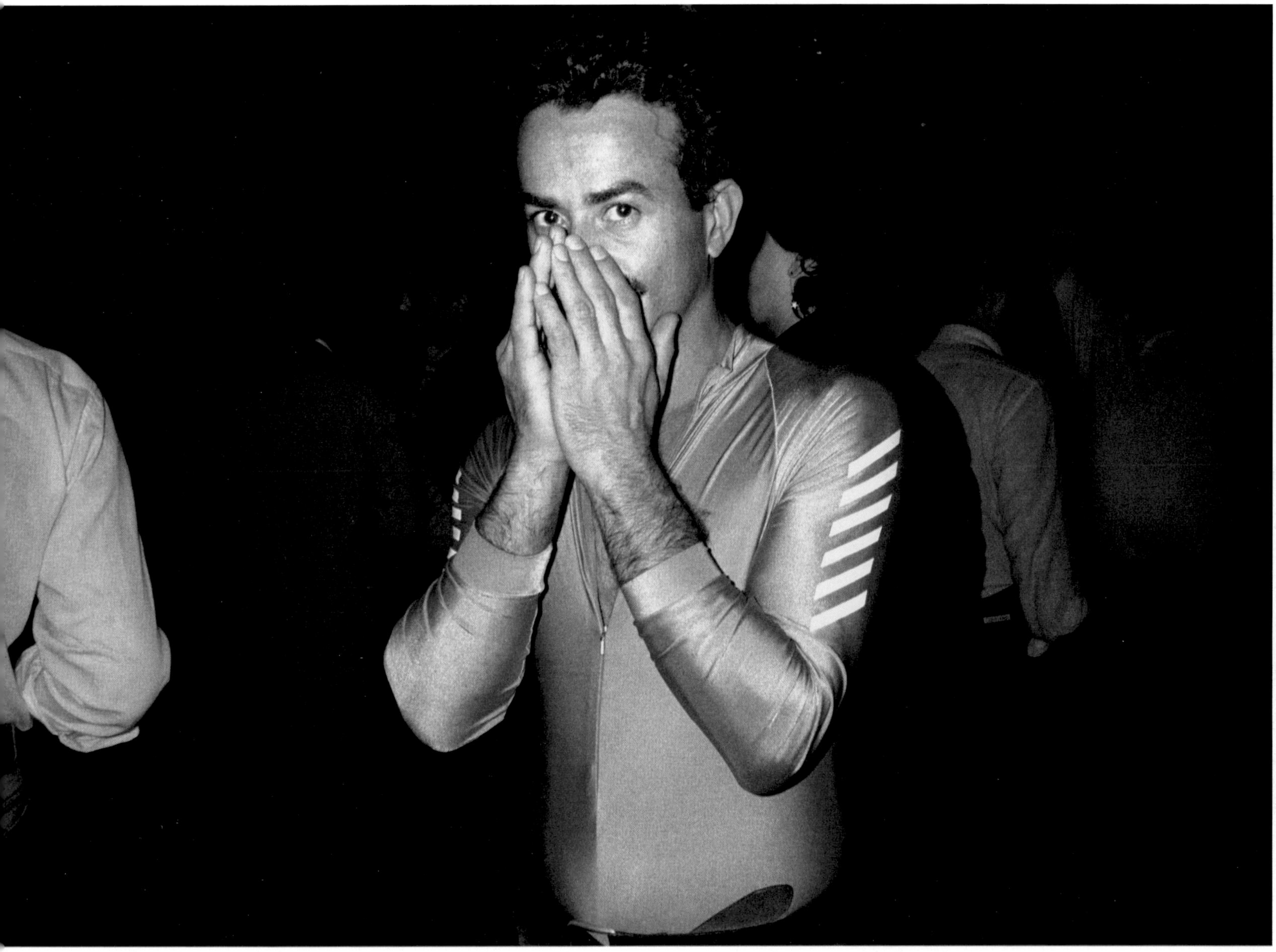

Victor Hugo at Area.
October 18, 1984

The 80s were a time of sex, drugs, and disco. The parties were wild, over the top, and beyond imagination--they were unlike anything you had ever seen before and there has been nothing like it since.

It was the era of excess, a time of hedonism, when people thought they could party forever. It was a very inspirational and creative time--I couldn't put my camera down!

Roxanne Lowit

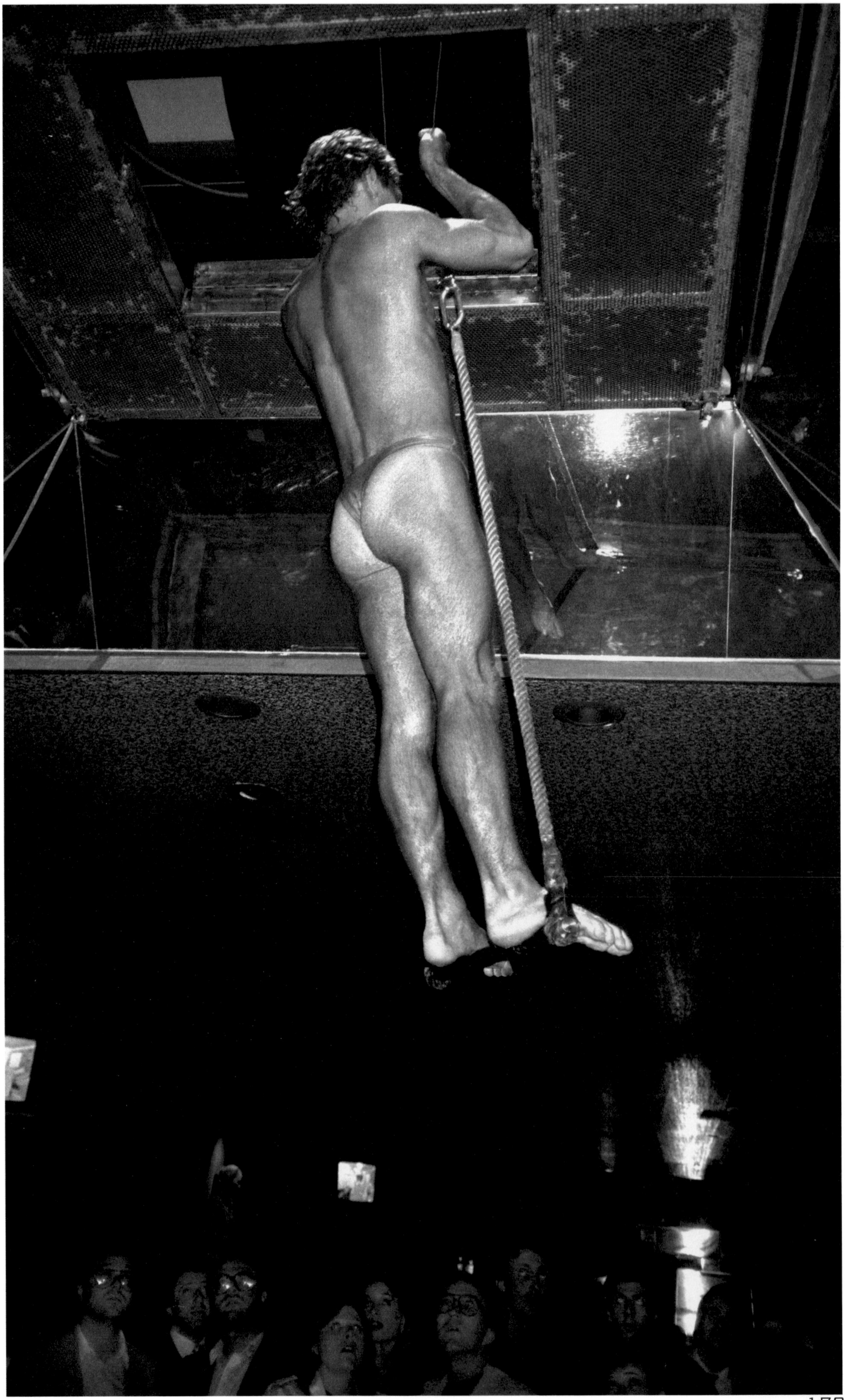

Performer on a swing at Esai Morales' birthday party at Visage. Tuesday, October 1, 1985

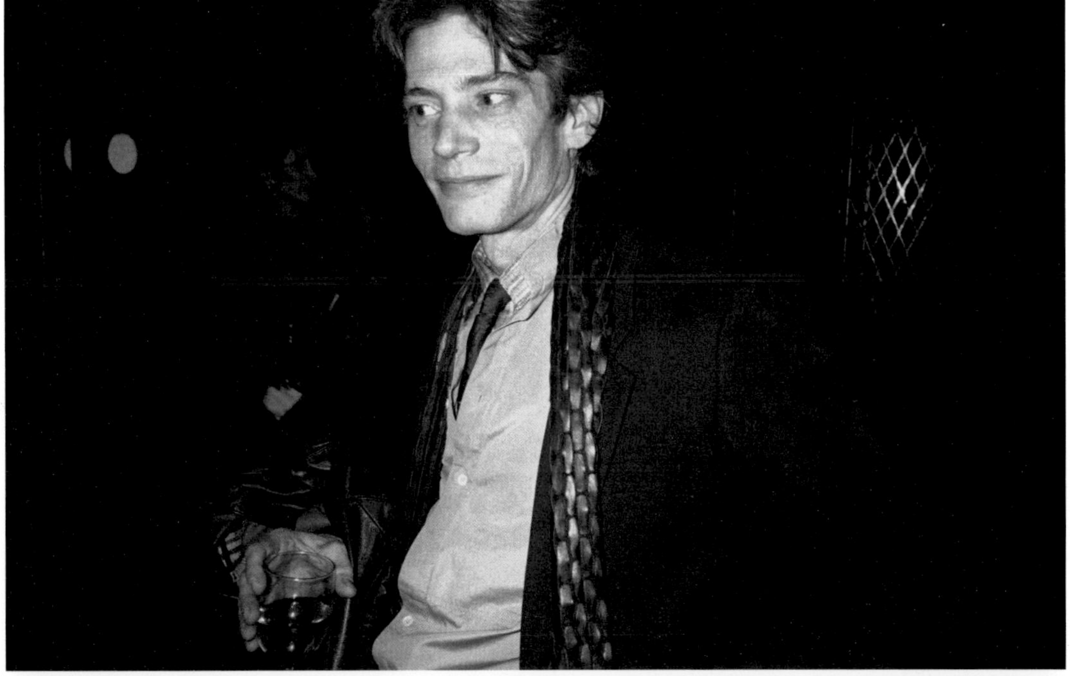

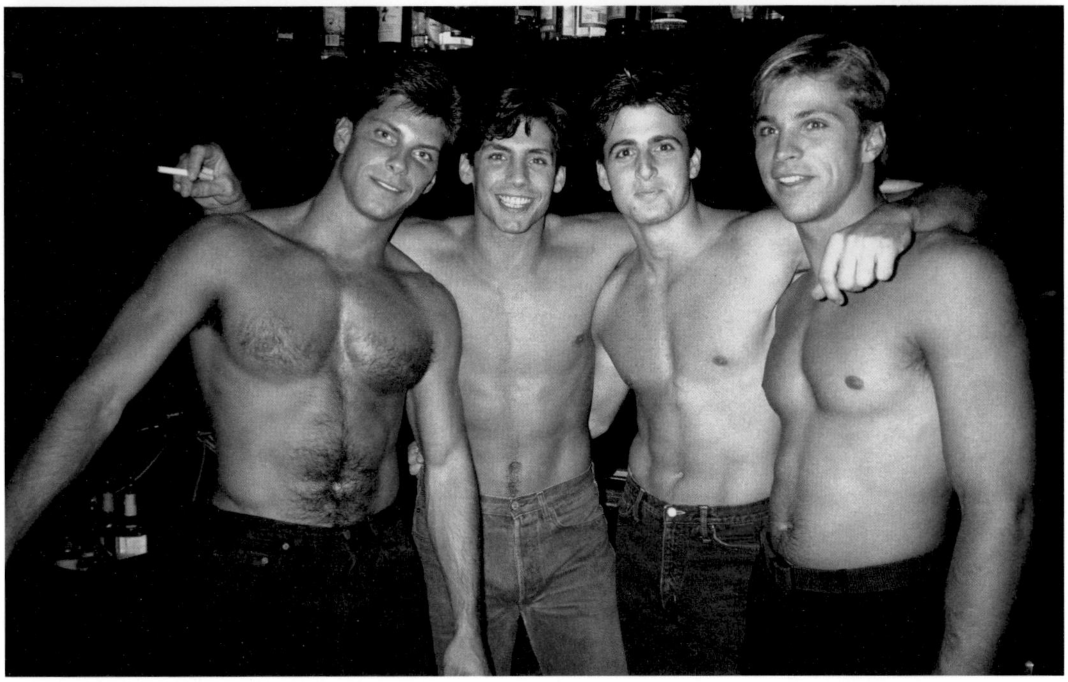

Top: Robert Mapplethorpe
at the Wool Bureau Party at Saint.
January 1985
Bottom: Bartenders at the Palladium.
September 29, 1985

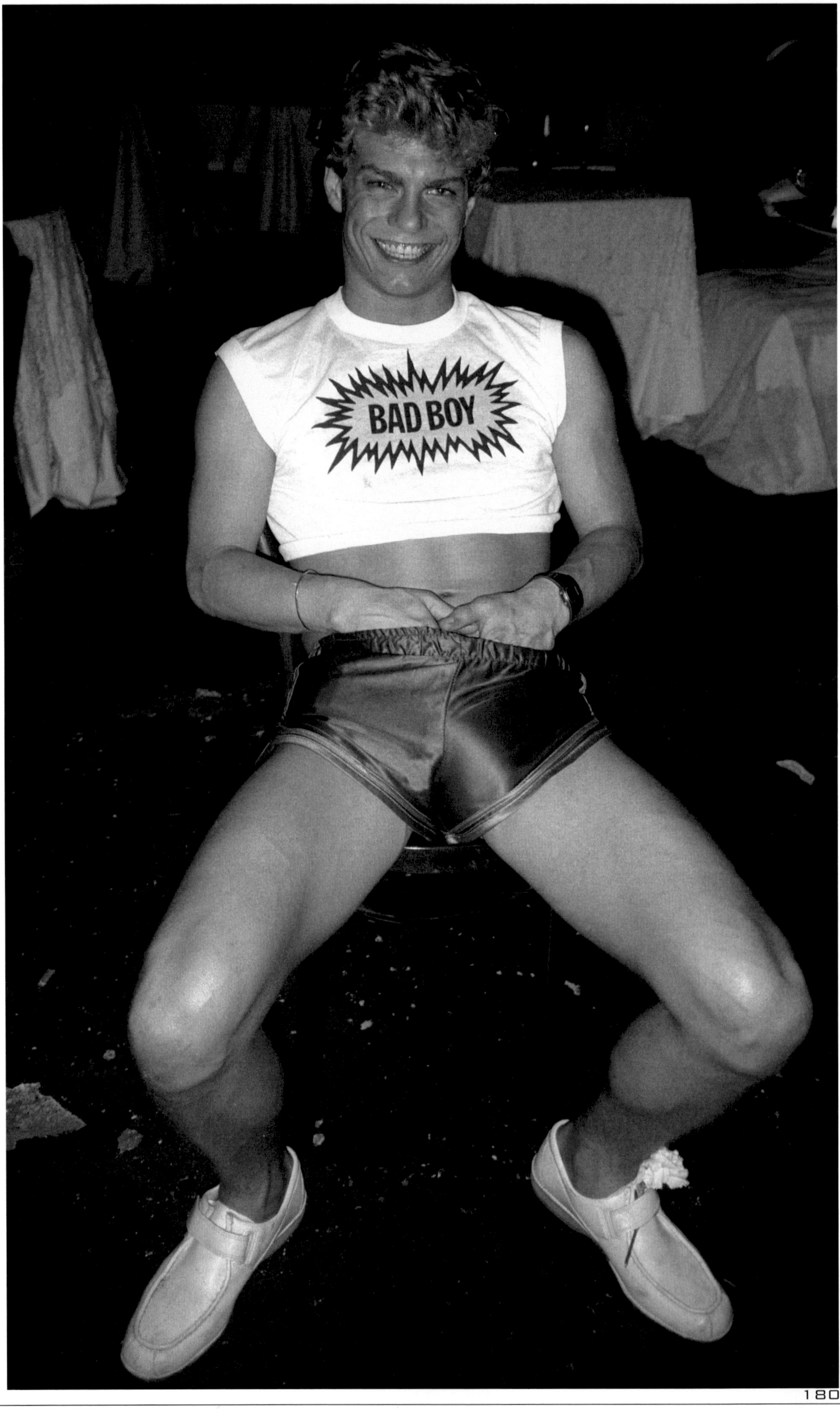

"Bad Boy"
at the Palladium.
June 20, 1985

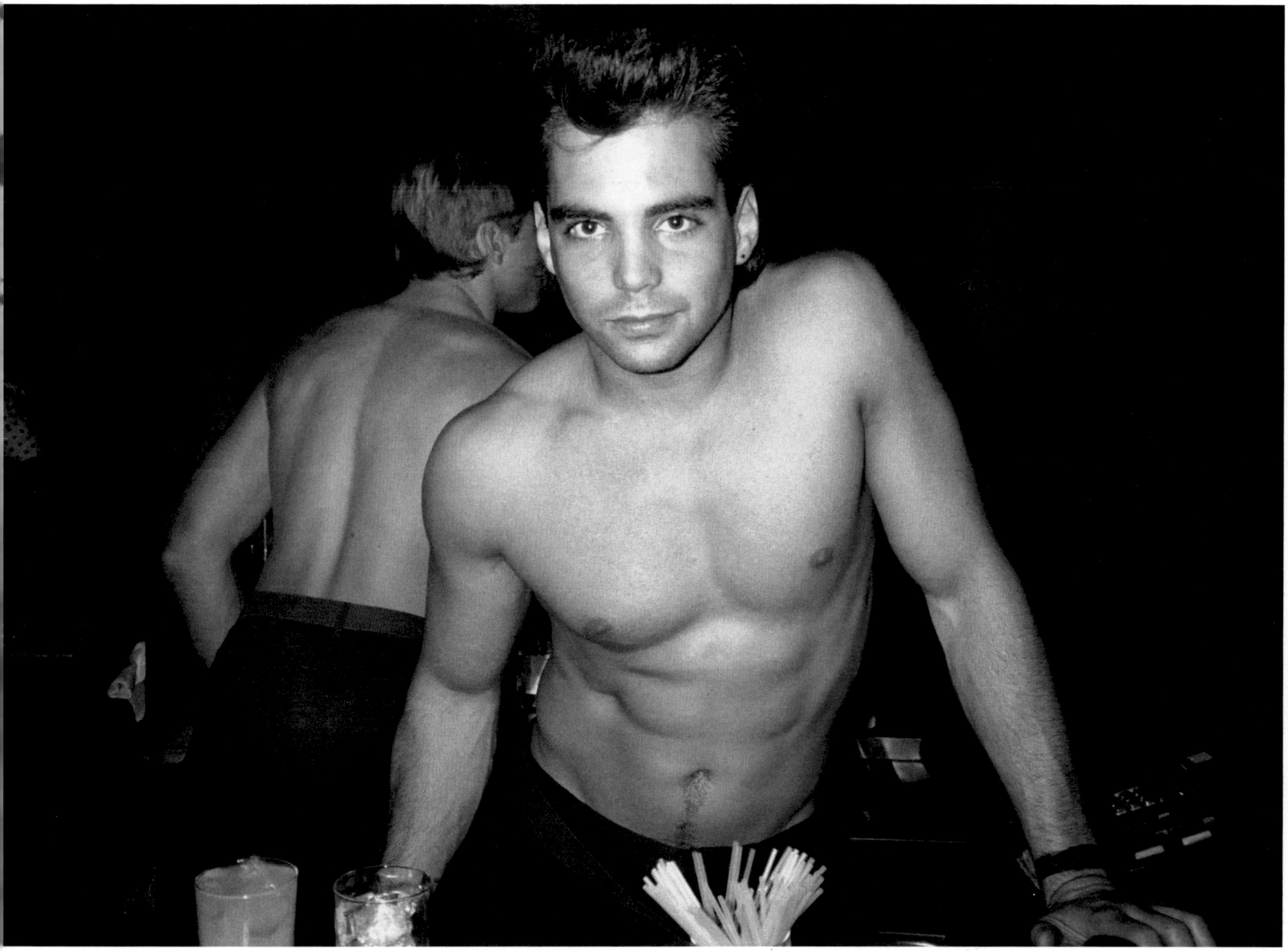

"I could not wait for the nightlife." Kevin Downs

Richard Grieco
bartending at the Palladium.
September 29, 1985

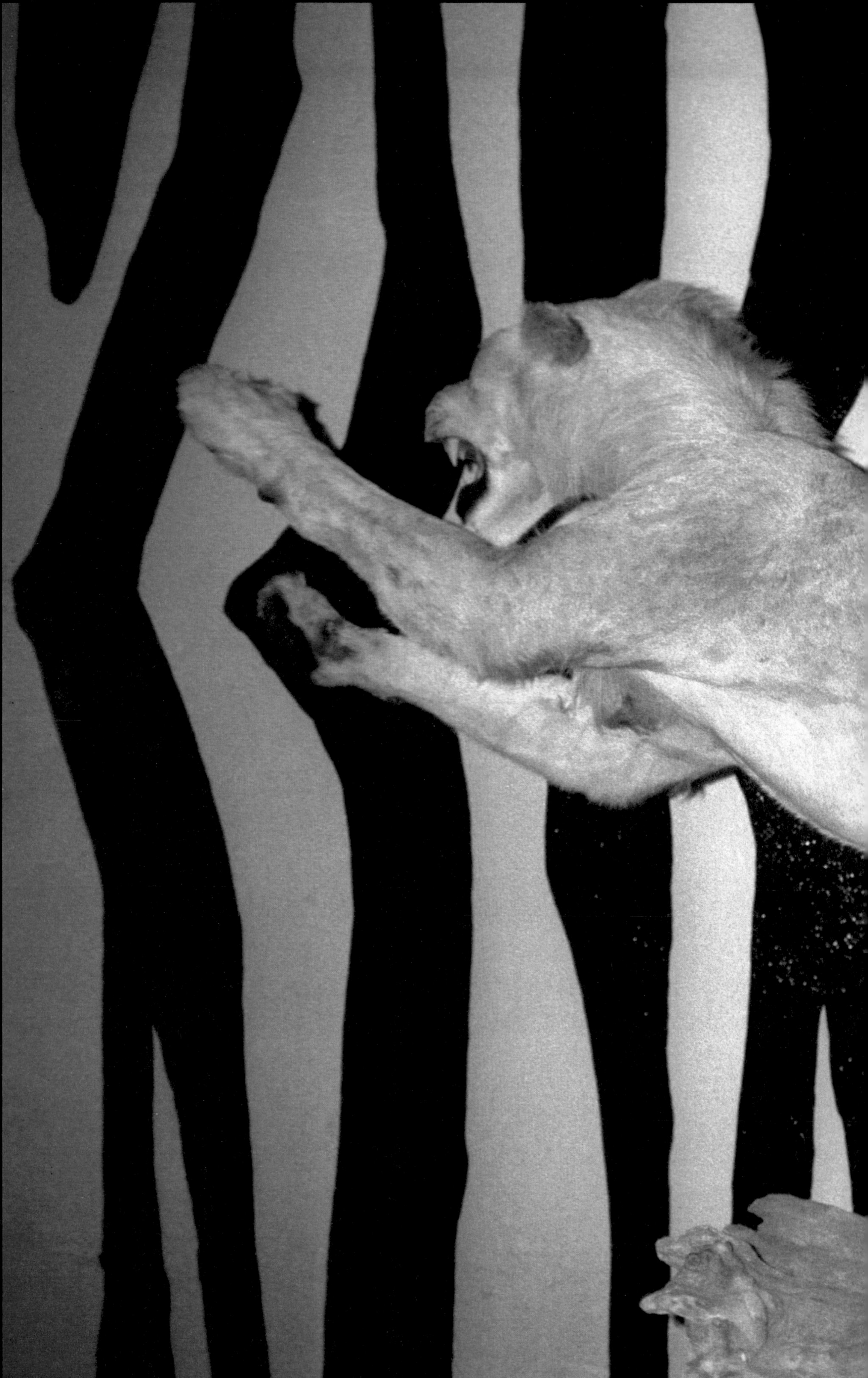

Christina Downing at the party for Yves Arman at Area. Wednesday, October 10, 1984

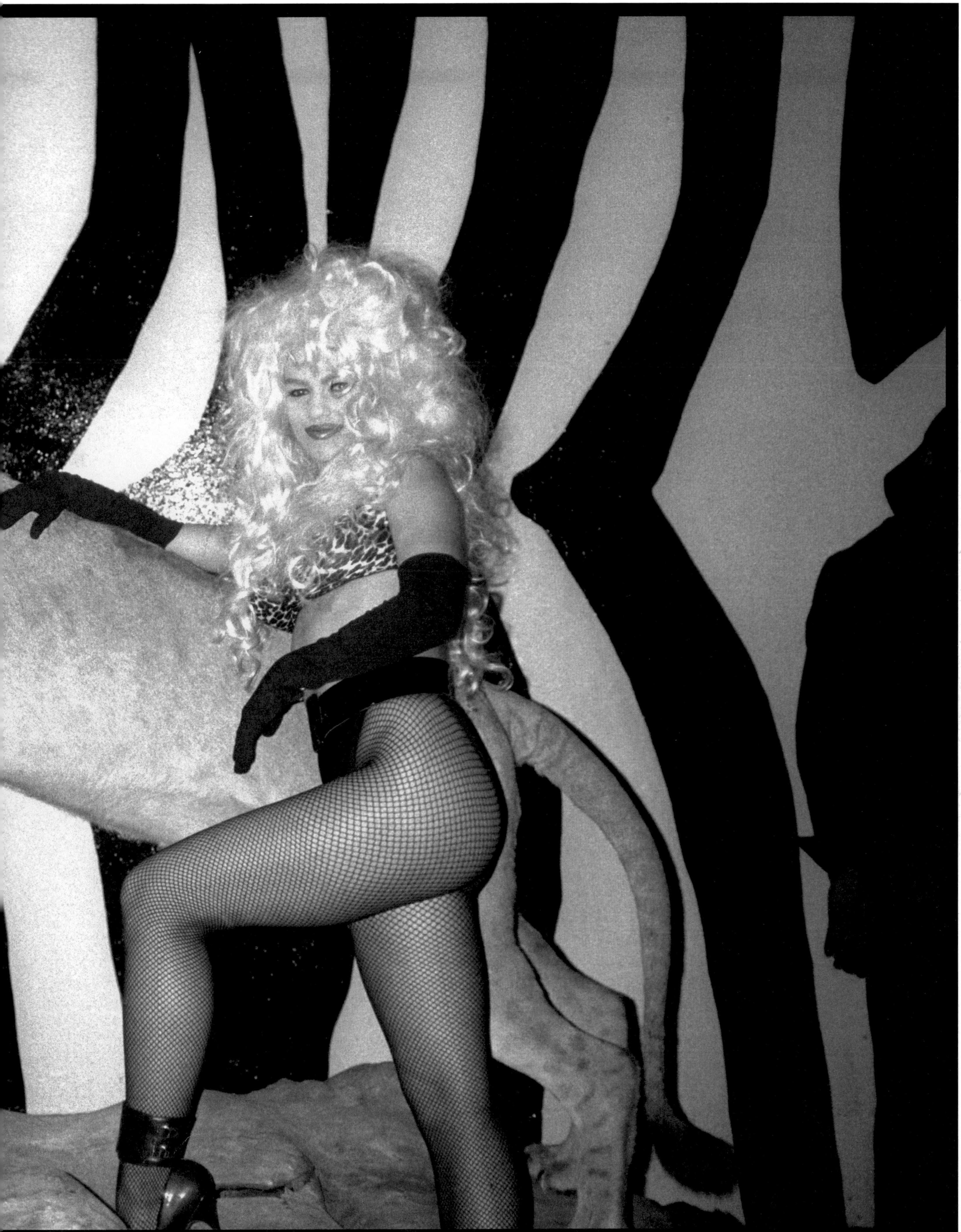

"The 80s. It came dressed in its best Armani, sniffed all the coke, drank the booze, fucked everything in sight, and when the last line was gone, dragged itself off to rehab in the 90s."
David Barton

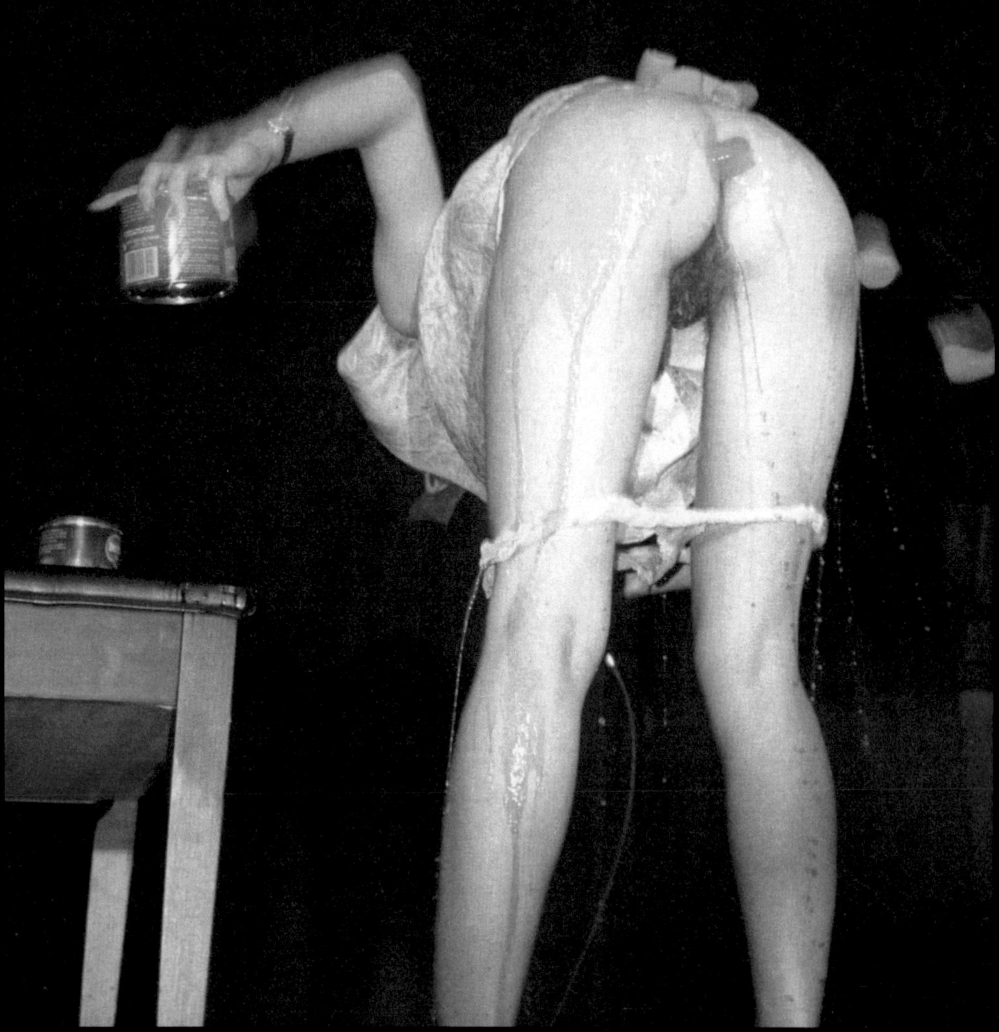

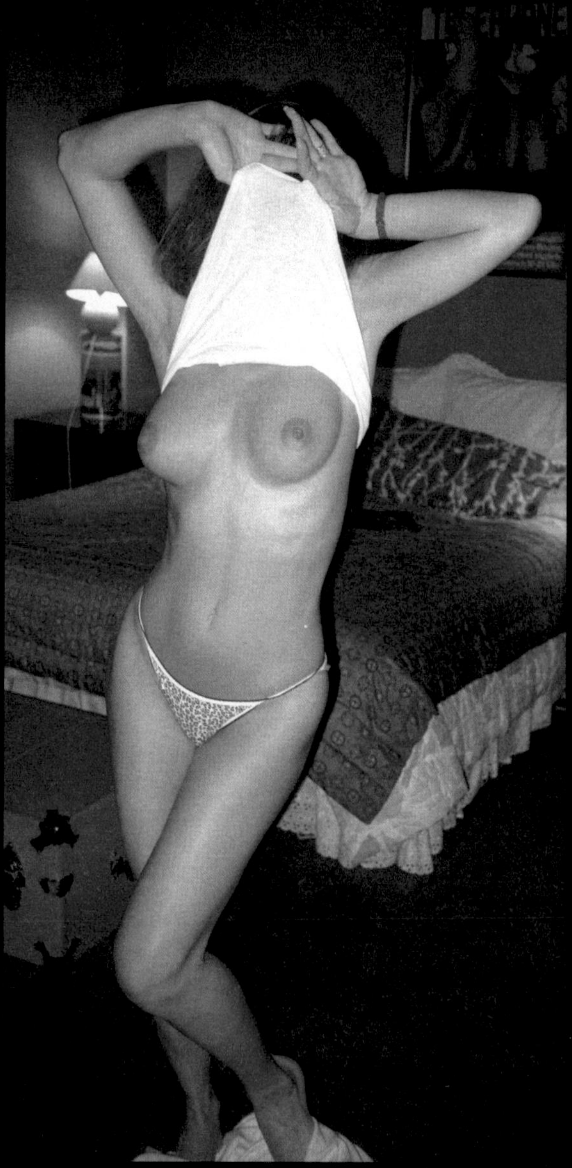

Top Left: Karen Finley and the canned yams
at the New York Talk party in the Mike Todd Room at the Palladium.
April 2,1986
Top Right: Jane Fredericks
Thursday, June 14, 1984

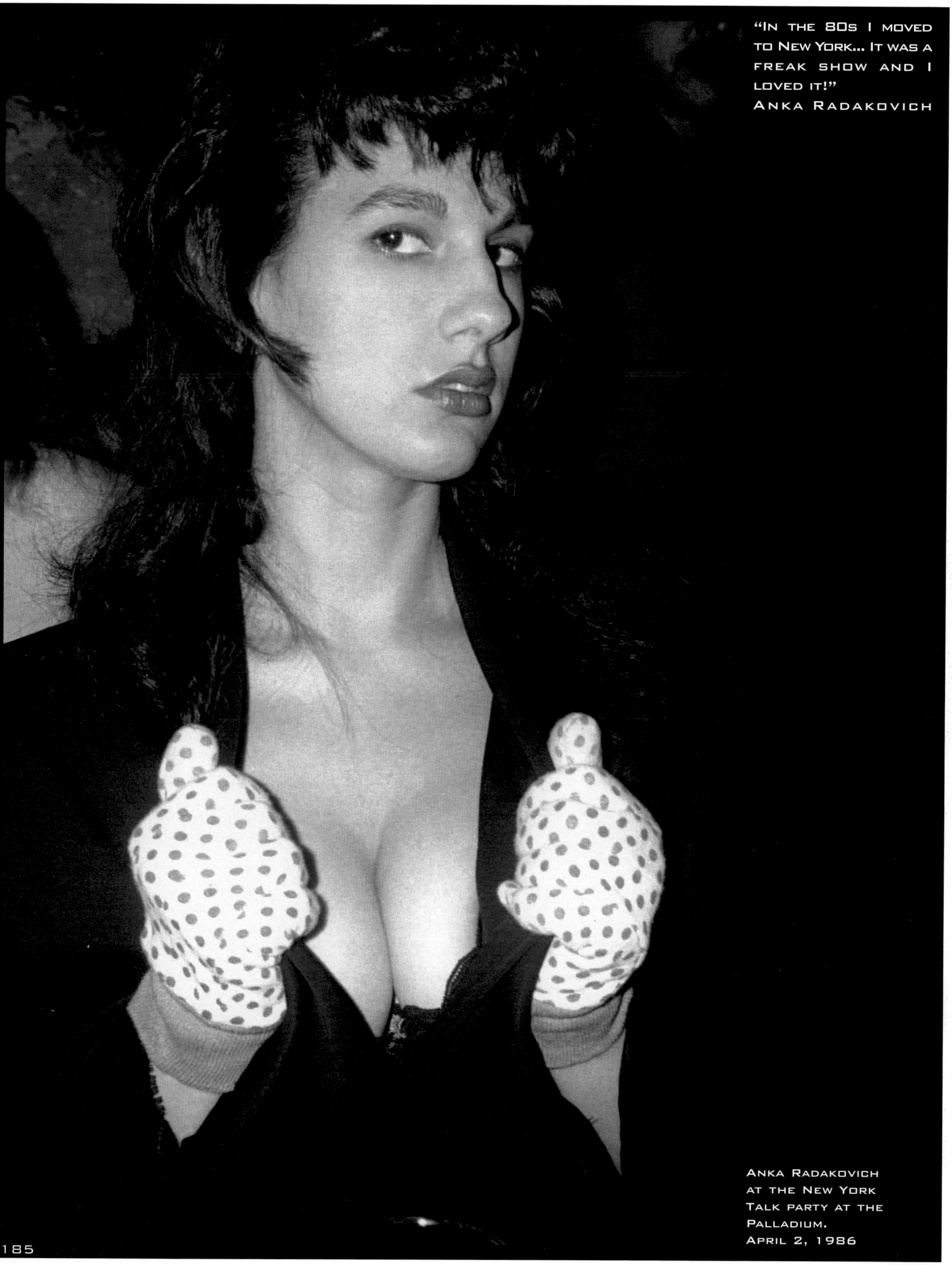

"IN THE 80S I MOVED TO NEW YORK... IT WAS A FREAK SHOW AND I LOVED IT!"
ANKA RADAKOVICH

ANKA RADAKOVICH AT THE NEW YORK TALK PARTY AT THE PALLADIUM.
APRIL 2, 1986

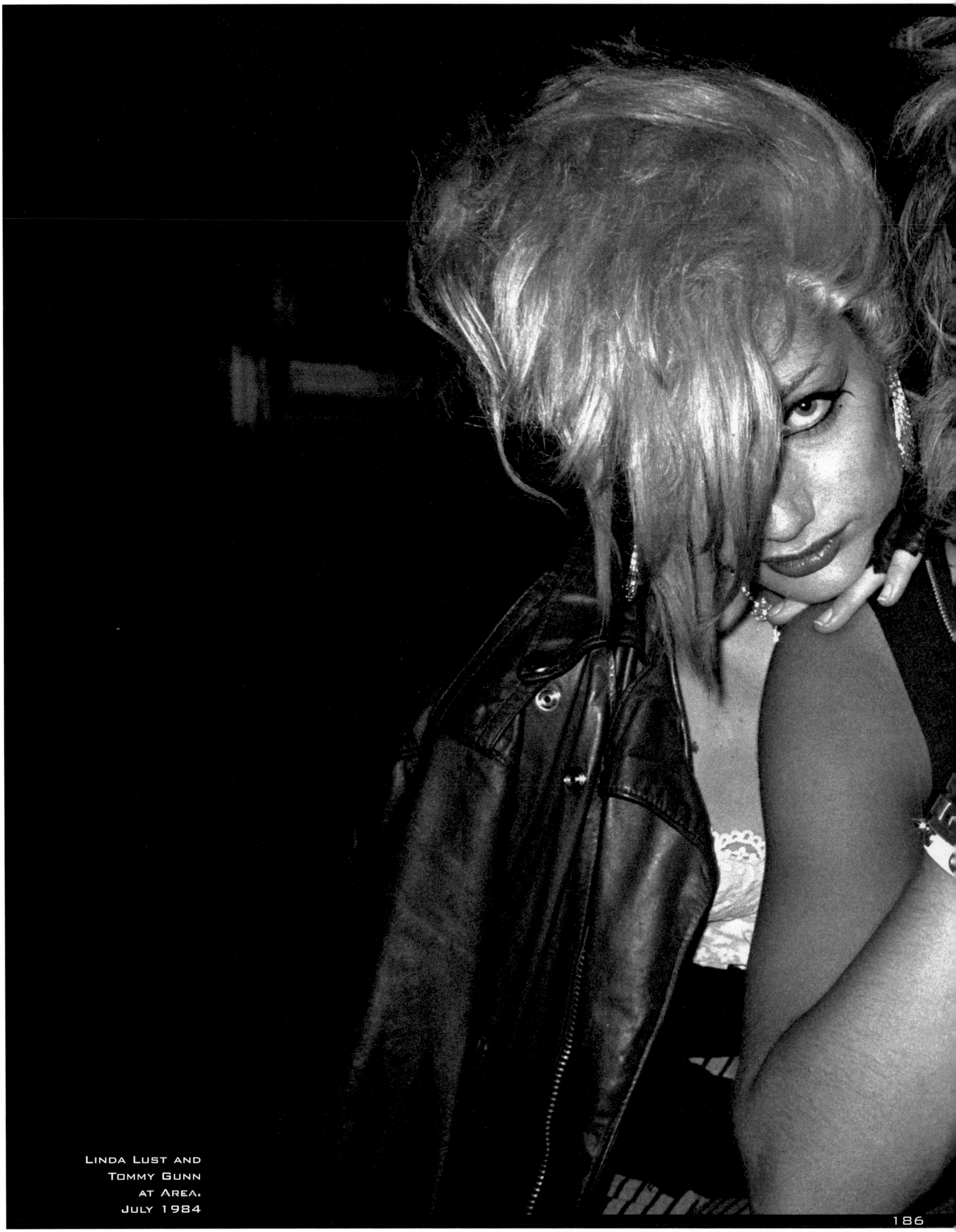

Linda Lust and
Tommy Gunn
at Area.
July 1984

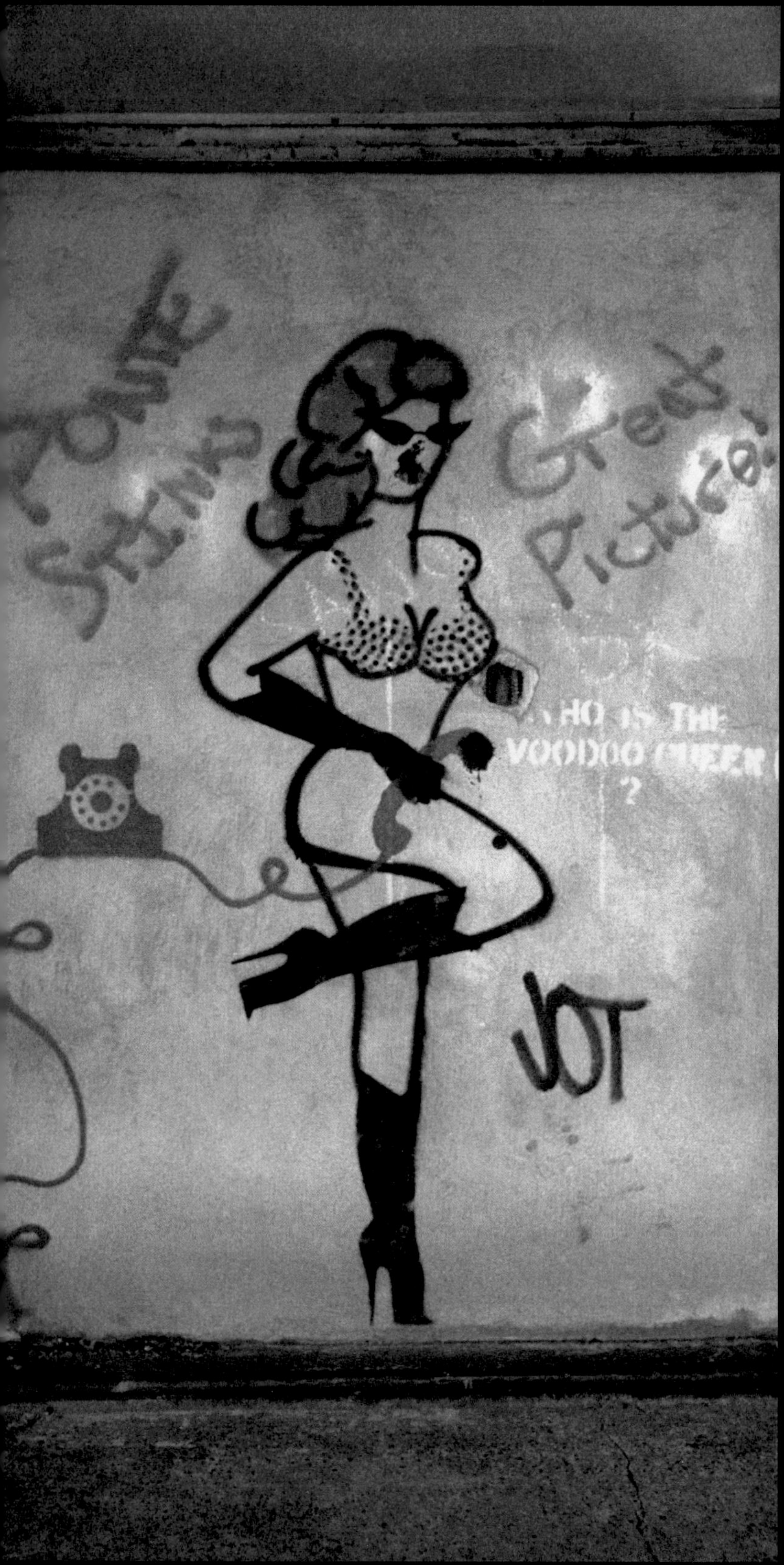

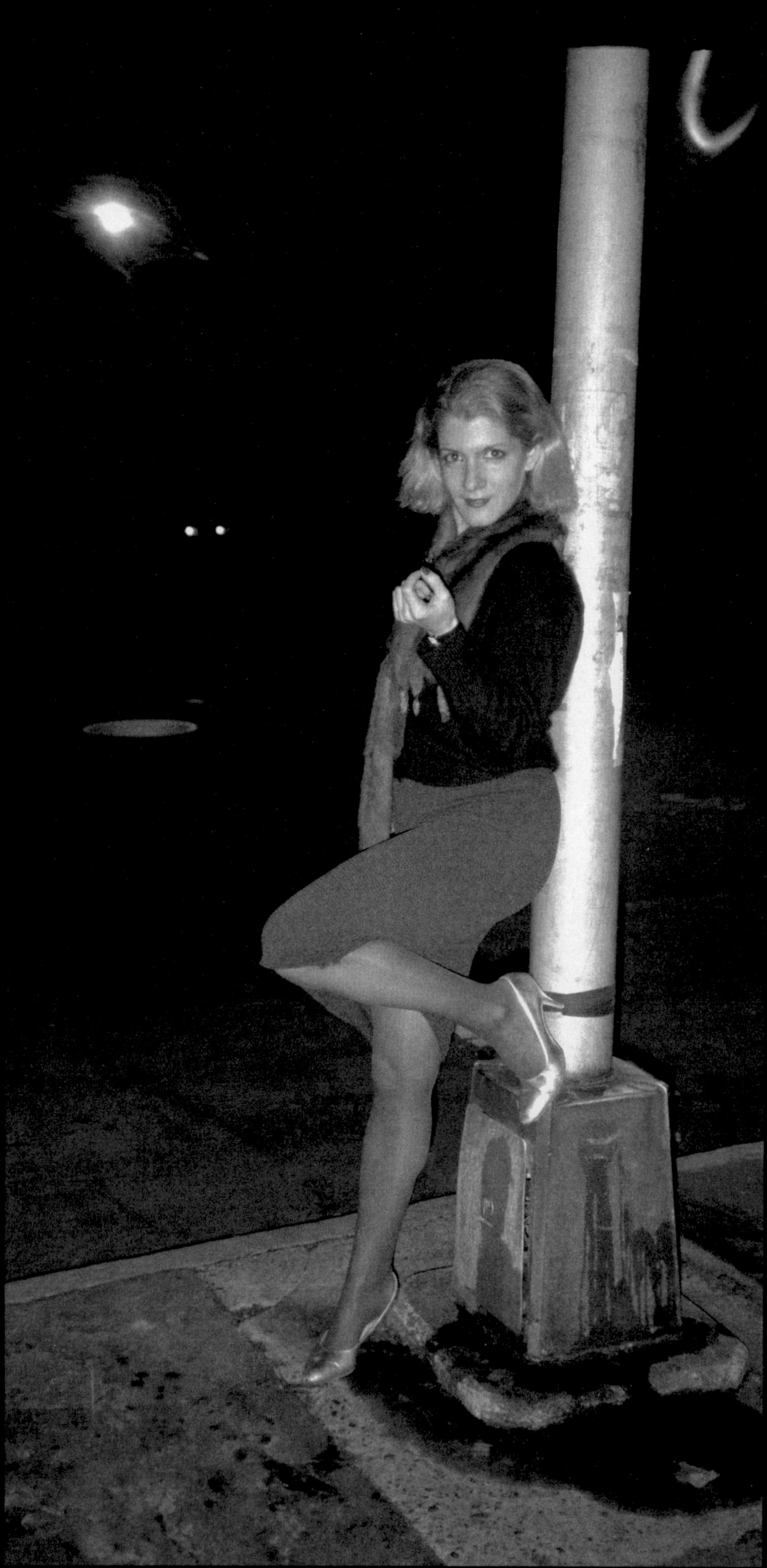

Top Left: "Hot Girl" graffiti. June 1984
Top Right: Chi Chi Valenti after hours on the street. December 18, 1984

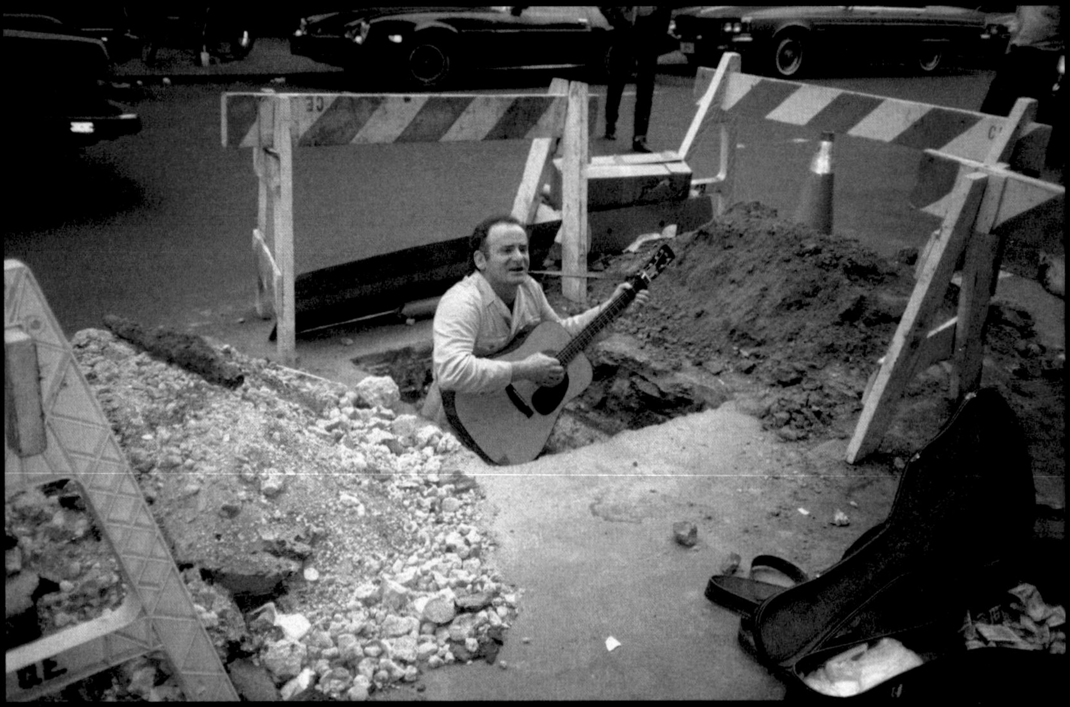

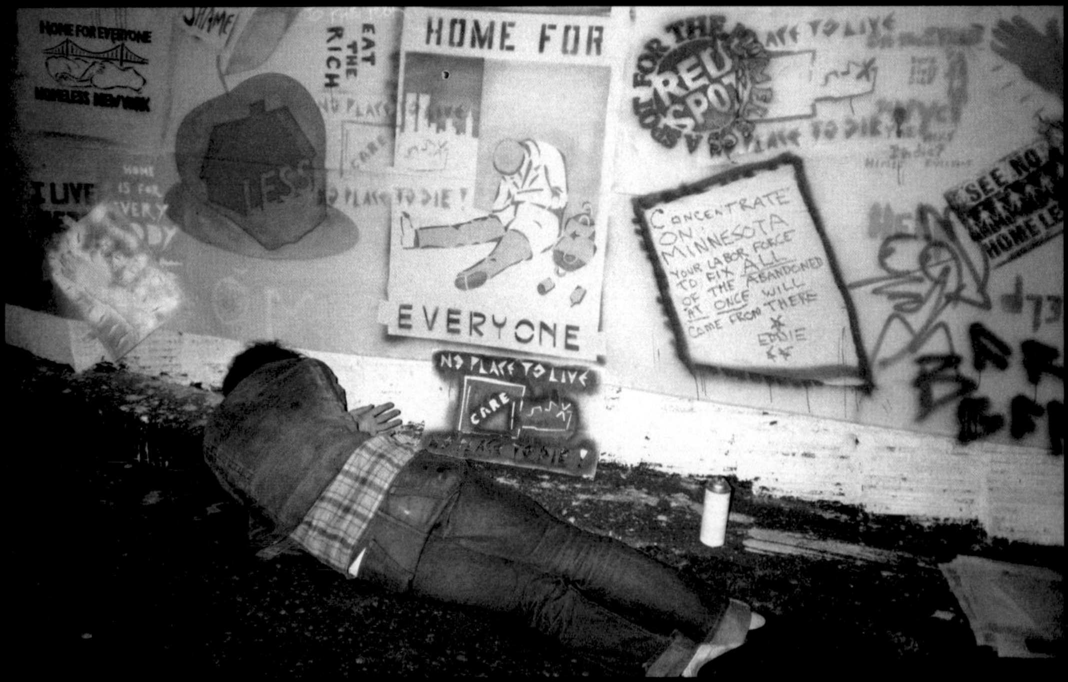

Top: Guitar player in construction ditch on 8th street.
October 15, 1984
Bottom: Man under graffiti
at the party outside Kamikaze for the homeless.
Thursday, October 3, 1985

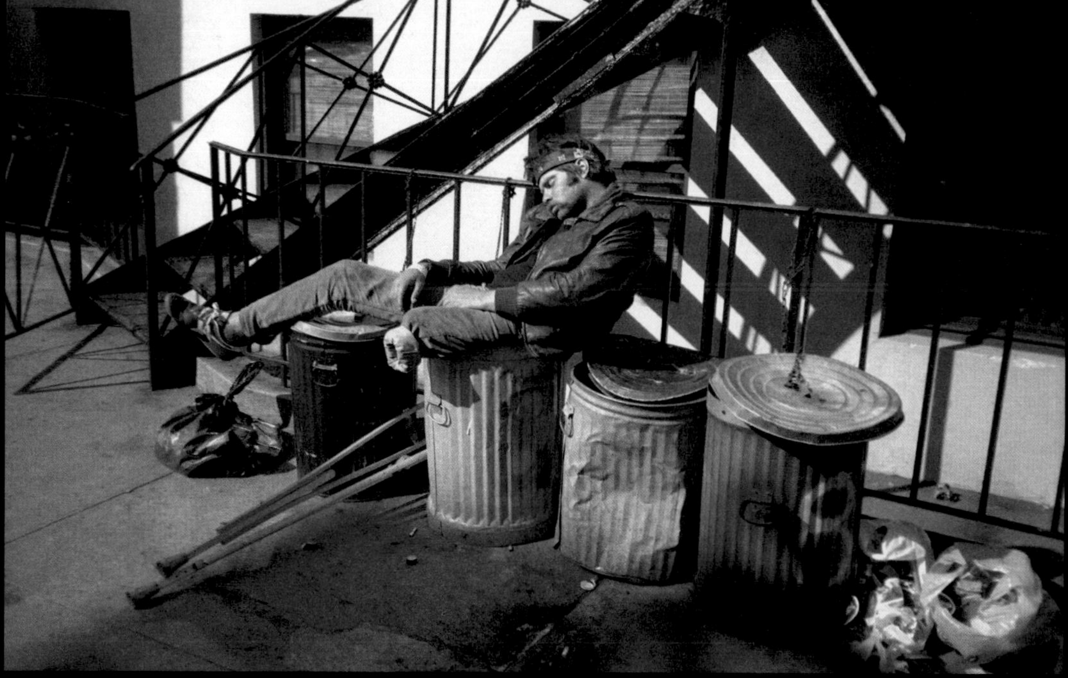

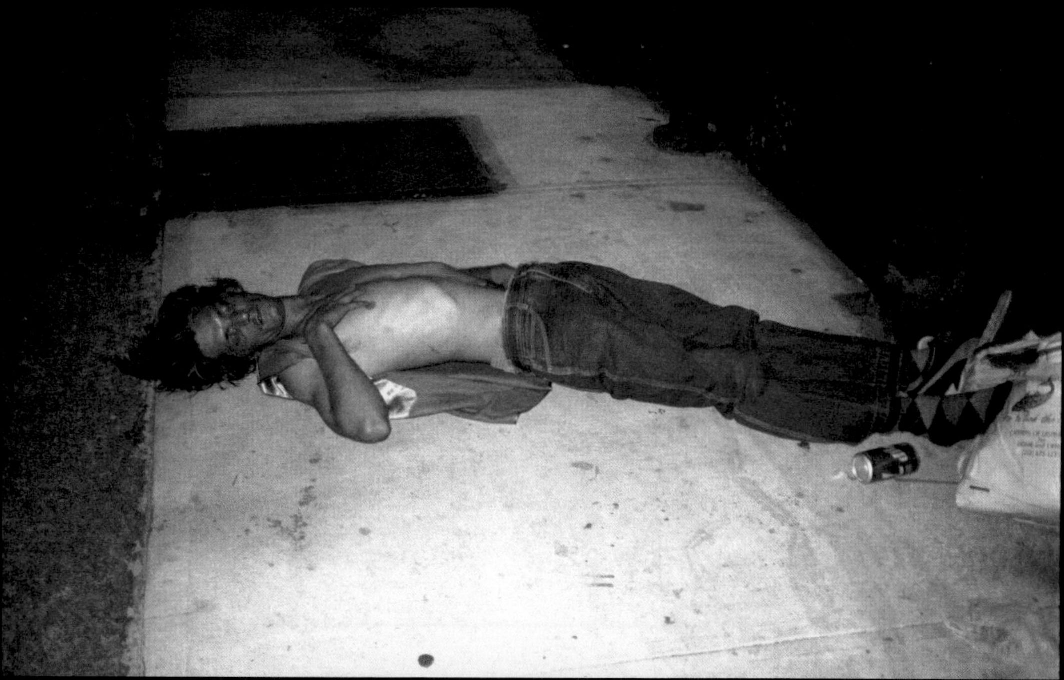

Top: Man on St. Marks Place. April 9, 1986
Bottom: Man sleeping on the street in the East Village. July 1984

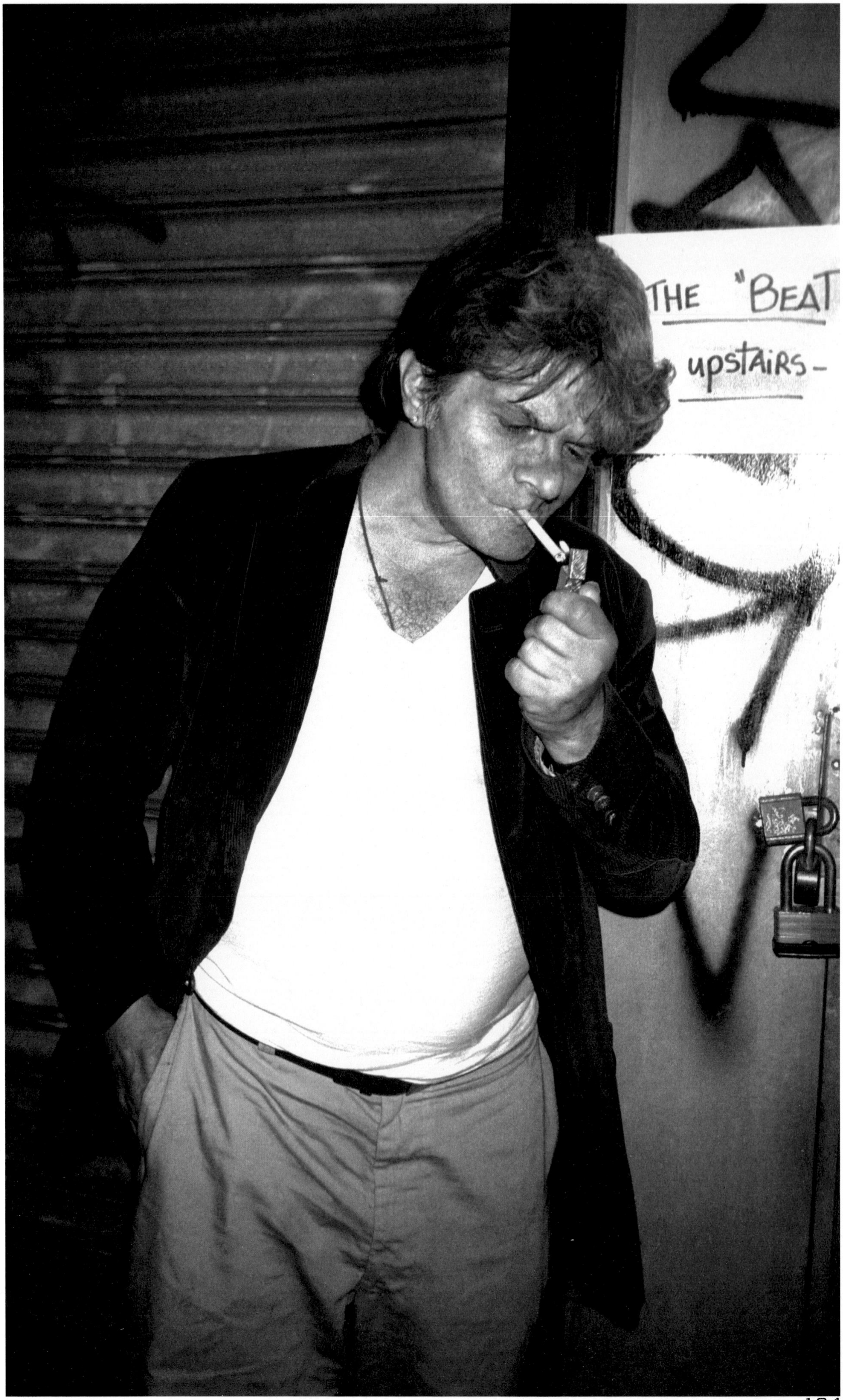

GREGORY CORSO
AT THE PALLADIUM
FOR THE BEAT LOUNGE.
THURSDAY,
NOVEMBER 21, 1985

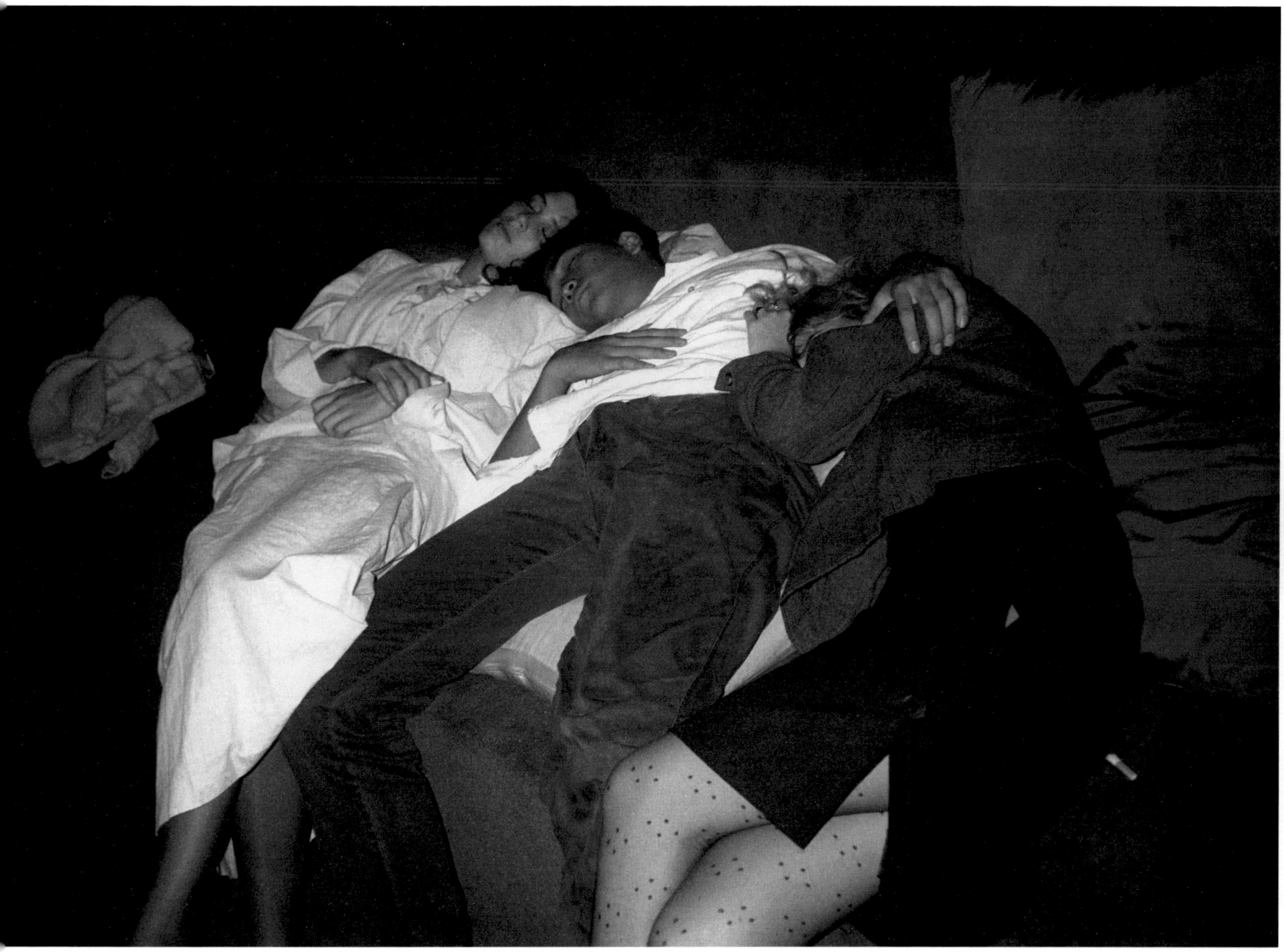

SLEEPING AT THE PALLADIUM.
OCTOBER 4, 1985

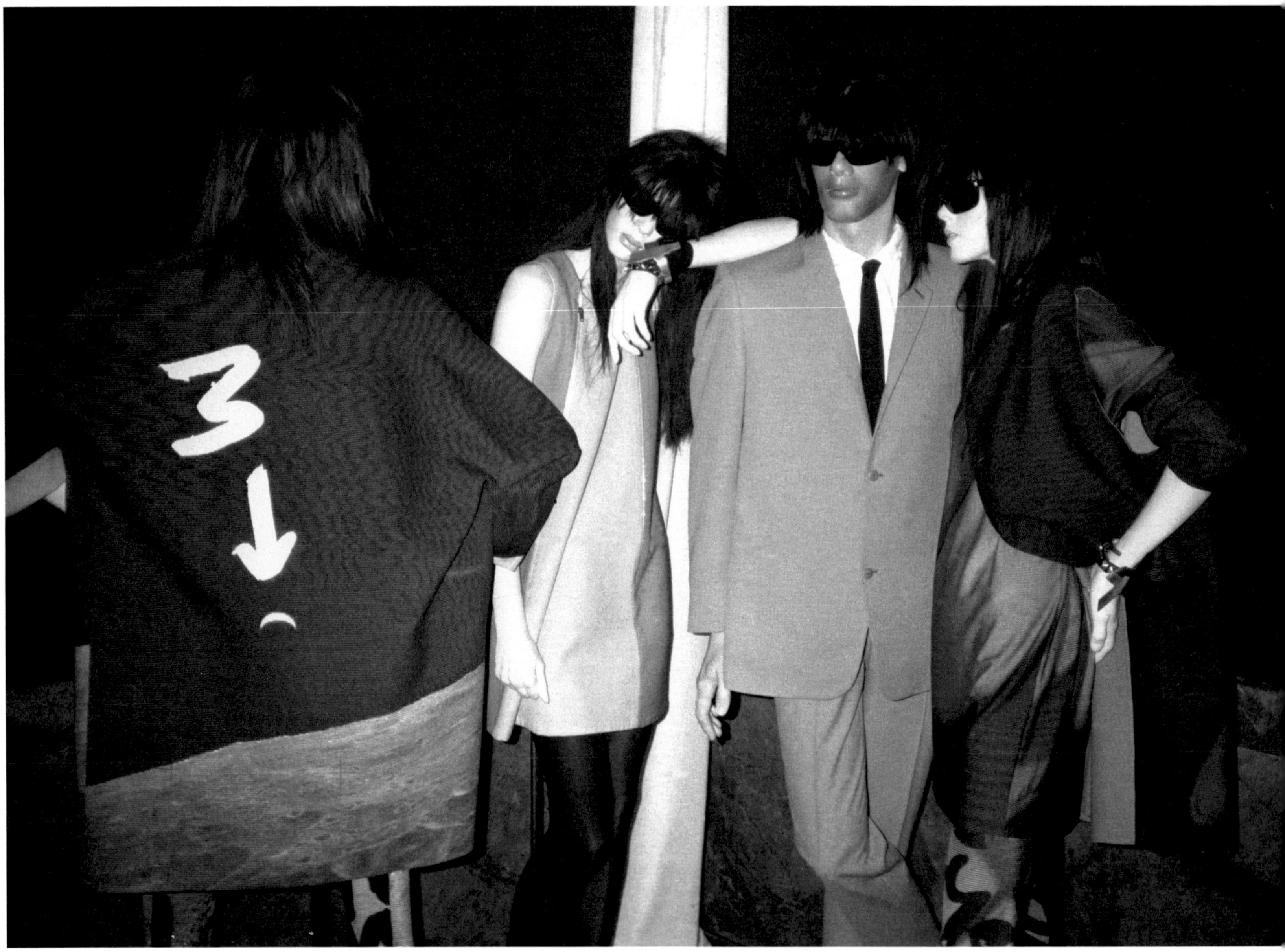

80s MANNEQUINS
AT THE WOOL BUREAU PARTY AT SAINT.
JANUARY 1985

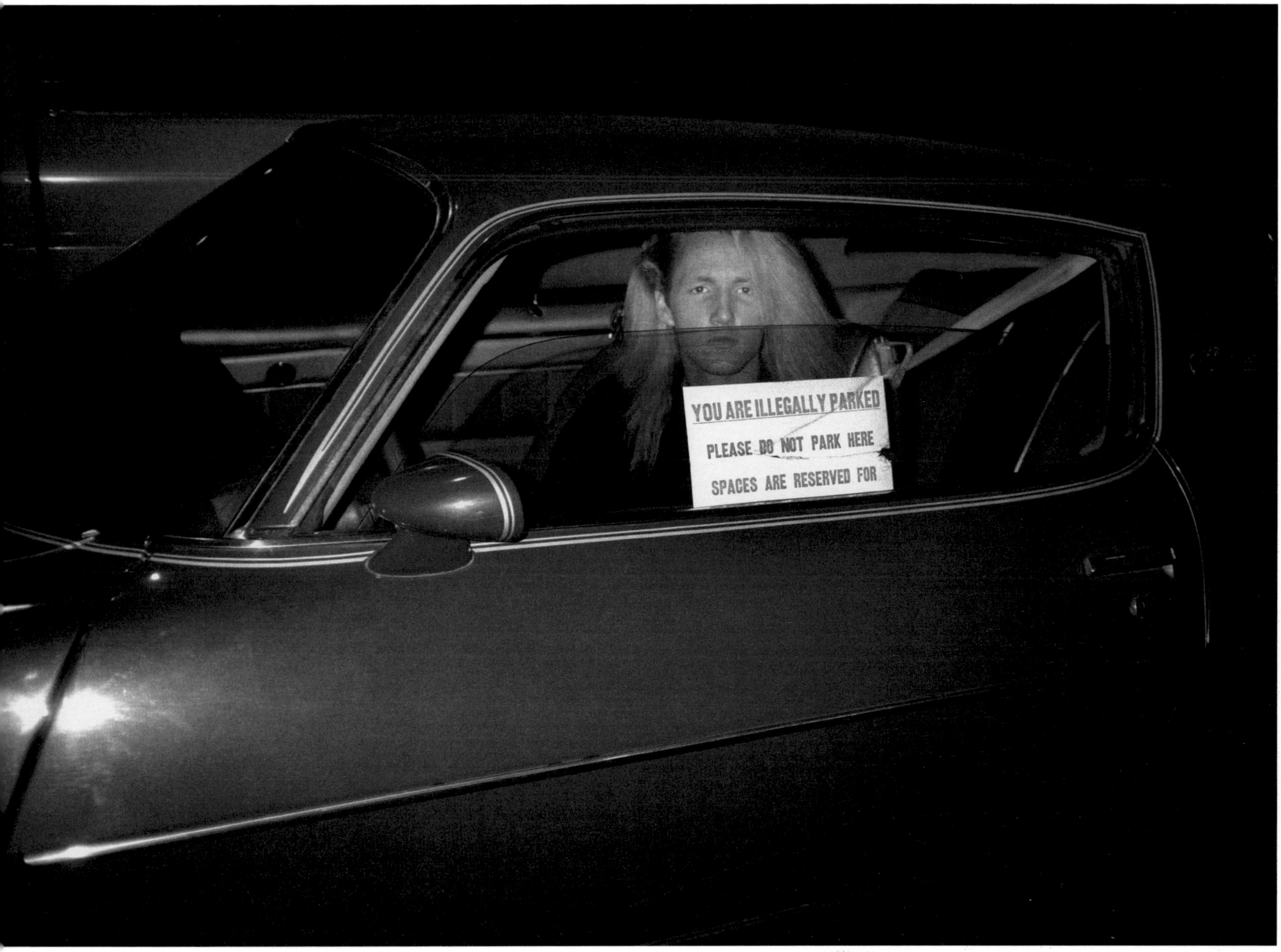

James St. James
Arriving at the XTC party at the Sensory Evolution Gallery.
August 20, 1985

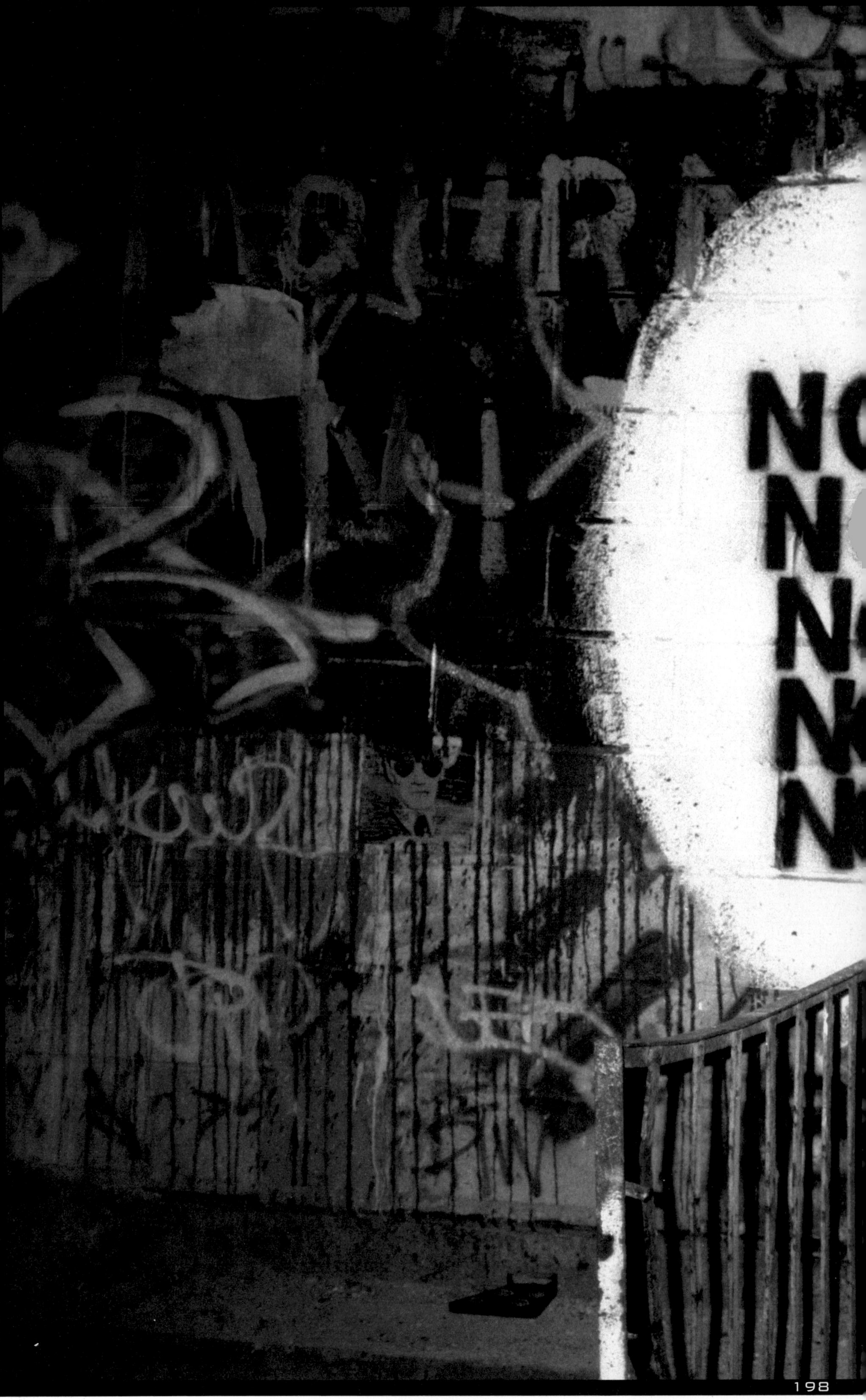

"Now Here" graffiti shot by Patrick for the NYC Nightlife story for The New York Times. October 1985

WHERE
WHERE
WHERE
W HERE
W HERE
PETRICK
1985

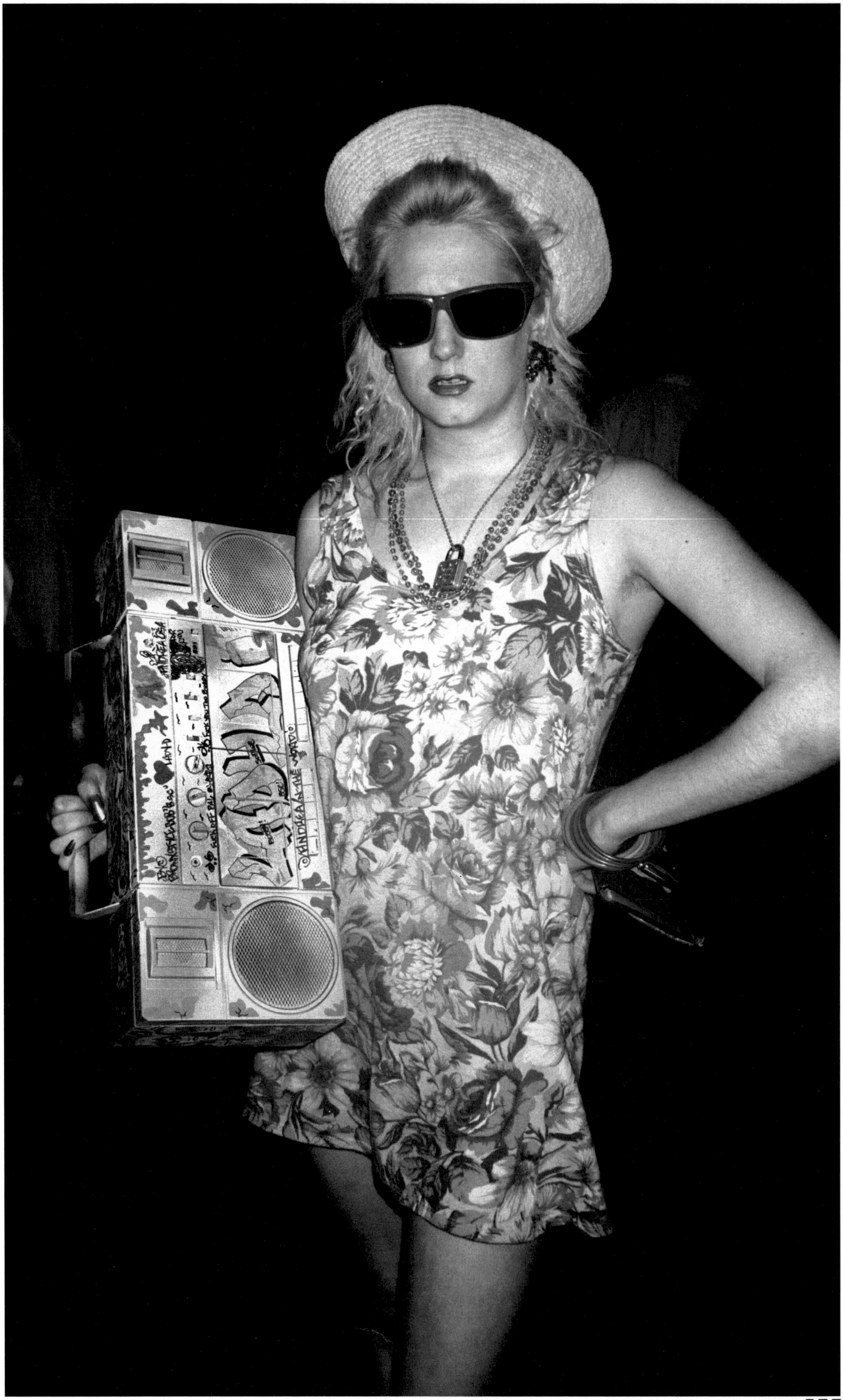

Andrea Bourgeois
at the Cat Club.
August 20, 1985

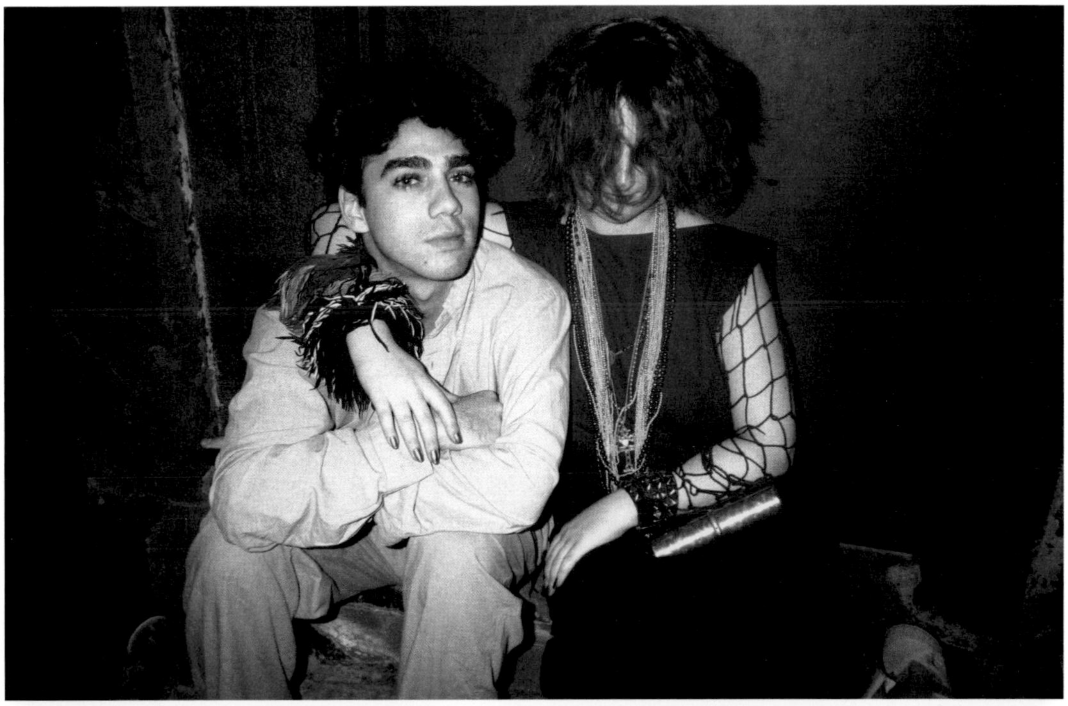

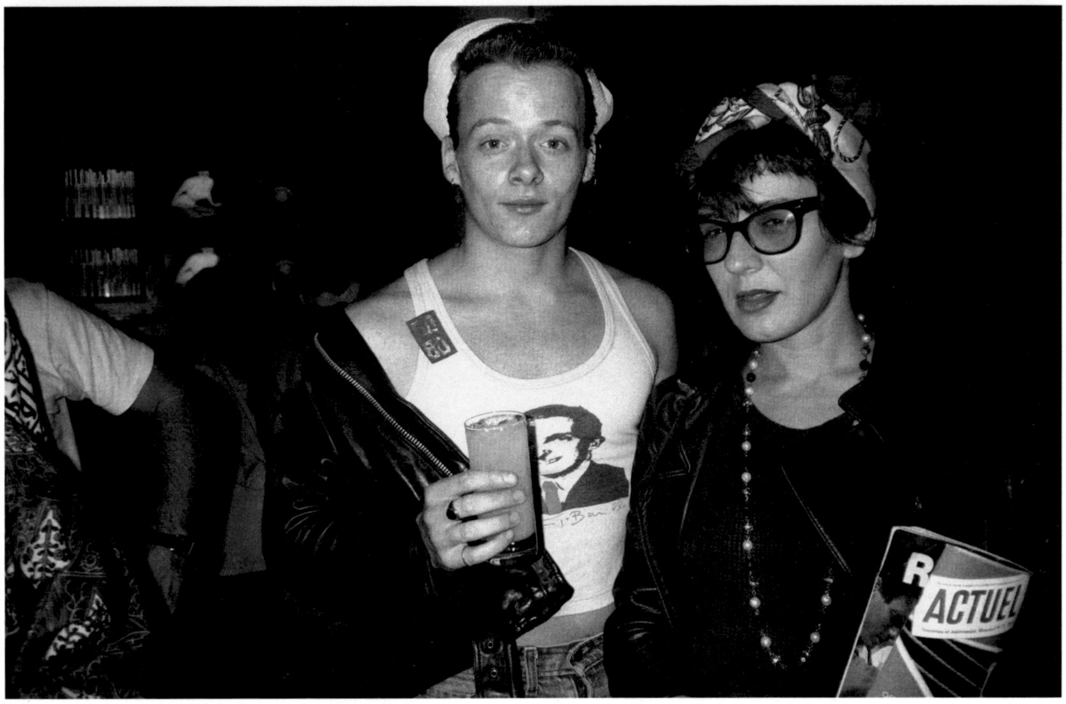

TOP: PETER OQUENDO AND MIRIAM BENDAHAN
AT THE XTC PARTY AT THE SENSORY EVOLUTION GALLERY.
AUGUST 20, 1985
BOTTOM: MARTIN BURGOYNE AND MARIPOL
AT THE JOHN "JELLYBEAN" BENITEZ PARTY AT PRIVATE EYES.
SEPTEMBER 29, 1985

The 80s were the greatest! I loved every exciting moment. The 80s was a time that everyone was adventurous, frivolous, and ready to party-- and party we did. New York became Party Central. People came from all over the world with one Idea in mind--can you get me into Studio 54?

You saw drag queens and princesses. While lots of people danced half naked, more than a few were overdressed. It was a phenomenon. The success of Studio 54 was a great factor in pulling N.Y. out of a major economic slump. Art, music, Pop Culture, fashion, and fun.... The music: "Last Dance," "Enough is Enough," "It's Raining Men," and "YMCA." Every restaurant was fancy and Chic. Skirts were short and shoulders were big. Andy Warhol was at the Factory, painting up a storm.

Cable was just coming in, no one had a fax or a cell phone. In the mid-80s no one ever heard of e-mail or e-anything. Let alone dot.com. No one had ever heard of AIDS. It was the last decade of innocence.

Nikki Haskell

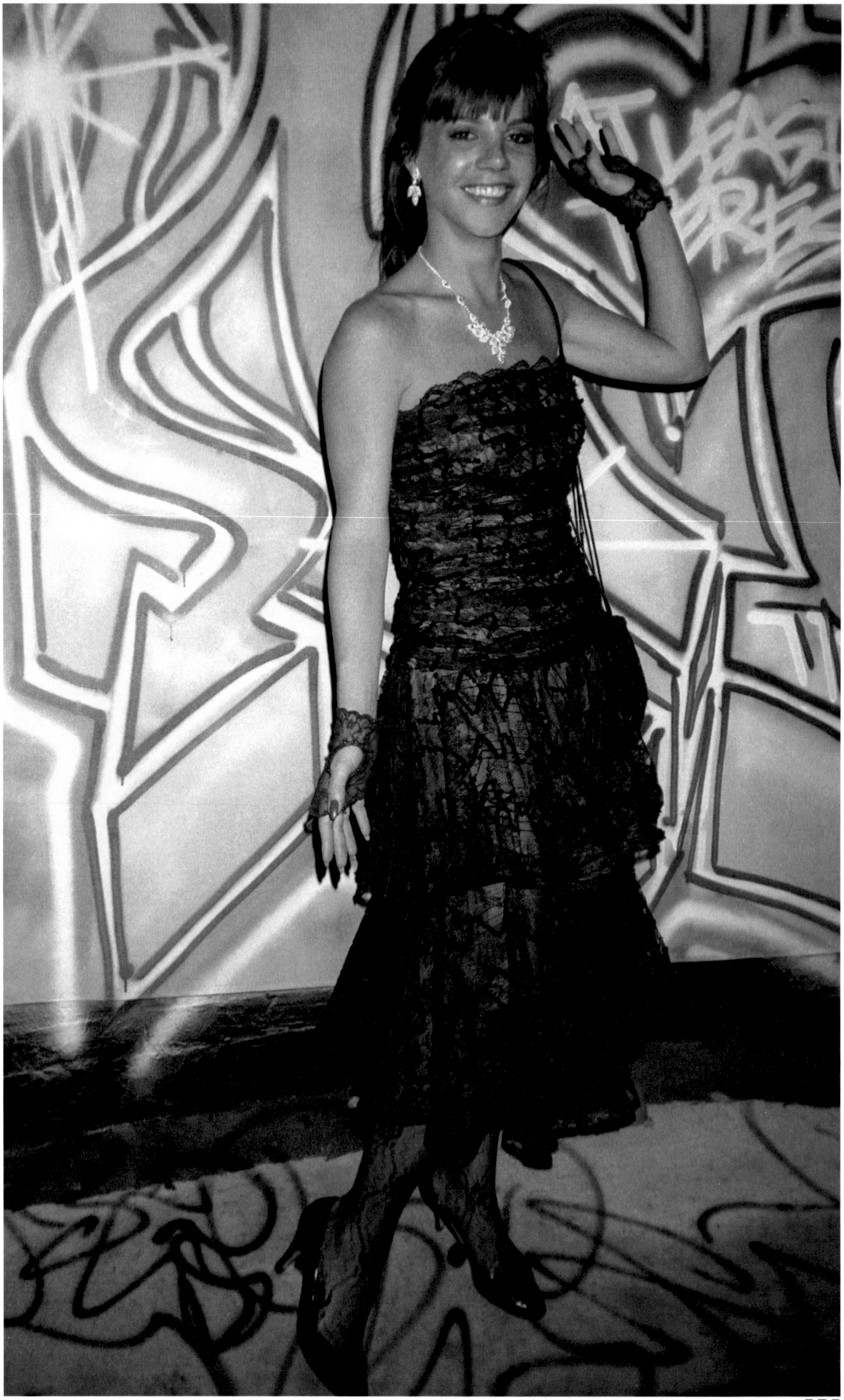

Nancy Pearson at the Benefit for Homeless Children at the World. June 18, 1986

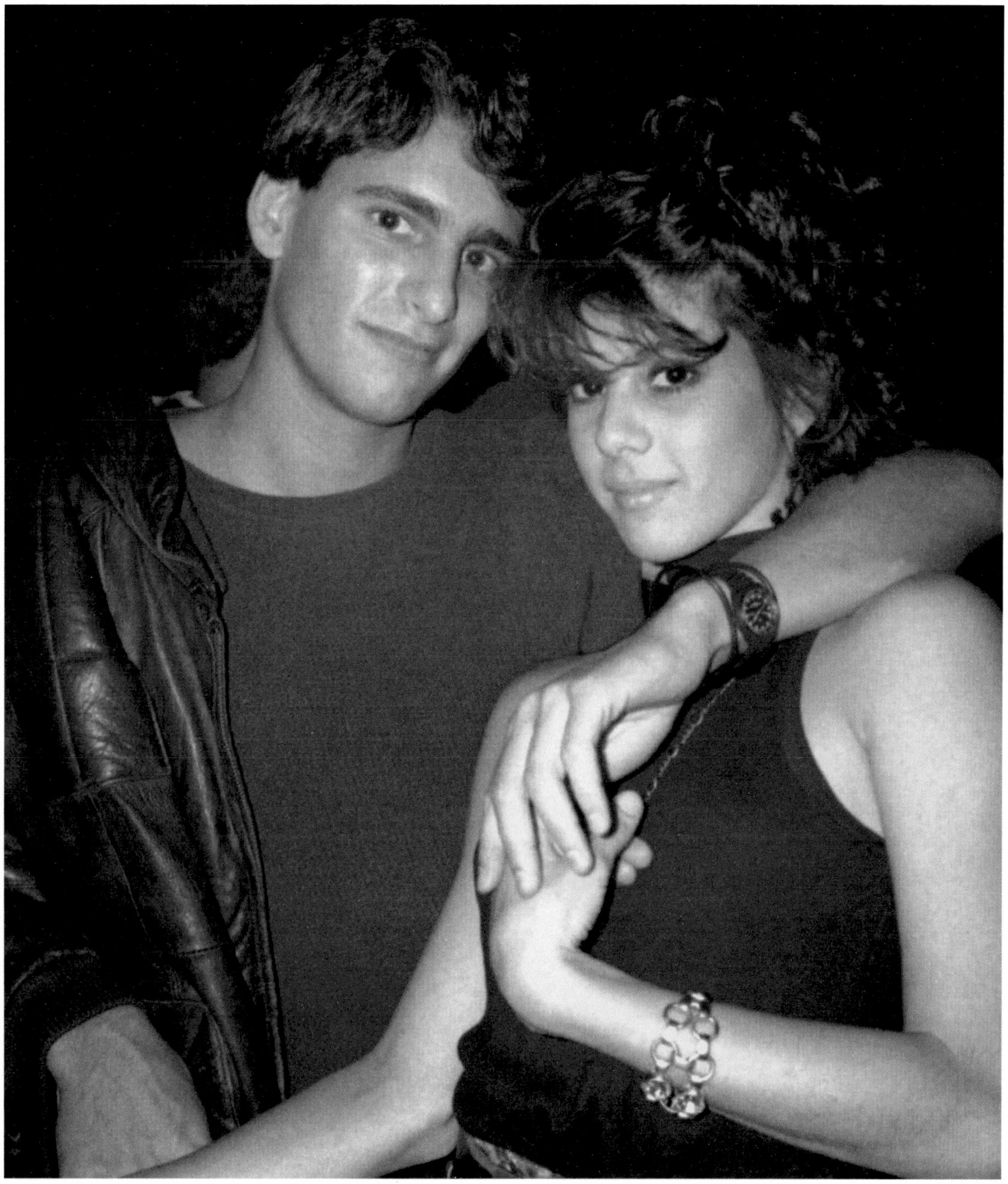

Dave Schlachet and Marisa Tomei
at Michael Grosner's party at Studio 54.
April 1985

"I THINK SOMETHING HAPPENED IN THE 1980s, BUT I CAN'T REMEMBER WHAT IT WAS."
DANNY FIELDS

DANNY FIELDS
DECEMBER 1985

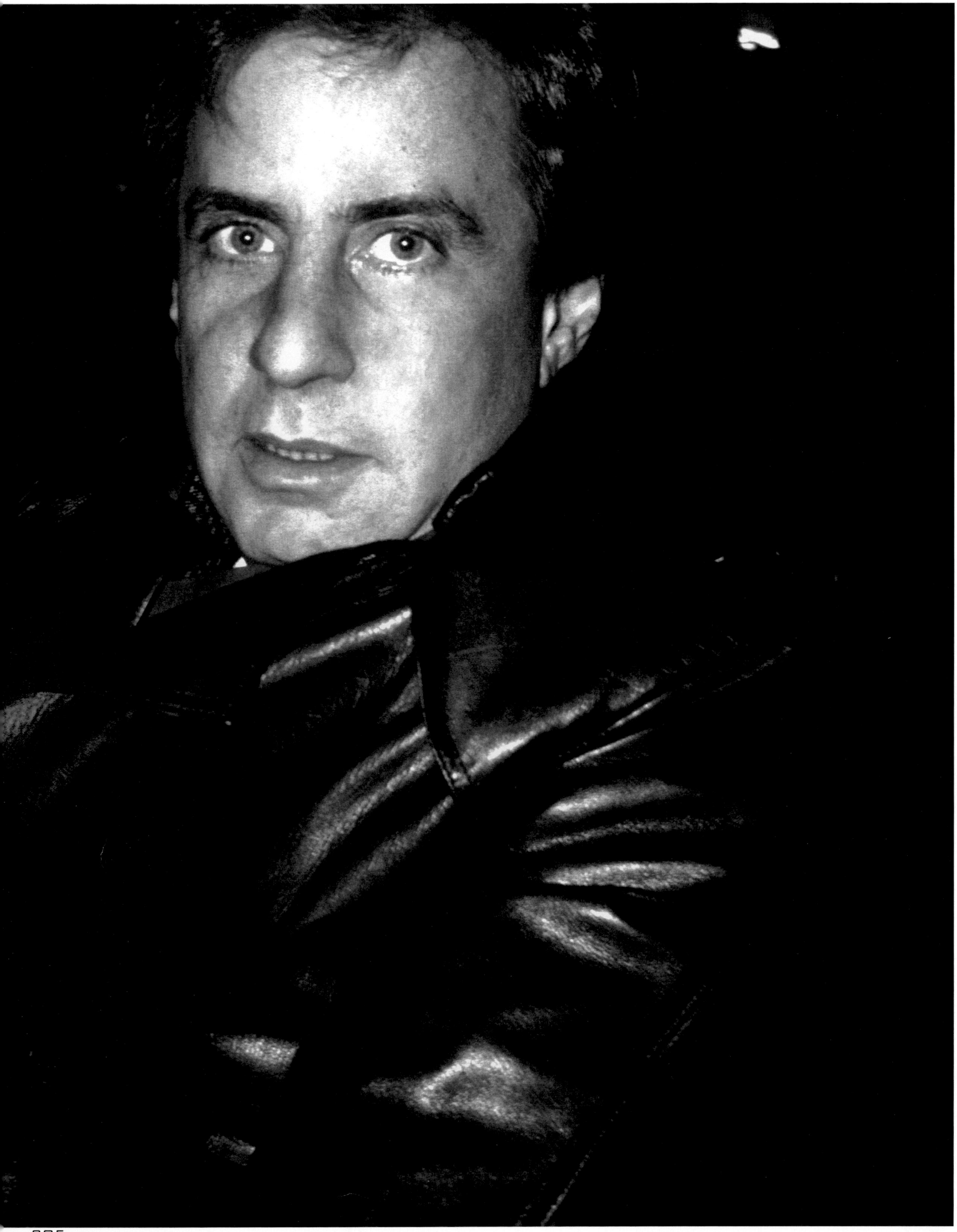

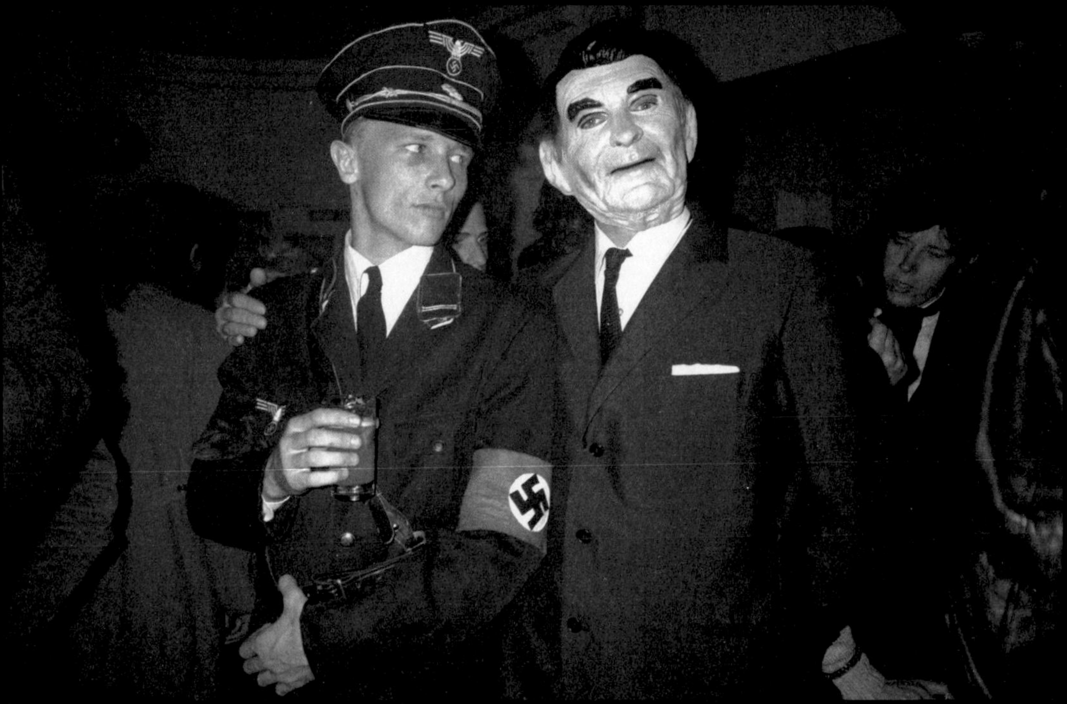

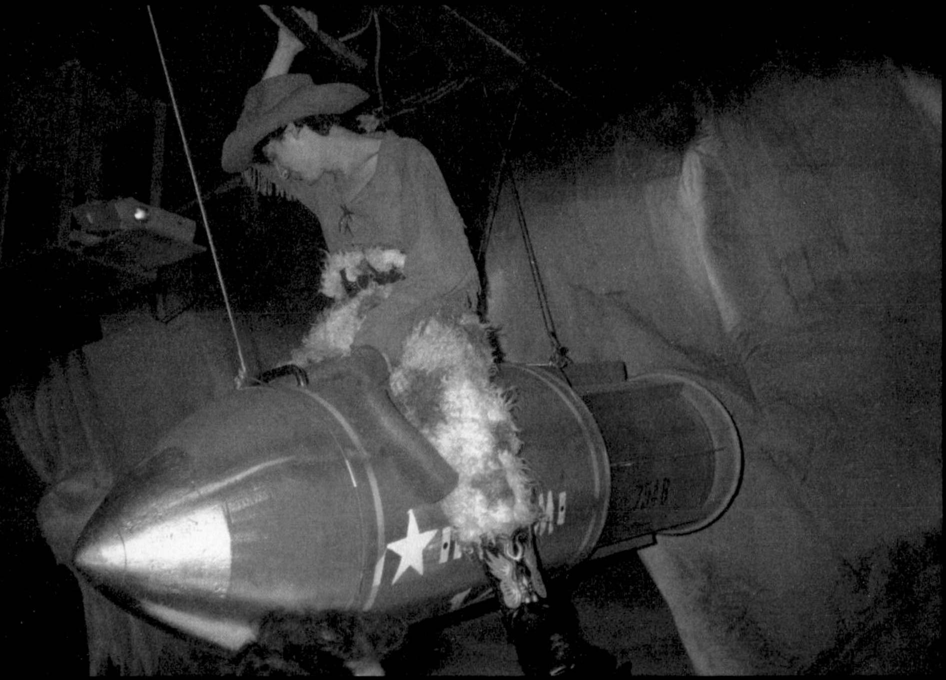

Top: Nazi and Reagan costumes at the War Party at Area. October 1984
Bottom: "Rocket Man" at the War Party at Area. October 1984

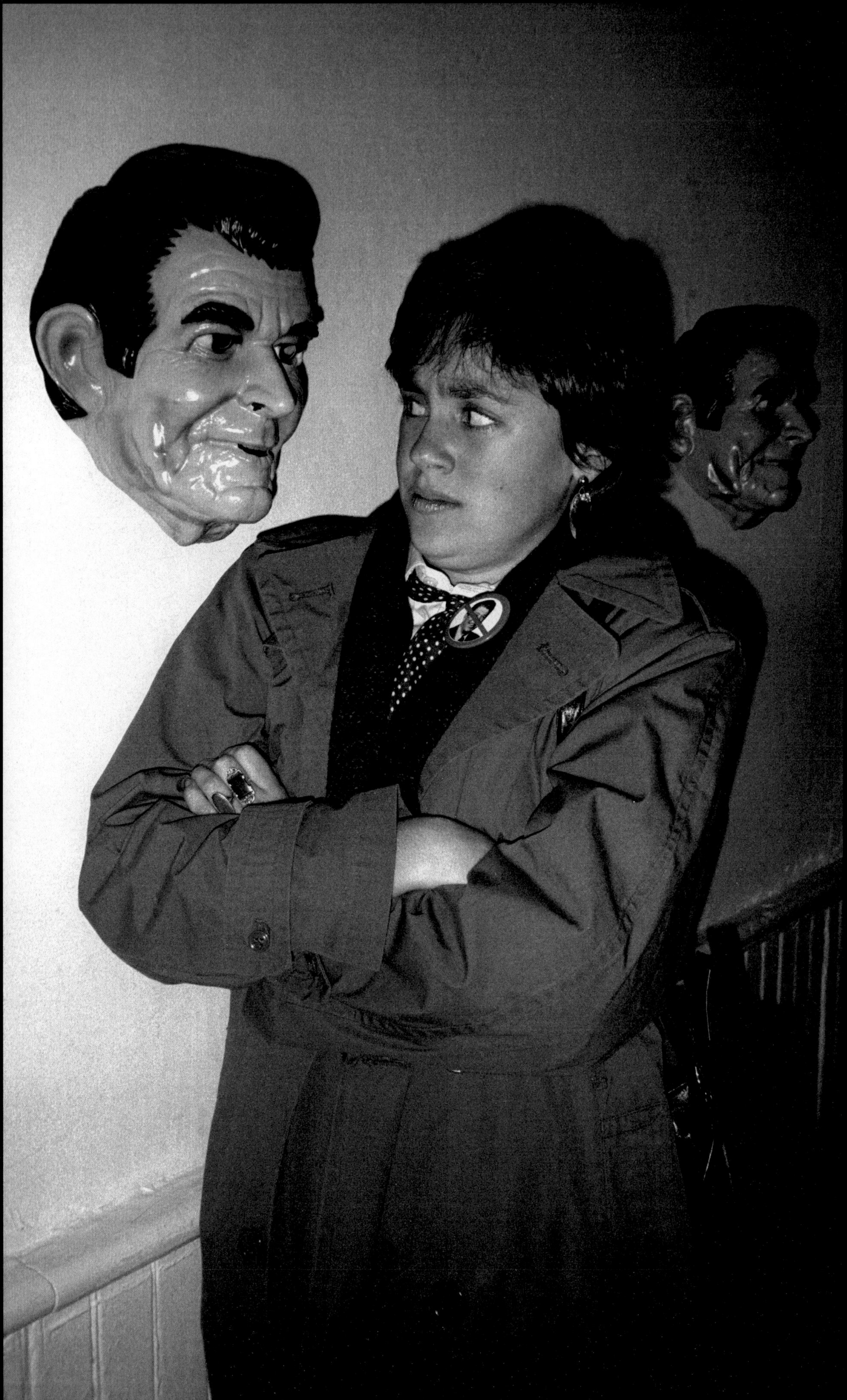

Maura Moynihan
at Limelight's party
for Gary Trudeaus.
Saturday, September 29, 1984

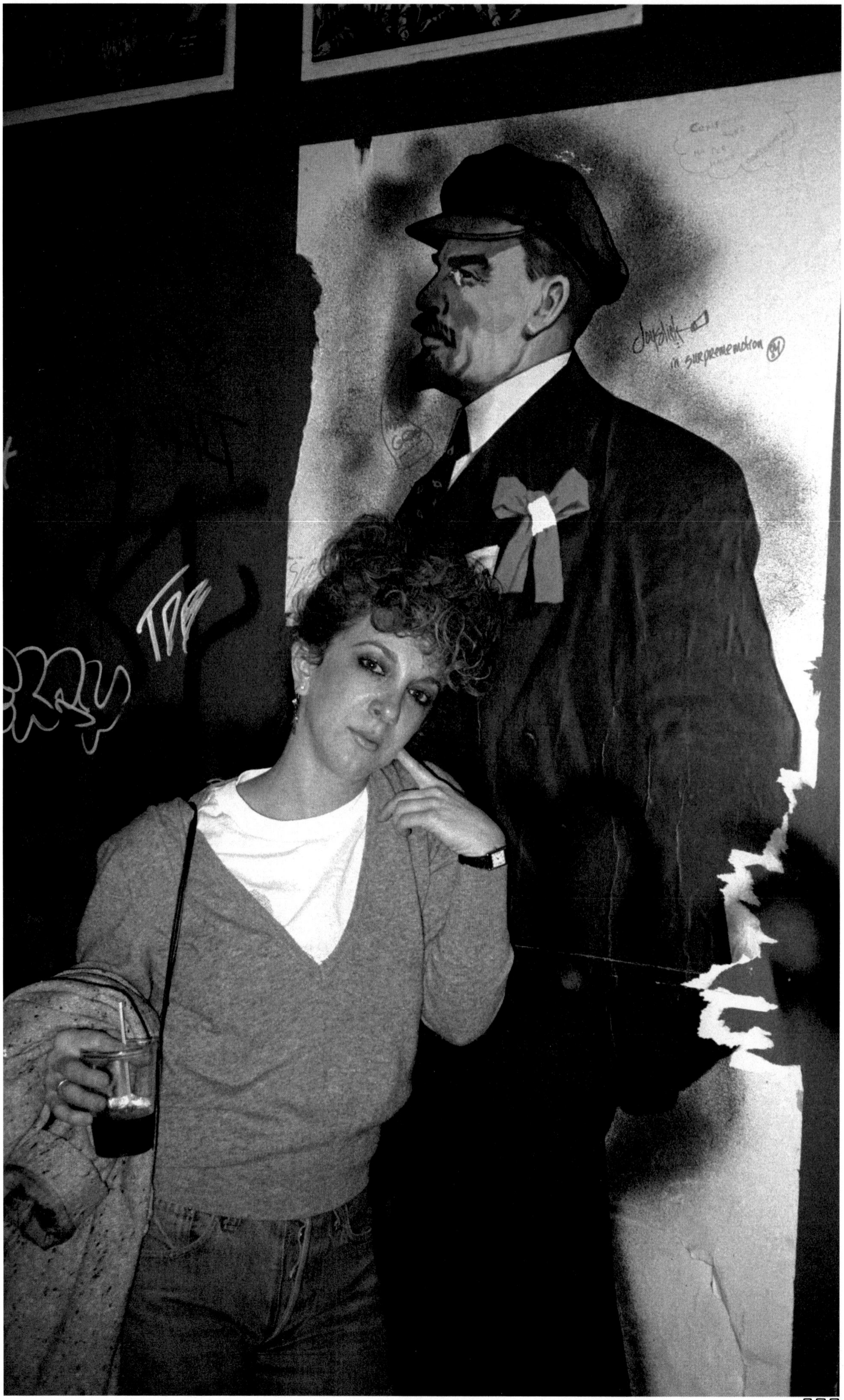

Karon Bihari
at the "I don't go out
much anymore" party
at Danceteria.
March 1984

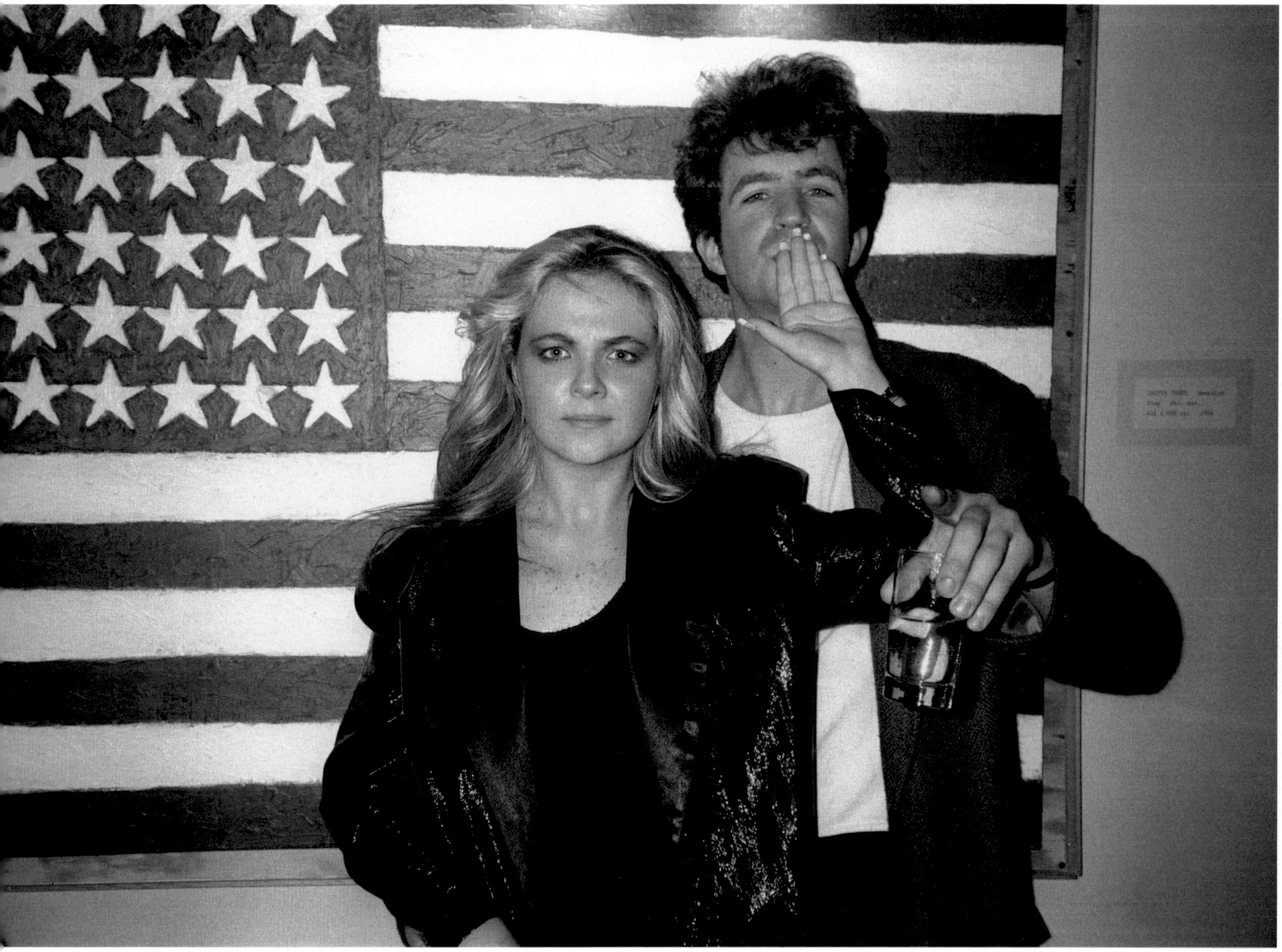

Cornelia Guest and Eric Goode
at Area.
May 11, 1985

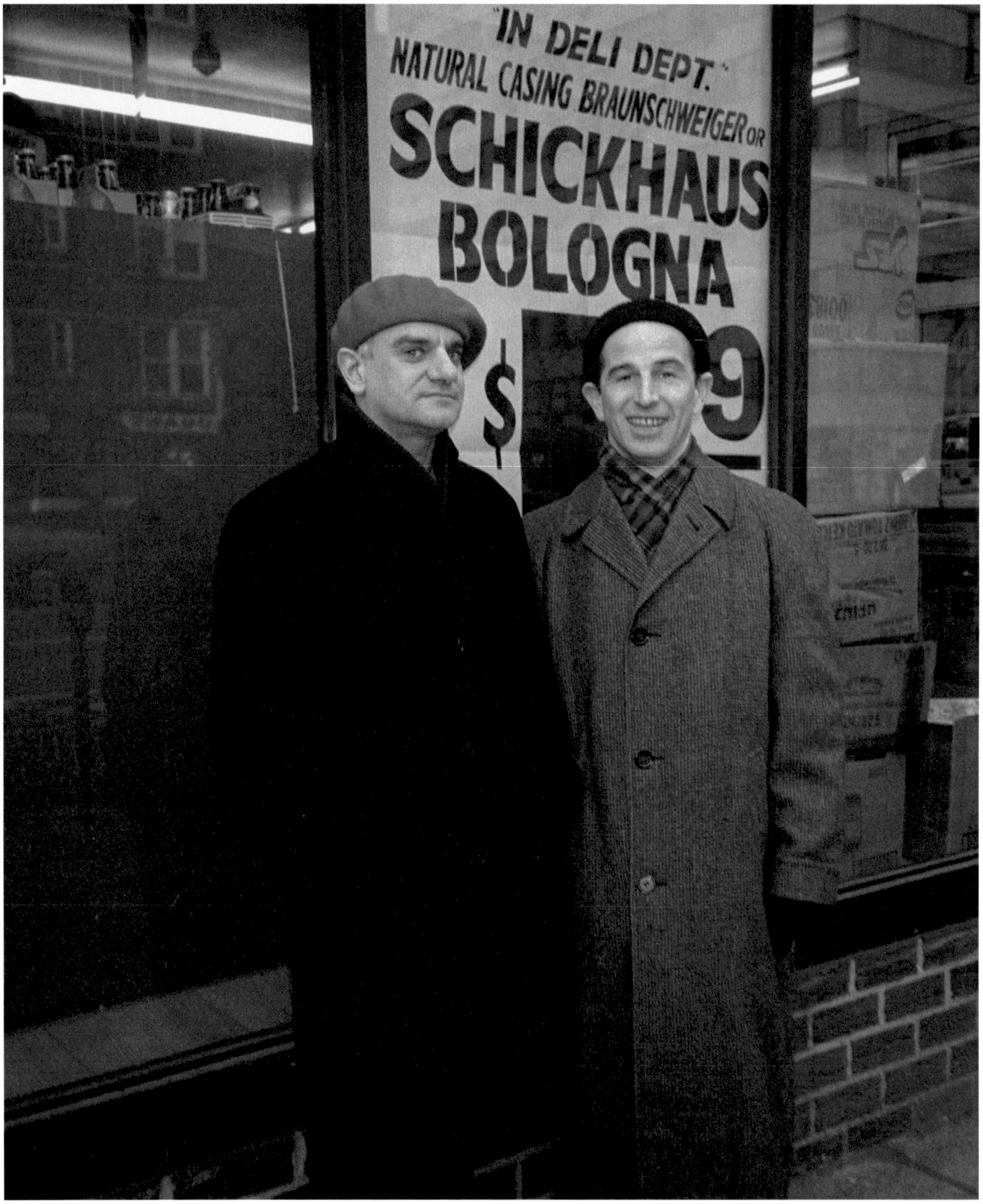

Charles Ludlam and Everett
Wednesday, March 5, 1986

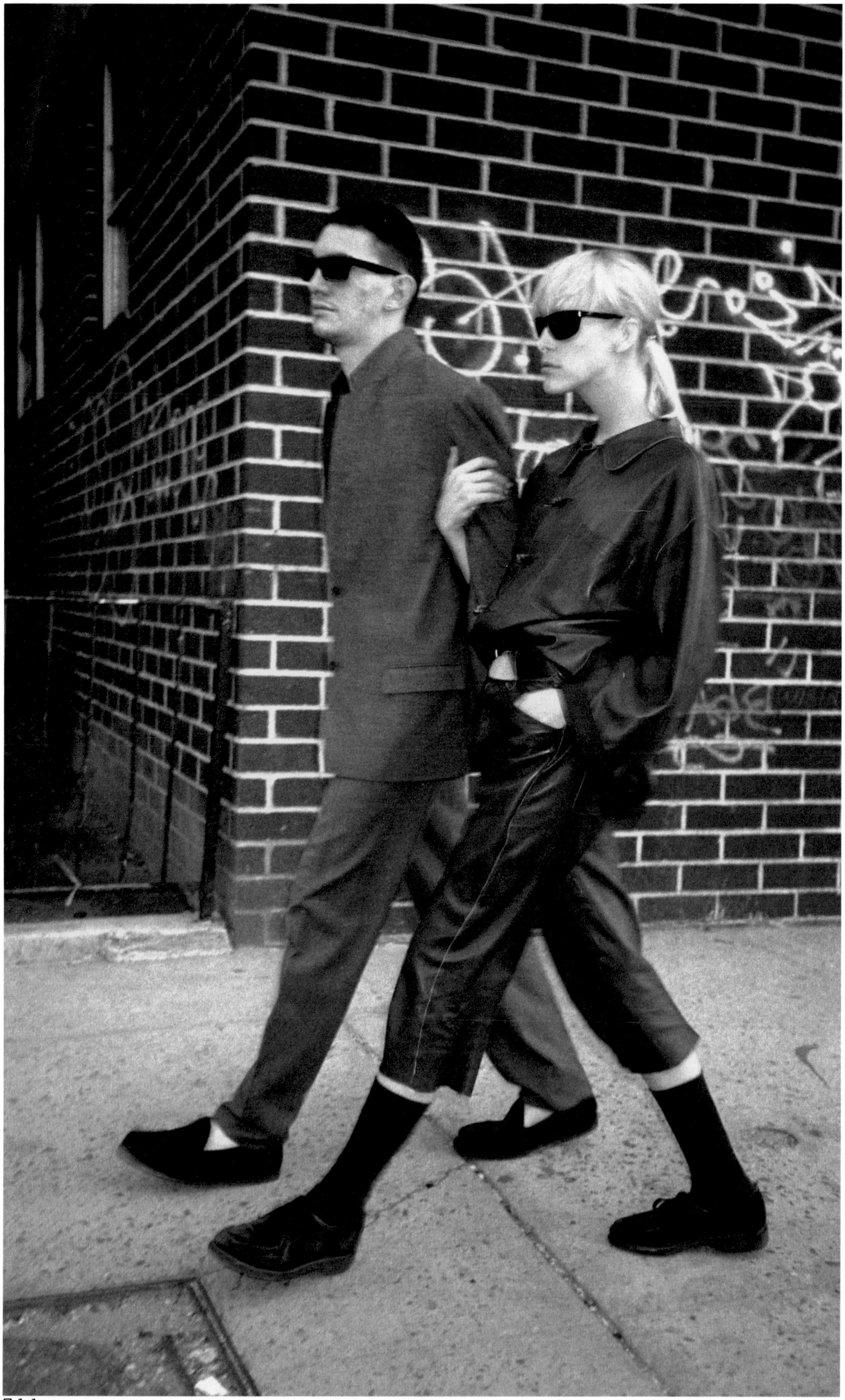

Patrick Fox
and Teri Toye
September 14, 1985

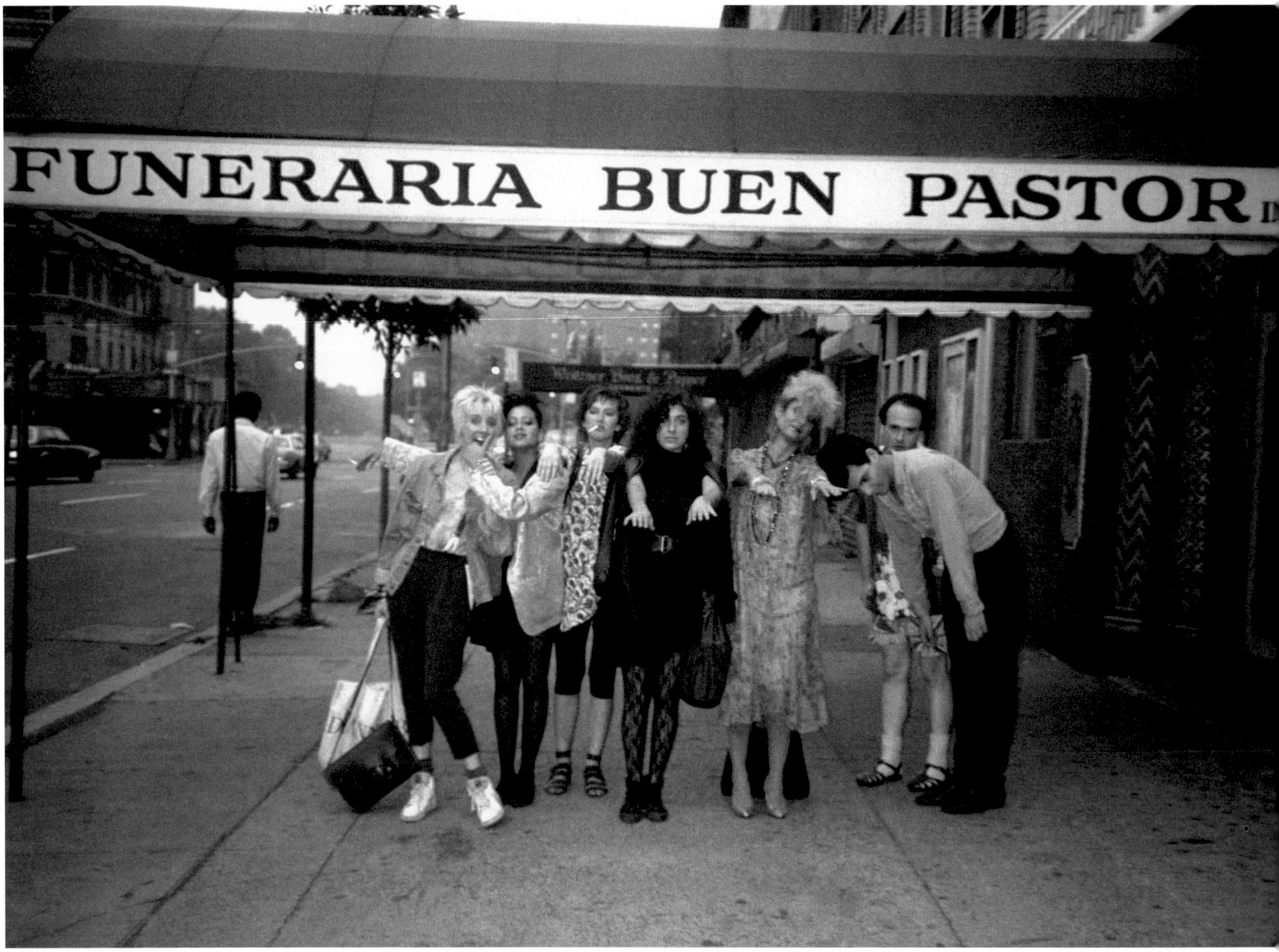

"We were called Celebutantes. Newsweek had dubbed James St. James a Celebutante (which I suppose by osmosis bled over onto me) in one of their nightlife columns. It was a mixture of Celebrity and Debutante of which we had been neither. But, despite no money, terrible clothes, worse hair-do's and unknown lineages--the name stuck."
Lisa Edelstein (Lisa E.)

Bonnie Vaughn, Name Unknown, Name Unknown, Lisa Edelstein,
Anita Sarko, Bobby Reed, and Michael Musto as "walking zombies" on
the streets after the party "Save the Robots."
July 1985

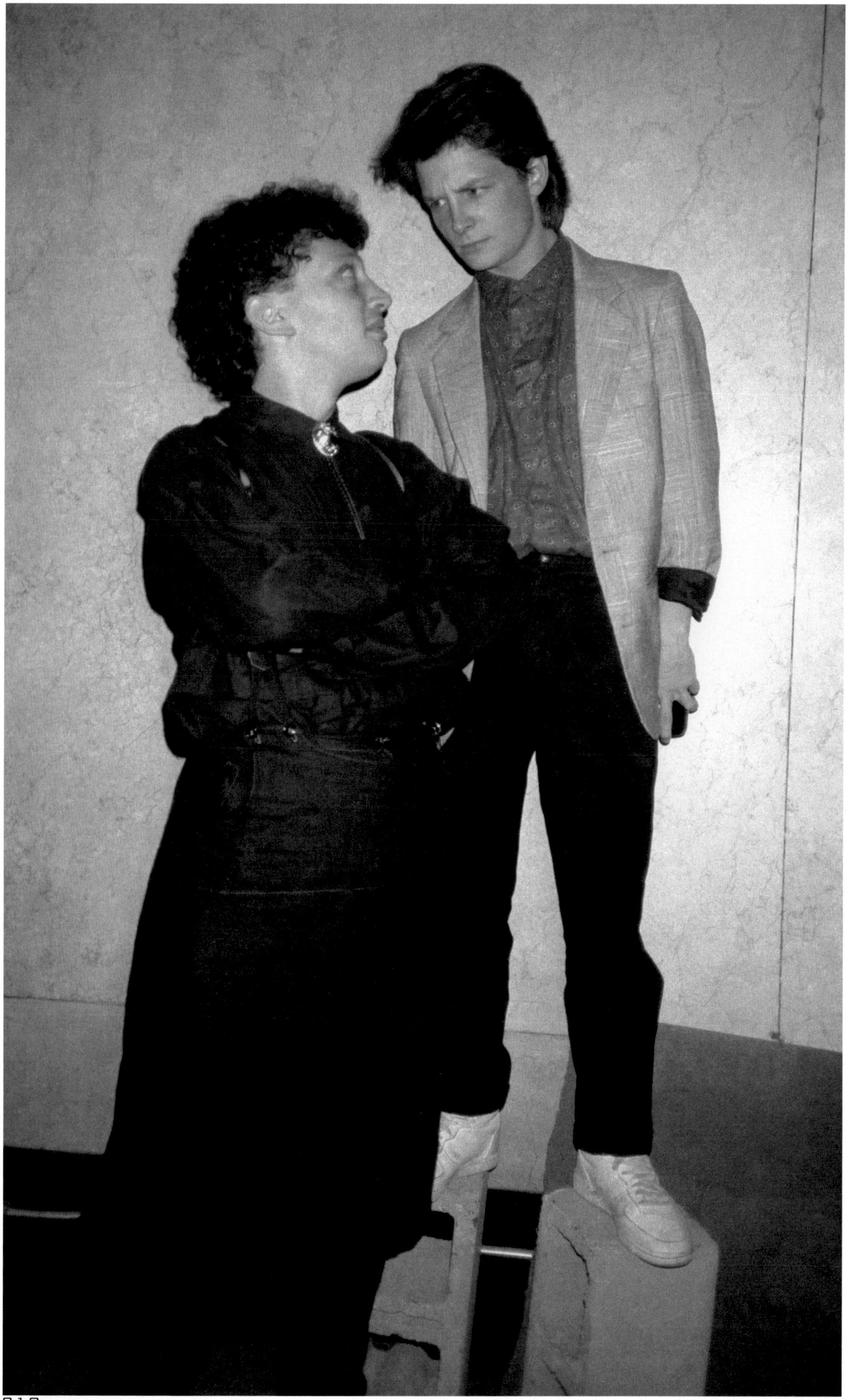

Haoui Montaug
and Michael J. Fox
at the Palladium.
September 23, 1985

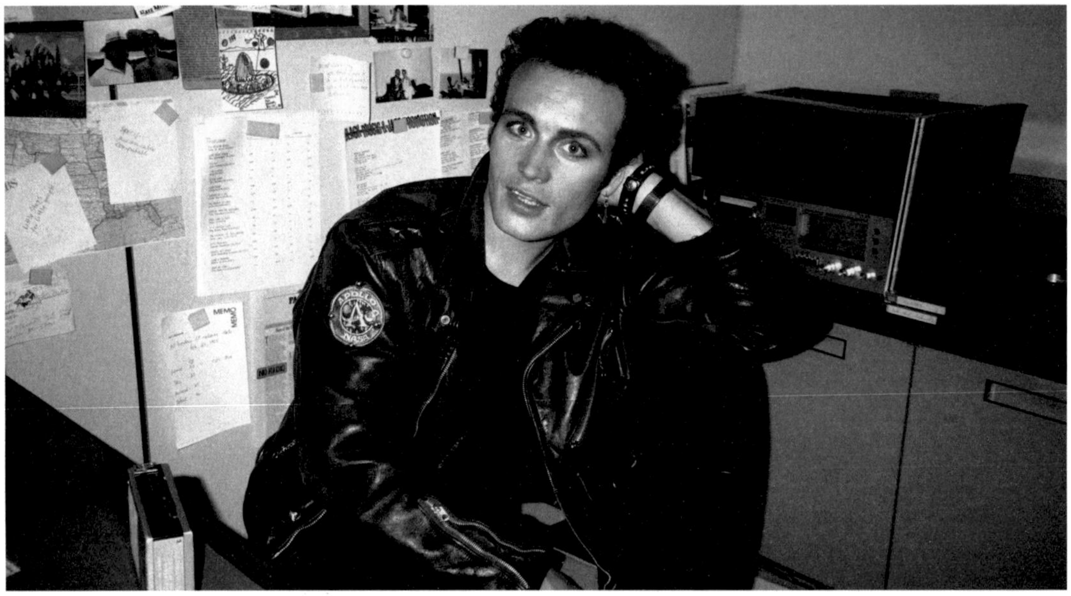

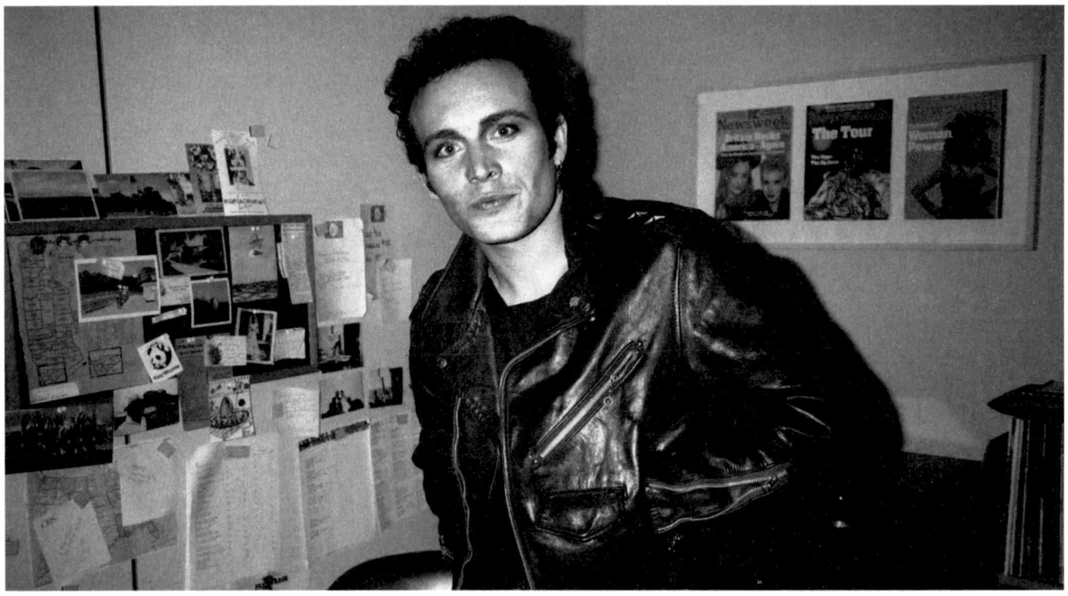

Adam Ant
at Susan Blond's office.
August 28, 1985

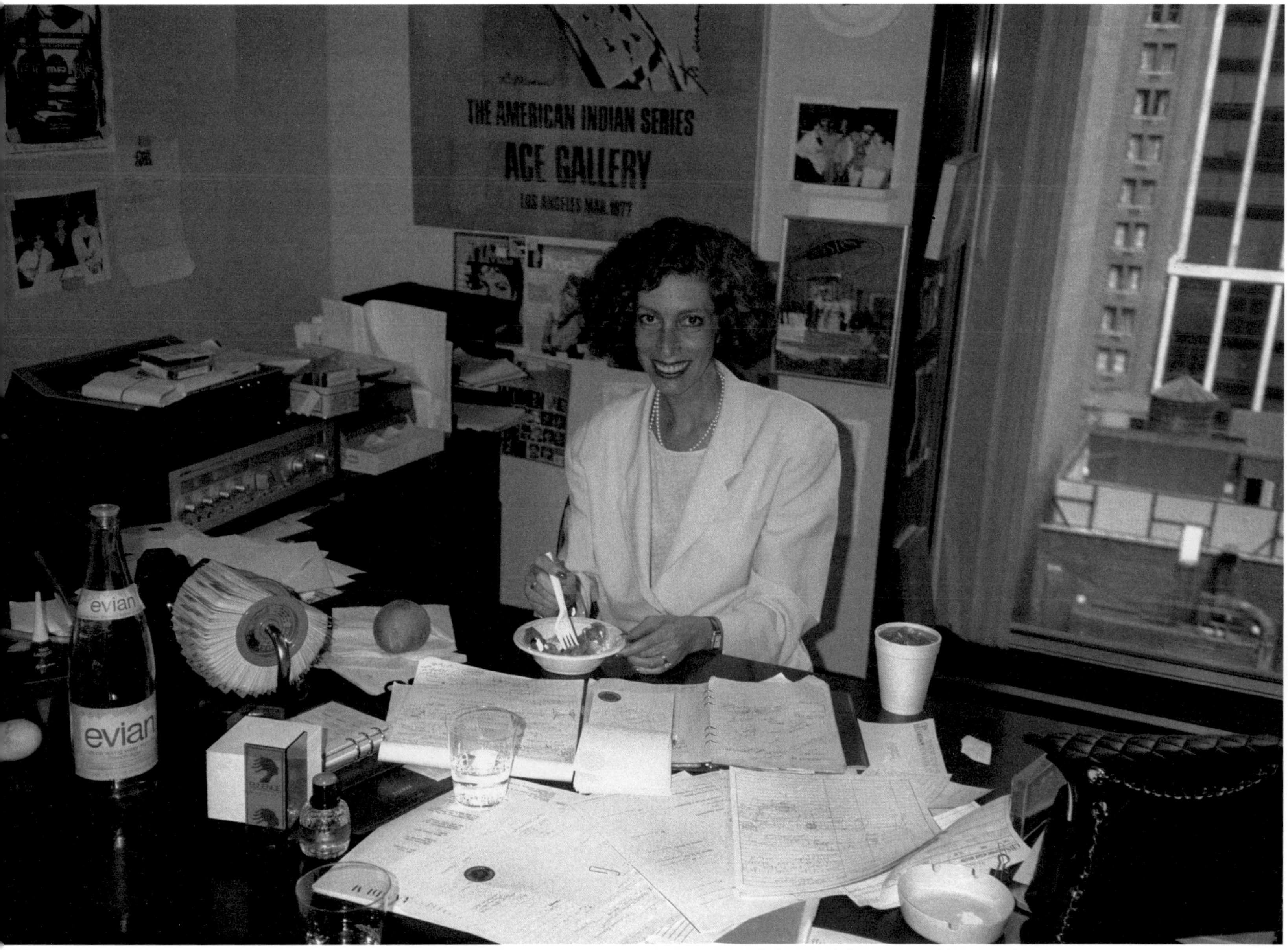

"Patrick was really there, part of it, not only physically, but his heart was with us and he made us look gorgeous--with someone like me that wasn't easy. He was always and will always be the best."
Susan Blond

Susan Blond in her office.
August 28, 1985

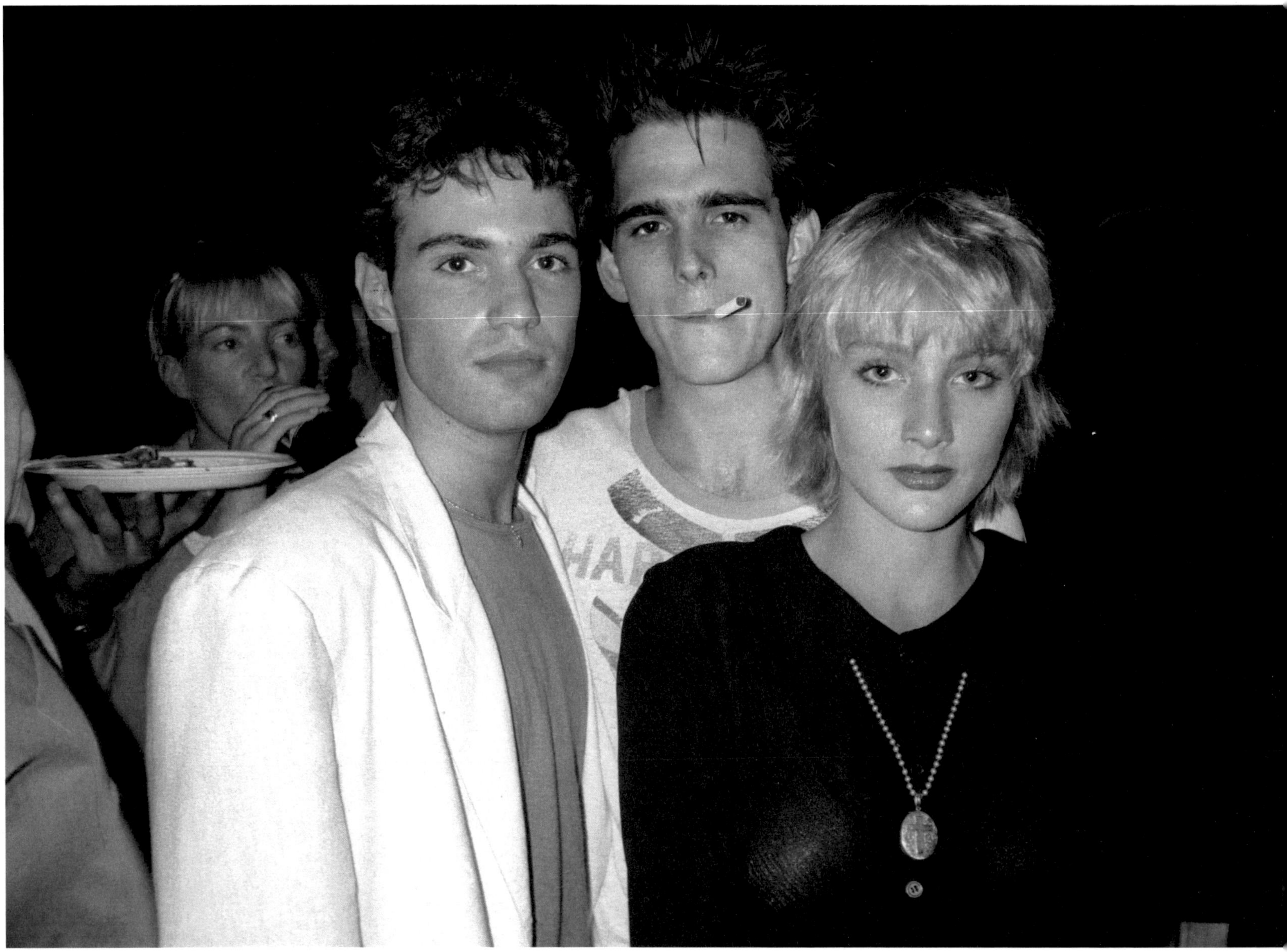

NEIL BARRY, MATT DILLON, AND JENNY WRIGHT
AT THE OUT OF BOUNDS PREMIERE PARTY HELD AT REVOLUTION.
JULY 23, 1986

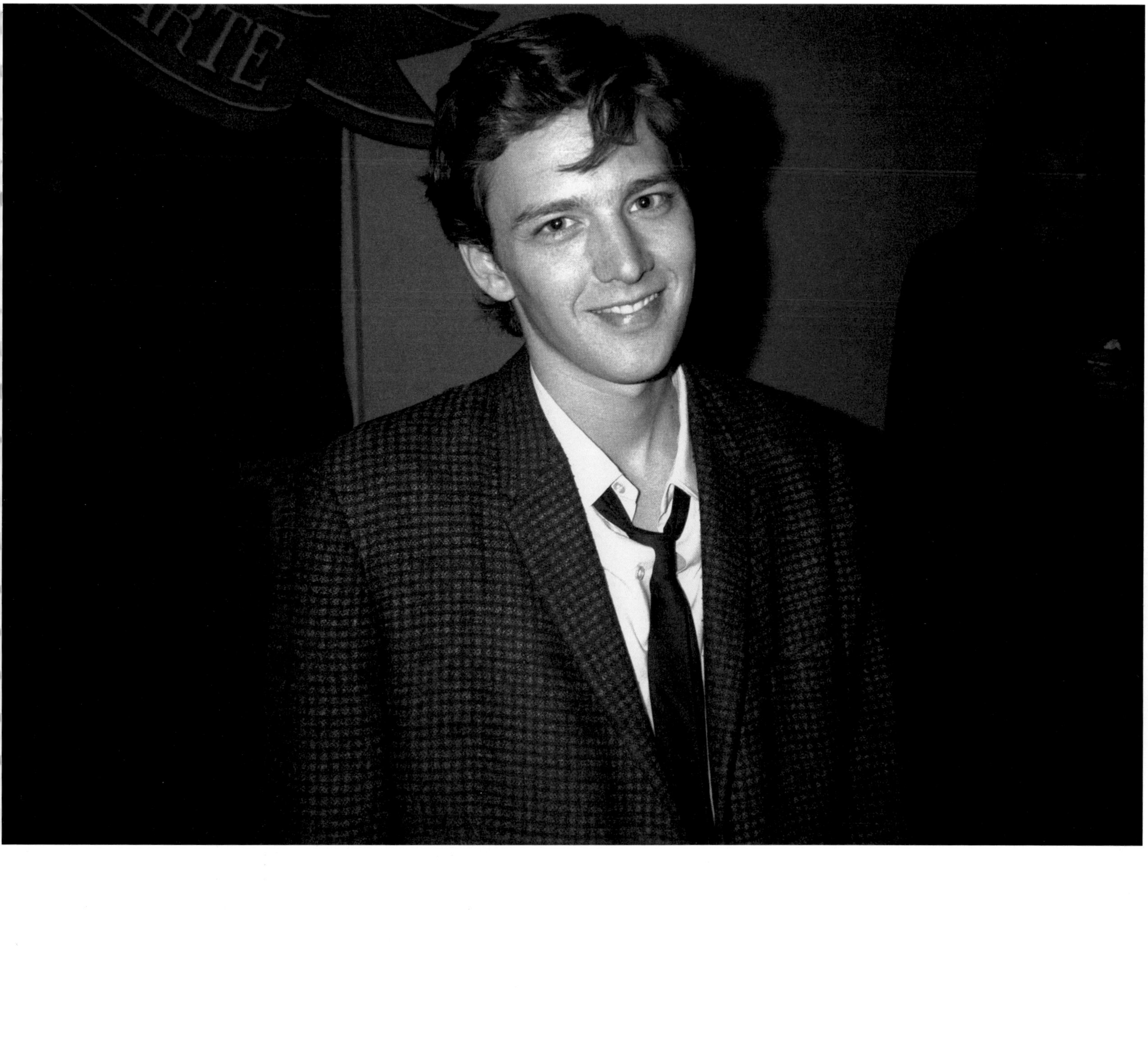

ANDREW McCARTHY
AT AREA.
MARCH 1985

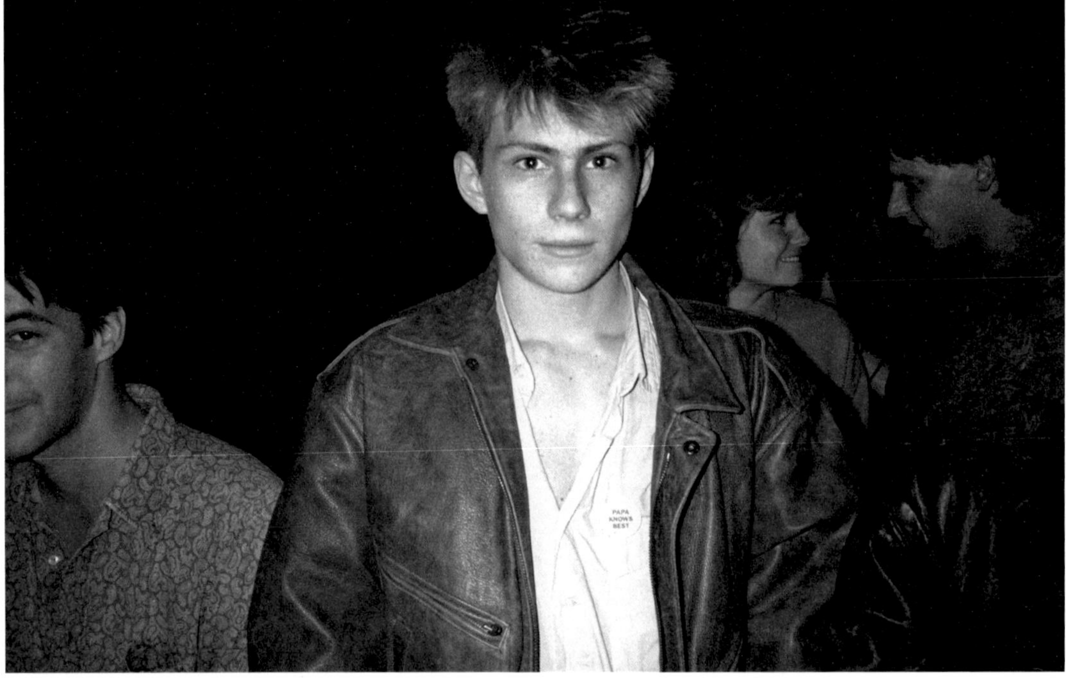

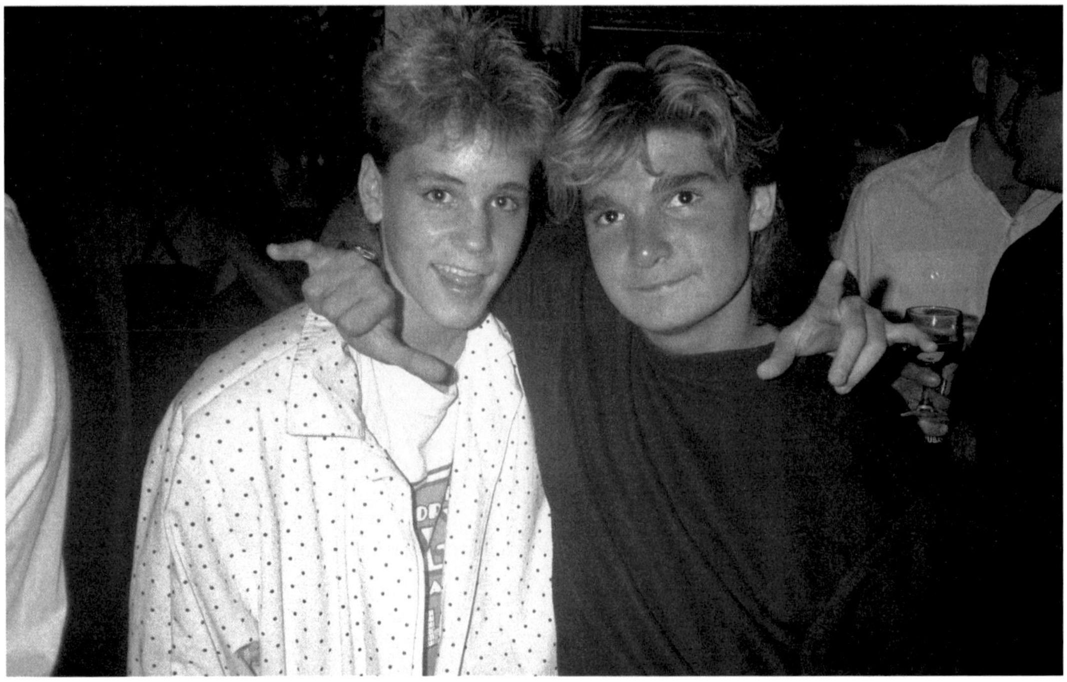

Top: Christian Slater
at Danny Aiello's party at Saint.
Thursday, November 6, 1986
Bottom: Corey Haim and Corey Feldman at the Tunnel.
July 29, 1987

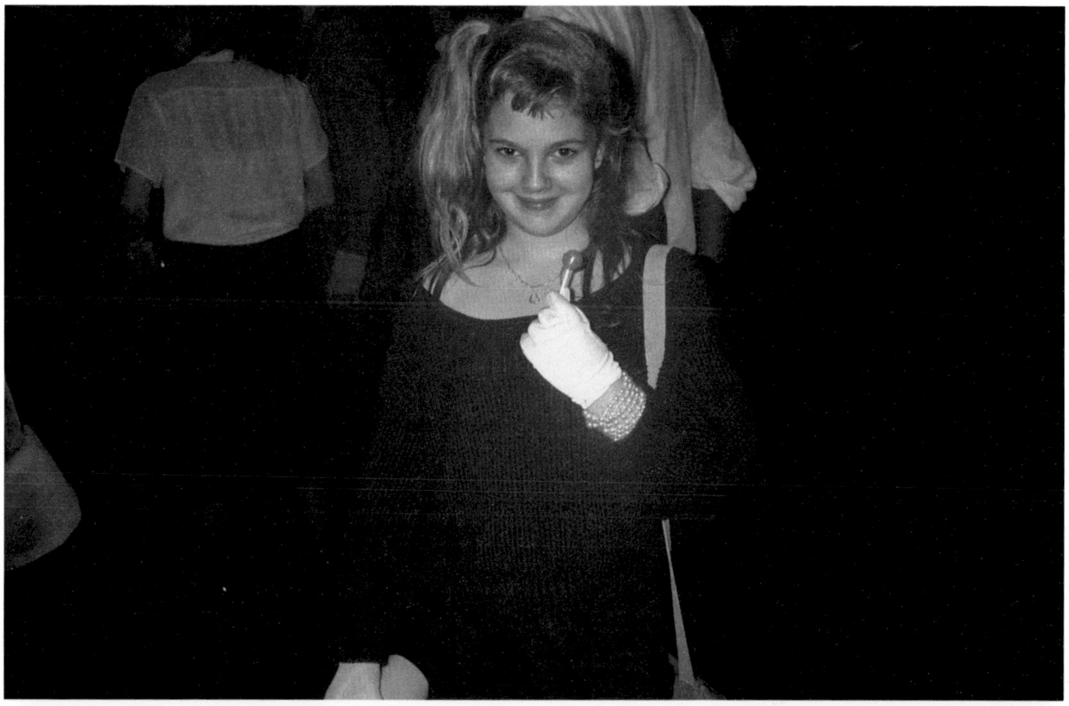

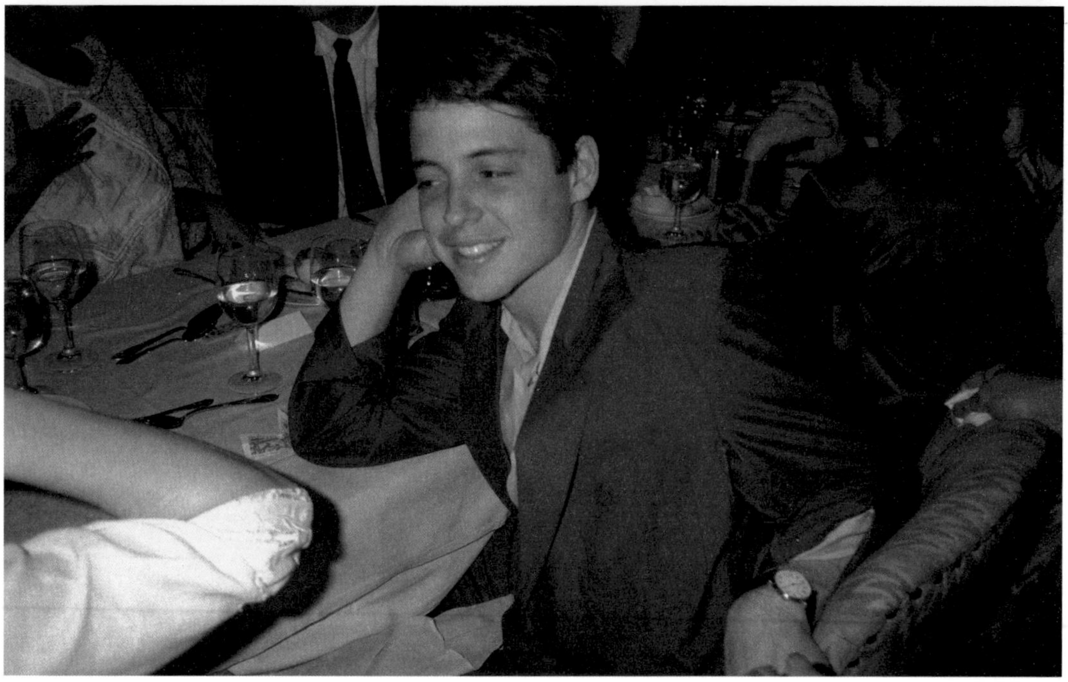

TOP: DREW BARRYMORE
AT PIA ZADORA'S PARTY AT THE PALLADIUM.
JANUARY 29, 1986
BOTTOM: MATTHEW BRODERICK
AT THE HORTON FOOTE AND CHRISTOPHER DURANG PARTY AT THE PAINTED DESERT.
MARCH 25, 1987

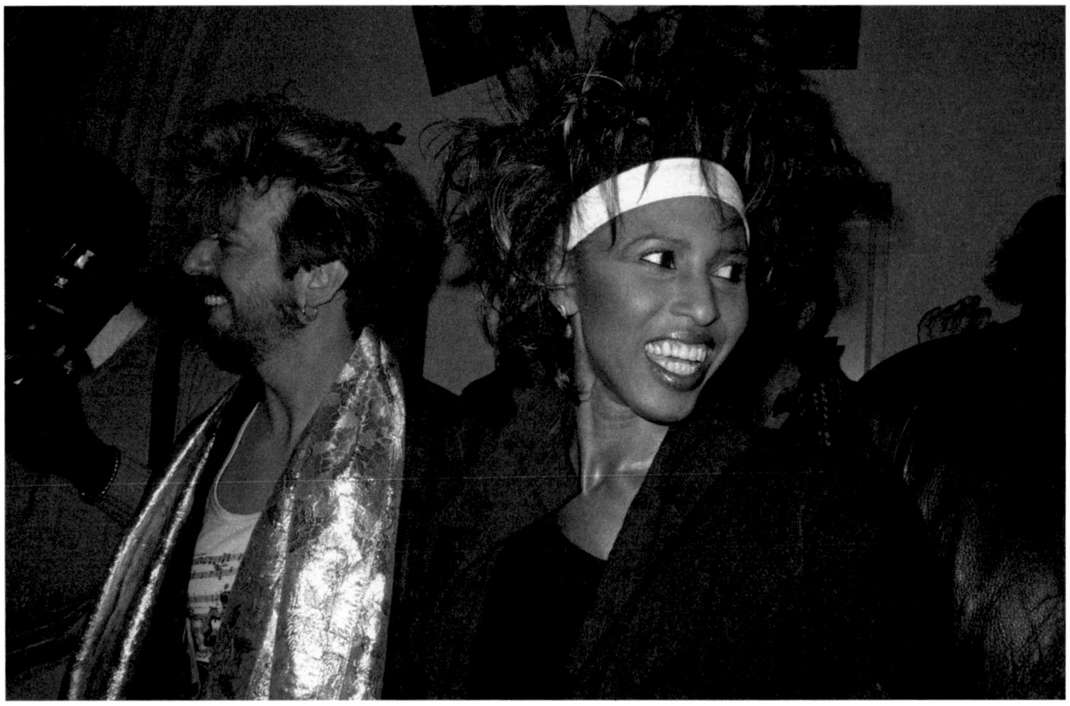

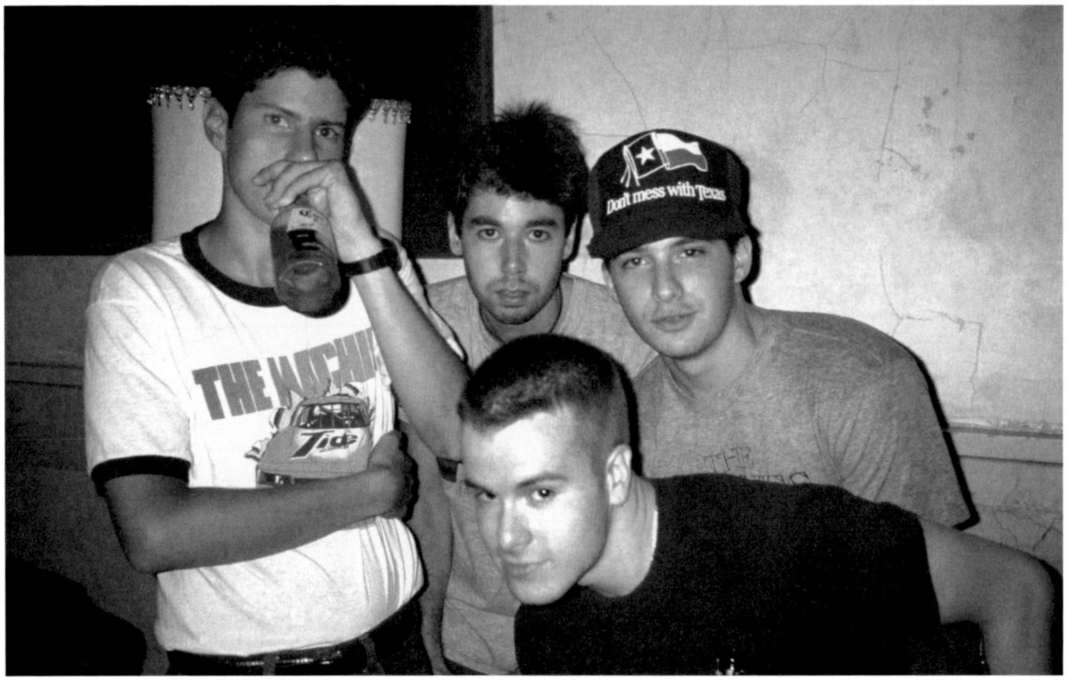

TOP: DAVE STEWART AND NONA HENDRYX
AT LIMELIGHT. MARCH 1984
BOTTOM: THE BEASTIE BOYS AT MK.
JUNE 1988

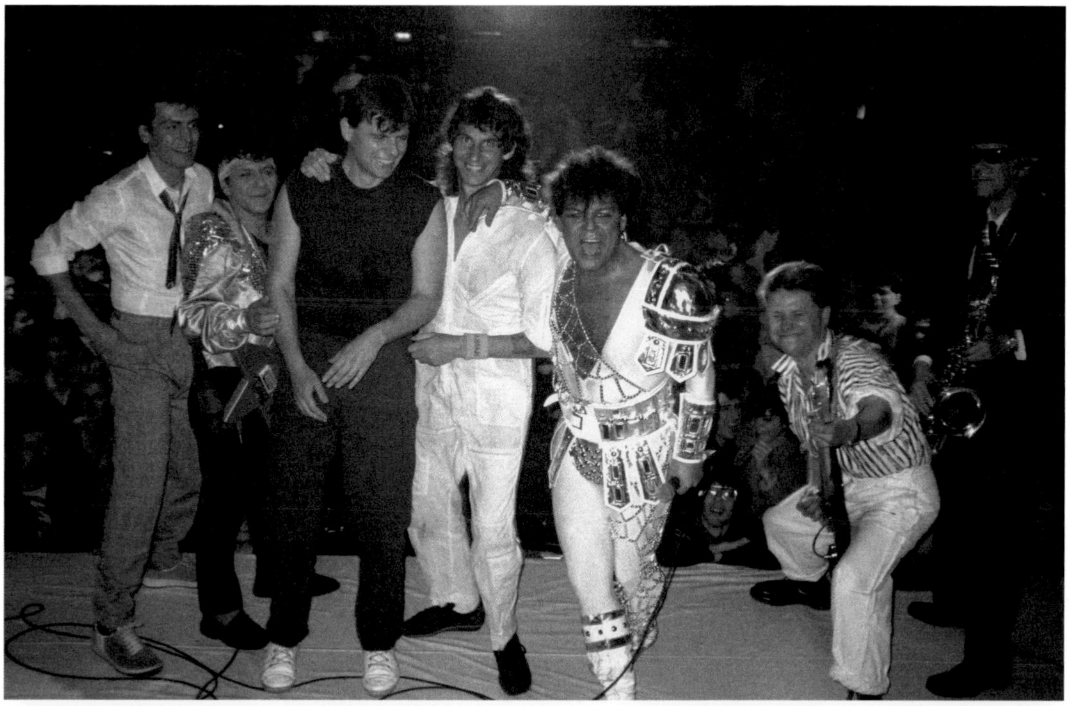

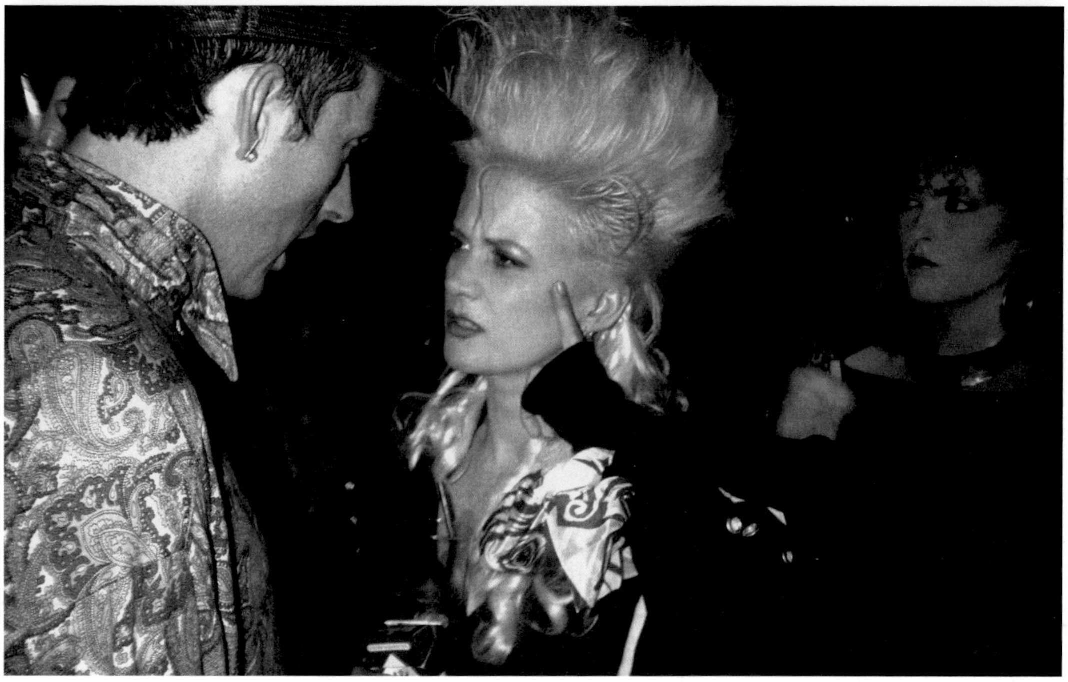

TOP: ONSTAGE WITH GARY GLITTER LIVE AT LIMELIGHT.
MAY 15, 1984
BOTTOM: ALANNAH CURRIE, OF THE THOMPSON TWINS
AT LIMELIGHT'S OPENING IN LONDON.
JULY 15,1986

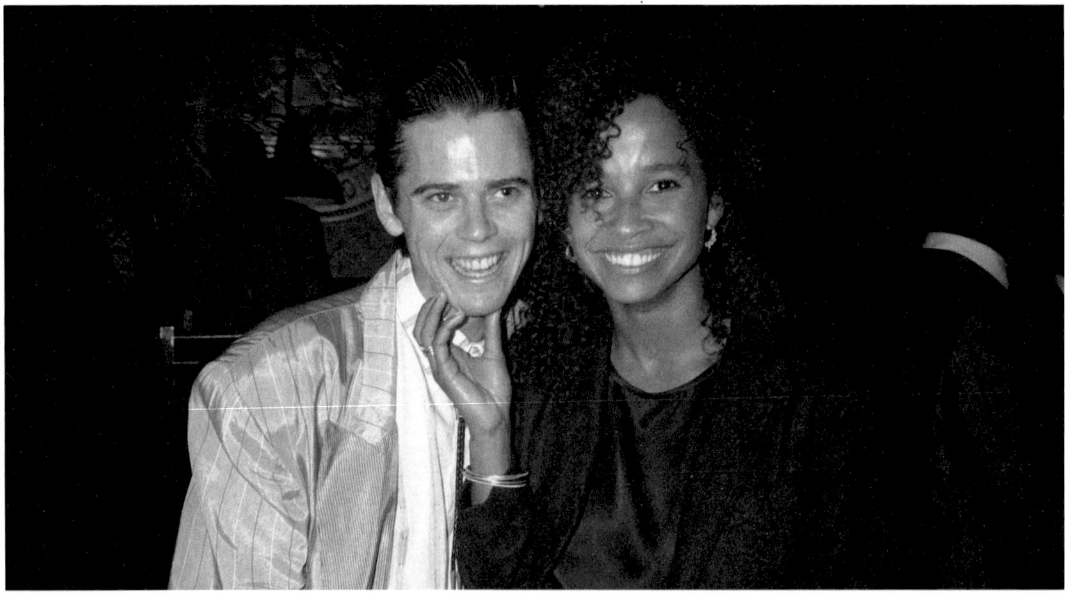

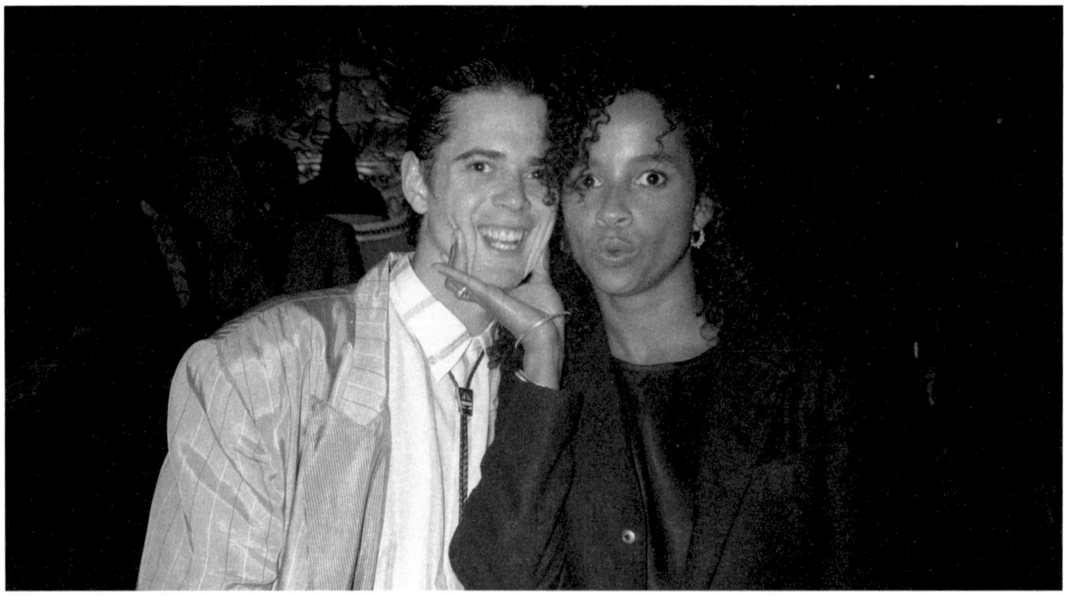

Costars C. Thomas Howell and Rae Dawn Chong
celebrate the release of their film Soul Man
at the Hard Rock Cafe.
September 10, 1986

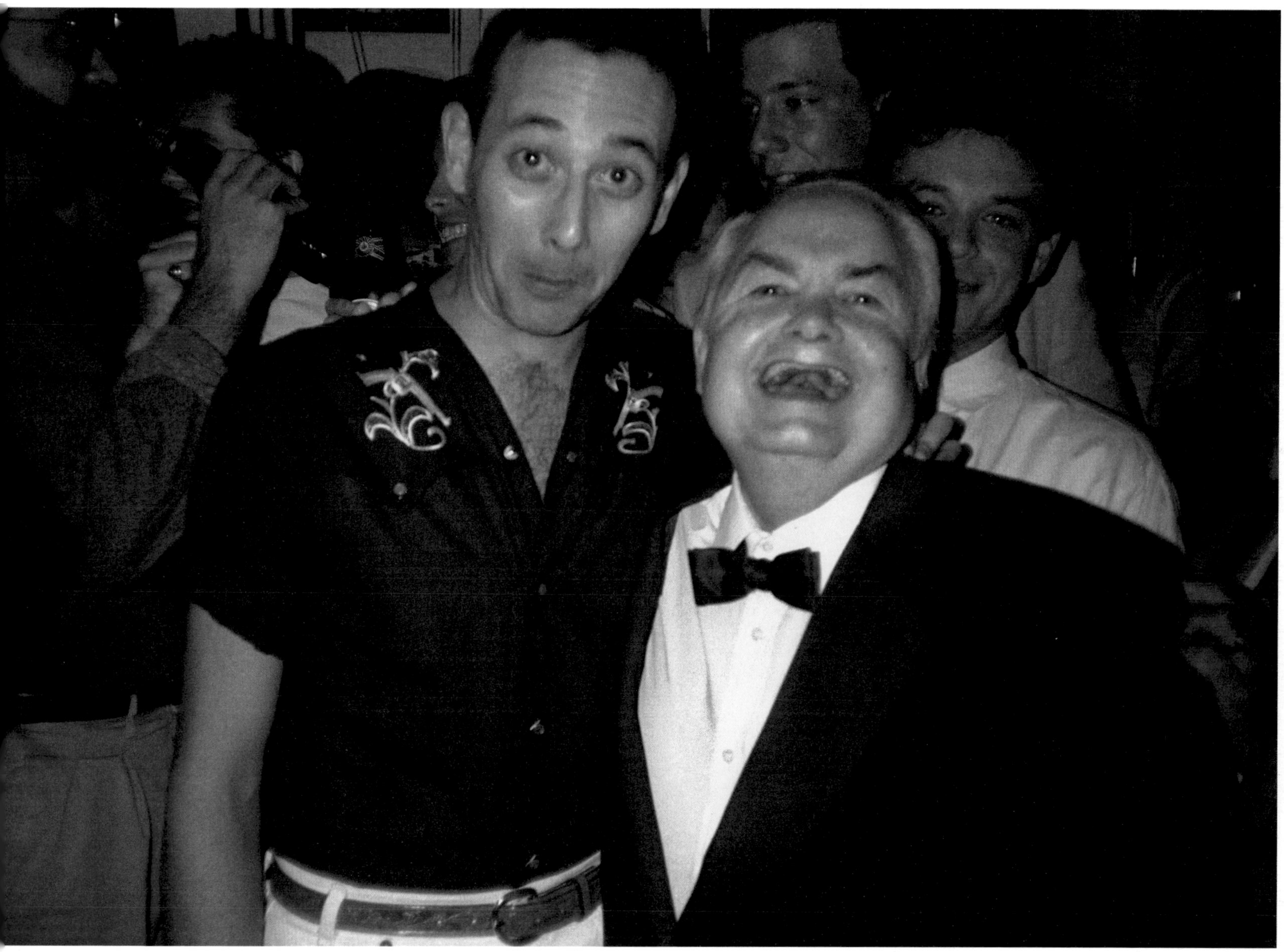

Pee-wee Herman (Paul Reubens) and Larry "Bud" Melman
at Larry "Bud" Melman's birthday party at the Key Cafe.
August 12, 1986

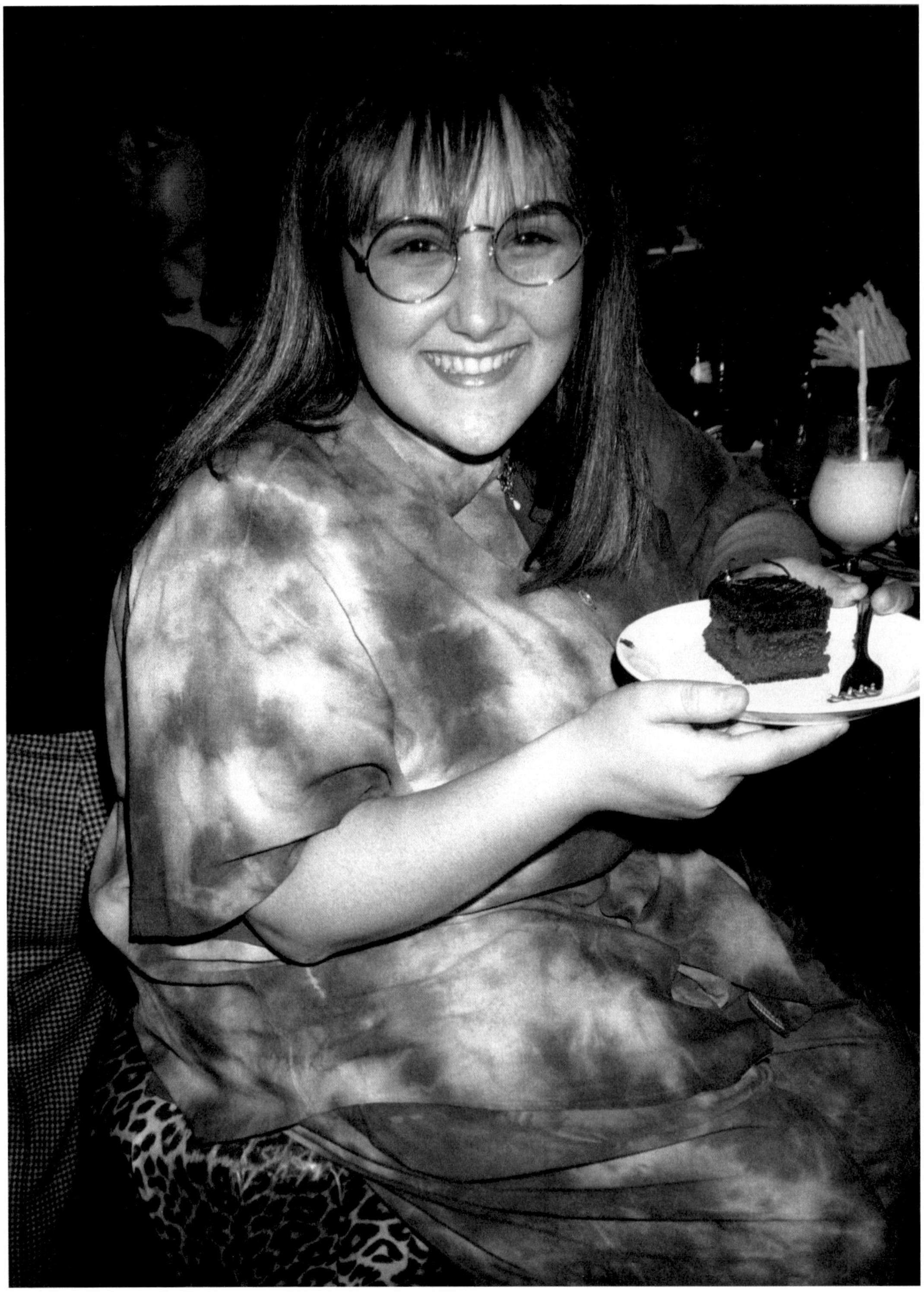

Ricki Lake
at Michael Musto's birthday party.
December 7, 1987

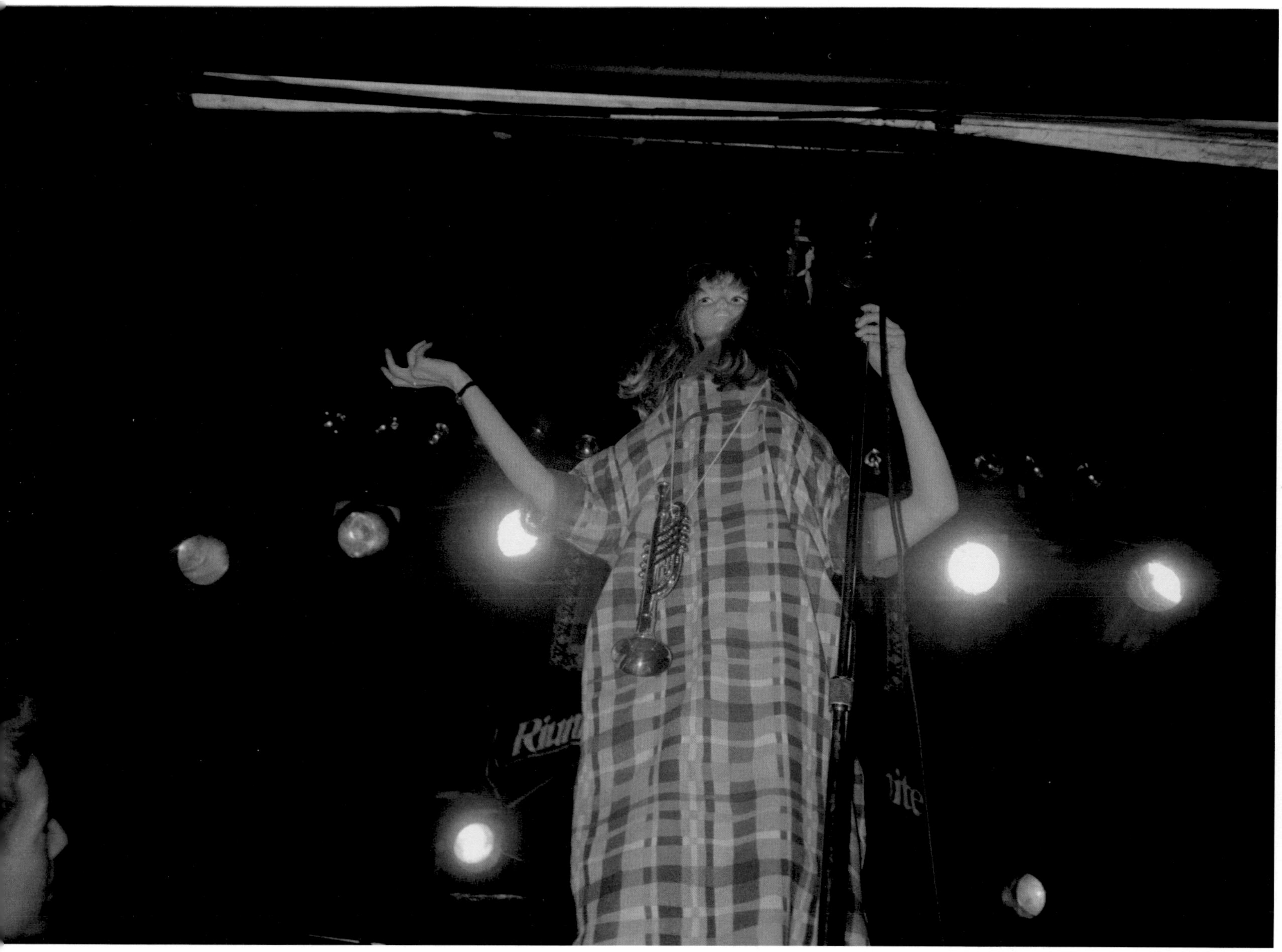

Frieda
at the "No Entiendes" party at Danceteria.
May 11, 1986

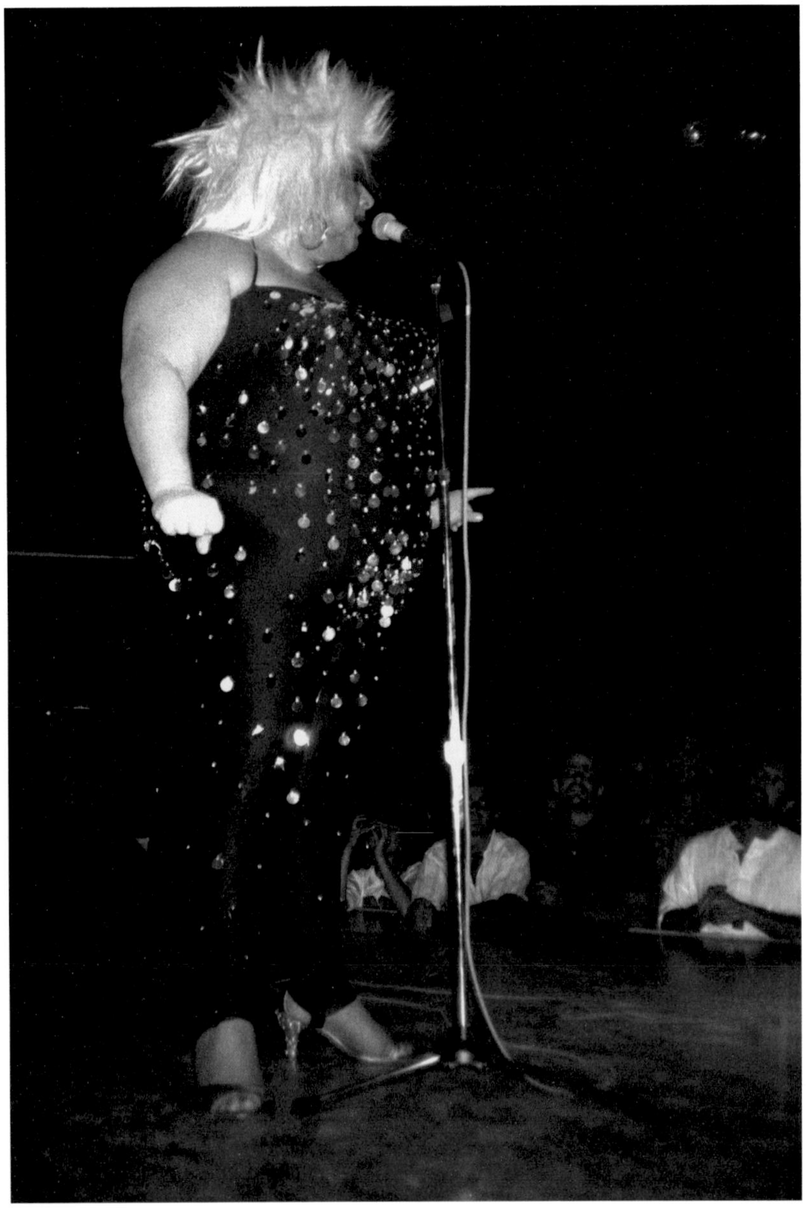

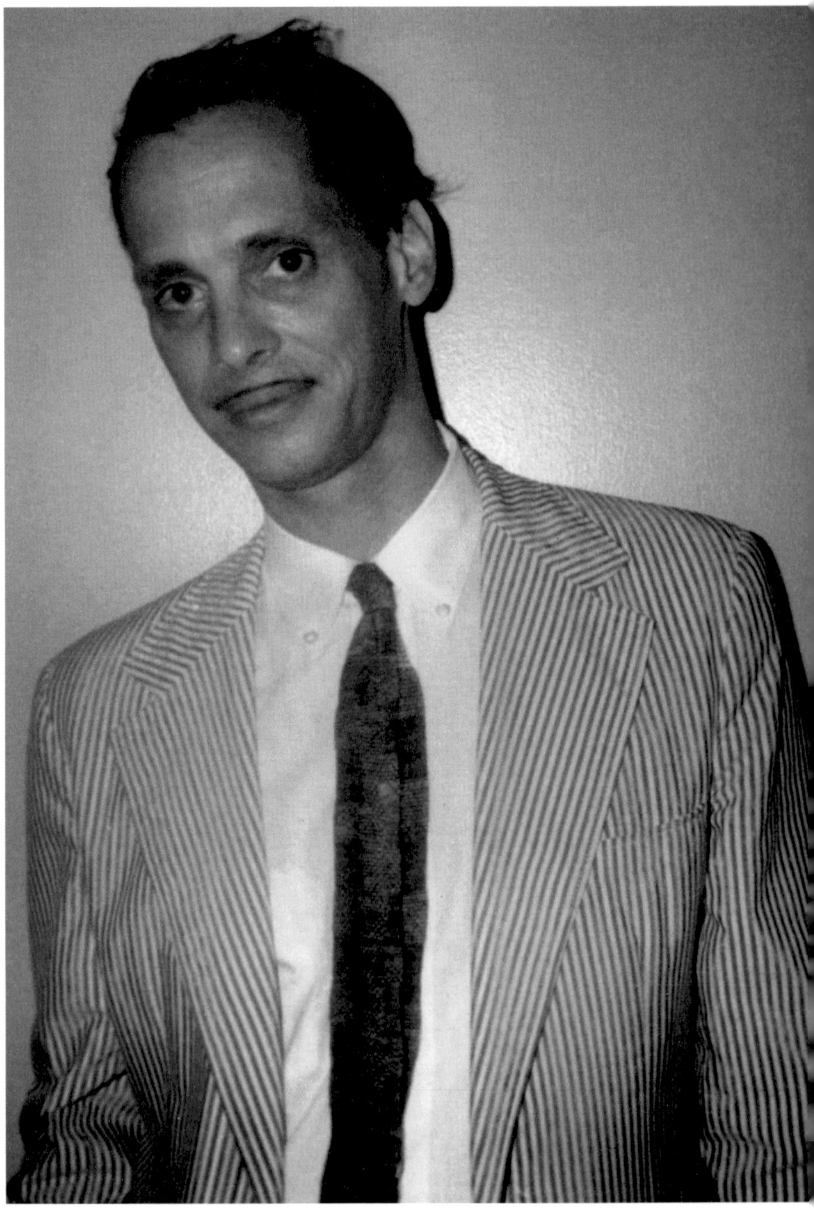

Top Left: Divine performing at 1018.
Thursday, August 27, 1987
Top Right: John Waters at the Fellini Party at Area.
June 10, 1985

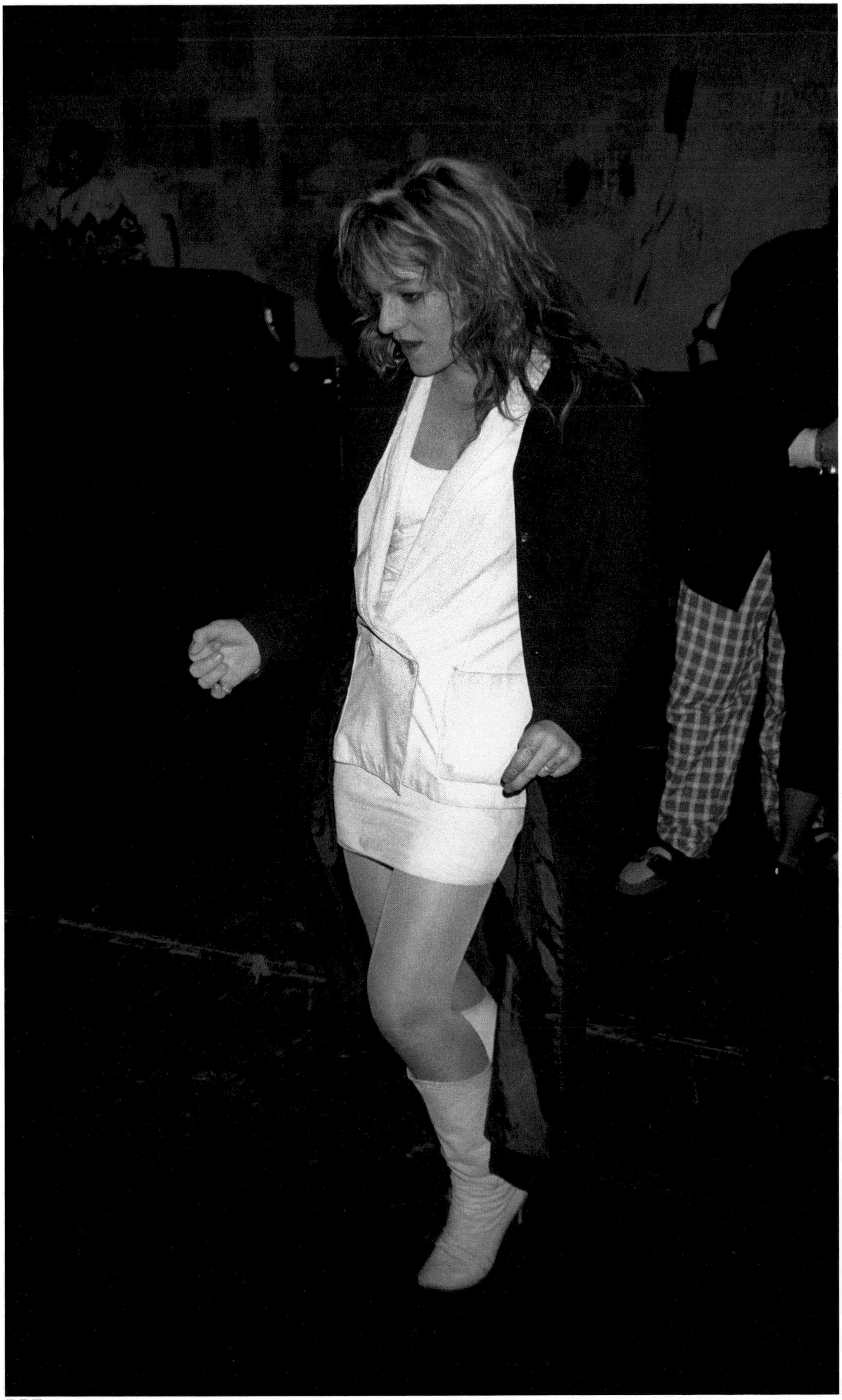

Cookie Mueller
at the Palladium.
April 10, 1987

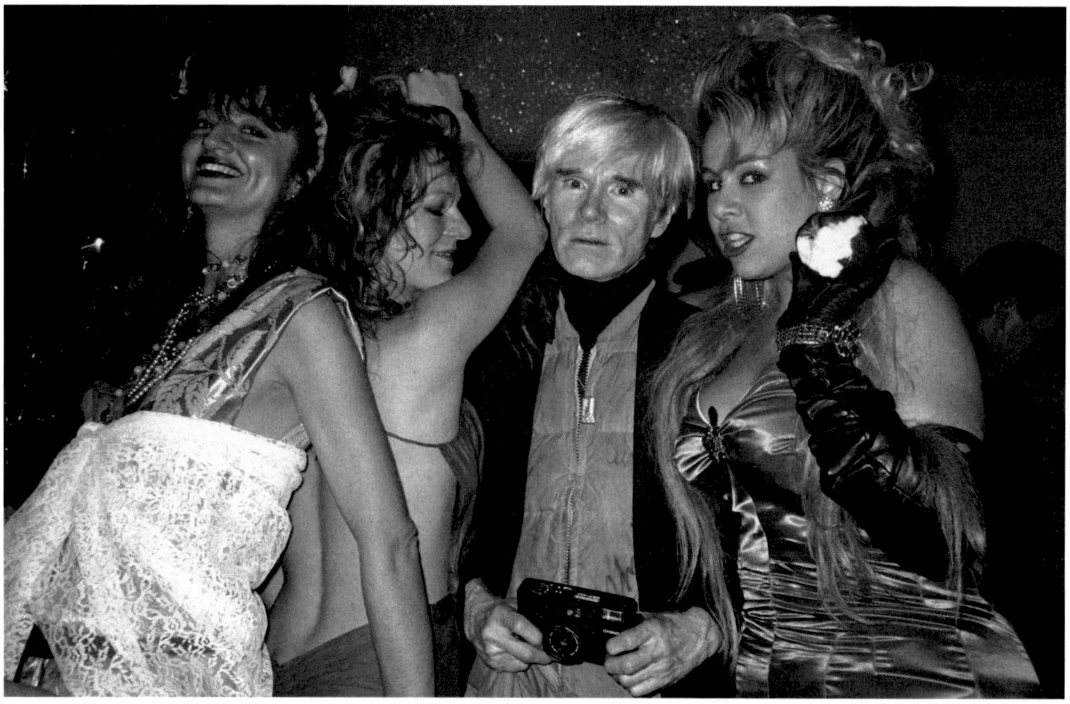

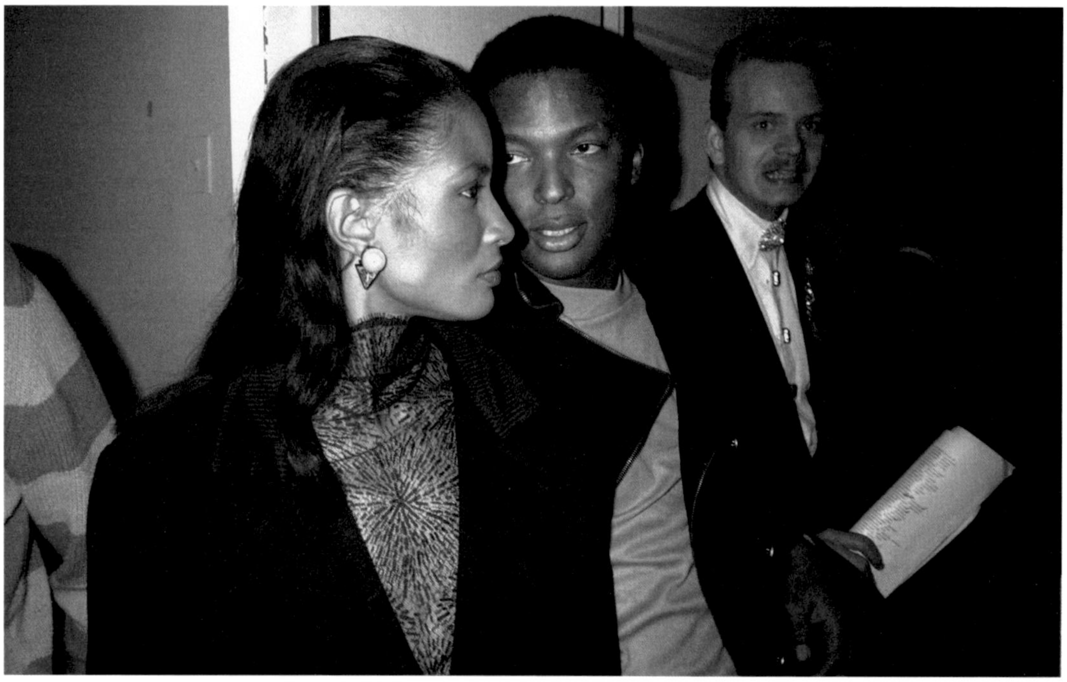

TOP: CARMILLE JOHNSON, COOKIE MUELLER, ANDY WARHOL, AND DIANNE BRILL
AT DIANNE BRILL'S BIRTHDAY PARTY AT DANCETERIA. APRIL 5, 1984
BOTTOM: BEVERLY JOHNSON AND CHRIS JONES AT MARISA BERENSON'S
DRESSING UP BOOK PARTY AT LIMELIGHT. NOVEMBER 19, 1984
RIGHT: CHARLES PIERCE AS BETTE DAVIS' CHARACTER MARGO CHANNING
FROM THE FILM ALL ABOUT EVE AT LIMELIGHT.
SUNDAY, MAY 20,1984

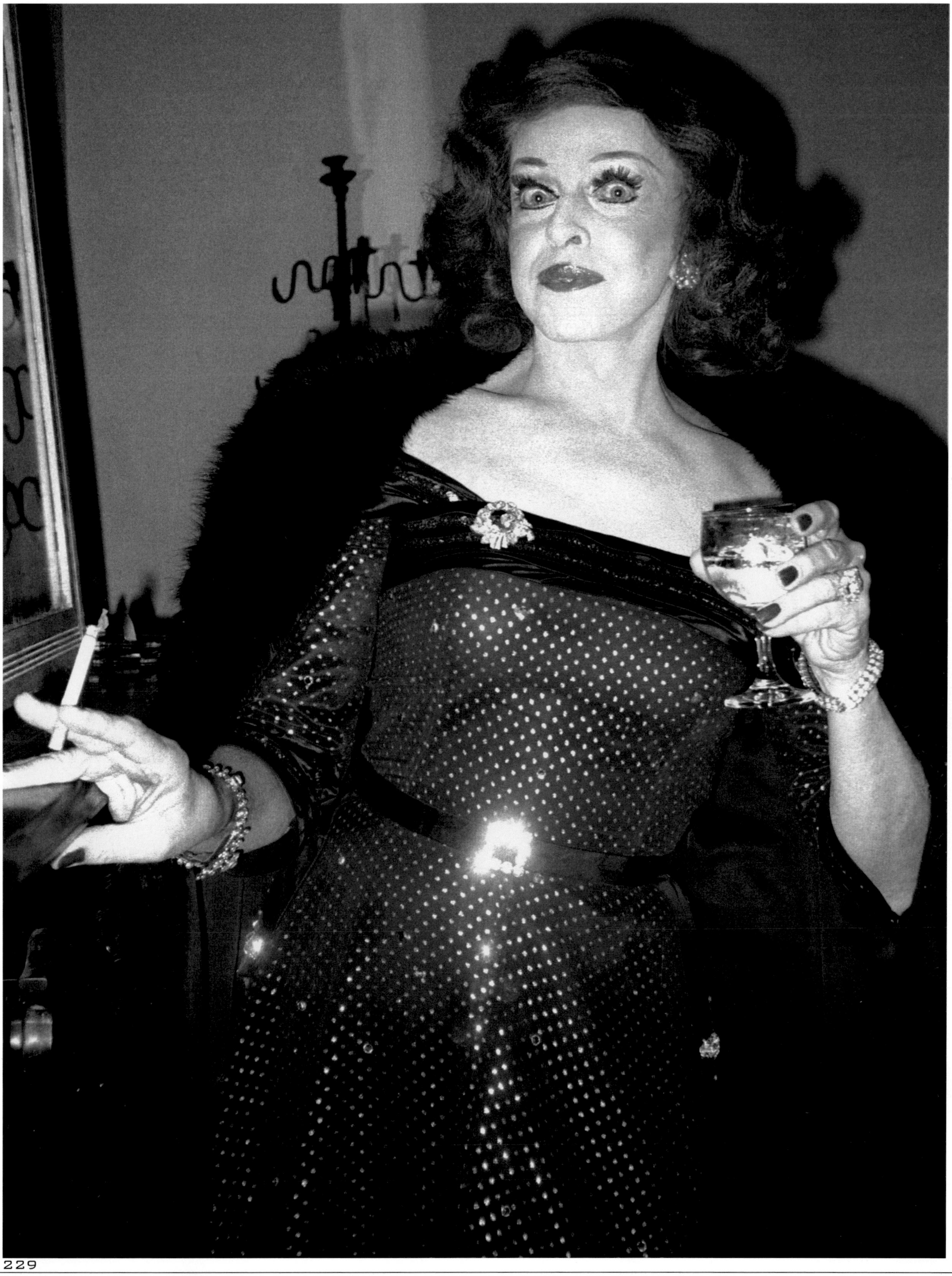

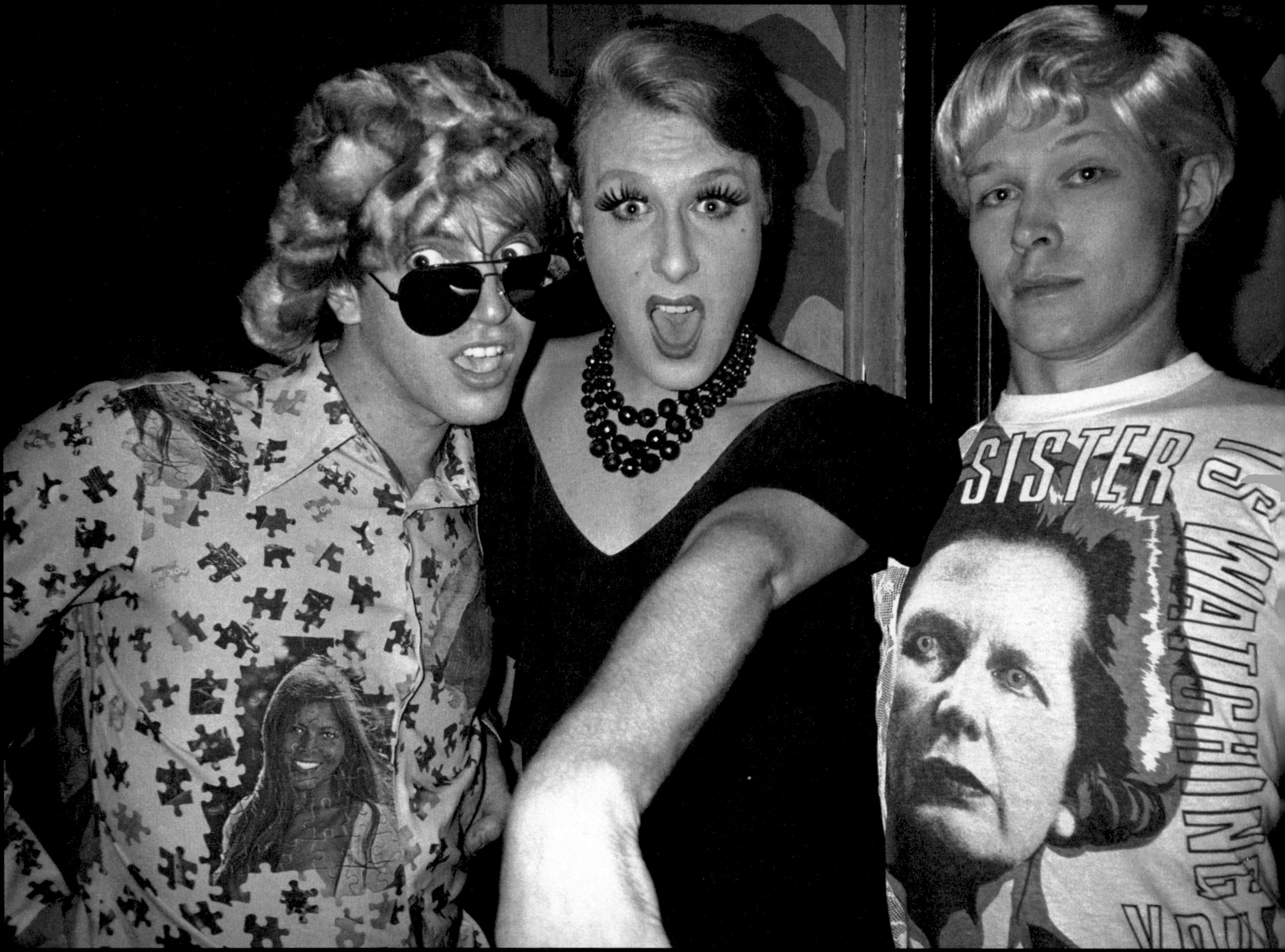

David Ilku, Lady Bunny, and Clark Render
at the benefit party for Martin Burgoyne at the Pyramid Club.
September 4, 1986

It was the best of times.
It was the worst of times.
The 80s nostalgia today reminds me of the 60s nostalgia in the 80s. Patrick was always there to let all of us exhibitionists have an audience. I never felt like he was documenting us, he was just part of the fun!"
Kenny Scharf
Los Angeles, 2003

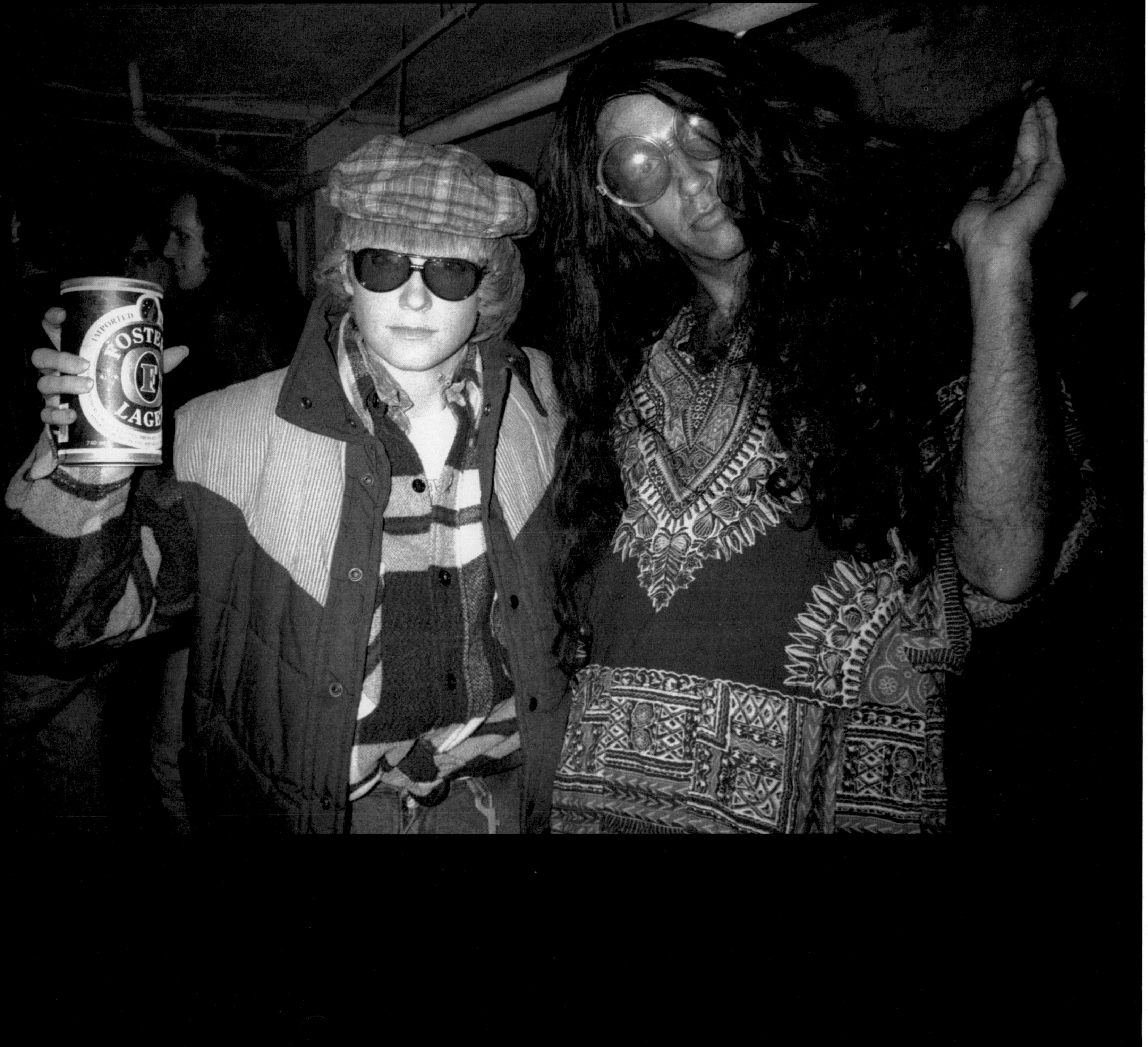

Ann Magnuson and Kenny Scharf in costume
at the benefit party for Martin Burgoyne at the Pyramid Club.
September 4, 1986

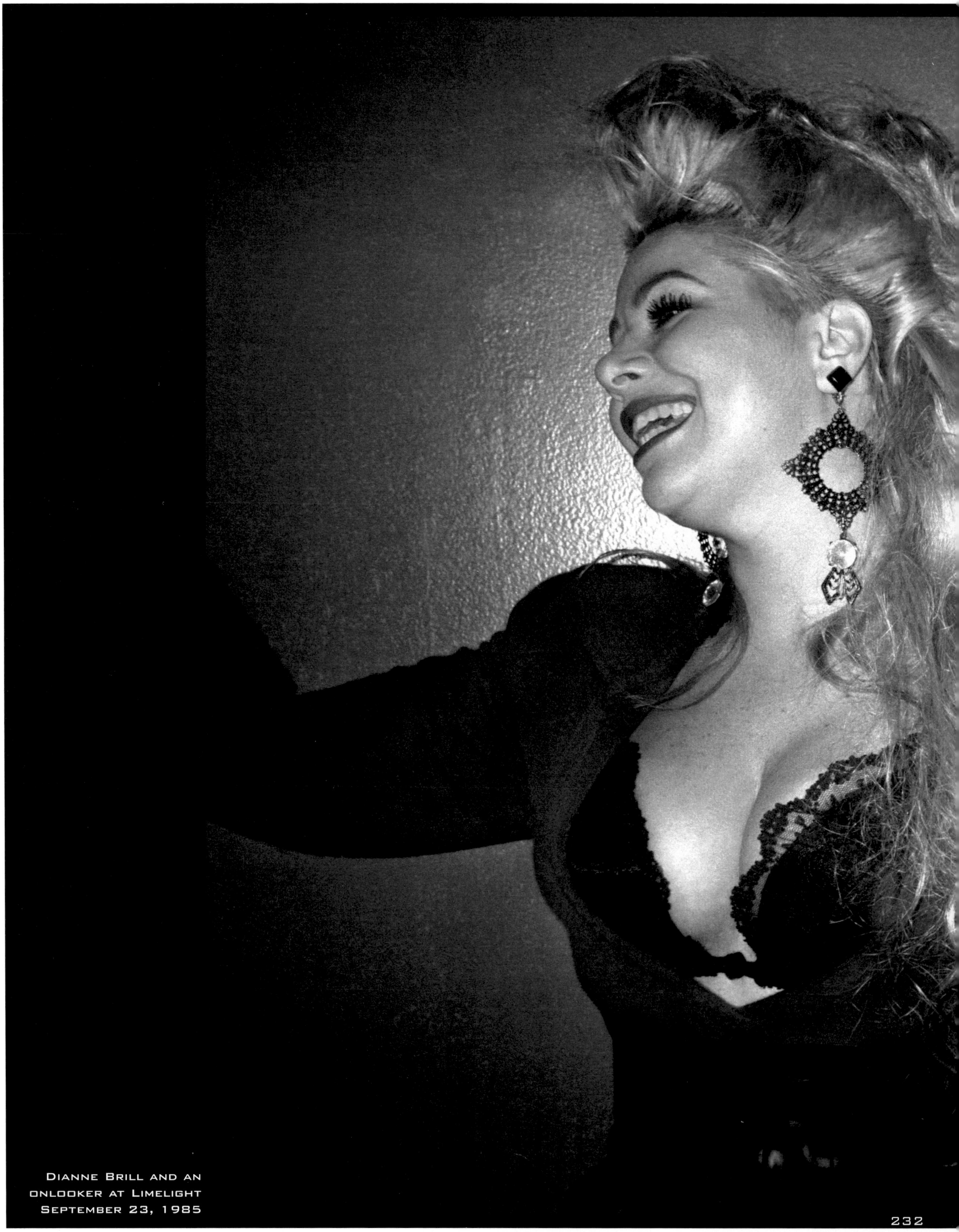

Dianne Brill and an
onlooker at Limelight
September 23, 1985

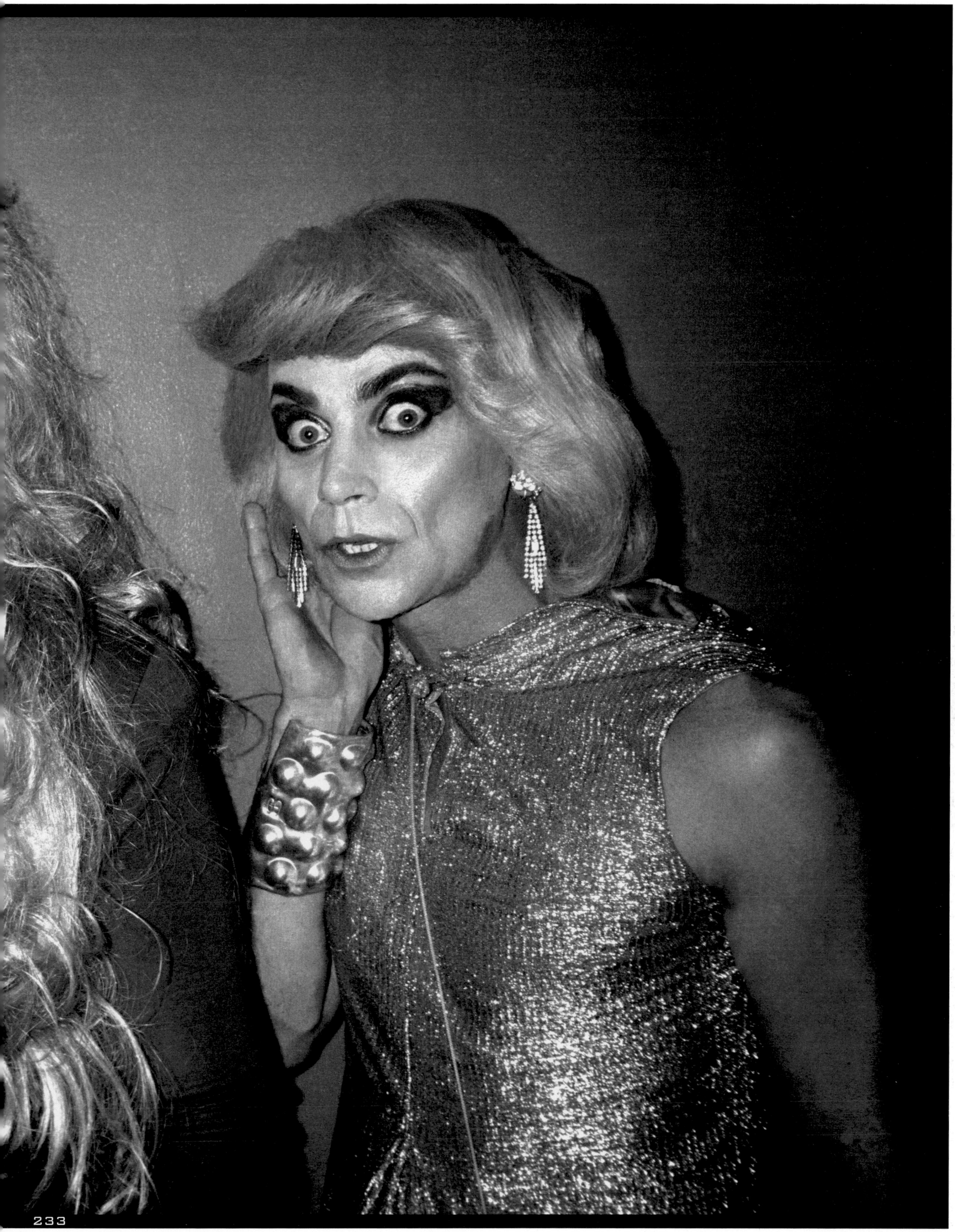

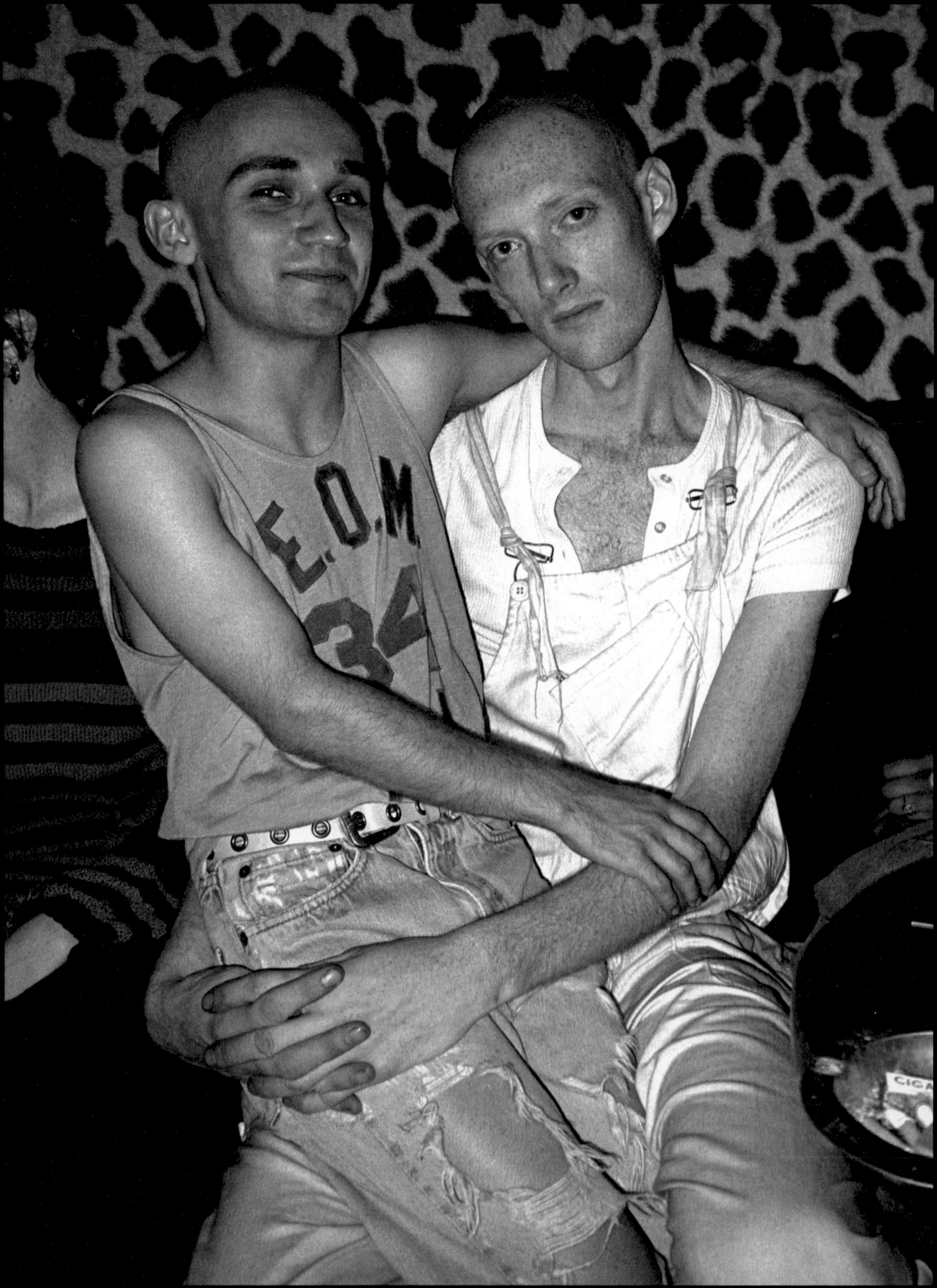

David Yarritu and Dean Johnson
at the Pyramid Club.
June 1984

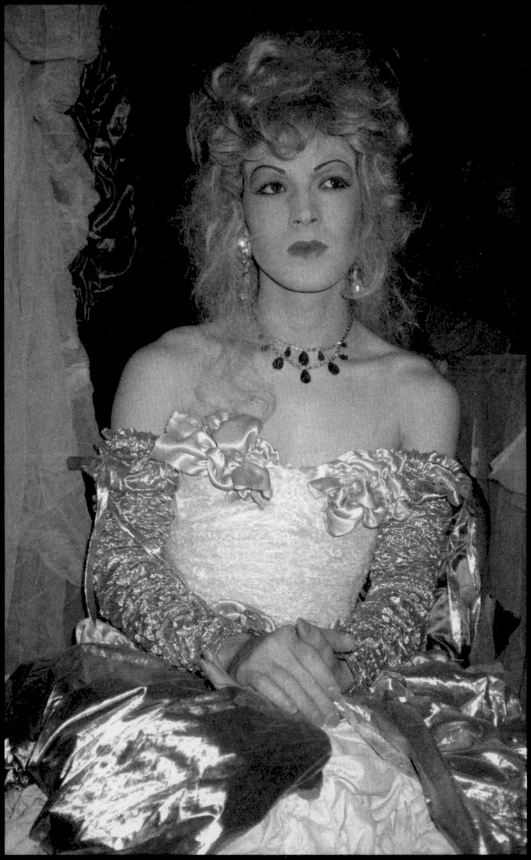
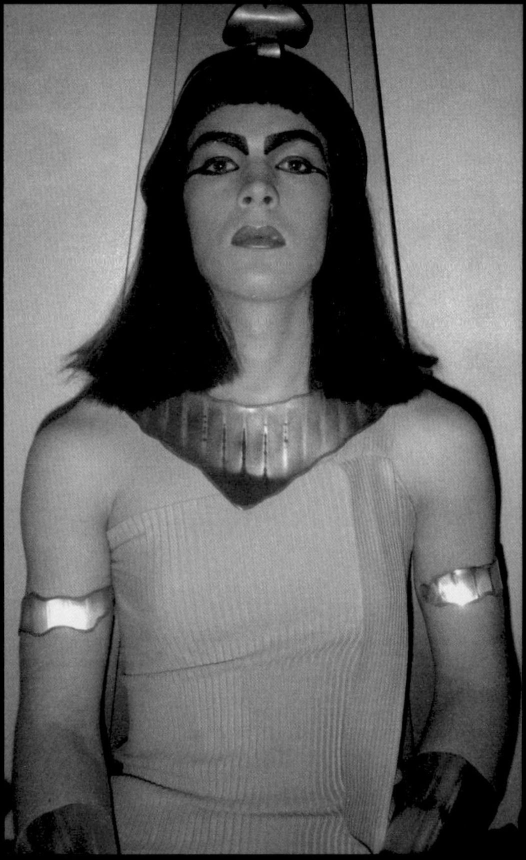
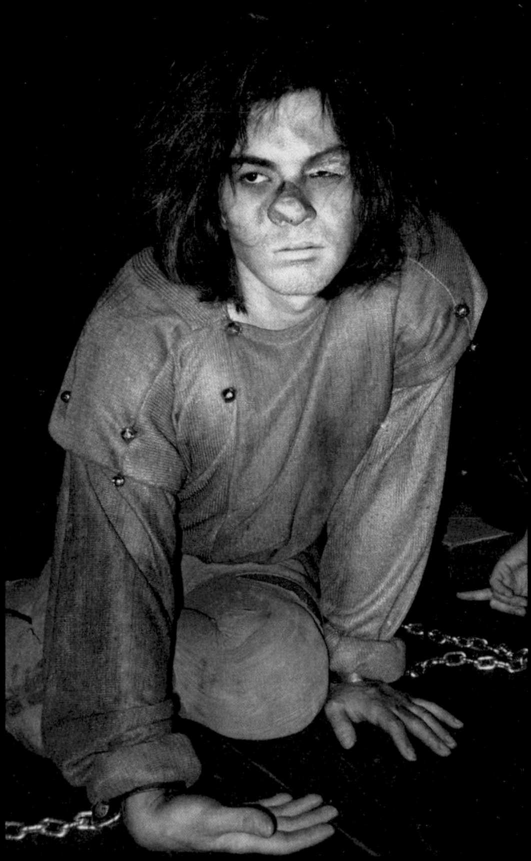
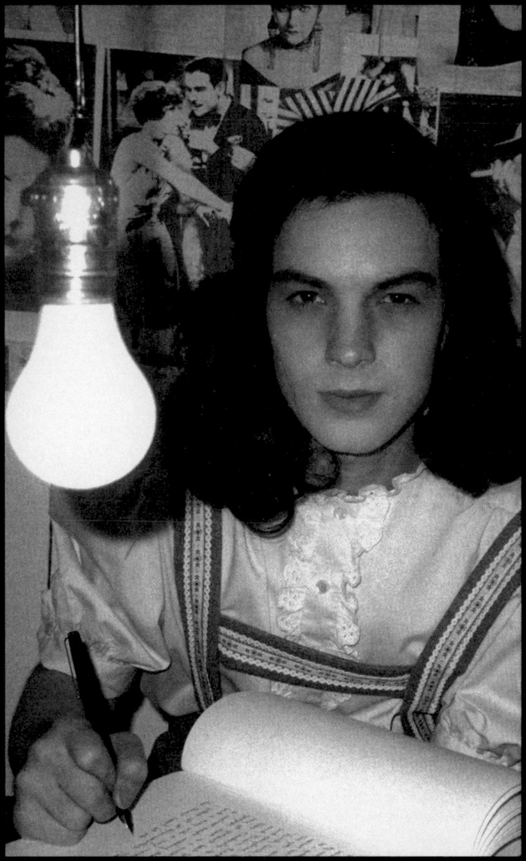

Top Left: Bernard Zette at Area. January 9, 1986
Top Right: Bernard Zette as Cleopatra
at the Details magazine party at Area. Early November 1984
Bottom Left: Bernard Zette as the Hunchback of Notre Dame
at the Boy Crazy book party at Area. May 11, 1984
Bottom Right: Bernard Zette as Anne Frank at Area. May 17, 1984

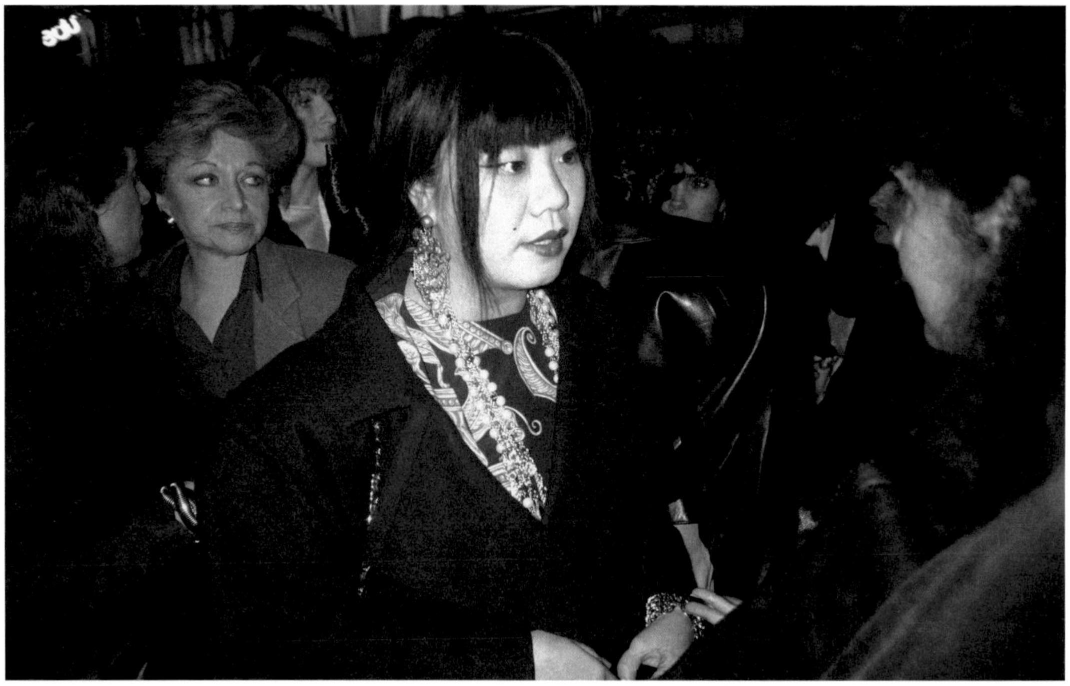

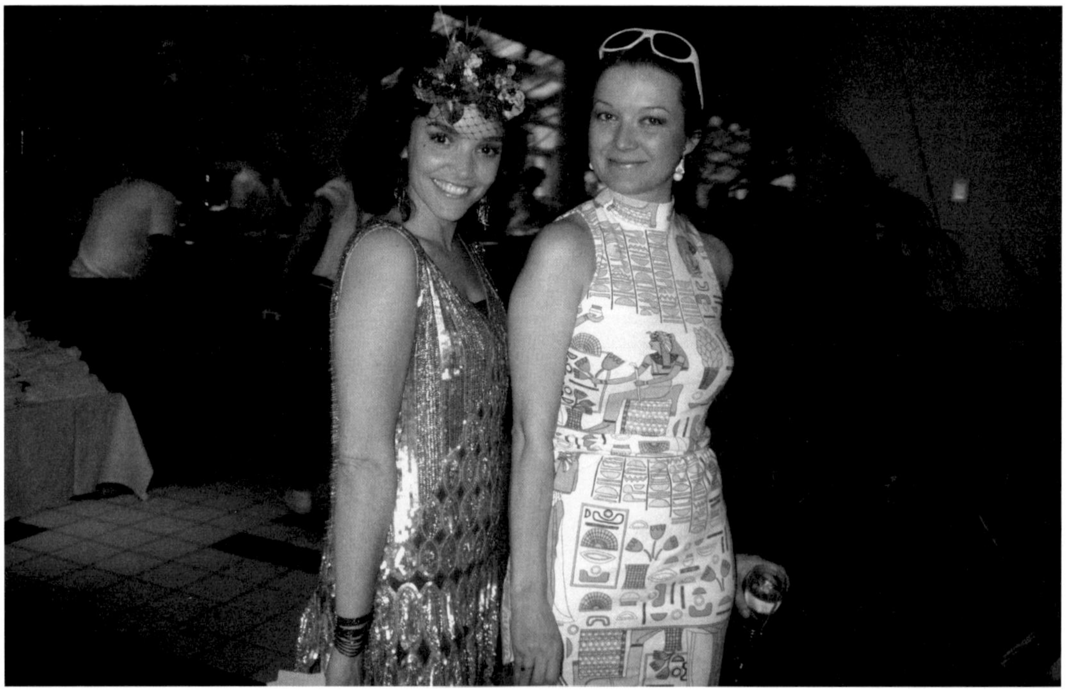

"The 80s were ecstatic, exhausting, and embarrassing."
Isaac Mizrahi

Top: Anna Sui talking with Annie Flanders at the opening of Le Chateau.
Wednesday, March 5, 1986
Bottom: Brooke Adams and Patti Astor
at the Green Plays Party at the Liberty Cafe in the South Street Seaport.
May 18, 1986
Right: Marc Jacobs and models
at the Francesco Scavullo benefit fashion show at the Ballroom.
Monday, June 3, 1985

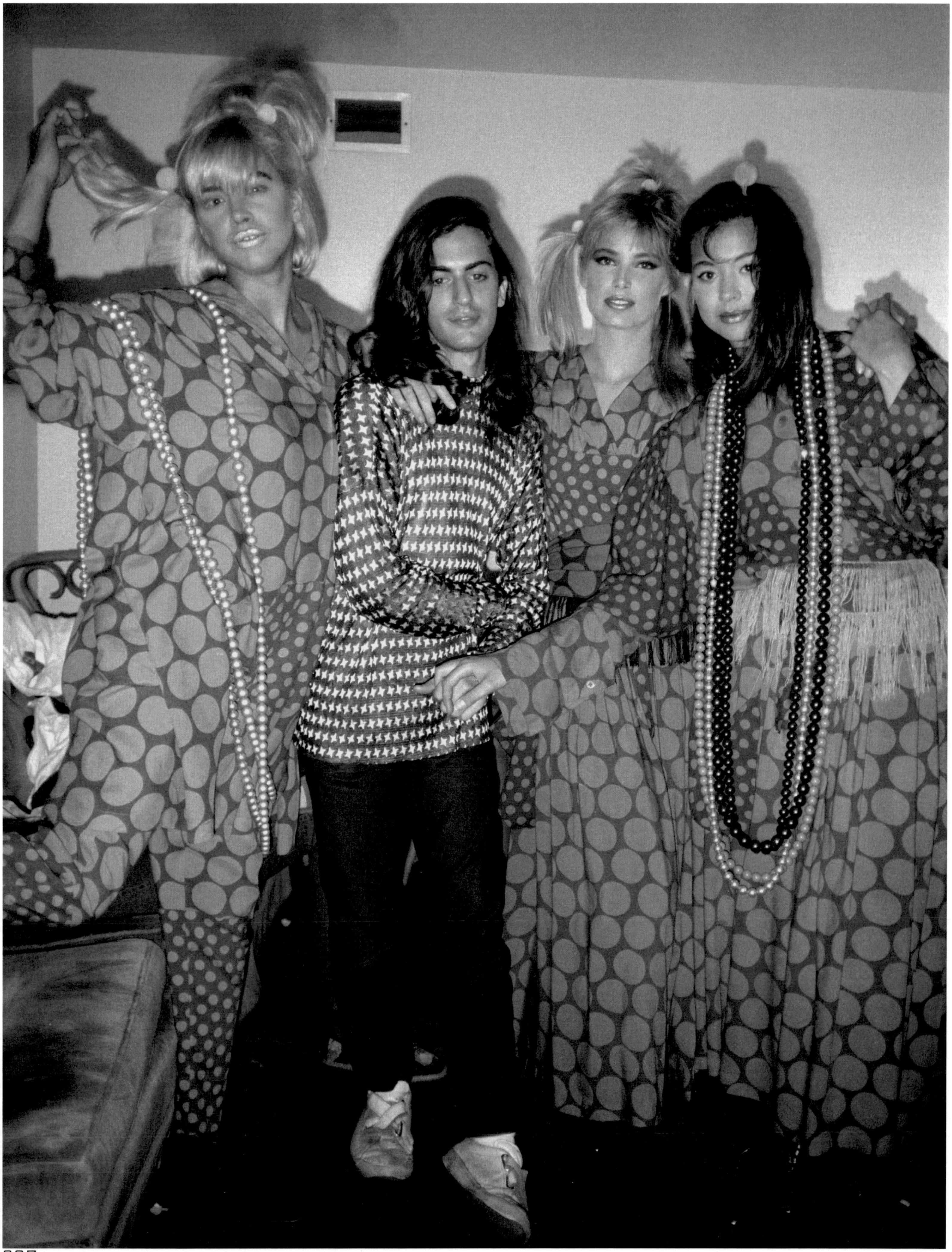

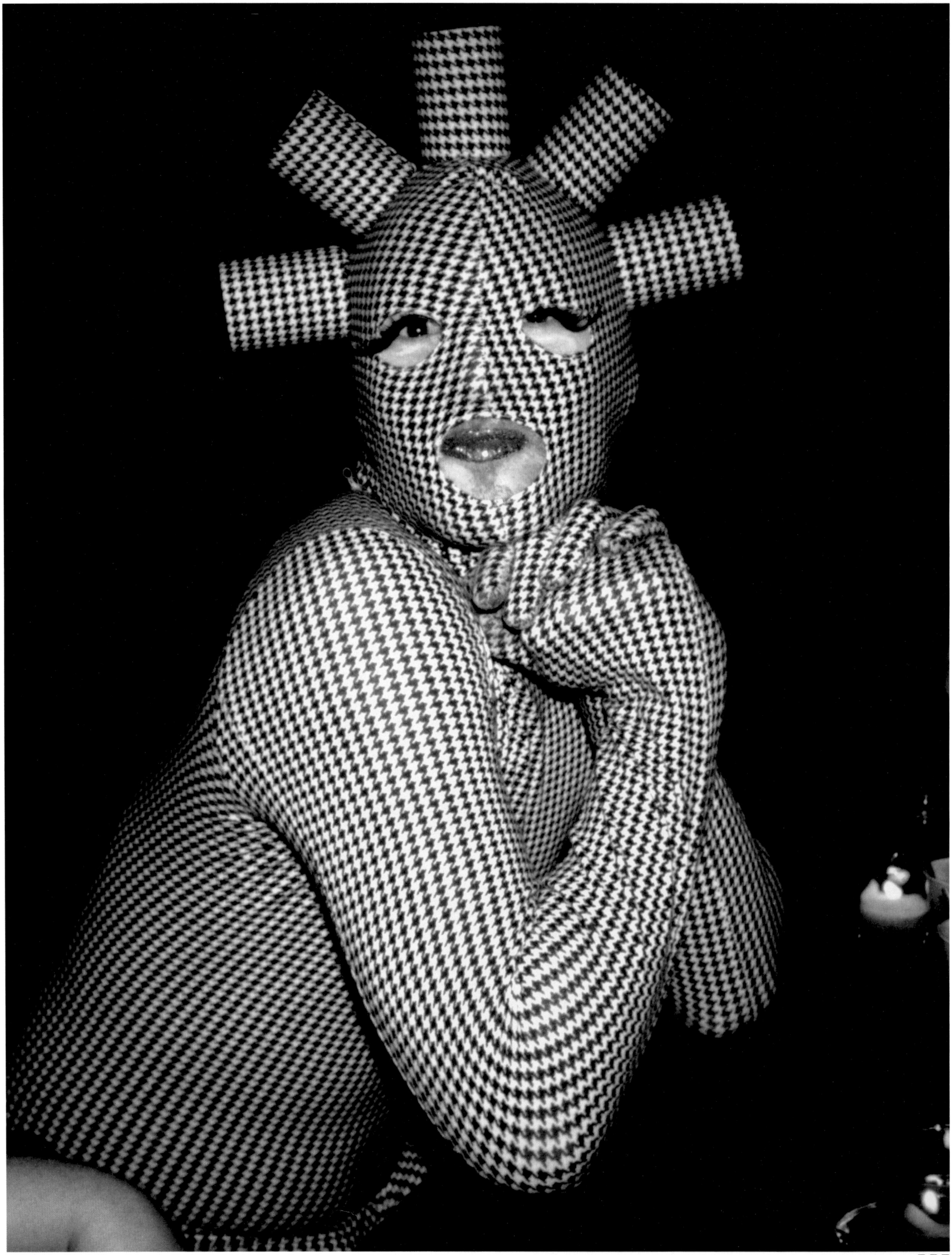

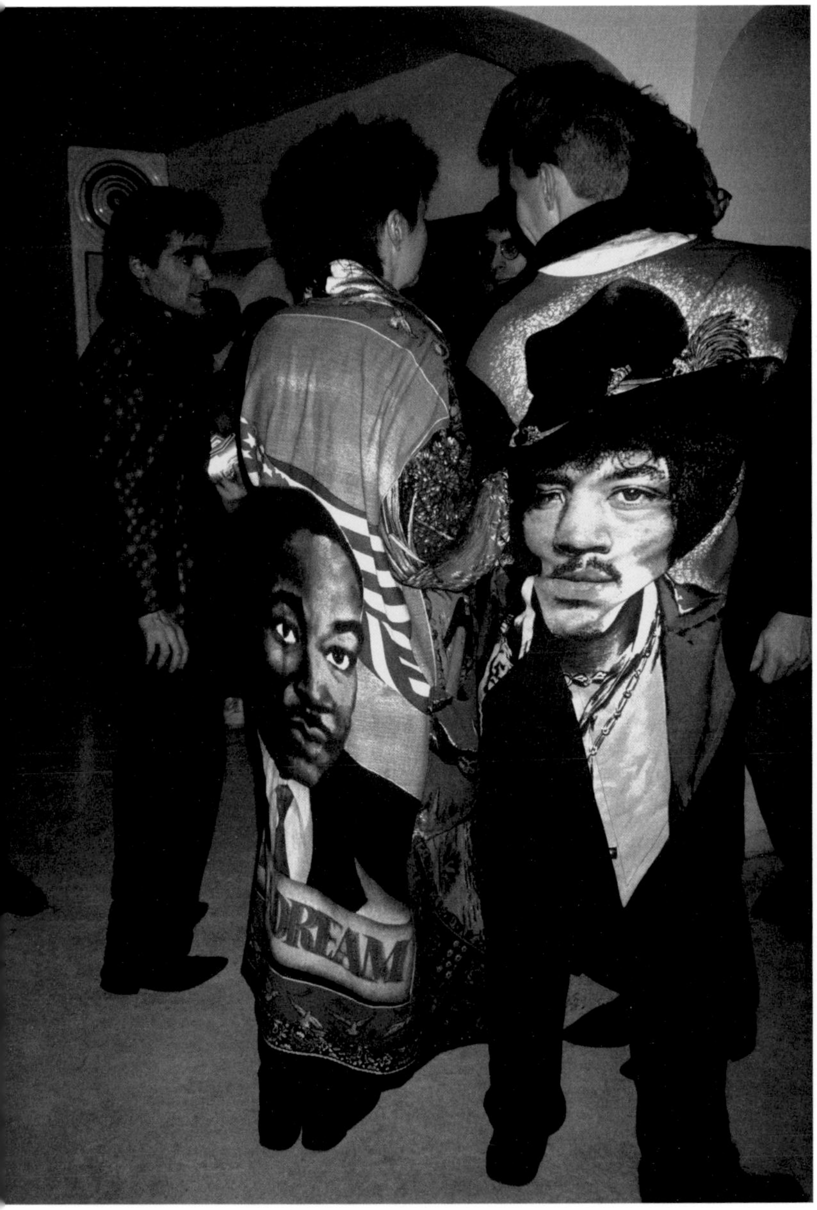

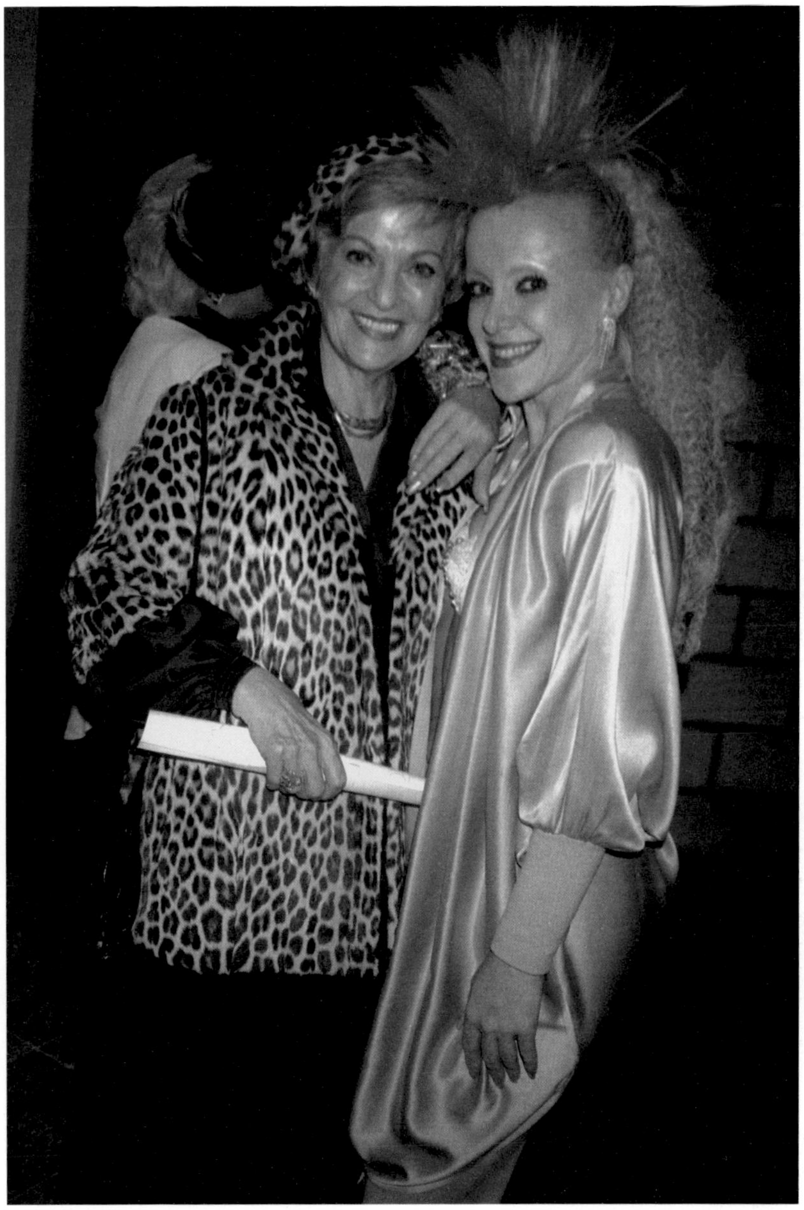

"No matter where I went or what I was doing in the 1980s Patrick McMullan was there, taking pictures. If I was playing in Washington Square Park with my girls on a Sunday afternoon Patrick would pop up and snap us. If we were having dinner at Texarkana, Patrick would be there too. Of course I expected to see him at each and every art opening and benefit, but it was the out of the way or boring events where he turned up that his fun loving enthusiasm helped ease the pain and with a flash, made me feel like a star."
Shelly Dunn Fremont

Left: James St. James as Leigh Bowery. 1985/86
Top Left: Martin Luther King and Jimi Hendrix coats brought together by Patrick at the Milk Bar. November 1985
Top Right: Baroness Sherry von Koerber-Bernstein and High Voltage at the 1018 Opening. Thursday, October 9, 1986

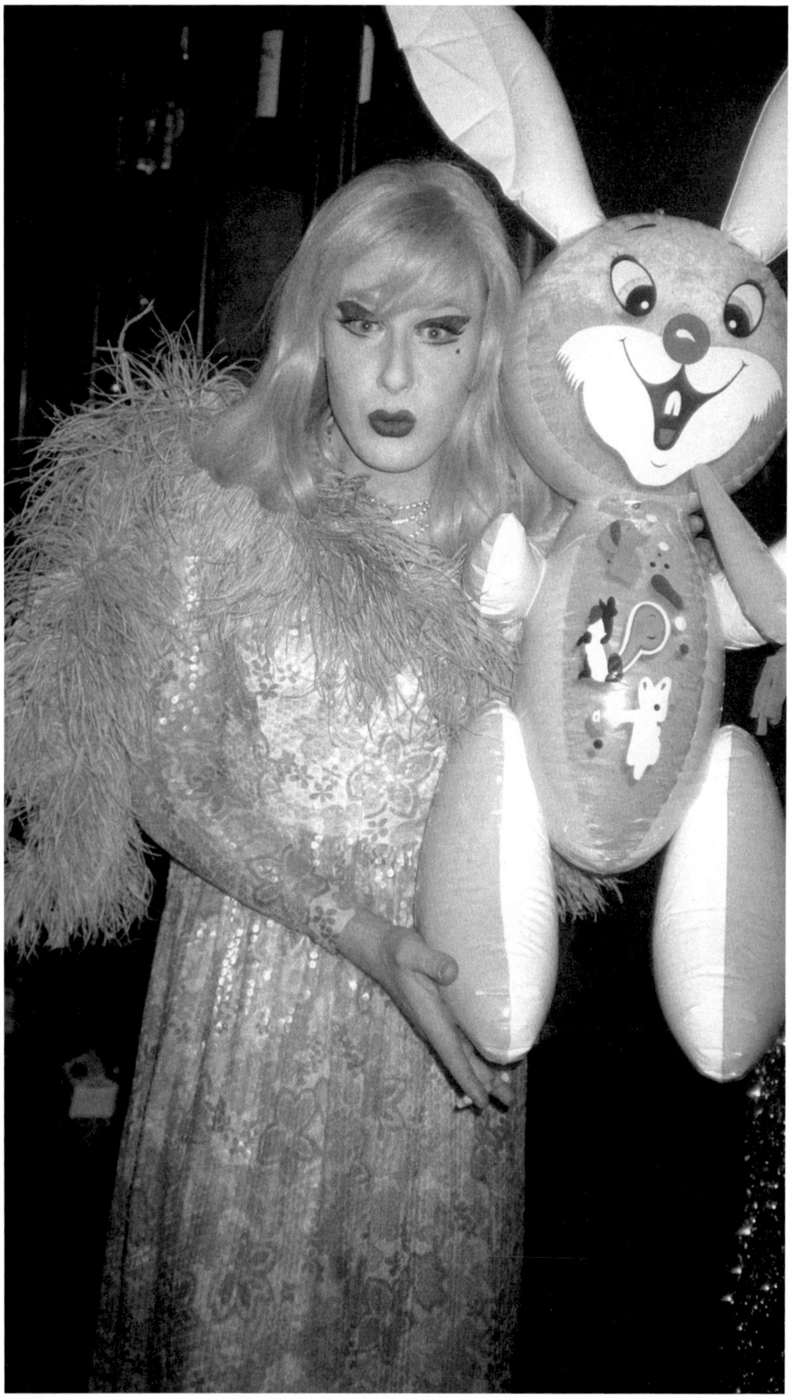

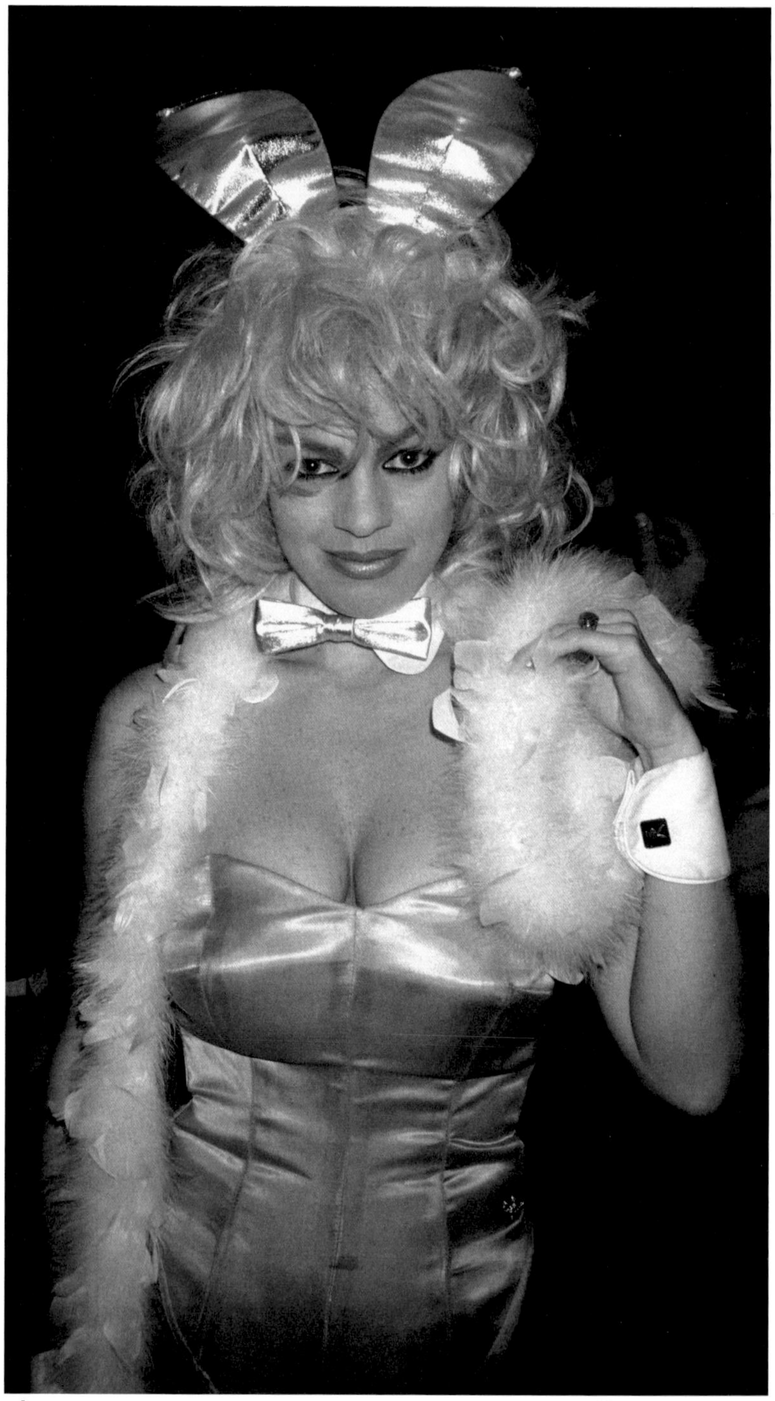

"The 80s were pretty messy on the club scene and I can't recall too much of it personally, so I'm grateful that Patrick's vibrant photos are around to document what was (I think) a very exciting time in NYC."
Lady Bunny, Drag Diva Extraordinaire

Top Left: Lady Bunny at Area.
January 9, 1986
Top right: Christina Downing
at Susanne Bartsch's party for Norman Parkinson at Area.
November 27, 1985

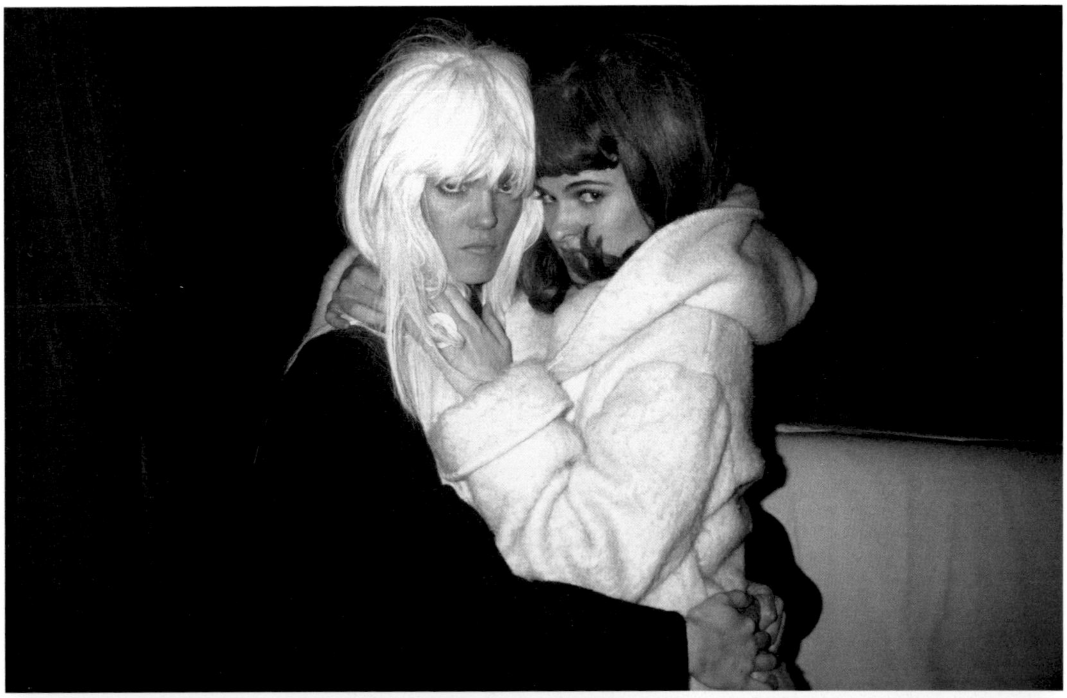

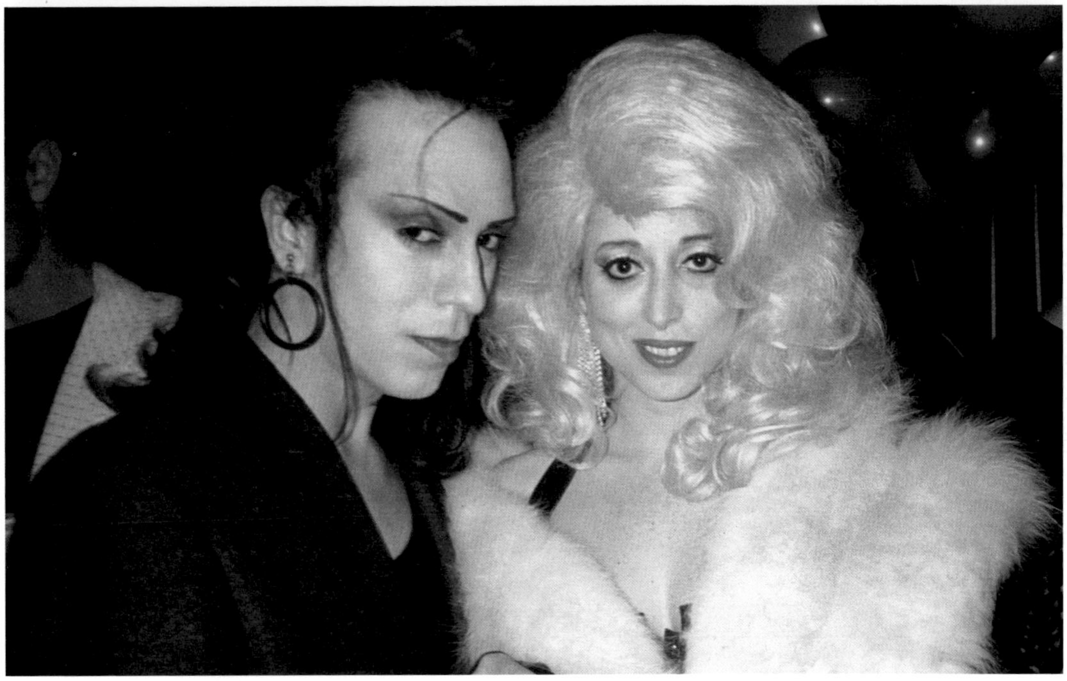

Top: Kate Harrington and Ellen Kinnally
at Grace Jones' party at the Palladium.
December 20, 1985
Bottom: Joey Arias and Katy K
at Pierce Brosnan's party at Limelight.
March 6, 1986

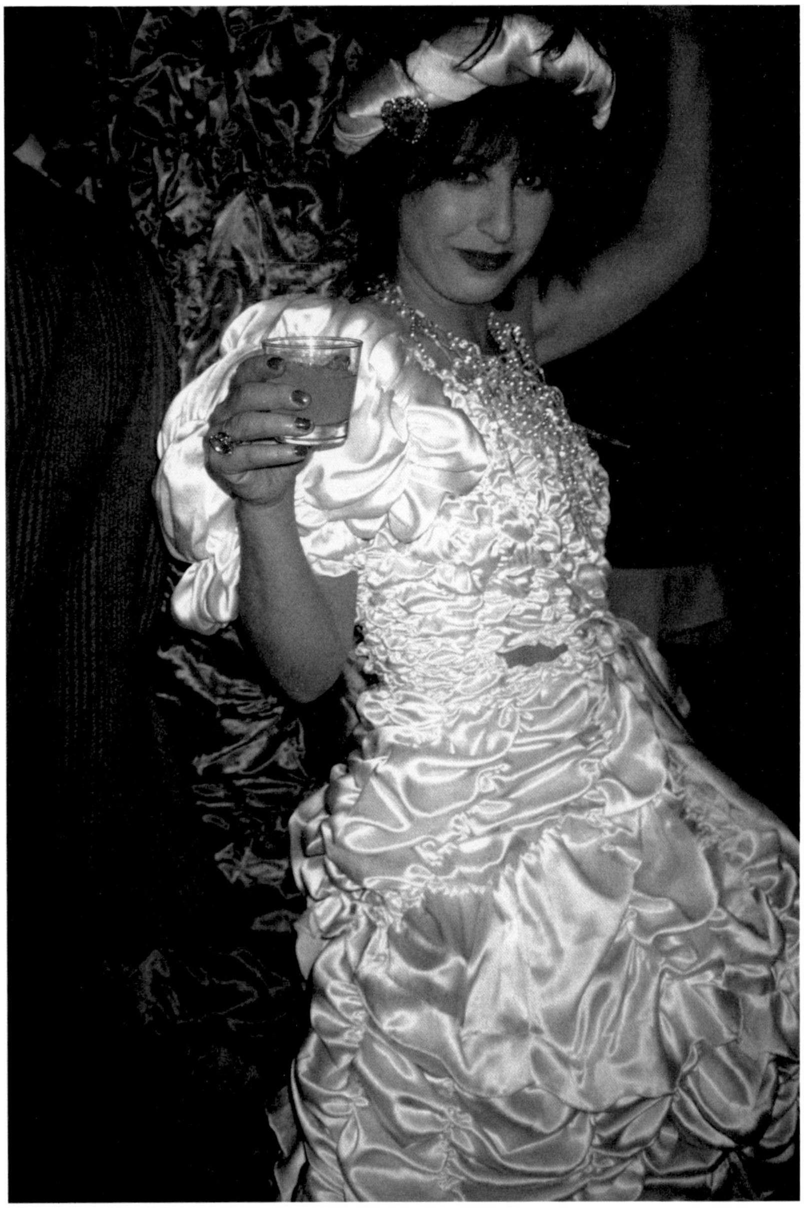

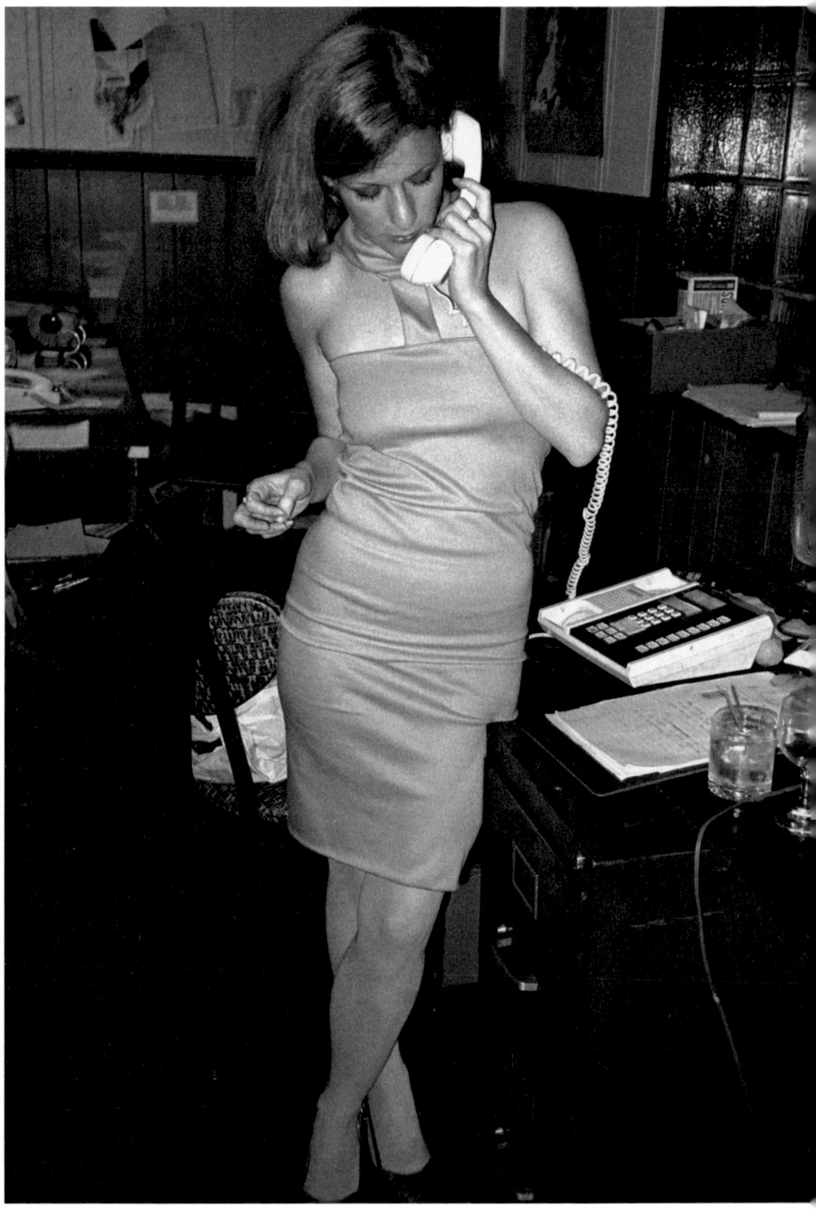

Top Left: Collette at Area. January 9, 1986
Top Right: Mavis (Bibi) Hume
at the Kamikaze office during the celebrity art show. 1984

"BIG HAIR, VINYL CLOTHES, AND TEFLON COATING UP YOUR NOSE." PERRI LISTER

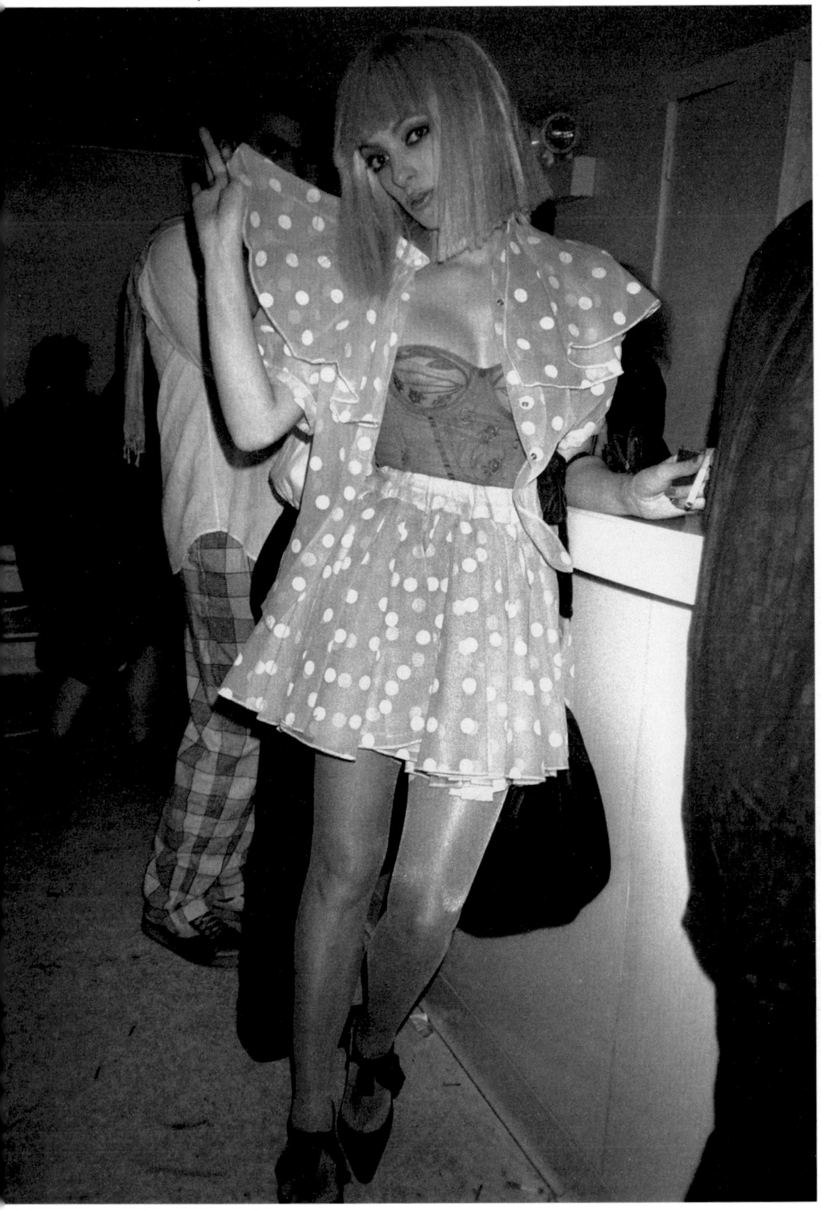

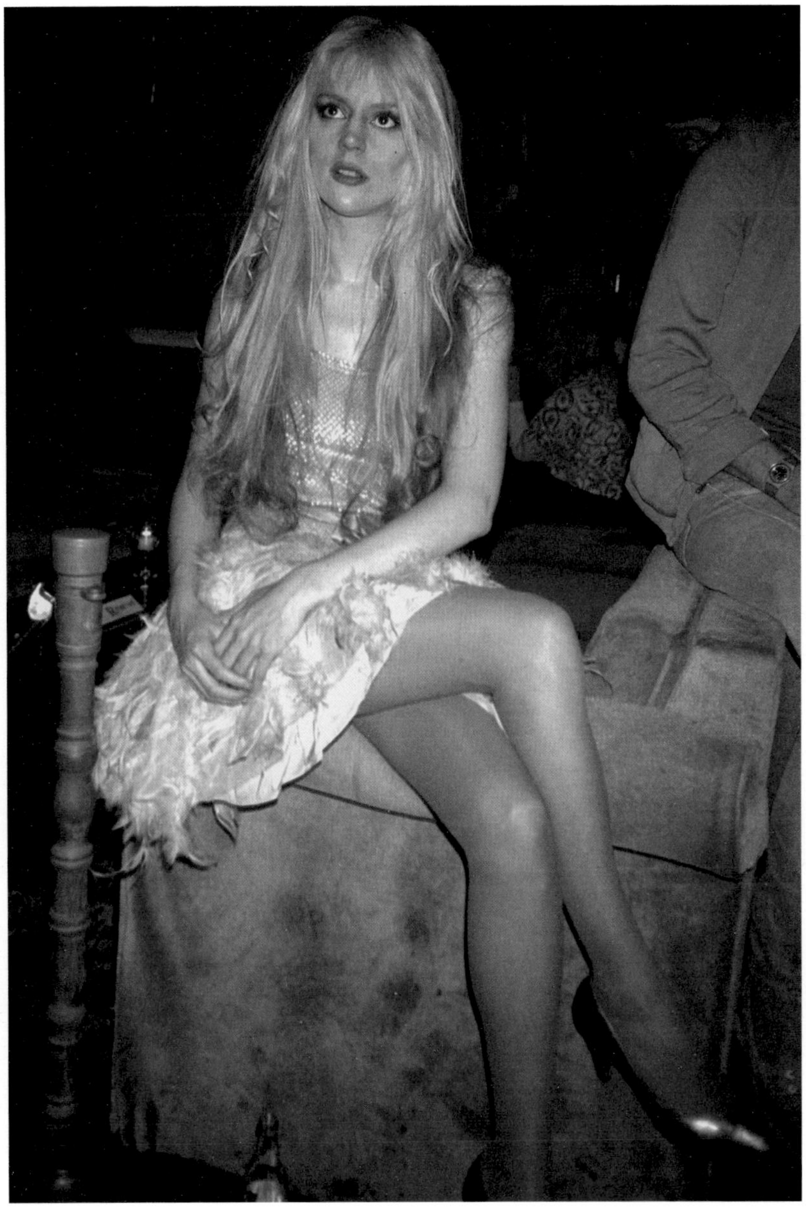

TOP LEFT: PERRI LISTER AT THE MILK BAR. NOVEMBER 1985
TOP RIGHT: PHOEBE LEGERE AT LIMELIGHT. NOVEMBER 1985

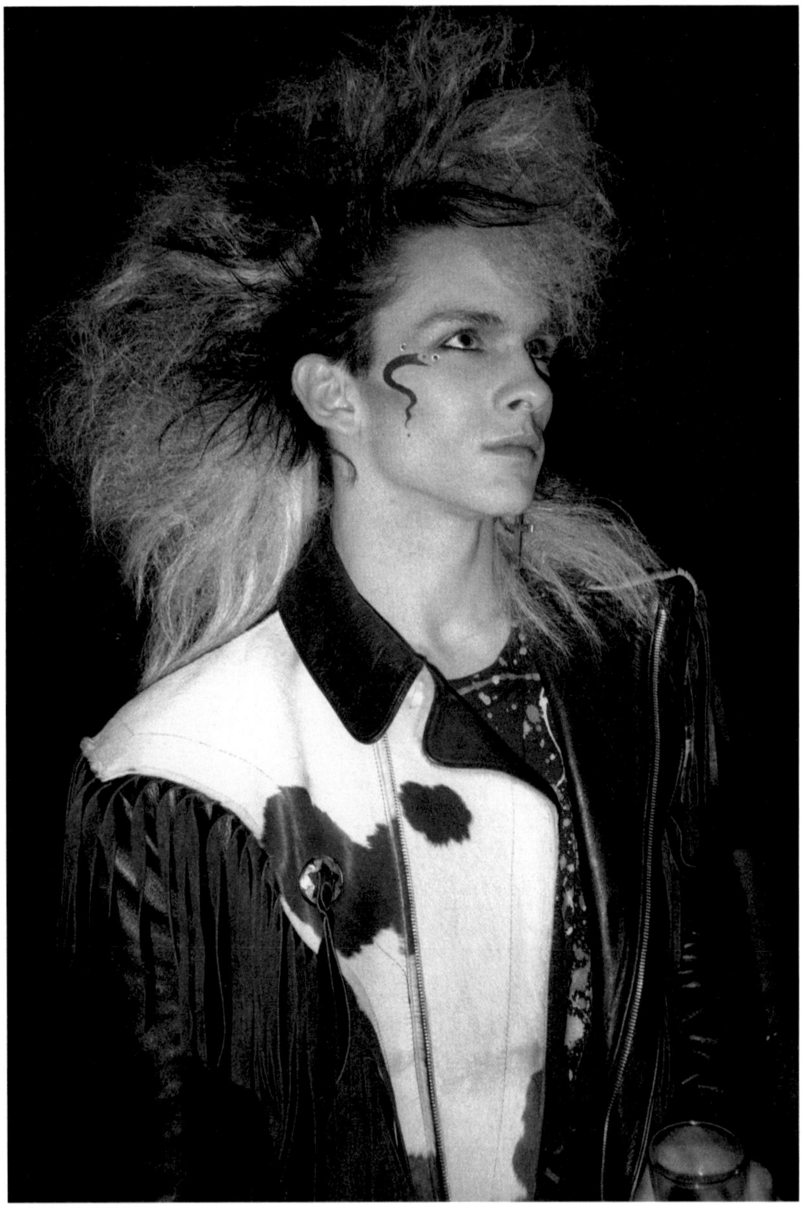

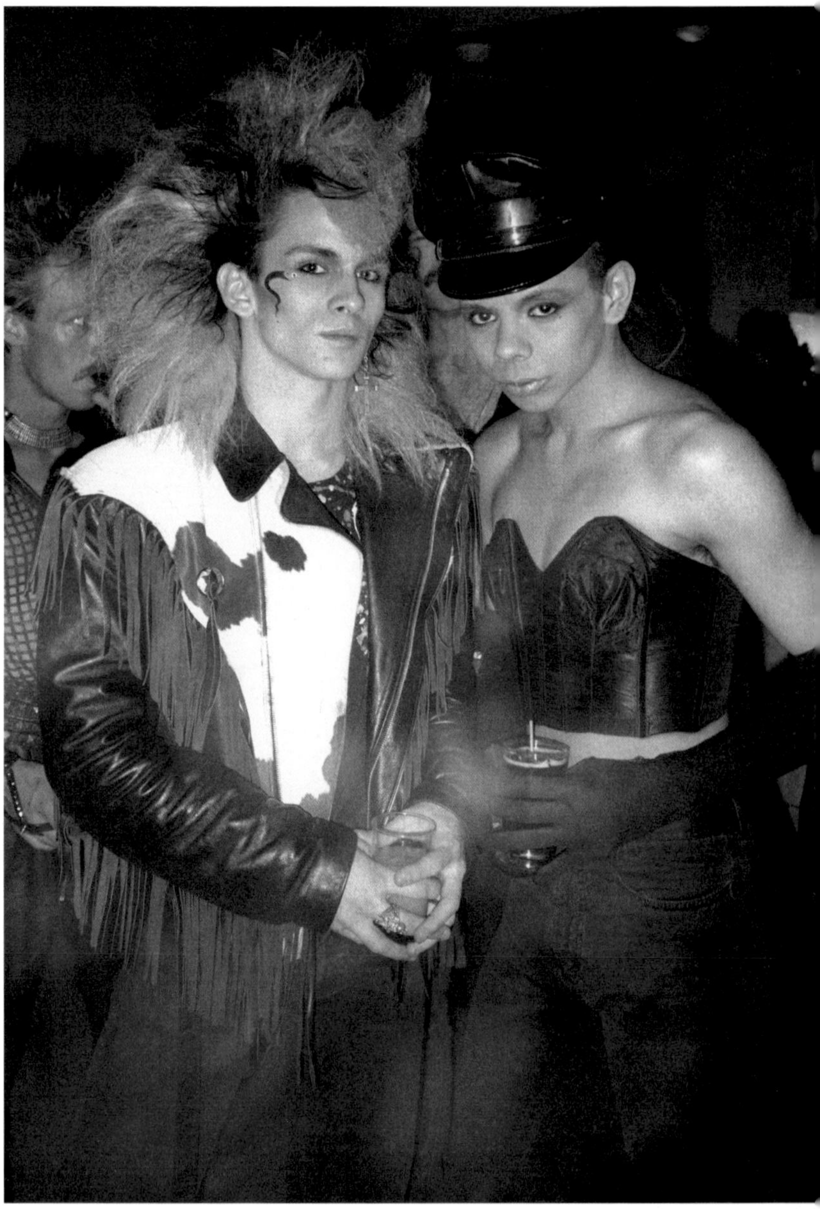

Top Left: Pat Di Giovanni at Area.
Top right: Pat Di Giovanni and Raven O at Area.
Saturday, May 4, 1985

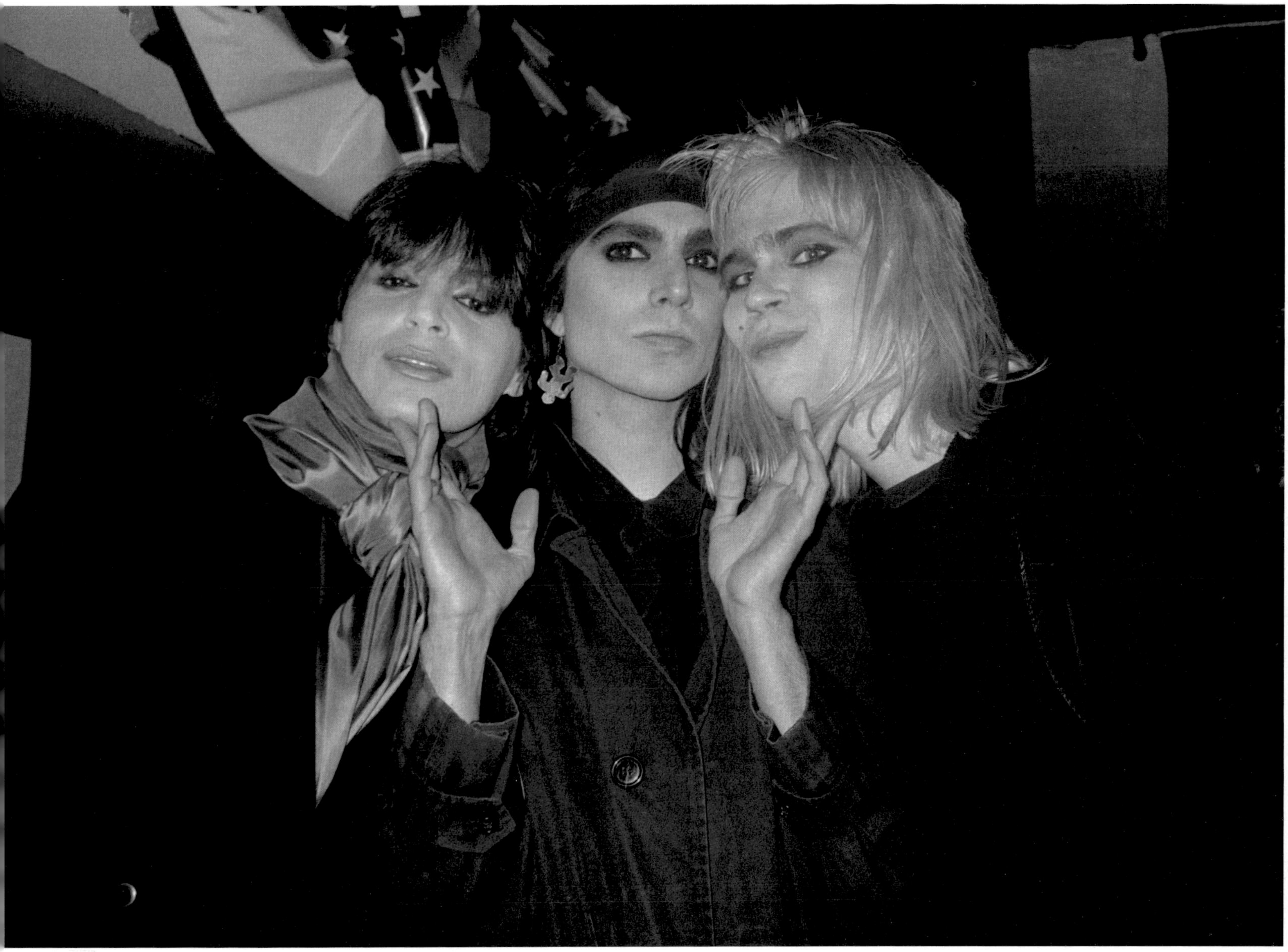

Way Bandy, Steven Meisel, and Jim Breese
at Dianne Brill's five year anniversary party for Rudolf at Danceteria.
February 1984

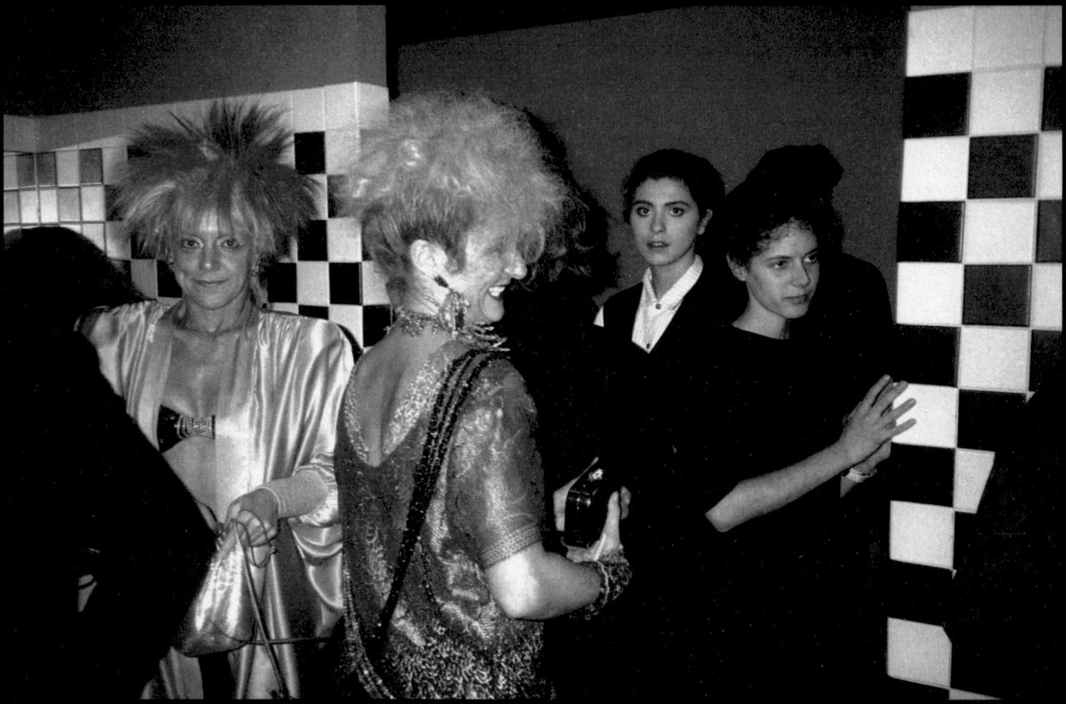

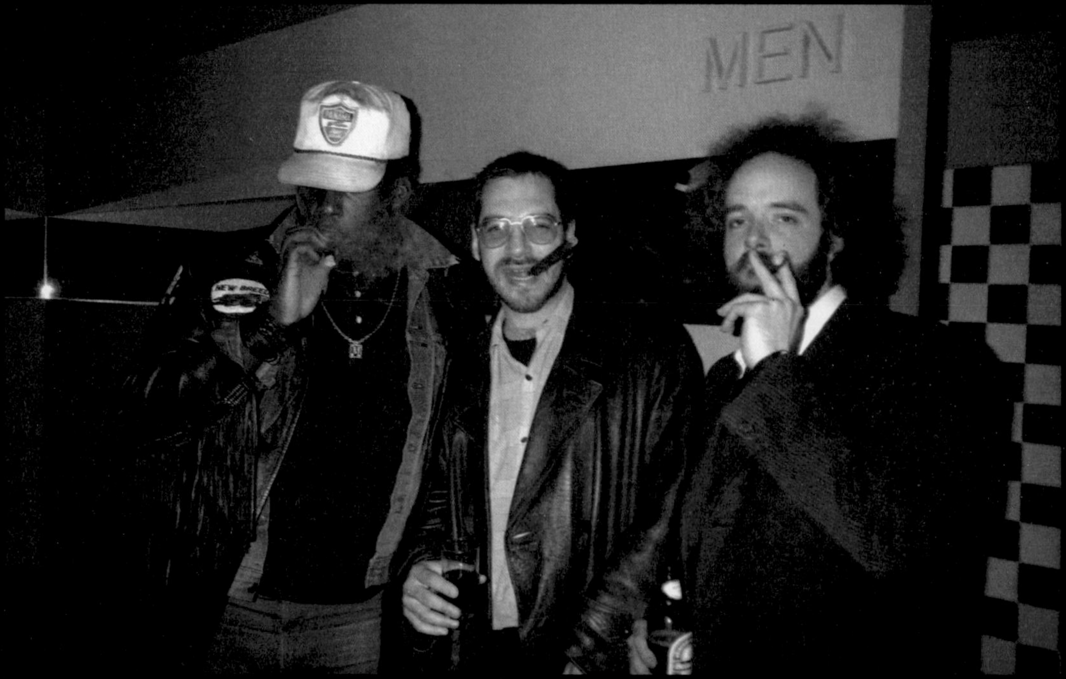

Top: Anita Sarko and party goers in the Palladium bathroom during the New York Talk magazine party. December 11,1985
Bottom: Mojo, Trigger, and Mark Moskin outside the Palladium bathroom. May 1, 1987

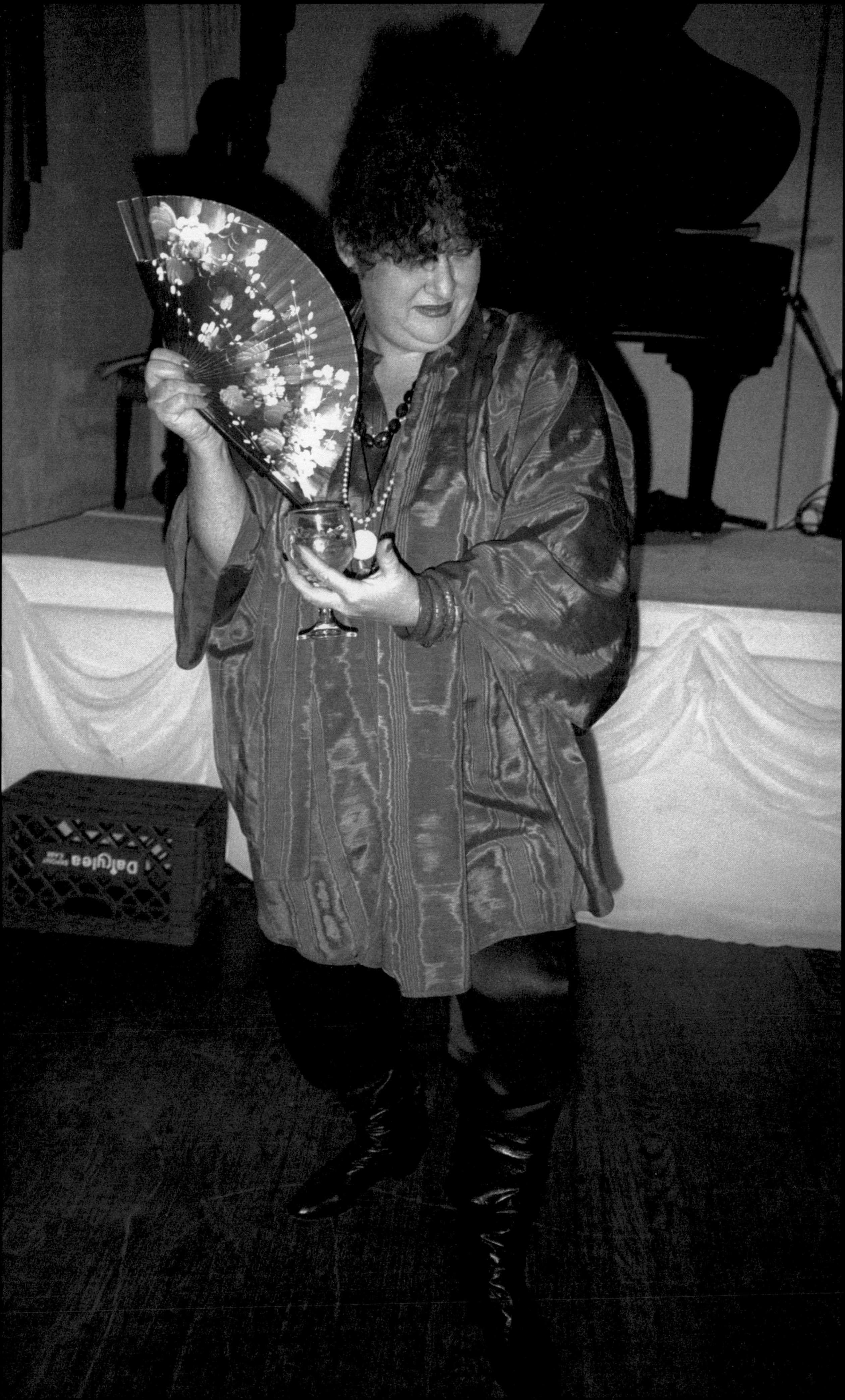

Pat Ast
at Marisa Berenson's
Dressing Up book
party at Limelight.
November 19, 1984

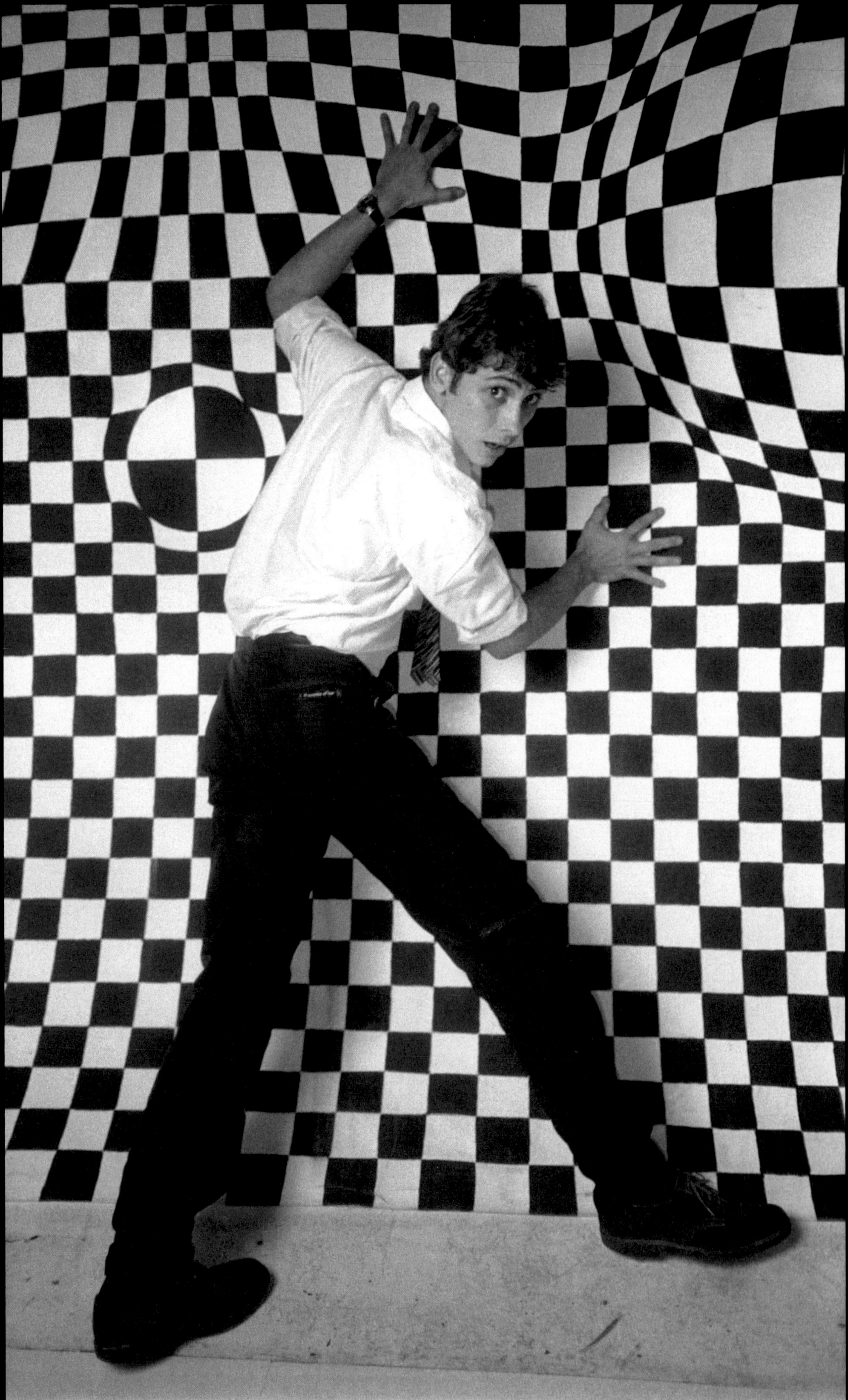

Eddie Suggs at Alan Rish's party for Hedy Klineman at Area. November 4, 1984

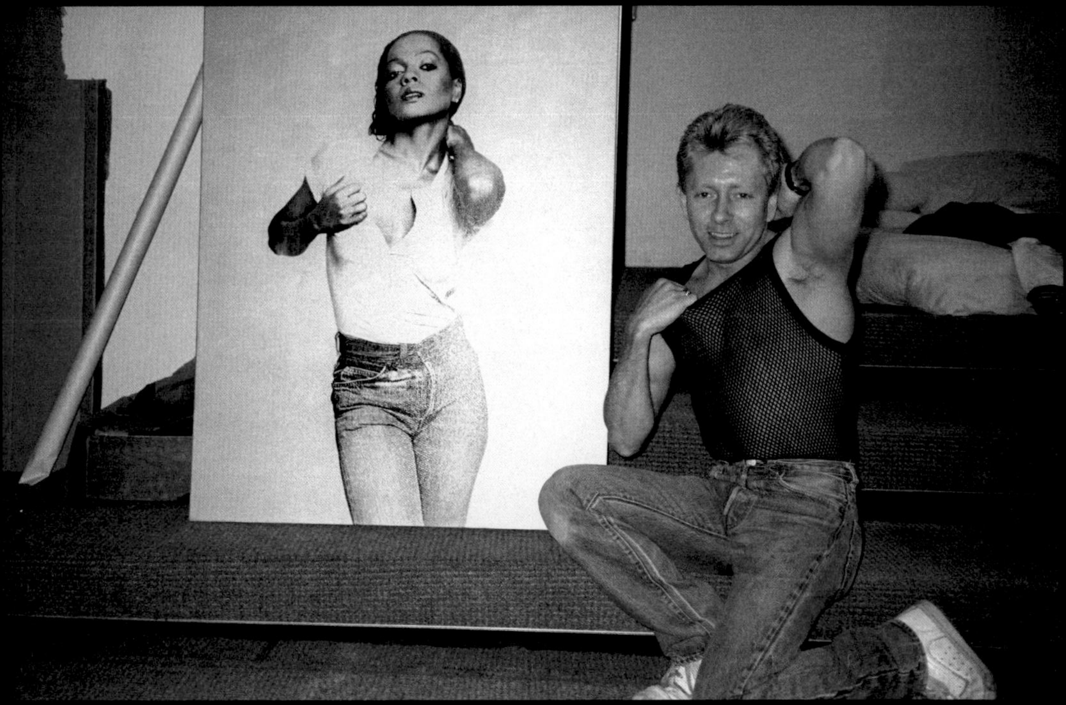

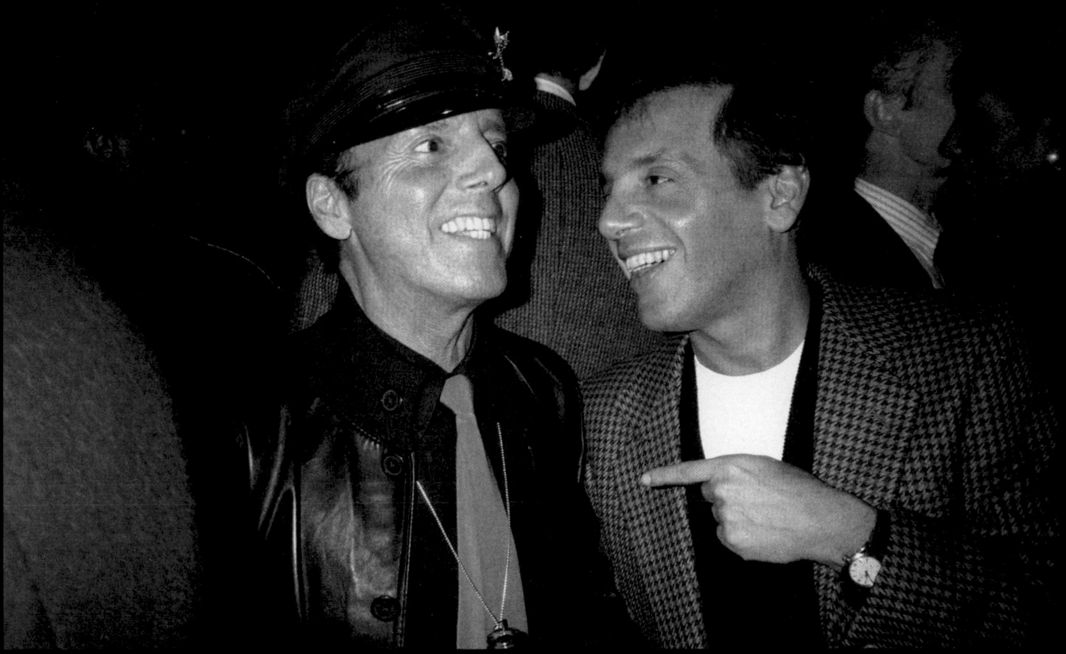

Top: Rupert Smith in his studio. June 1984
Bottom: Francesco Scavullo and Steve Rubell
at Marisa Berenson's Dressing Up book party at Limelight.
November 19, 1984

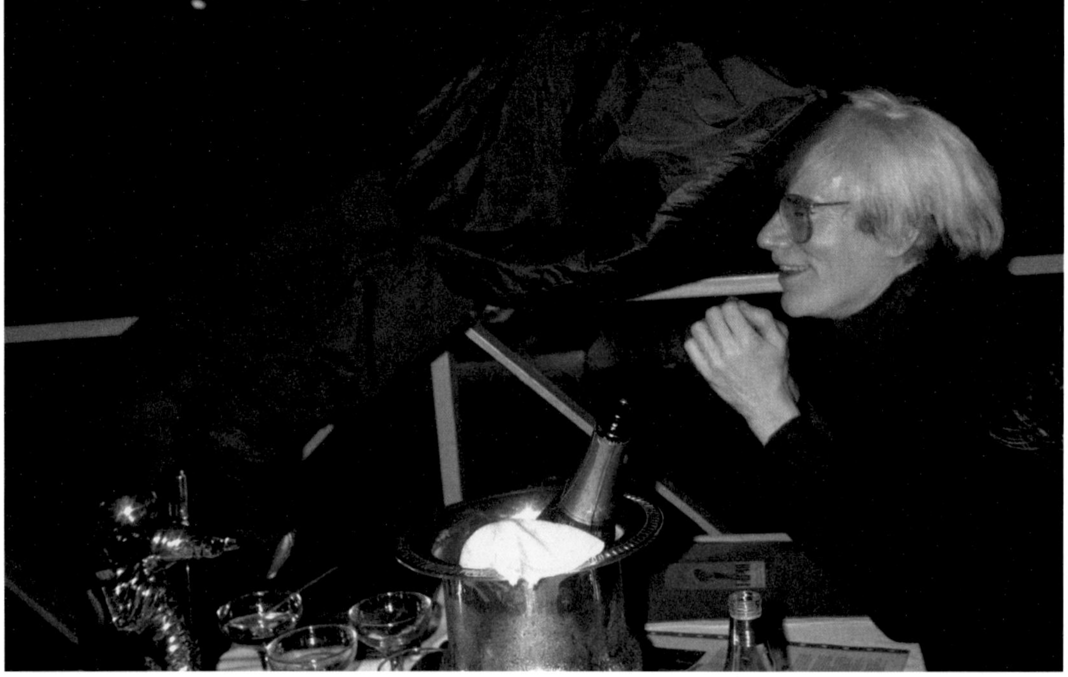

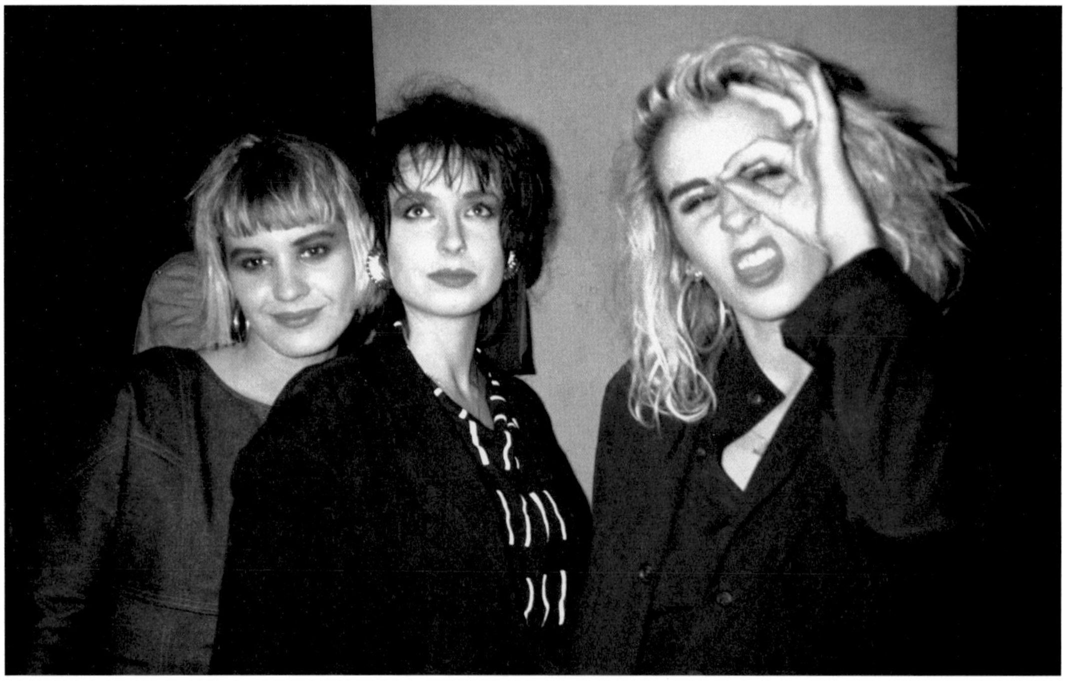

Top: Grace Jones and Andy Warhol
Bottom: Bananarama
at the 1986 MTV Music Awards at the Palladium.
Friday, September 5, 1986

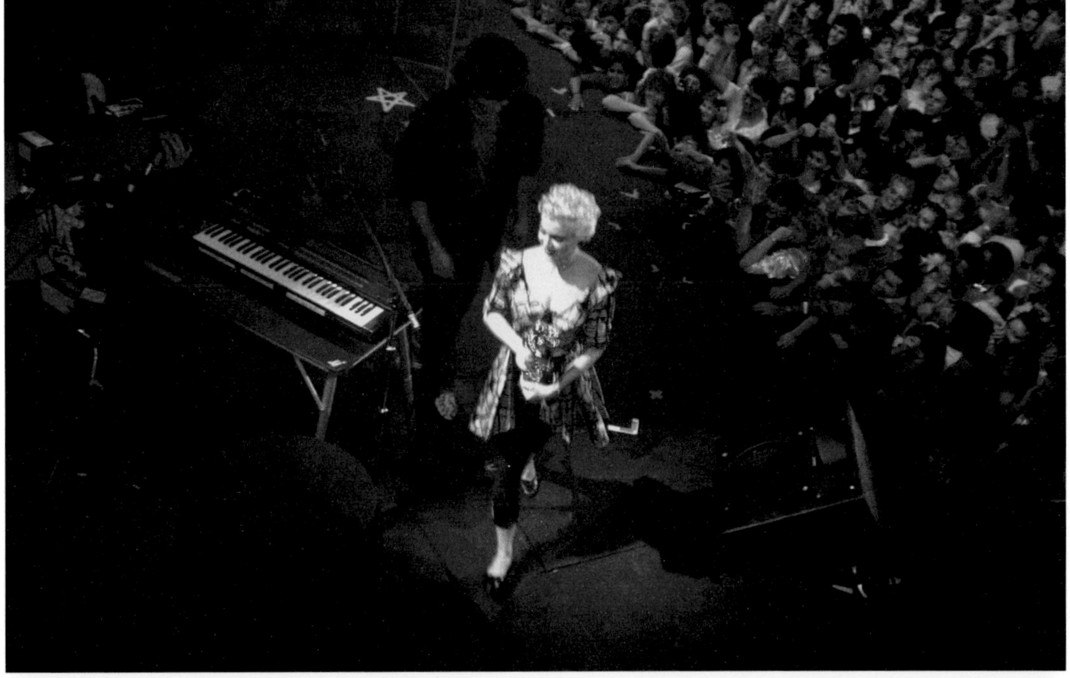

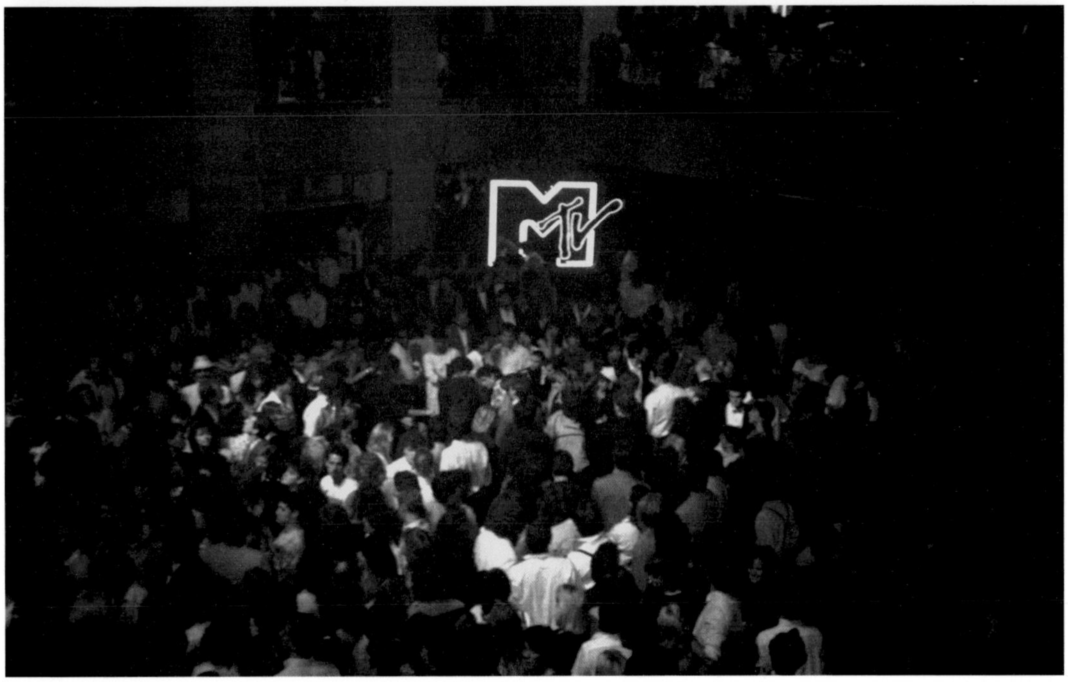

Top: Madonna on stage accepting
the Video Vanguard Award for Career Achievement.
Bottom: Overlooking the crowd
at the 1986 MTV Music Awards at the Palladium.
Friday, September 5, 1986

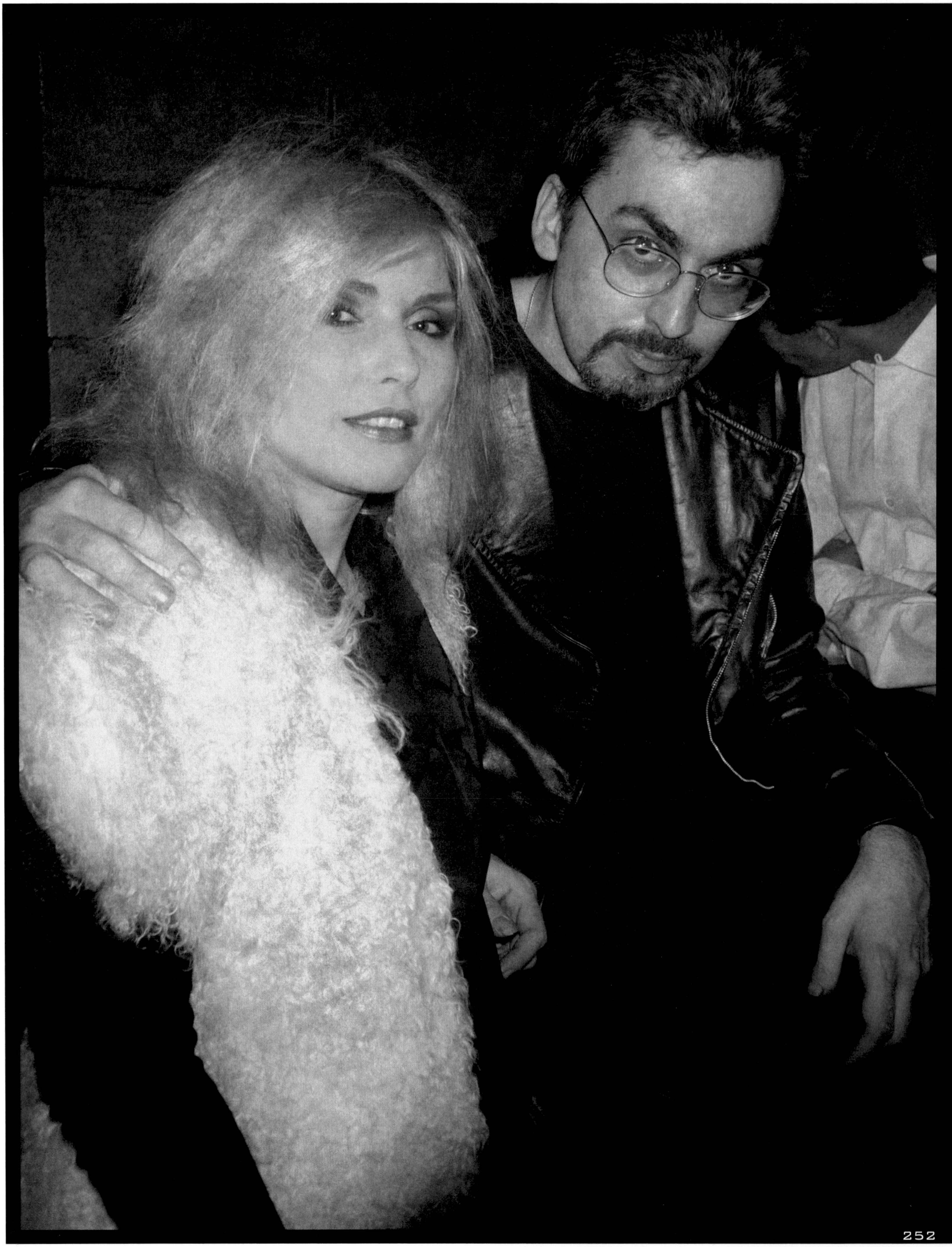

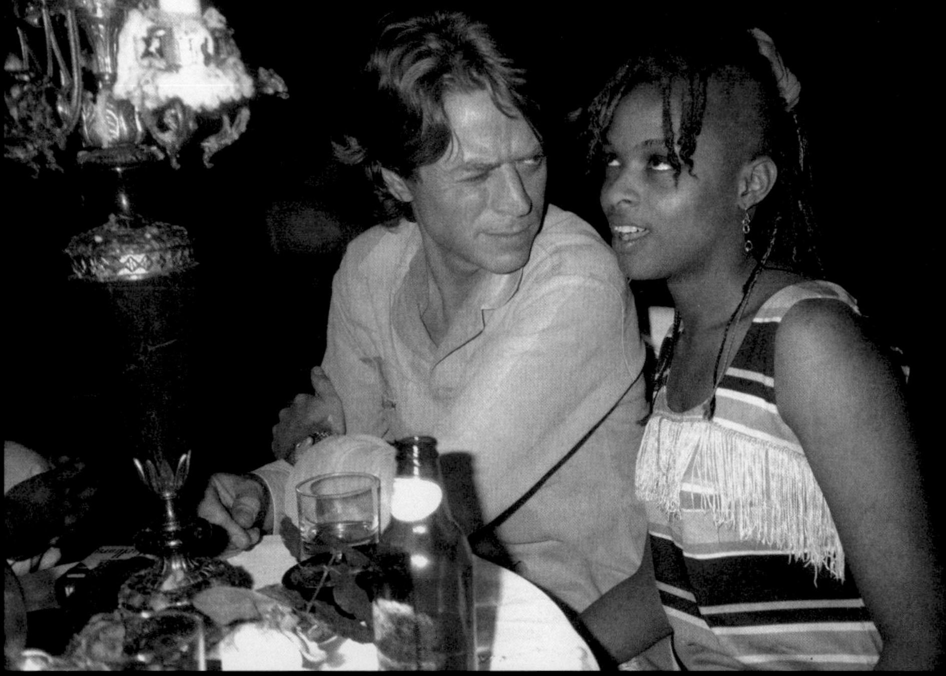

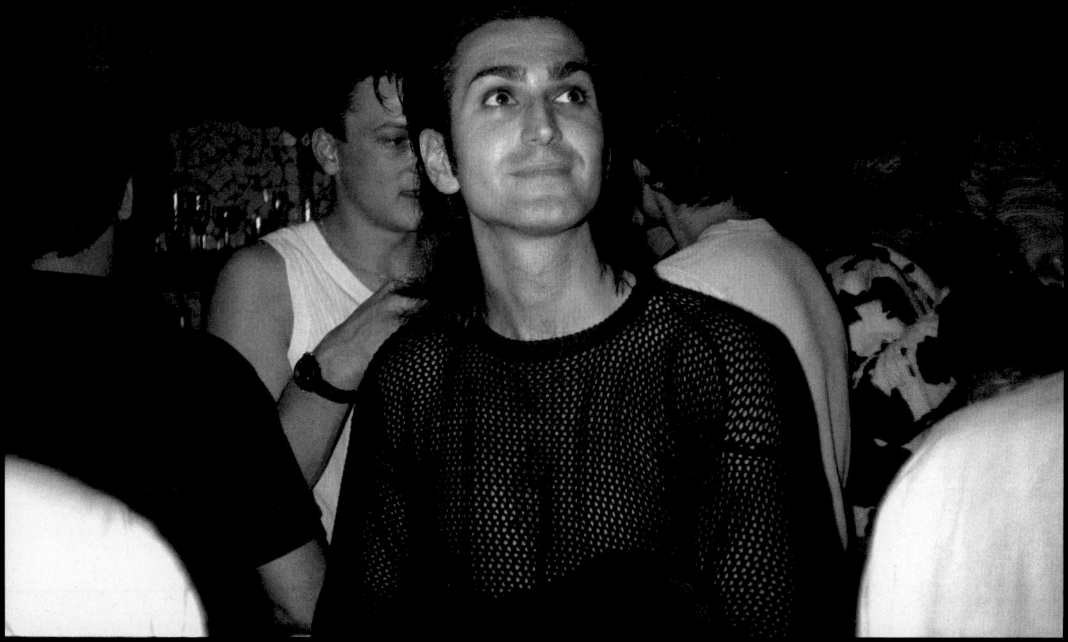

Top: Robert Palmer and Sheba
at the Palladium for the St. Elmo's Fire party. June 12, 1985
Bottom: Paul King at Limelight's opening in London. July 15, 1986
Left: Debbie Harry and Chris Stein
at Stephen Saban's birthday party at 1018.
December 12, 1986

"Happy New Year"

A frame flash-frozen in the mind: December 31, 1985, 11:50 p.m. The back seat of a limo, speeding up the West Side Highway. Grace Jones is squinting into a mirror, deftly painting her maquillage.

We are en route to a disco, that big one on West 56th Street, where Grace is being paid $10,000--not to sing, not to dance, but to stand on a balcony and wave to the revelers. She is the featured attraction--if she arrives before 1986 does. "Eat the red light," I advise the driver.

When the car lurches up to the back door, with two minutes to spare, the owner is ashen-faced, but Grace is cool as a crème brûlée. She leads the countdown to midnight, hoists a flute of champagne, brandishes her incisors, pockets the ten grand, and heads off to the next party.

Eight hours later, when the sun blasts into her loft overlooking the Hudson, Grace is playing her new demo for Dolph Lundgren, Rob Lowe, Melissa Gilbert, Katie Wagner, and Richard Bernstein.

Nobody wants to go home. It is the apogee of an era when too much is never enough, and nothing exceeds like excess.

Richard Turley

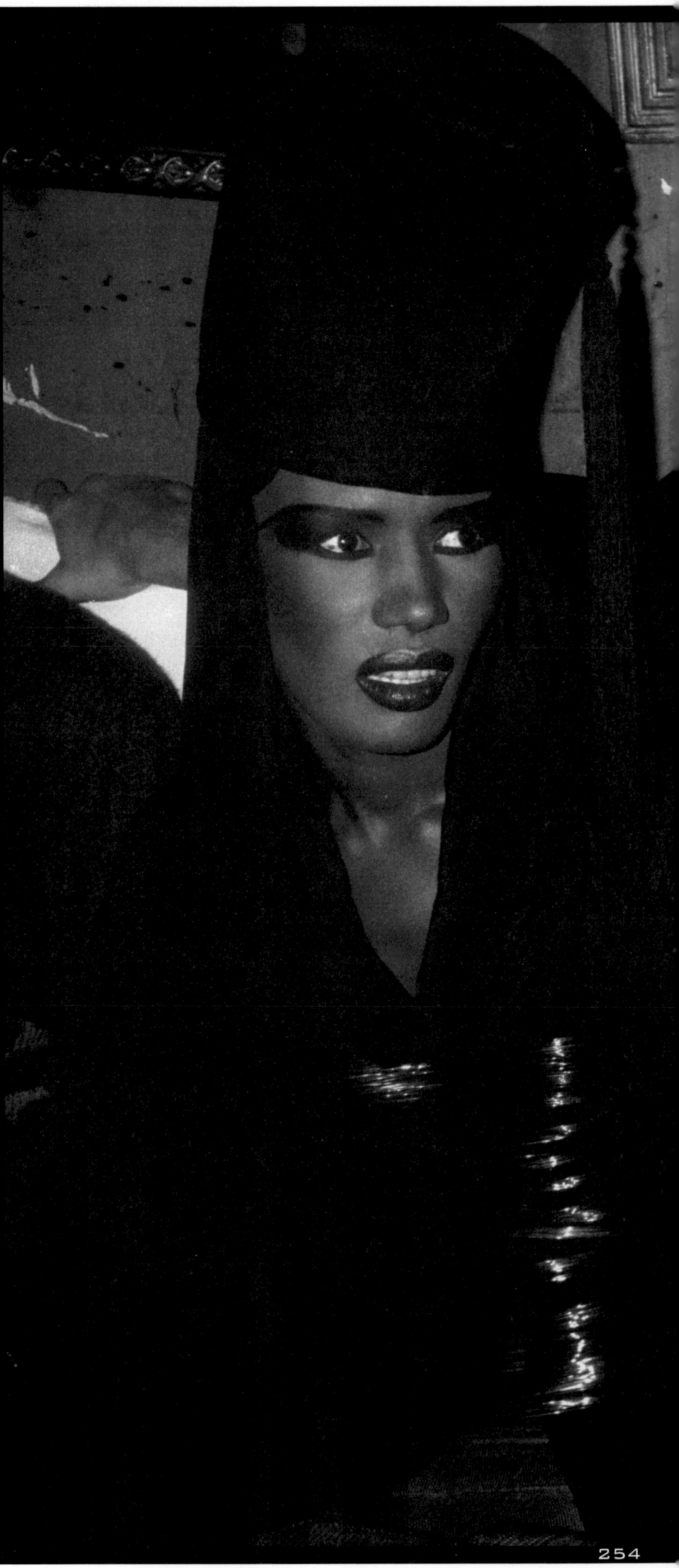

Grace Jones and Dolph Lundgren
at Grace Jones' party at the Palladium.
December 20, 1985

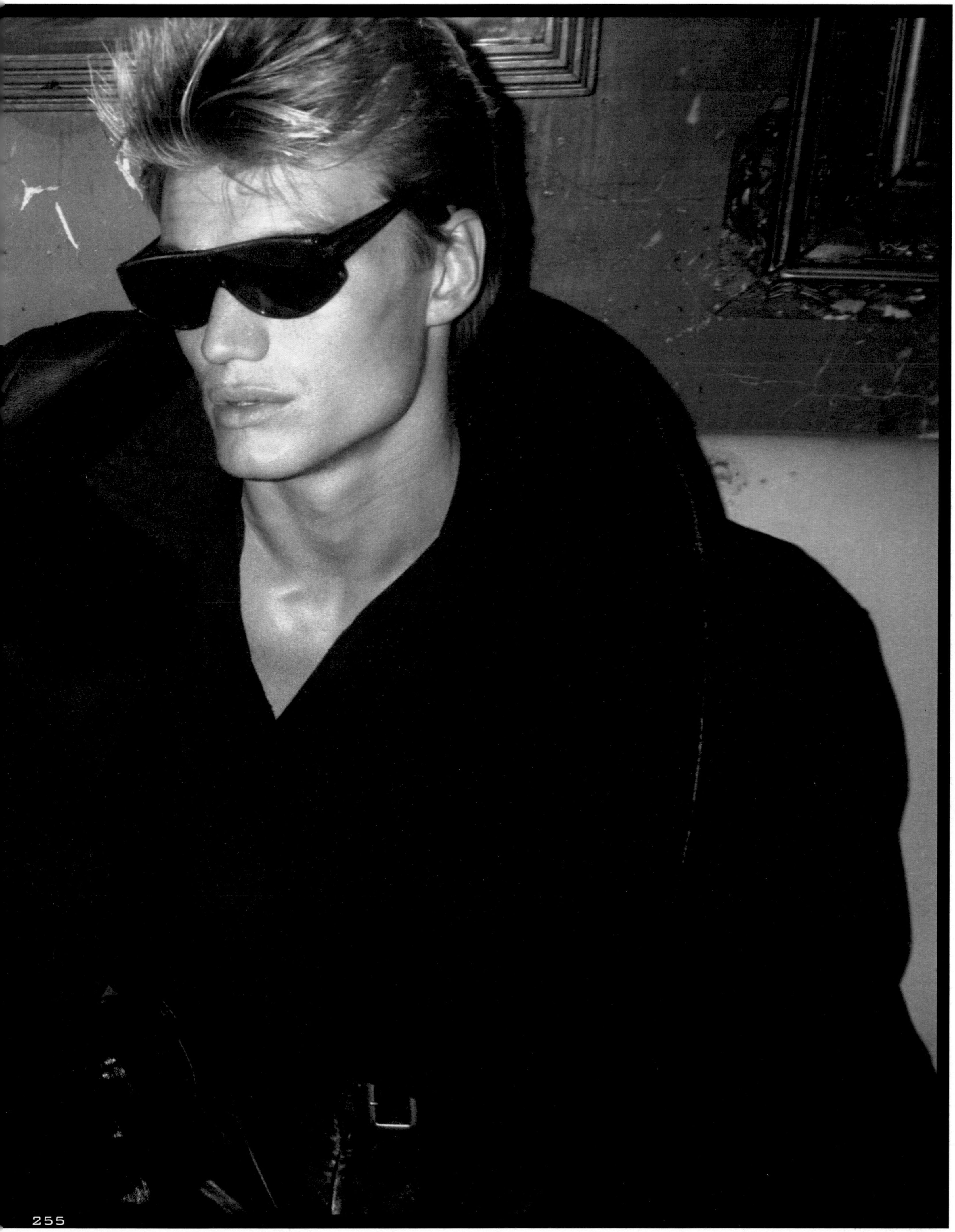

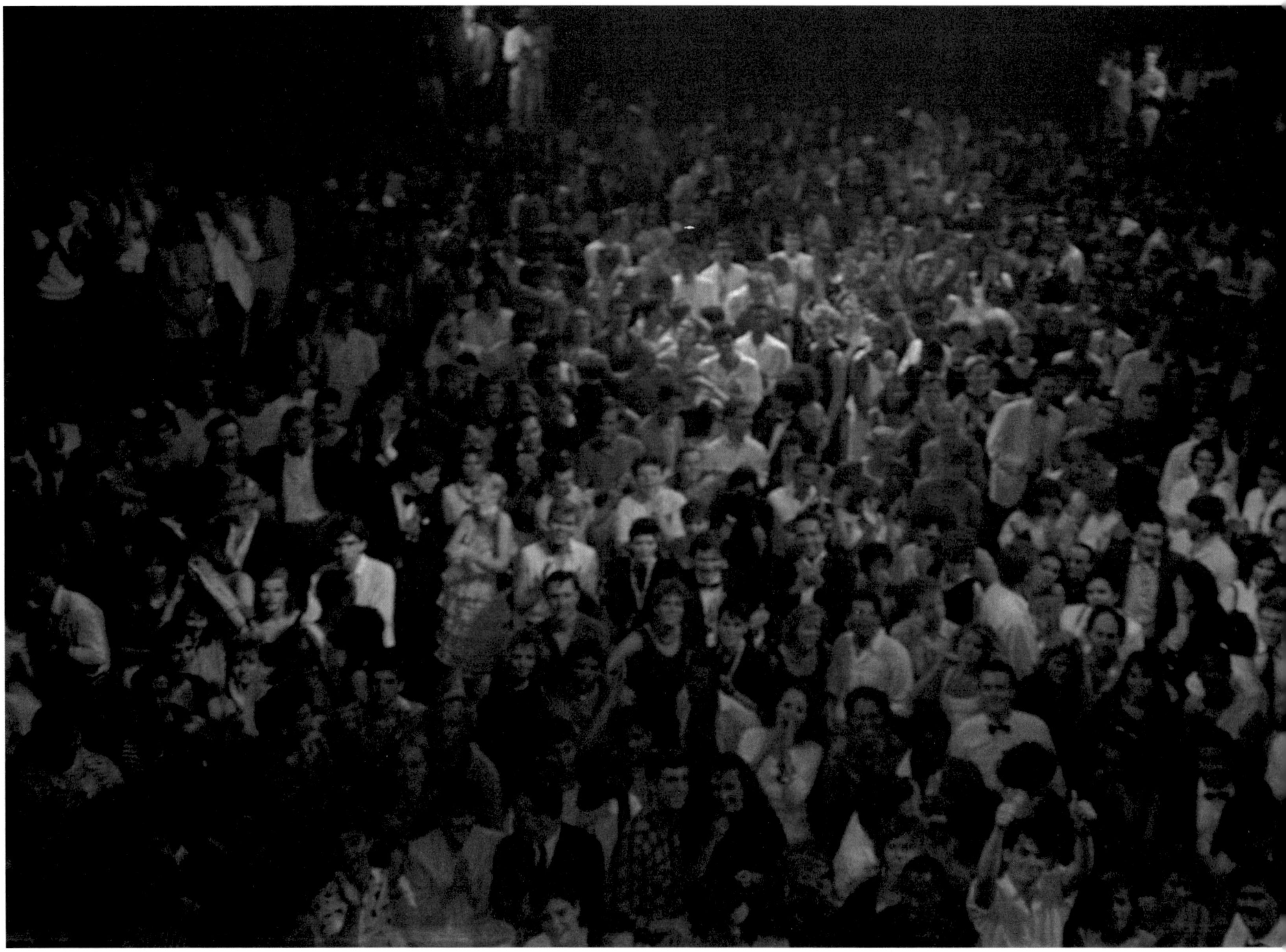

Crowd at the birthday party for
Patrick McMullan and Sally Randall at the Palladium.
July 10, 1985

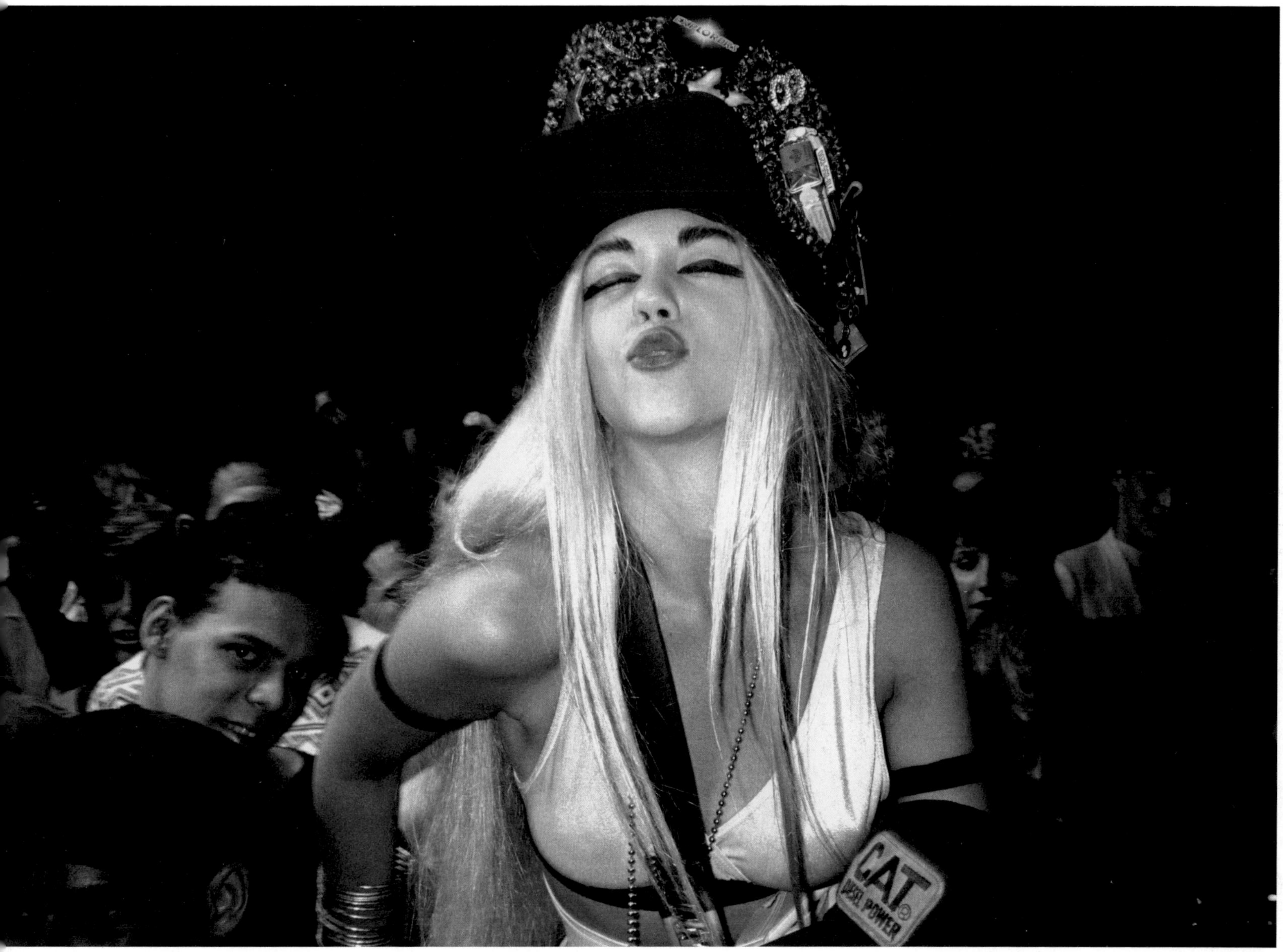

"IT ALL STARTED WITH NAIVE IDEALISM IN THE EARLY 80s--WHEN YOU COULD AFFORD AN APARTMENT ON A PART TIME JOB AND STILL HAVE TIME TO MAKE ART. NYC WAS A HOTBED OF CREATIVITY AND FILLED WITH YOUNG ARTISTS AND MUSICIANS. NIGHTCLUBS WERE WHERE WE ALL MET AT NIGHT TO PLAY. THEY WERE OUR ART GALLERIES AND OUR LIVING ROOMS. AFTER THE EAST VILLAGE ART BOOM IT BECAME POPULAR TO BECOME PART OF THIS ENCLAVE, AND WITH IT CAME THE RICH, THE FAMOUS, AND THE ENTITLED. YOU EITHER WENT ALONG FOR THE RIDE OR QUIETLY BOWED OUT. I WENT FOR THE RIDE FOR JUST LONG ENOUGH TO GET UTTERLY AND COMPLETELY CONFUSED ABOUT WHAT I WAS IN IT FOR. IT WAS A WILD AND FUN RIDE THAT WAS NEVER MEANT TO GROW INTO A FRONT PAGE NEWS STORY."
SALLY RANDALL

SALLY RANDALL BEING LIFTED ABOVE THE CROWD
AT THE BIRTHDAY PARTY FOR PATRICK MCMULLAN AND SALLY RANDALL AT THE PALLADIUM.
JULY 10, 1985

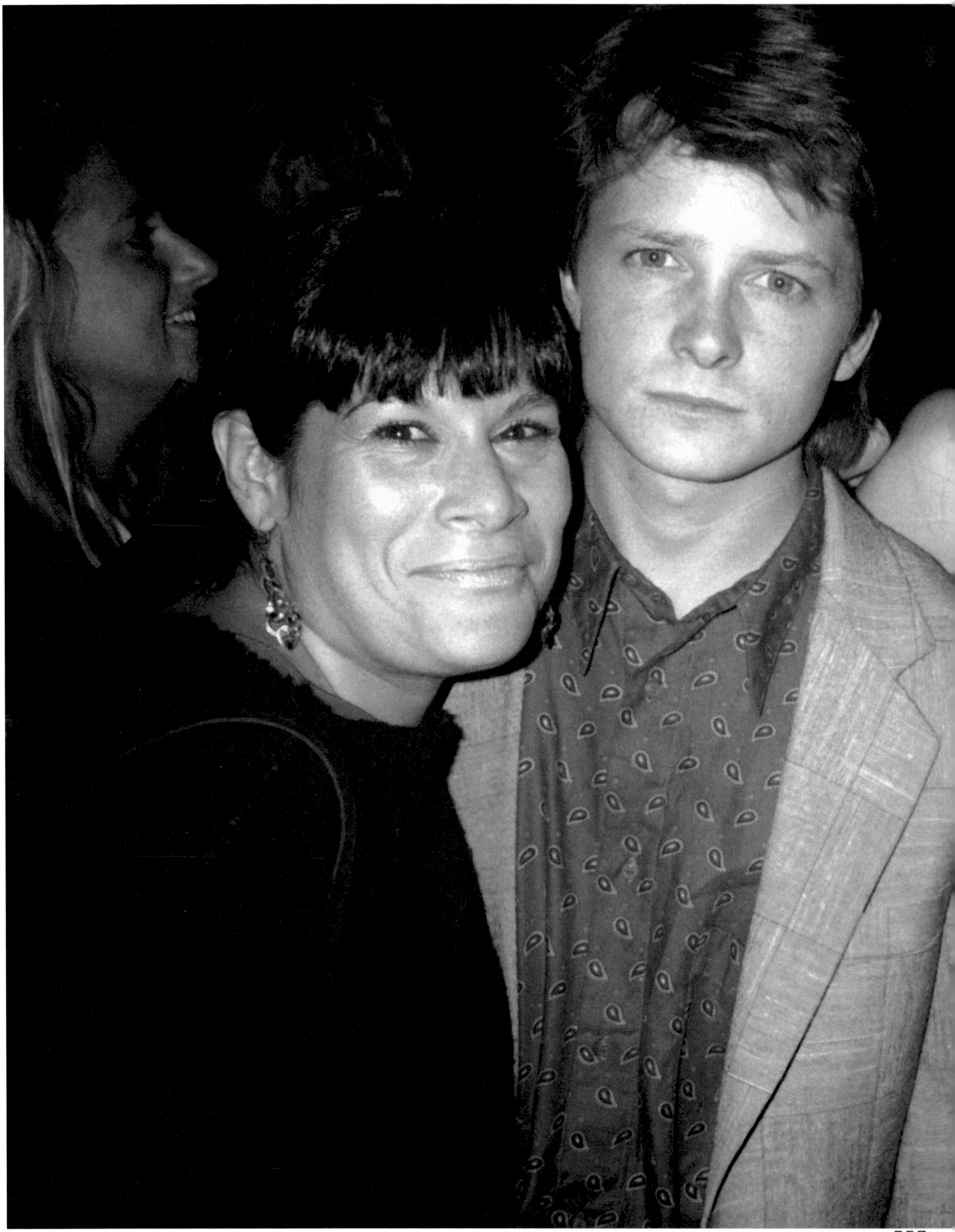

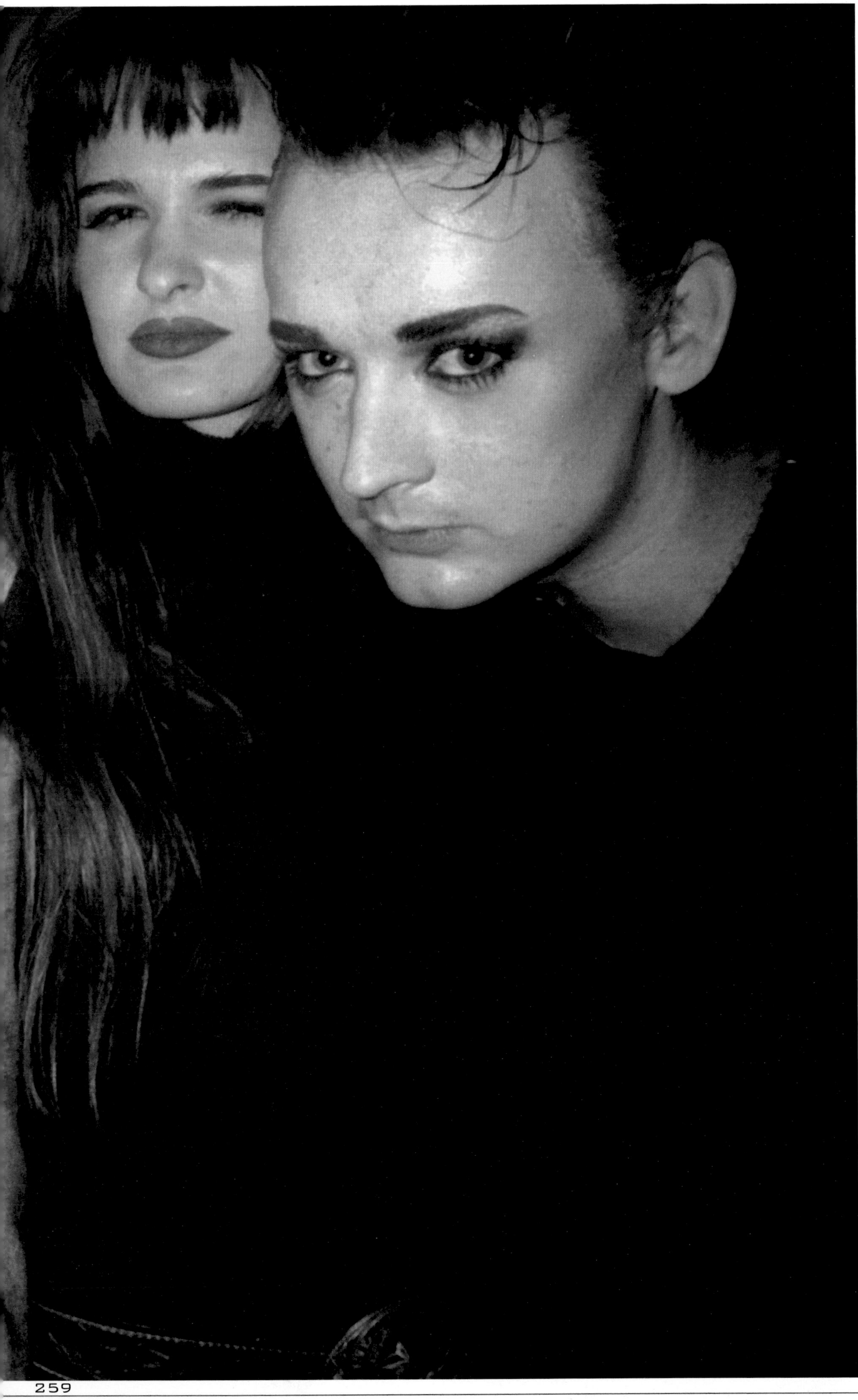

LINDA STEIN, MICHAEL J. FOX, ELLEN KINNALLY, AND BOY GEORGE AT AREA. SEPTEMBER 23, 1985

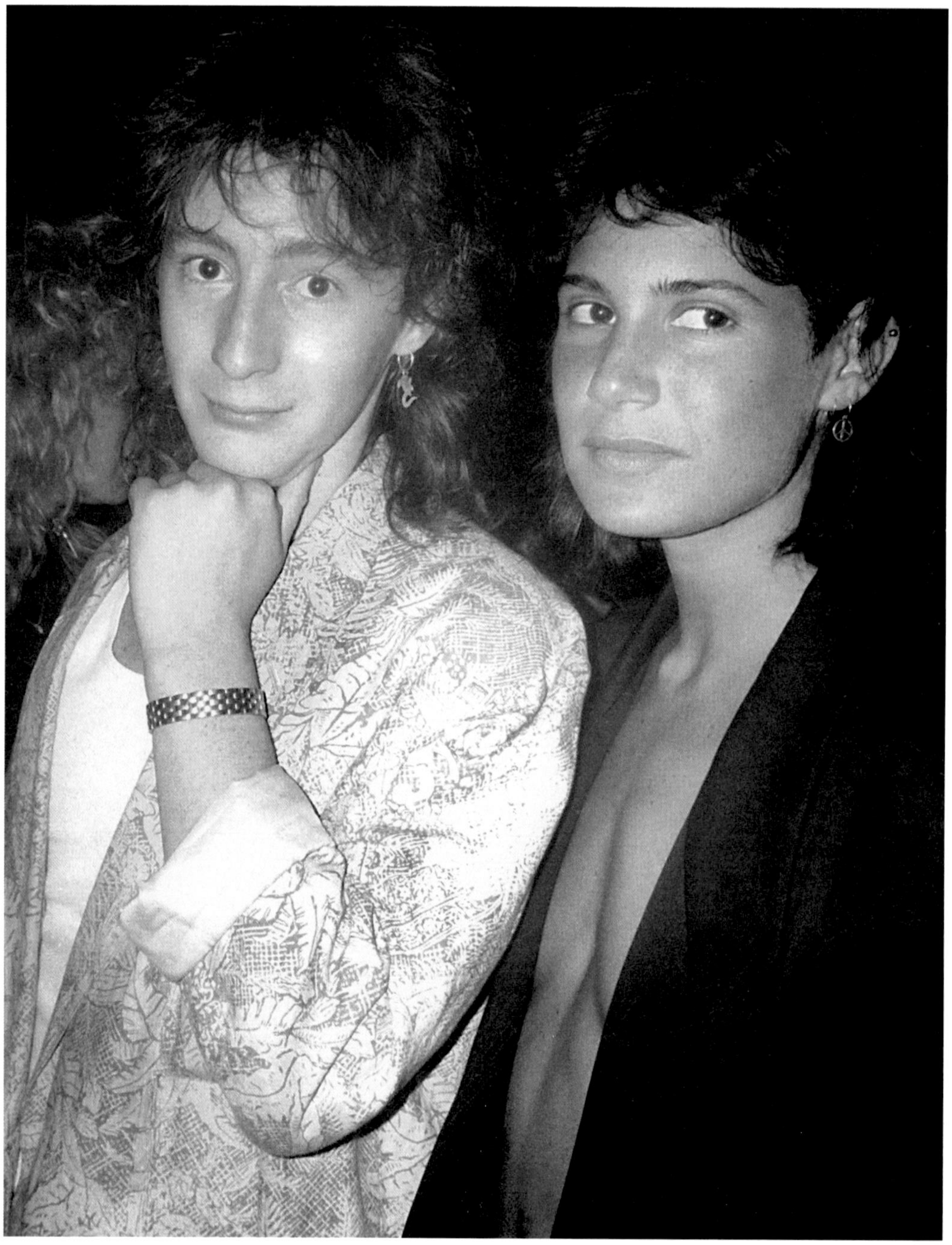

Julian Lennon and Elizabeth Saltzman
at Limelight.
July 29, 1985

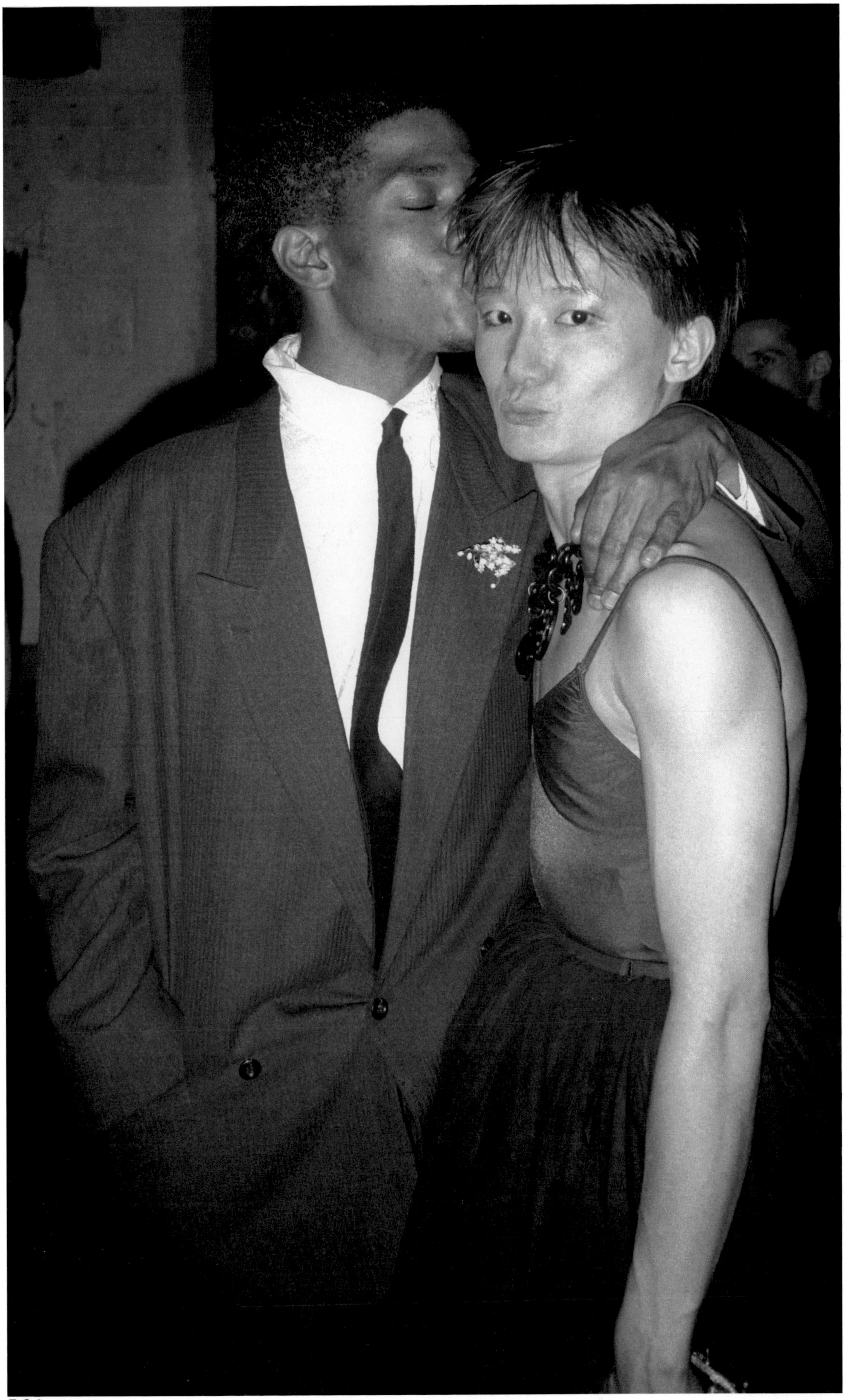

Jean-Michel Basquiat and Benjamin Liu as "Ming Vauze" at the opening night of the Palladium. May 14, 1985

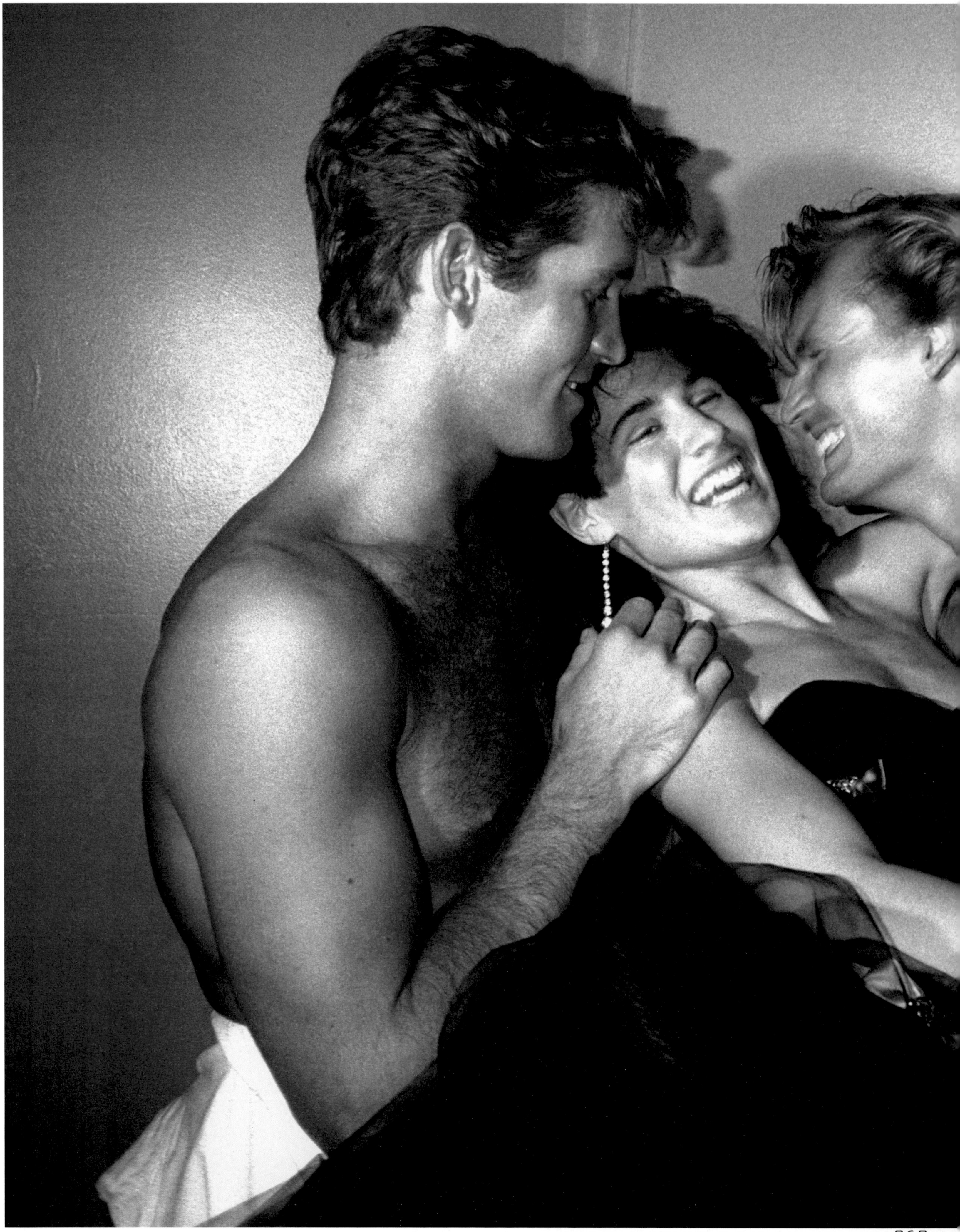

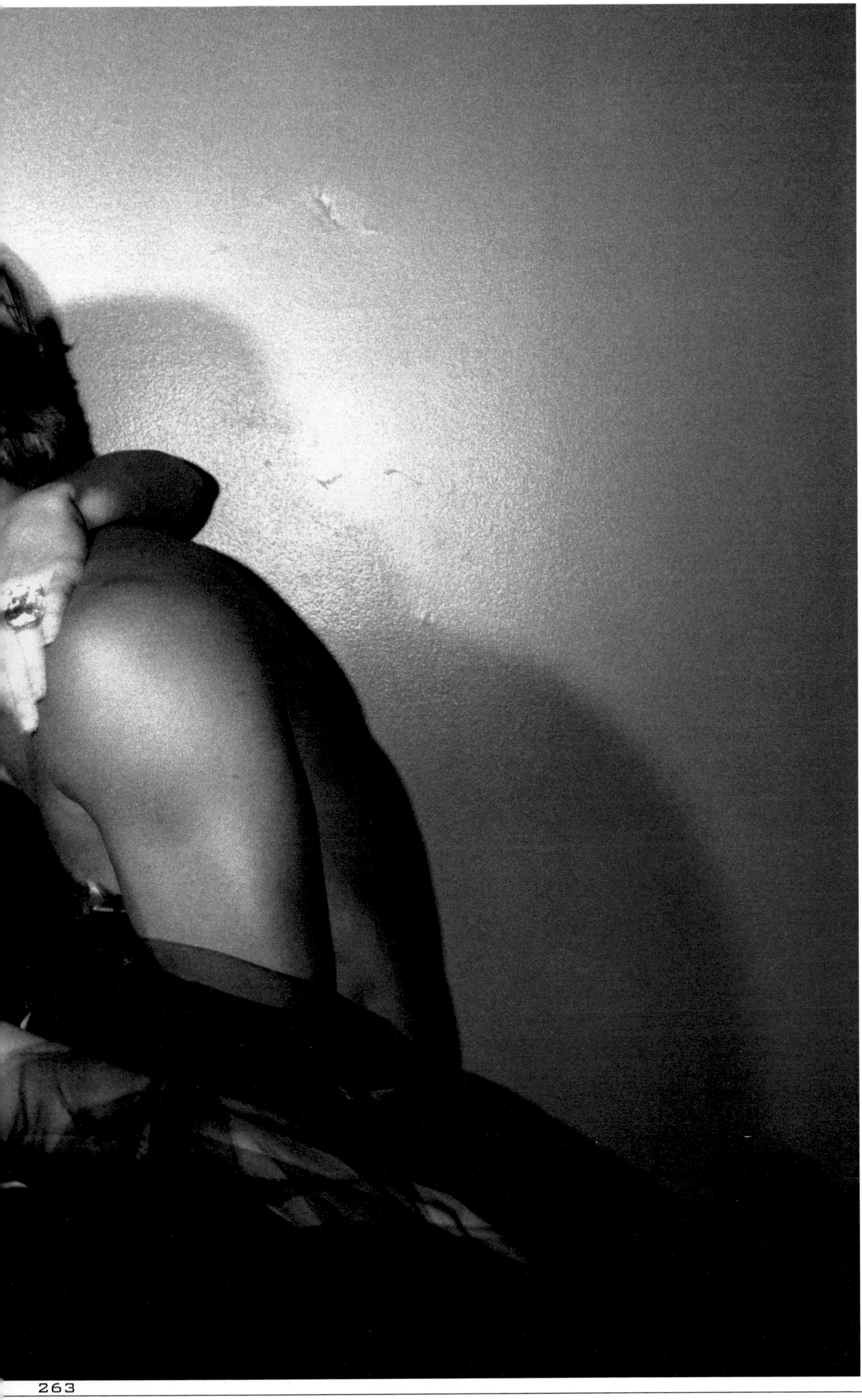

"The 80s were fun... frivolous...fantasy-filled, and fantastic. Thank heavens I survived so I can live on the fond memories and embarrass my children with them for the next twenty years."
Elizabeth Saltzman

Elizabeth Saltzman and the boys at her birthday party at Area. June 20, 1985

1
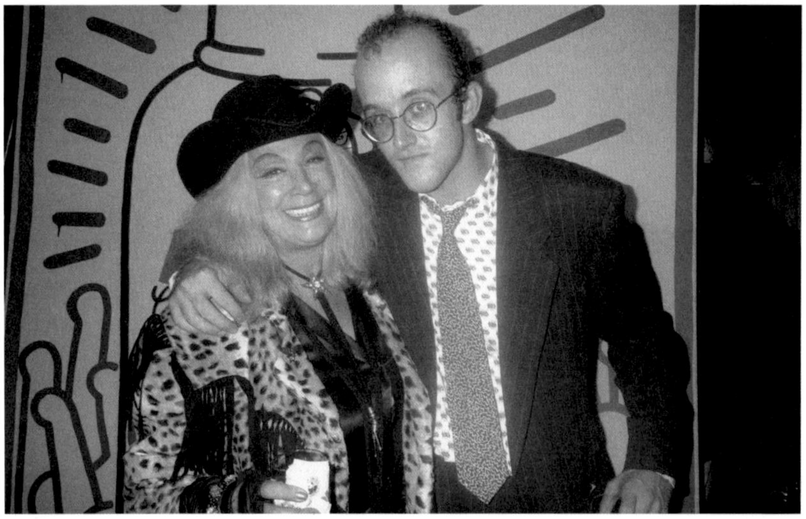
2
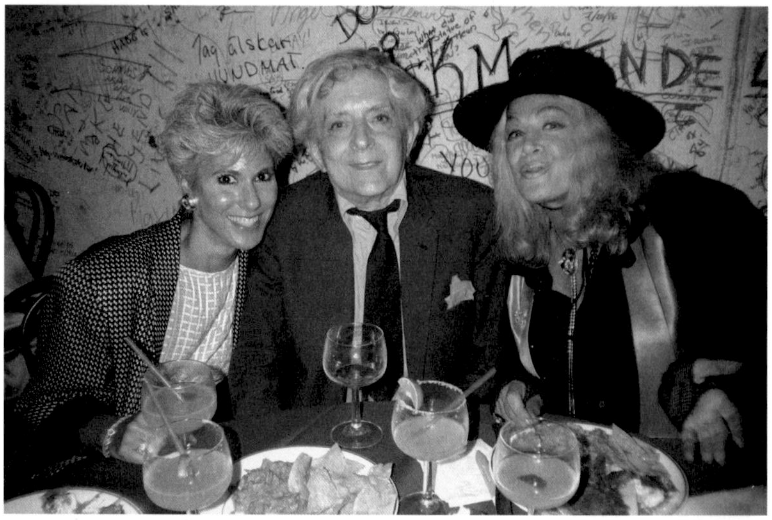
3
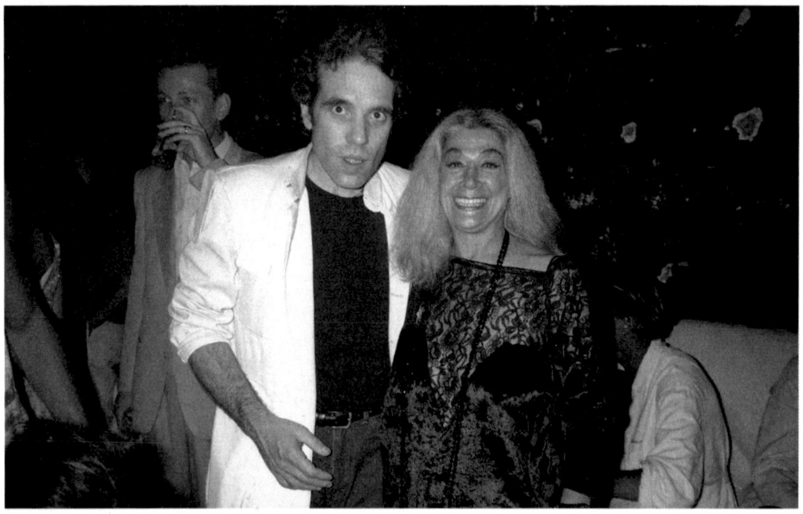
4
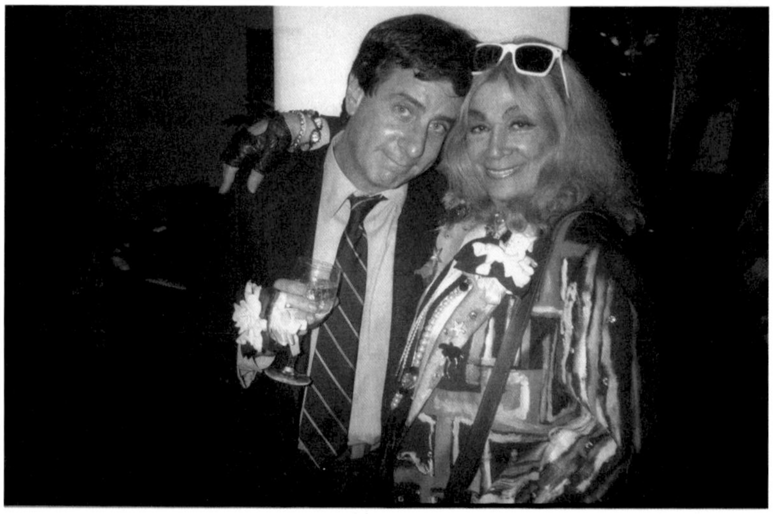
5
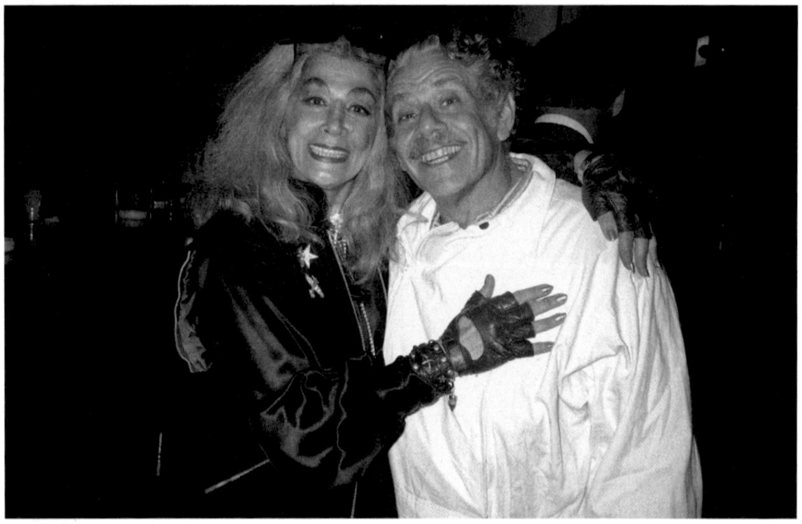
6
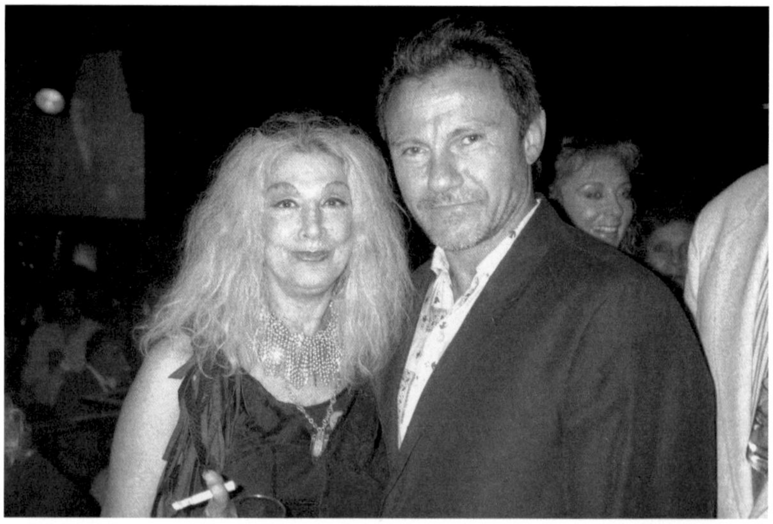
7
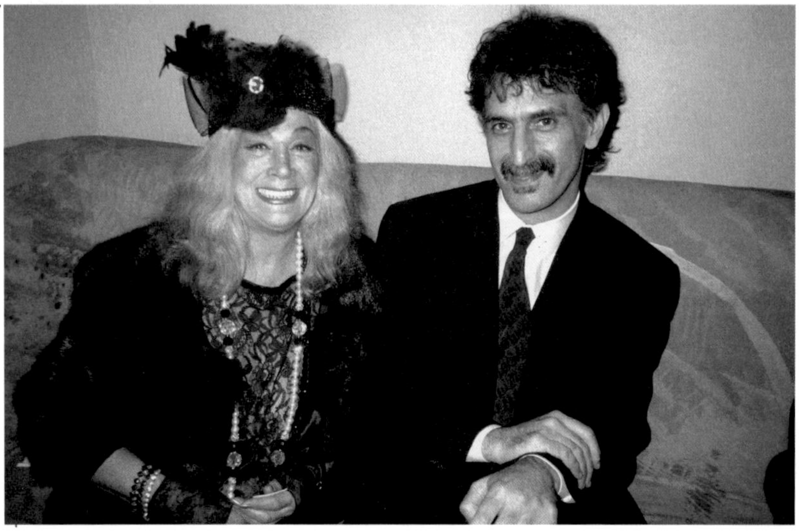
8
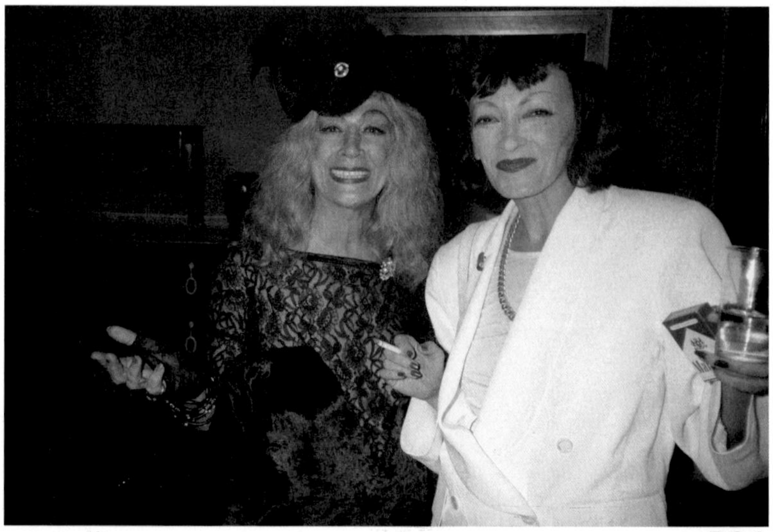

"The 80s, wow! A lot of hustling, a lot of bustling. A lot of yuppies, and a lot of buppies. A lot of stock market sharking, a lot of illegal diplomatic parking. Thank God that it's 2003, I'm alive, and had the time to make this rhyme."
Most humbly, Sylvia Miles

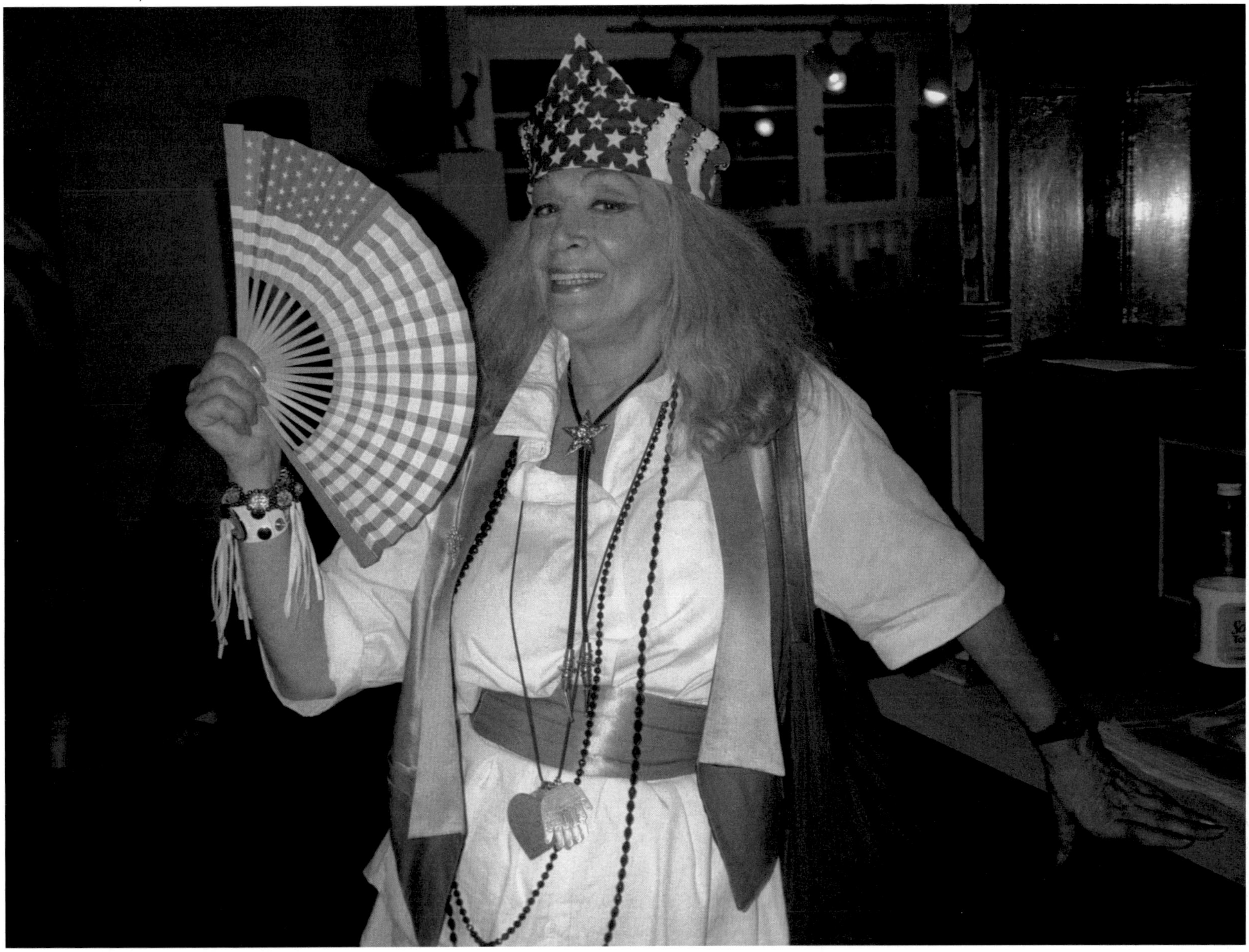

Above: Sylvia Miles at Steven Styles' birthday party at Hedy Klineman's house in East Hampton. Saturday, June 28, 1986

1. Sylvia Miles and Keith Haring at Absolut Vodka's party for Keith Haring at the Whitney Museum of American Art. Thursday, October 2, 1986 2. Jamie deRoy, Quentin Crisp, and Sylvia Miles at Dallas Boesendahl's party at the Cadillac Bar. July 28, 1986 3. Abel Ferrara and Sylvia Miles at the birthday party for Patrick McMullan and Sally Randall at the Palladium. July 10, 1985 4. Danny Fields and Sylvia Miles at the dinner party hosted by Susan Blond for Ozzy Osbourne held at Mr. Chow's. April 21, 1986 5. Sylvia Miles and Jerry Stiller at Esai Morales' birthday party at Visage. Tuesday, October 1, 1985 6. Sylvia Miles and Harvey Keital at Eddie Fisher's birthday party at Stringfellows. Wednesday, August 10, 1988 7. Sylvia Miles and Frank Zappa at the Mirror Rep Benefit. October 27, 1986 8. Sylvia Miles and Larissa at the surprise birthday party for Susanne Bartsch at the Rainbow Roof, 30 Rockefeller Plaza. Thursday, September 19, 1985

"The 80s--Andy, Halston...what an amazing time to have been in New York." Jane Holzer

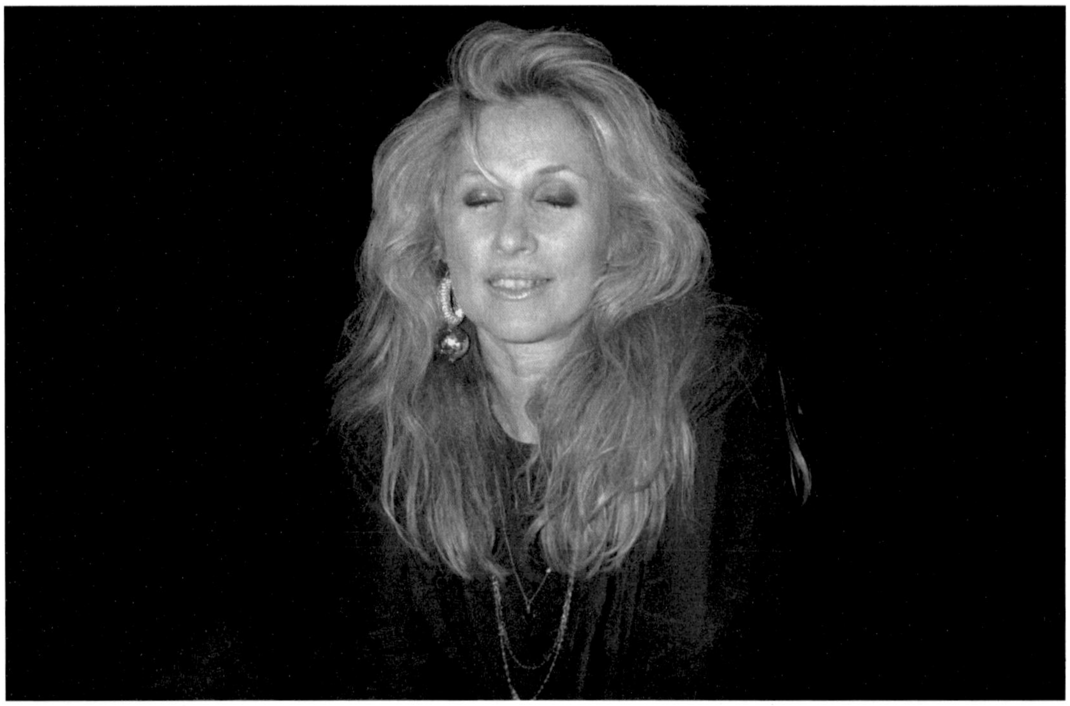

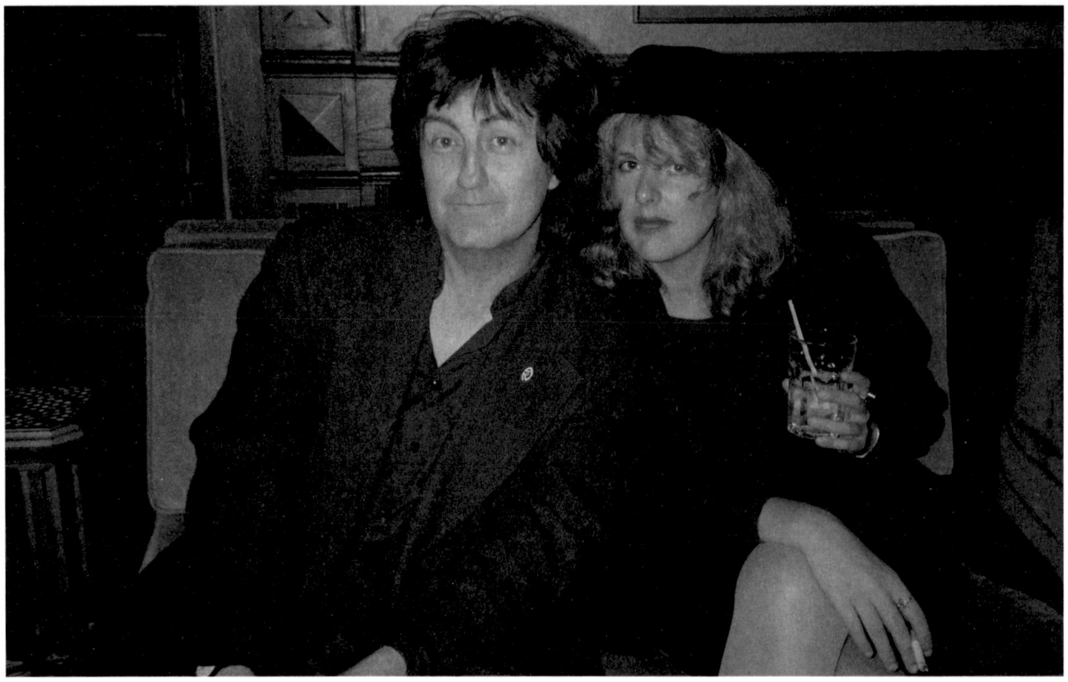

Top: Jane Holzer
at Sugar Reef for a dinner party.
Friday, June 27, 1986
Bottom: Stephen Saban and Cynthia Heimel at Limelight.
Monday, September 8, 1986

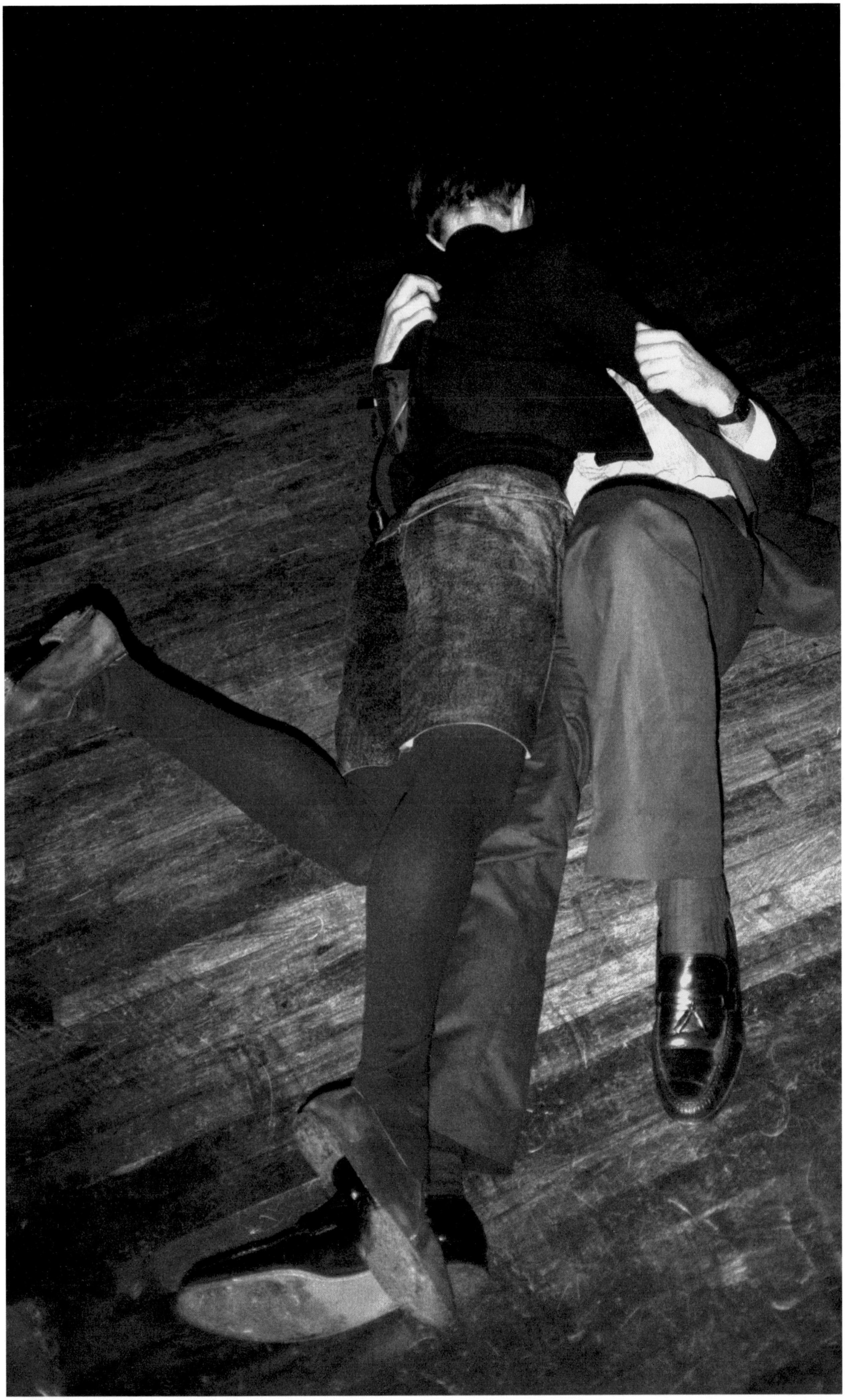

On the floor at Alan Rish's party for artist Hedy Klineman at Area. November 4, 1984

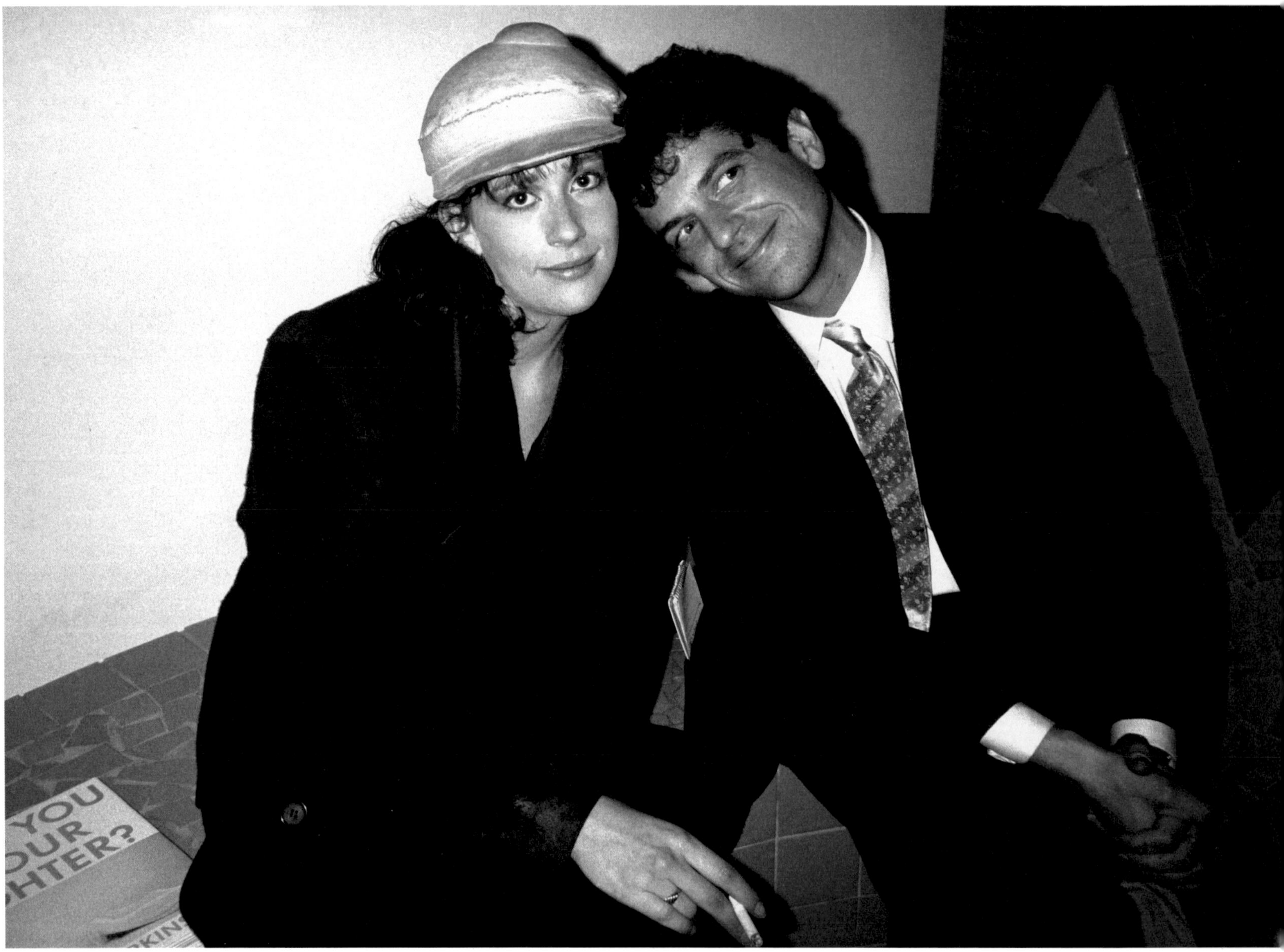

Justine Harari and Michael Gross
at Susanne Bartsch's party for Norman Parkinson at Area.
November 27, 1985

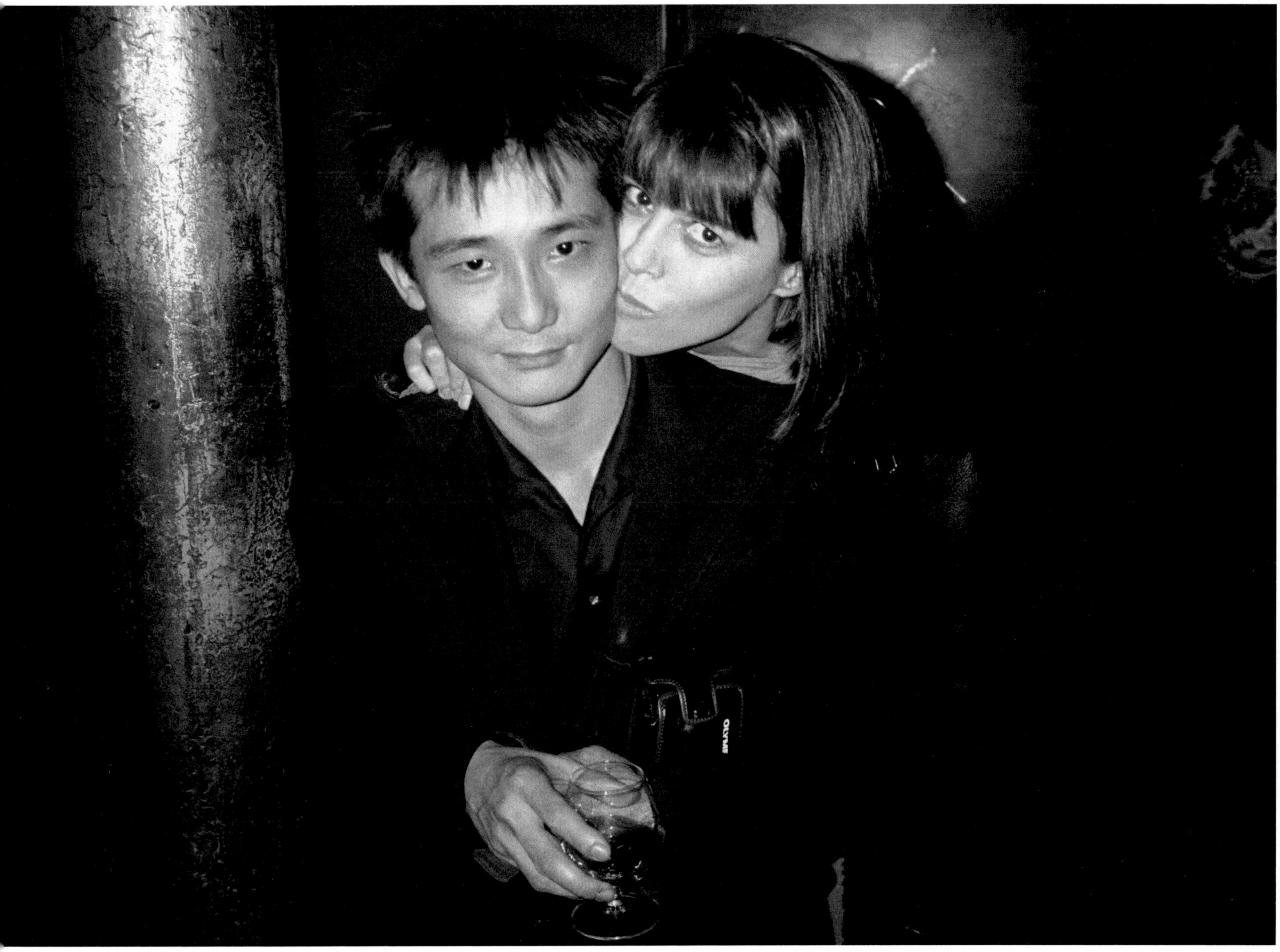

"There's a certain amount of professionalism about the decade, all the night crawlers have day jobs."
Benjamin Liu

Benjamin Liu and Paige Powell
at Area.
November 27, 1985

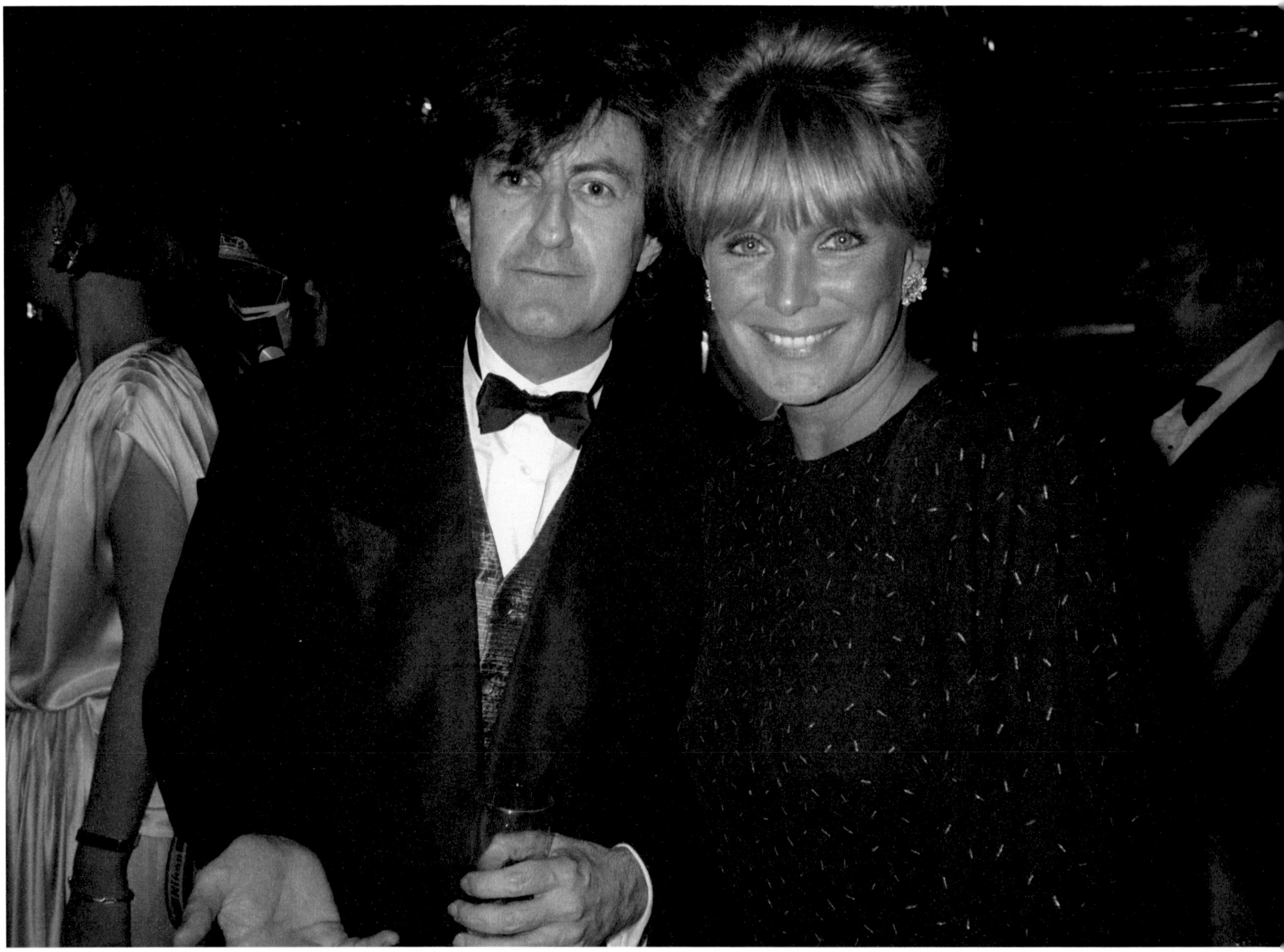

STEPHEN SABAN AND LINDA EVANS
AT THE DYNASTY DINNER AT REGINE'S.
OCTOBER 1985

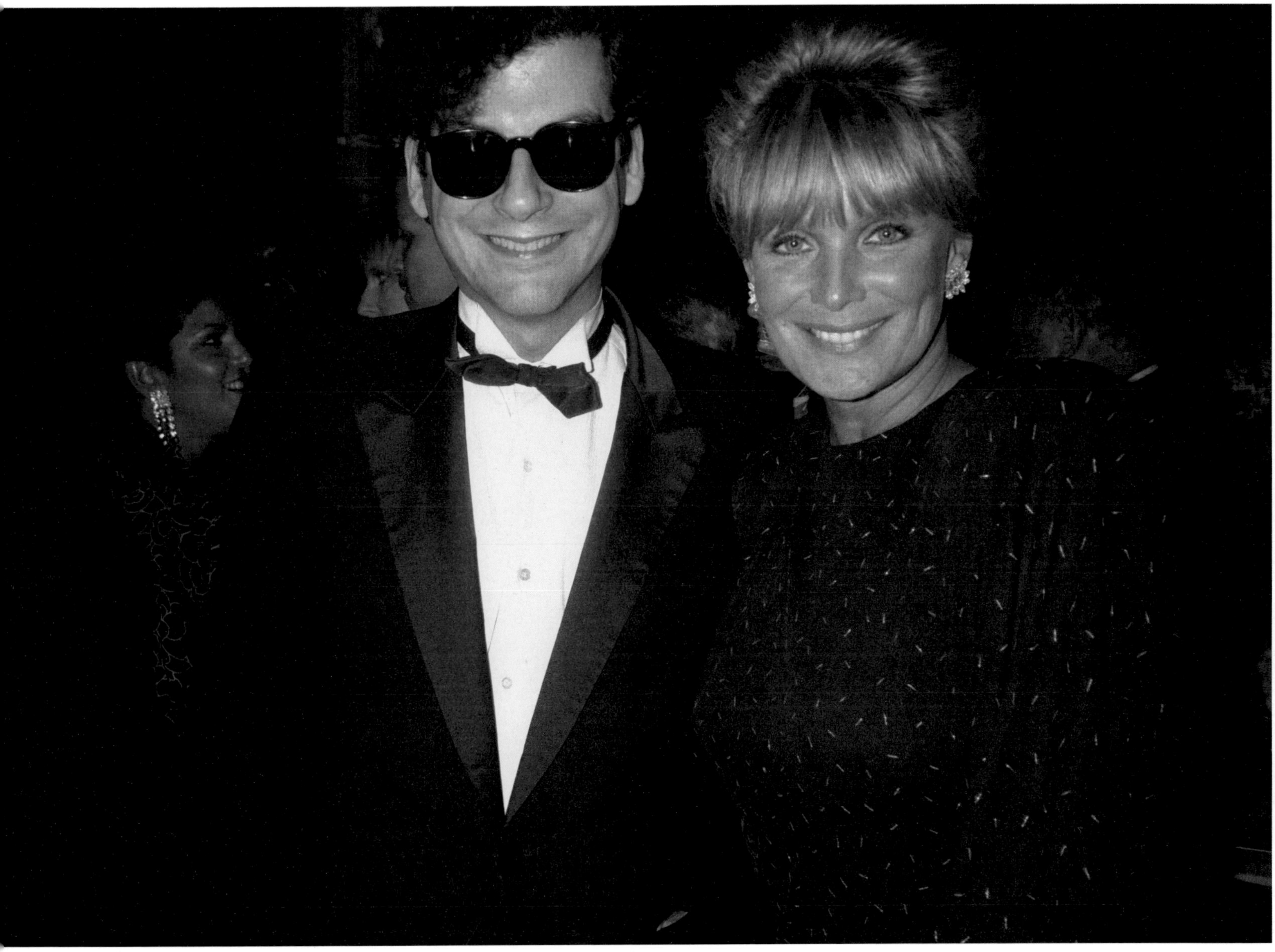

Michael Musto and Linda Evans
at the Dynasty dinner at Regine's.
October 1985

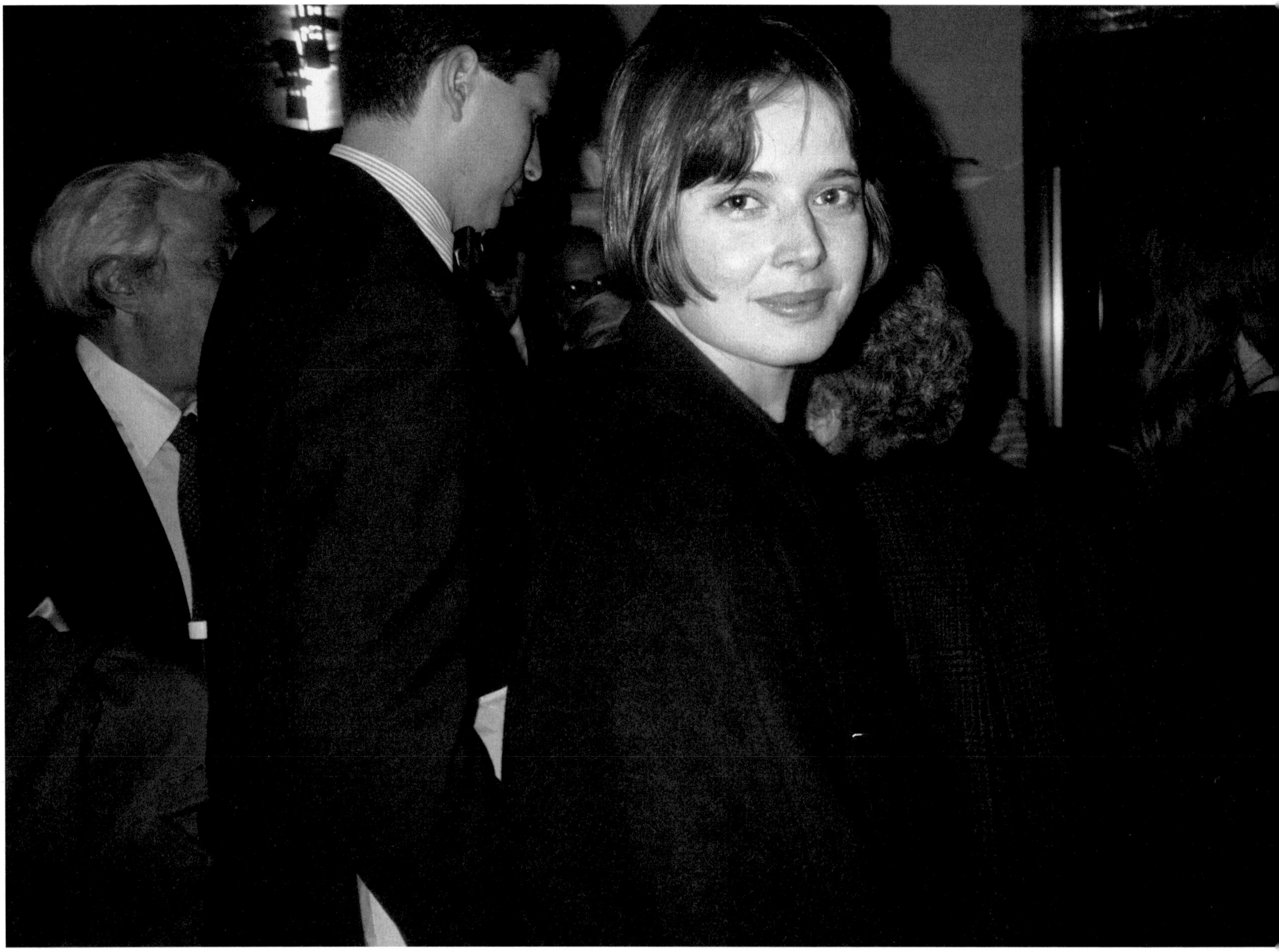

Isabella Rossellini
at Federico Fellini's film premiere of Fred and Ginger
at the Museum of Modern Art.
March 26, 1986

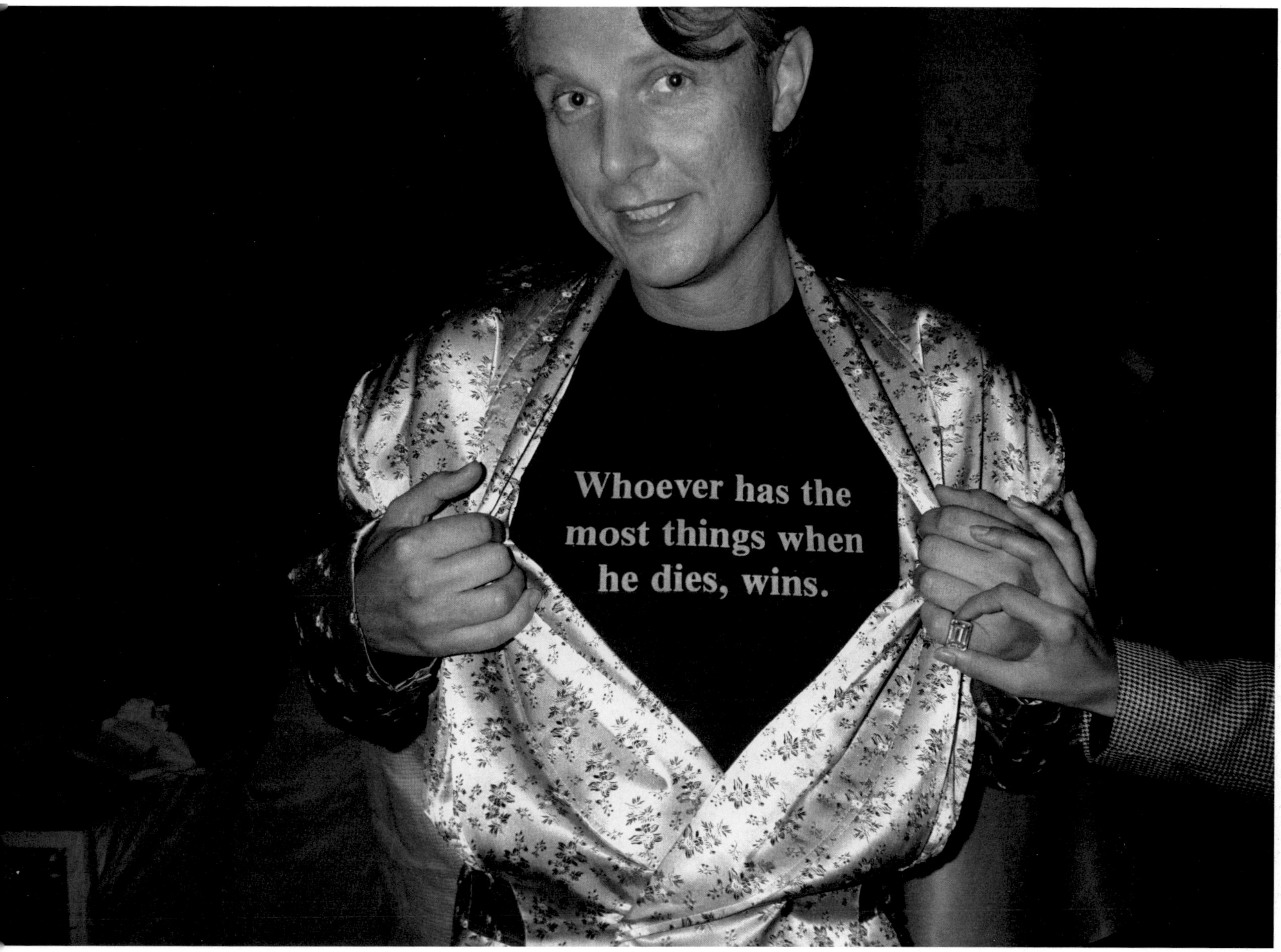

..I STARTED AT DANCETERIA IN '82 I THINK. PYRAMID, BERLIN...YOU NAME IT. I ALSO REMEMBER HANGING OUT AT THE PARADISE GARAGE (SAW GRACE JONES PERFORM) AND ROXY. I GOT HIRED BY RUDOLF FOR MY JOB AT DANCETERIA WHILE HANGING OUT WITH HIM AT ROXY ONE NIGHT.

RUDOLF... "I LIKE THE WAY YOU LOOK. CAN YOU BARTEND?"
ME... "NO, BUT I CAN DRINK."
RUDOLF... "GOOD, GO DO YOUR HOMEWORK AND BE AT THE CLUB ON TUESDAY NIGHT."
JULIE LANKE

RUDOLF
AT THE CHRISTOPHE DE MENIL FASHION SHOW AT THE PALLADIUM.
1985

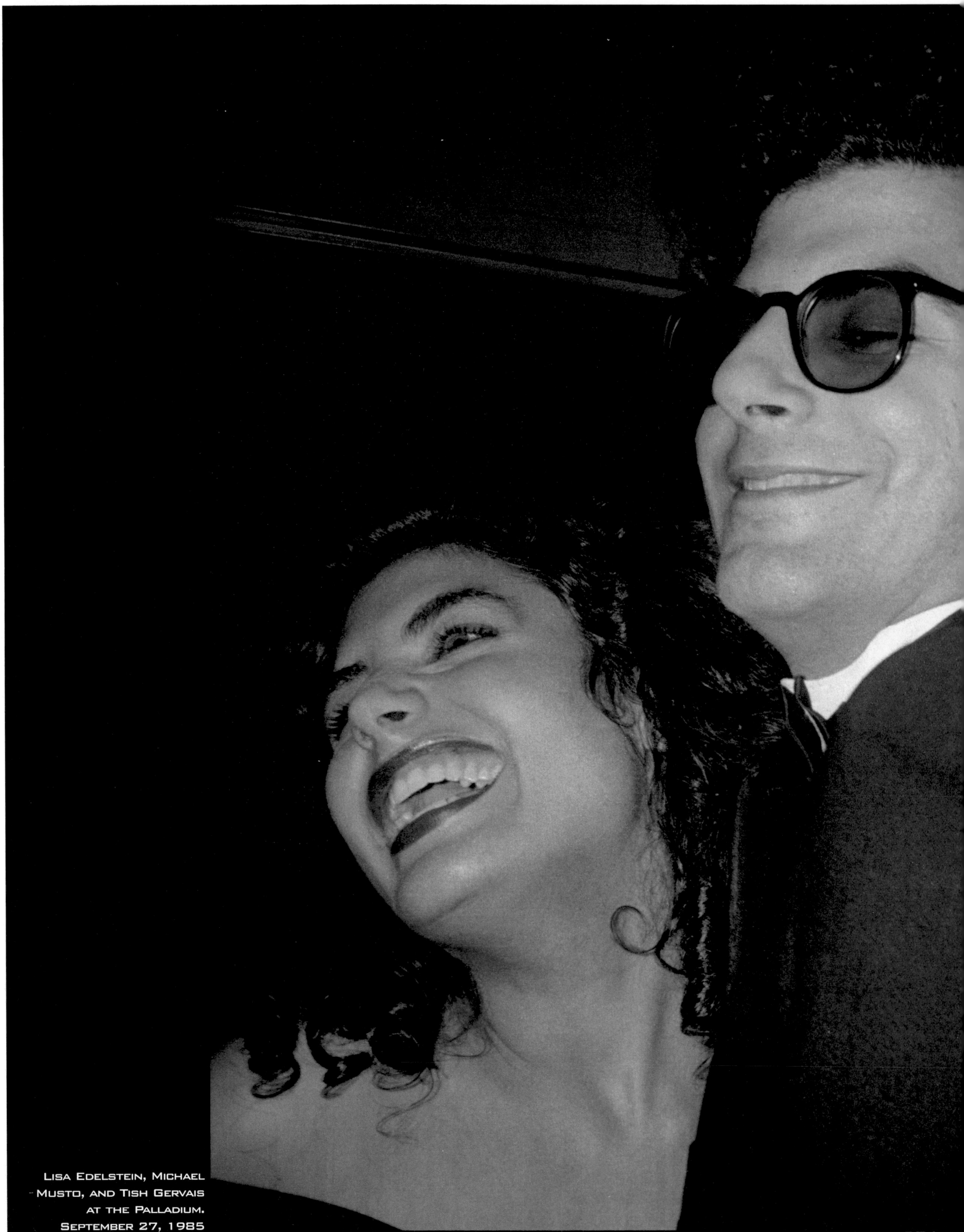

Lisa Edelstein, Michael Musto, and Tish Gervais at the Palladium. September 27, 1985

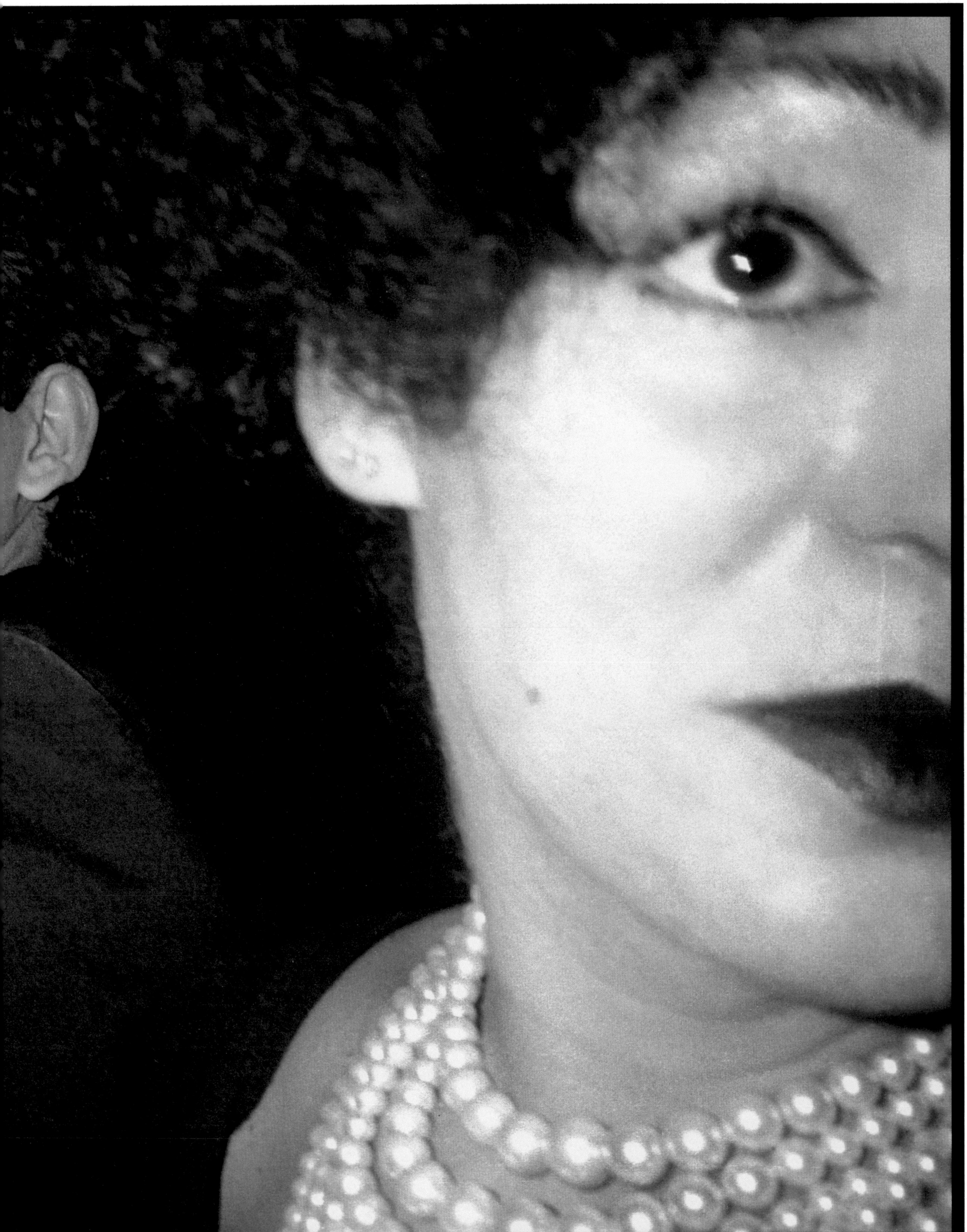

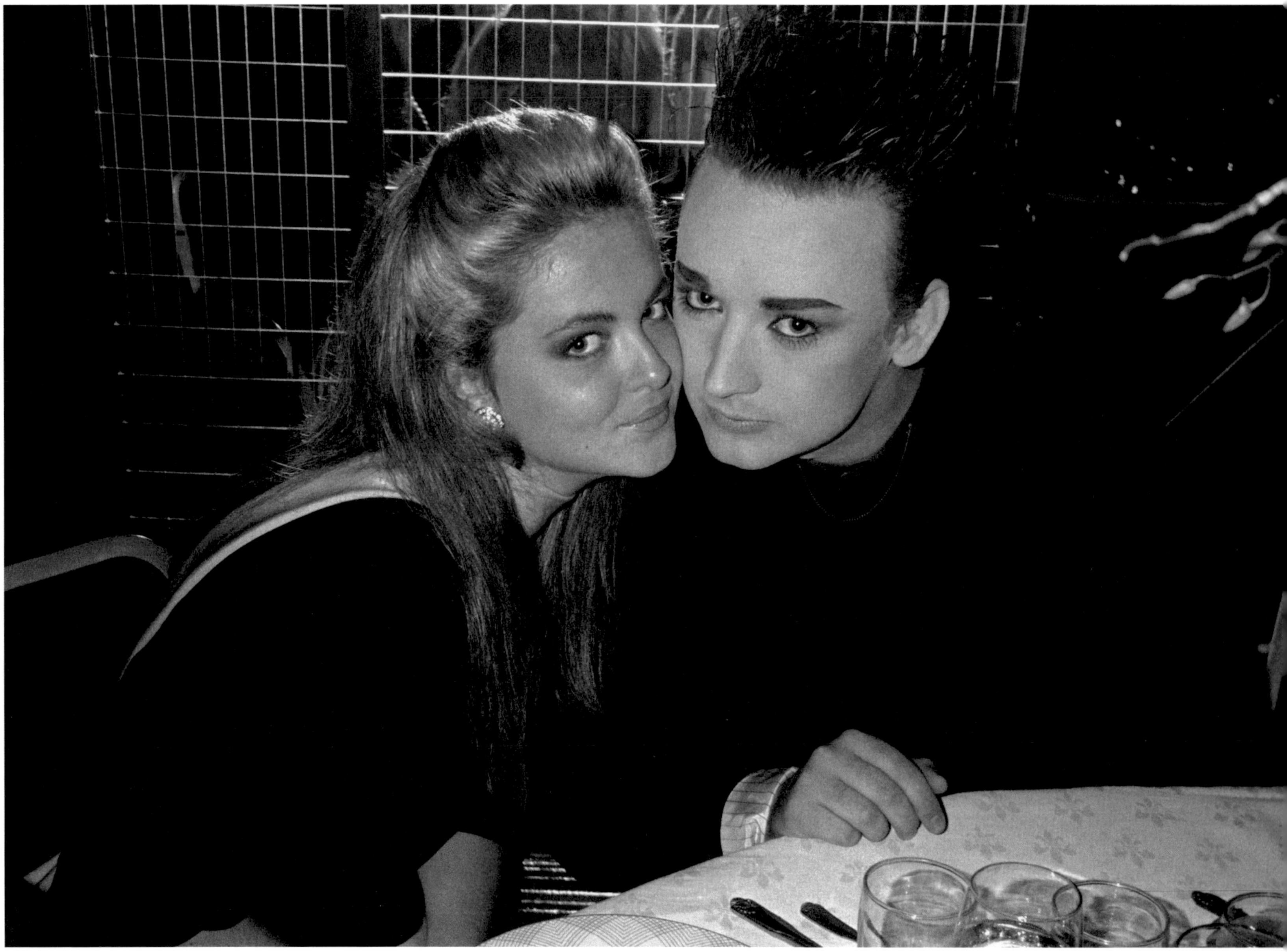

Cornelia Guest and Boy George
at the Dynasty dinner at Regine's.
October 1985

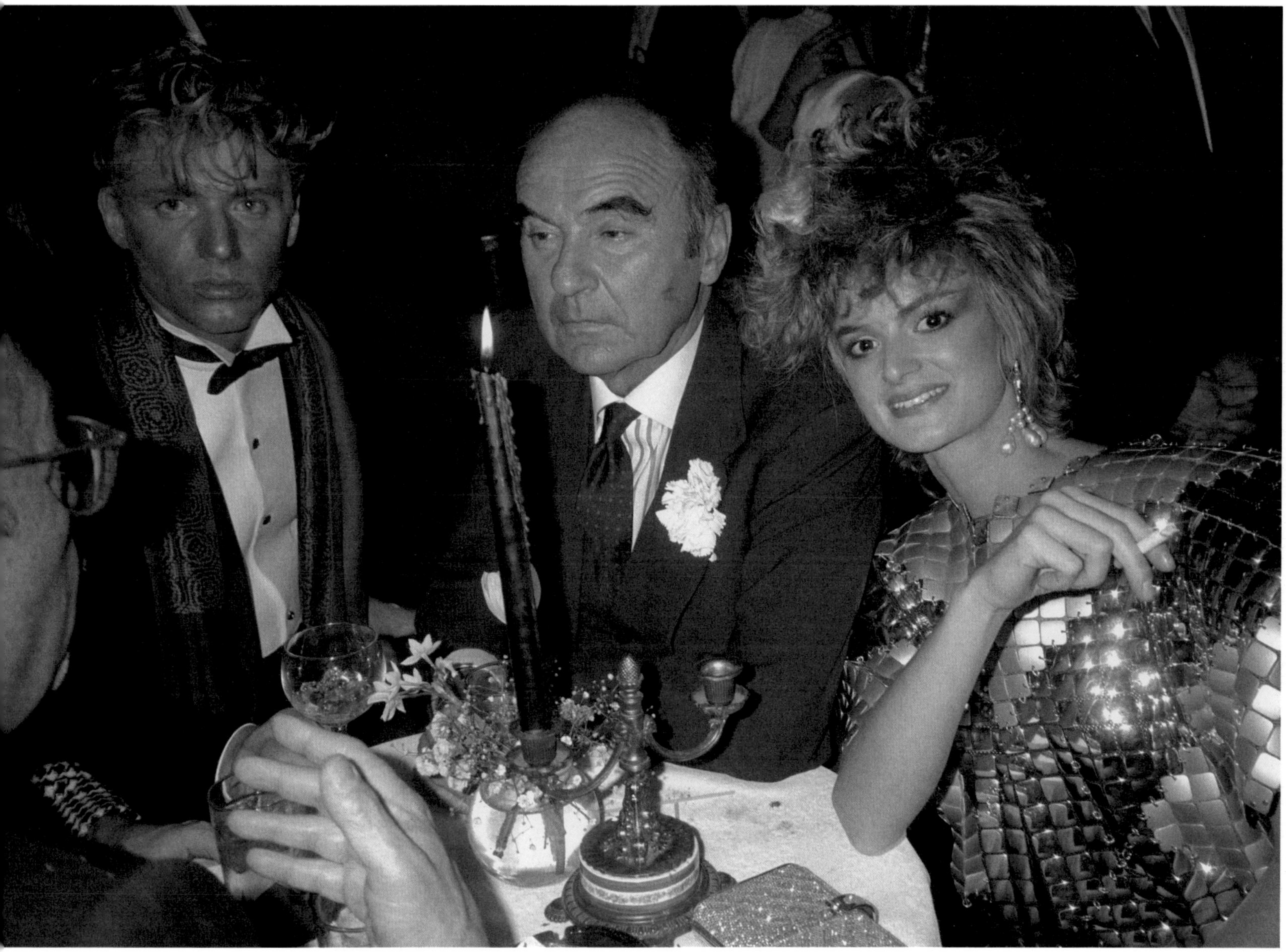

Ahmet Ertegun, Name Unknown, Prince Johann, and Princess Gloria von Thurn und Taxis
at the party in her honor at the Palladium.
October 30, 1985

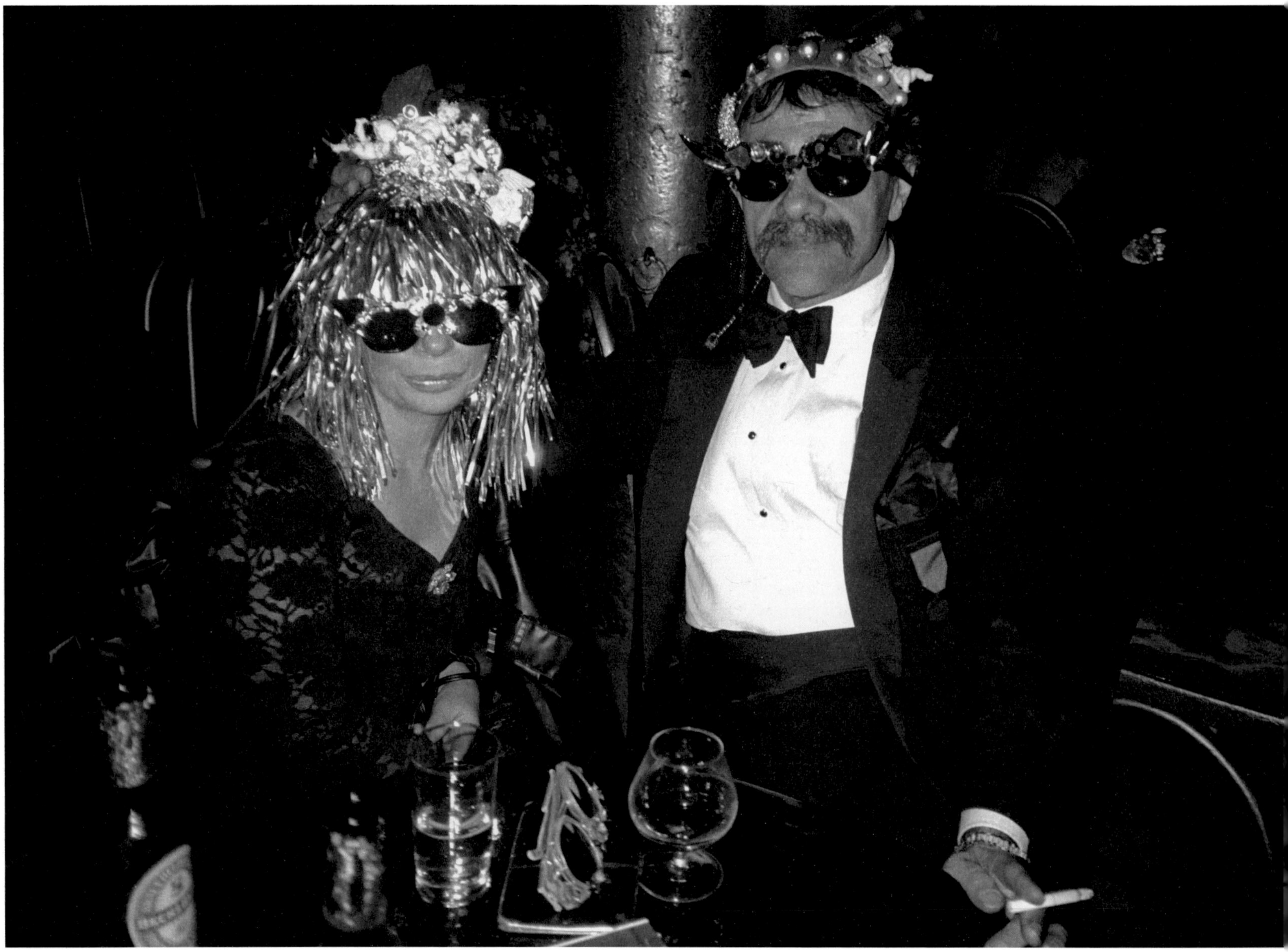

Disguised party guests at the Patricia Field's Hat Party at Area.
Monday, October 28, 1985

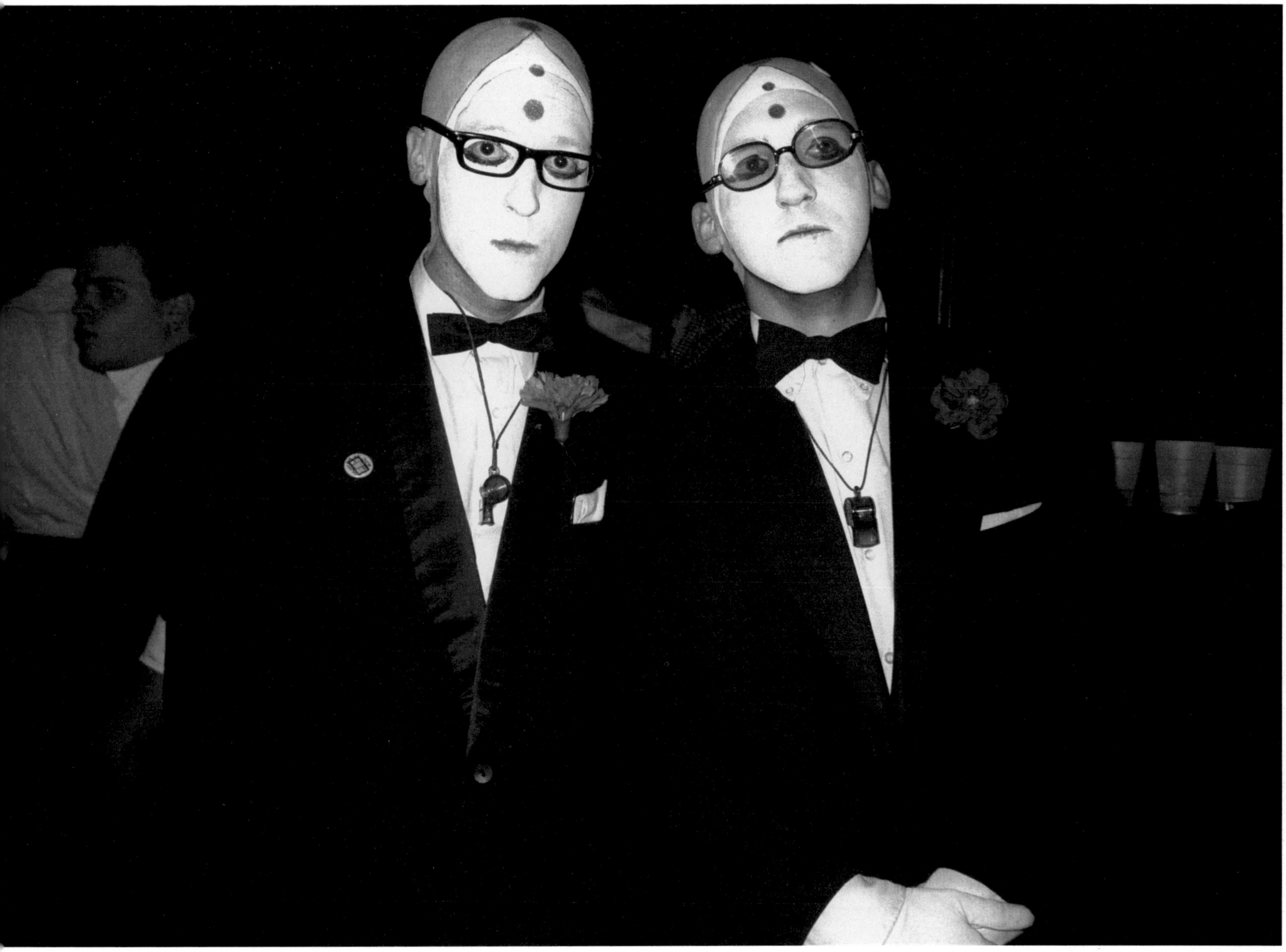

Costumes at The Ritz
for the WLIR Radio Costume Ball.
Thursday, April 11, 1985

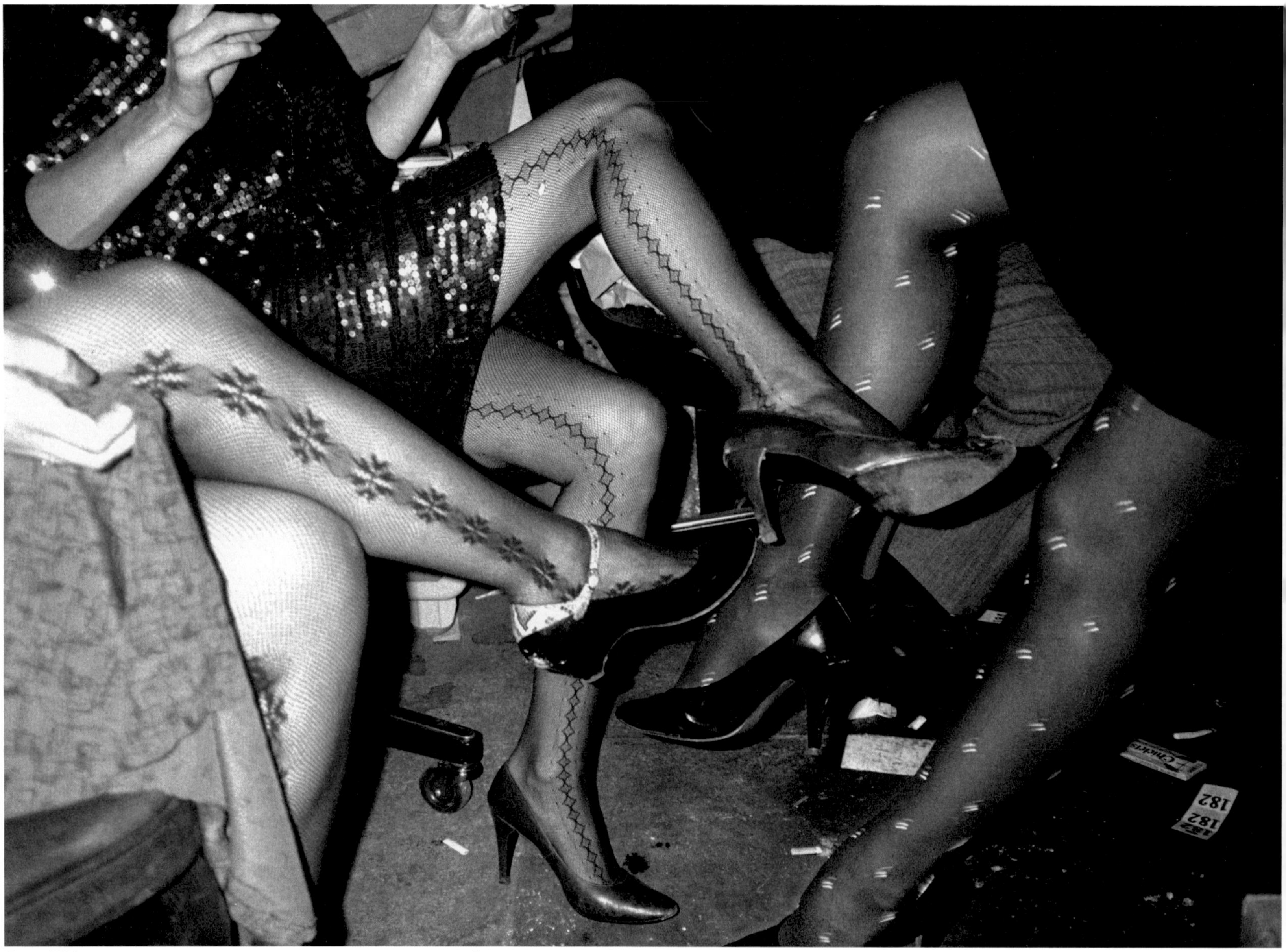

The 80s were the happiest time of my life. I was newly married, and the mother of a growing family of three children. Funny story...I was working with "The Donald," to help create the magic of changing the old Commodore Hotel into the dynamic Hyatt at Grand Central Terminal. I was working as Executive Vice President, and in charge of all interior designs. I worked, and I worked, and I worked...until one week before the birth of one of my children. The crew were thrilled that I had given birth and would be out for weeks, if not months. Ha! The joke was on them...I was back at work in 3 days and the hotel opened on time. It was a magical time for us.
Ivana Trump

Legs, including Tinkerbelle's,
at Vito Bruno's birthday party at Area.
Wednesday, October 3, 1984

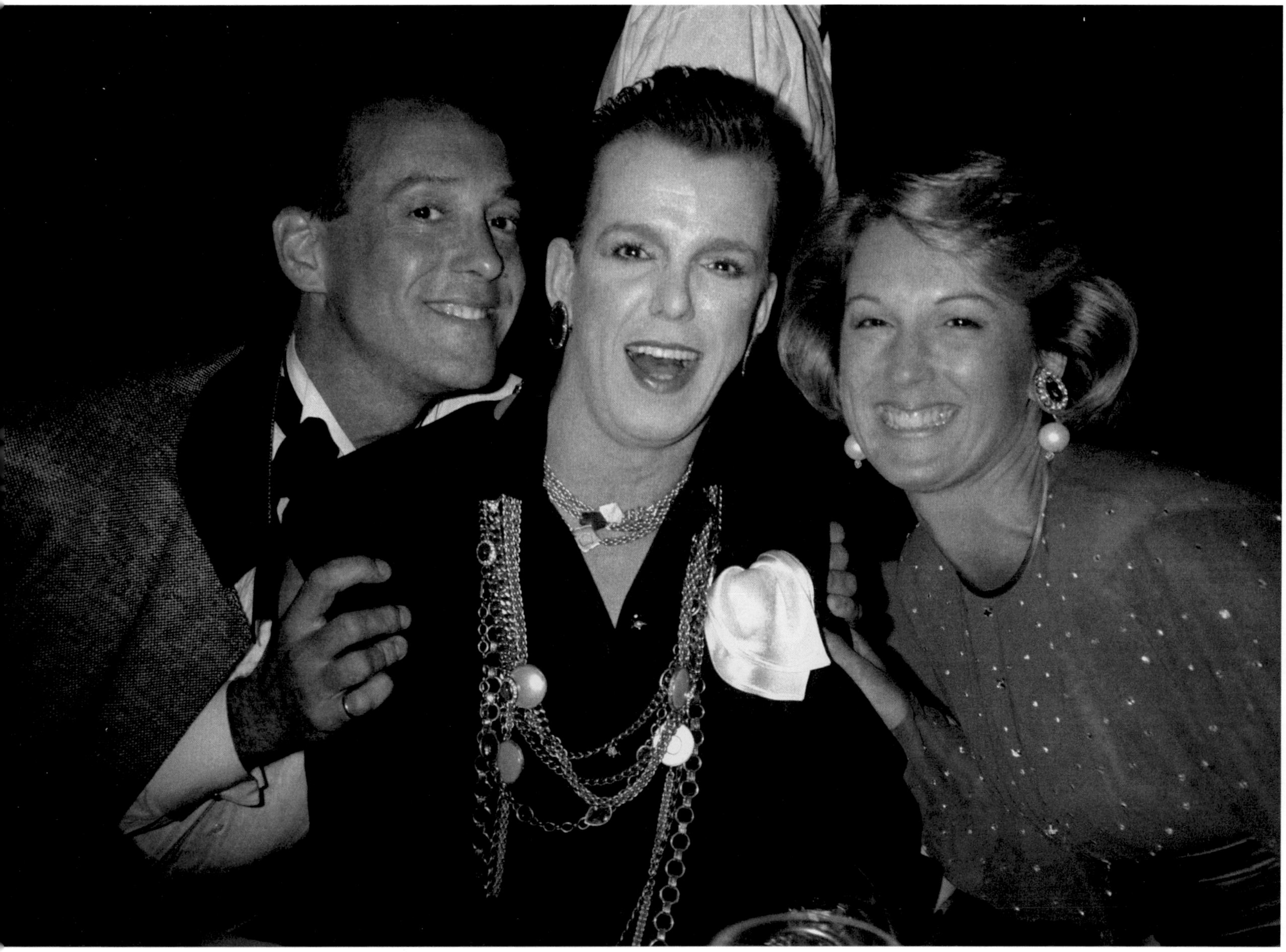

Michael Katz, Kevin Boyce, and Sydney Biddle Barrows
at Sydney Biddle Barrow's dinner party at Stringfellows.
September 10, 1986

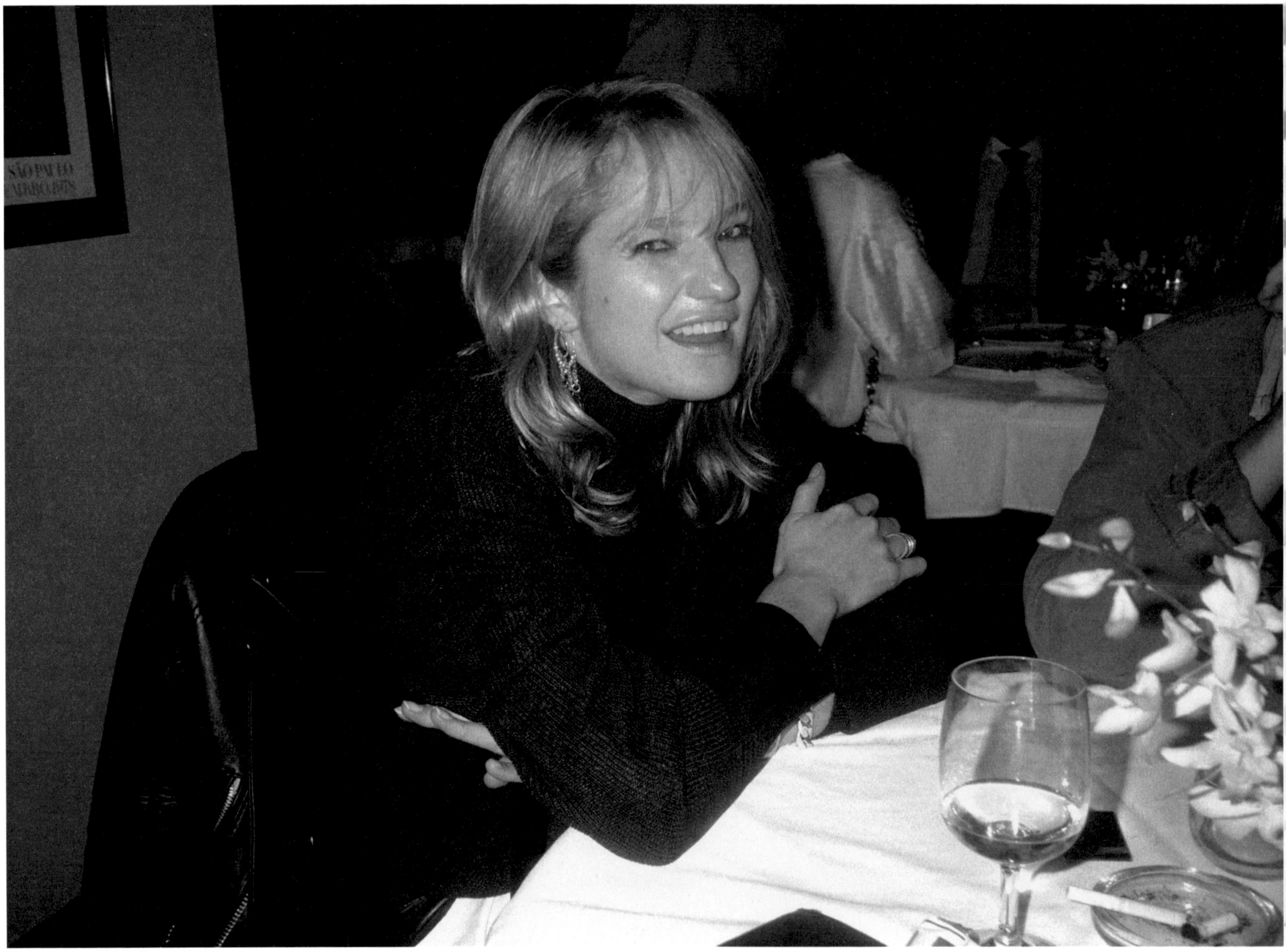

Ellen Barkin
at the Fellini Party at the Trump Towers.
March 26, 1986

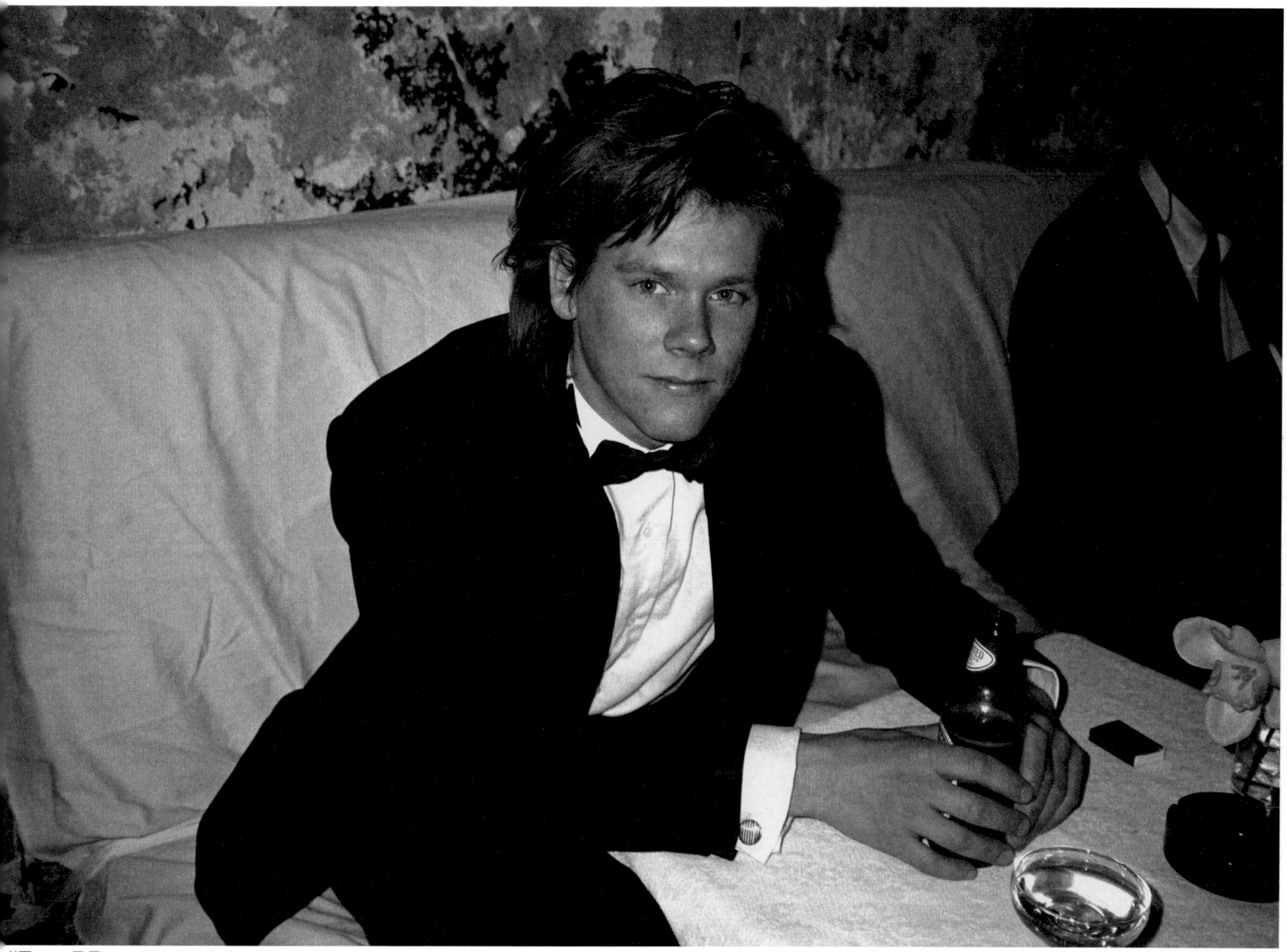

"THE 80S WERE A VERY TRANSITIONAL TIME FOR ME. THE PARTY WAS OVER AND IT WAS TIME TO CLEAN MY HOUSE. FAME, LONELINESS, BIRTH, DEATH, MARRIAGE. A LOT OF RUNNING AND A LOT OF CHANGE."
KEVIN BACON

KEVIN BACON
AT THE GREAT PEACE MARCH DINNER HELD AT THE PALLADIUM.
JANUARY 1986

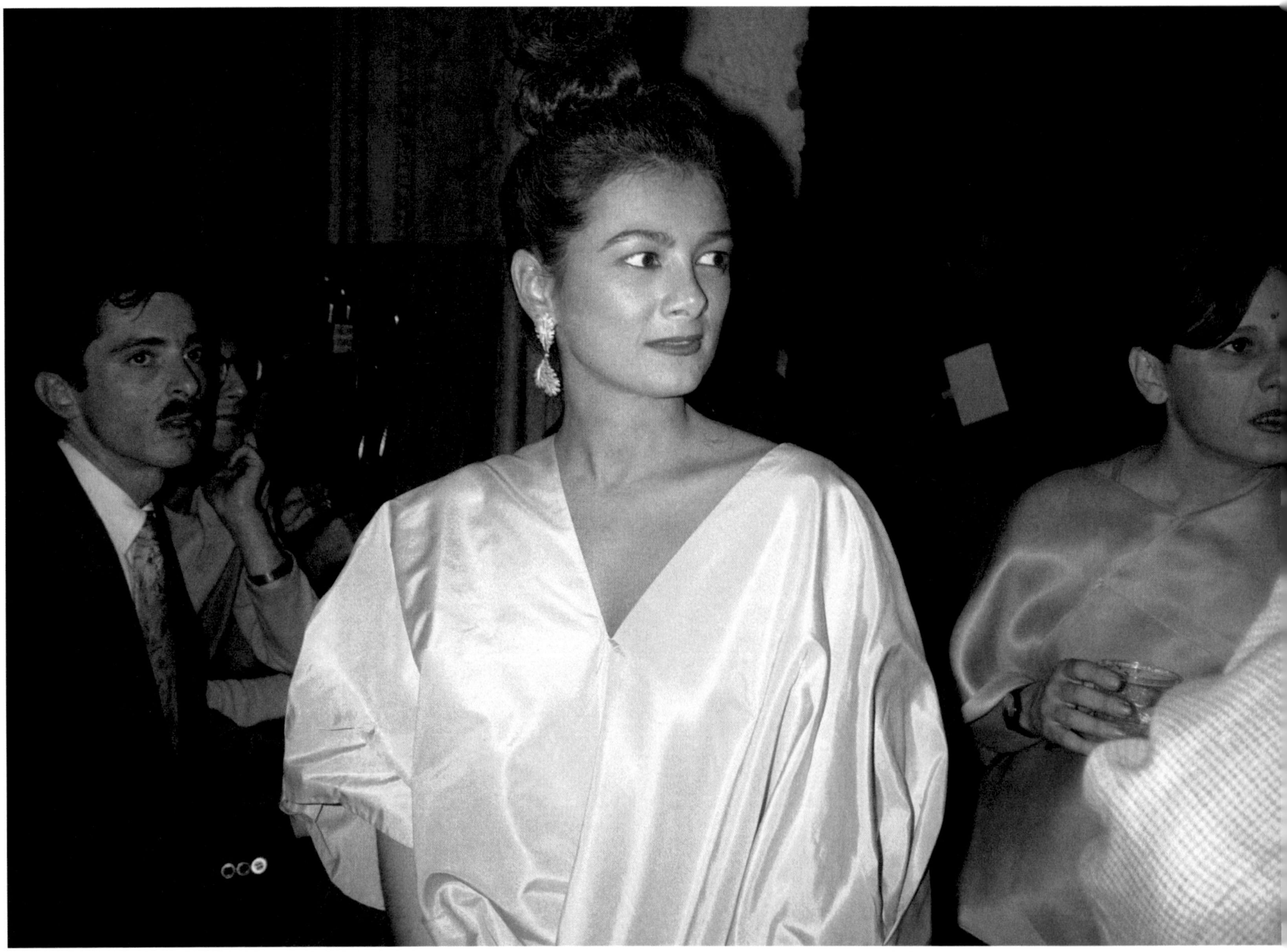

"In contrast to the greed and corruption often associated with this decade, the 80s were exciting because of talent and innovation. Patrick McMullan was there to help us remember those times."
Mary Boone

Mary Boone
at the Christophe de Menil Fashion Show at the Palladium.
1985

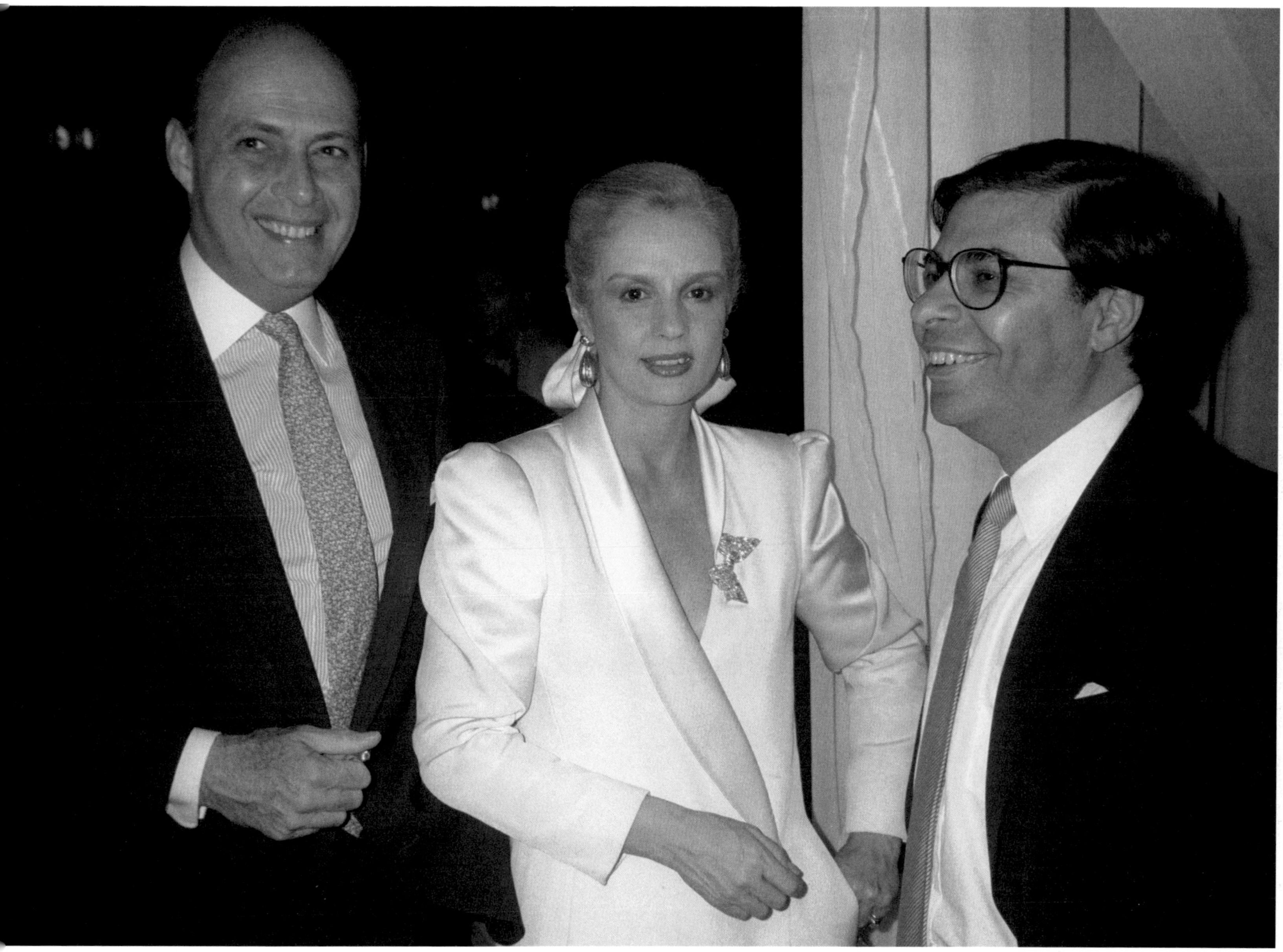

Reinaldo and Carolina Herrera, Bob Colacello
at the opening night of the Palladium.
May 14, 1985

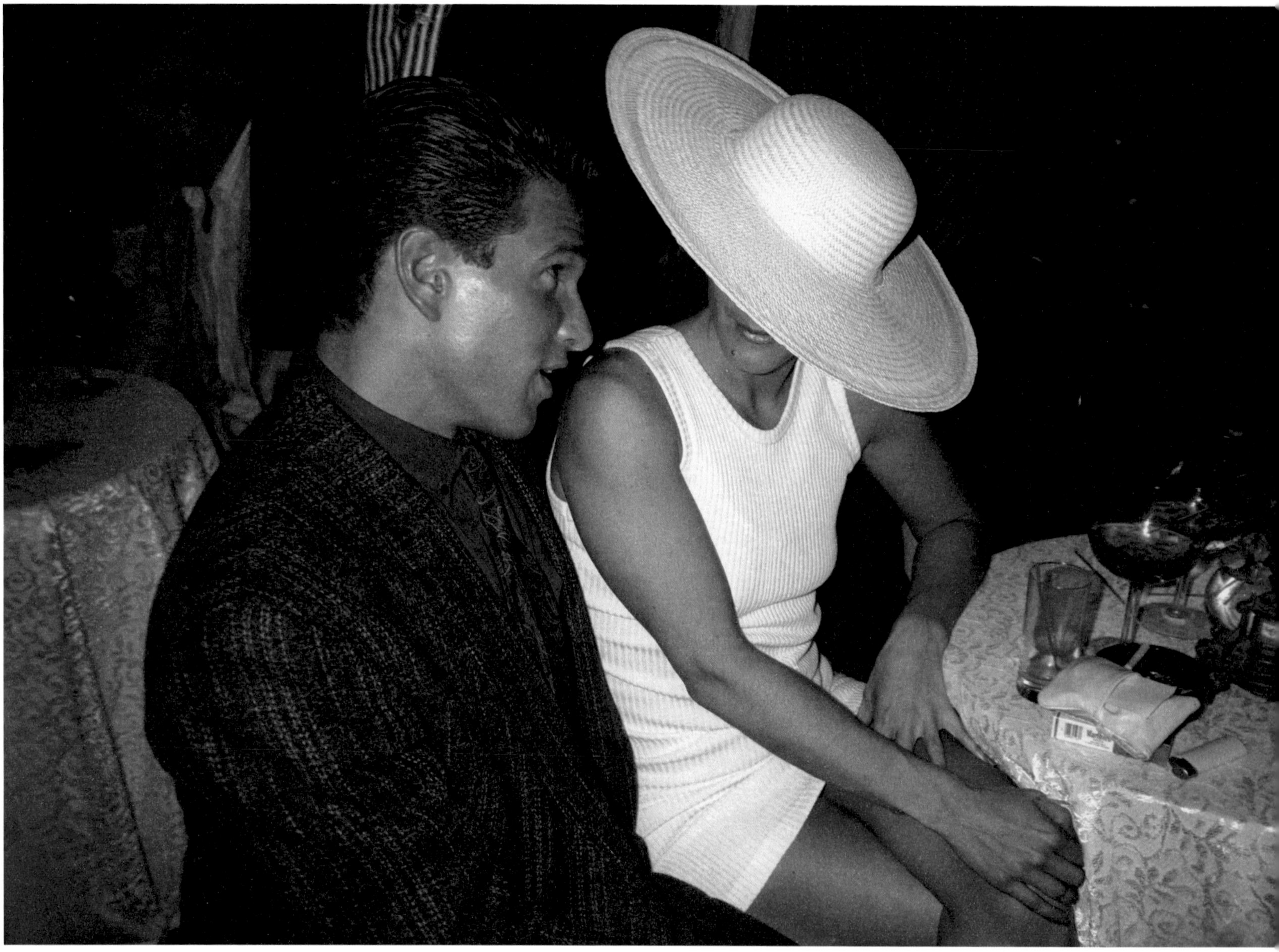

LEFT: DAVID BURNS AND CHI CHI VALENTI
AT THE OPENING NIGHT OF THE PALLADIUM. MAY 14, 1985
RIGHT: MORGAN FAIRCHILD AND LINDA EVANS
AT THE FRAGRANCE AWARDS, HELD AT LINCOLN CENTER. JUNE 4, 1985

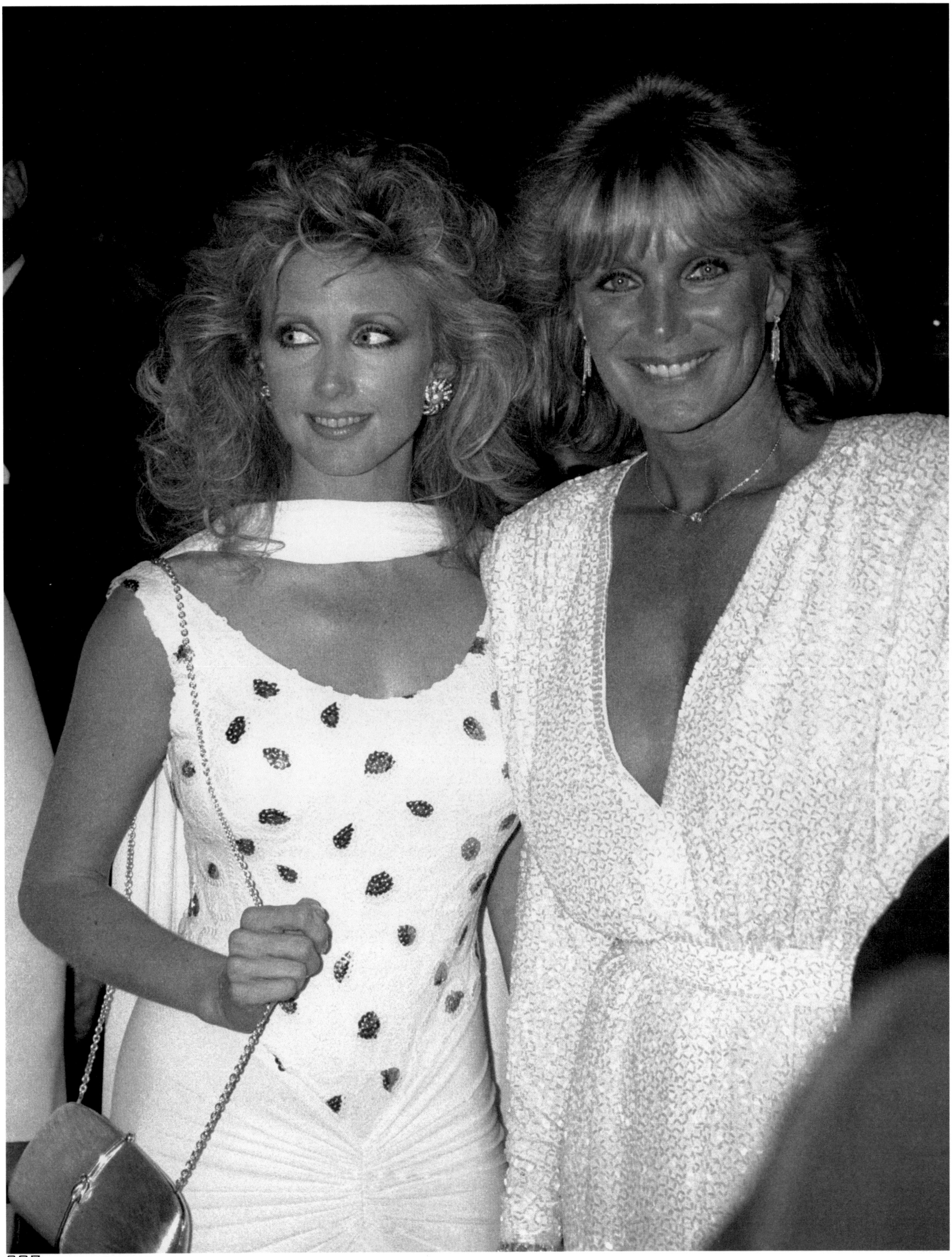

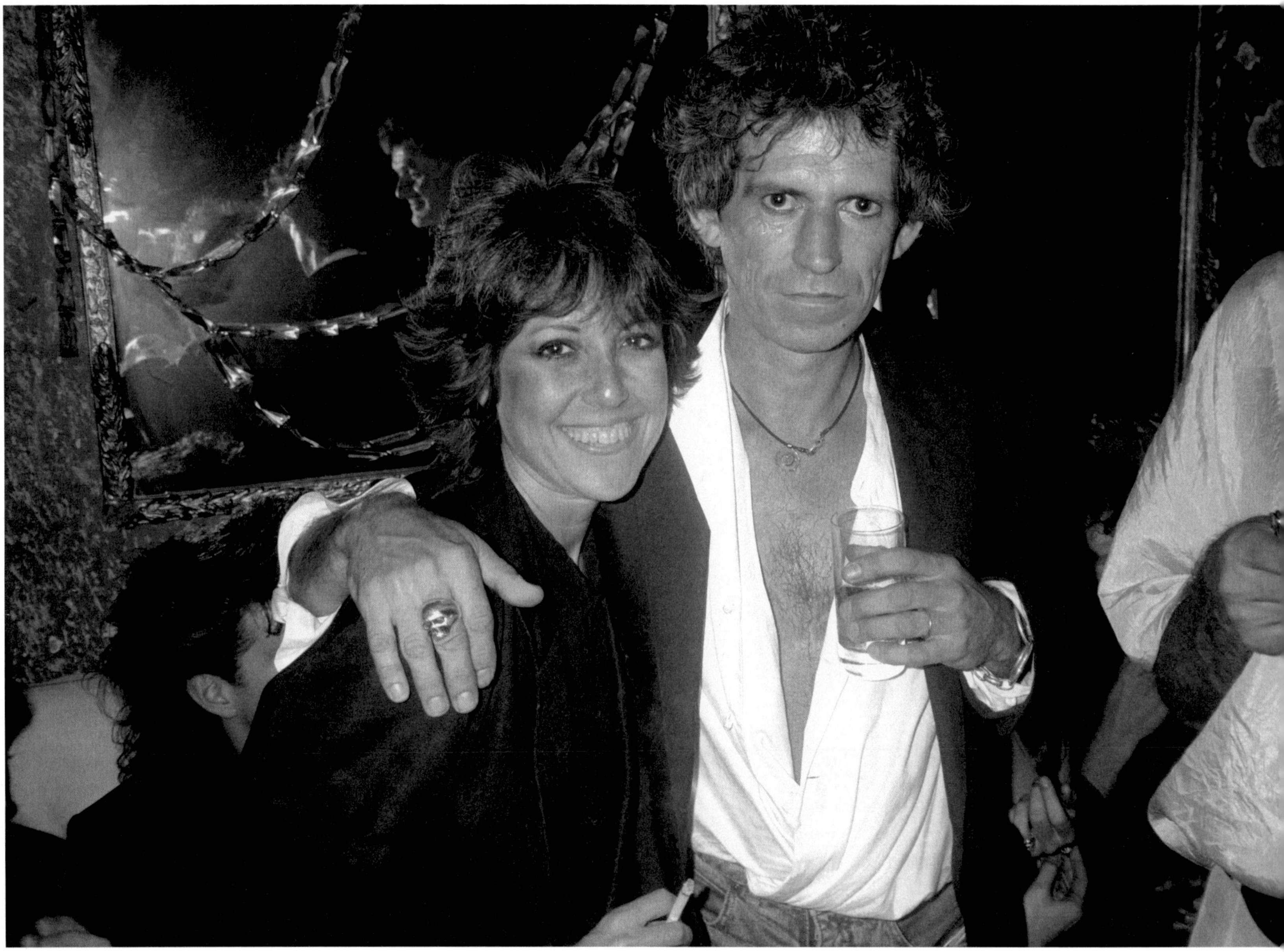

Lisa Robinson and Keith Richards
at Mick Jagger's birthday party at the Palladium.
August 1985

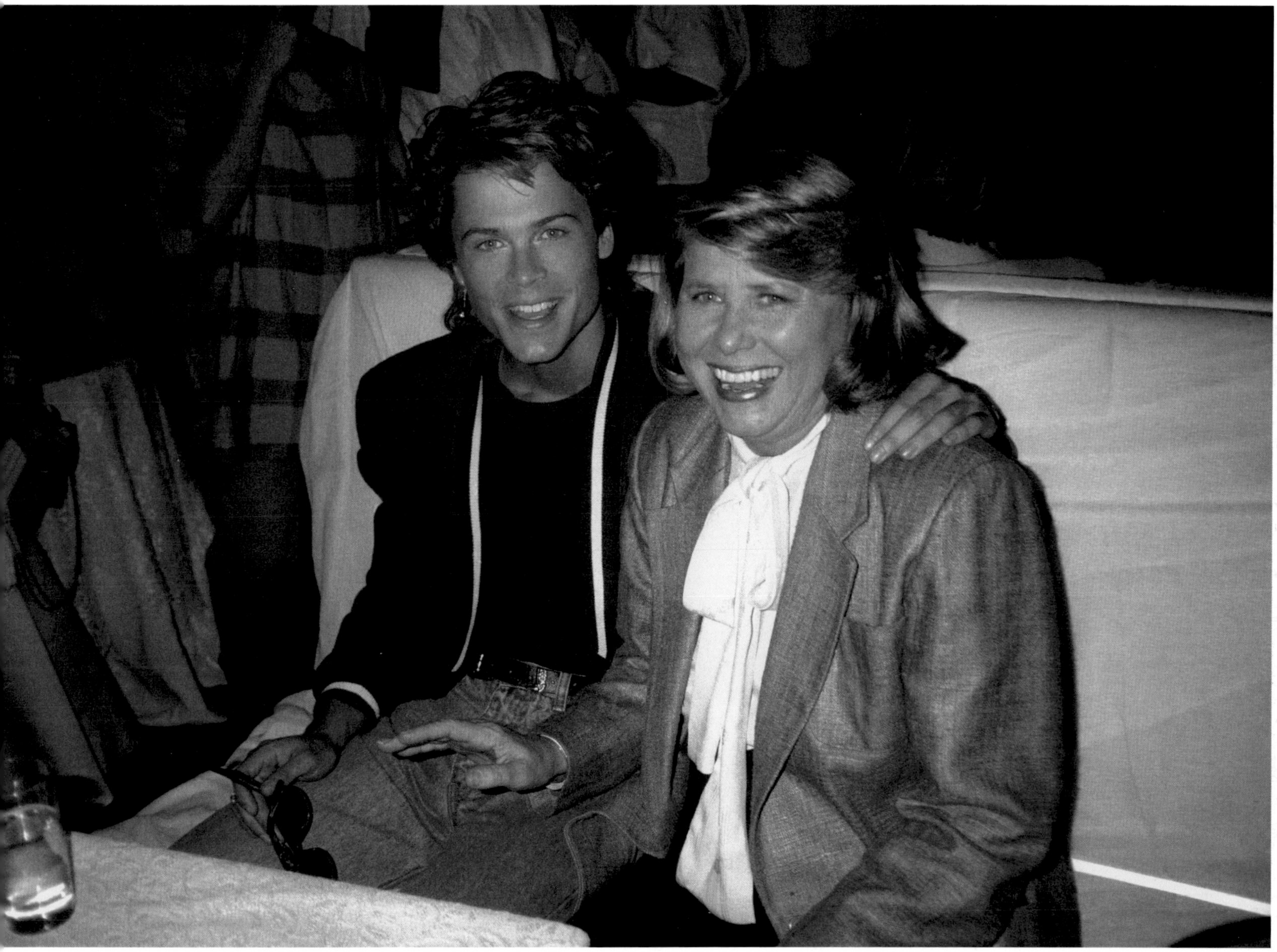

"You don't need to have lived through the 80s; all you have to do is look at so80s: A Photographic Diary of a Decade by that friend to VIPs and the famous, Patrick McMullan. When you see him at a party or gathering, you know it's on the record. The 80s were horrible, wonderful, exhausting, exhilarating. This book captures all of that!"
Liz Smith

Rob Lowe and Liz Smith
at the Palladium for the St. Elmo's Fire party.
June 12, 1985

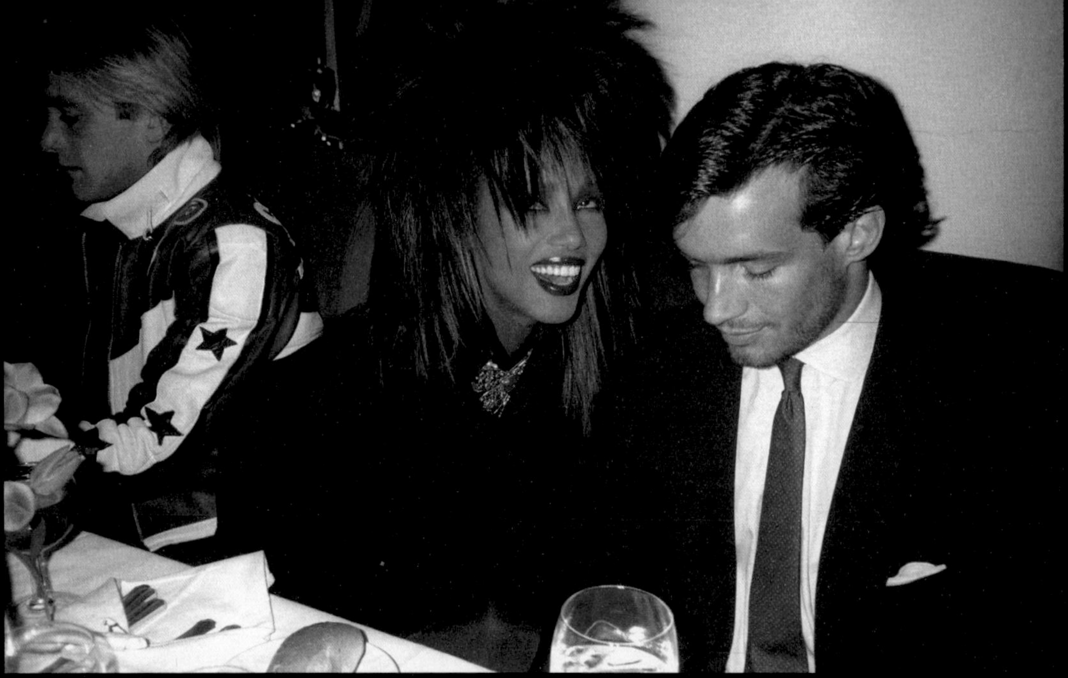

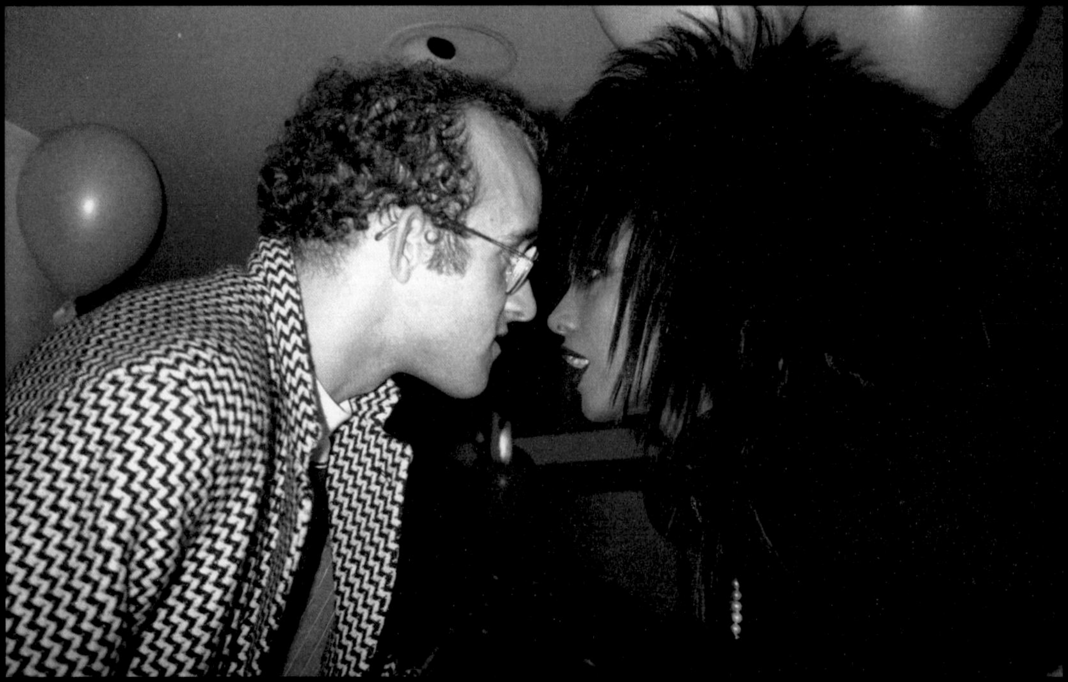

TOP: IMAN AND WILL REGAN
BOTTOM: KEITH HARING AND IMAN
AT THE GRACE JONES DINNER PARTY AT LES TULERIES.
APRIL 5,1986
RIGHT: GRACE JONES AT THE DINNER PARTY IN HER HONOR.
APRIL 5, 1986

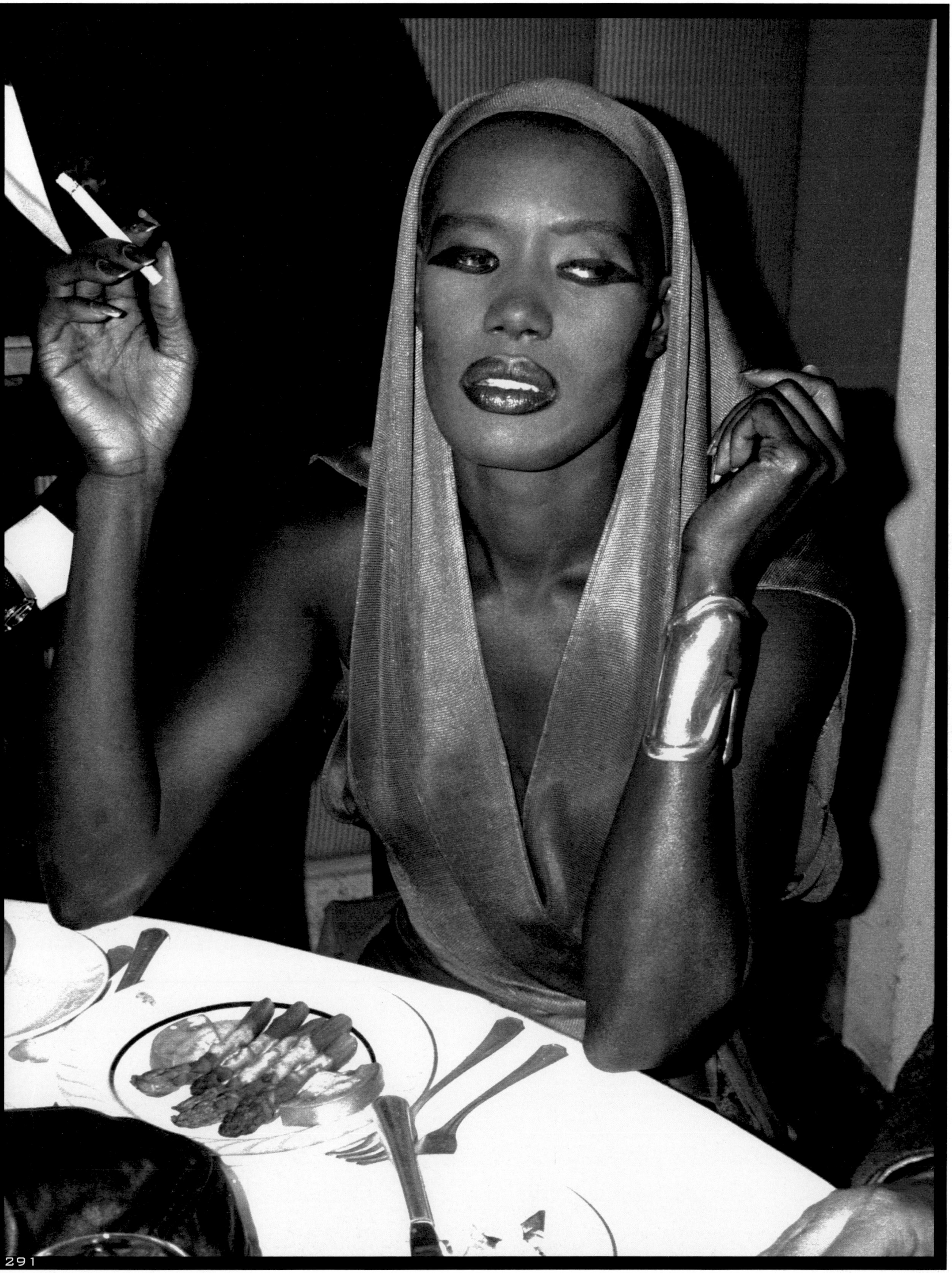

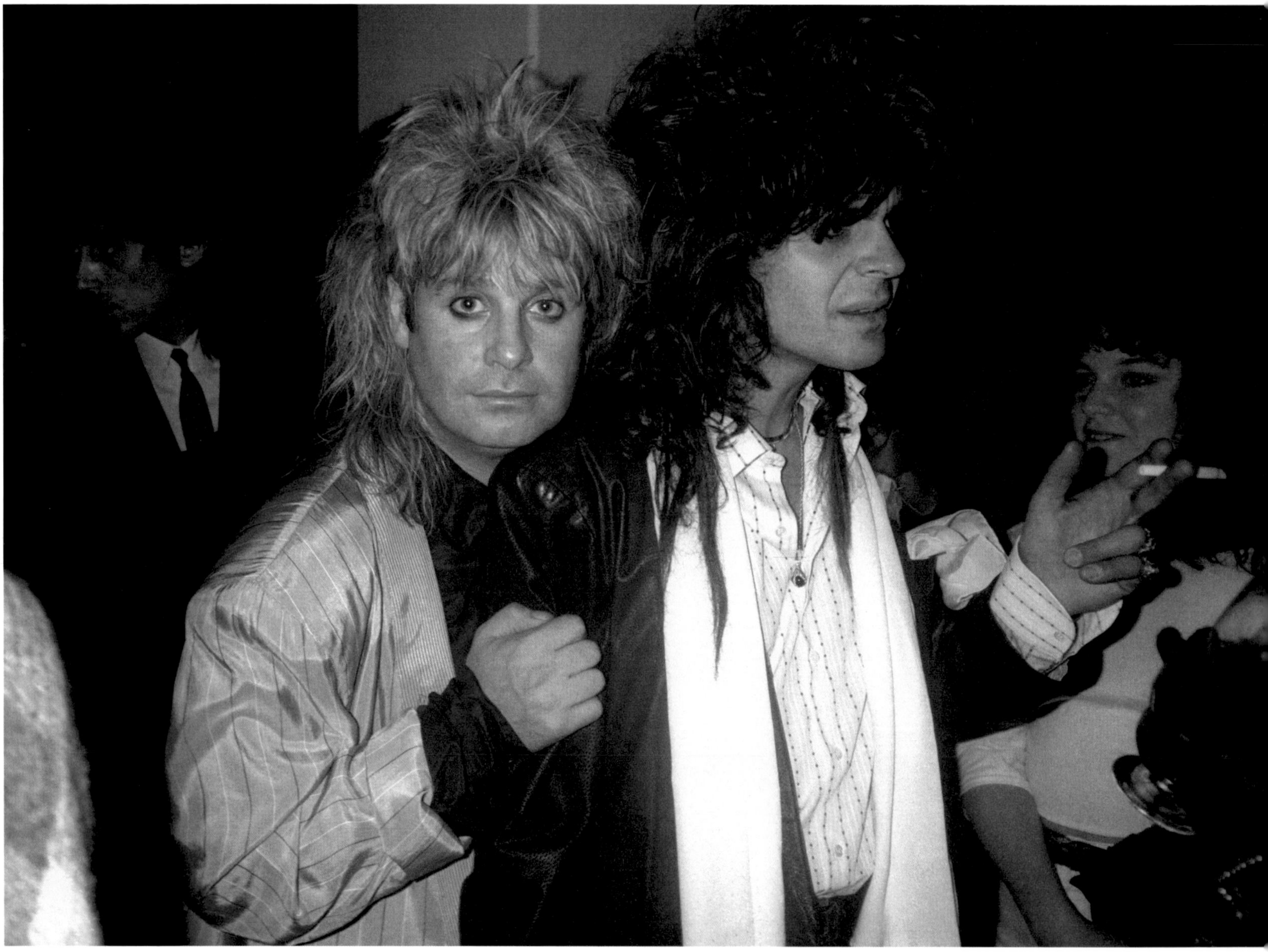

Ozzy Osbourne at Susan Blond's dinner party in his honor at Mr. Chow's.
April 21, 1986

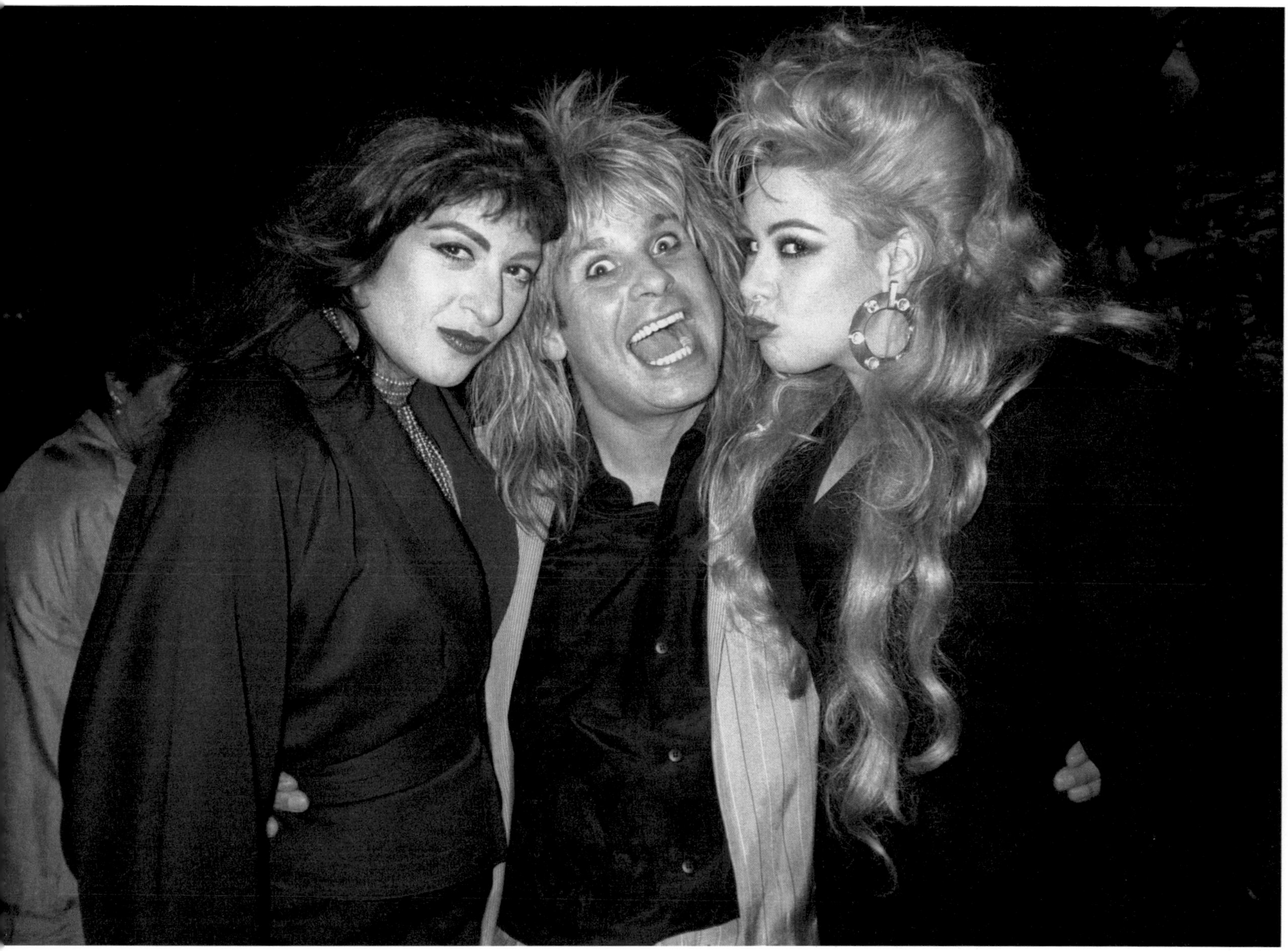

"It was all about the arrival.
Dianne was the glamorous blonde and I was the sultry brunette." Janis Savitt

Janis Savitt, Ozzy Osbourne, and Dianne Brill
at Susan Blond's dinner party for Ozzy Osbourne at Mr. Chow's.
April 21, 1986

THE HOST OF THE PARTY LOOKED SAD. HE WAS SITTING IN THE CORNER ON THE GRAY WALL-TO-WALL INDUSTRIAL CARPETING WATCHING HIS SHIMMERING, GILDED, CELEBRATED GUESTS WITH HIS SLOE EYES FULL OF APATHY AND HIS OFT-KISSED LIPS FROZEN INTO A DISINGENUOUS SMILE. HE WAS IGNORING HIS FAMOUS GUESTS, IGNORING THE SAMBAS AND TANGOS FROM THE TWELVE–MEMBER MARIMBA BAND, IGNORING LA DOLCE VITA HUMMING ON THE MAMMOTH ADVENT VIDEO SCREEN, IGNORING PEALS OF LAUGHTER FROM THE GROUP FROLICKING IN HIS JACUZZI, IGNORING THE NEBUCHADNEZZARS OF CHAMPAGNE, THE MR. CHOW-CATERED FOOD, EVEN IGNORING THE BAD MANNERS OF THE TWO FRENCH POSEURS, DRESSED IN FASHION-CASUALTY DRAG OF BLACK-AND-RED PLAID SHIRTS AND LEOPARD-SKIN TROUSERS, WHO WERE ON TOP OF A TABLE CROUCHING OVER THE KILO OF BELUGA CAVIAR THAT ALBA CLEMENTE HAD PRESENTED THE HOST AS A PARTY GIFT. THESE AWFUL FROGS WERE RIGHT ON THE TABLE, RIGHT IN THE LETTUCE LEAVES, EATING CAVIAR BY THE TABLESPOONSFUL, AS IF IT WERE CHEAP LIVESTOCK OATMEAL.

THE HOST WAS UNRUFFLED. HE BATTED NOT ONE BAMBI-LIKE LASH.

IT WAS A GOOD PARTY, YOU COULD TELL BY THE PARTY BAROMETER MAN, ANDY WARHOL. ALL THE STARS WERE CRUSHING IN, BUBBLY, PERFUMED, CRACKLING WITH SPARKS, BUT THE HOST WAS JUST LOOKING MELANCHOLY. AND WHEN HE WASN'T LOOKING WISTFUL, HE WAS LOOKING BORED AND SULLEN. HE EVEN YAWNED A FEW TIMES.

I THOUGHT HE MIGHT PERK UP WHEN I SAW THE GAGGLE OF GORGEOUS GIRLS AND THE BEVY OF BLONDE BOMBSHELL BEAUTIES CLUSTER AROUND HIM, ATTEMPTING TO TITILLATE HIM, BUT THIS DID NOTHING TO AROUSE HIM. HE WAS MONOSYLLABIC IN HIS ANSWERS TO THEIR GIGGLY QUESTIONS.

YES, OUR HOST, JEAN-MICHEL BASQUIAT, THE BRIGHT GRAFFITI ARTIST TURNED SUDDENLY WILDLY SUCCESSFUL GENIUS PAINTER, WAS IN A HO-HUM KINDA MOOD.

WATCHING HIM, I FILLED IN THE BLANKS MYSELF. MAYBE HE WAS, FOR THE FIRST TIME, THINKING WHAT A SHAM THIS SUCCESS NONSENSE WAS. MAYBE HE WAS ASKING HIMSELF IF THIS WAS ALL THERE WAS. WHERE WAS THE JOY THAT'S SUPPOSED TO COME WITH FAME AND MONEY? WASN'T LIFE SUPPOSED TO BE FUN AND GLAMOROUS AND FULFILLING AFTER ONE WAS SUCCESSFUL AND RICH AND HAD A BEAUTIFUL HOME, FAMOUS FRIENDS, LOVERS, ESTEEM, RESPECT? WHEN WAS THE REAL DEAL GOING TO START? WHEN CAME THE FUN AT THE TOP STUFF? WHEN WAS THE PANORAMA UP THERE GOING TO LOOK BETTER THAN ANY OTHER VISTA? WHEN WAS IT GOING TO MEAN SOMETHING?

Maybe Jean-Michel had found that packing for the trip was better than getting there, the climb more rewarding than the summit. True, Basquiat had always seemed more vital and happier, more involved, bright-eyed and bushy-tailed when he was just a poor graffiti artist crashing on friends' floors. He used to laugh a lot.

Looking at him now. I wanted to shake him and say, "Don't you appreciate all this, Jean? Don't take this success jive so seriously. It's just a ball, it's all a party, enjoy it. It's all a façade...you're the one that has to give it depth."

But maybe that's exactly what he was discovering while watching his party drama unfold around him, while he was just sitting on the floor in the Party Pooper Corner. But whatever was on his mind, he was light-years away from where his body was, he was just a Jean-Michel Basquiat shell sitting there. His genius, which he so deftly displayed on canvas, was somewhere else.

Looking at him, I began to feel somehow protective, but kind of angry and sort of sorry for him too.

It was later in the evening, around 3 a.m., after people had eaten and drunk and were whipped up and sweating in samba frenzies, when I looked up from my dancing partner's face and saw Jean quietly slipping out the door. No one noticed that the host himself was leaving. No one noticed because the party was that good, it was ripping, one of the year's best. No one noticed and half the crowd, the hollow party people, the ones that appear uninvited at every party not even knowing who the host might be, didn't care an iota.

The host had had enough of his own party. Let them eat cake, the guests, let them laugh and dance and slop drinks all over the floor, whatever. The host was going out into the night. A gust of wind bearing a few gold and red leaves and a stray piece of newspaper blew in after him and that was all. The door closed behind him and as Chuck Berry had said in one of his songs, the host was gone..."gone like a cooool breeeeeeeze."

Cookie Mueller
November 1988

Published with the permission of the Estate of Cookie Mueller, and its Executor, Richard Turley

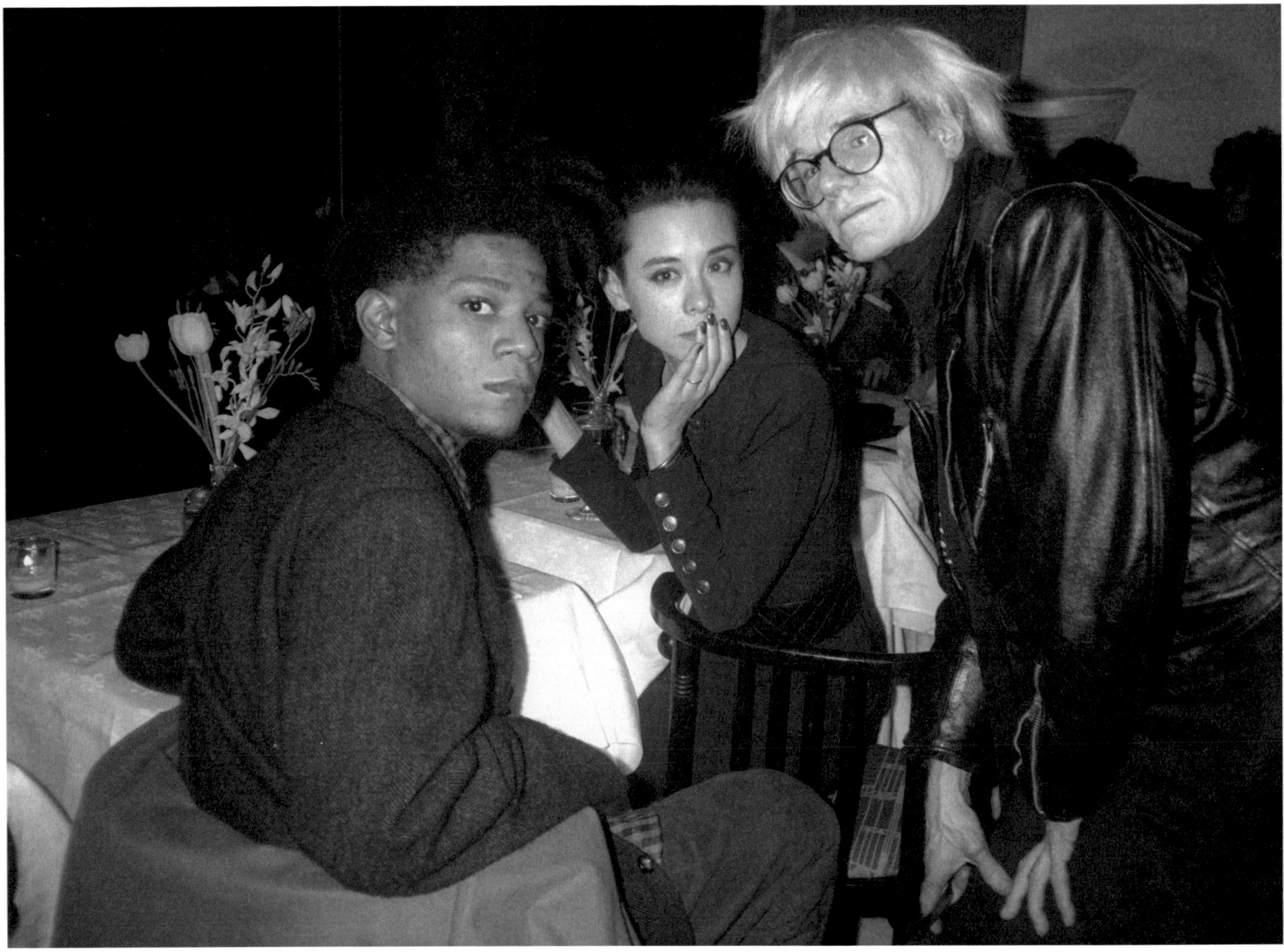

Jean-Michel Basquiat, Tina Chow, and Andy Warhol
at Susan Blond's dinner party for Ozzy Osbourne at Mr. Chow's.
April 21, 1986

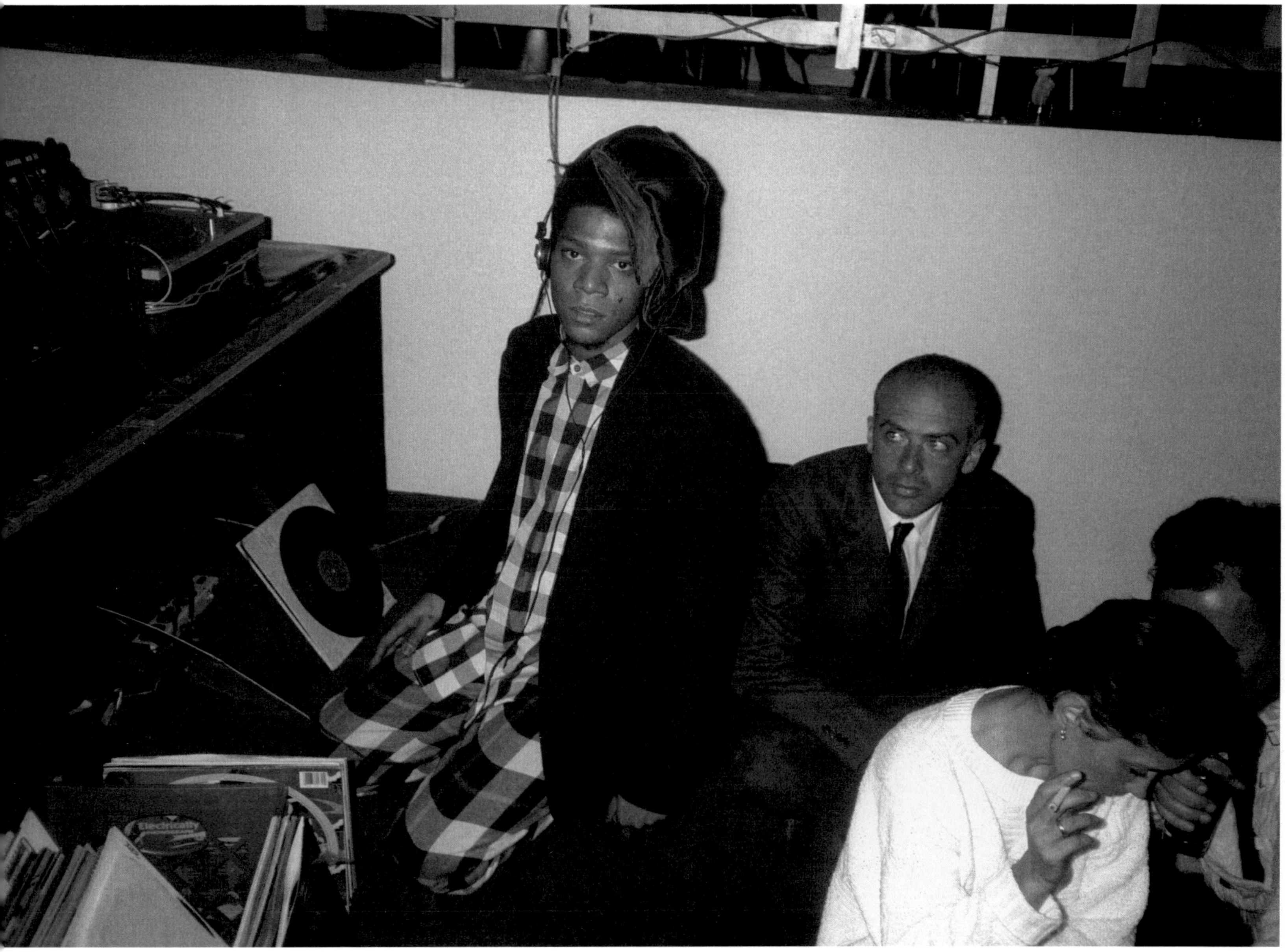

JEAN-MICHEL BASQUIAT AND FRANCESCO CLEMENTE
AT THE AREA PARTY FOR KEITH HARING'S NEW STORE: THE POP SHOP.
THURSDAY, APRIL 17, 1986

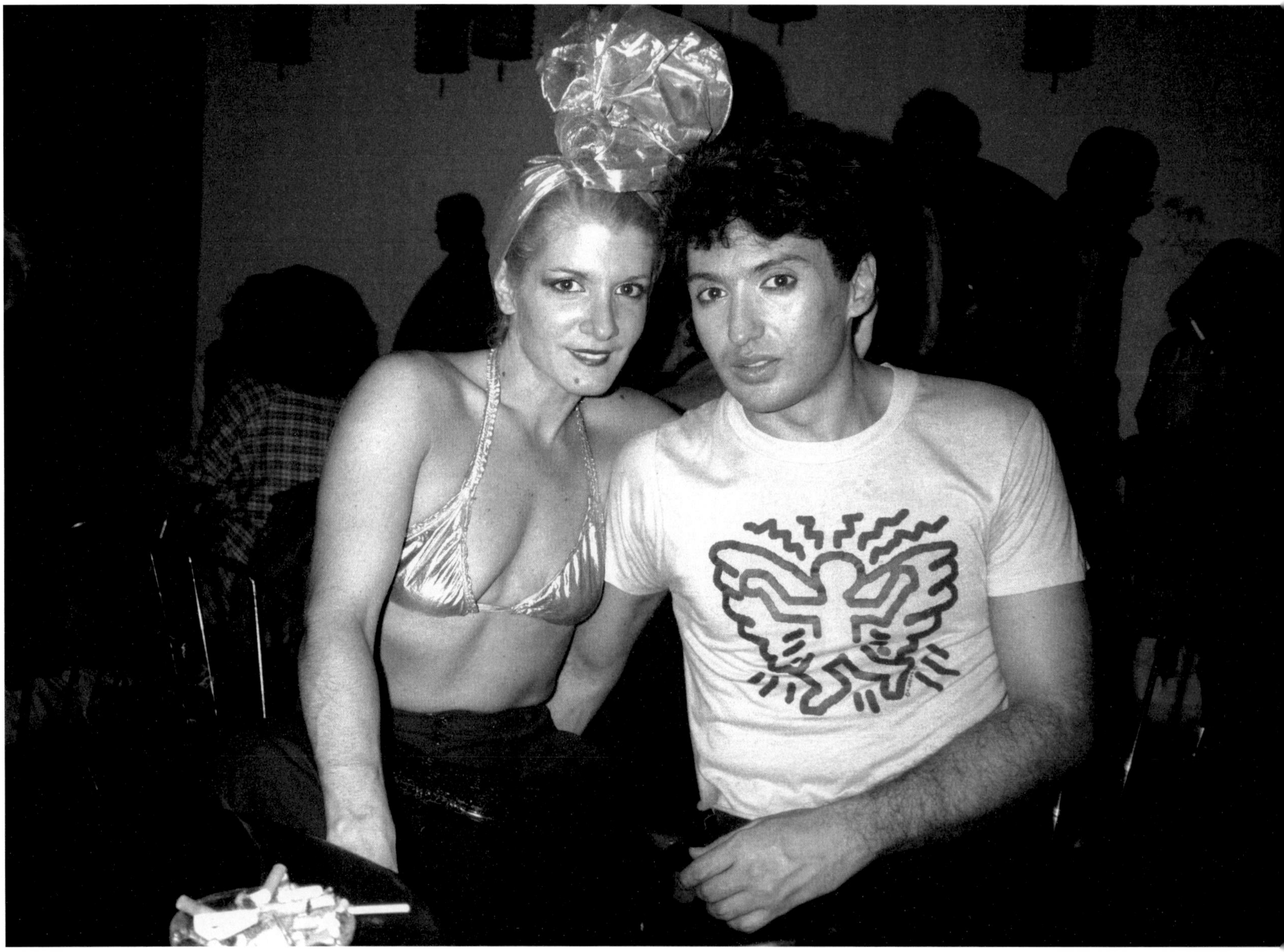

CHI CHI VALENTI AND JOHNNY DYNELL
AT THE AREA PARTY FOR KEITH HARING'S NEW STORE: THE POP SHOP.
THURSDAY, APRIL 17, 1986

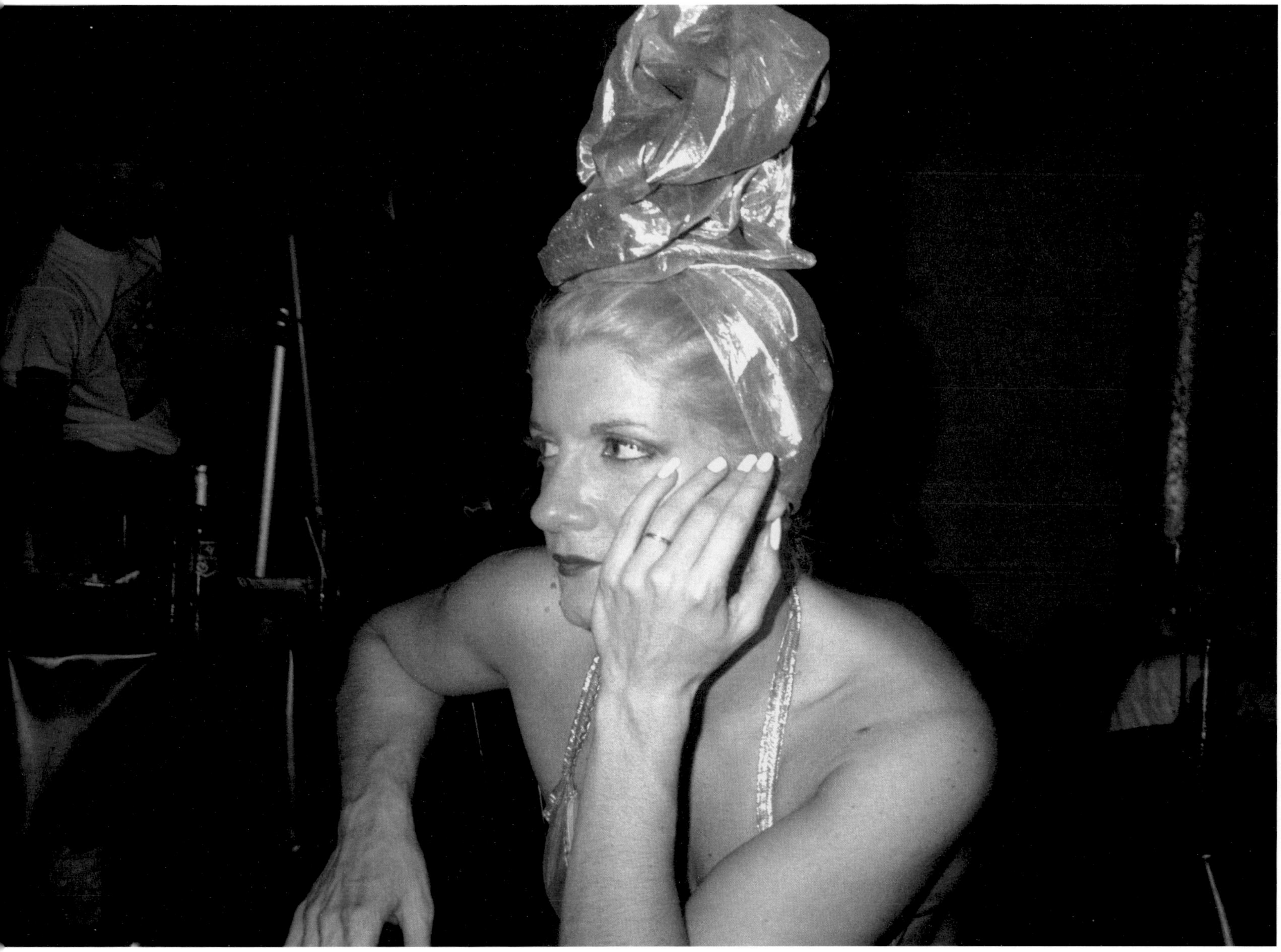

Chi Chi Valenti
at the Area party for Keith Haring's new store: the POP shop.
Thursday, April 17, 1986

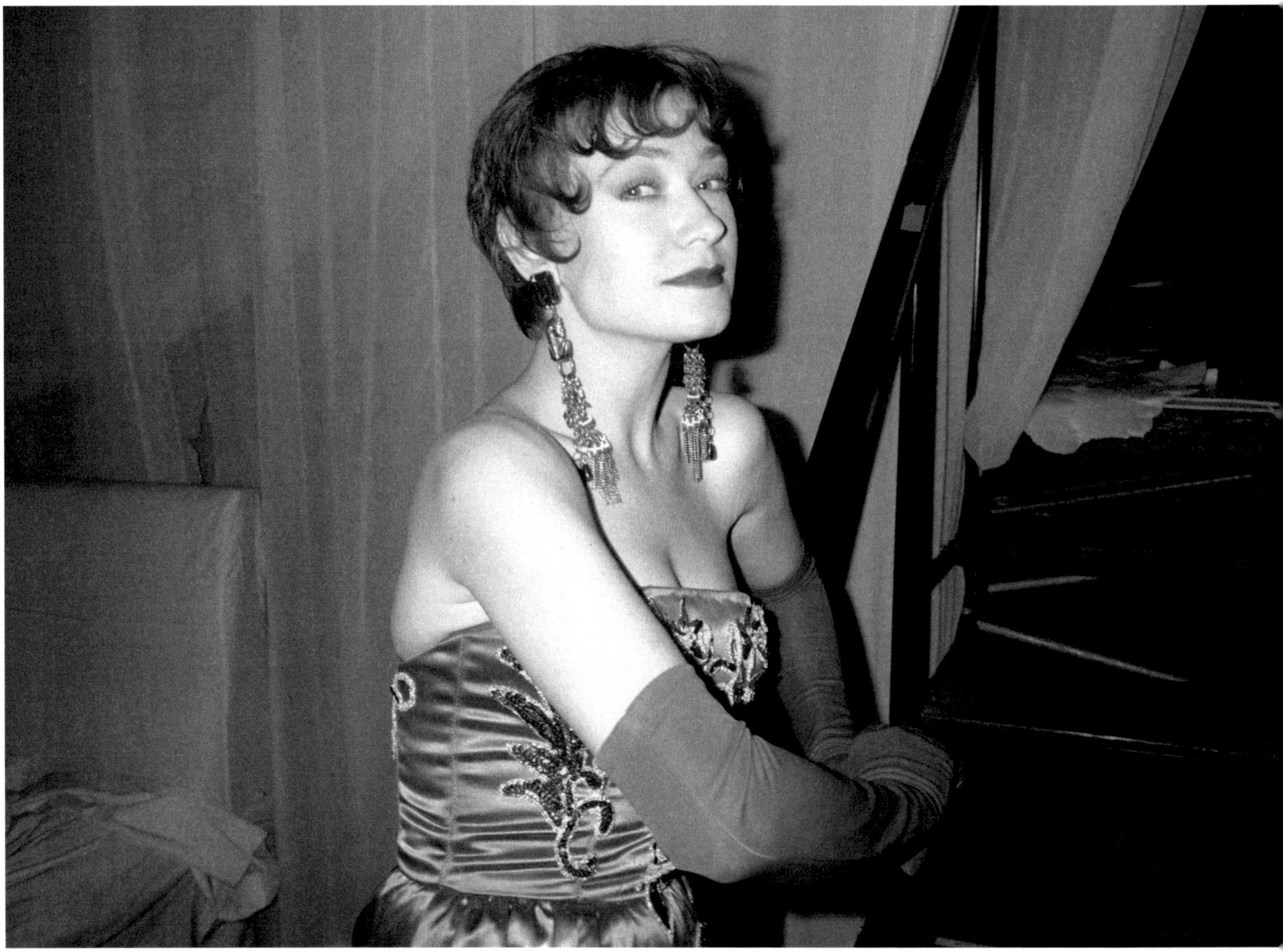

"We lived to put on a show." Ann Magnuson

Ann Magnuson
at the New York Talk party held in the Mike Todd Room at the Palladium.
April 2,1986

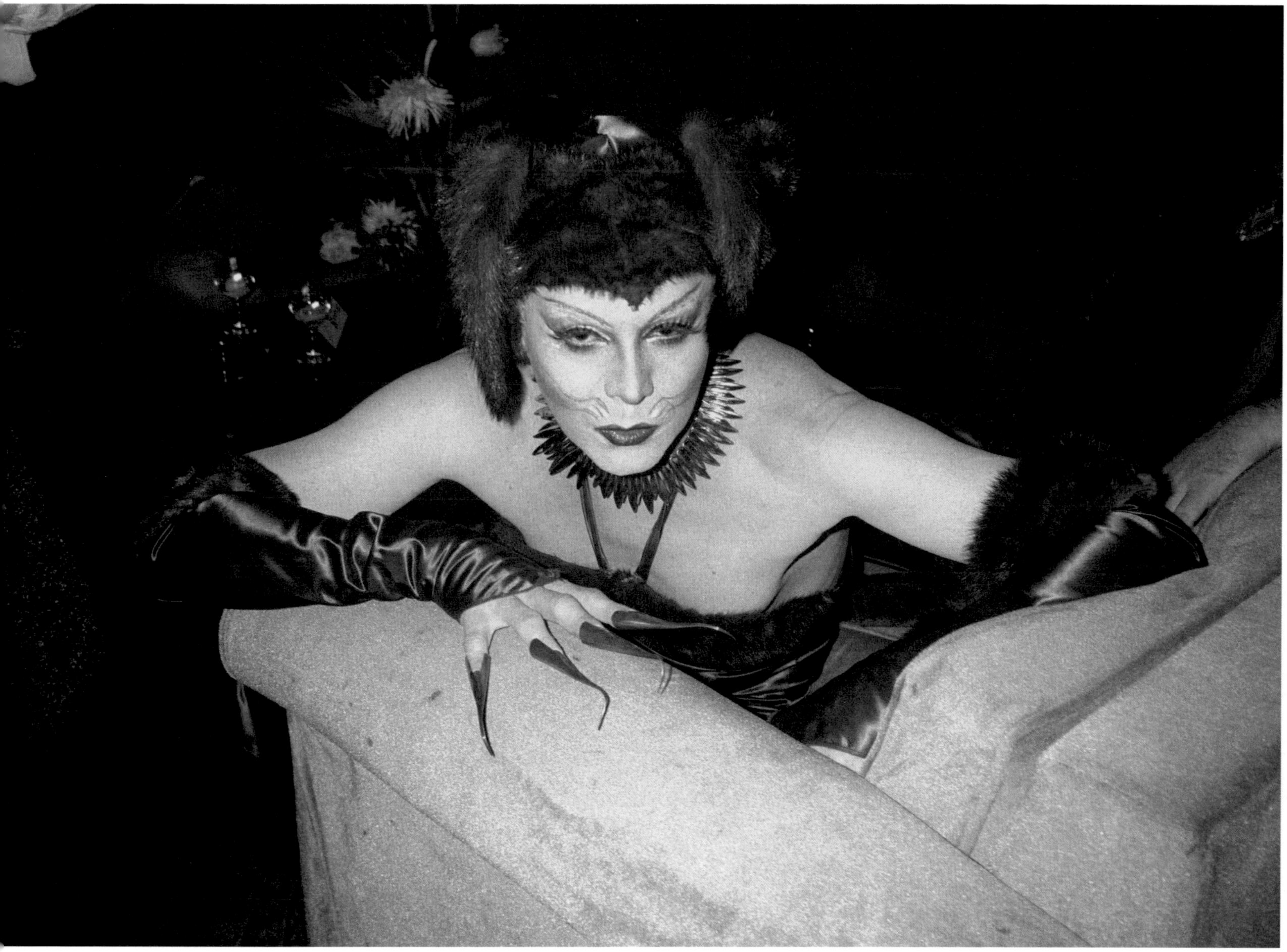

Alexis DeLago
at Scott Whitman's Once Upon A Time party at Limelight.
March 2,1986

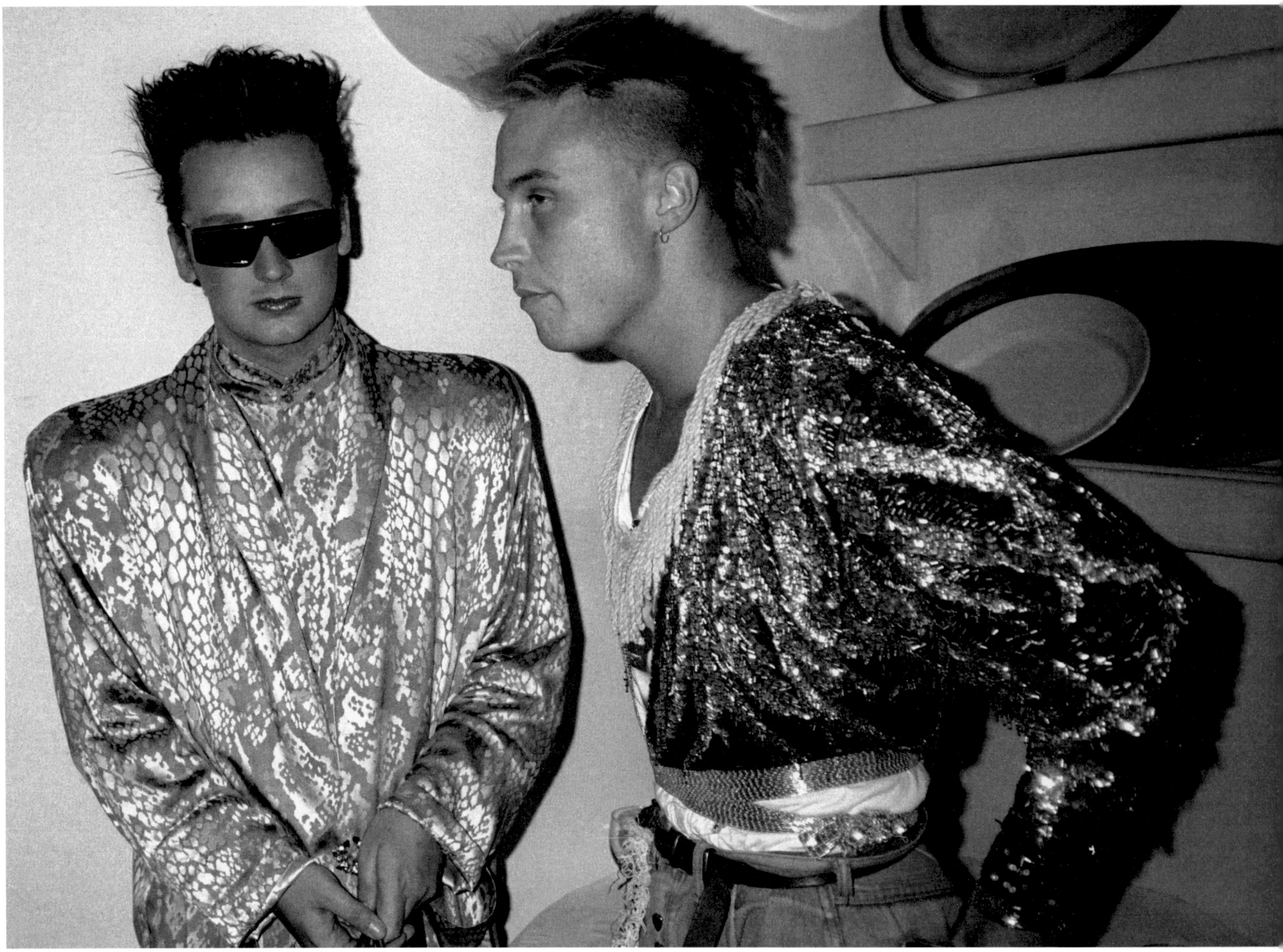

Boy George and Marilyn
at the Francesco Scavullo Benefit at the Ballroom.
Monday, June 3, 1985

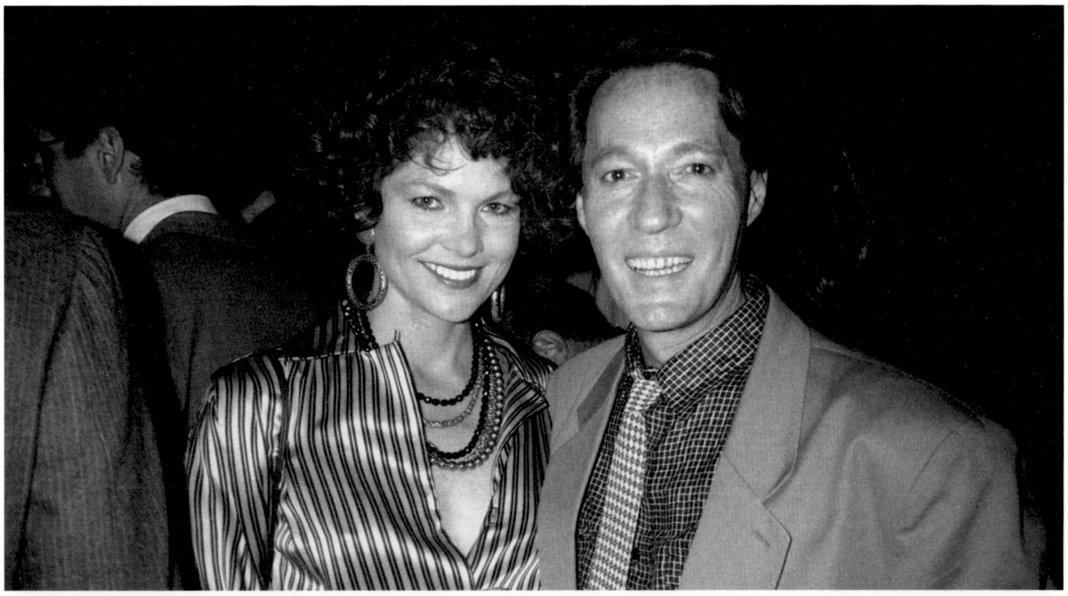

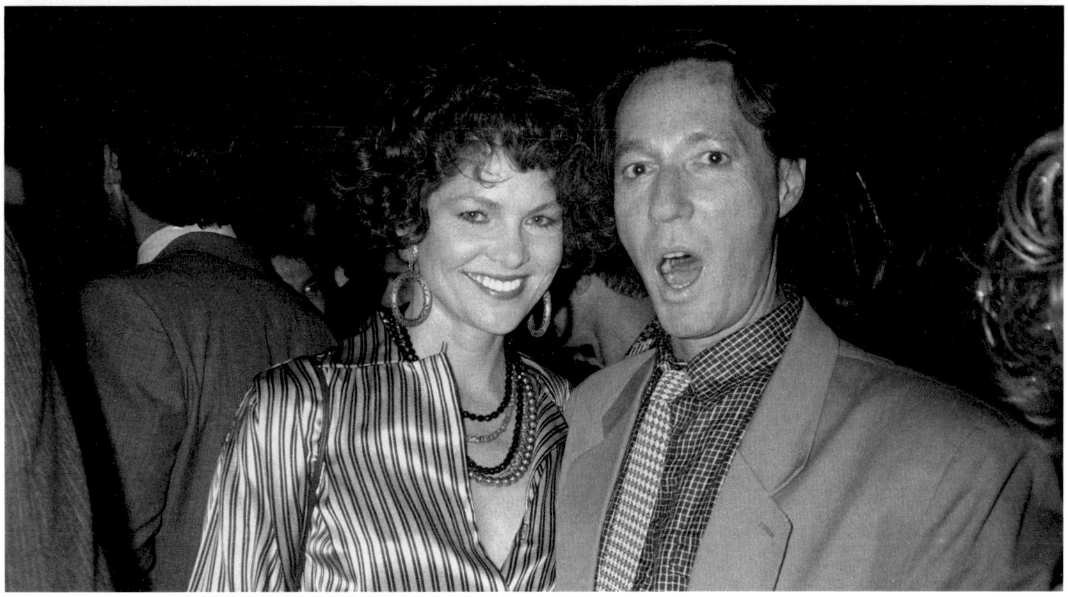

Lois Chiles and Maury Hobson
at Teri Toye and Patti Hansen's party for Maury Hobson at Area.
Friday, September 20, 1985

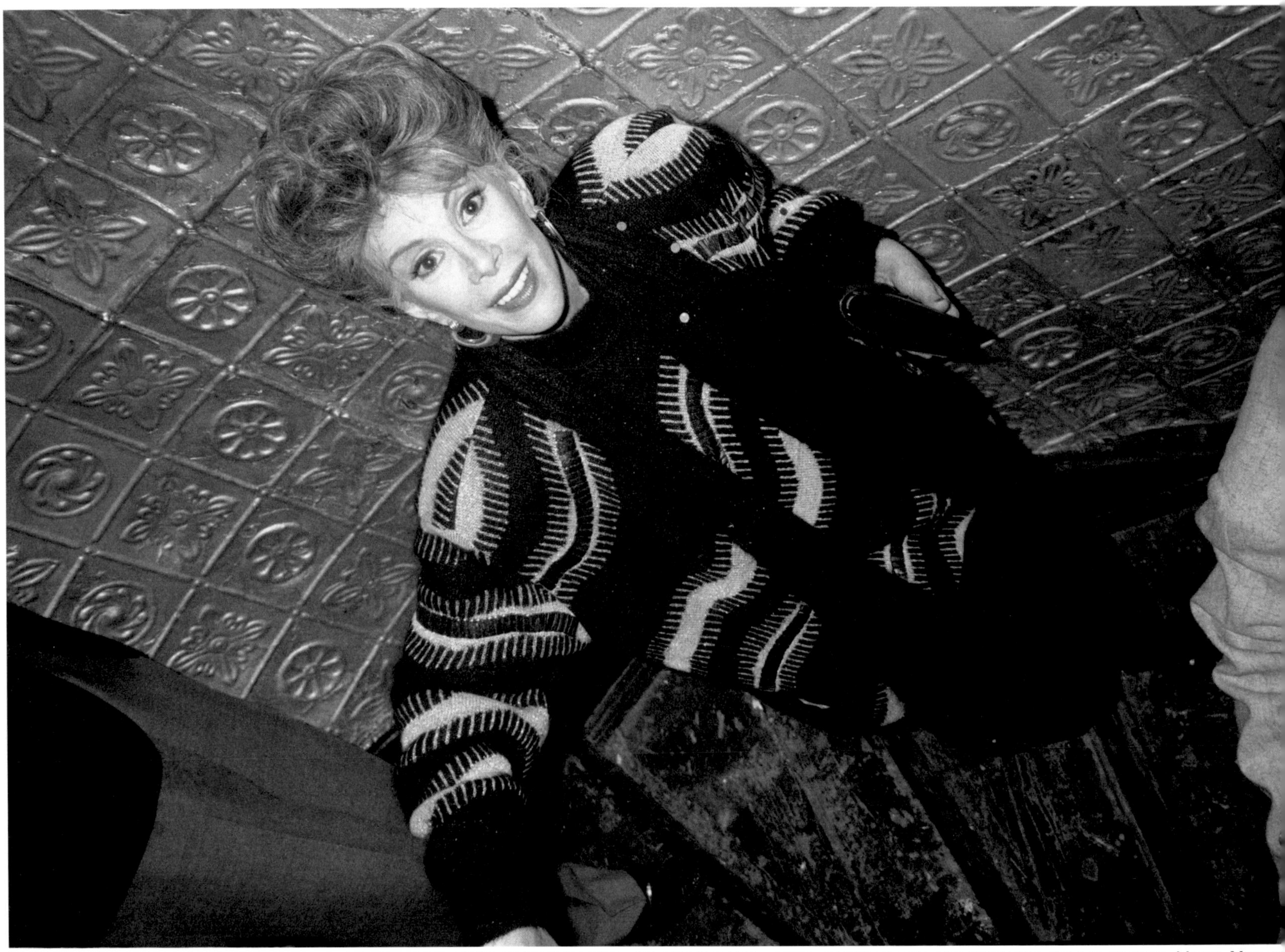

"Seeing these pictures makes me miss the turbulent, glamorous, and decadent nightlife that made New York so exciting in the 80s."
Joan Rivers

Joan Rivers
at the Halloween party at the World.
October 31, 1987

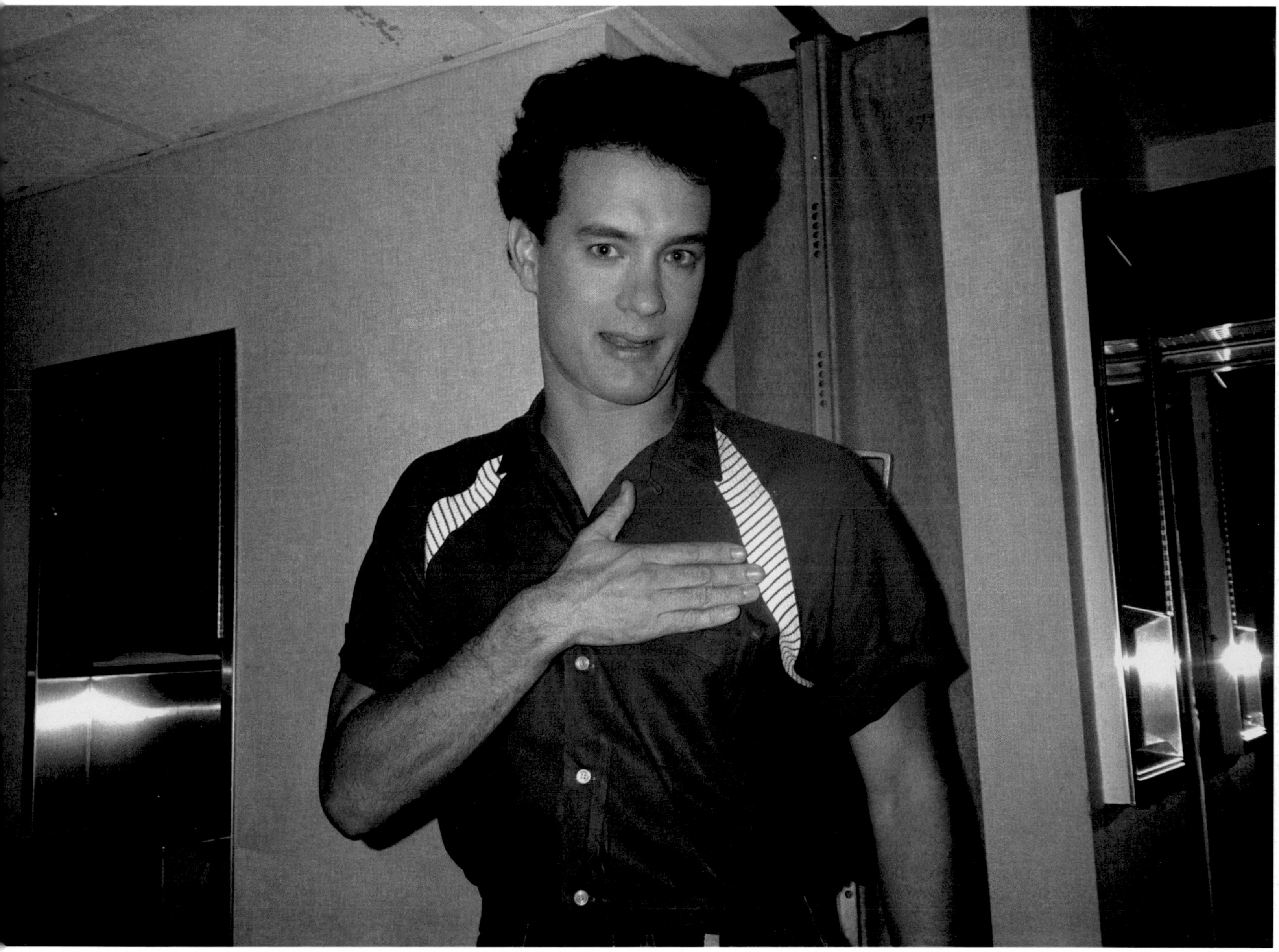

TOM HANKS
BACKSTAGE AT THE "LATE SHOW" WITH DAVID LETTERMAN.
AUGUST 20, 1985

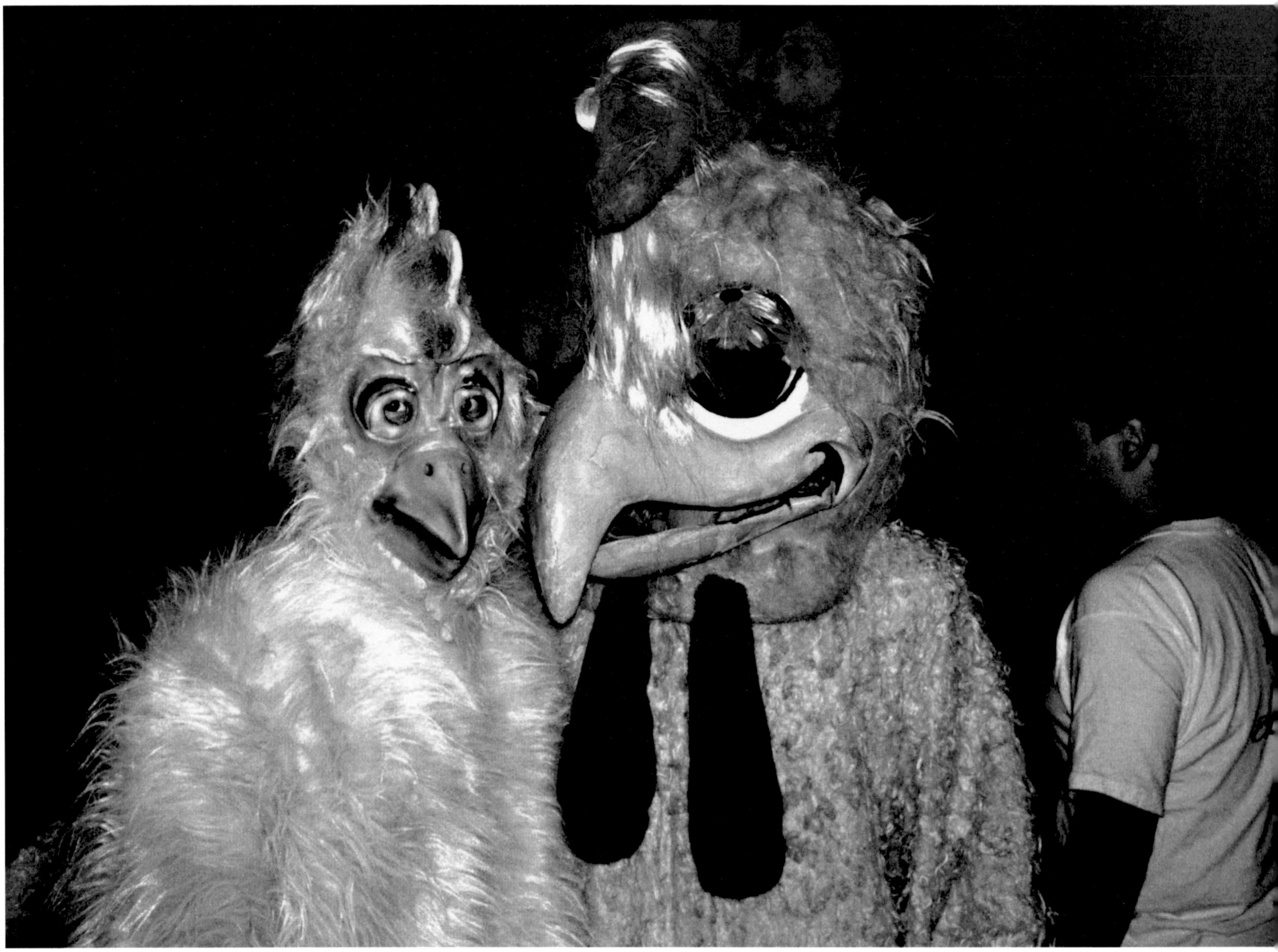

Chickens introduced by Patrick
at an outlaw party.
1988

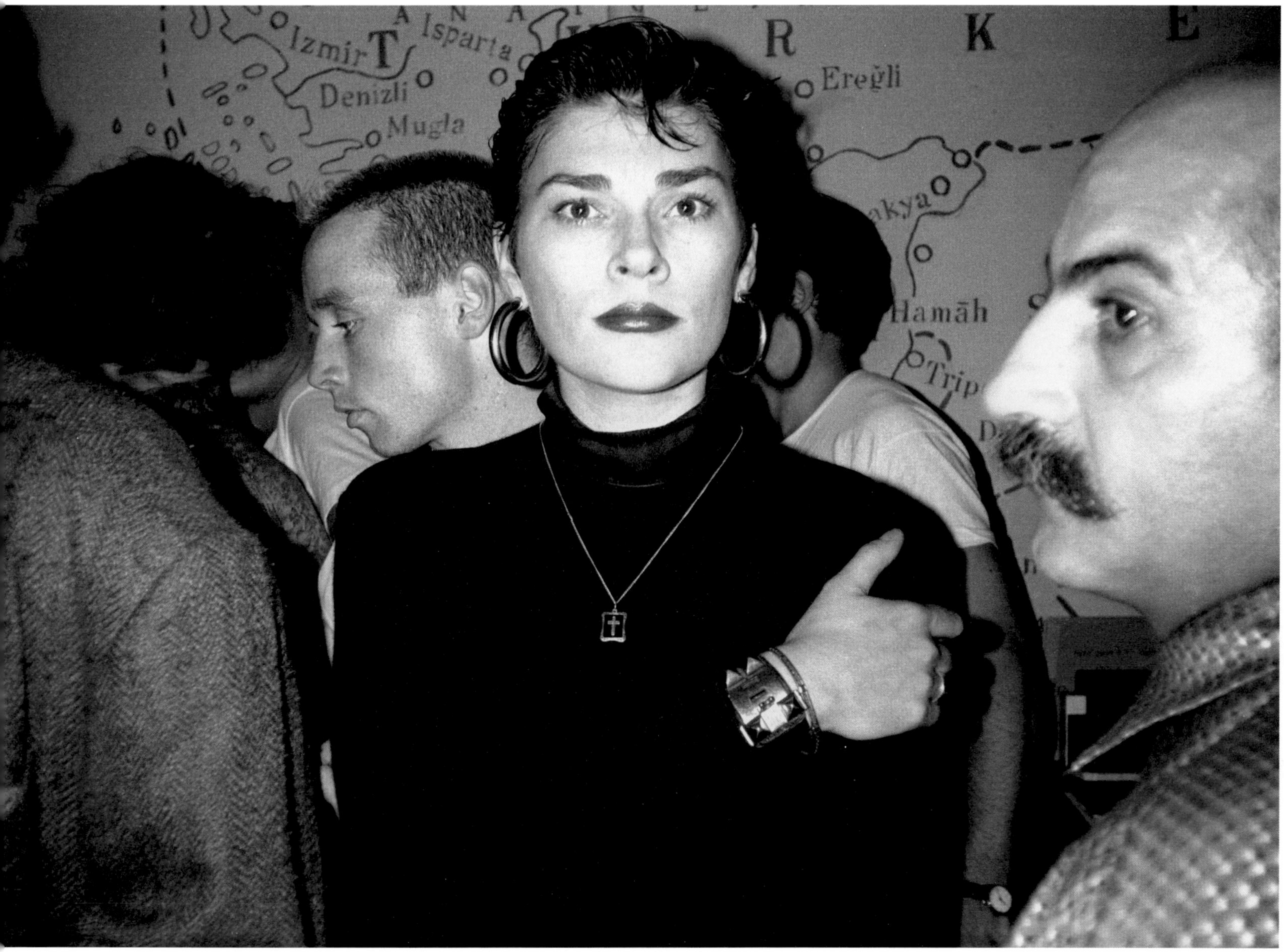

EDWIGE
AT RESTAURANT.
JULY 29,1986

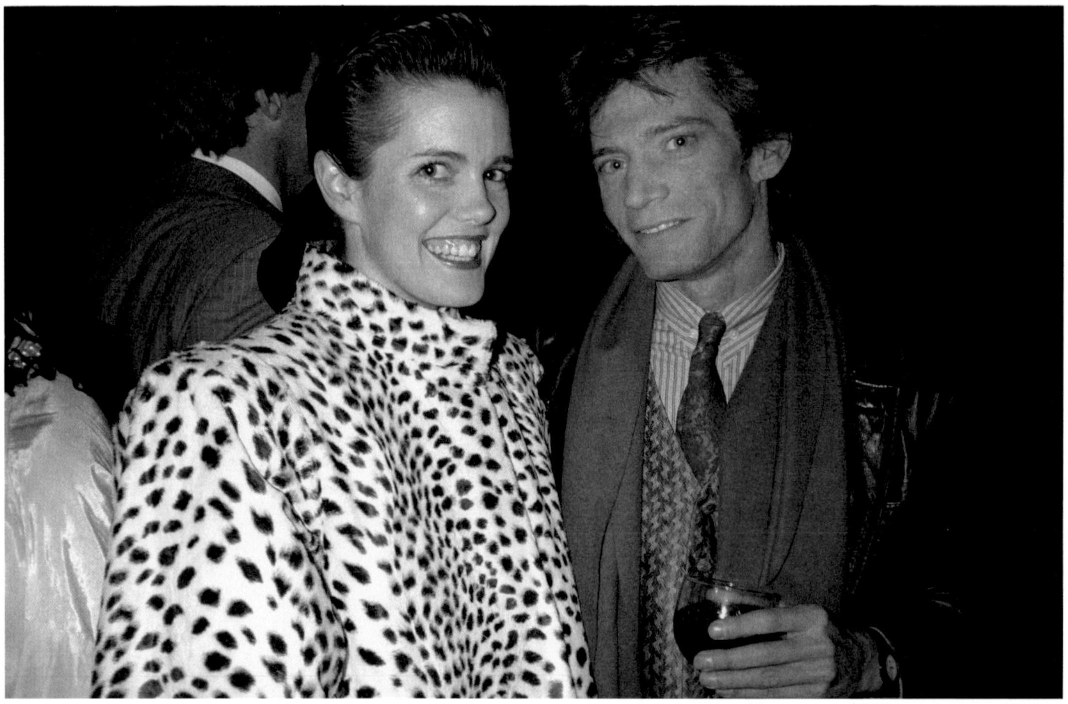

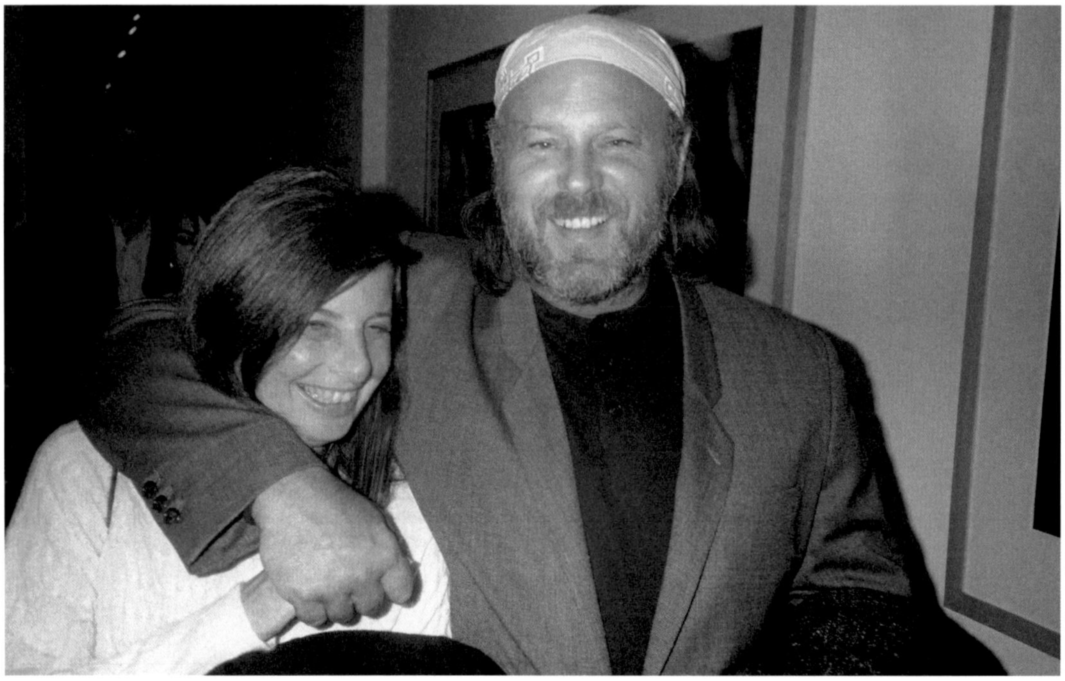

TOP: KATE HARRINGTON AND ROBERT MAPPLETHORPE
AT THE DINNER PARTY FOR PAUL KING AT THE WATER CLUB.
FRIDAY, APRIL 11, 1986
BOTTOM: NAN BUSH AND BRUCE WEBER
AT THE ROBERT MILLER GALLERY.
JUNE 1985

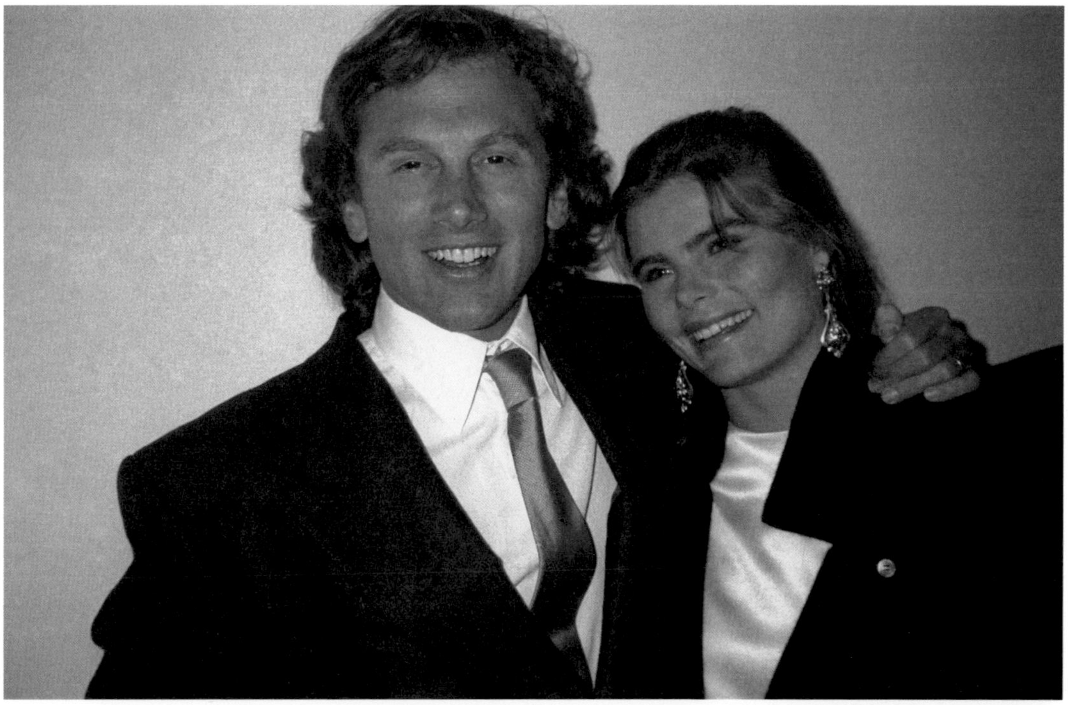

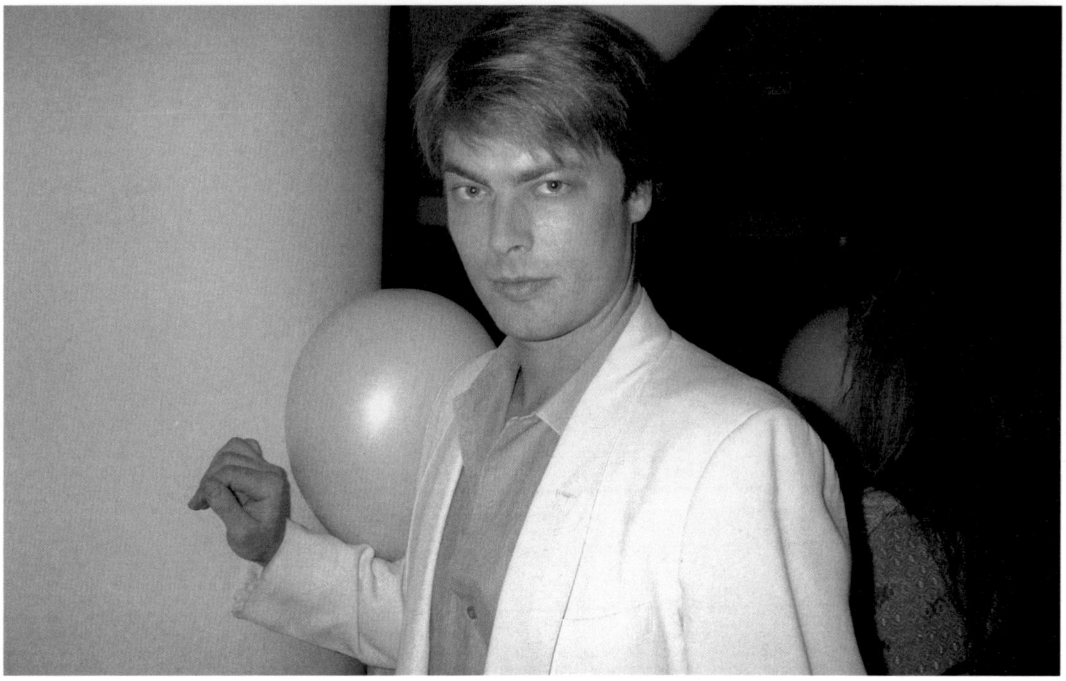

Top: Steve Crisman and Mariel Hemingway
at Sam's Restaurant.
January 24, 1986
Bottom: Richard Johnson
at the Grace Jones dinner party held at Les Tuleries.
April 5, 1986

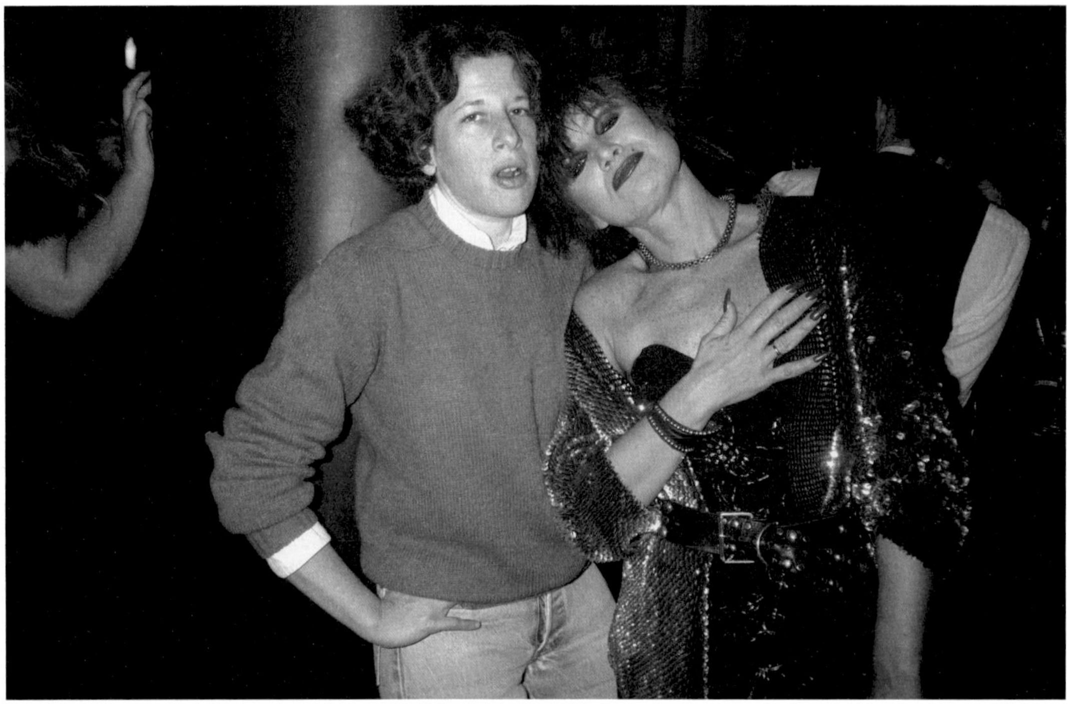

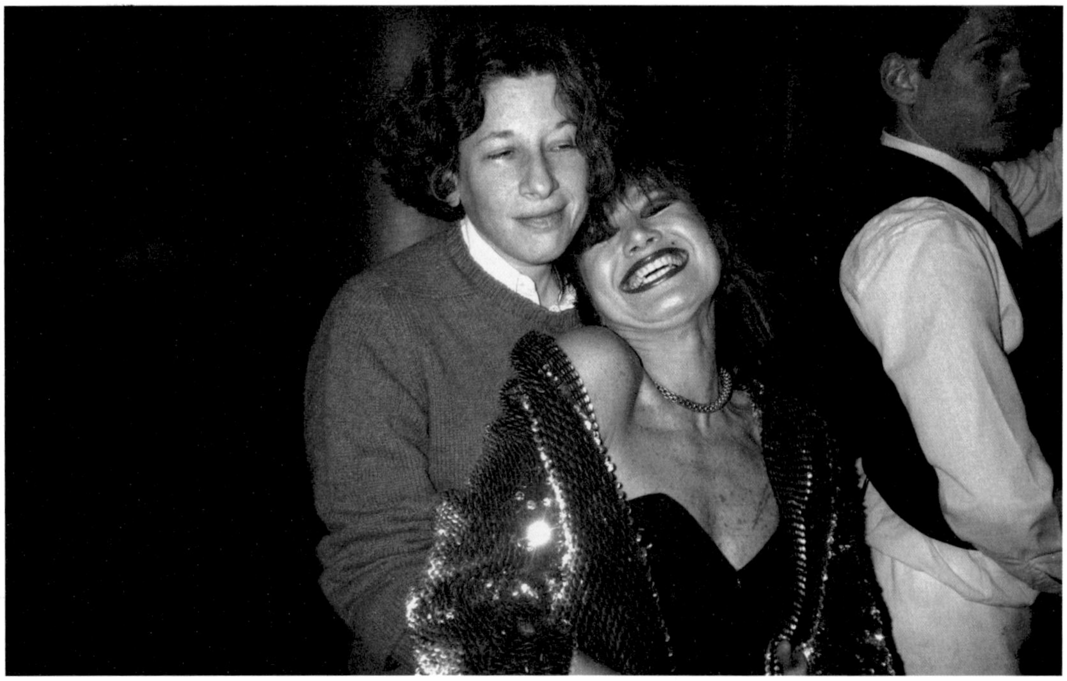

FRAN LEBOWITZ AND BETSEY JOHNSON
AT DIANNE BRILL'S BIRTHDAY DINNER PARTY AT CAFE SEIYOKEN.
APRIL 16, 1986

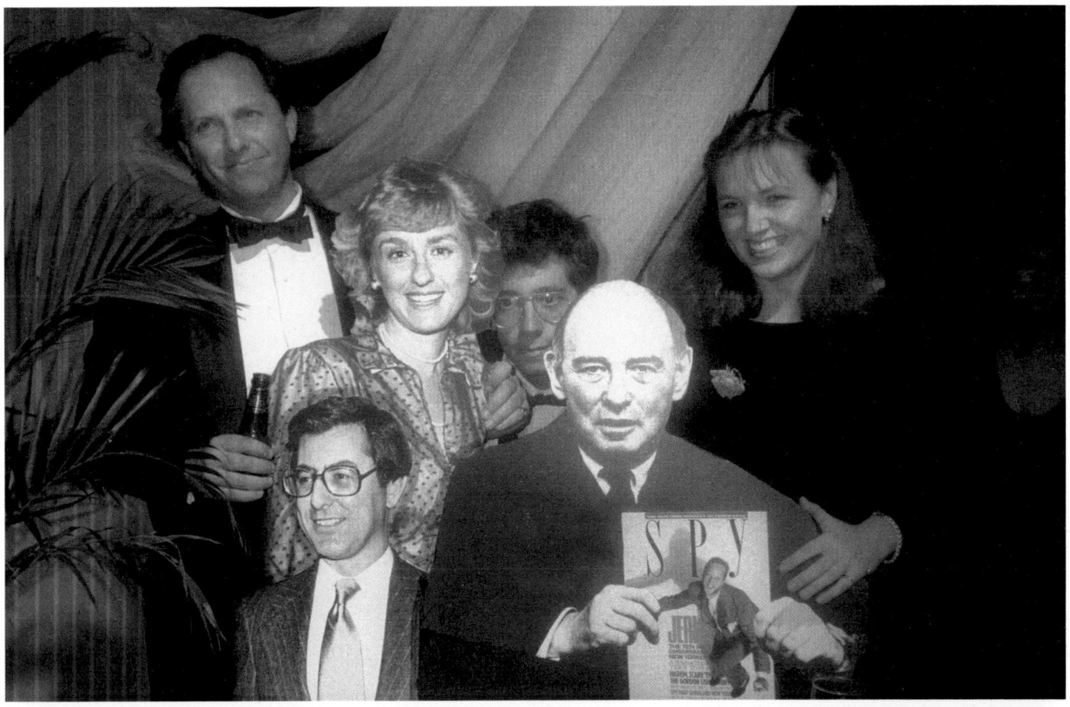

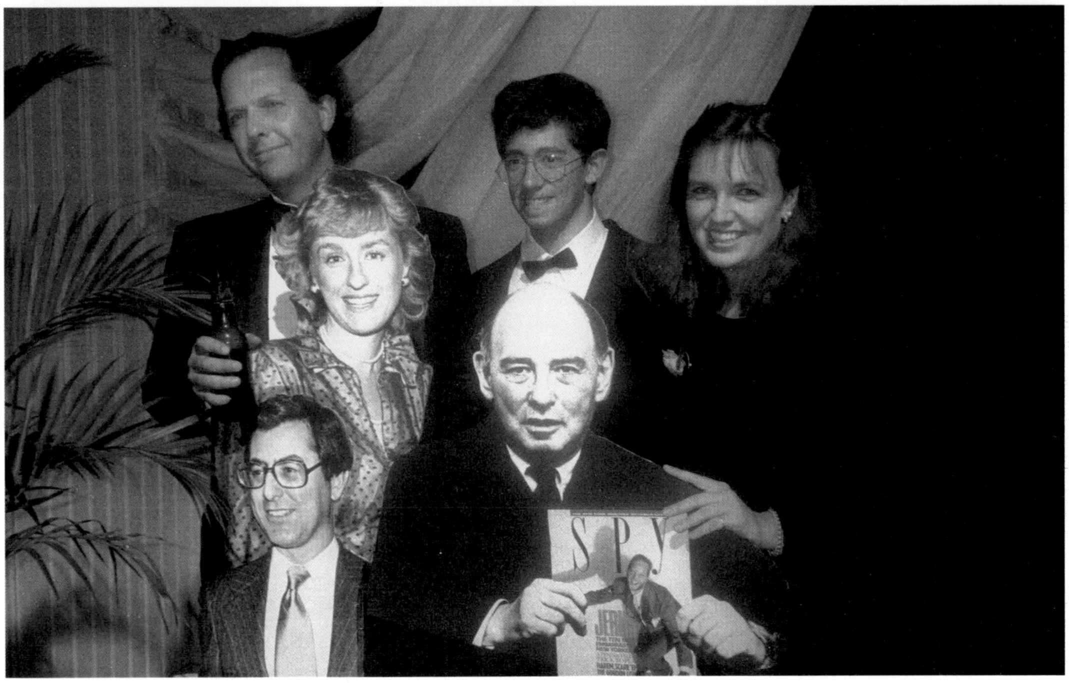

Graydon Carter, Eric Kaplan, and Susan Morrison
behind cardboard cut-outs of Tina Brown, Ed Kosner (Editor of New York Magazine), and William Shawn (Editor of The New Yorker) holding an issue of SPY magazine at the Spy magazine party at the Puck Building.
October 1, 1986

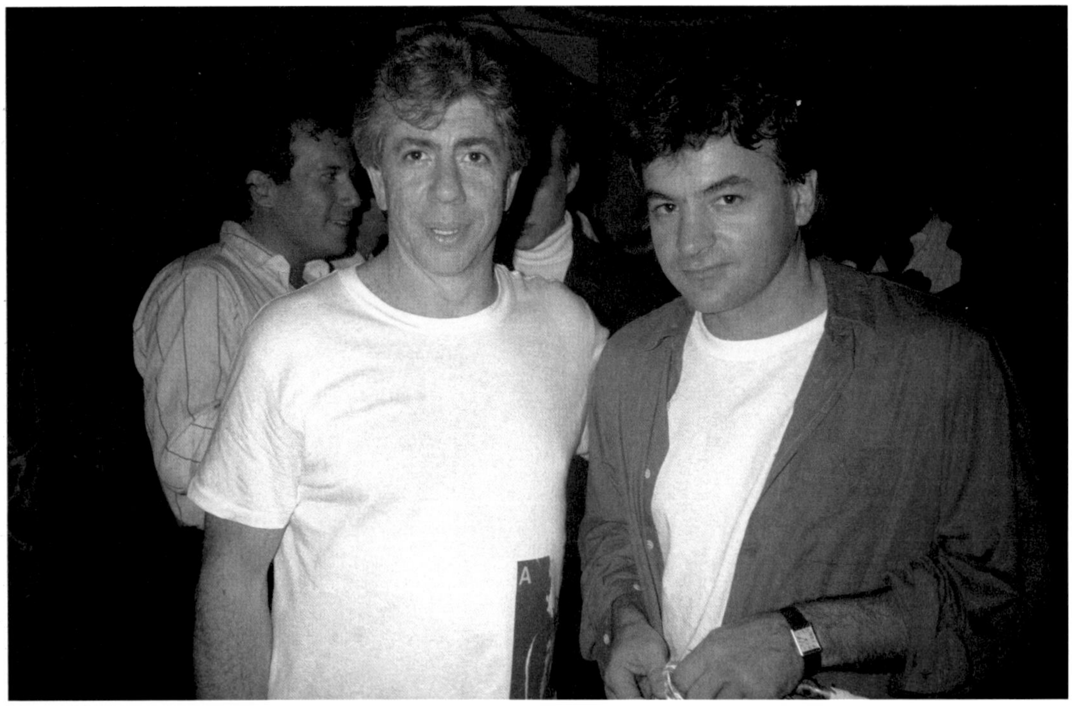

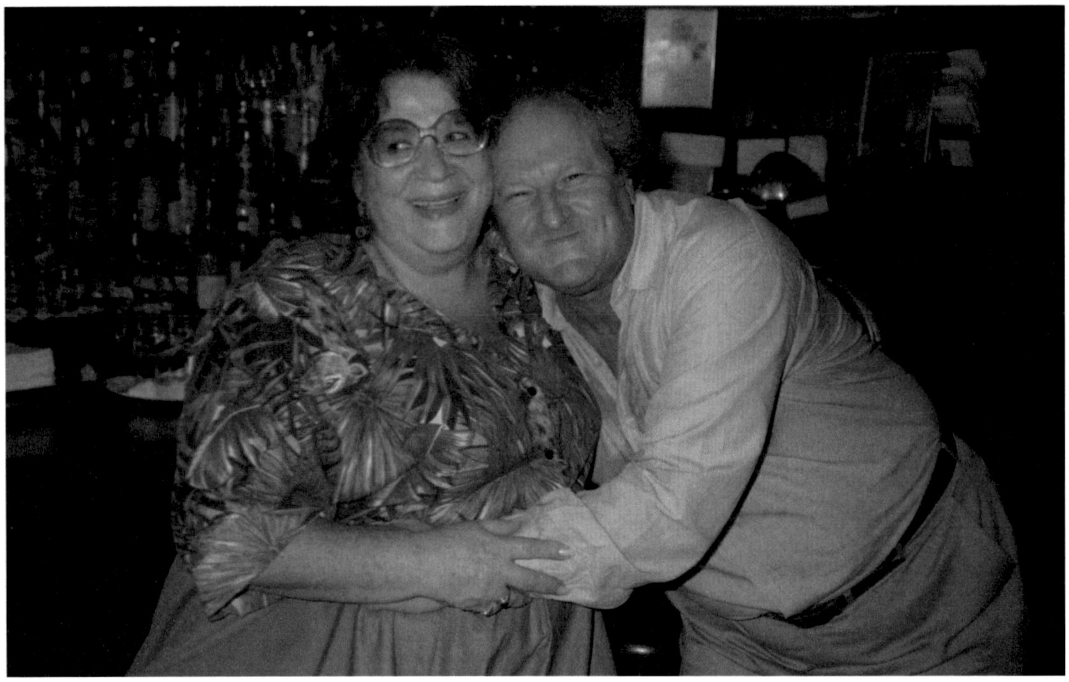

Top: Carl Bernstein and Brian McNally
at Area's third anniversary party.
September 24, 1986
Bottom: Elaine Kaufman and Bobby Zarem
at the luncheon for Jane Powell for her book: The Girl Next Door.
Wednesday, June 13, 1988

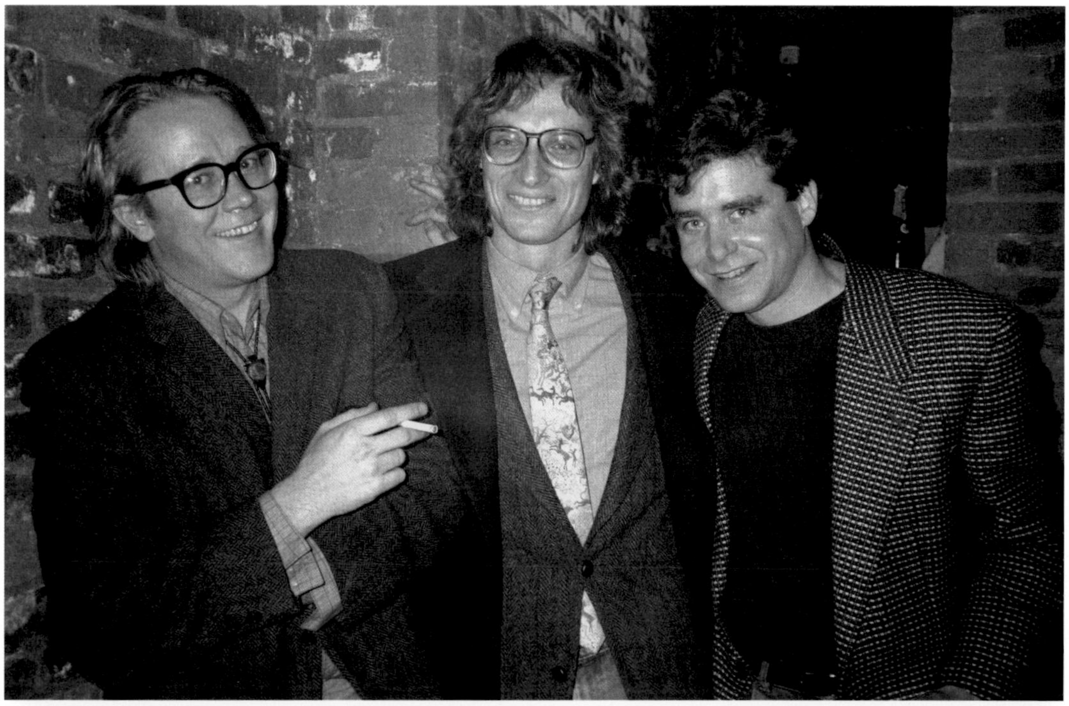

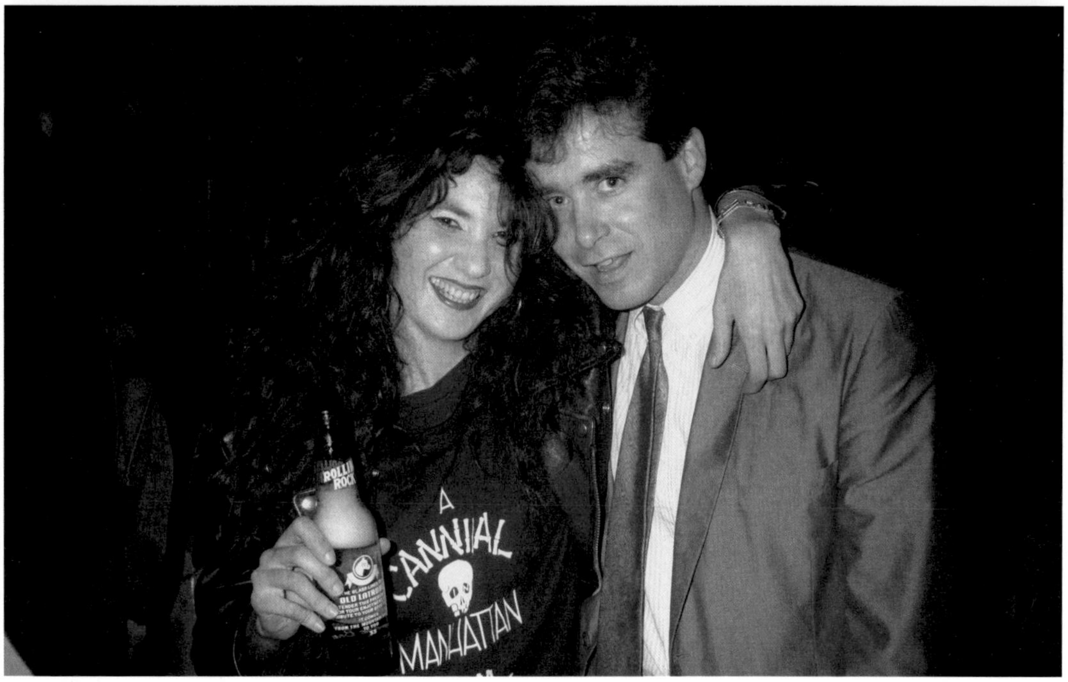

Top: Gary Fisketjon, Morgan Entrekin, and Jay McInerney
at the Tunnel. January 1987
Bottom: Tama Janowitz and Jay McInerney
at the Saint party in their honor. May 21, 1987

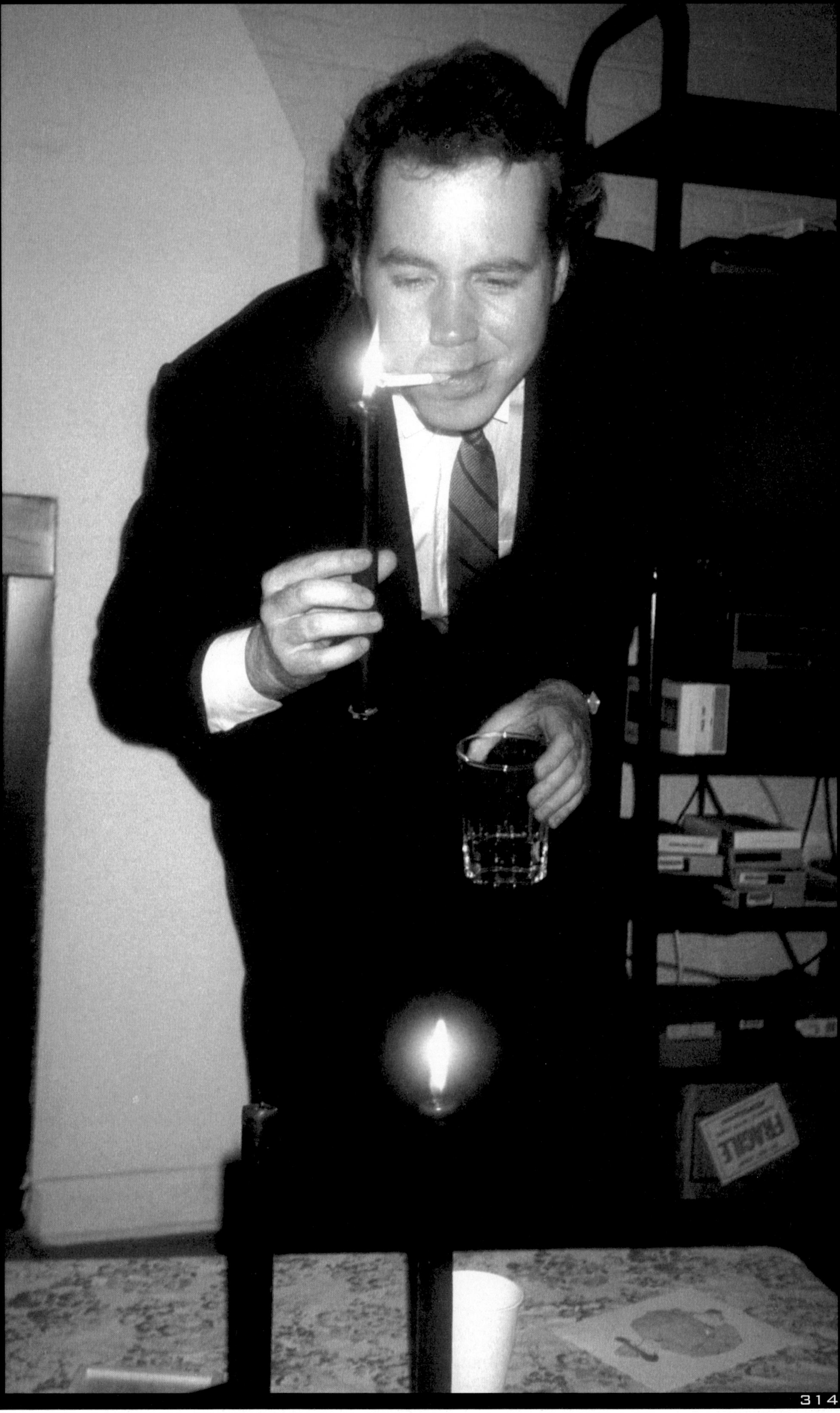

Bret Easton Ellis
April 1989

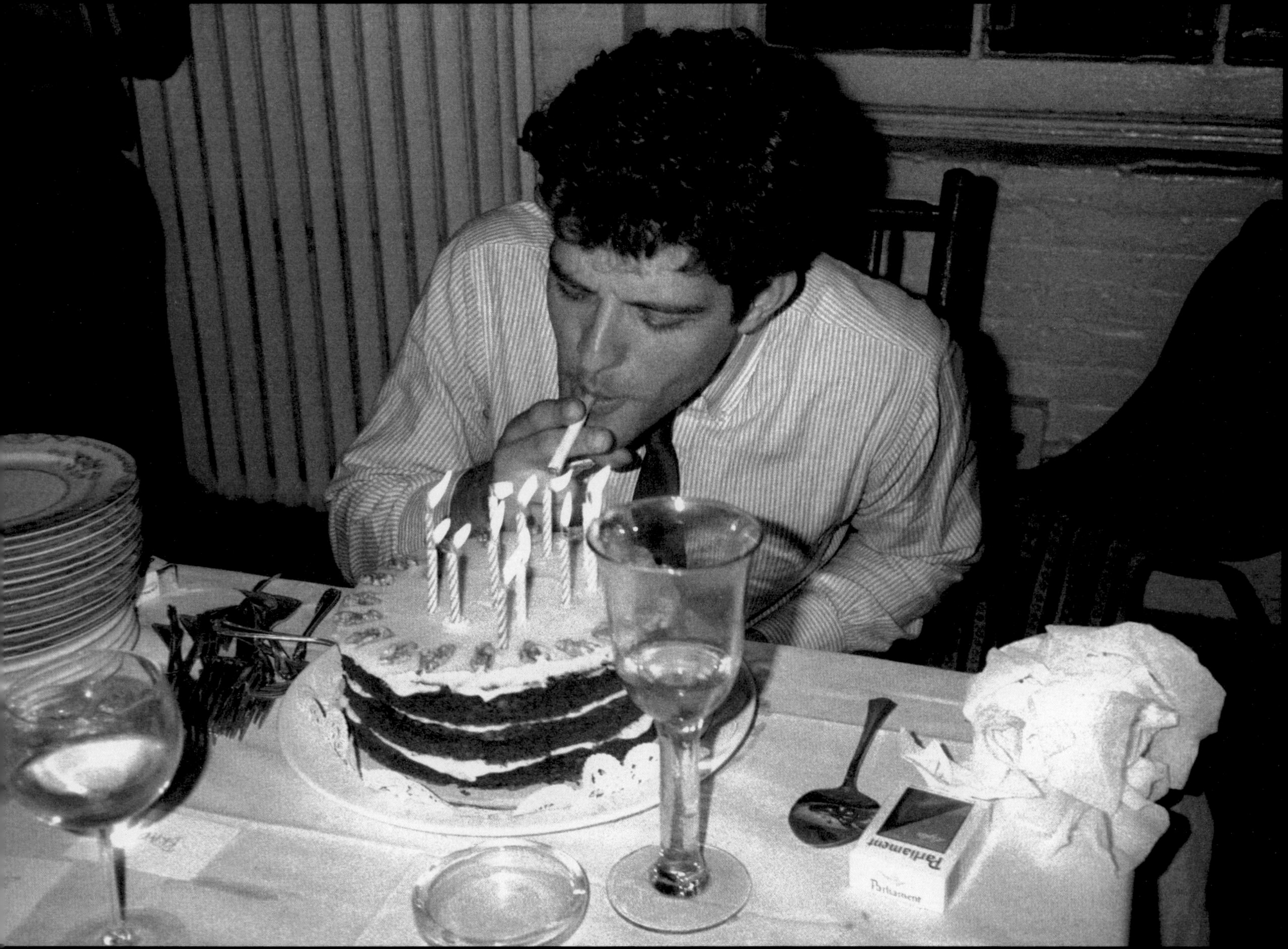

"In the 70s, I was a nice poet. In the 80s, I went through a makeover: as a padded-shouldered thing, I rode in tinted cars, took drugs at Save the Robots, wore sunglasses at night, worked as a B-model in Paris, Milan, and New York, and wasn't at ease unless I looked around and saw Andy, Rudolf, or Anita. What was I thinking??"
Brad Gooch

Brad Gooch
at his birthday party.
Wednesday, January 28, 1987

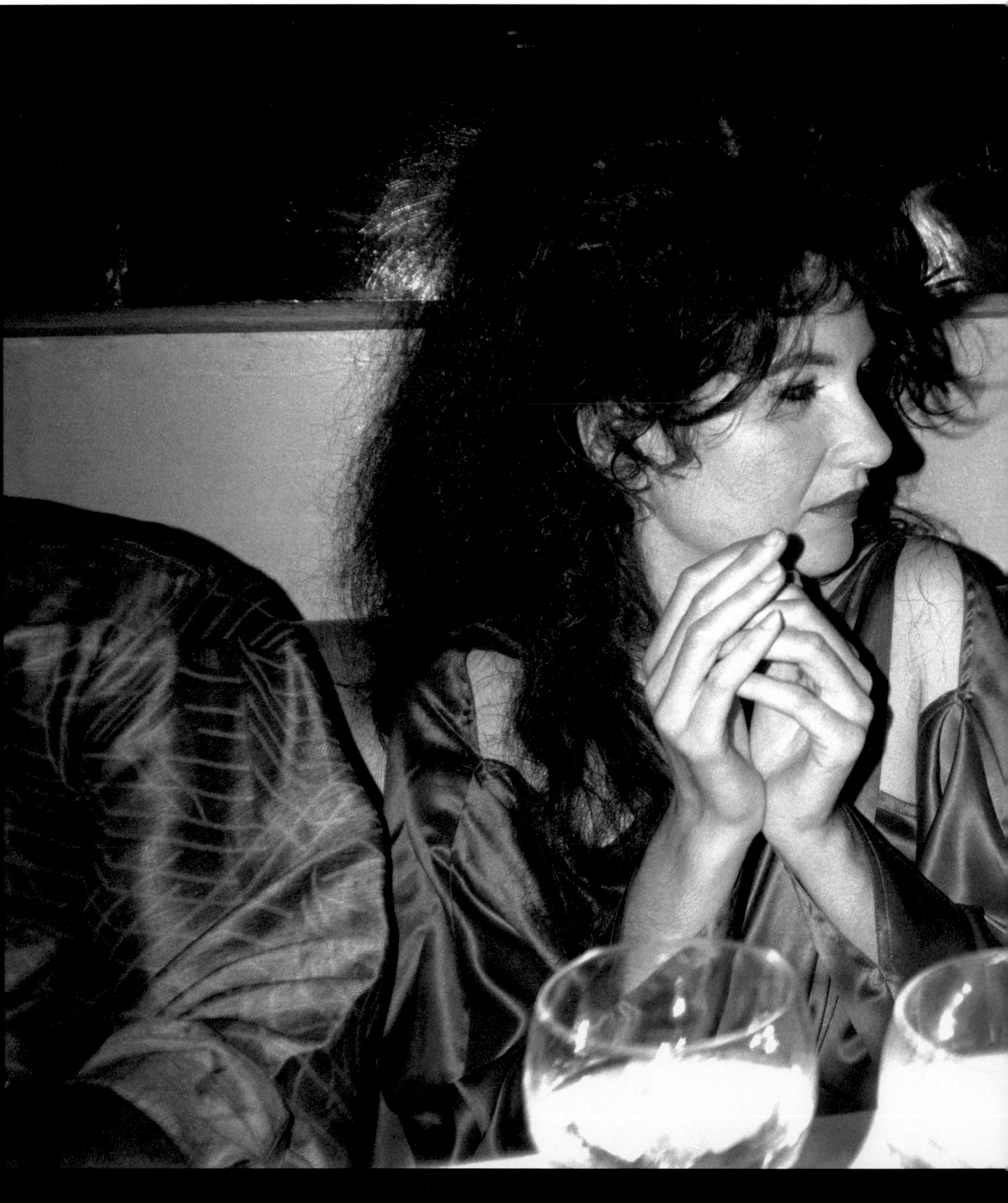

TAMA JANOWITZ AND ANDY WARHOL
AT THE TAMA JANOWITZ DINNER PARTY, HOSTED BY ALAN RISH TO CELEBRATE THE SUCCESS OF HER BOOK: SLAVES OF NEW YORK HELD AT PETALUMA.
AUGUST 19, 1986

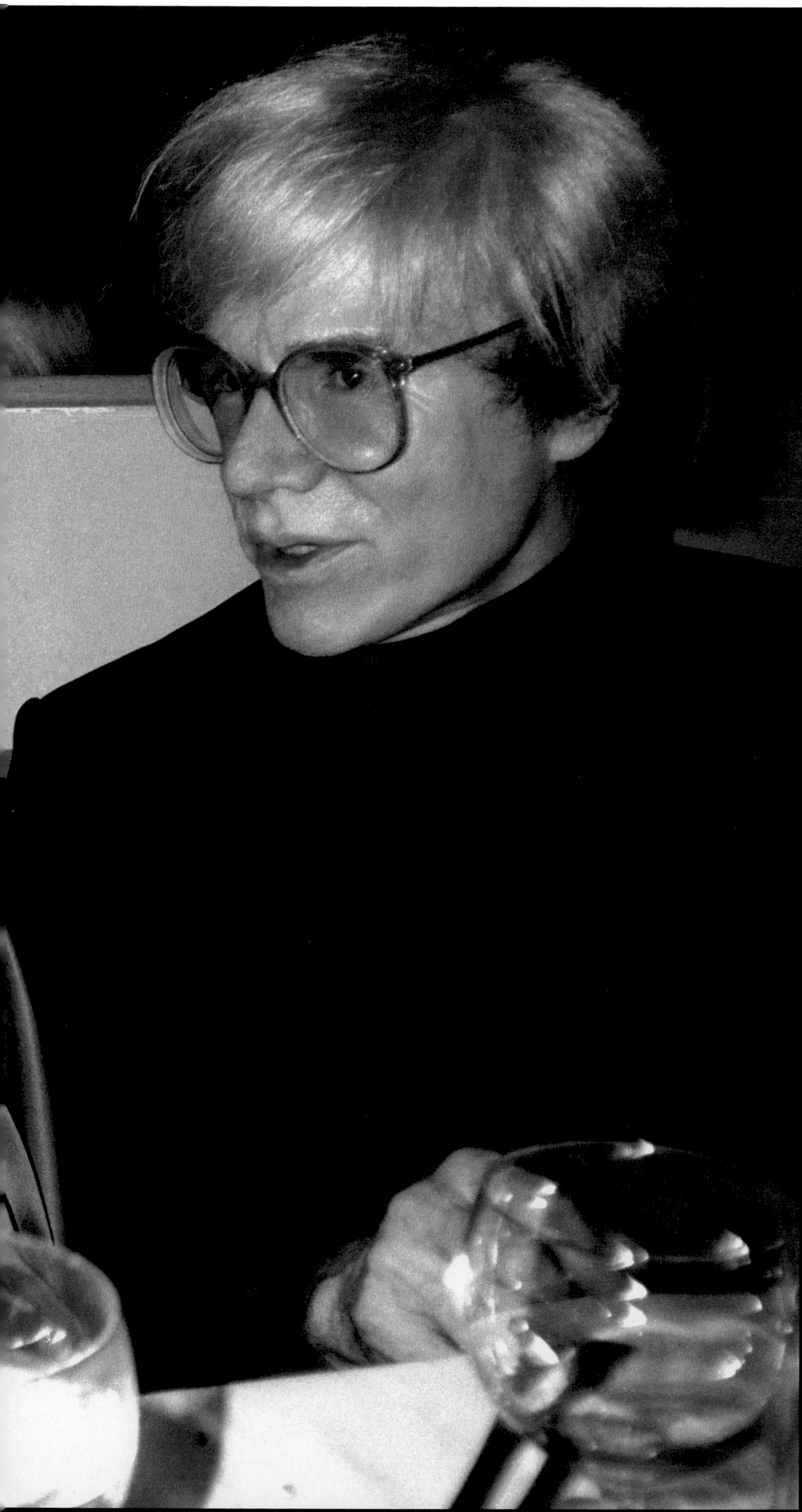
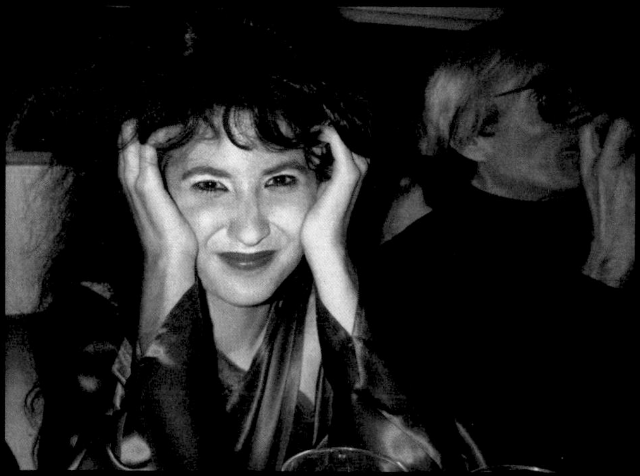
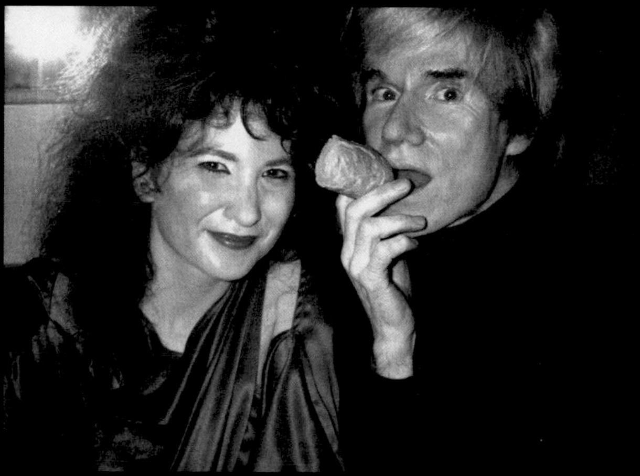
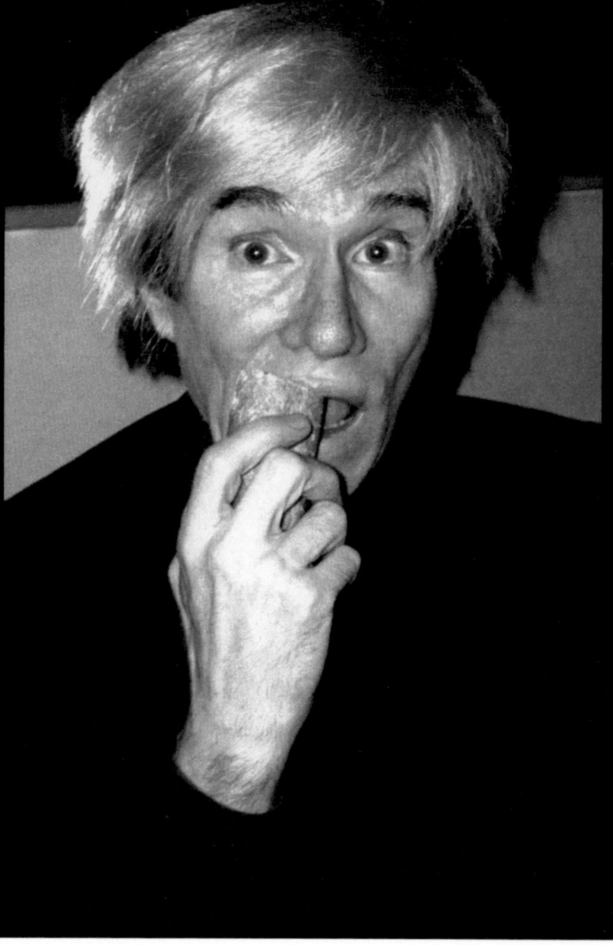

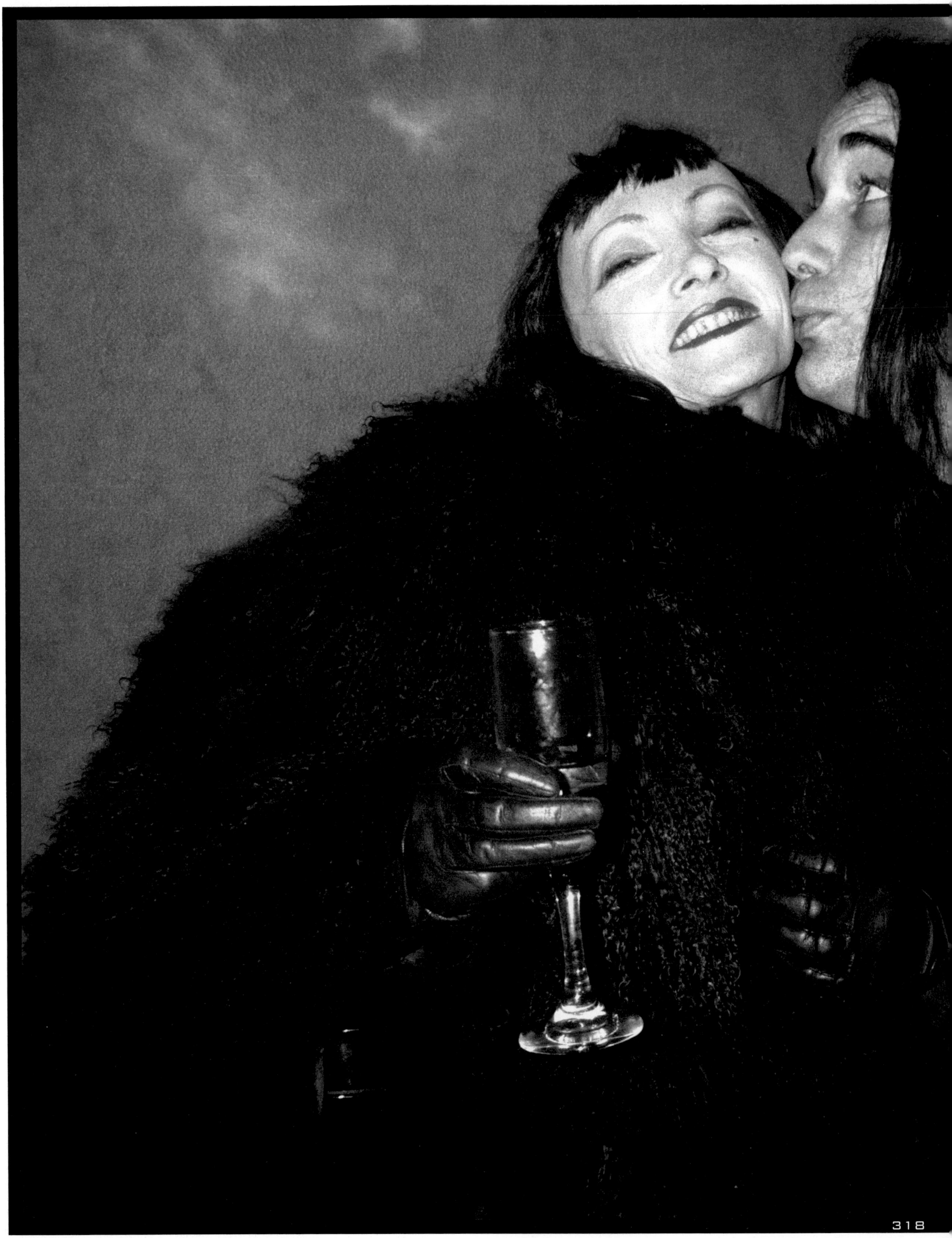

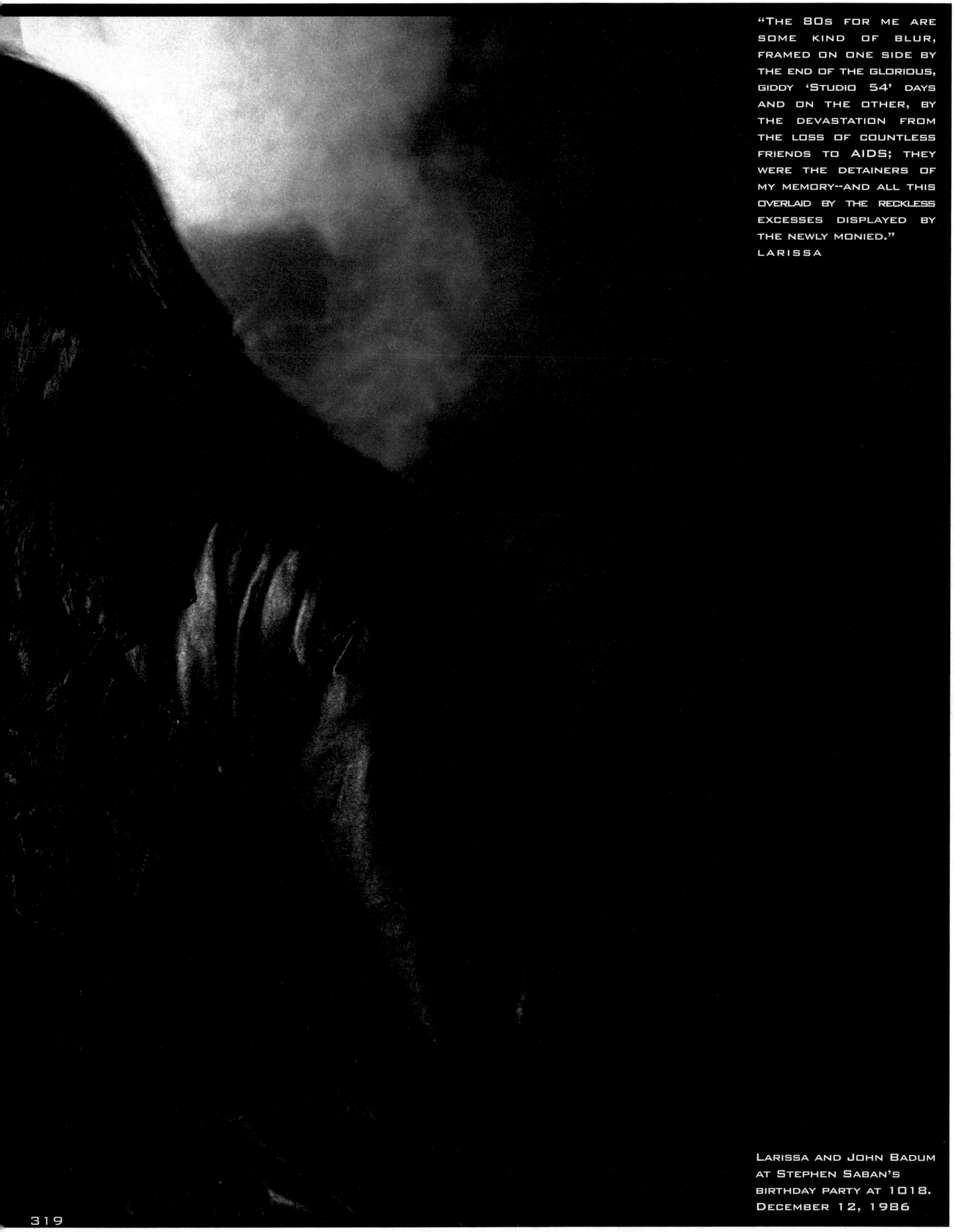

"THE 80s FOR ME ARE SOME KIND OF BLUR, FRAMED ON ONE SIDE BY THE END OF THE GLORIOUS, GIDDY 'STUDIO 54' DAYS AND ON THE OTHER, BY THE DEVASTATION FROM THE LOSS OF COUNTLESS FRIENDS TO AIDS; THEY WERE THE DETAINERS OF MY MEMORY--AND ALL THIS OVERLAID BY THE RECKLESS EXCESSES DISPLAYED BY THE NEWLY MONIED."
LARISSA

LARISSA AND JOHN BADUM
AT STEPHEN SABAN'S
BIRTHDAY PARTY AT 1018.
DECEMBER 12, 1986

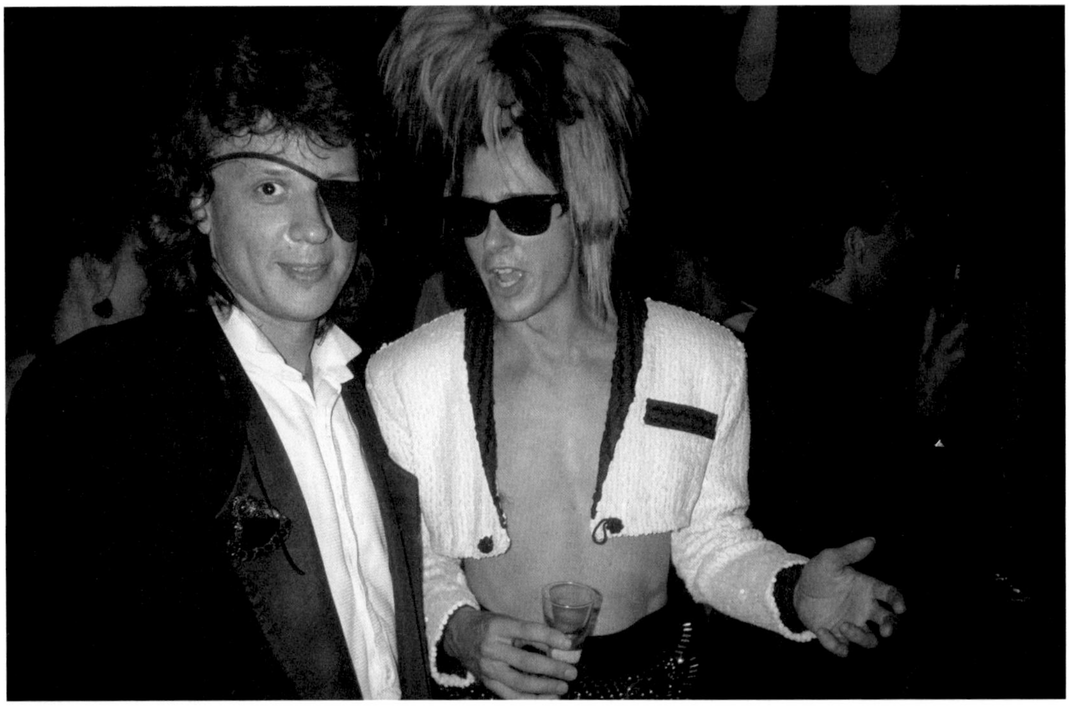

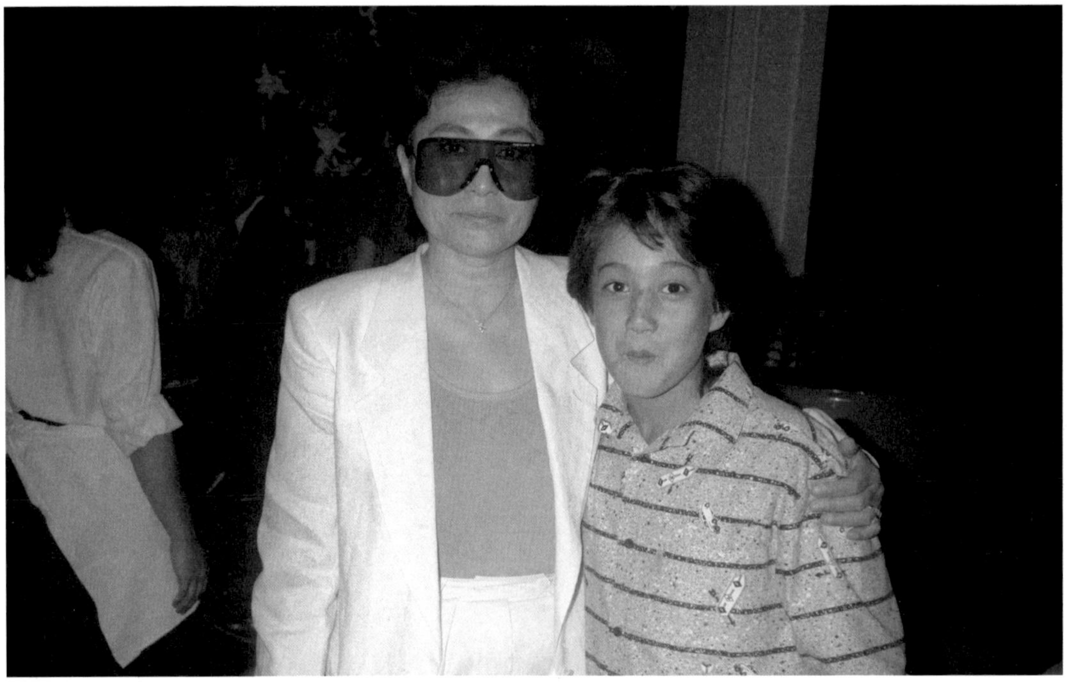

Top: Peter Gatien and Tony James from Sigue Sigue Sputnik
at Limelight's opening in London.
July 15, 1986
Bottom: Yoko Ono and Sean Lennon
at the Green Plays party at the Liberty Cafe in South Street Seaport.
May 19,1986
Right: Sylvester Stallone and Eddie Murphy
at Eddie Murphy's party at 4D.
Thursday, December 10, 1986

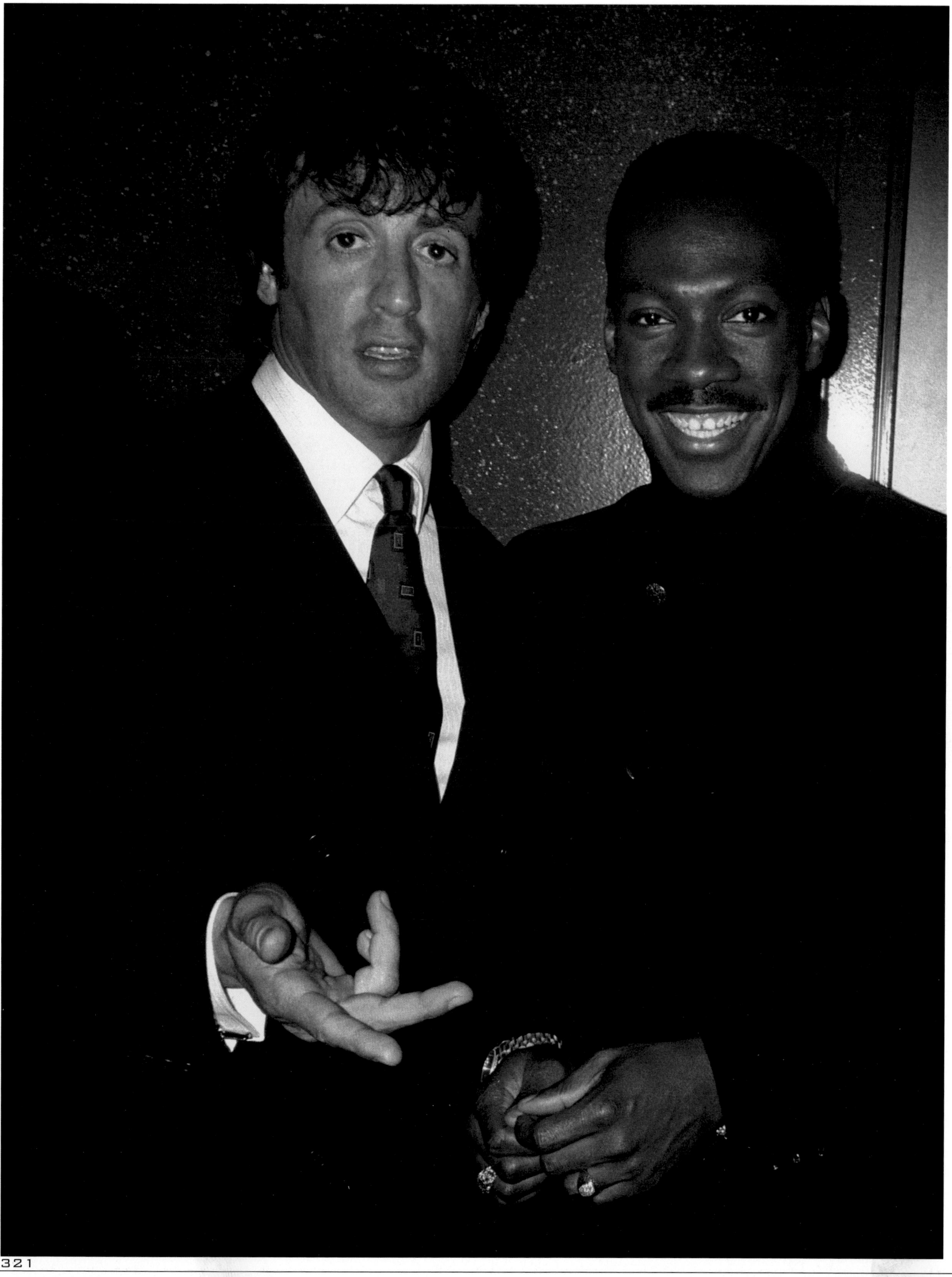

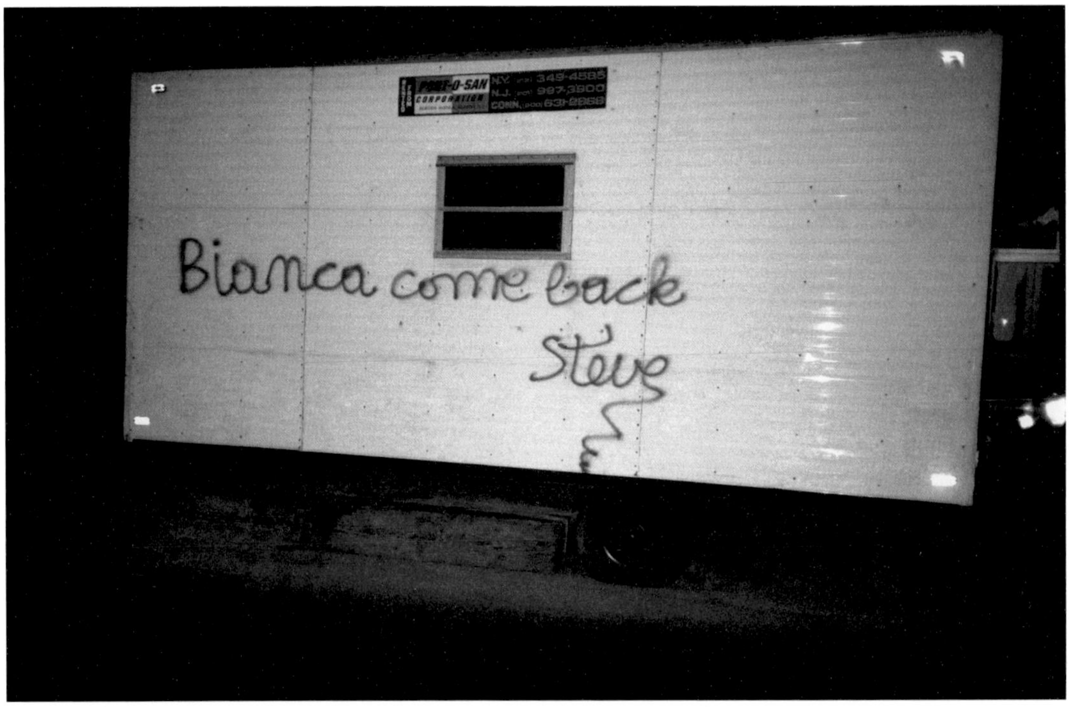

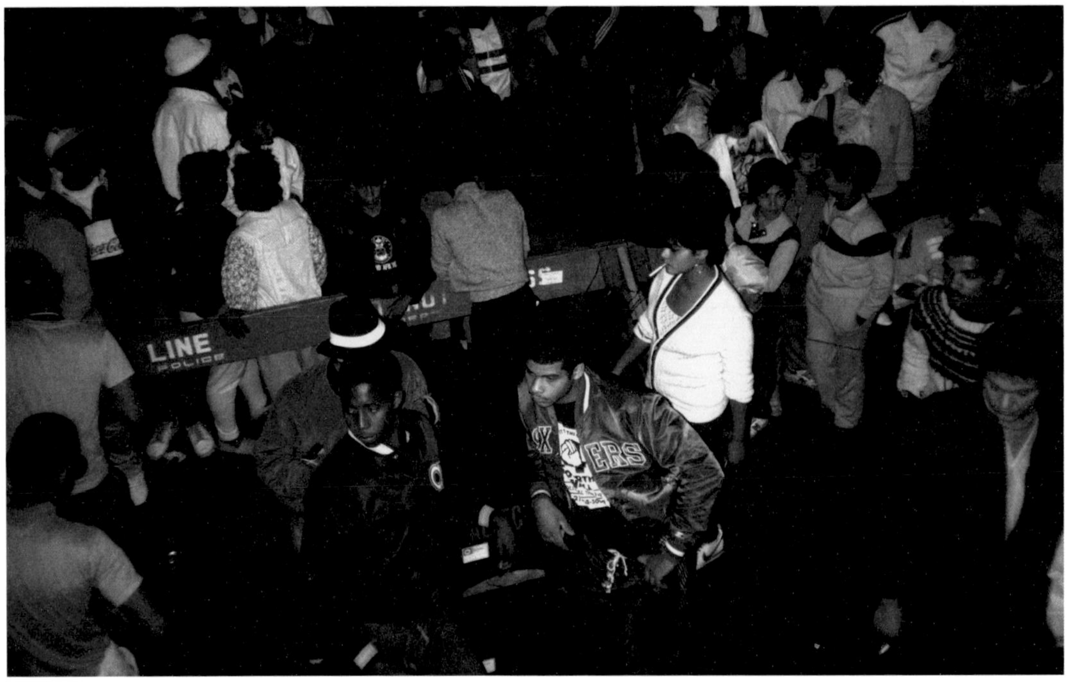

Top: "Bianca Come Back" graffiti
Thursday, November 13, 1986
Bottom: Crowd at Vito Bruno's party for Sally Randall
and Patrick McMullan under the Brooklyn Bridge.
August 28, 1986

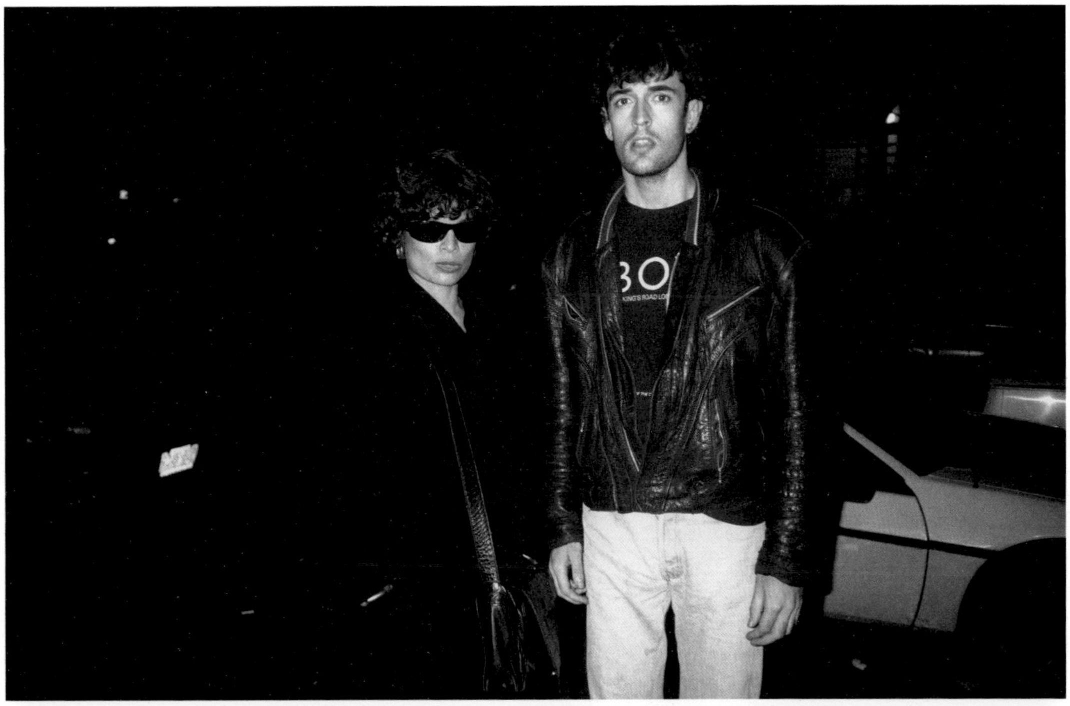

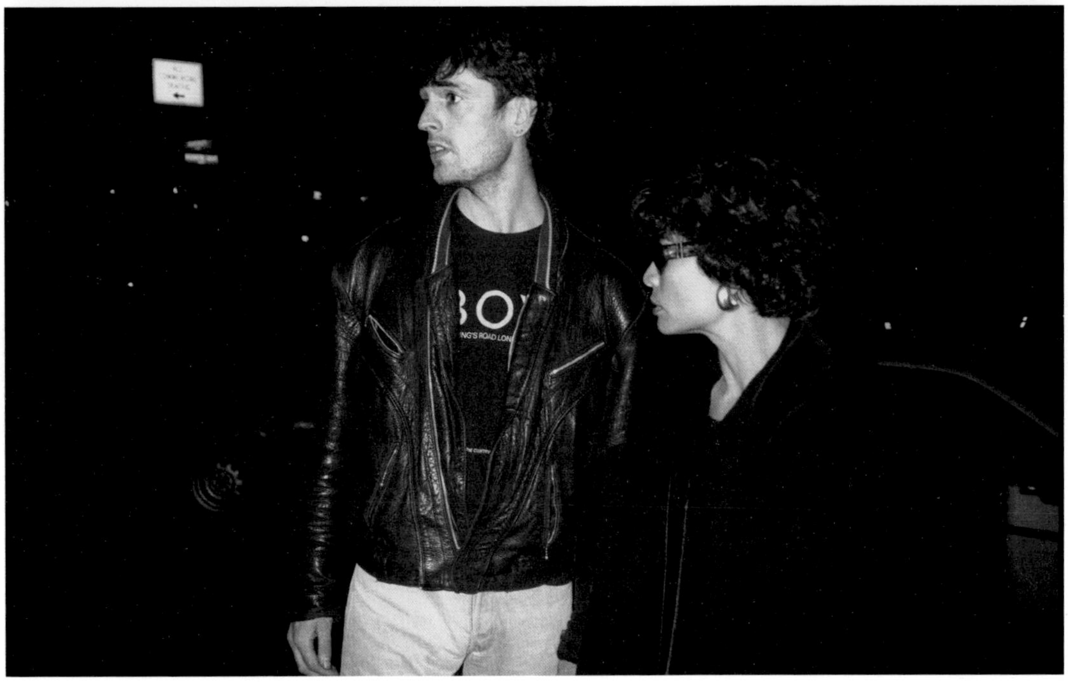

Bianca Jagger and Rupert Everett
Before Angela Janklow Harrington's Columbus Day
party held at Revolution. Monday, October 13, 1986

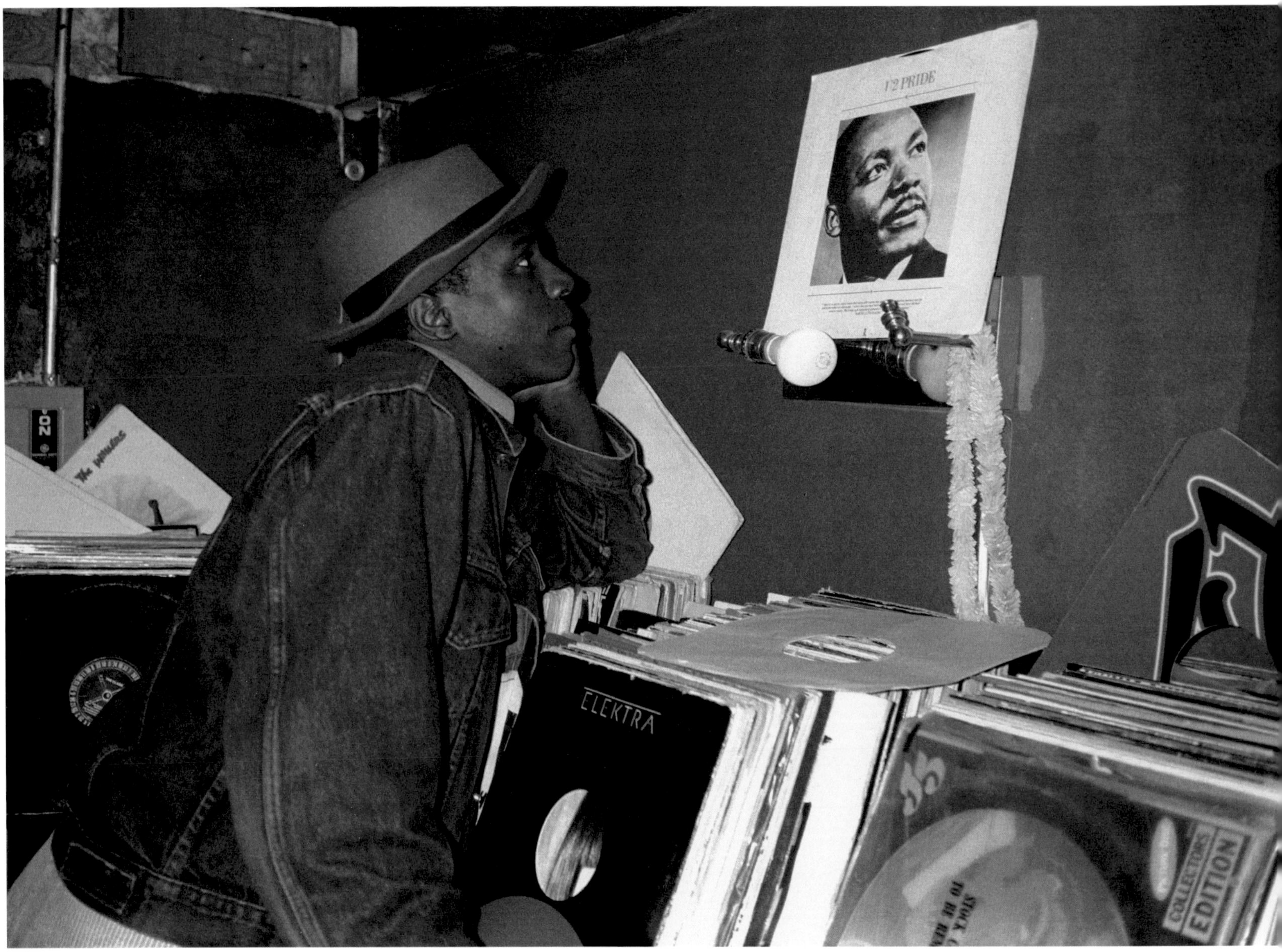

40 Worth DJ
at Richard Johnson's birthday party at 40 Worth.
Saturday, January 16, 1988

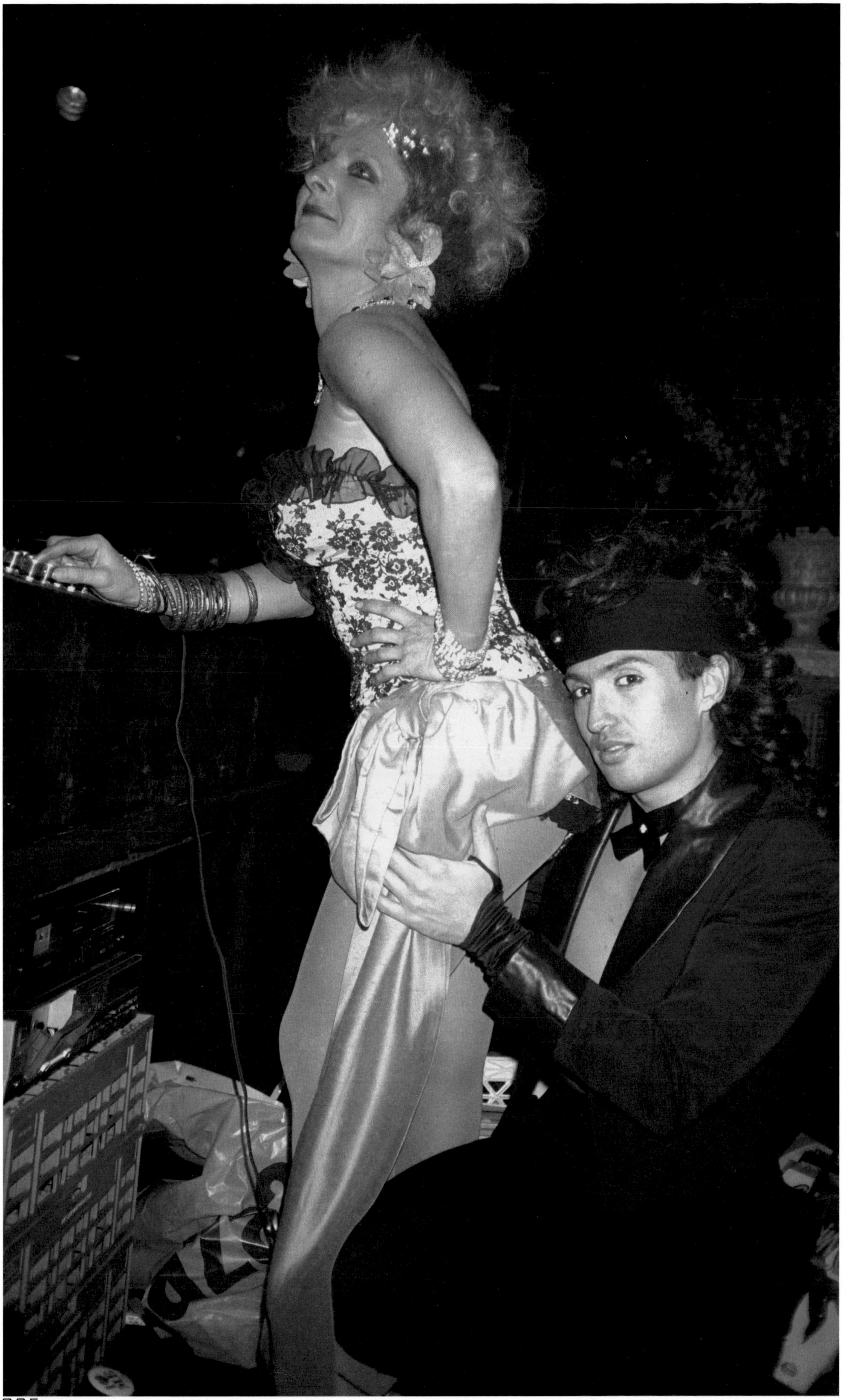

When I DJ'd the opening night of Nell's I quickly saw that things would never be the same.

The big club was dead. Area, the last of the golden clubs would be replaced by the now ubiquitous restaurant/ lounge. Crazy home-made outfits would be replaced by business suits and little black cocktail dresses. Even the temple, Studio 54, became nothing more than an after work networking party. coke would be replaced by cappuccino and dance music would be drowned out by cell phones.

In the 80s, adults acted like kids. After the 80s, kids acted like adults.
Johnny Dynell

Anita Sarko and Johnny Dynell at Stephen Saban's party for Stephen Lupino at the Palladium. March 5,1986

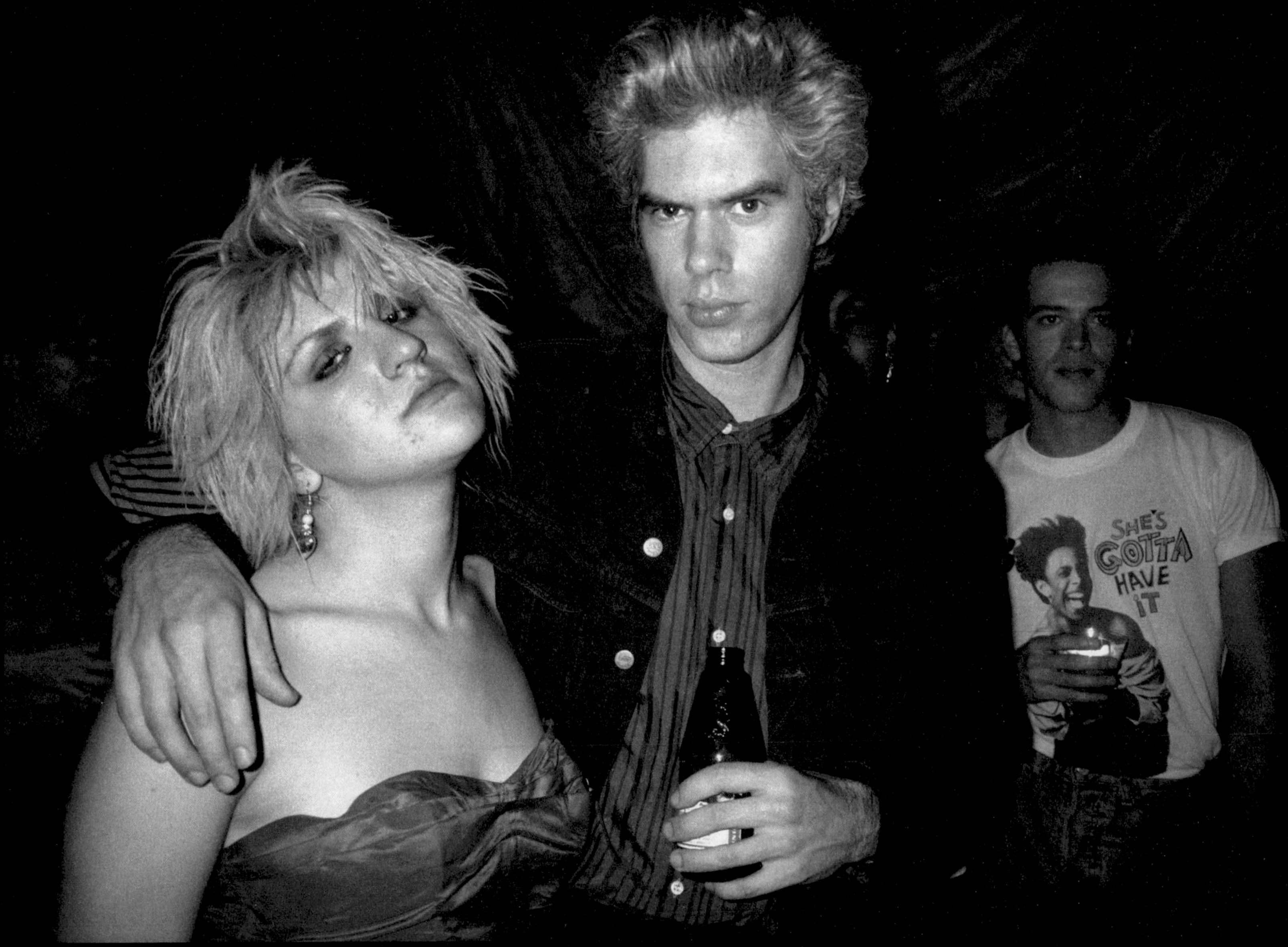

LEFT: COURTNEY LOVE AND JIM JARMUSCH
AT THE SID & NANCY FILM PARTY AT THE PUCK BUILDING.
SATURDAY, OCTOBER 4, 1986
RIGHT: IGGY POP AT DIANNE BRILL'S BIRTHDAY DINNER PARTY
AT CAFE SEIYOKEN. APRIL 16, 1986

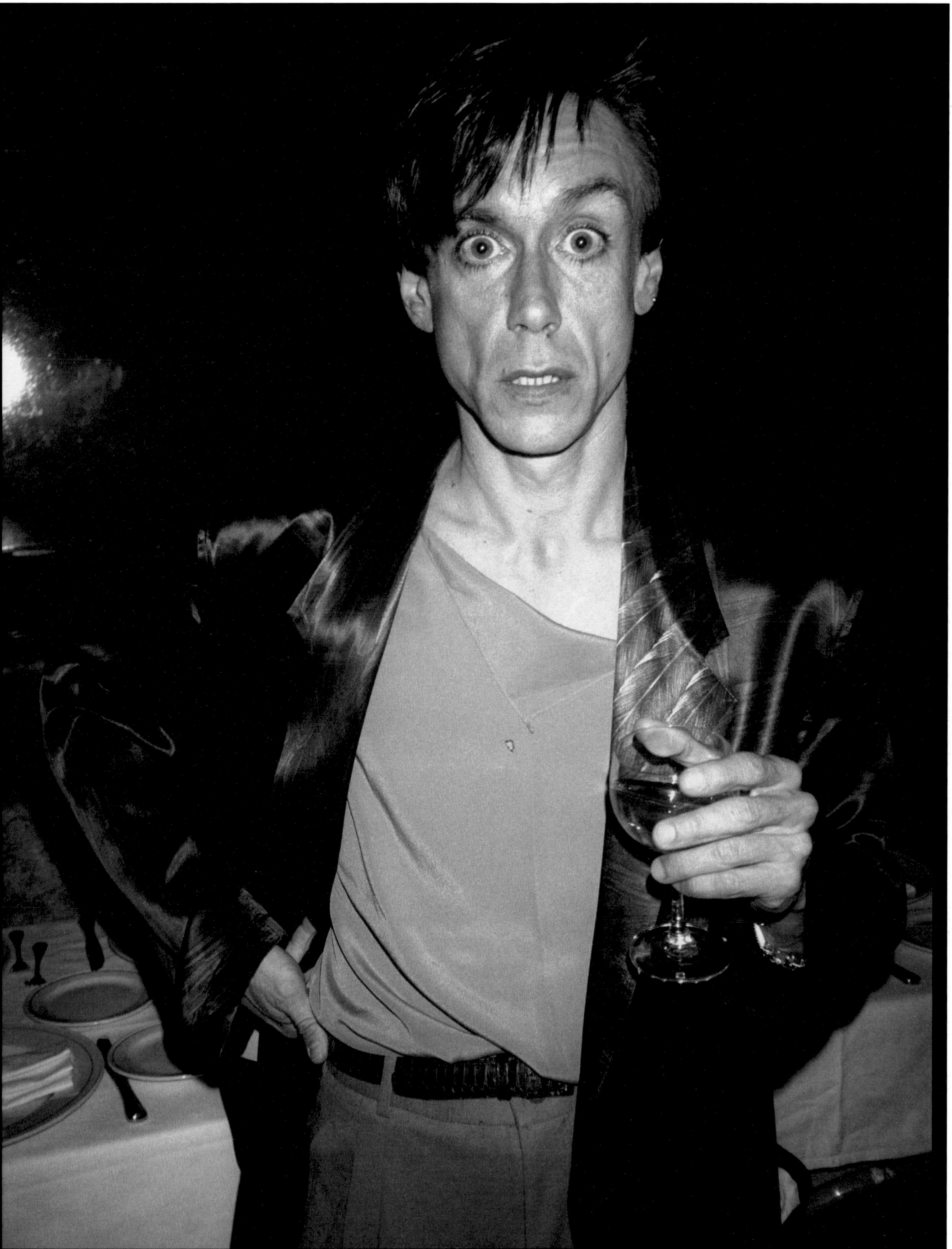

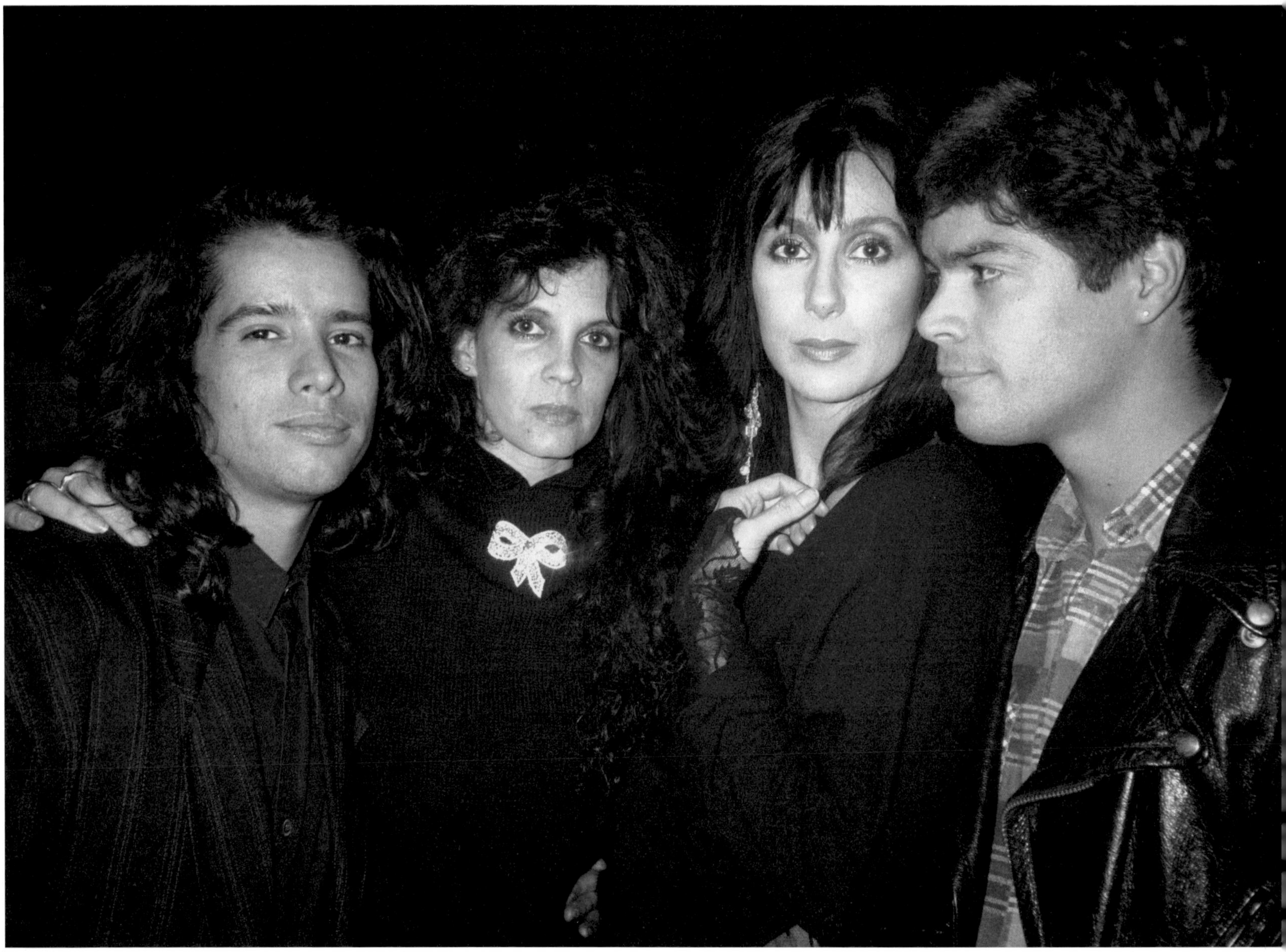

John "Jellybean" Benitez, Loree Rodkin, Cher, and Esai Morales at the Palladium.
January 1987

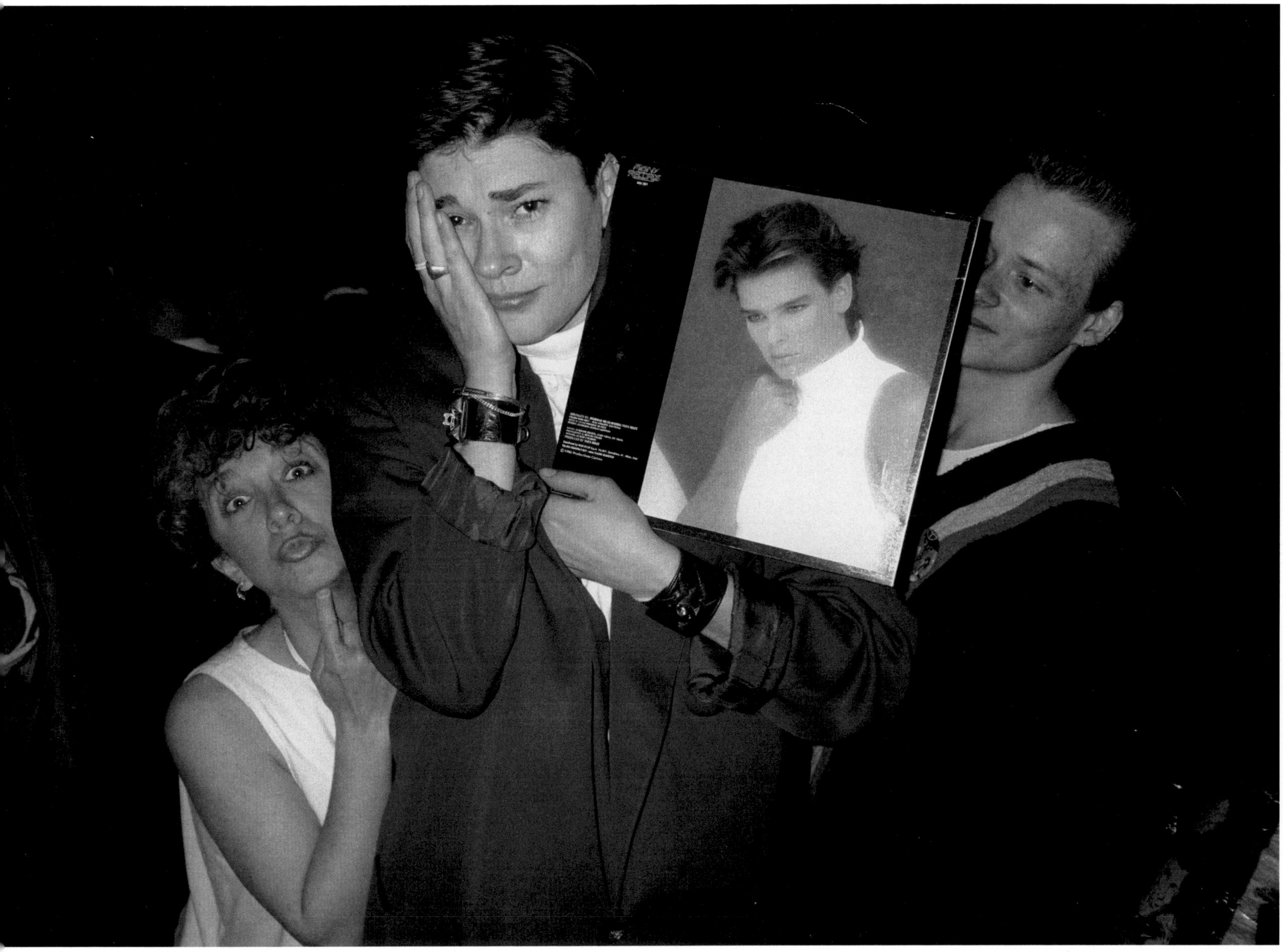

KARON BIHARI, EDWIGE, AND MARTIN BURGOYNE
HOLDING PRINCESS STEPHANIE OF MONACO'S RECORD
AT MICHAEL MUSTO'S DOWNTOWN BOOK PARTY AT THE PALLADIUM.
WEDNESDAY, MAY 28, 1986

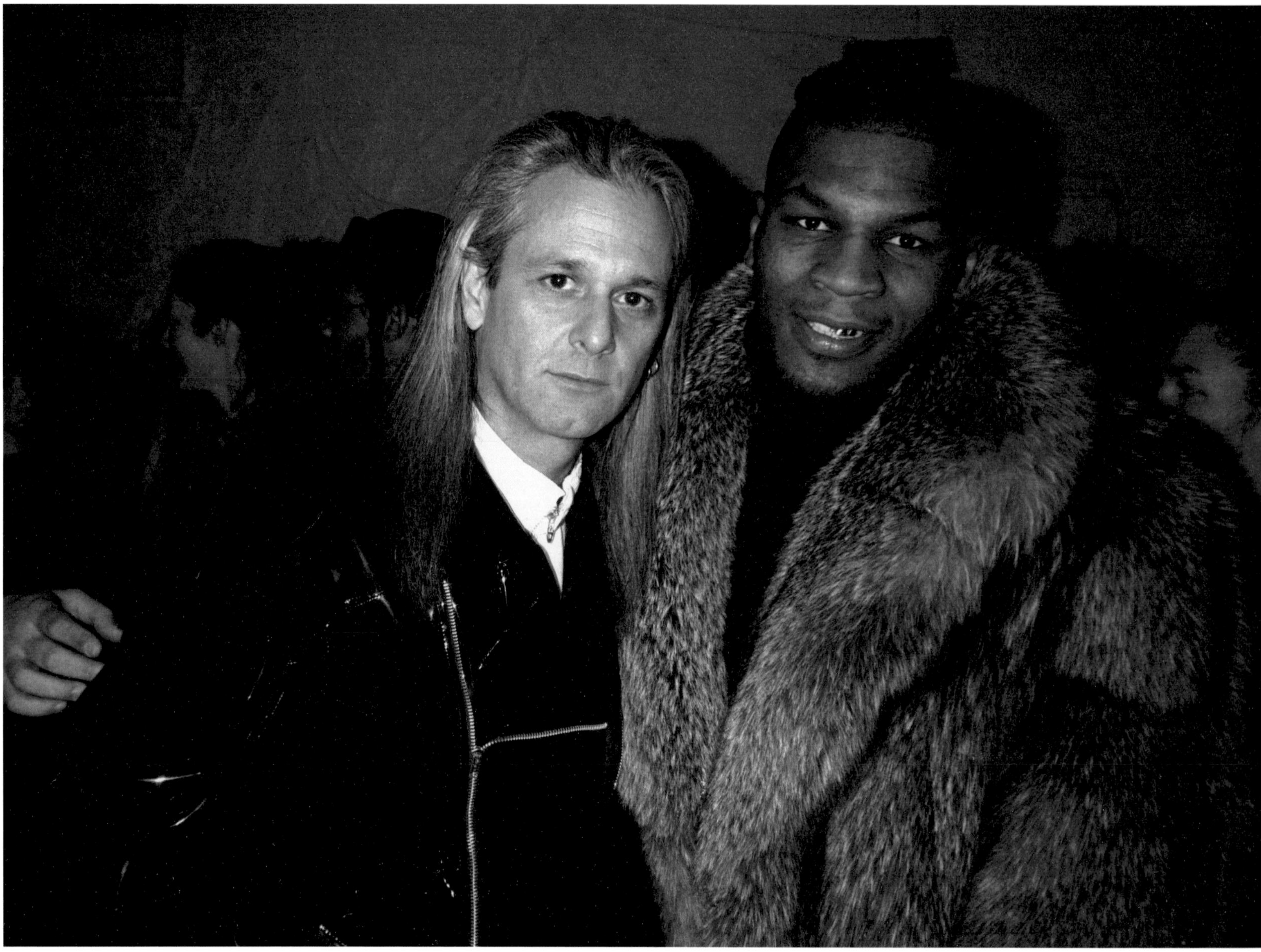

FRANK ROCCIO AND MIKE TYSON
AT THE DETAILS MAGAZINE CHRISTMAS PARTY AT THE WORLD.
DECEMBER 16, 1987

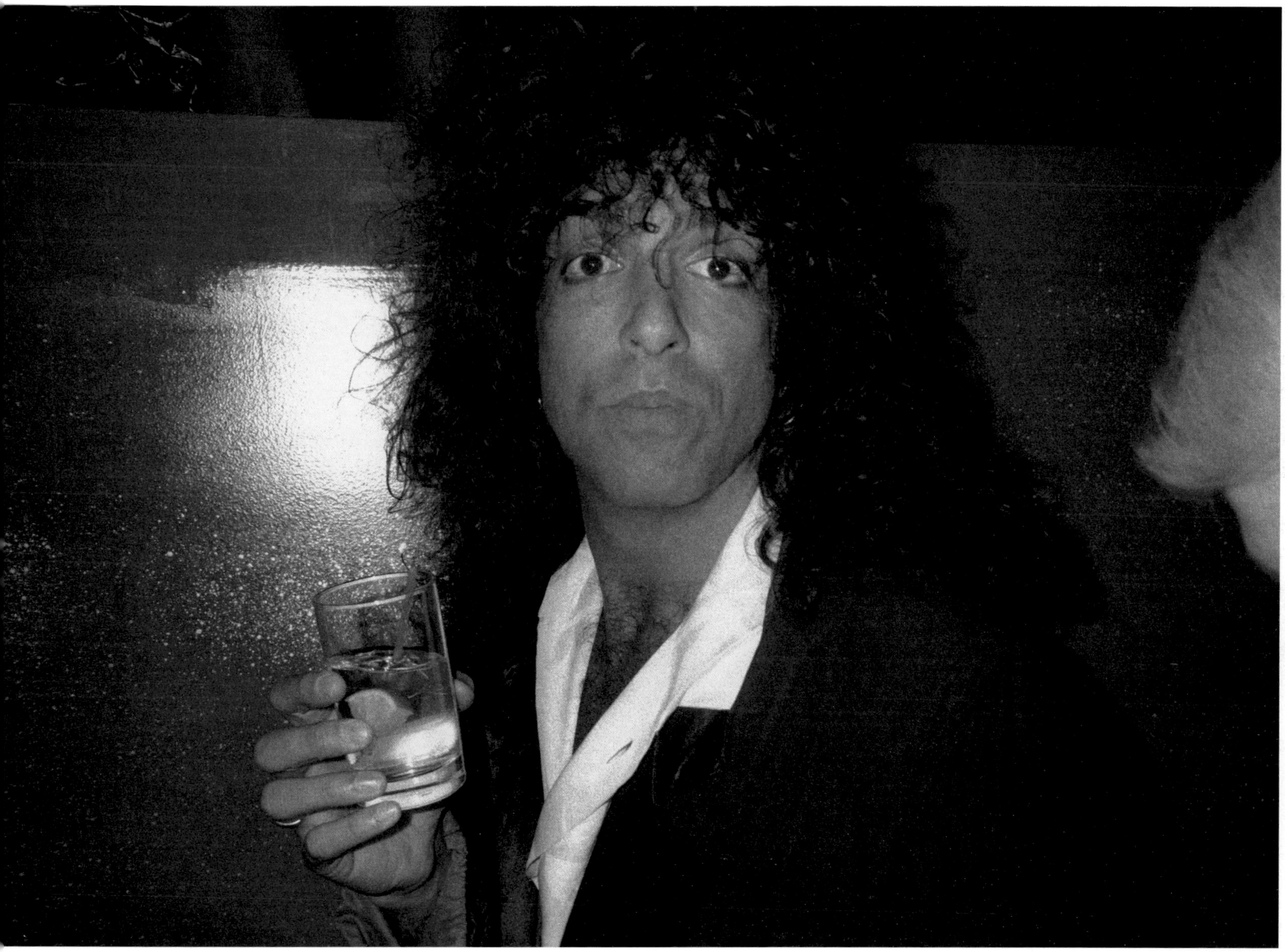

Paul Stanley of KISS
at the opening of 4D.
Tuesday, September 16, 1986

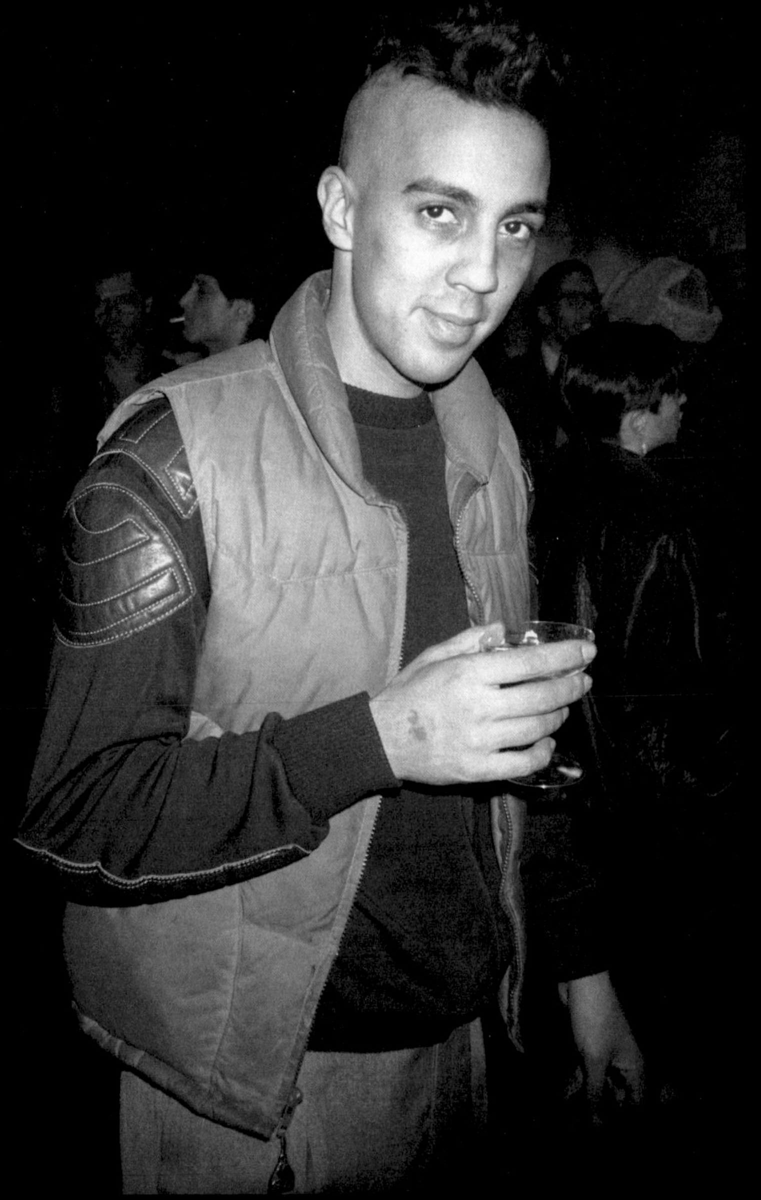

Ooooooooh La La Zee 80s...
The 80s to me were about SoHo lofts, Matt Dillon at art openings french kissin' with me and every other girl in Lower Manhattan at one time or another, graffiti boyz at parties at Jean-Michel's, eating endlessly at Mr. Chow's, Norbert at the door at Area in all his blonde European glory, the Munson and the beautiful, yet funny Garcia brothers, Richie and Paul, adorable Johnny Sex, Wendy Wild, Edwige and me doing James Bond shows everywhere downtown, my neighbor Madonna banging on my door early in the mornings to borrow a pan to make breakfast, exercise with her to her new records, or watch herself on my TV, Danceteria and Palladium and Limelight and Roxy and Paradise Garage every night, Michael Byron, gorgeous Michael Byron fragile artiste, Cookie Mueller and her hilarious writing and her exquisite spirit, Patti Astor, Keith Haring, detox, Fab 5 Freddy, Futura, Dondi, Revolt, and, of course, Zephyr and wild times at the Fun Gallery, the Beat cocktail lounge, Suzanne Mallouk, Metta Madsen, the Mandelbaum pirates, Dante Ross and Ethan, Hawaii 5-O, Pretty Debbie M, Ronnie Cutrone, Marcus Leatherdale's wonderful birthday parties, and Patrick with us all taking the best pictures we could ever imagine to remind of dayz gone by....
Ooooooooh La La Zee 80s, lots' fun...
Karon Bihari

Futura 2000
at 4D for the opening of the Futura Room.
Thursday, November 13, 1986

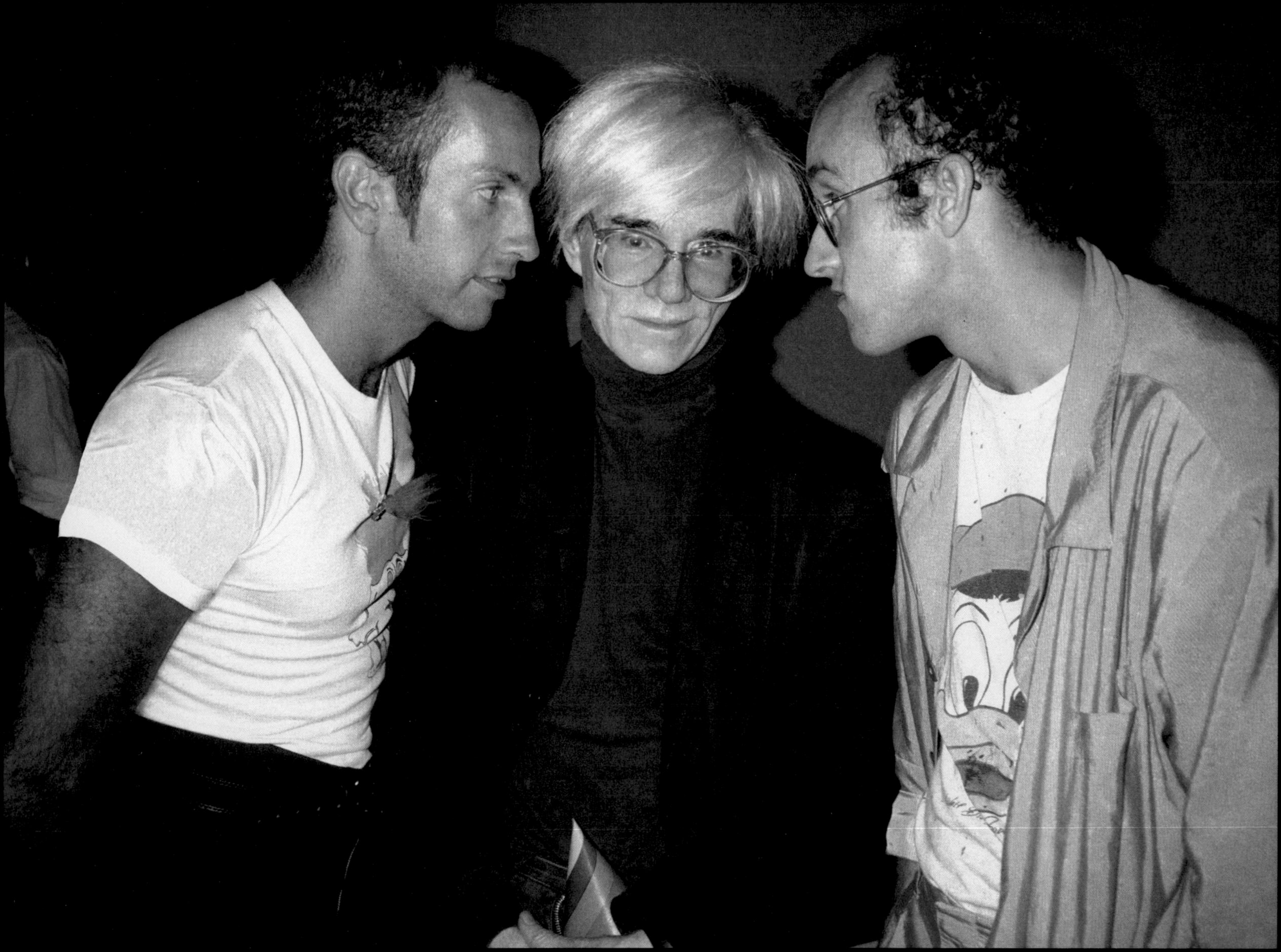

Kenny Scharf, Andy Warhol, and Keith Haring
at Elizabeth Saltzman's birthday party at Il Cantinori.
June 16, 1986

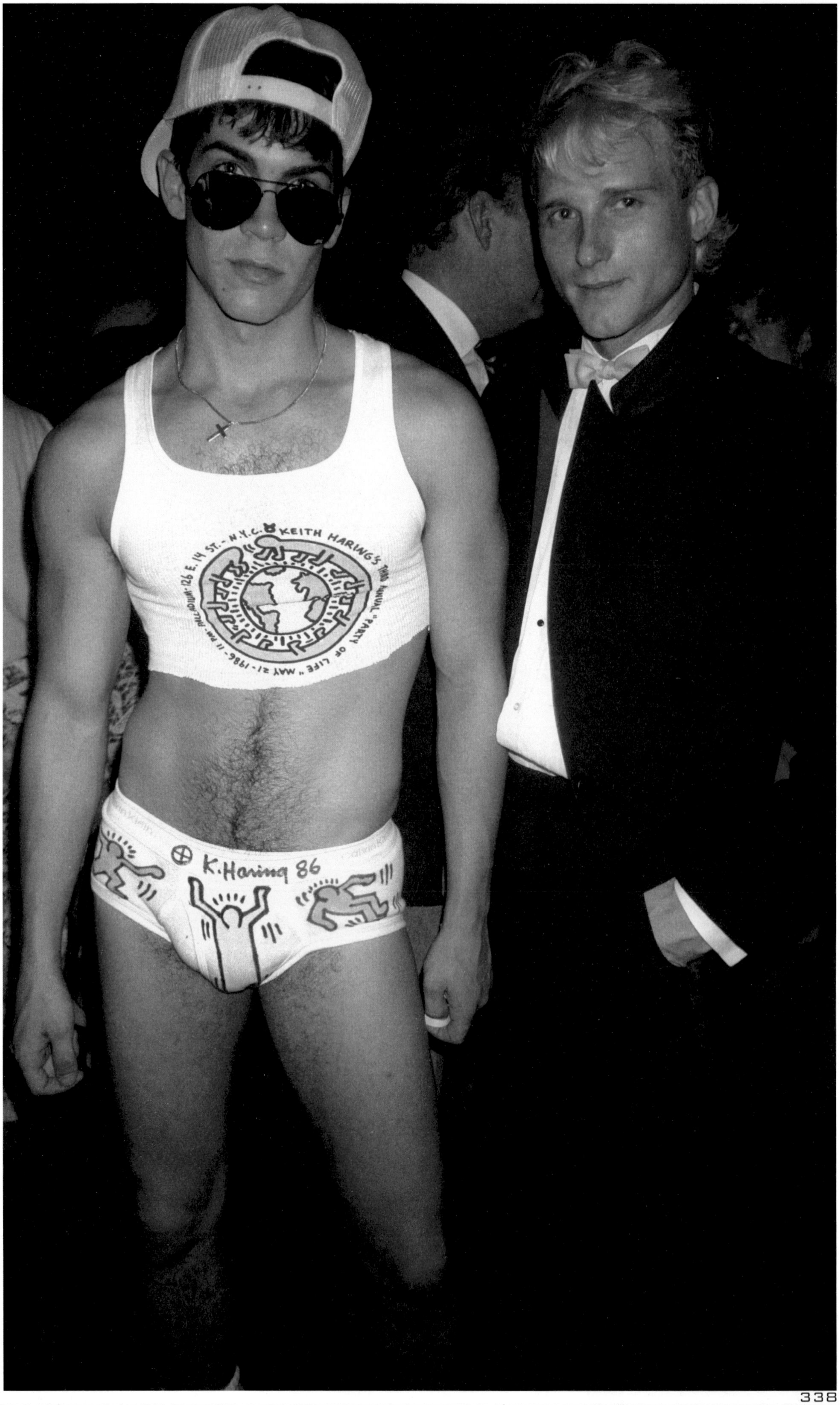

JOE DIETRICH AND LEO FORD AT KEITH HARING'S PARTY OF LIFE AT THE PALLADIUM. MAY 21, 1986

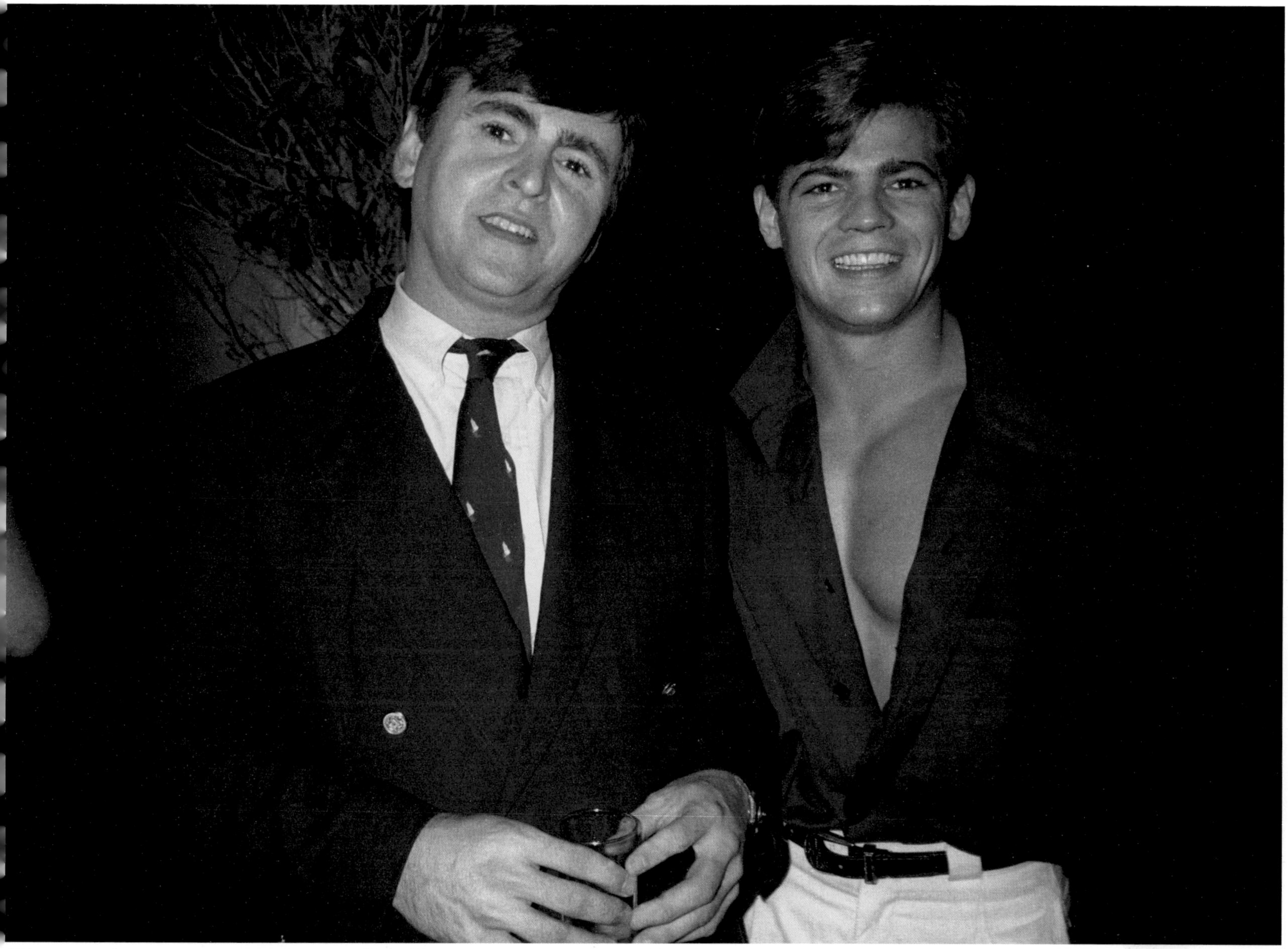

"Studio may have been gone, but New York was still magic. The Odeon and Palladium were hopping, everyone had cash, and Andy's lunches at the Factory were always fun."
Ron Wanless

Ron Wanless and Jeff Stryker
at the Palladium.
Sunday, April 26, 1987

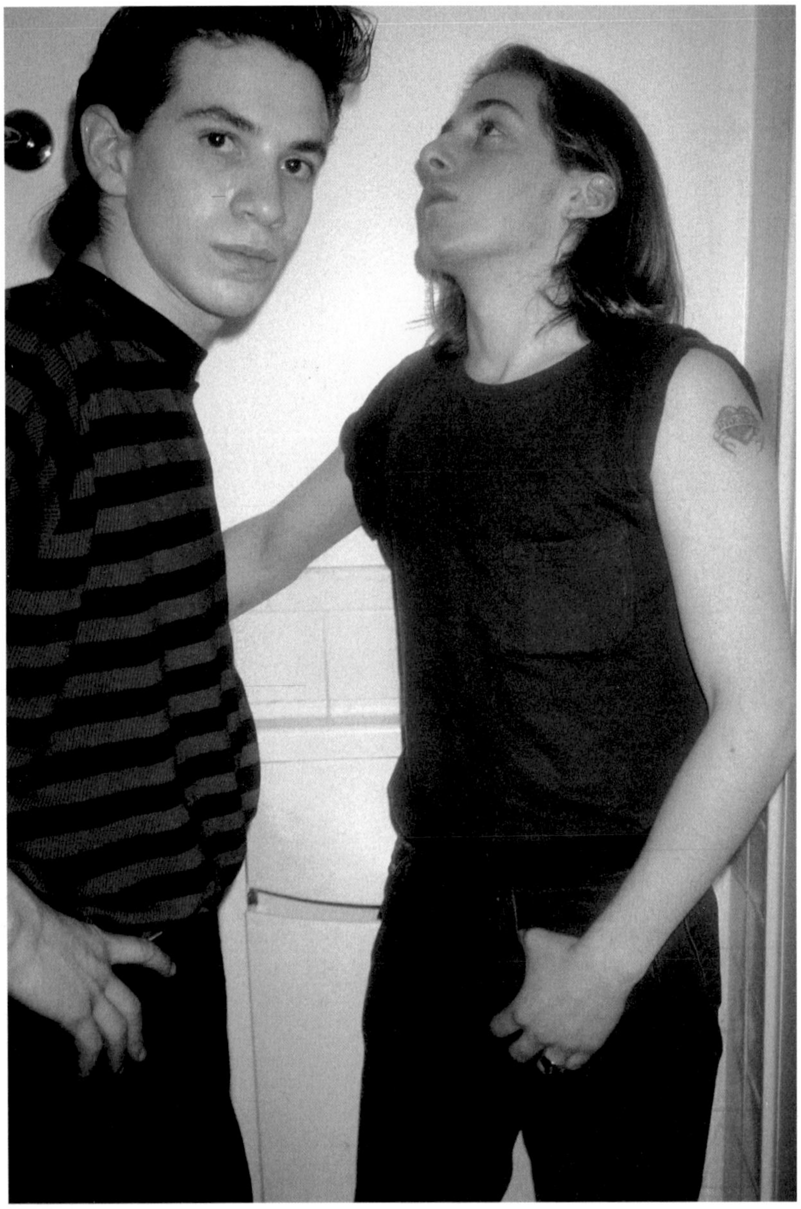

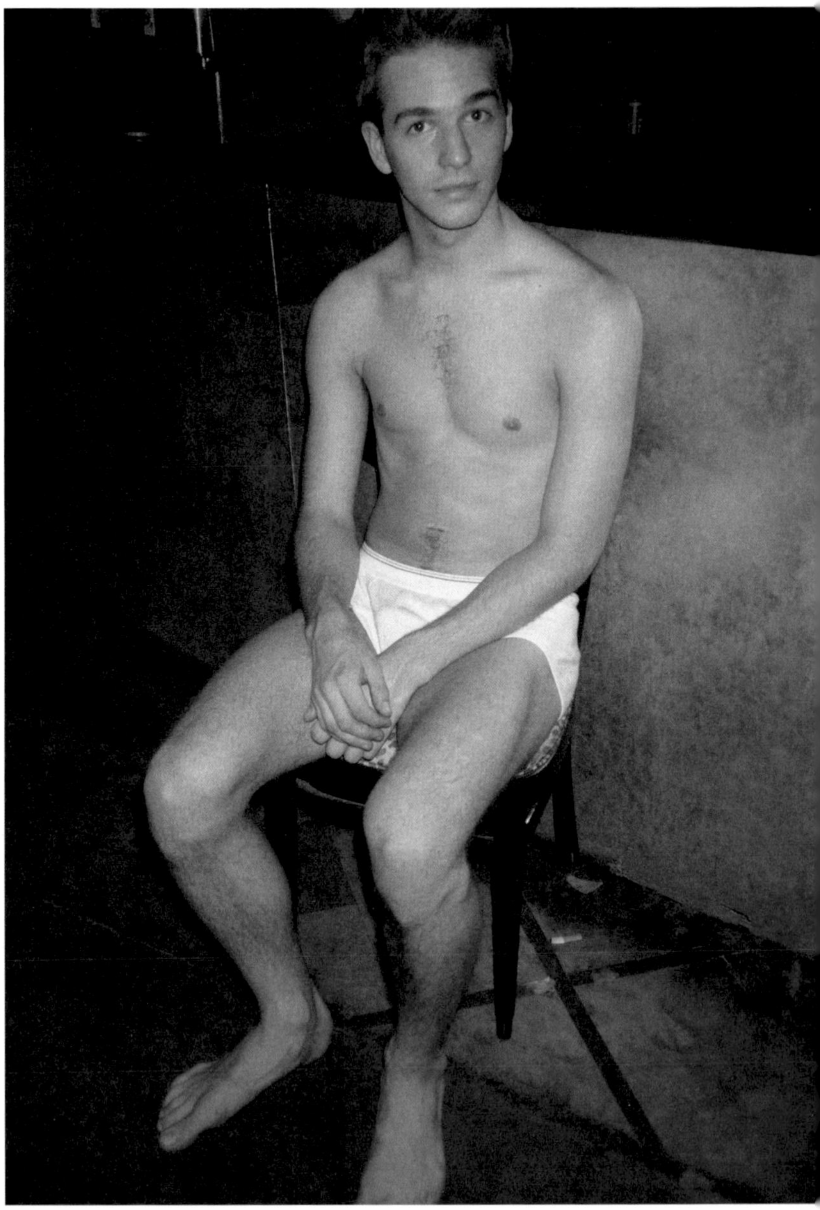

Top Left: Mark Altschuler and Jesse Cohen
March 1989
Top Right: Michael Alig
at Keith Haring's Party of Life at the Palladium.
May 21, 1986

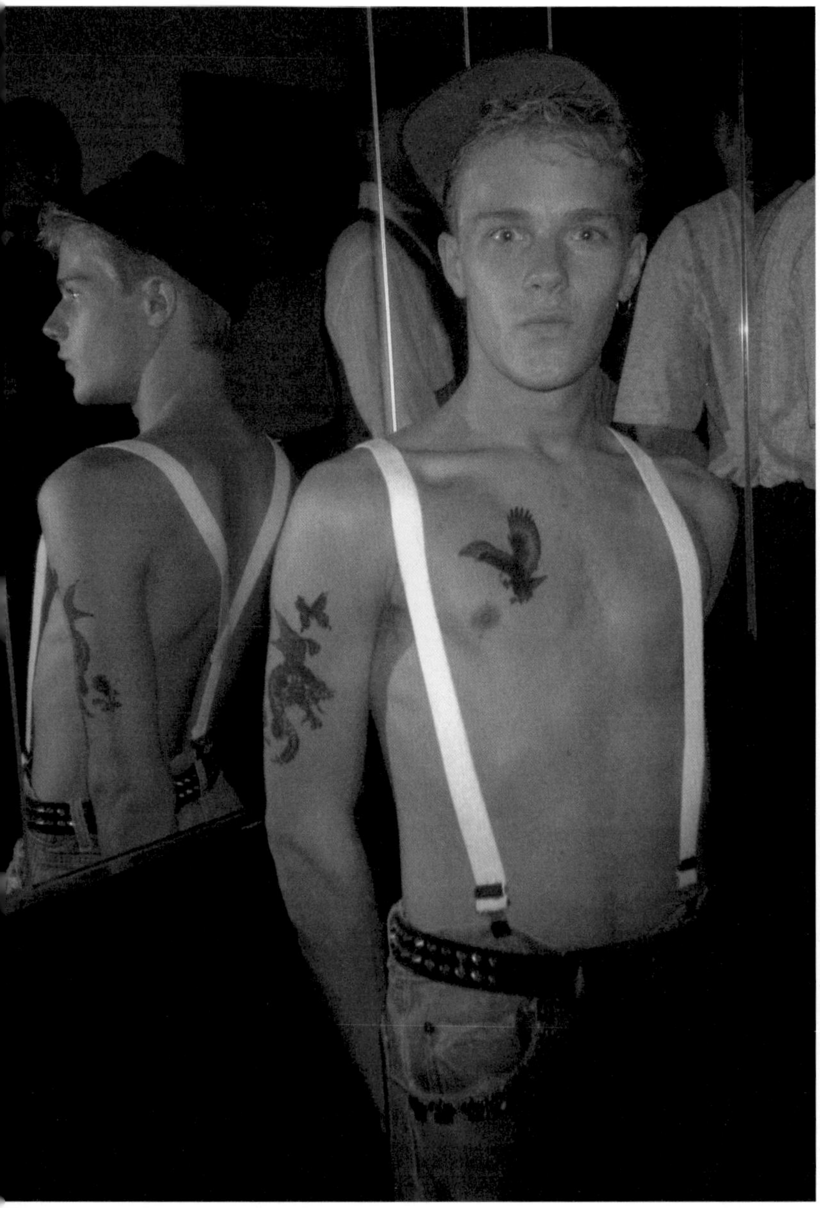

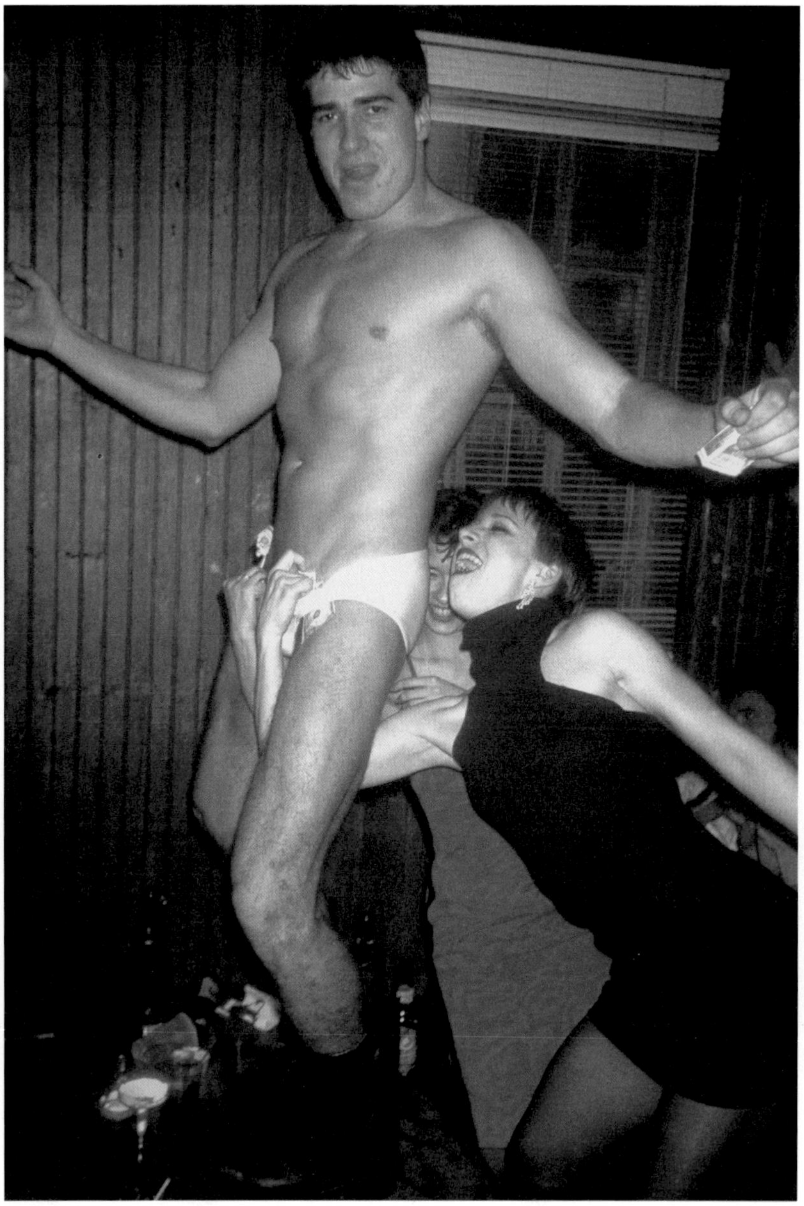

Top Left: Ty Bassett at the World.
Wednesday, June 29, 1988
Top Right: Trade at Mars.
March 1989

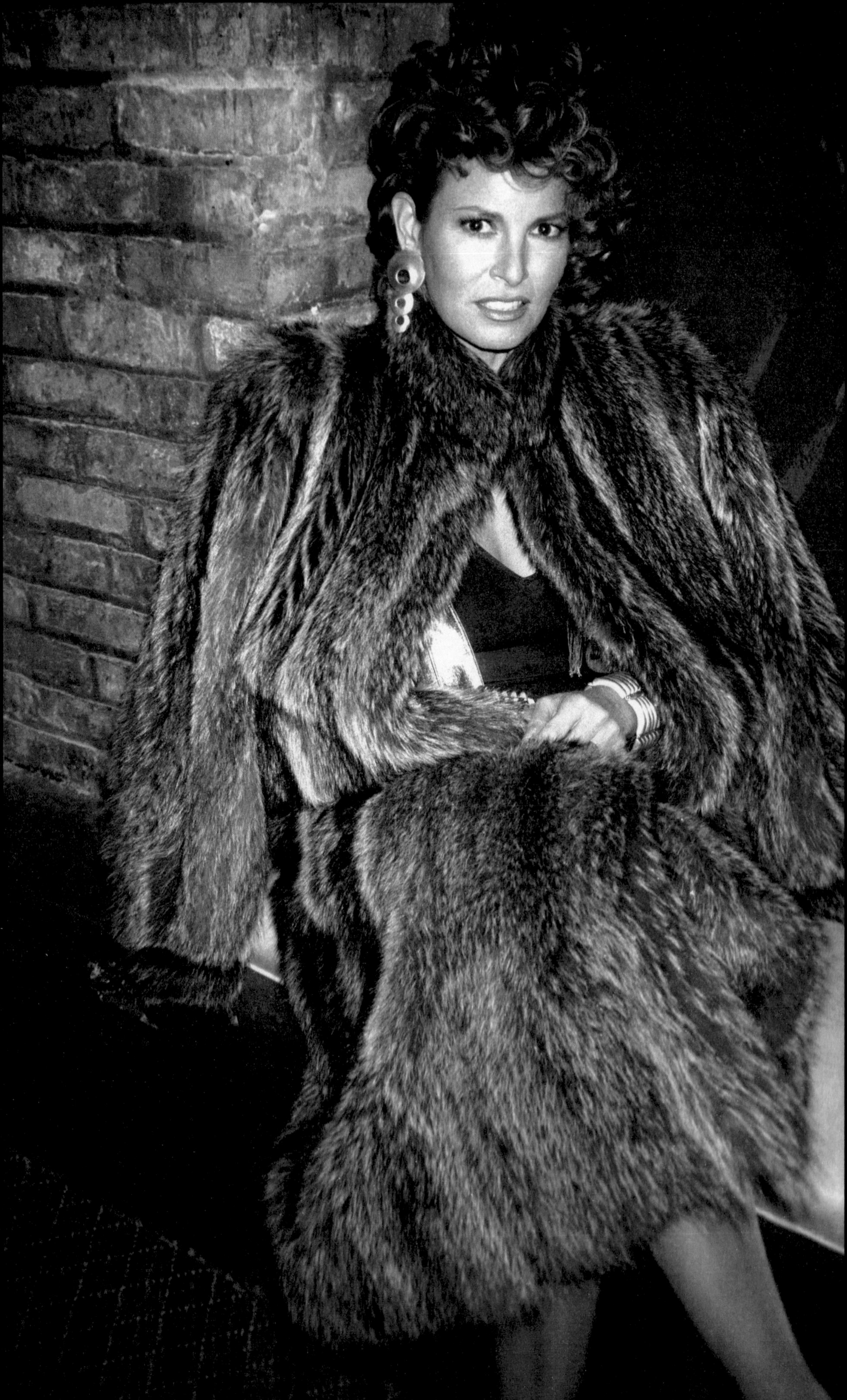

RAQUEL WELCH
AT THE TUNNEL.
NOVEMBER 10, 1987

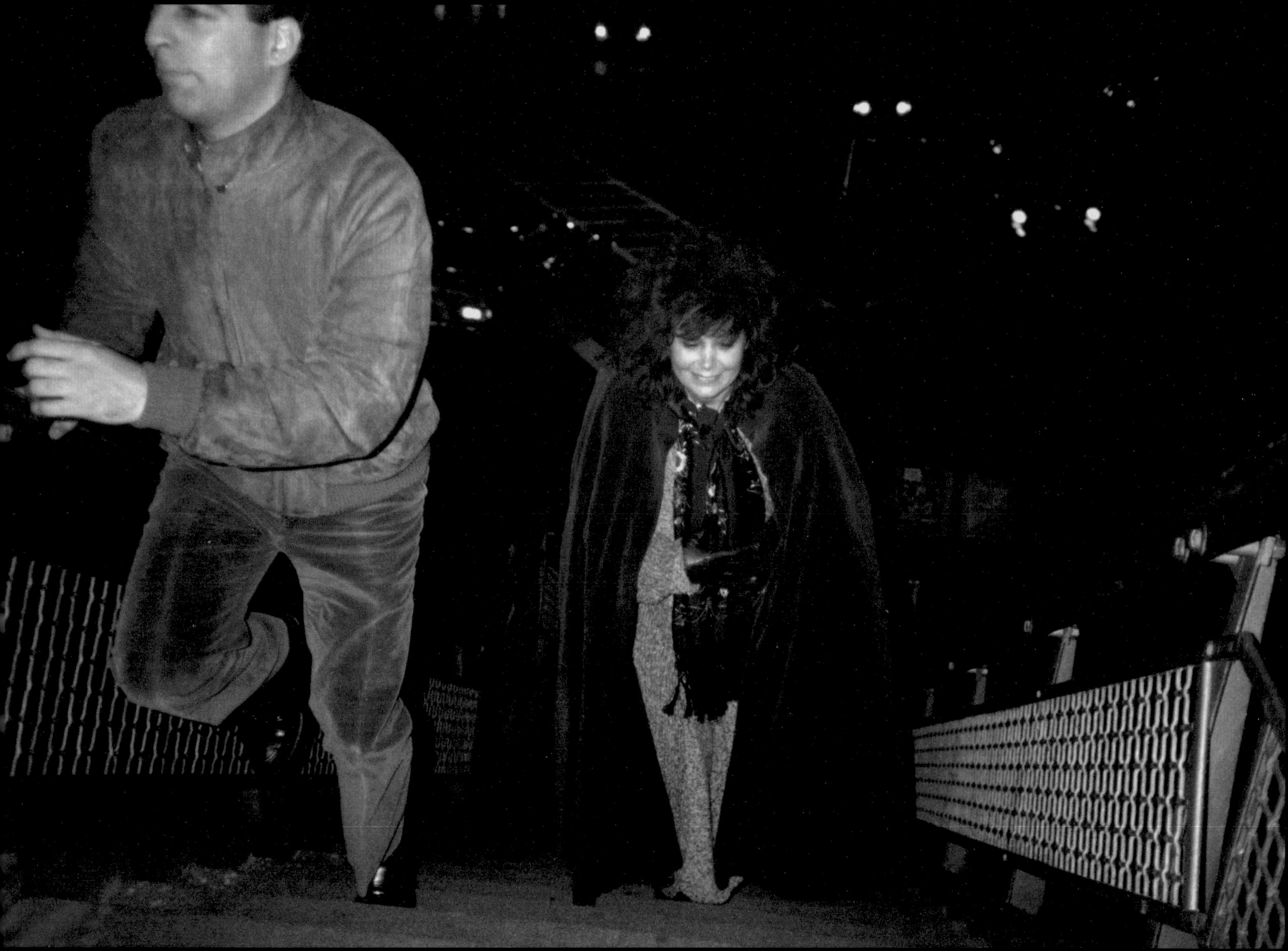

Annie Flanders
heading towards Area.
1986

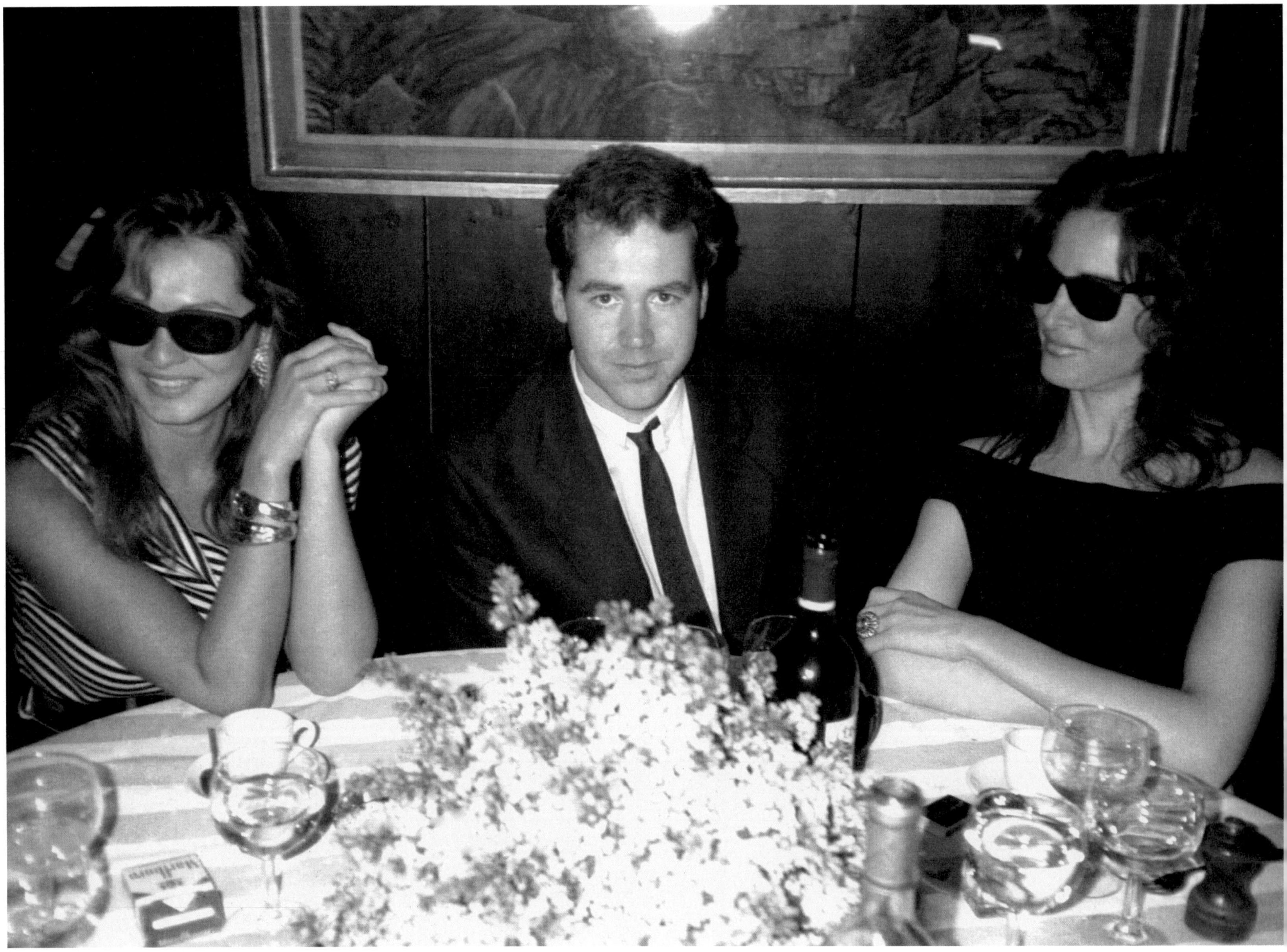

Kimberly DuRoss, Bret Easton Ellis, and Maria Snyder
at Hedy Klineman's luncheon at Mortimer's.
Saturday, May 9, 1987

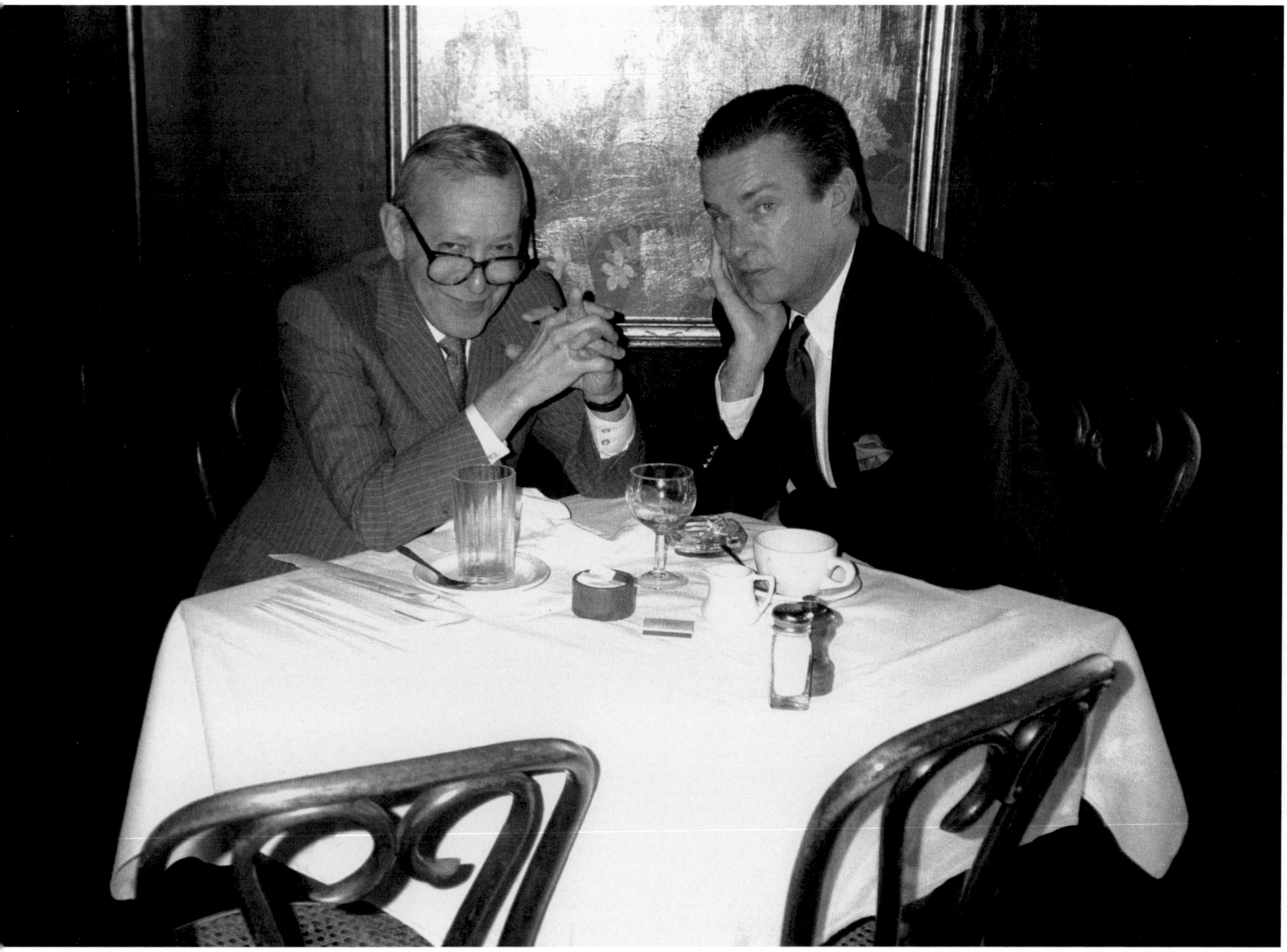

GLENN BERNBAUM, OWNER OF MORTIMER'S, AND PAUL WILMOT
AT HEDY KLINEMAN'S LUNCHEON AT MORTIMER'S.
SATURDAY, MAY 9, 1987

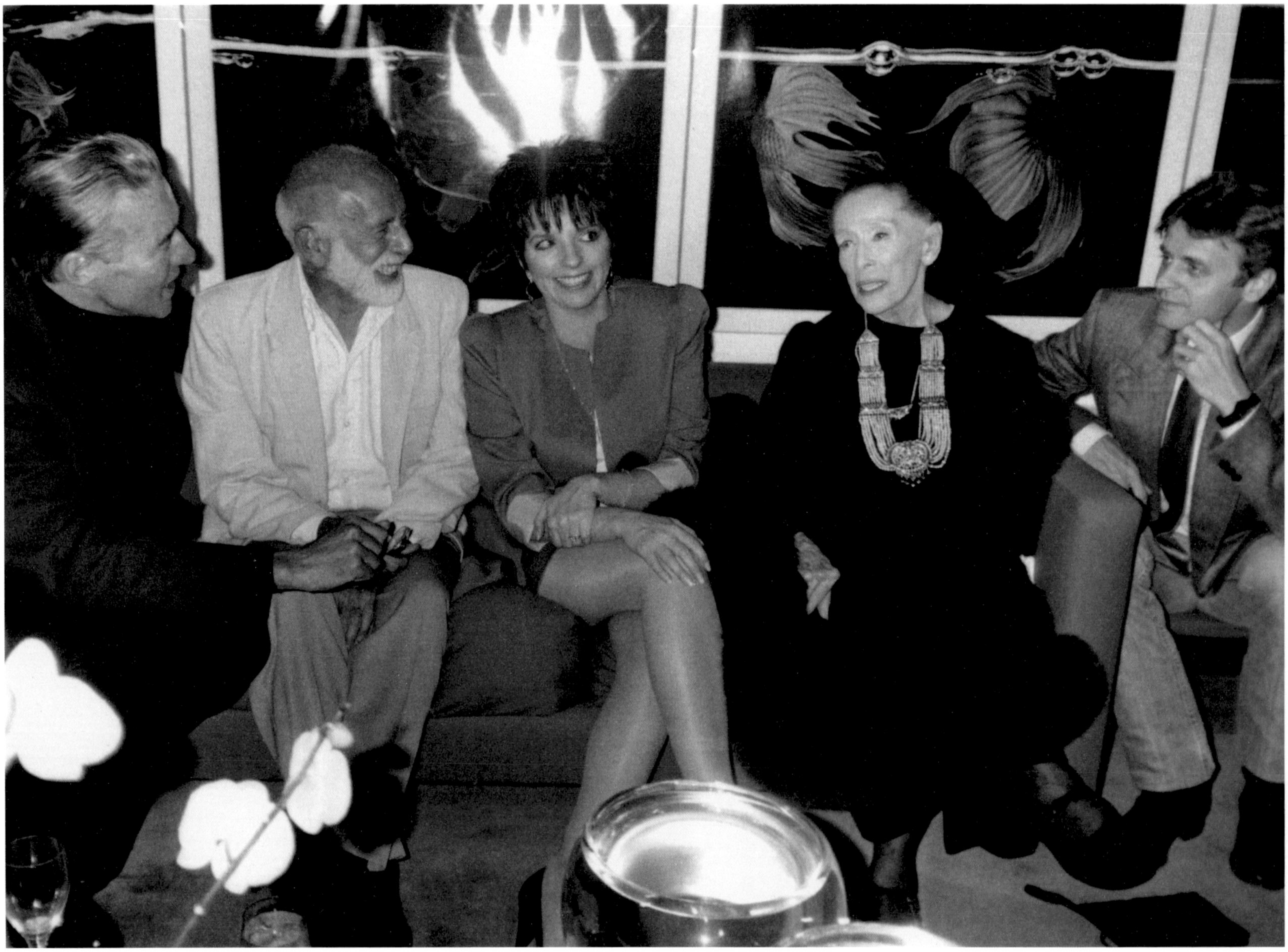

Halston, Jerry Robbins, Liza Minnelli, Martha Graham, and Mikhail Baryshnikov
at Halston's house.
September 1987

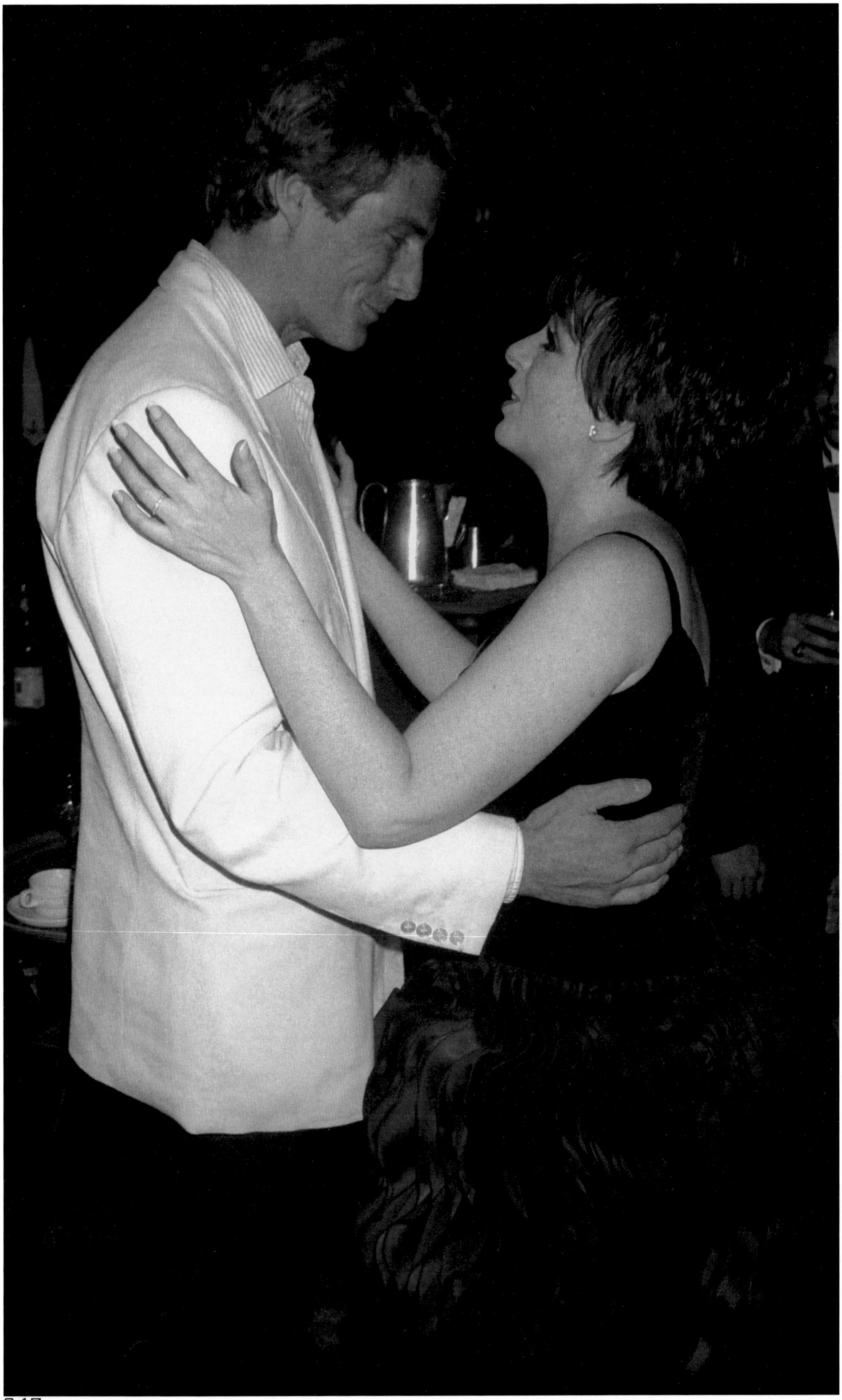

Christopher Reeve
and Liza Minnelli at
her opening night party.
May 28, 1987

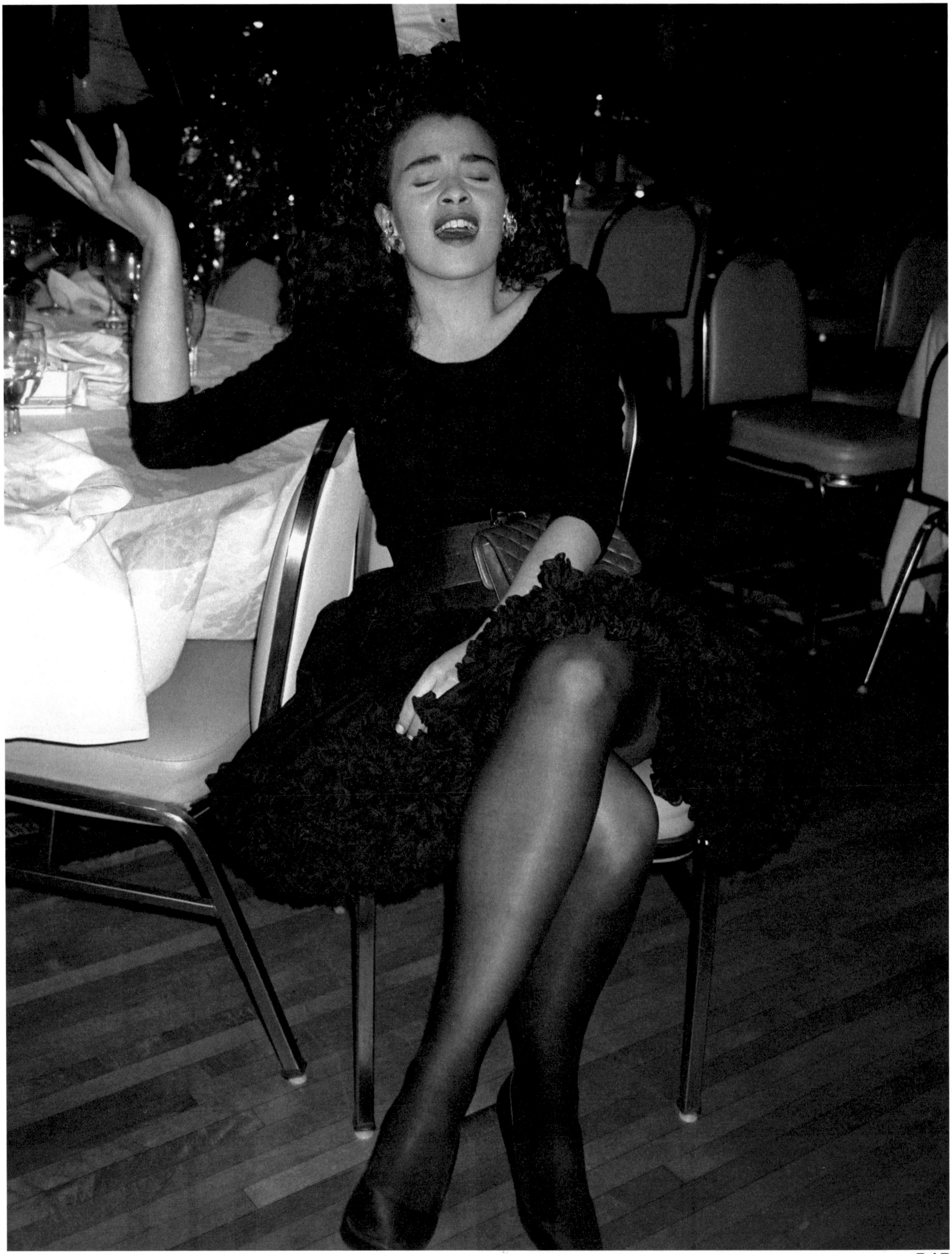

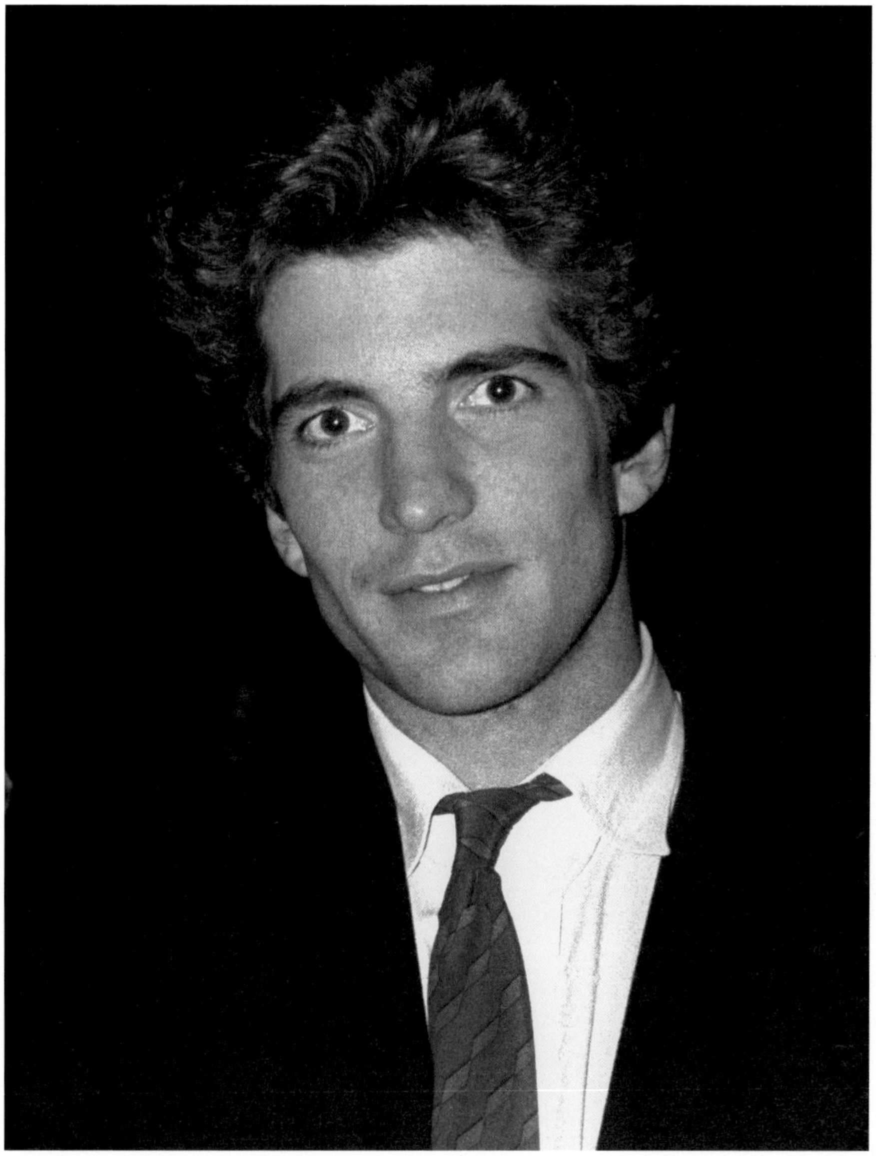

"...EVERY INCH, THE SEXIEST MAN ALIVE...HIS GENIUS GENEALOGY. IT WAS REALLY TRUE GOD CREATED MAN, HE THEN HE CREATED JOHN JOHN KENNEDY...HE WAS INDEED THE POST-MODERN MICHELANGELO COME TO LIFE.
GEORGE WAYNE

TOP: JOHN F. KENNEDY, JR.
AT THE "NIXON GOES TO CHINA" PARTY AT THE CHINA GRILL
FOR THE BROOKLYN ACADEMY OF MUSIC.
FRIDAY, DECEMBER 4, 1987
LEFT: JENNY LUMET AT THE AMERICAN MUSEUM
OF THE MOVING IMAGE: SALUTE TO ELIA KAZAN.
JANUARY 20, 1987

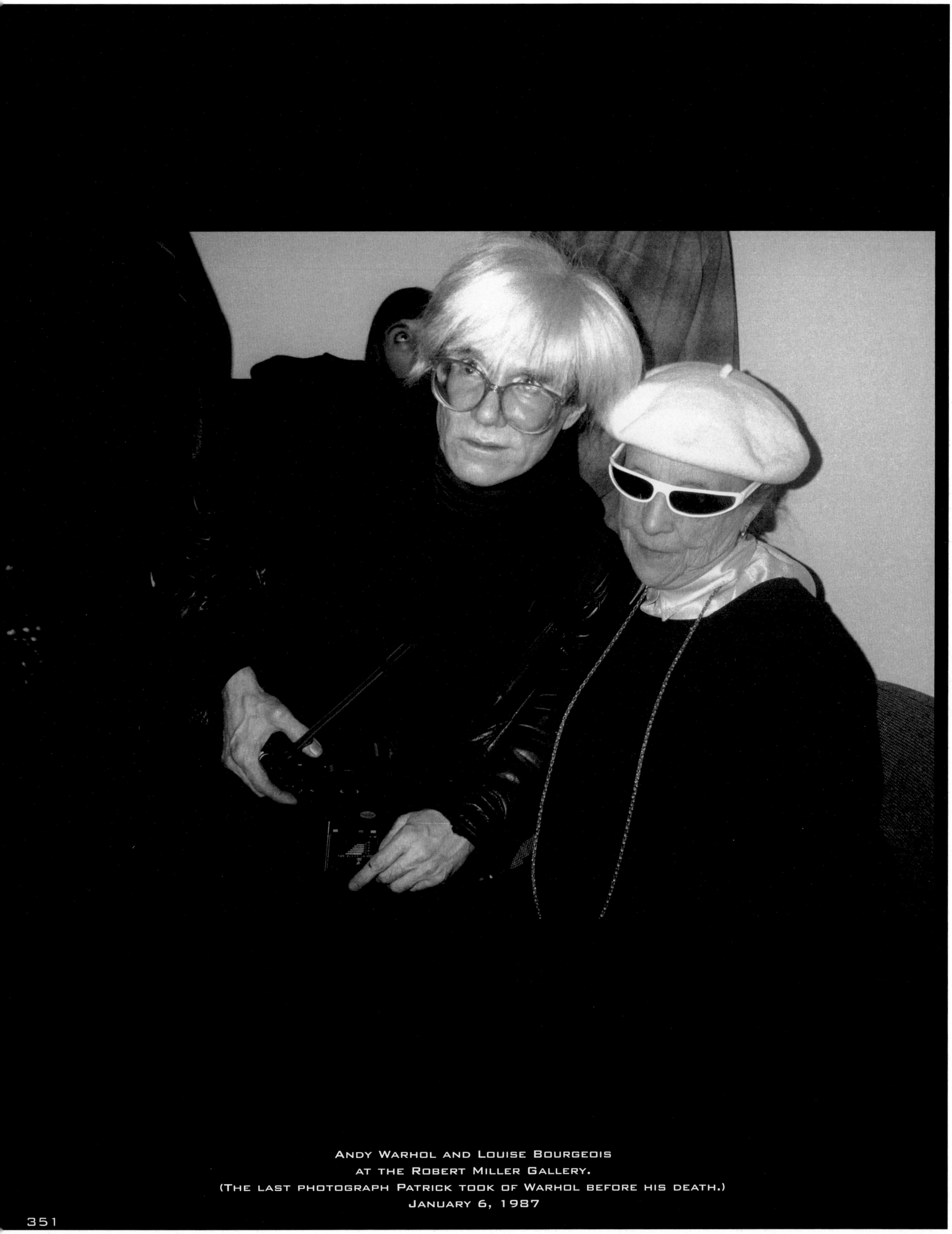

Andy Warhol and Louise Bourgeois
at the Robert Miller Gallery.
(The last photograph Patrick took of Warhol before his death.)
January 6, 1987

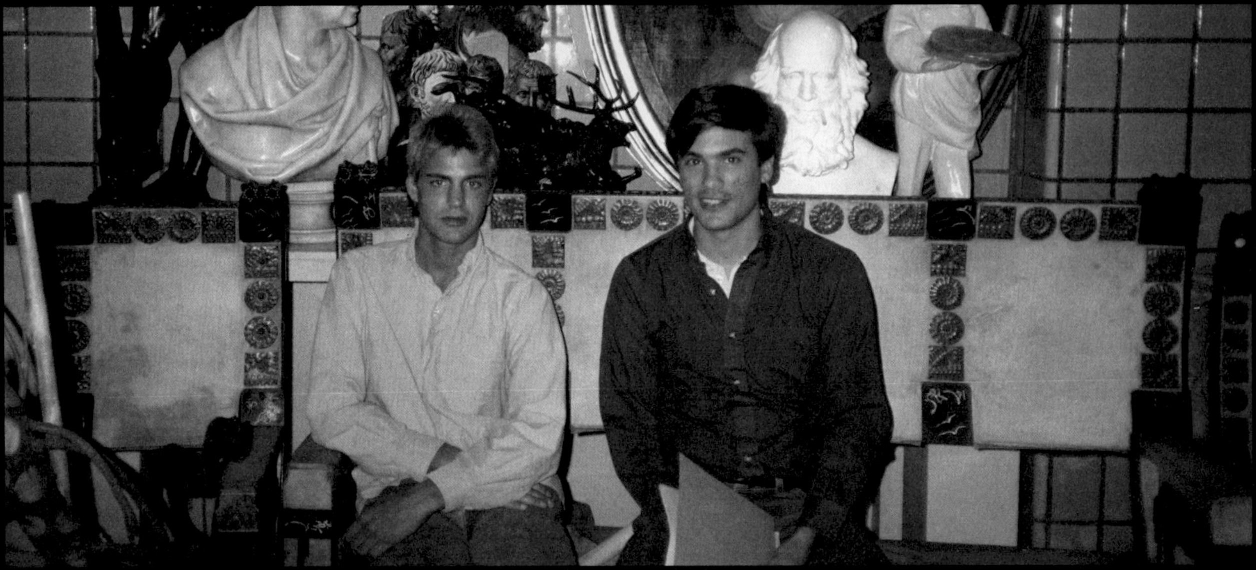

Yo, 80s: The Wigged-Out Era

For party-going celebs, the 1980s was the final Warhol decade. Today, the mark of an interesting party in Manhattan is whether or not party photographer Patrick McMullan has made an appearance.

But twenty years ago, the benchmark was if you had spotted Andy Warhol's fluffy white wig (fakes didn't count). It just meant that you had accepted the correct invitation that night.

Back in 1983, after graduating from Yale, I was living in southern Florida. I flew to Manhattan one weekend to go out on the town with Marcie Klein (Calvin's daughter) and her friends from Dalton. It was scary fun. Marcie, who had been kidnapped once, had a bodyguard. And her buddies, young Wall Street scions, raced their dads' massive, German four-doors to clubs.

We ended up at the nightclub Area, and when Marcie brought us over to meet Warhol, he didn't pay much attention to us but asked in great detail about her recent shopping jaunts.

In 1985, shortly after my cousin Tama Janowitz (Slaves of New York) got me a job at Interview, Warhol's magazine, she brought me to the Andy's Valentine's Day party at Area. Starstruck, my heart raced when I spotted Alexander Godunov cheek-to-cheek with Ursula Andress on the dance floor. They were both incredibly voluptuous. And I bonded with Tama's designer friend Stephen Sprouse, who wore his hair in a long, black shag back then. We used to share cabs back to the East Village after Interview outings, like, say, going skating with Debbie Harry at Wollman Rink.

At the office, one of my chores included schlepping a tiara back from Fred Leighton in a paper bag for some lesser von Furstenberg princess who dated Claus Von Bulow after Andrea Reynolds dropped him. I spent hours one afternoon searching for back issues for Bianca Jagger. She never even came to pick them up. But I would have done anything for her back in the day; in person, she exuded an uncanny sensuality.

Odd jobs were my specialty. One day, I was asked to take Sydney Biddle Barrows (the Mayflower Madam) on a tour of our offices. Another day, Matt Dillon came to lunch (Patrick McMullan brought his two-week old son Liam to meet him). Liam's now a Ford model.

And one day, after Andy had appeared on The Love Boat, I practically fell out of my chair when Jill Whelan, Captain Stubing's daughter on the show, who was visiting Andy, walked up and introduced herself. I was hearing The Love Boat theme song so loud inside my head, I could barely speak.

During lunch, I answered phones. One time, Jean-Michel Basquiat called for Andy from a pay phone at a disco in Germany. He sounded like he was on something, and the music was so loud, he couldn't hear anything I said. After Shirley MacLaine had appeared on the cover and we'd called her a bitch in the intro, she rang and asked for the home phone number of our then-editor, Gael Love. I started sweating when I picked up the phone and her conversation with me began: "This is Shirley MacLaine. May I speak to Gael Hate?"

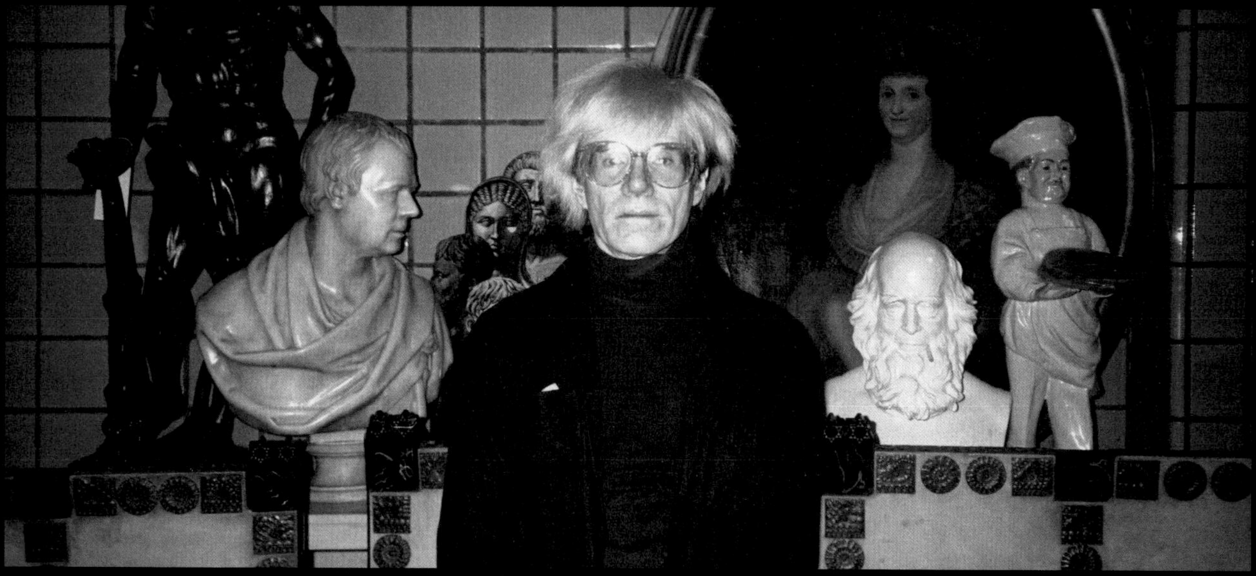

Once in a while, Andy took us out to the Odeon or Serendipity 3 after a movie. Before I went, I always emptied my bank account at a cash machine in case I had to pay. That never happened. One night we all ended up on a group blind date at the Odeon. Paige Powell, Andy's best friend, was wearing a short, pink chiffon tent dress by Sprouse. Tama's dark hair was piled up high, and every time she came back from the bathroom, it was piled a little higher.

Andy adored Tama, but I never heard him sound quite so excited as when he suddenly deadpanned, "Oh my God, it's Barbara Eden." Paige let out a shrill yelp when she spotted Eden at the next table. The rest of the night, I kept looking and saying, "Where?"

Actually, I was looking for Barbara Egan, the then-wife of one of our columnists, Glenn O'Brien. She also worked at Interview at that time. Whoops.

A few years later, I was coming back from a business trip for Interview, riding a bus across town when the driver happened to tell someone that Warhol was dead. That's how I heard the news. I remember getting off at the next stop and wandering for blocks, sobbing.

For me, the rest of what I remember about the 80s is a bit maudlin. In August of 1988, I was with Paige Powell at her house in Quogue when Alba Clemente, Francesco's wife, called to tell us that Paige's old boyfriend, Jean-Michel Basquiat, had overdosed. He was dead.

Paige was still asleep, and she'd been so upset when Andy died, I didn't want to wake her. I just didn't know how to tell her.

Then I recall being at a house the Clementes had rented in Southampton for one of their children's birthday parties. A plumpish Henry Geldzahler, the curator who had discovered Warhol, was wearing a grass skirt while still managing to look like Santa Claus. He had brought a beautiful coffee table book about ancient Roman glass with him to the house.

At a sun-drenched, wooden table in the backyard, Andy's close friend Keith Haring, who already had AIDS, slowly pored over images of the exquisitely delicate ancient art. Nearby, on a blanket, on the vivid green lawn, the tiny Clemente twin baby boys looked like miniature Roman bankers.

I remember feeling queasy with the knowledge that Andy's world, an exuberant, rich, though apparently fragile era, was in rapid decline.

Jeffrey Slonim
NYC, 2003

Top Left: Sam Bolton and Jeffrey Slonim at the Factory.
Tuesday, September 16, 1986
Top Right: Andy Warhol at the Factory.
Tuesday, September 16, 1986

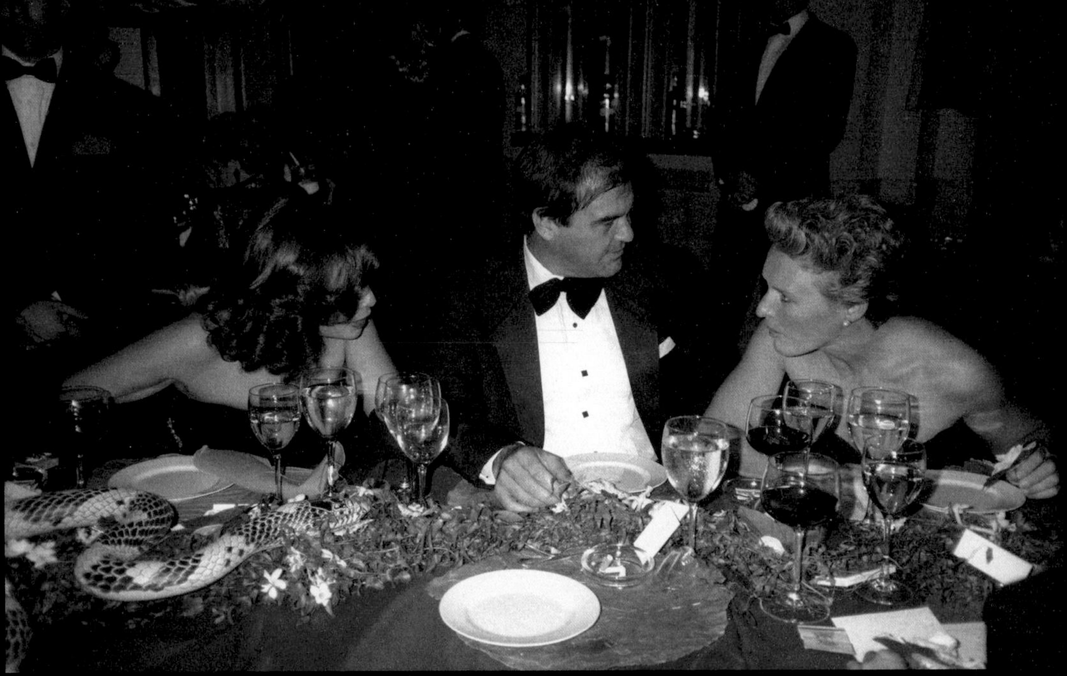

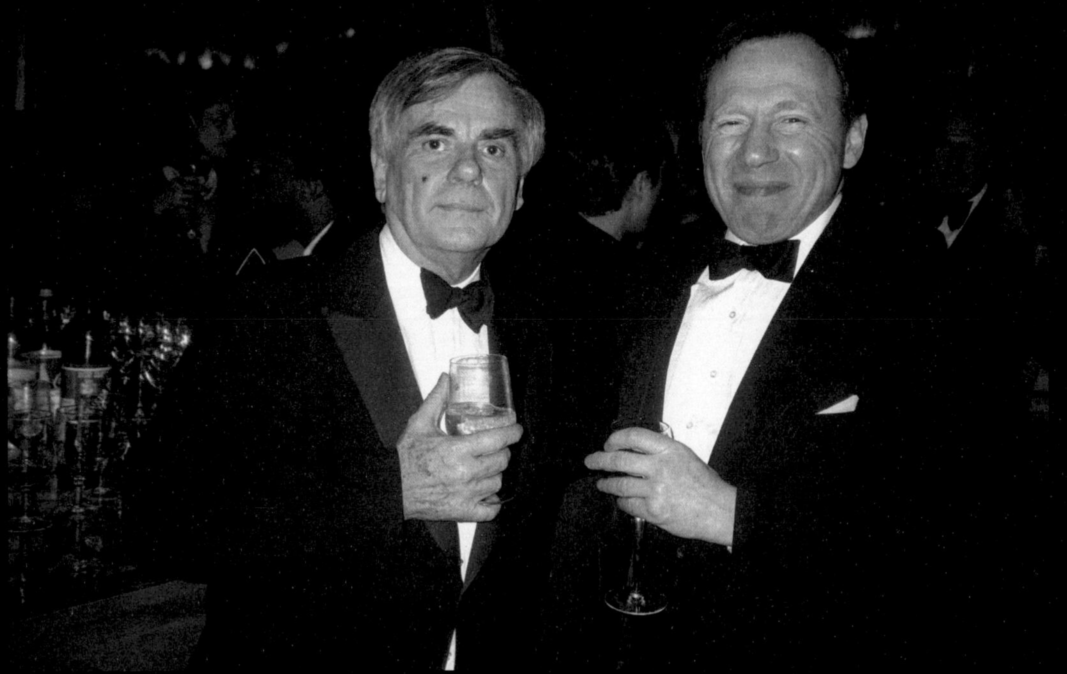

Top: Bianca Jagger, Oliver Stone, and Glenn Close
at the opening night gala at the Brooklyn Academy of Music.
October 14,1987
Bottom: Dominick Dunne and Anthony Haden-Guest
at the Vanity Fair party.
February 29, 1988

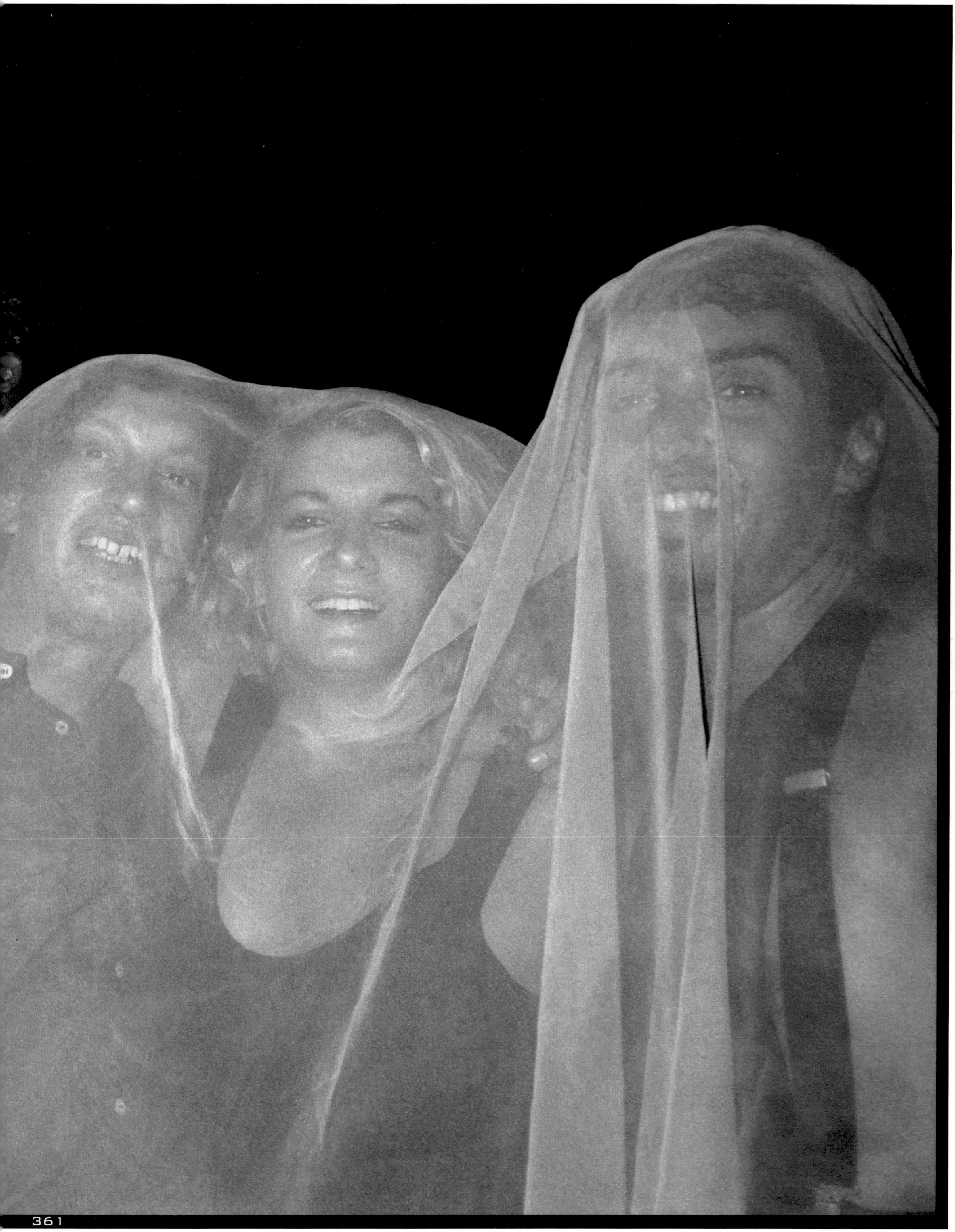

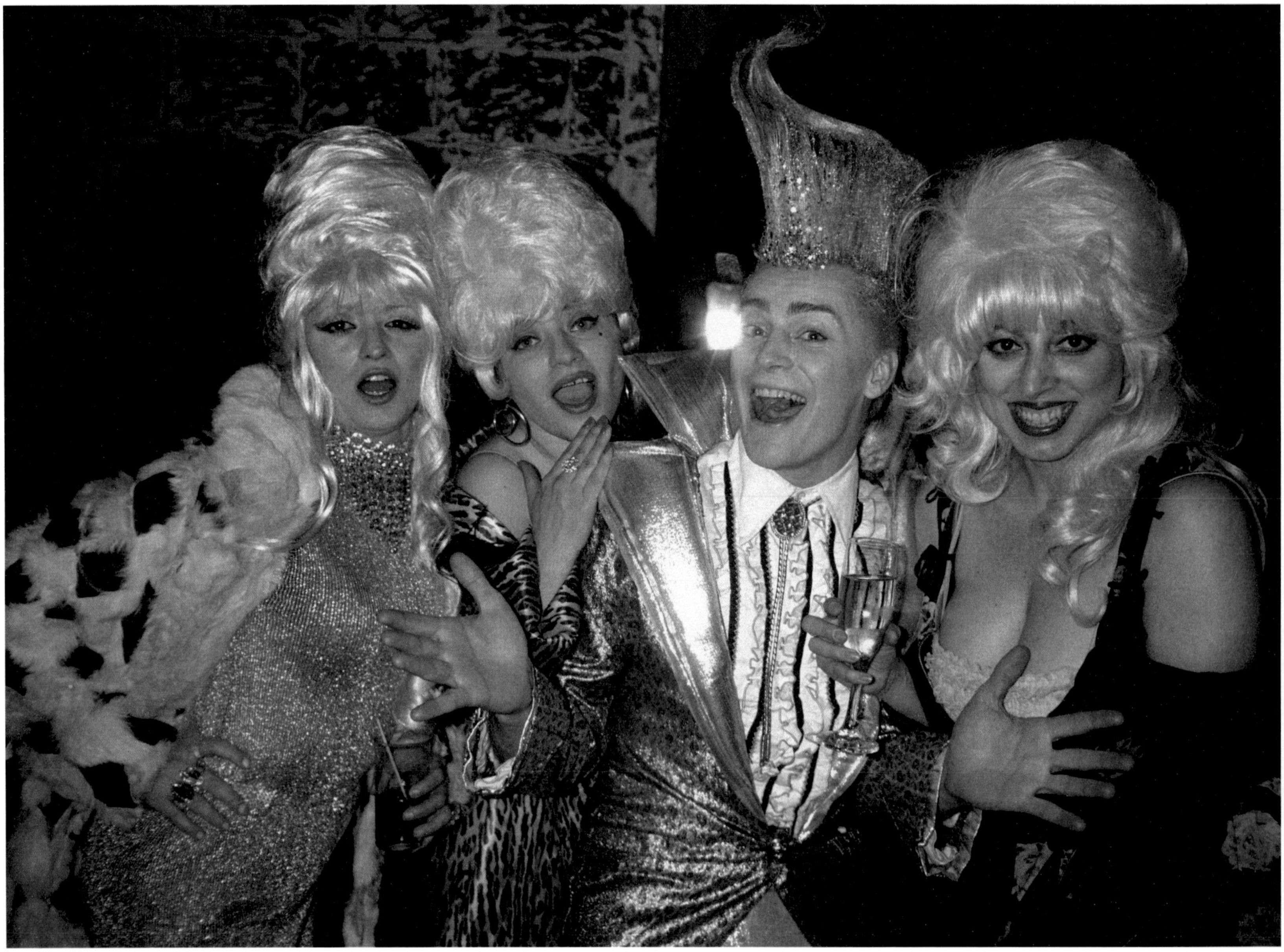

THE DECADE LAUNCHED ART AND FASHION AS "ENTERTAINMENT." ARTISTS AND MODELS BECAME "SUPERSTARS," MORE IF YOU LIKE. THEIR CLOTHES AND OBJECTS FROM THEIR LIVES BECAME COMMODITIES TO BE DISPLAYED, AUCTIONED AND SOLD.

HEDY KLINEMAN'S, "FASHION PORTRAIT" PAINTINGS WERE CREATED WITH CELEBRITIES' CLOTHES AND OBJECTS, COMMISSIONED BY THE SUBJECTS OR ASKED FOR BY THE ARTIST. ANDY WARHOL--GAVE HER HIS GLASSES, BETSEY JOHNSON--HER BUSTIER AND BOOTS, MICHAEL JACKSON--THE BOOTS HE WORE IN THE "BAD" VIDEO, JULIAN SCHNABEL--HIS PAINTING CLOTHES AND SHOES, ETC., PATRICK MCMULLAN--HIS FAVORITE, "GOING OUT" JACKET, CAMERA, AND PHOTOS FOR A LIFE-SIZE, THREE-DIMENSIONAL PORTRAIT.
HEDY KLINEMAN

TOP: WENDY WILD, APRIL PALMIERI, JOHN SEX, AND KATY K
AT JOHN SEX'S BIRTHDAY PARTY AT THE TUNNEL.
APRIL 11, 1987
RIGHT: MARY MCFADDEN AND THE GUARDIAN ANGELS.
NOVEMBER 1987

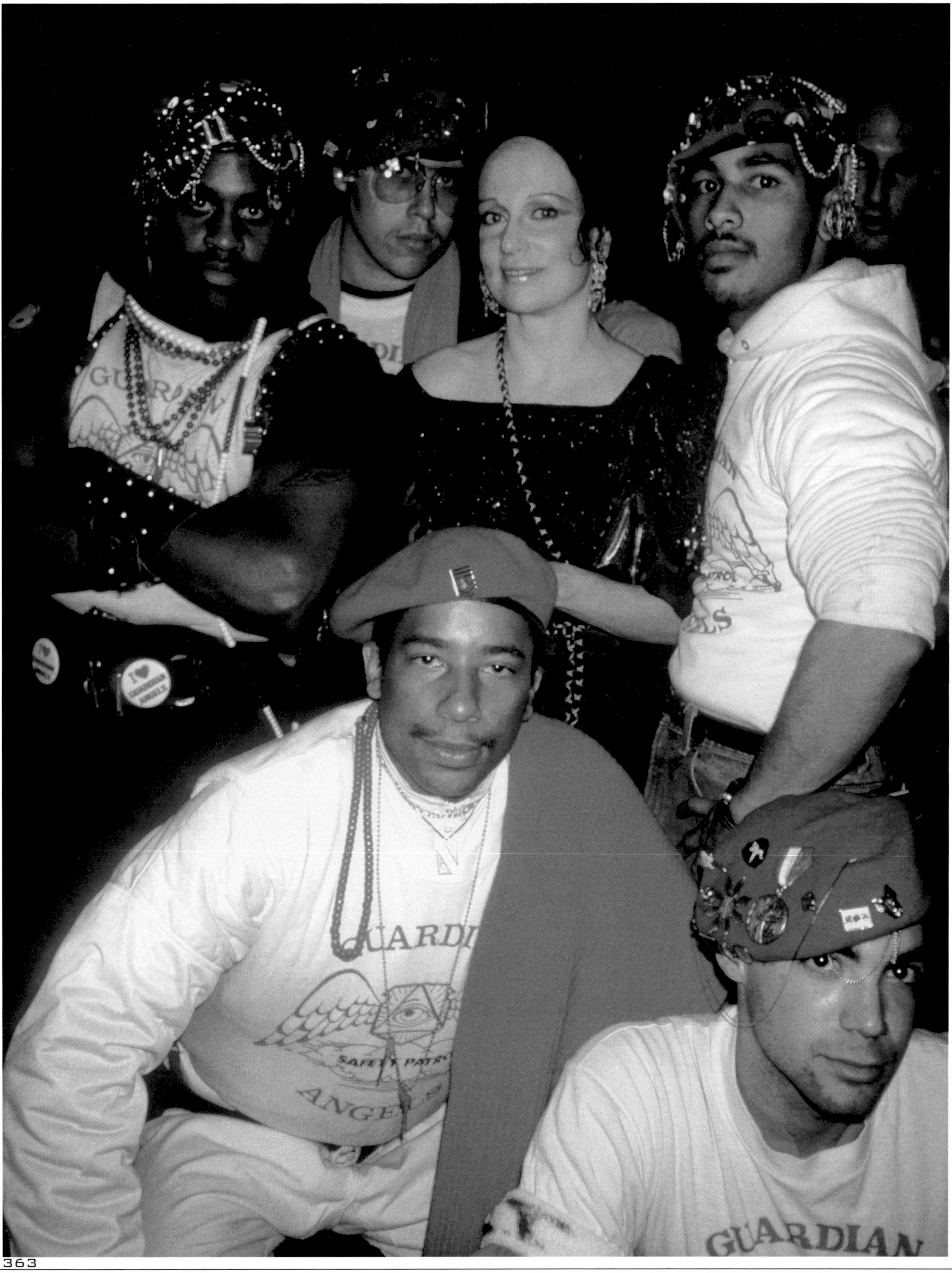
GUARDIAN
SAFETY PATROL
ANGELS
GUARDIAN

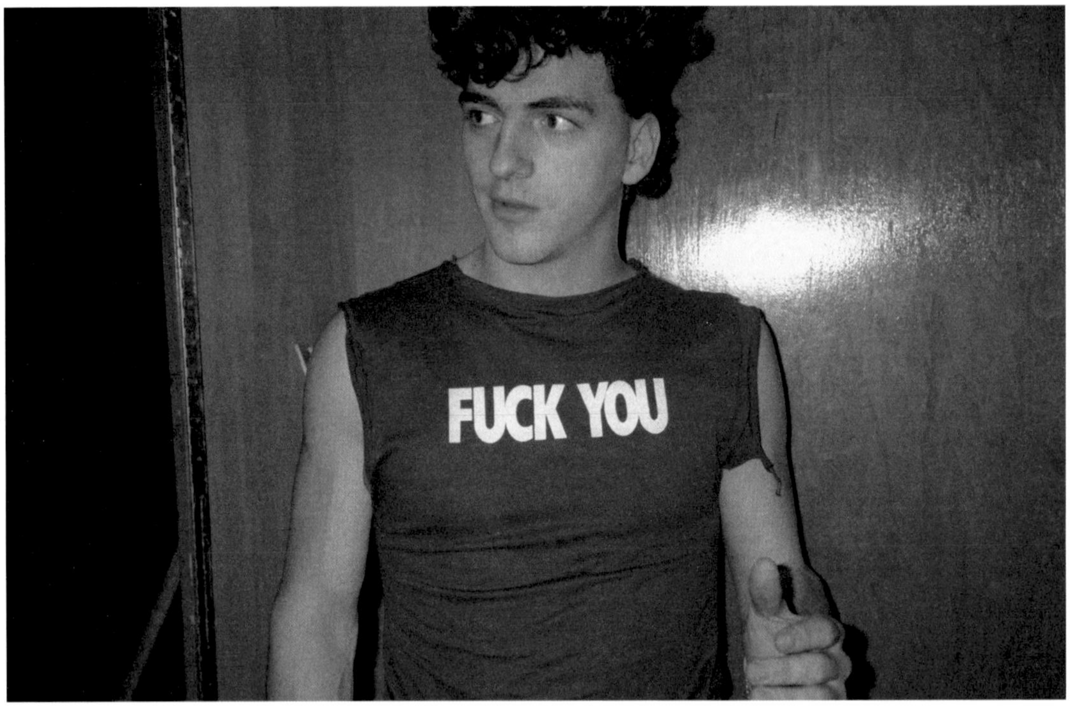

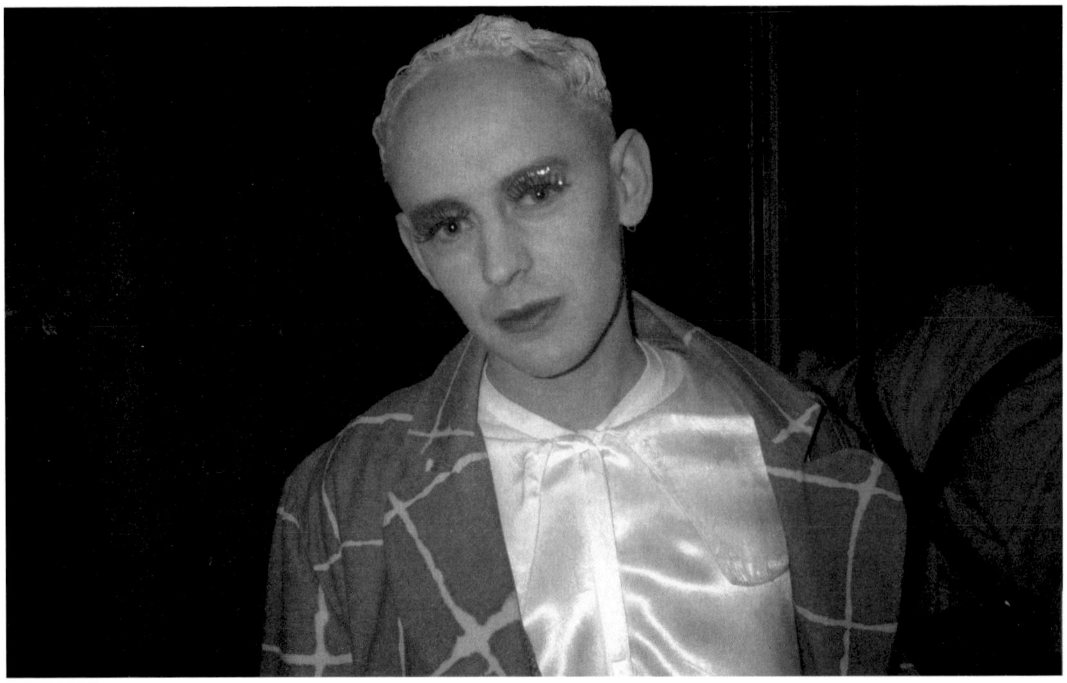

Top: Handsome lad at the Mondo New York party at the World.
April 21, 1988
Bottom: Kenny Kenny at the World.
April 21, 1988

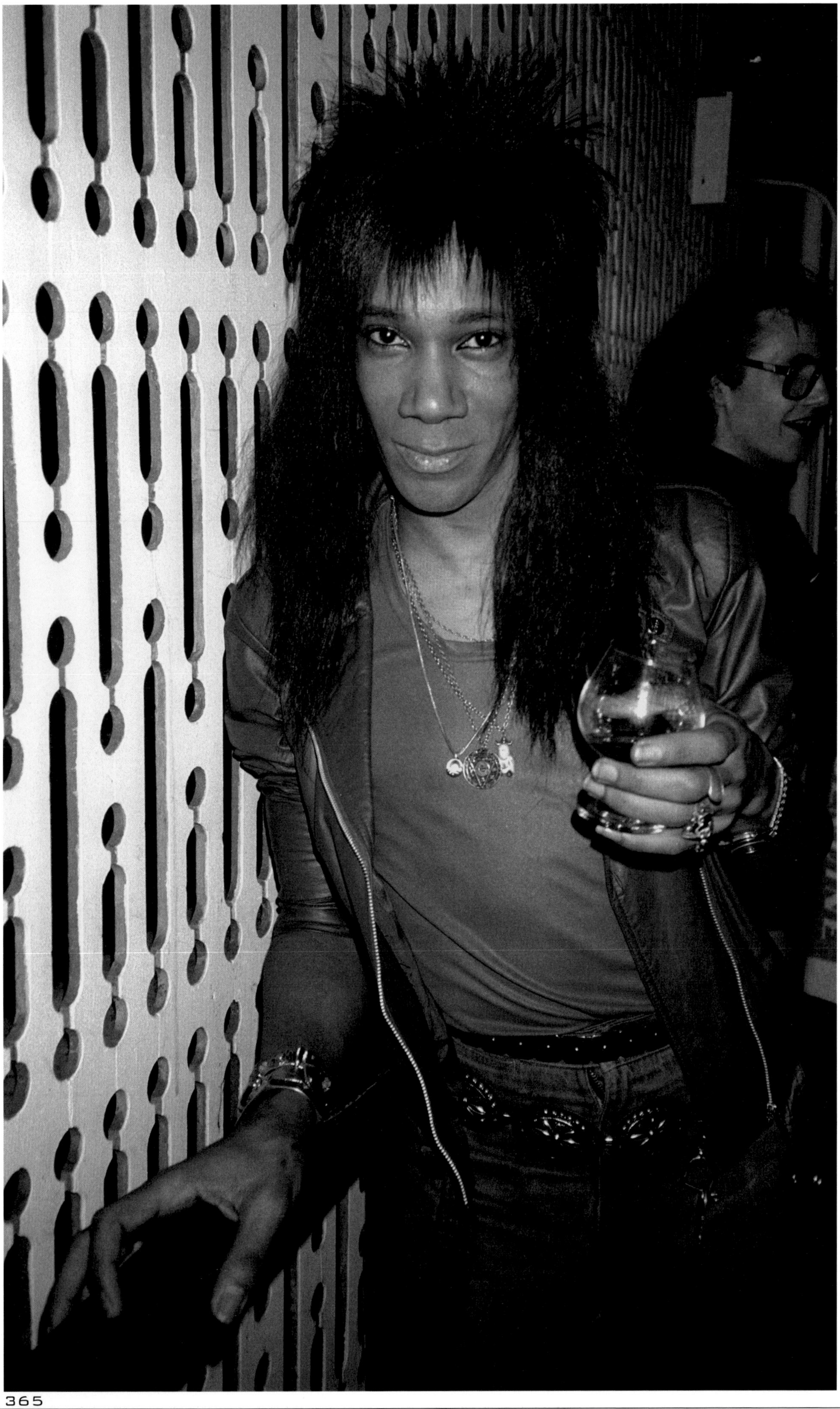

Neon Leon at Perri
Lister's birthday party
at Limelight.
Tuesday, April 7, 1987

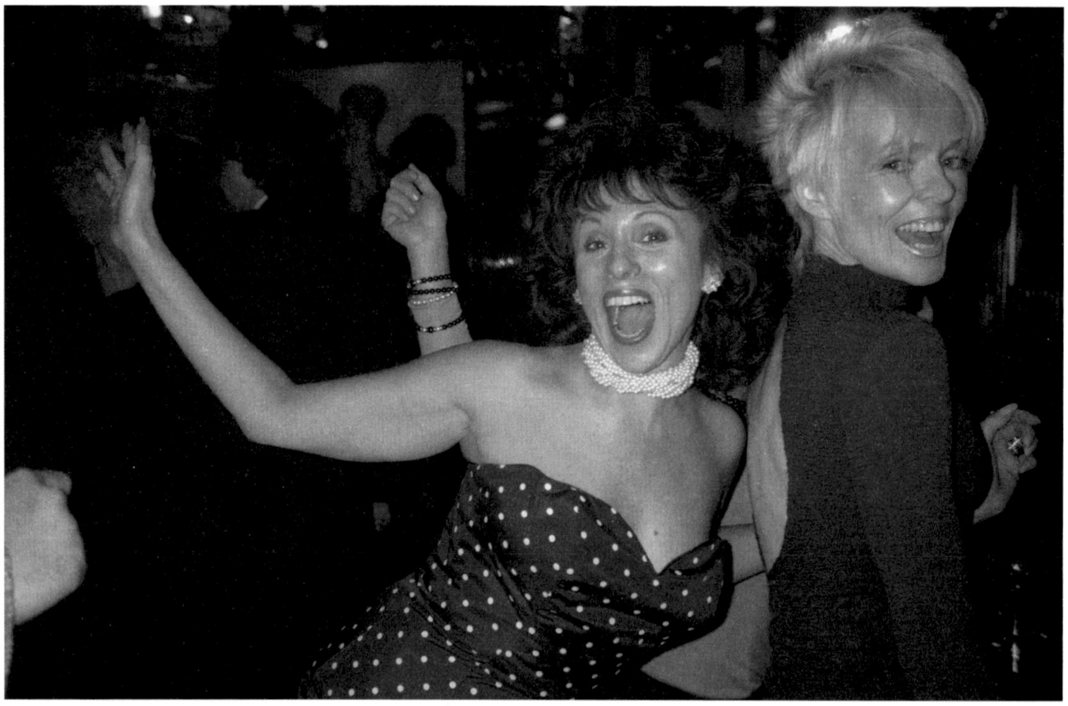

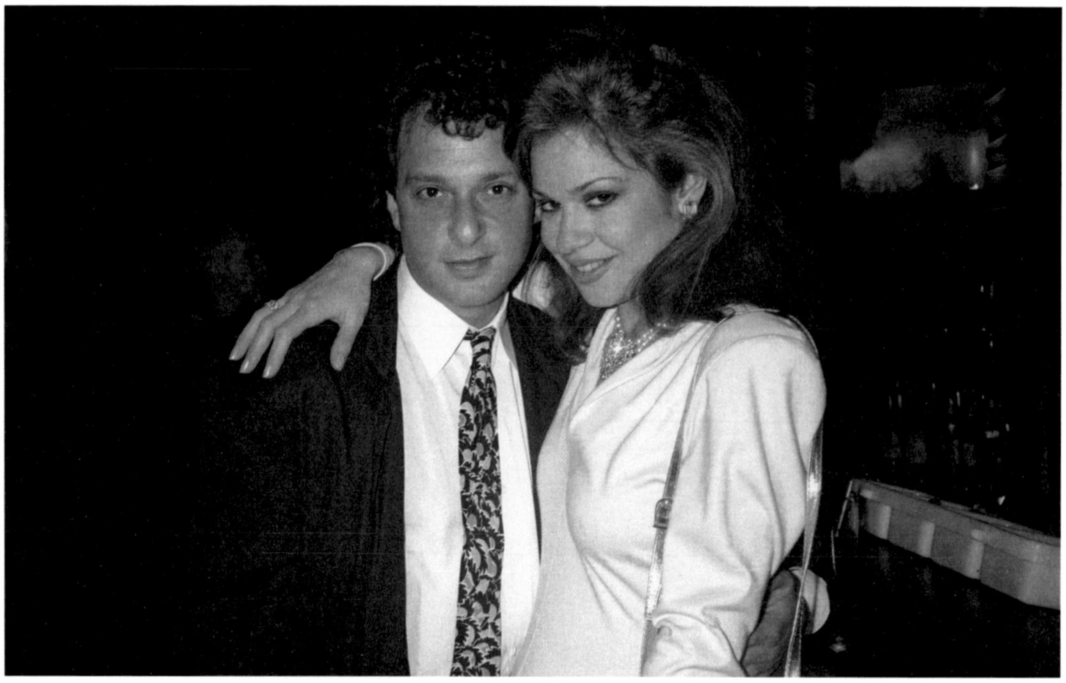

Top: Nikki Haskell and Joey Heatherton
at Paul Jabara's party for "Hair" at Regine's.
May 26, 1988
Bottom: Paul Jabara and Jane Fredericks
at the party for Paul Jabara at Studio 54.
February 6, 1986

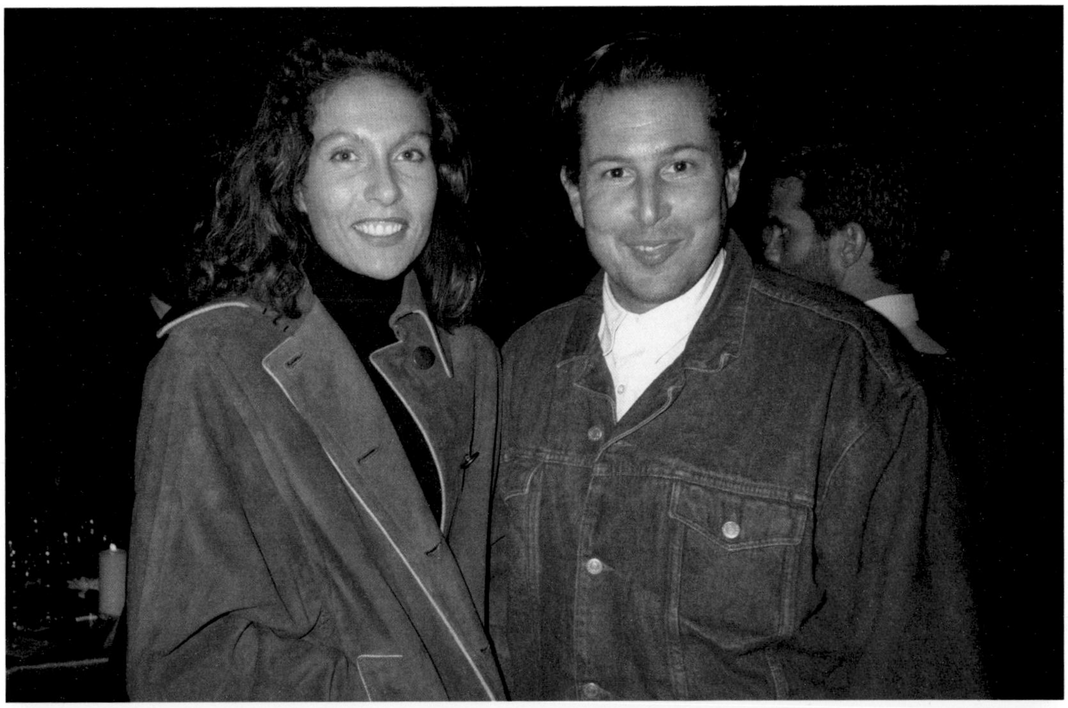

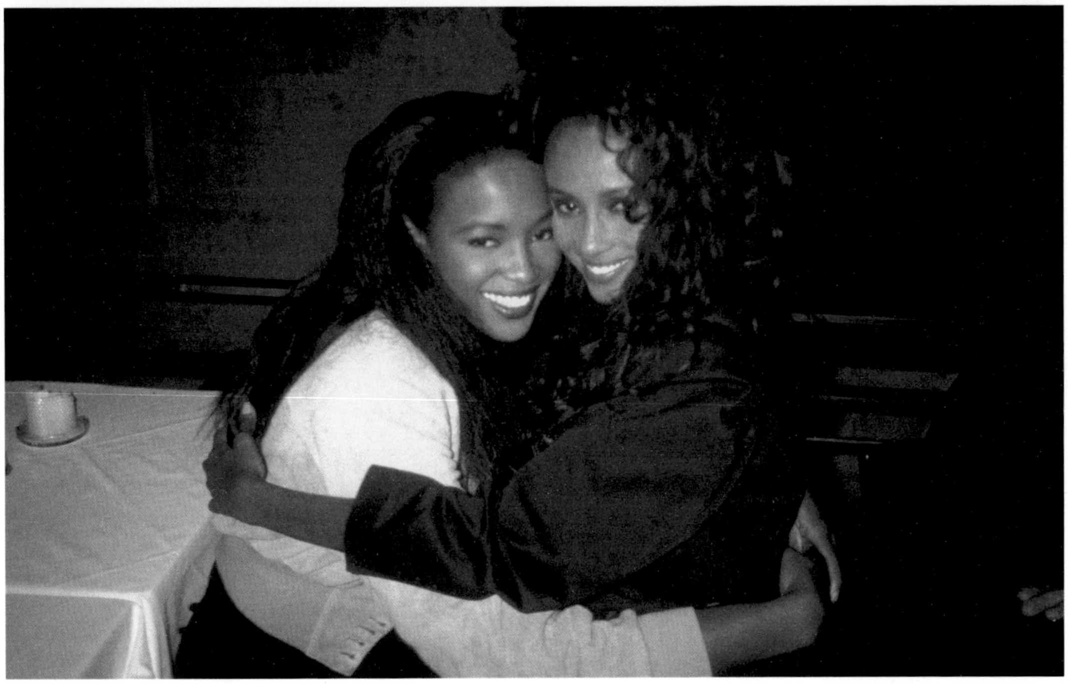

"I FONDLY REMEMBER THE 80S AS THE DECADE FOR BIG HAIR AND BIGGER SHOULDER PADS...FROM SUPERMODELS TO THE MASTERS OF THE UNIVERSE...FROM FAST CARS OR LIMOS TO FASTER GIRLS...FROM HIGH POWERED SOCIETY (LADIES AND GENTS) MARCHING TO THEIR OWN BEAT ON MARCHING POWDER. THE DECADE WHICH IS NOW KNOWN AS THE 80S SEEMS LIKE A CENTURY AGO...OH, YEAH...IT WAS LAST CENTURY! SO80S!!!! WHO COULD CAPTURE IT BUT ONLY THAT LOVABLE FLY ON THE WALL...PATRICK MCMULLAN!!!"
LOVE, IMAN

TOP: JAQUELINE AND JULIAN SCHNABEL
AT THE OPENING NIGHT GALA AT THE BROOKLYN ACADEMY OF MUSIC.
OCTOBER 14,1987
BOTTOM: NAOMI CAMPBELL AND IMAN AT MK.
SEPTEMBER 1988

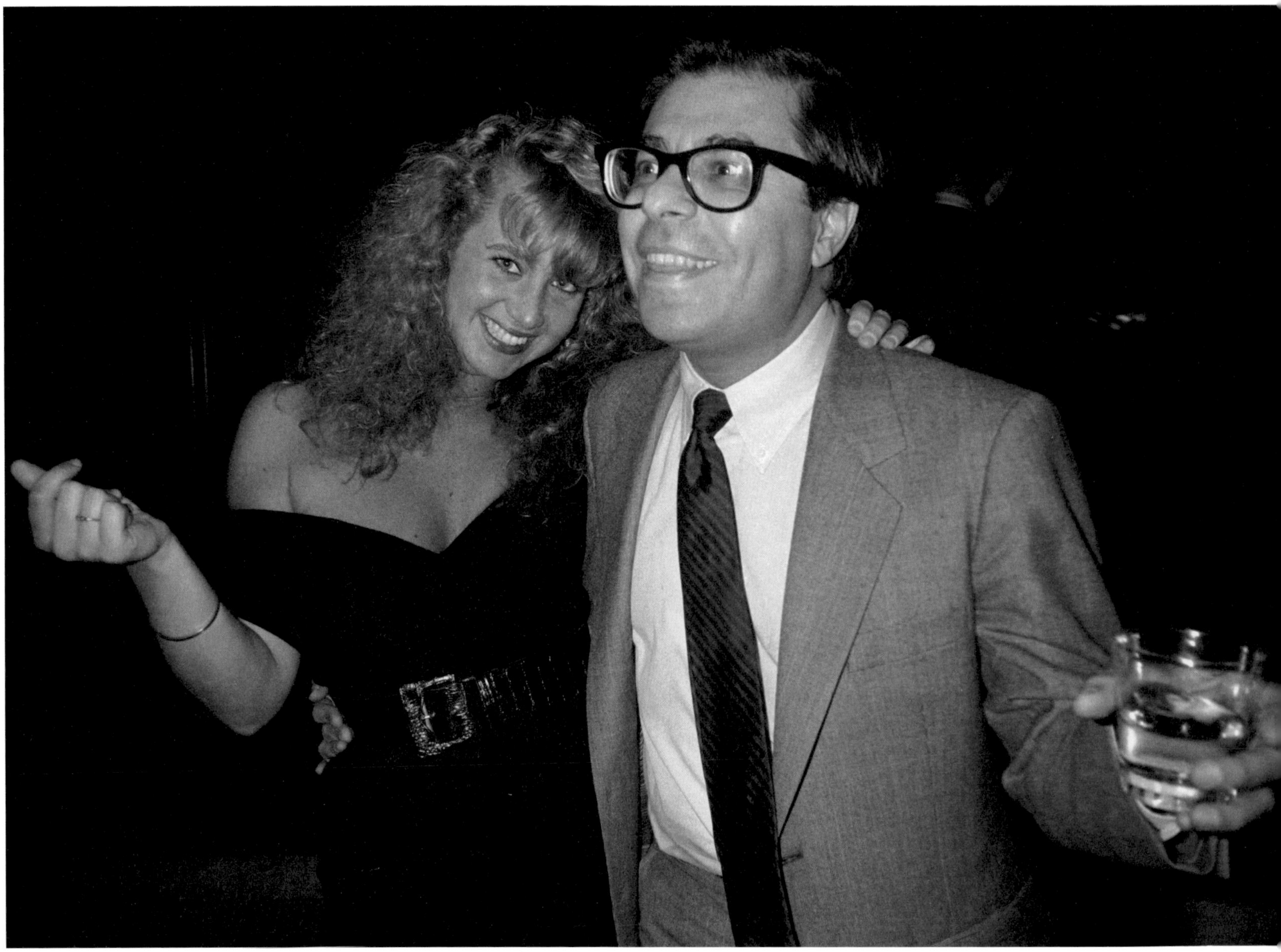

Angela Janklow Harrington and Bob Colacello
at her "Welcome Home" dinner at 40 Worth.
November 25, 1987

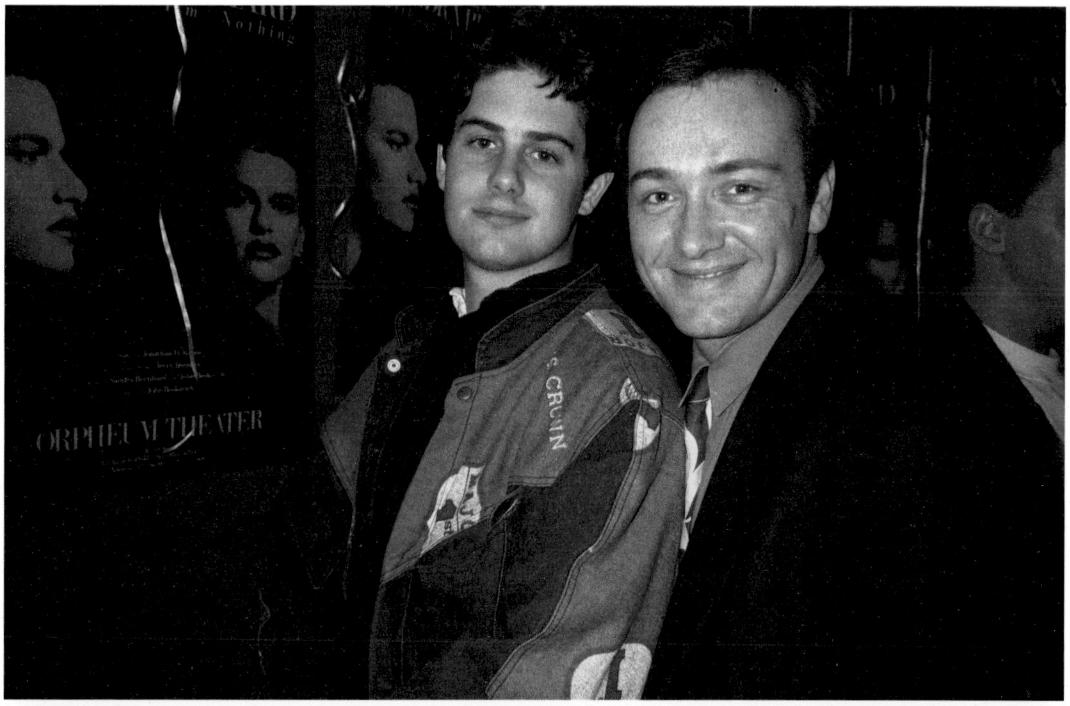

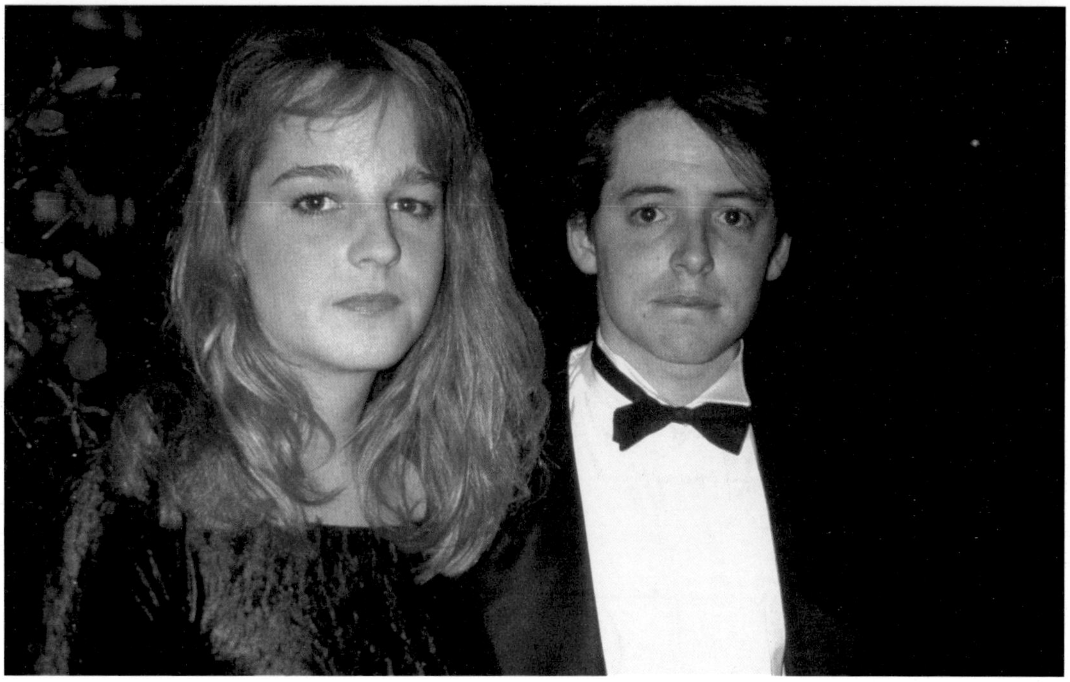

Top: Zach Galligan and Kevin Spacey
at 40 Worth for Sandra Bernhard.
March 31, 1988
Bottom: Helen Hunt and Matthew Broderick at The Metropolitan Opera.
December 1989

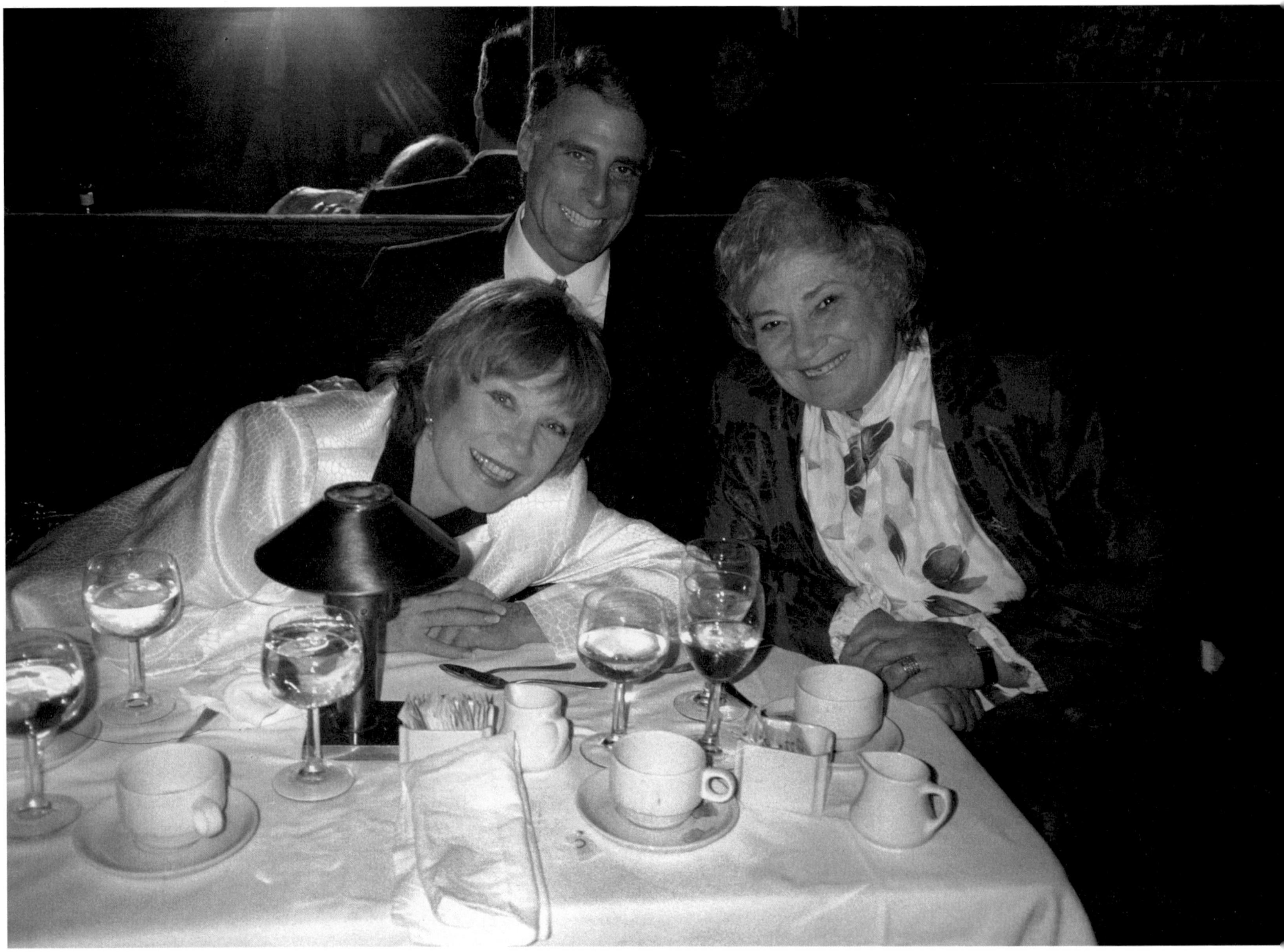

Shirley MacLaine, Andrew Stein, and Bella Abzug at Green Street Cafe.
May 21, 1987

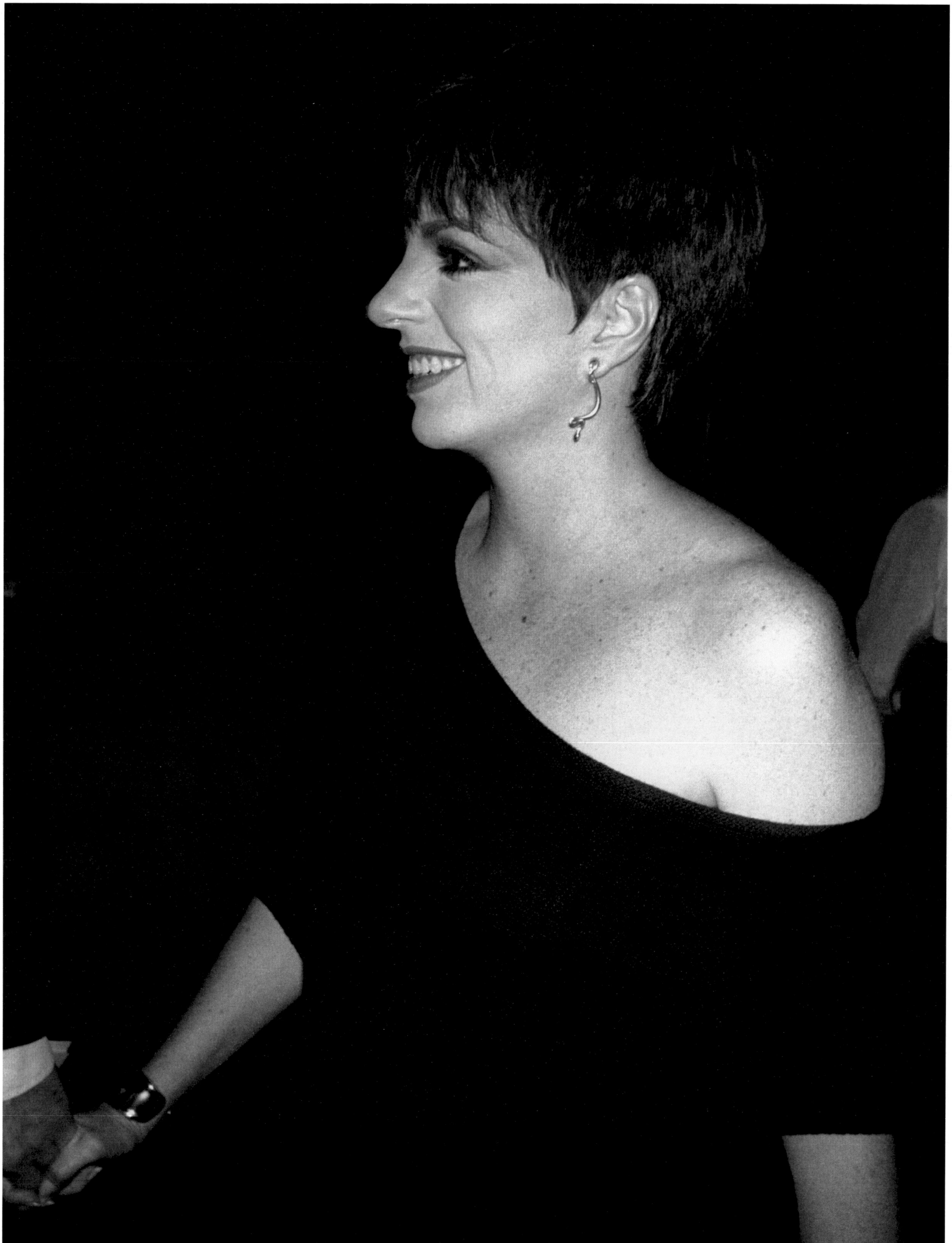

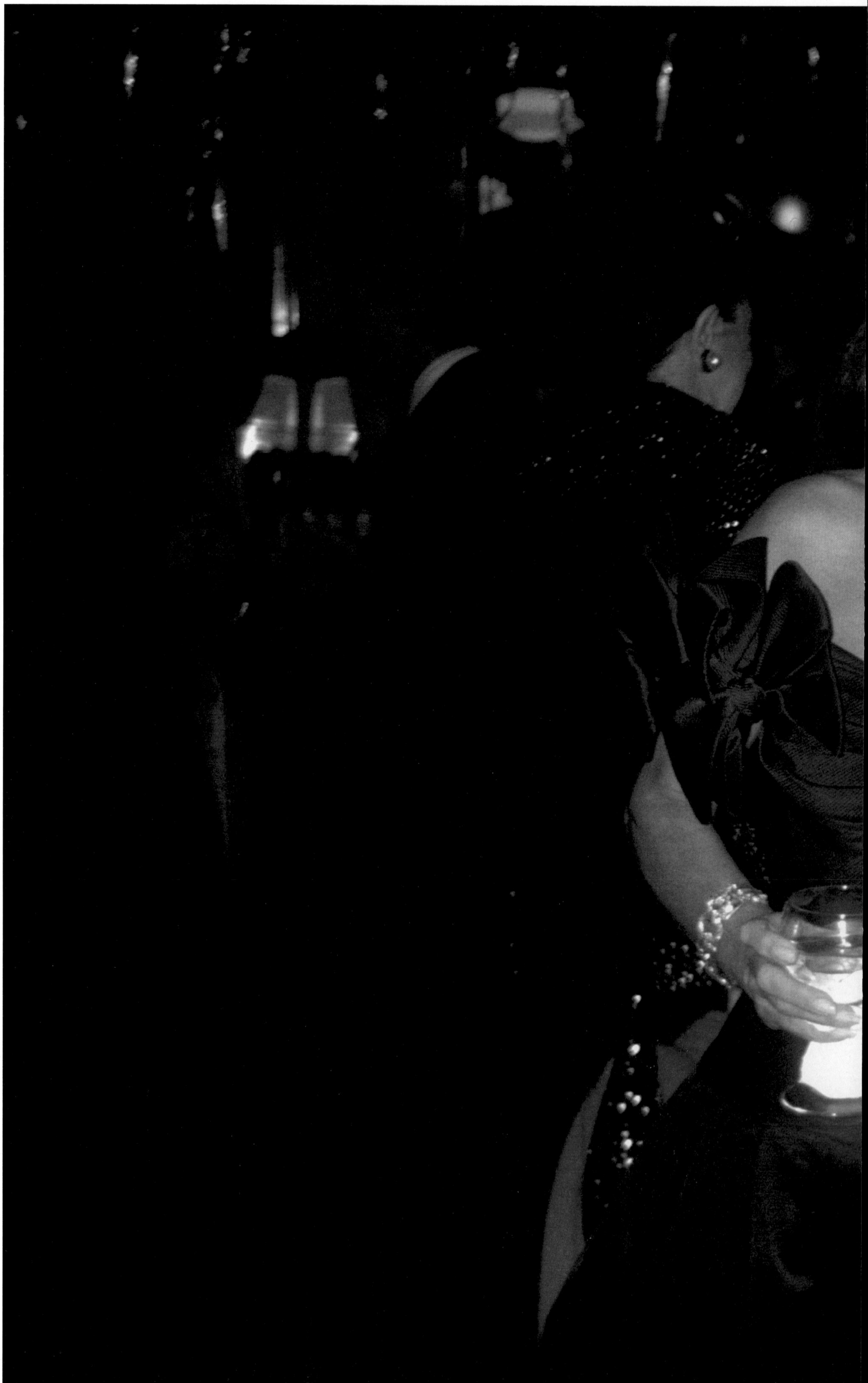

Joan Collins and Swifty Lazaar at Mortimer's. October 1989

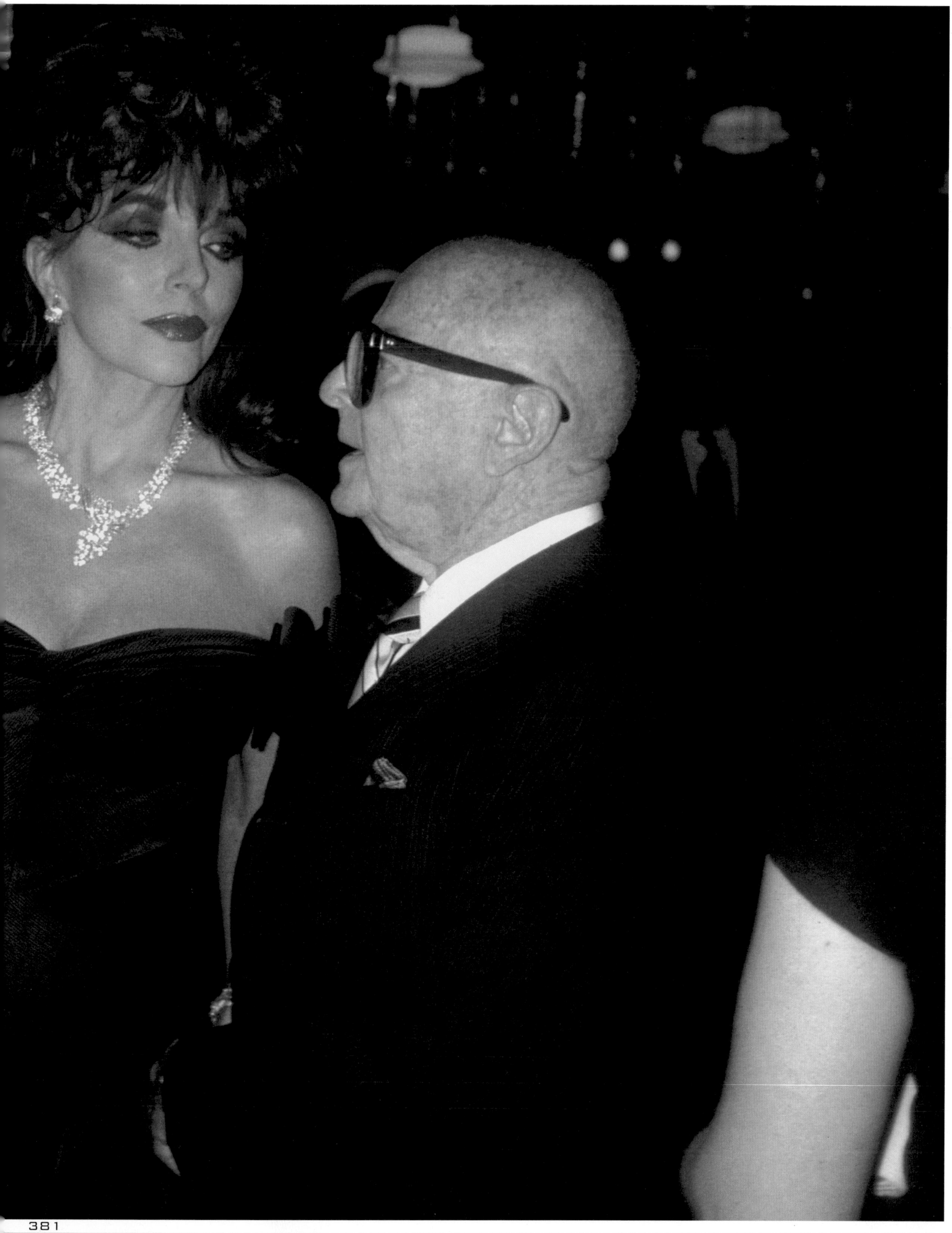

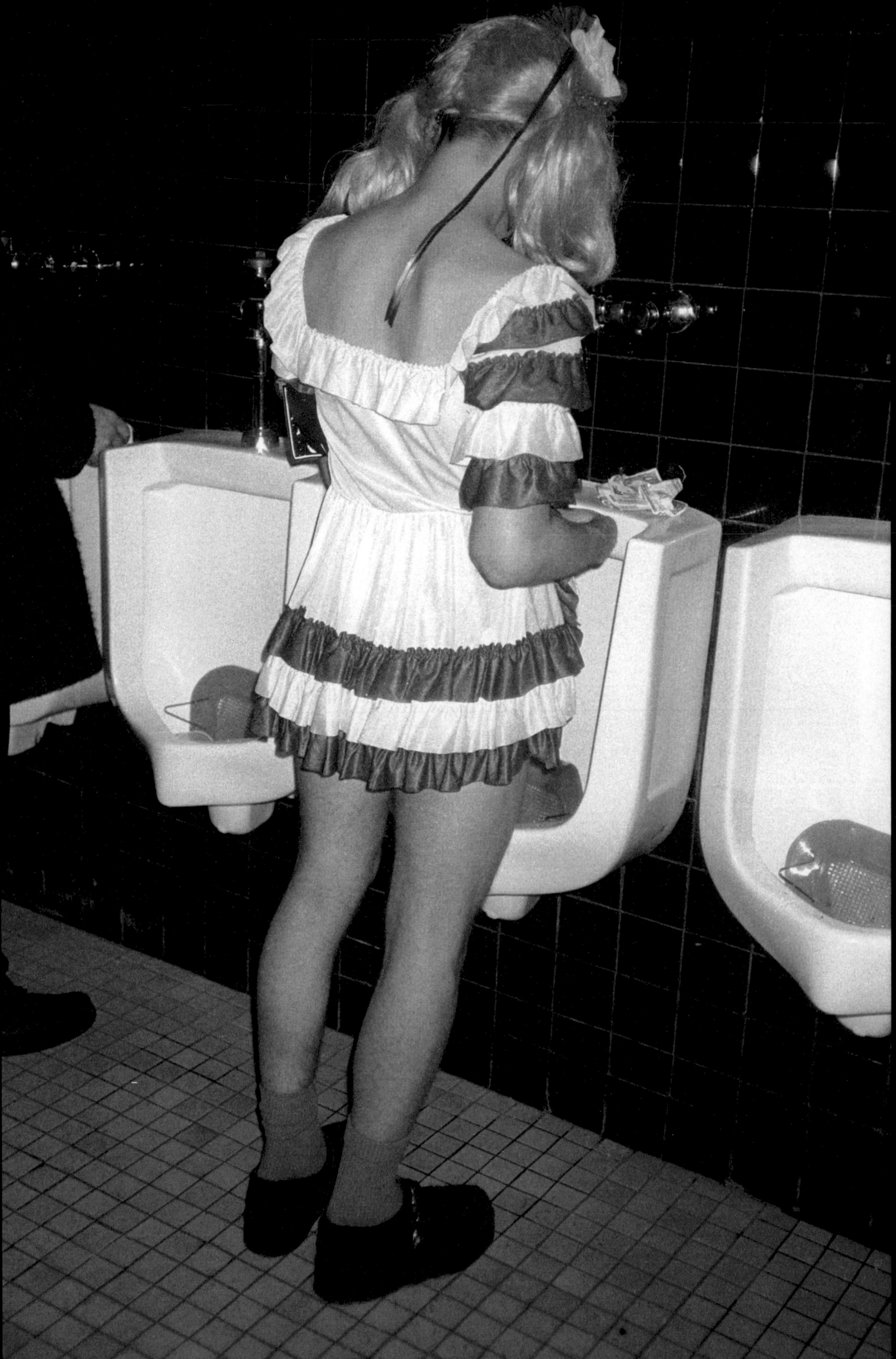

Michael Alig
in the bathroom
at Rudolf's birthday
party at the Tunnel.
February 27, 1988

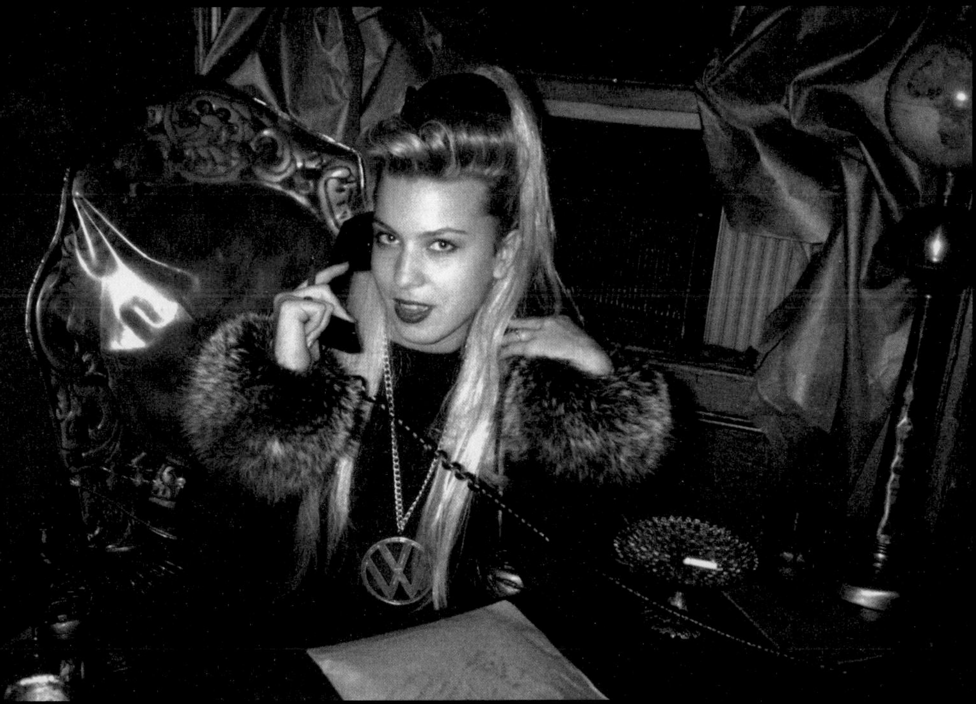

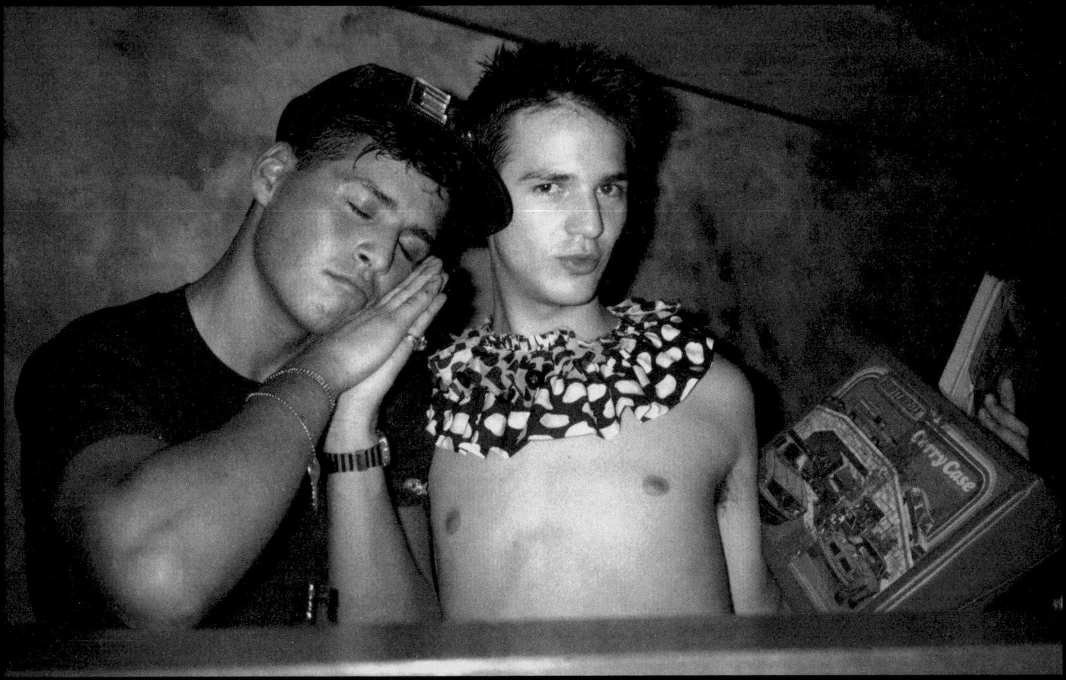

Top: Julie Jewels at the World.
Wednesday, July 27,1988
Bottom: Keoki and Michael Alig at the World.
Wednesday, August 27, 1988

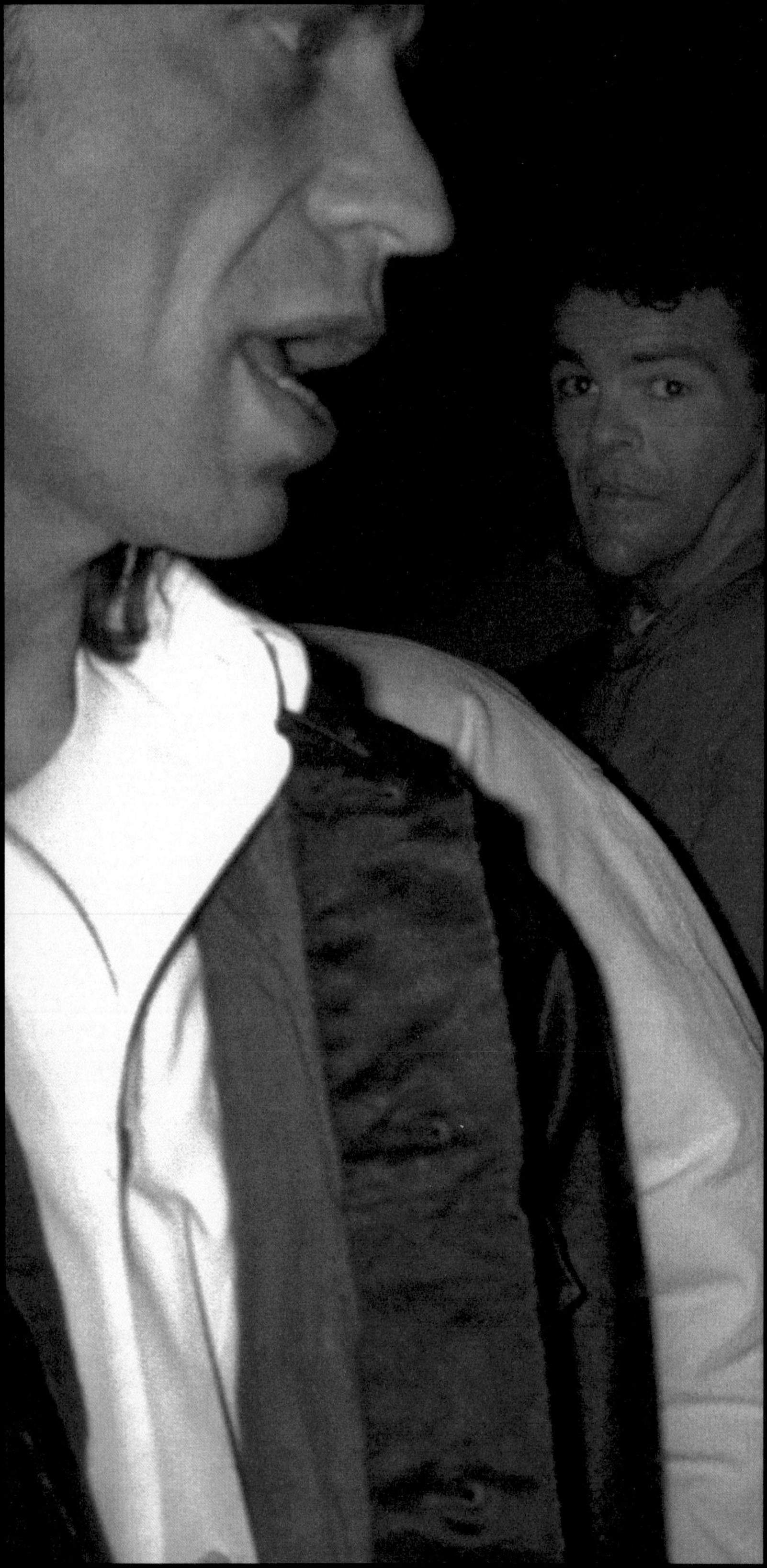

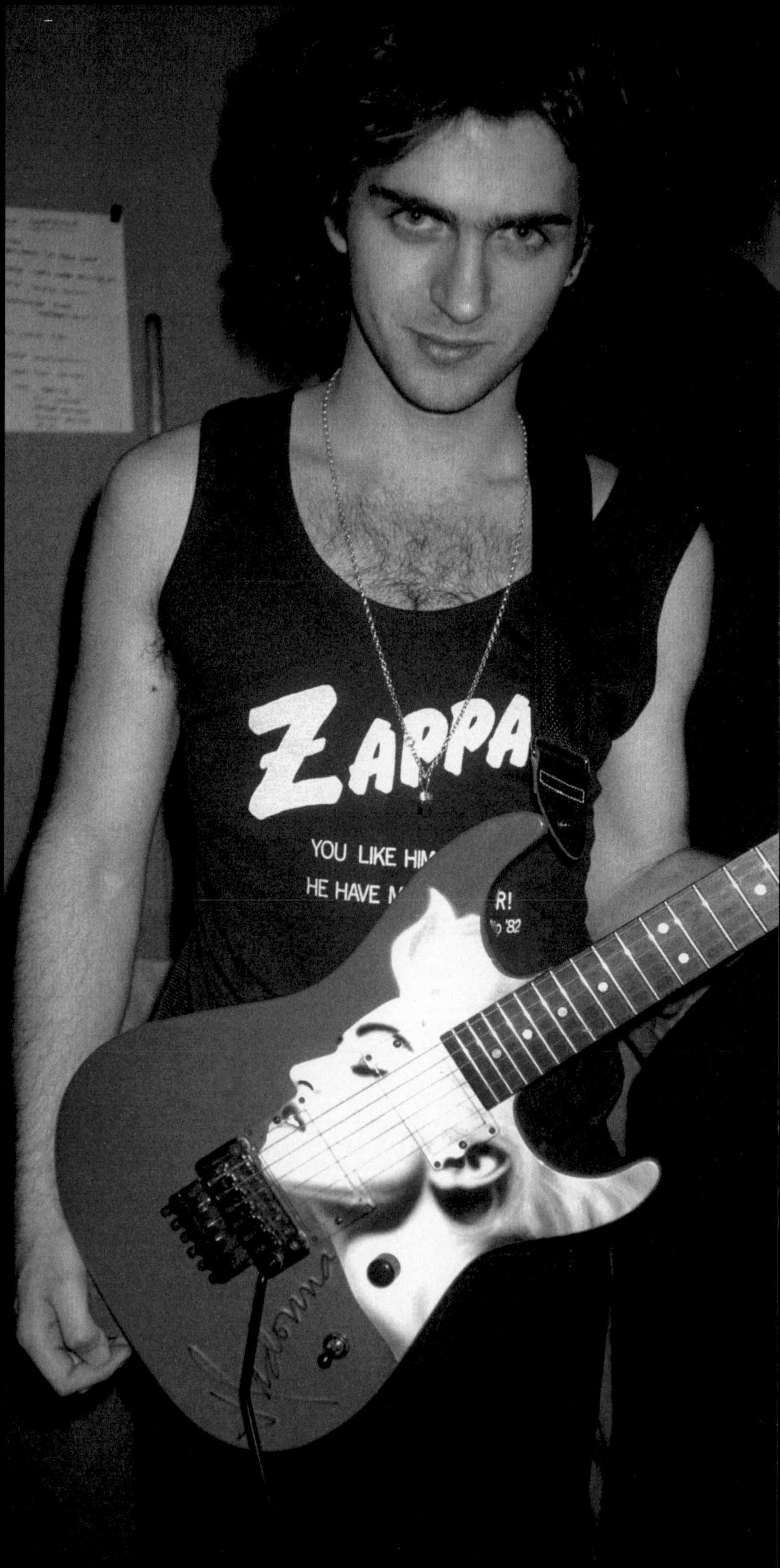

Top Left: Mick Jagger at the World.
April 21, 1988
Top Right: Dweezel Zappa with Madonna guitar
at the Grammy Awards pre-party at the Palladium.
March 1, 1988

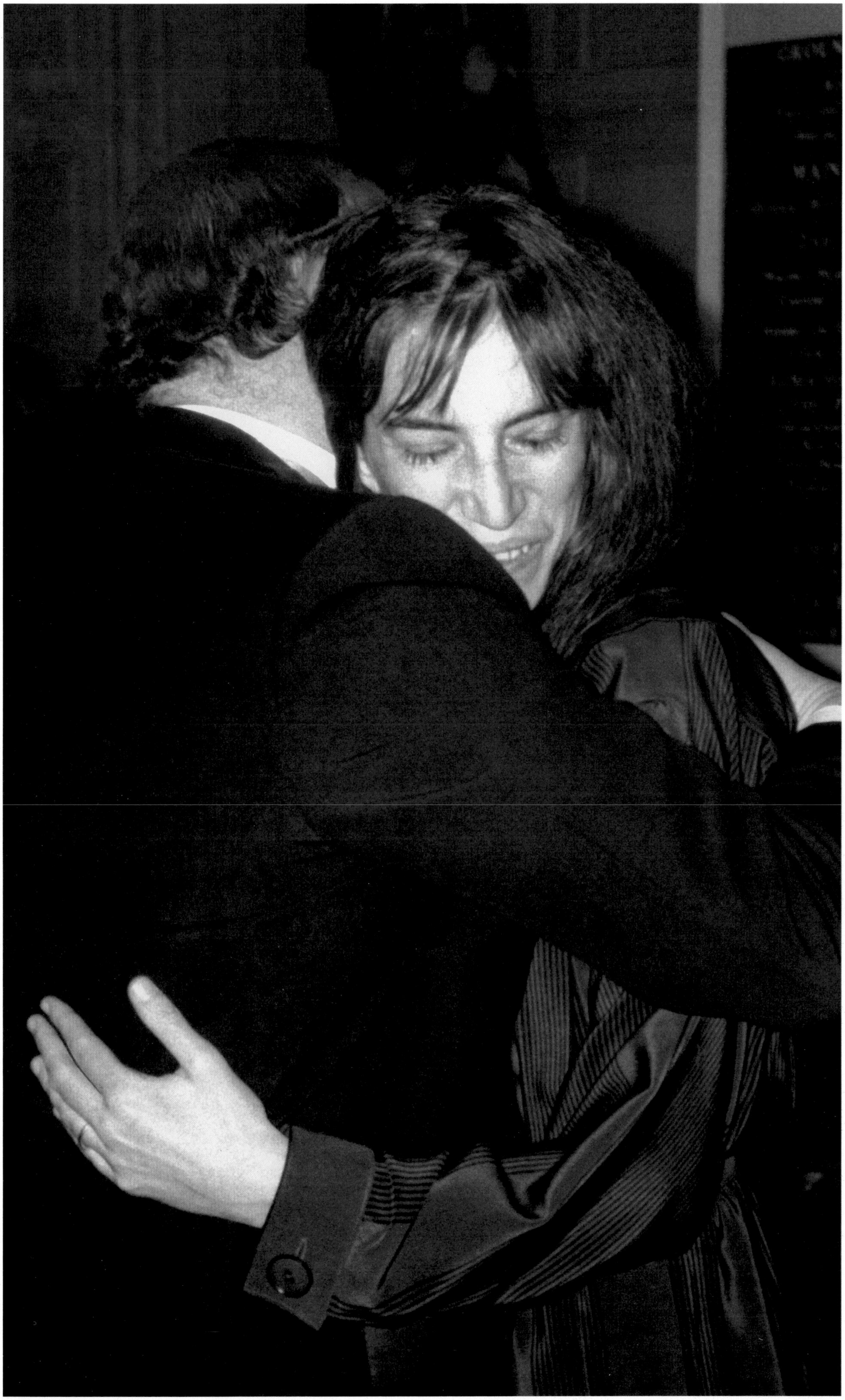

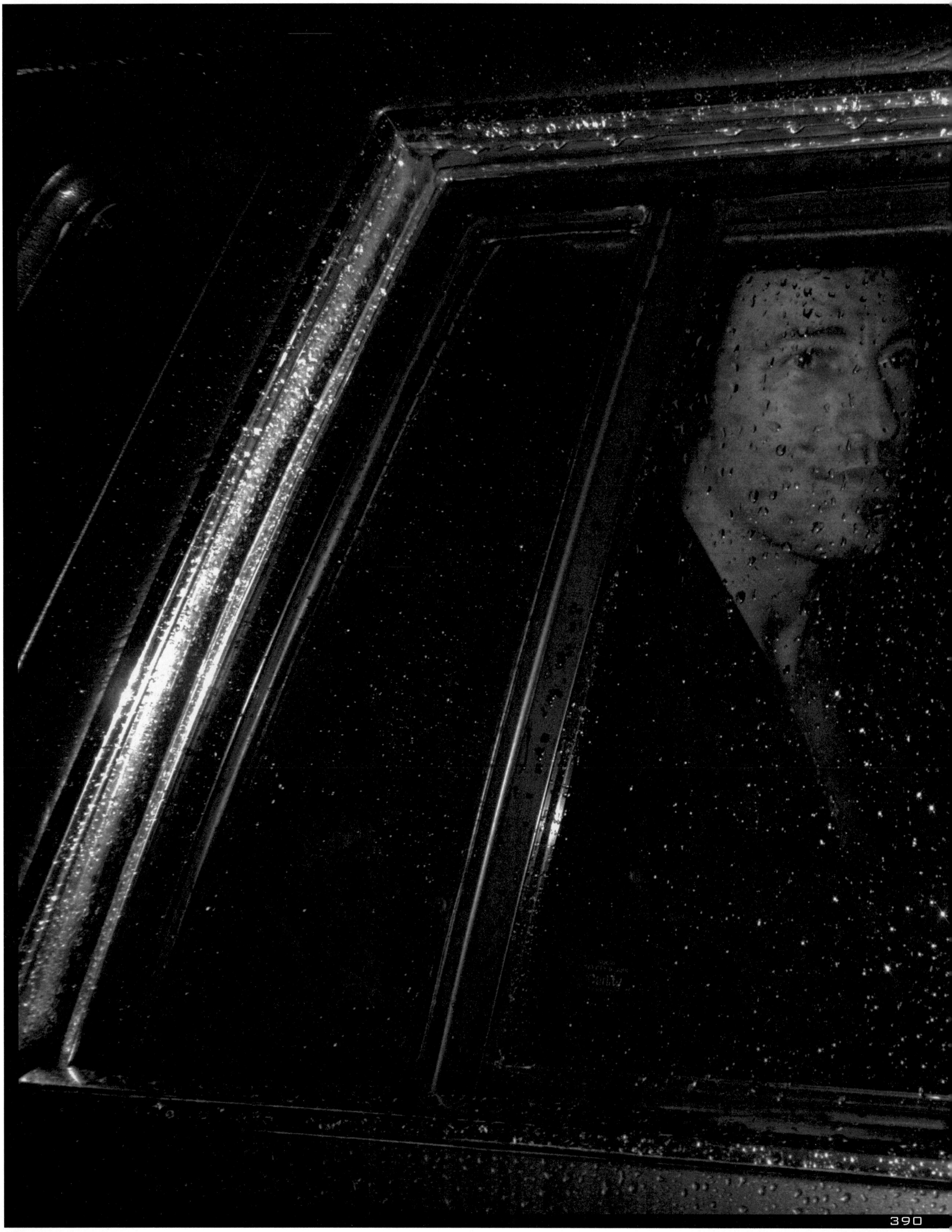

Bruce Springsteen
August 1988

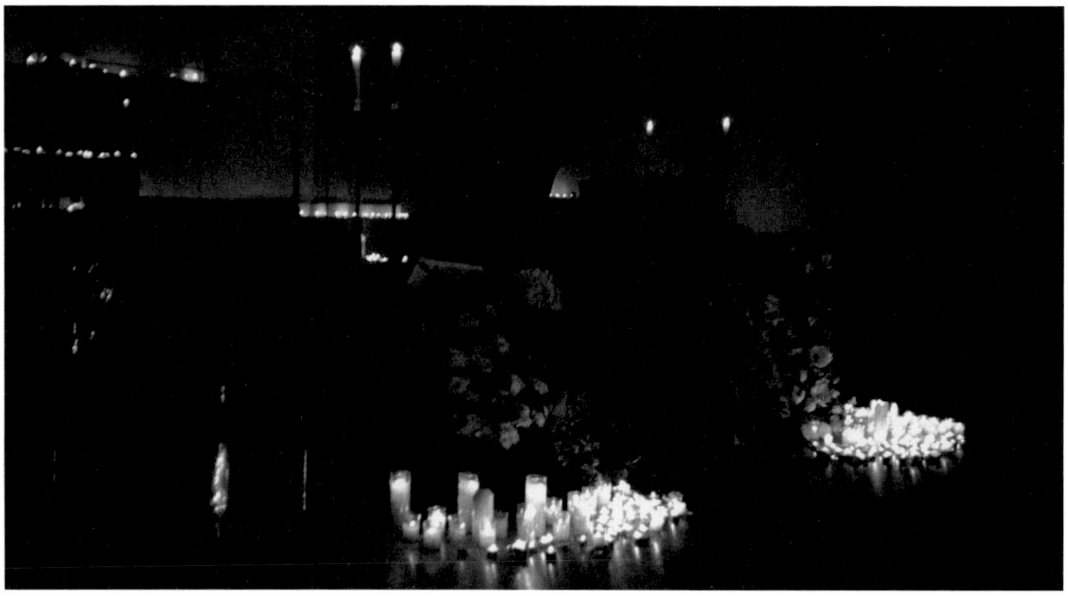

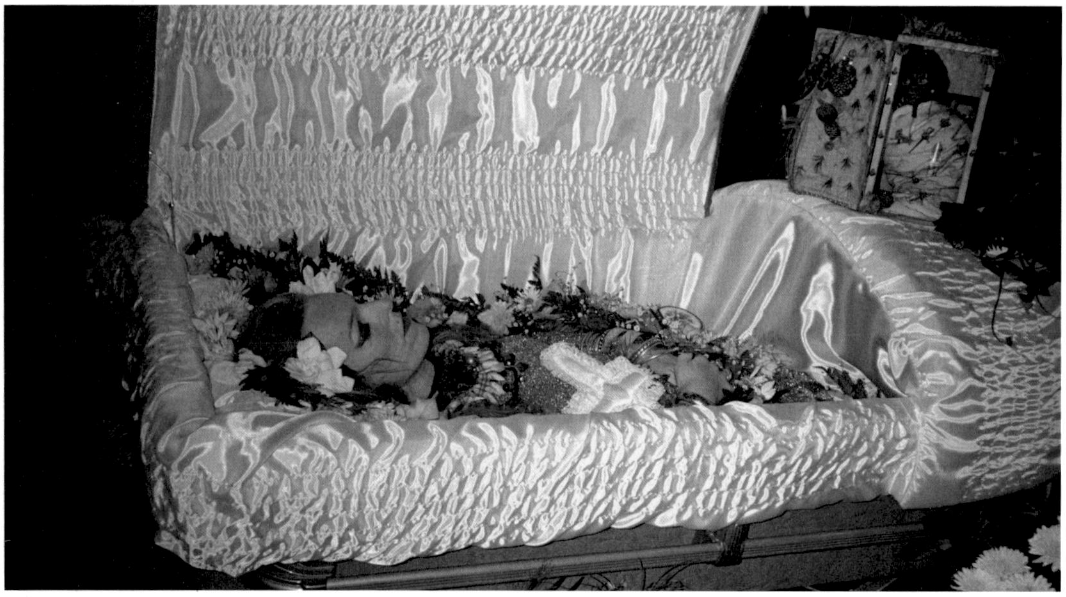

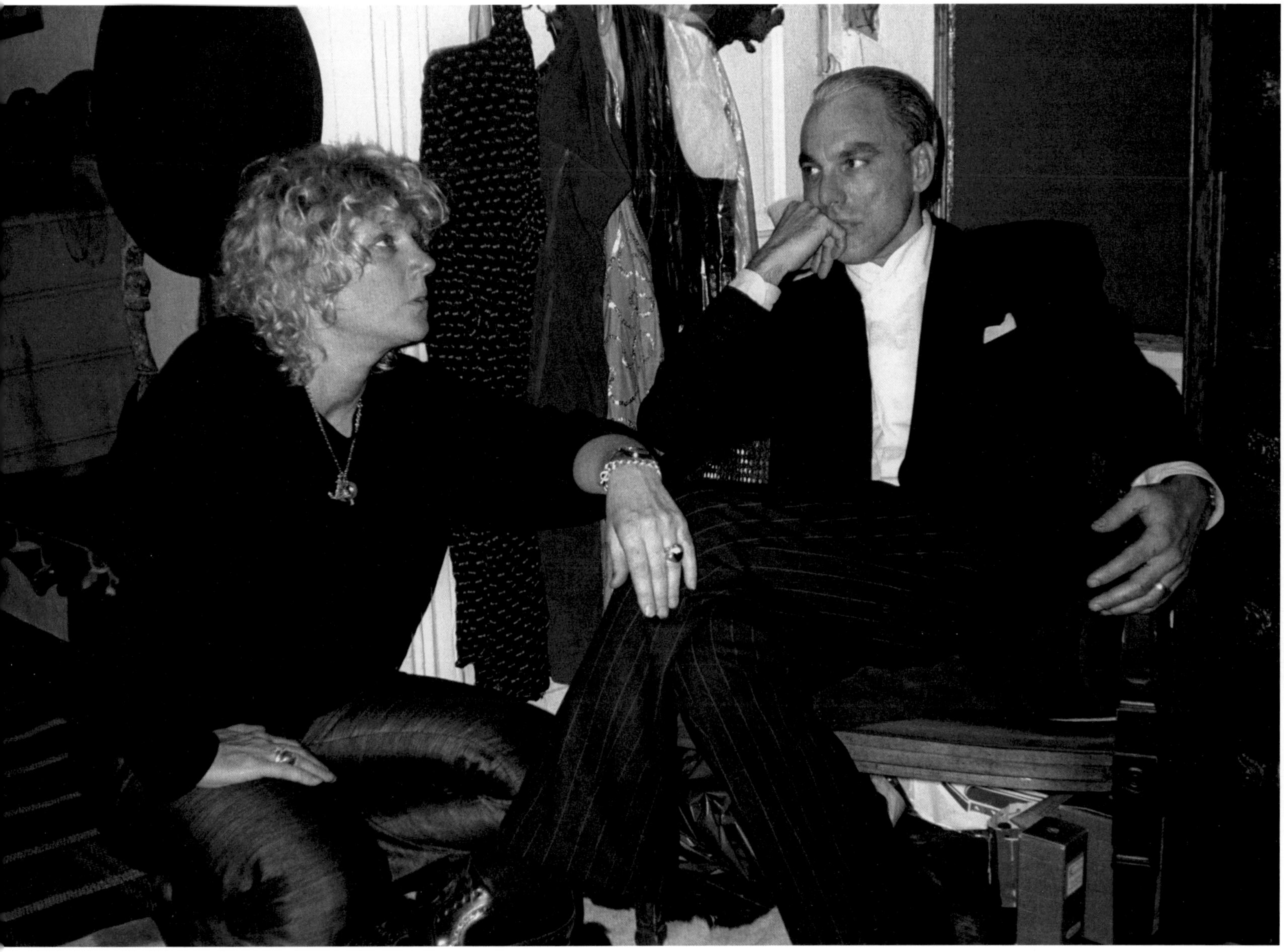

Top: Sharon Niesp and Richard Turley at Cookie's home.
Left: The funeral for Cookie Mueller at St. Marks Church.
Wednesday, November 15, 1989

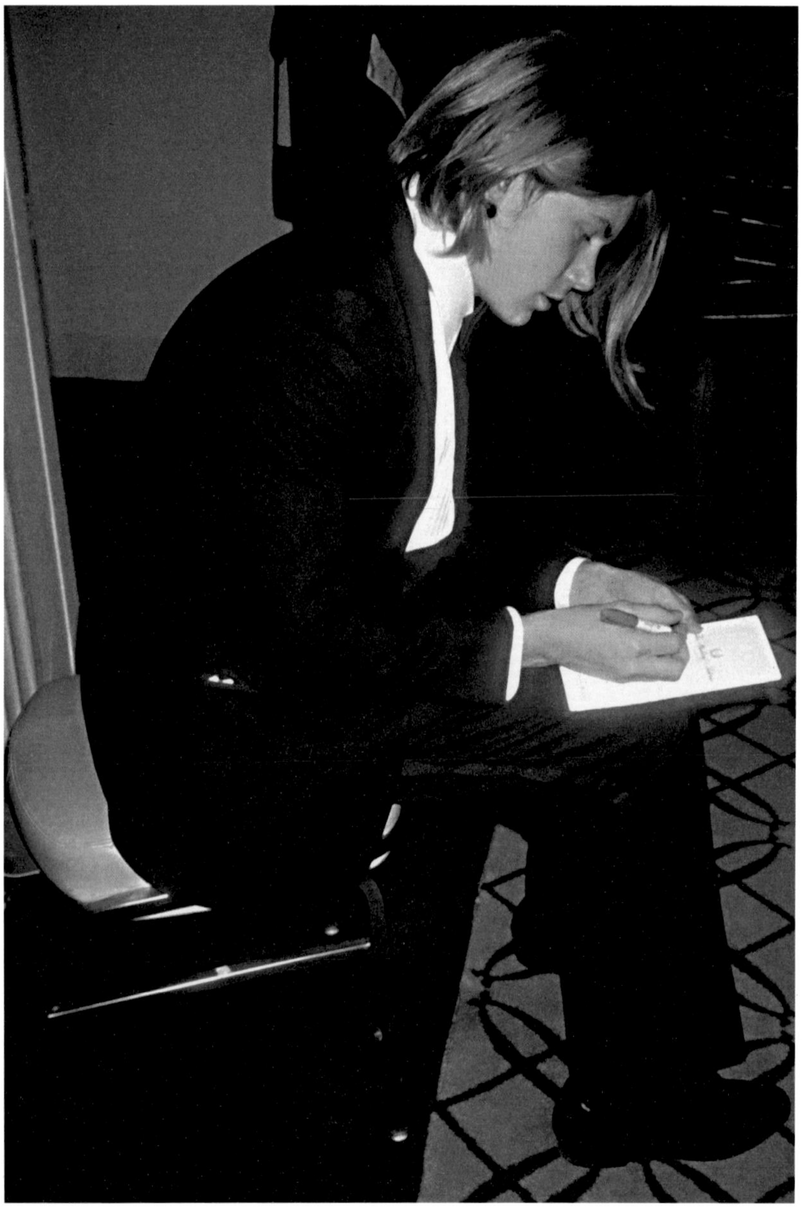

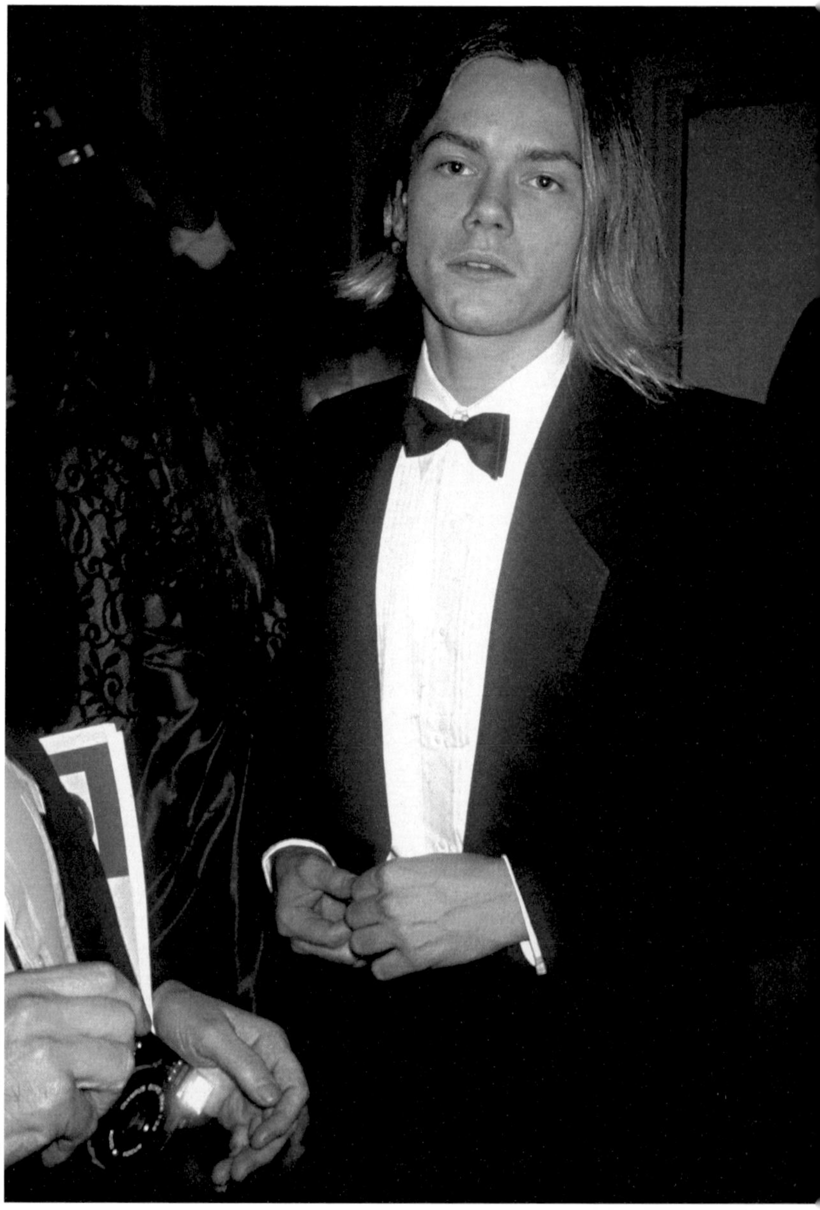

River Phoenix
at the American Museum of the Moving Image
salute to Sydney Poitier gala at the Waldorf Astoria.
March 1989

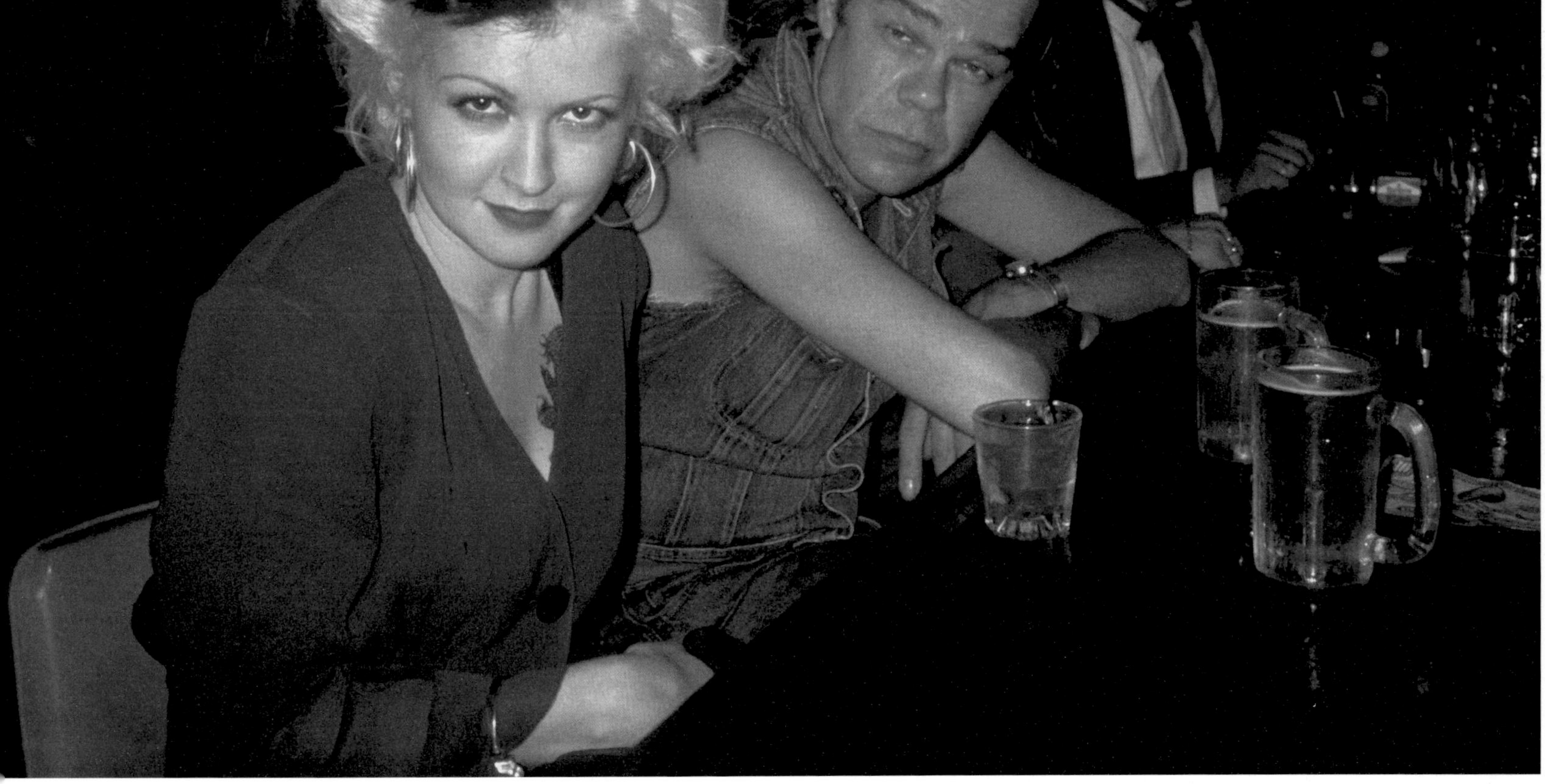

Cyndi Lauper and David Johansen
at a bar after the Z100 Party at the Palladium.
August 2, 1989

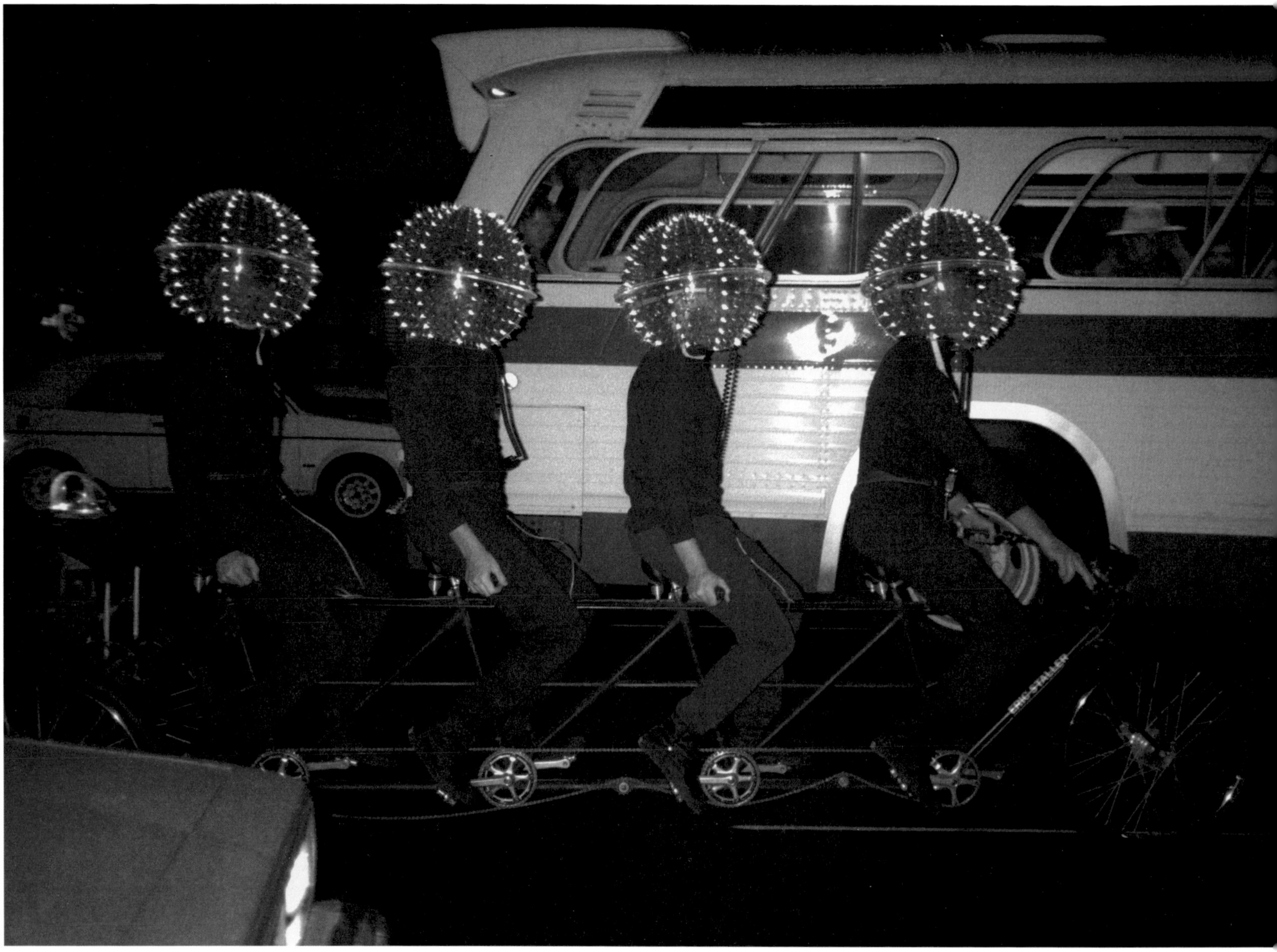

"Head Lights"
outside, after the Robert Mapplethorpe opening
at the Whitney Museum of American Art.
Wednesday, July 27, 1988

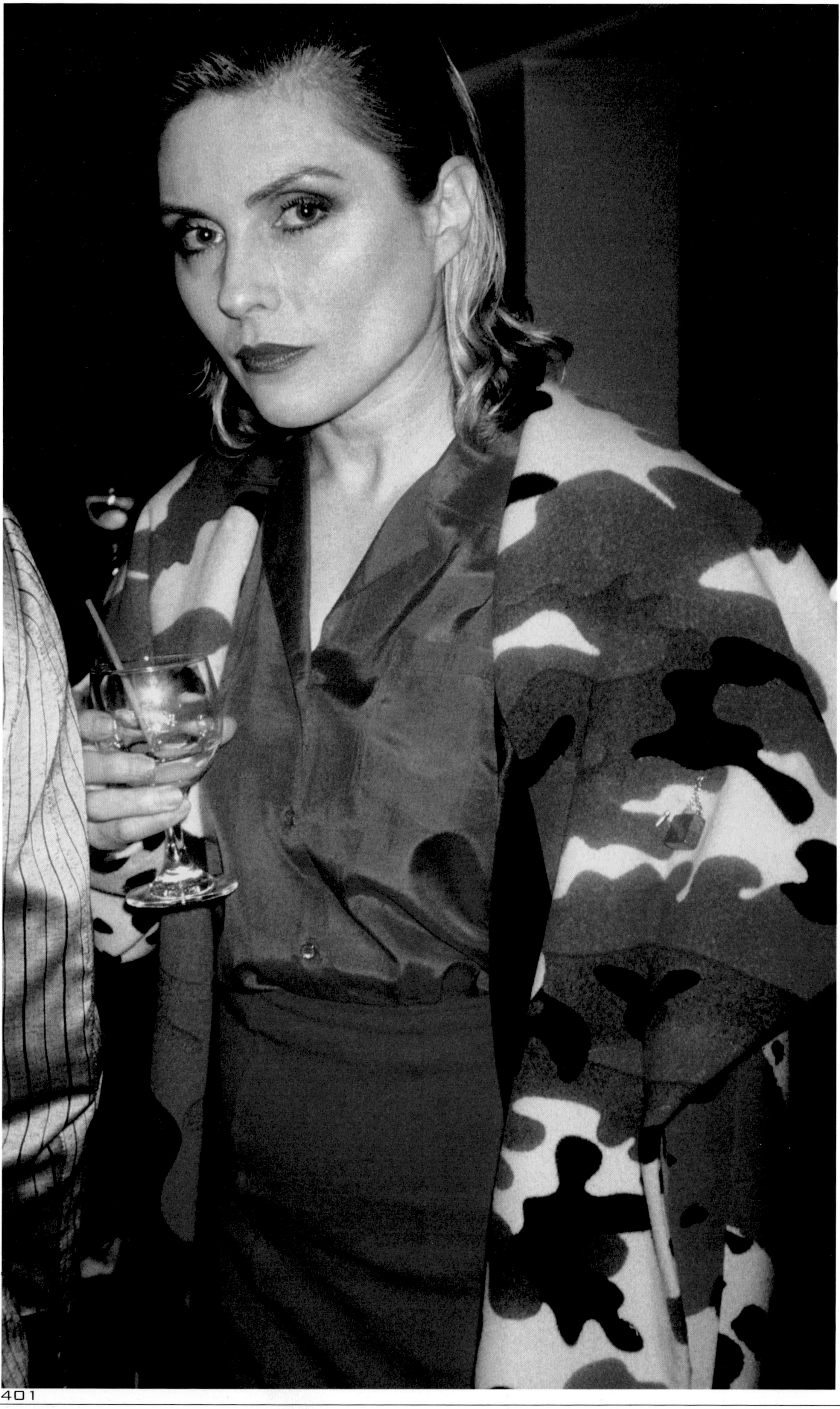

DEBBIE HARRY AT THE OPENING OF THE STEPHEN SPROUSE STORE.
1989

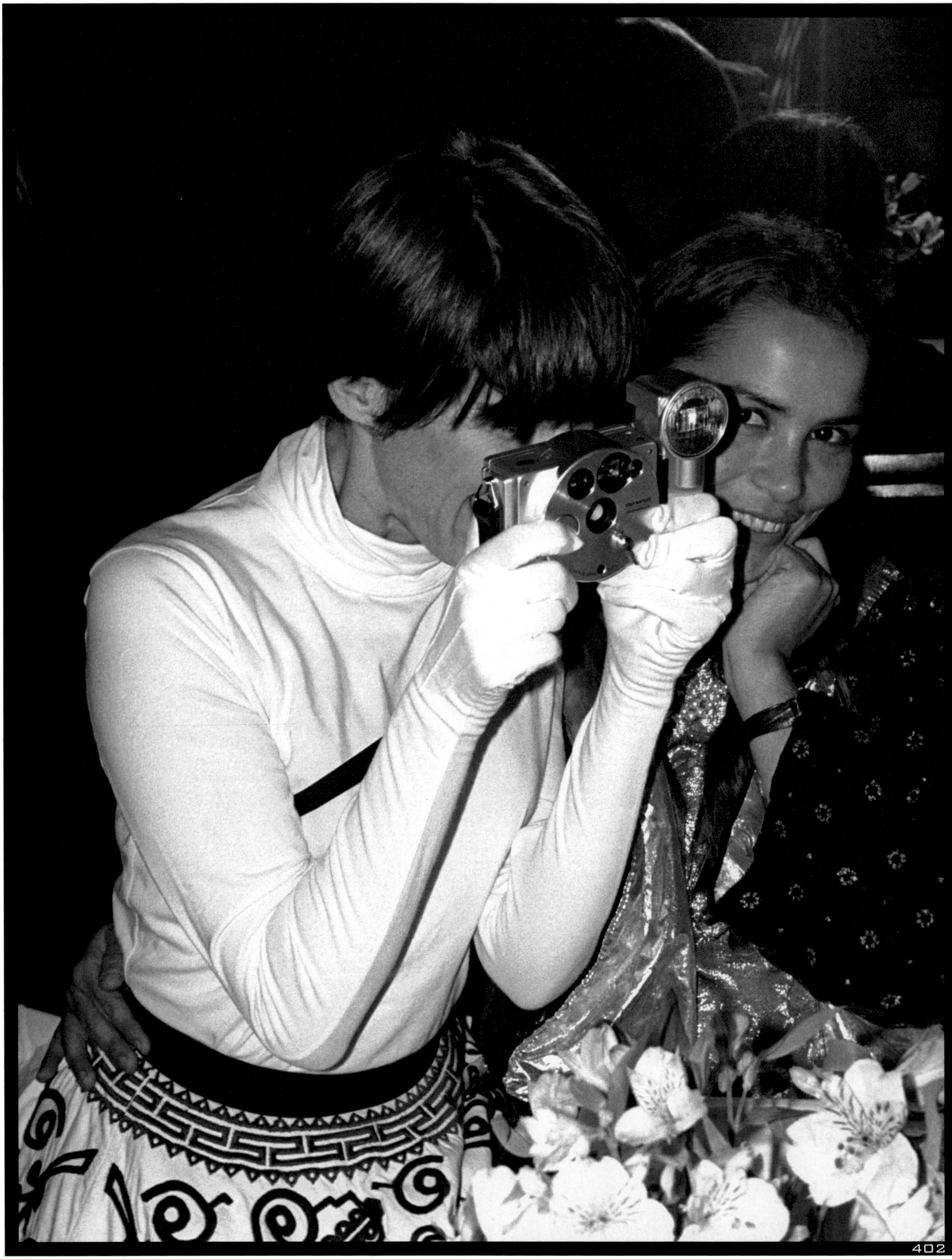

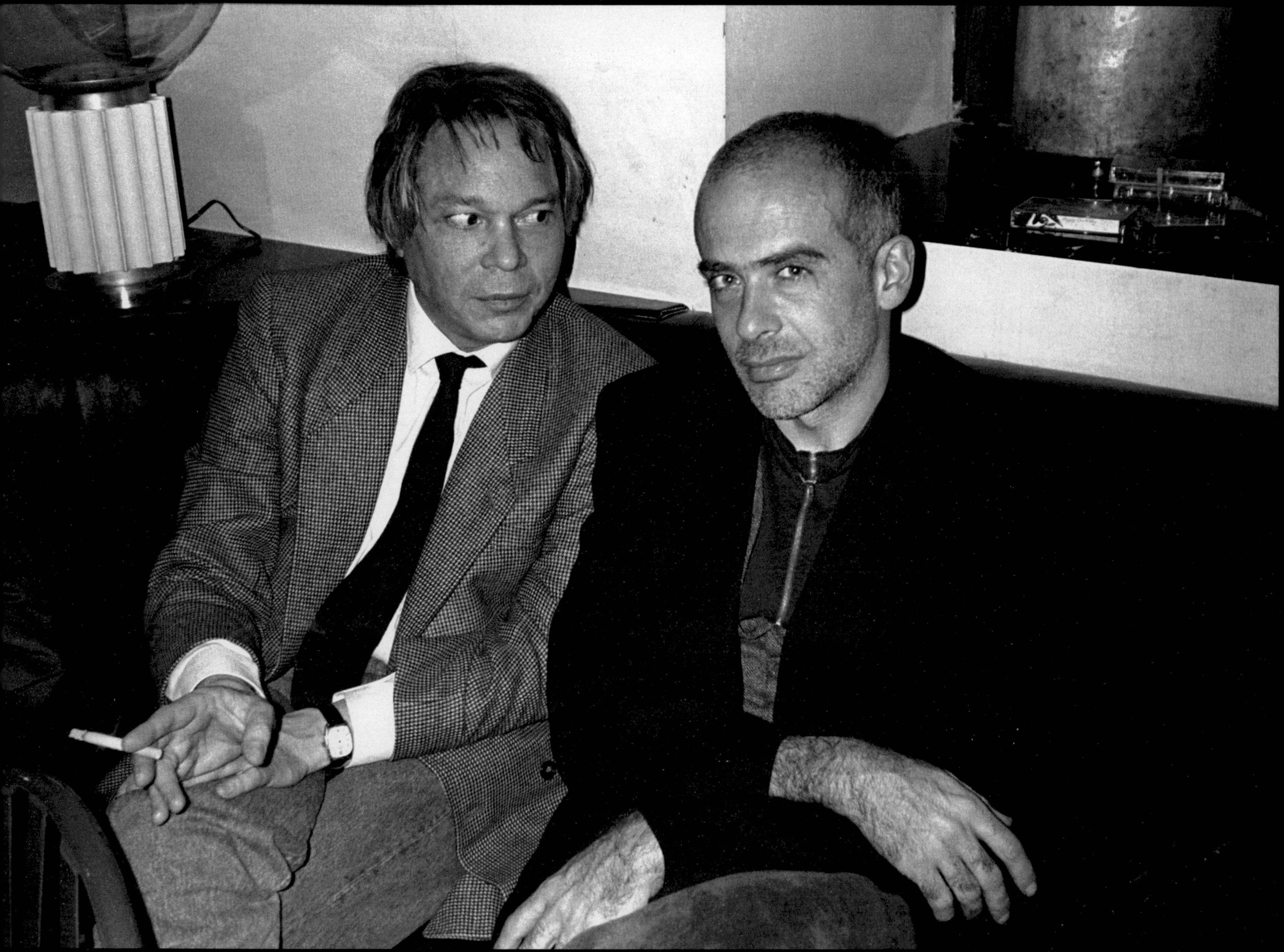

TOP: JOHN B. REINHOLD AND FRANCESCO CLEMENTE
LEFT: PAIGE POWELL AND TEREZA SCHARF
AT KENNY SCHARF'S BIRTHDAY PARTY HELD AT MR. CHOW'S.
1989

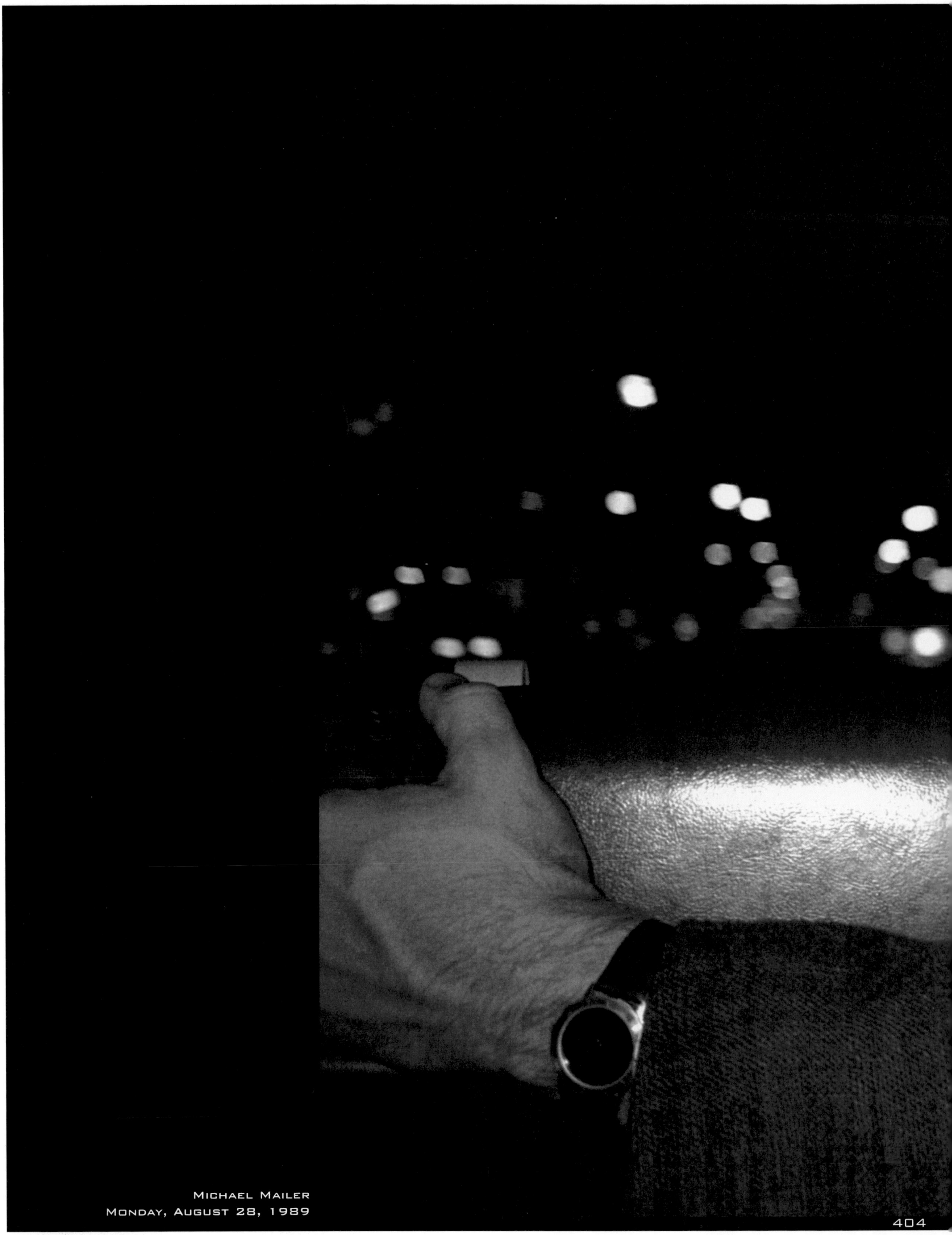

Michael Mailer
Monday, August 28, 1989

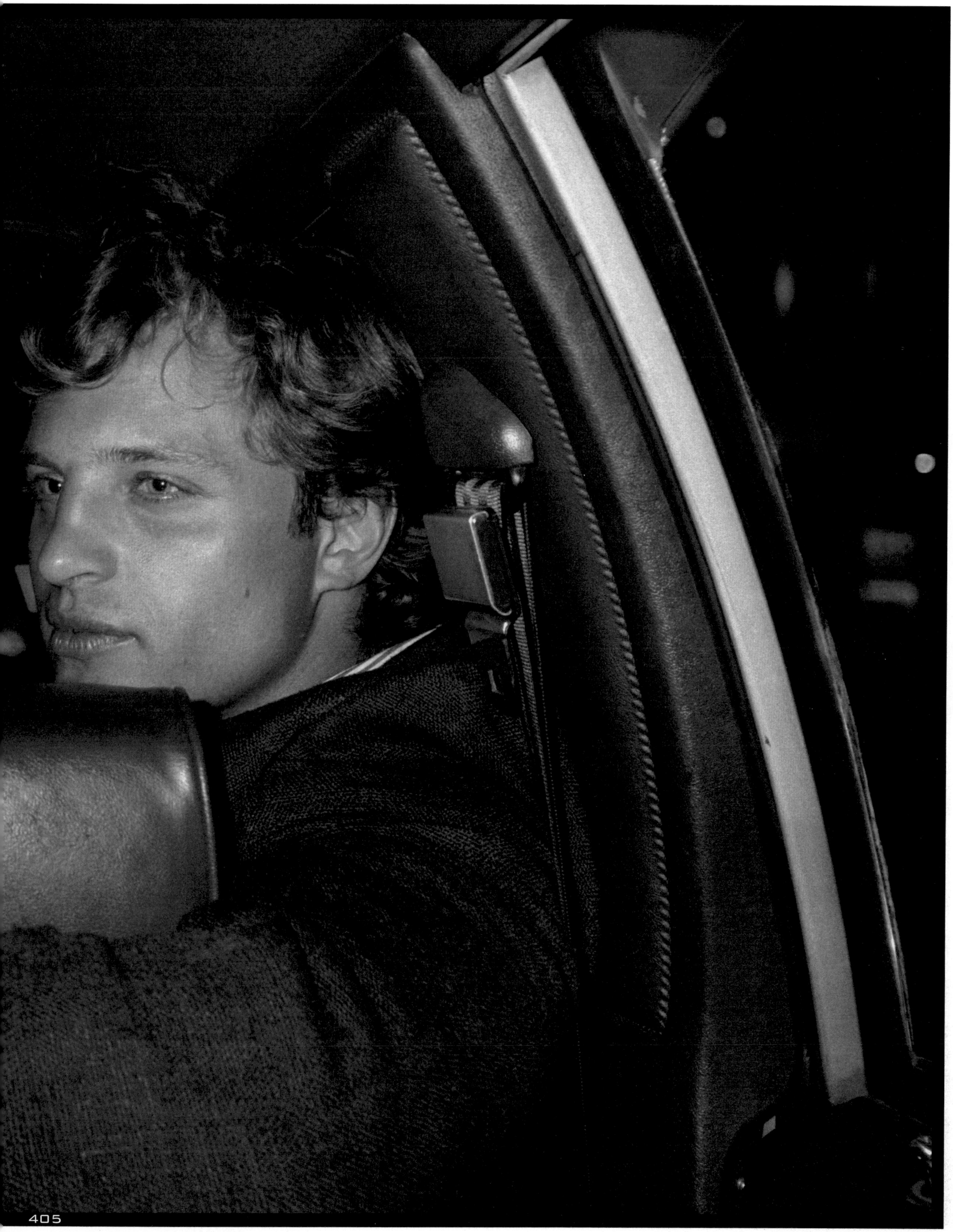

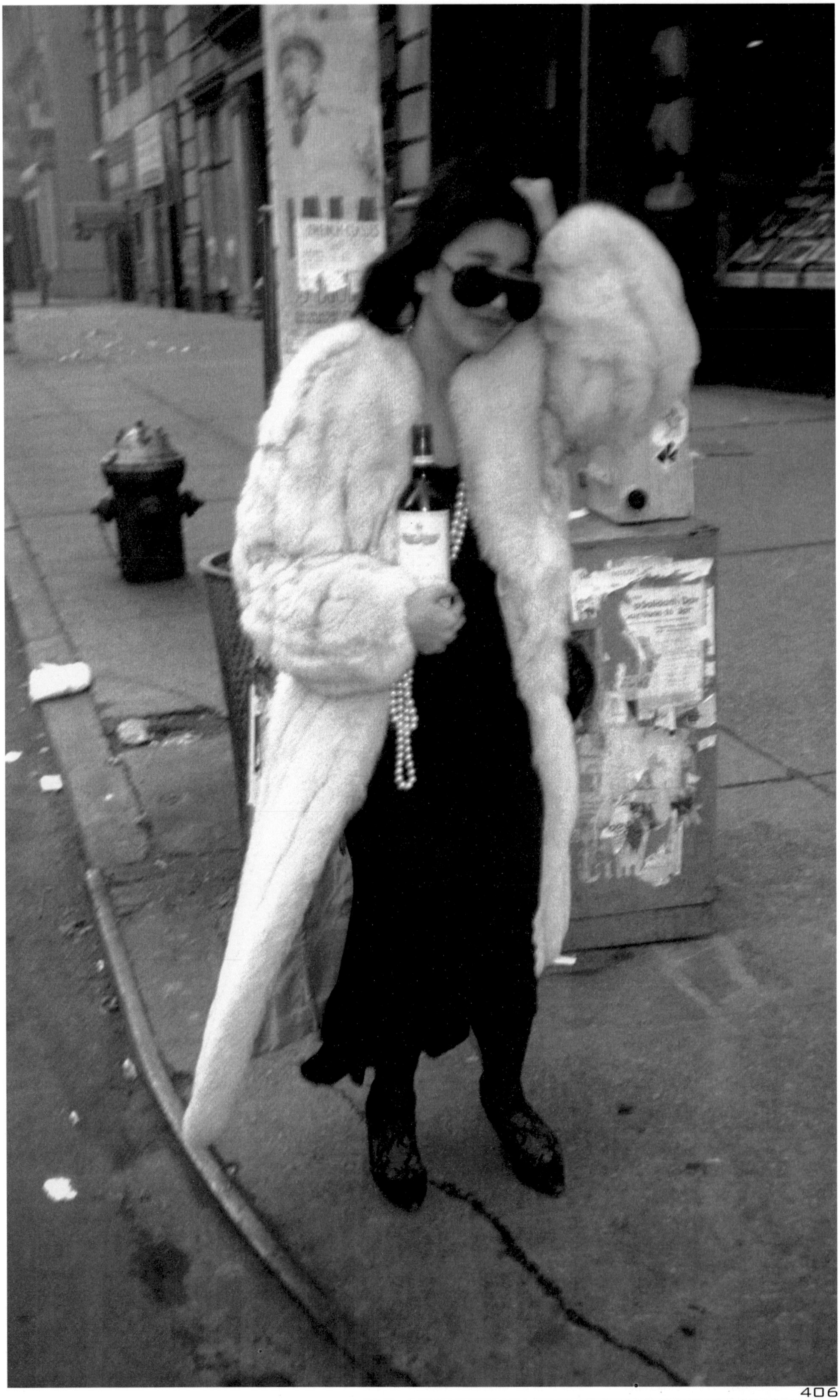

MIKIKO GILL
ON NEW YEAR'S DAY.
JANUARY 1, 1986

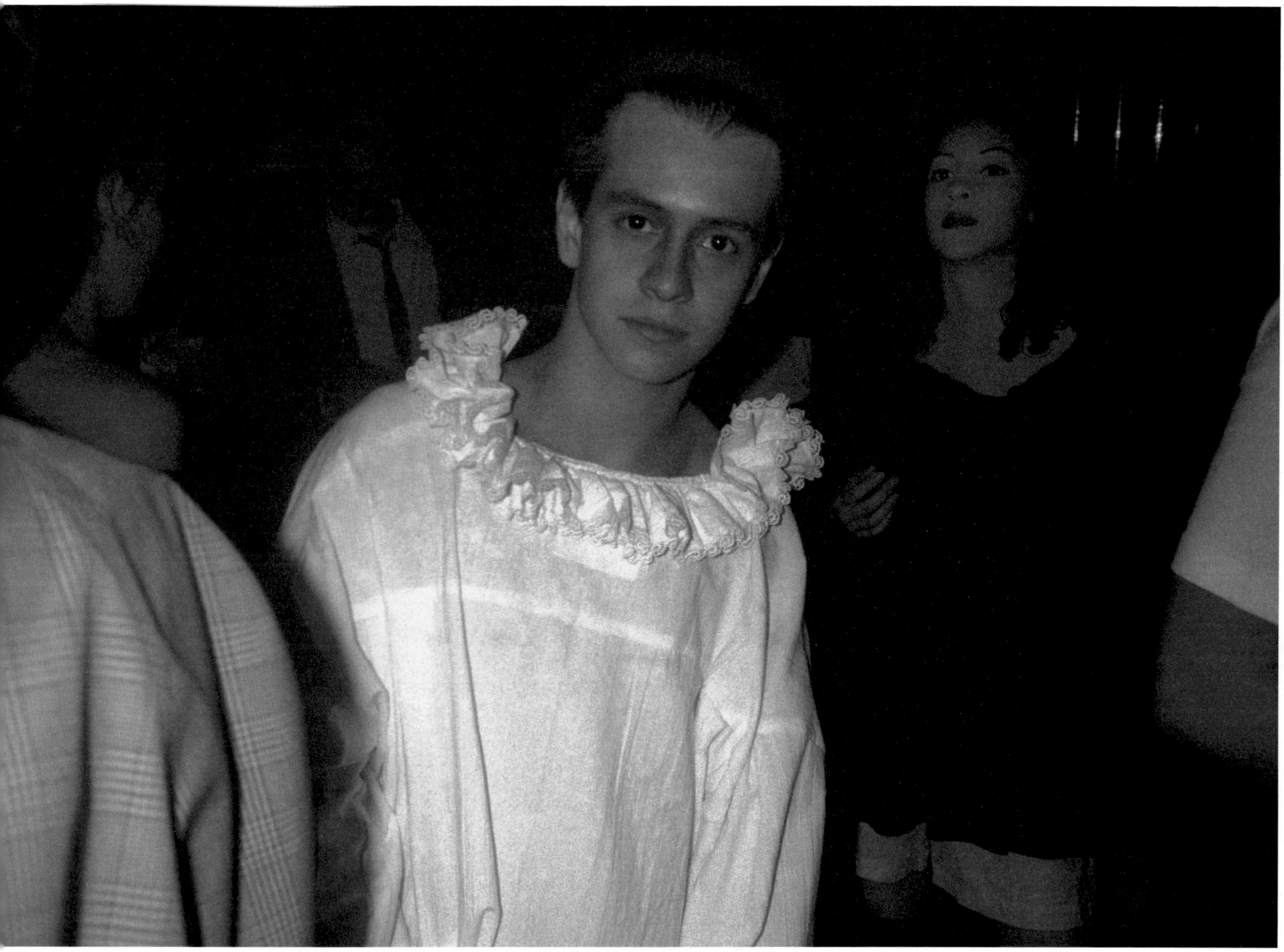

Angel Melendez
at the World.
Wednesday, June 29, 1988

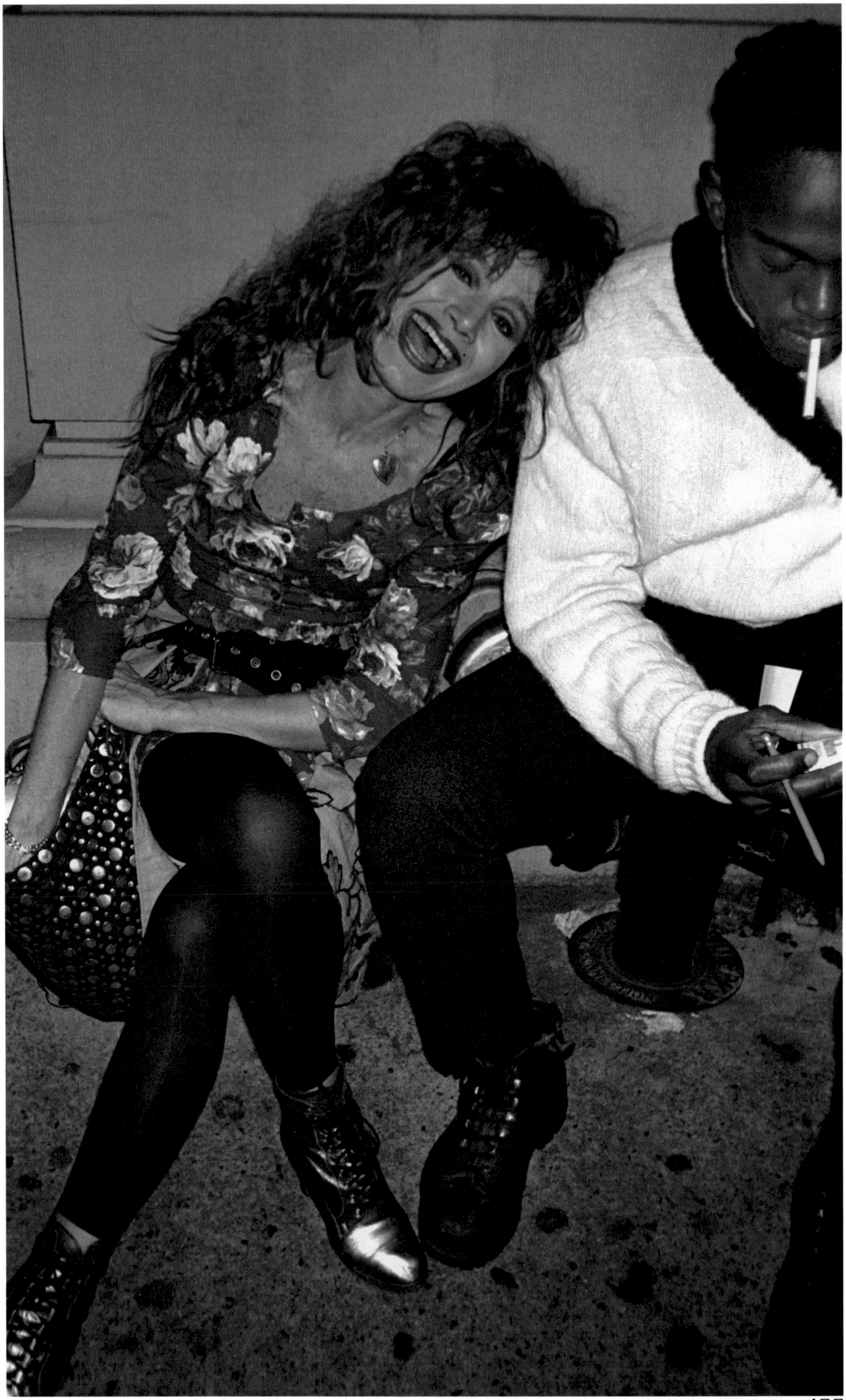

Betsey Johnson
and Name Unknown
outside MK.
Saturday,
October 26, 1989

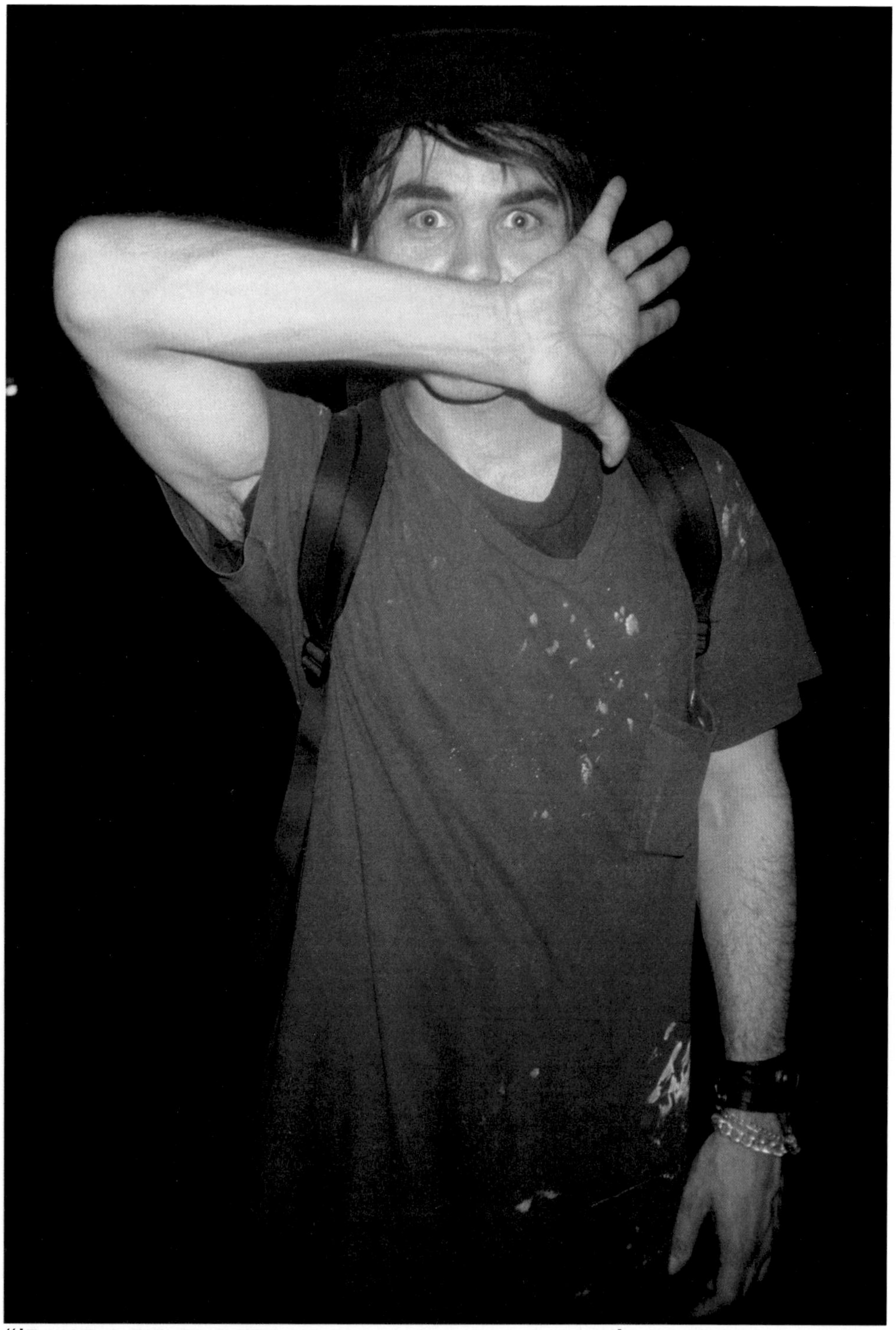

"It was a big time for me creatively, but it wasn't my favorite decade. I like the 90s and 2000 except for the terrorism and war."
Stephen Sprouse

Stephen Sprouse
on the street after the Sunny Baks studio.
Saturday, July 11, 1987

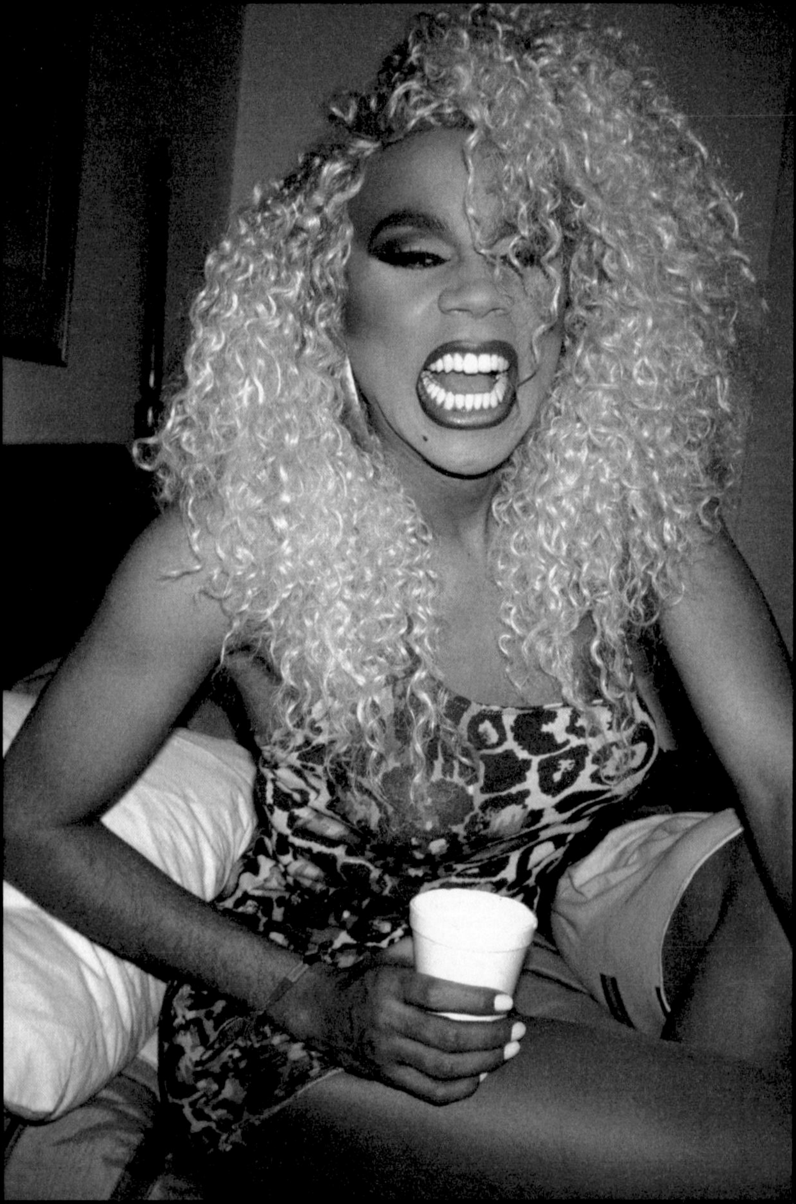

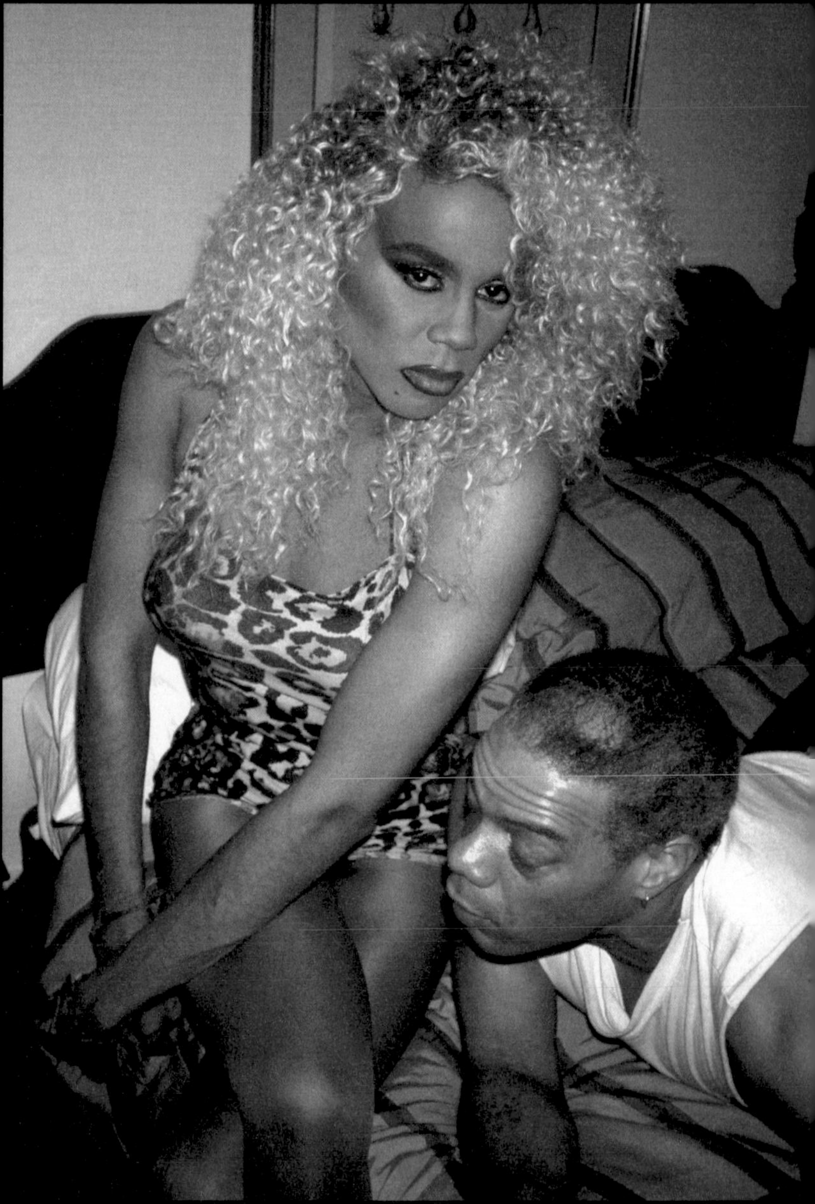

Top Left: RuPaul
Top Right: RuPaul and Gilbert
after hours in a Chicago hotel following the opening of Limelight.
December 1989

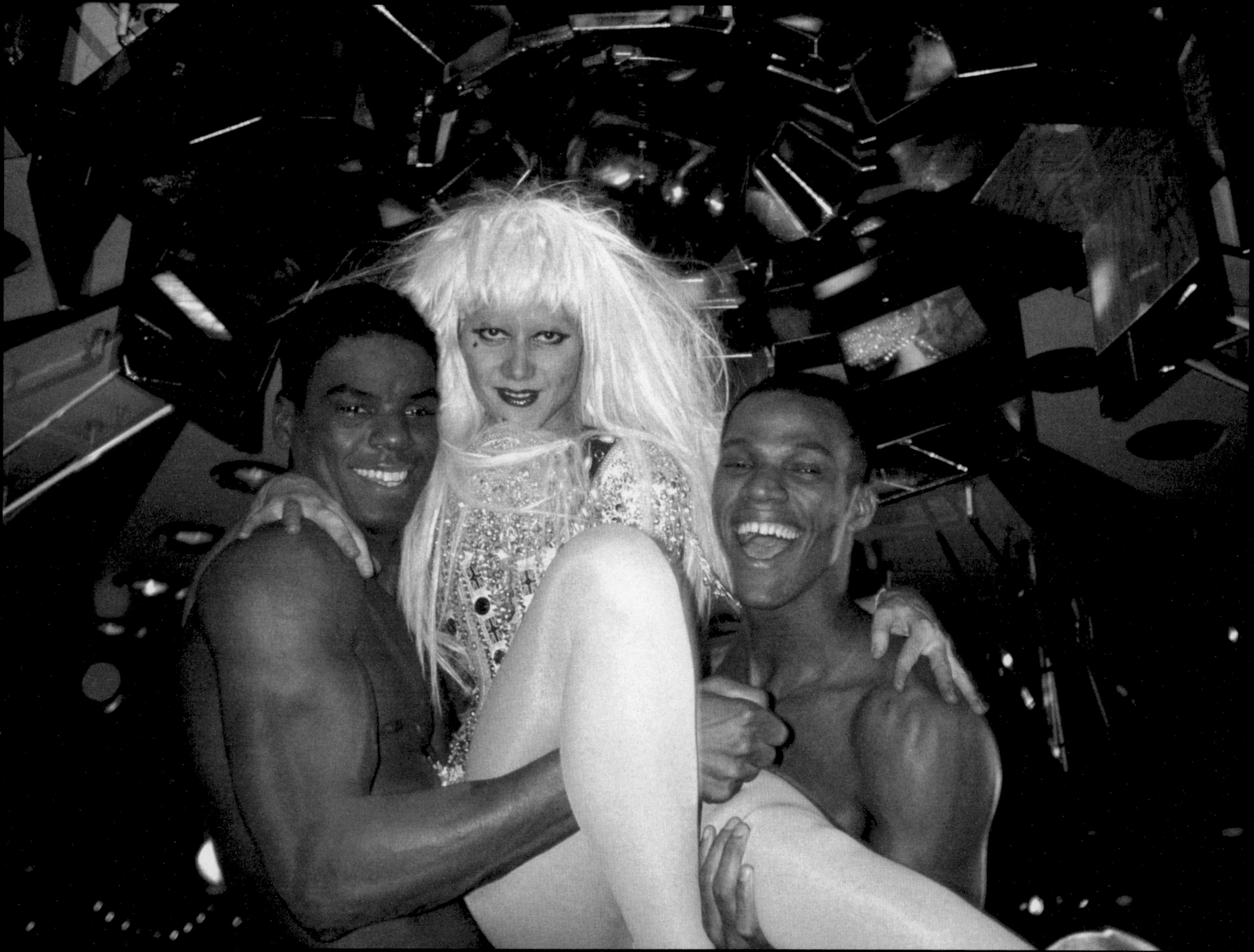

"Pull out that wig girl! The 80s were very creative, exciting, full of big highs, big lows, and tons of fashion. Every Monday there was a million dollar deal. Come Friday it all fell through, but there was always another Monday."
Susanne Bartsch

Susanne Bartsch with dancers
at the Copacabana.
November 1989

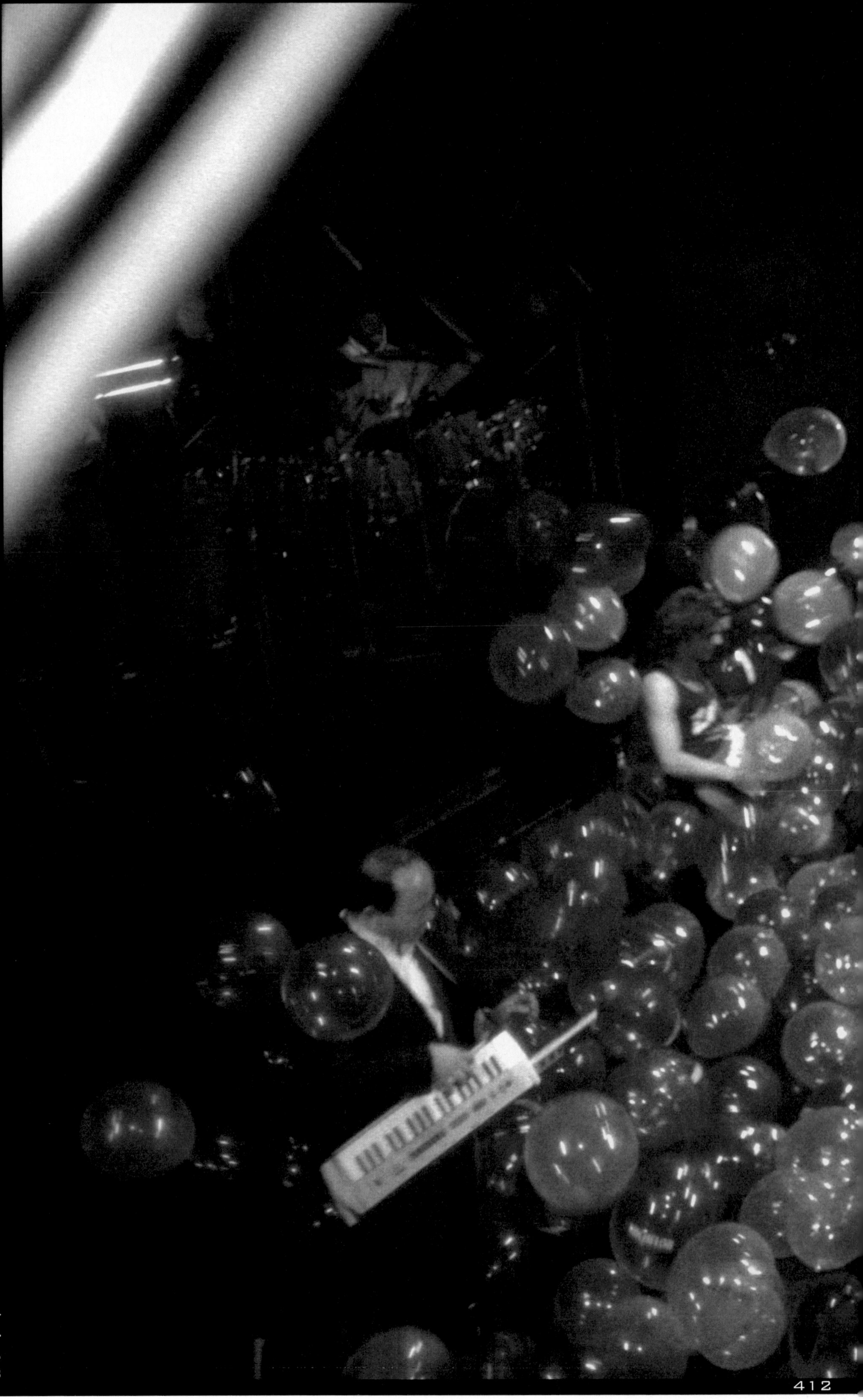

BALLOONS ON STAGE AT THE GRAMMY AWARDS PRE-PARTY AT THE PALLADIUM. MARCH 1, 1988

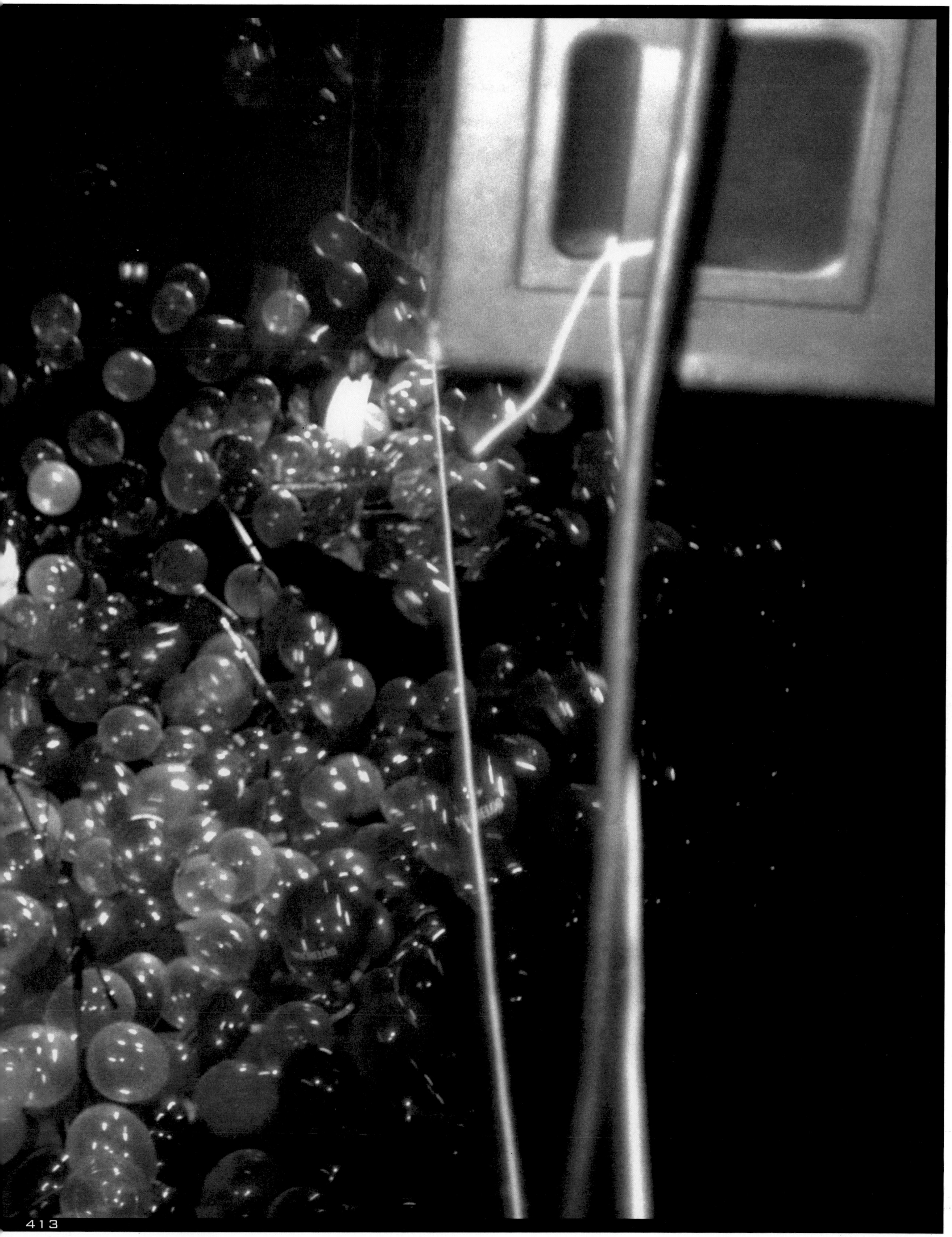

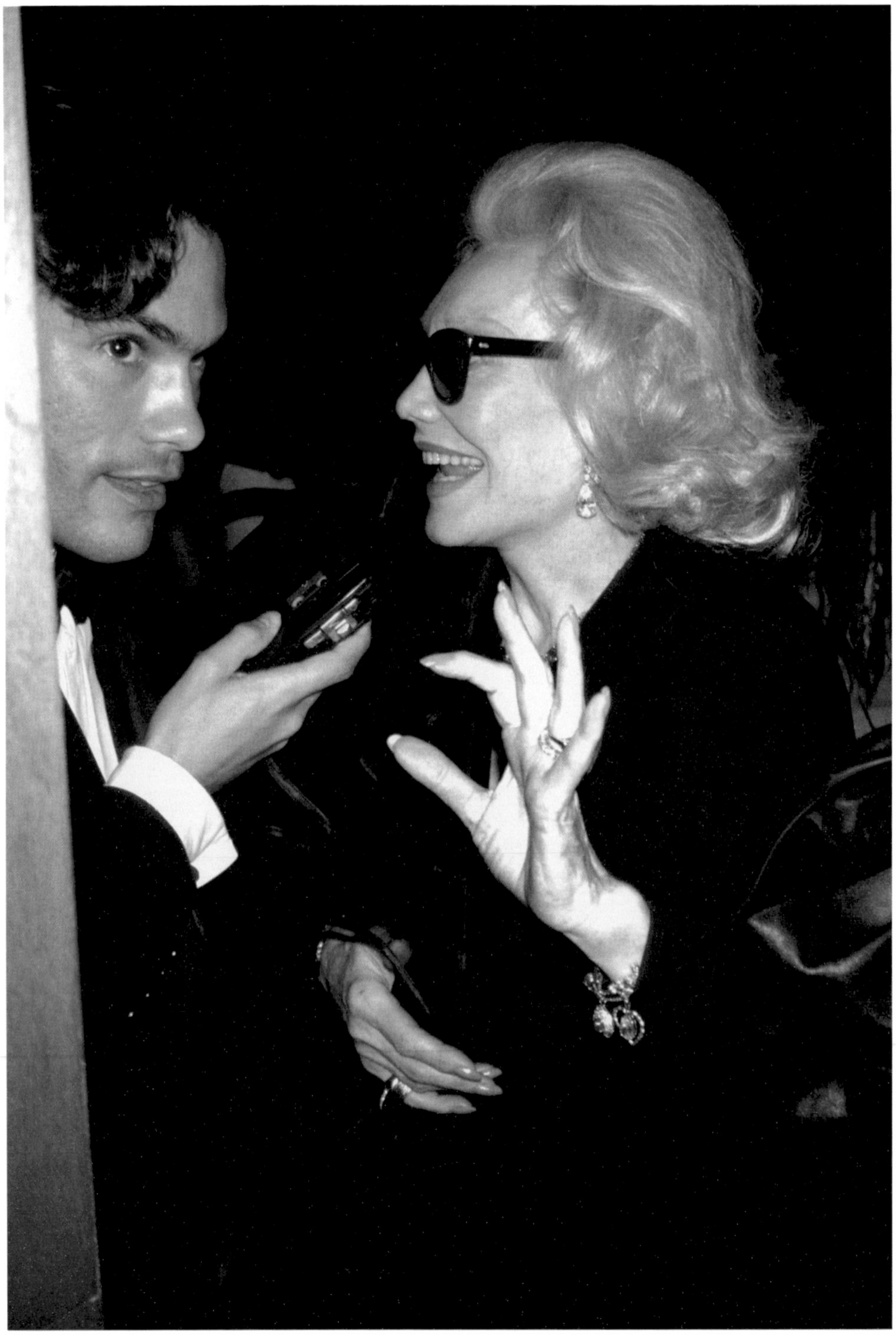

TOP: JEFFREY SLONIM AND ANNE SLATER.
1989
RIGHT: SUSANNE BARTSCH AND OLYMPIA AT THE COPACABANA.
1989

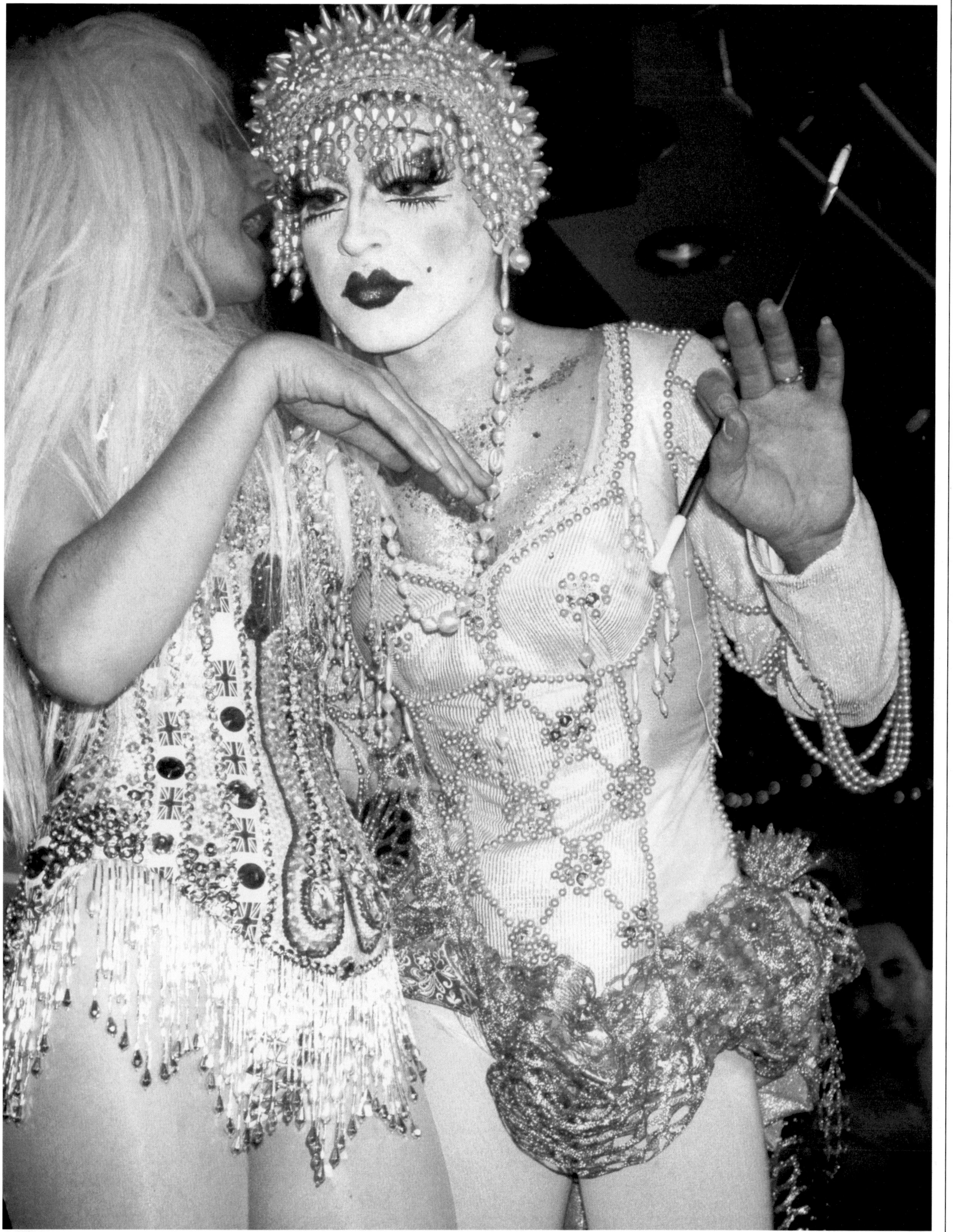

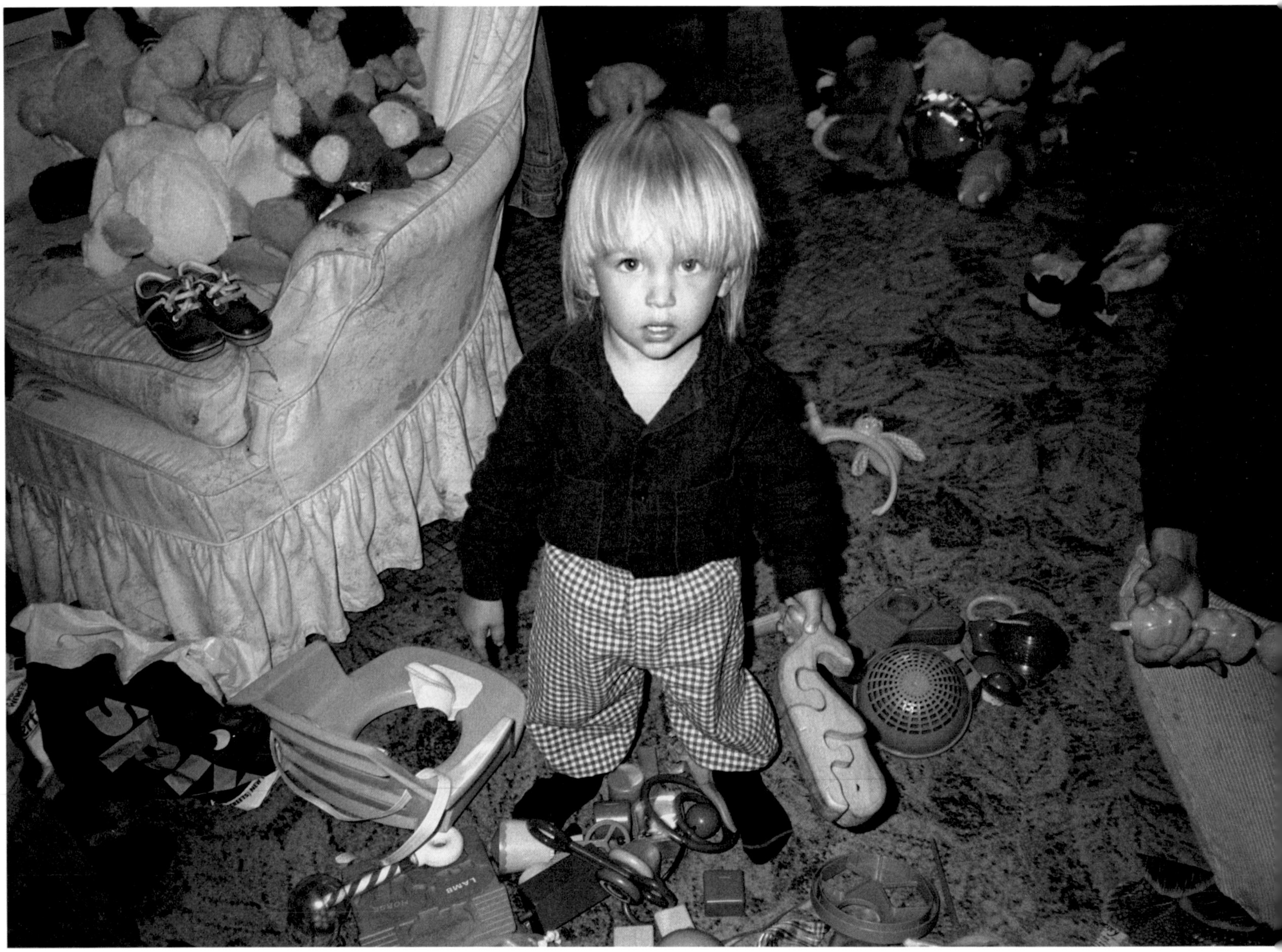

Liam McMullan
at home at Patrick's apartment.
September 30, 1989

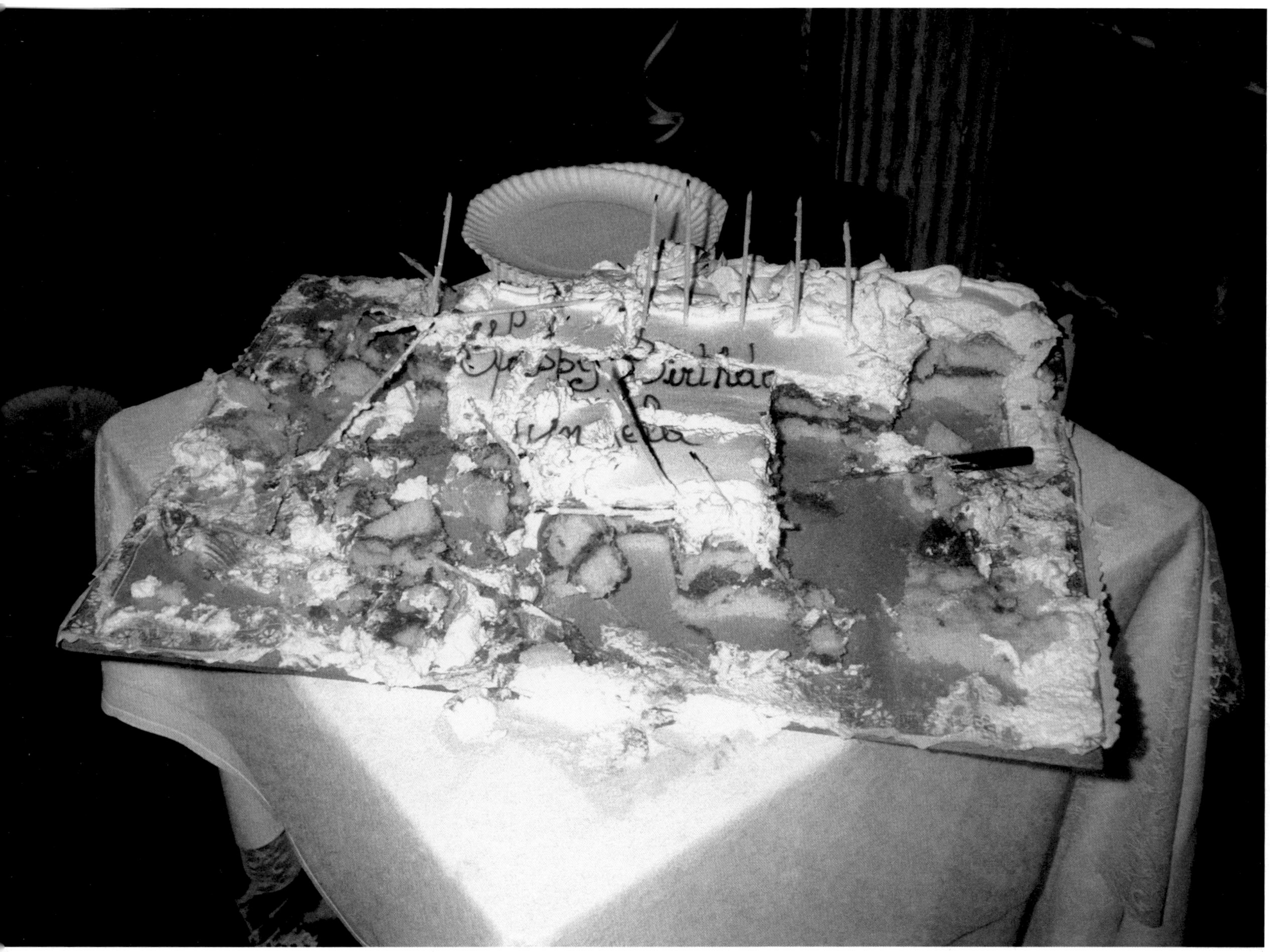

Angela's left over cake
at Angela Janklow Harrington's birthday party
in the Mike Todd Room at the Palladium.
Wednesday, June 4, 1986

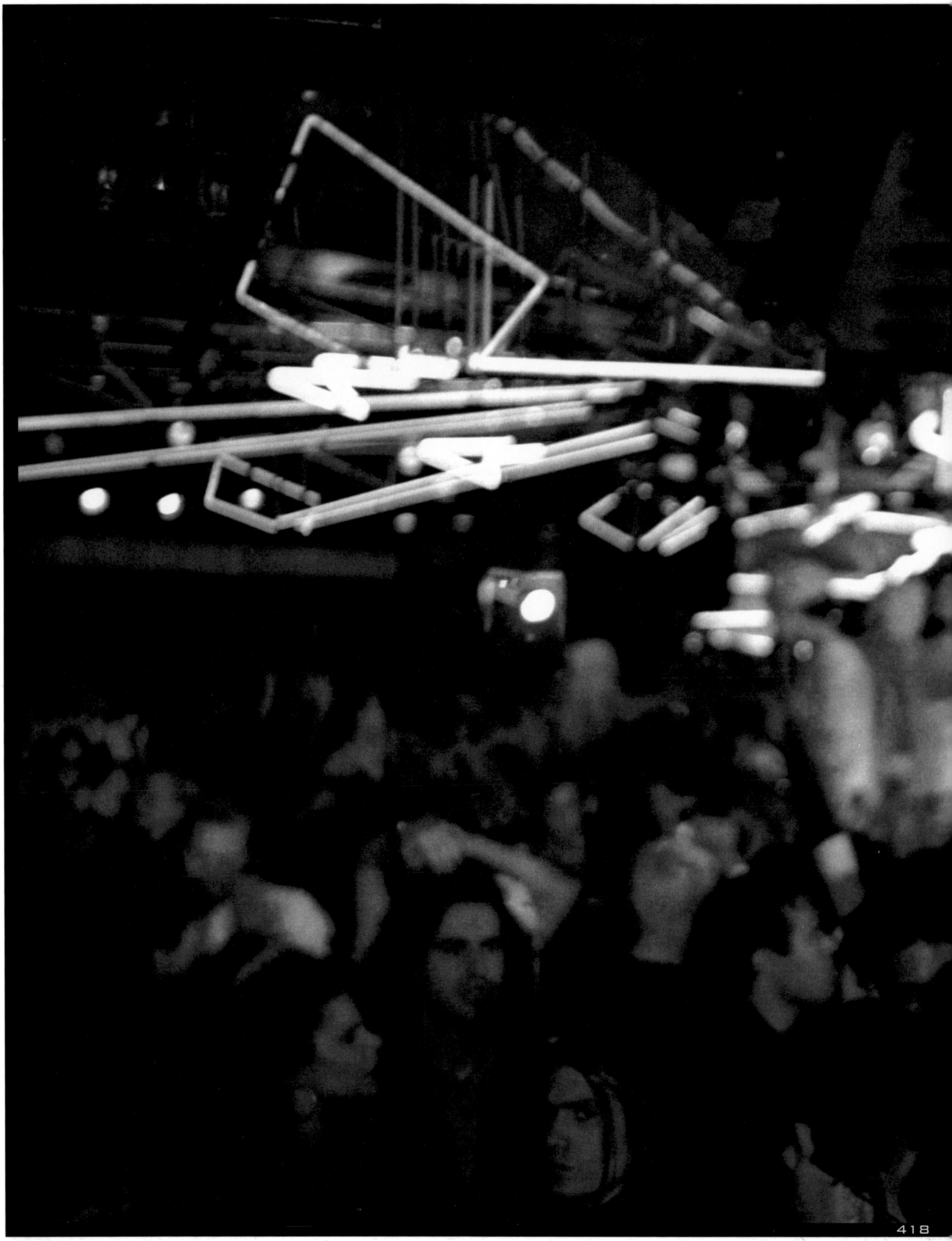

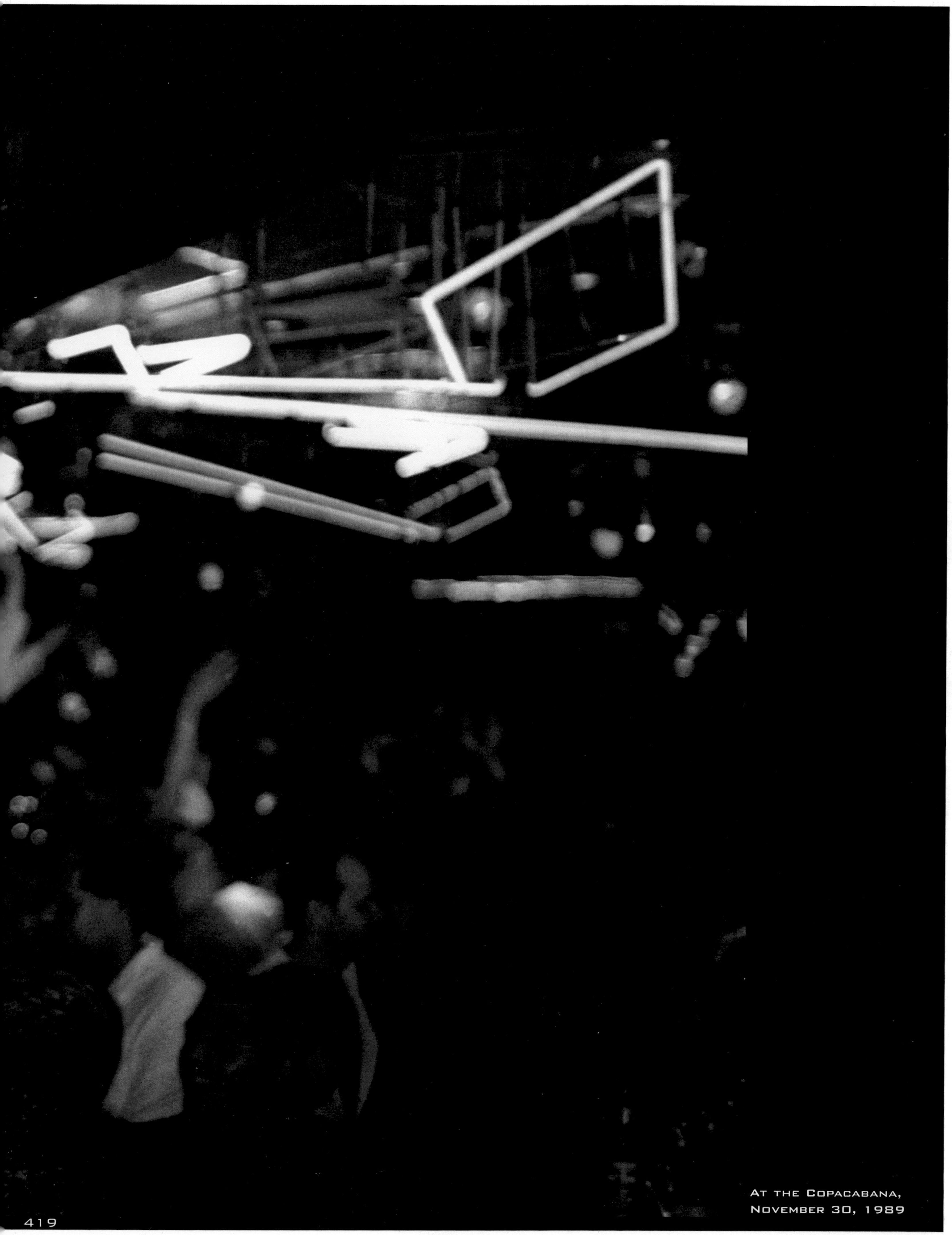

At the Copacabana,
November 30, 1989

SooooPatrick

I don't know how I met Patrick but I do know it was a short time after I moved to New York City in the early 80s. Whenever I saw him he always made me feel good. He was like a big friendly dog (well, okay, I prefer dogs to people, mostly) with a tail that started wagging whenever he saw you. I mean this only in the best way. Patrick always seemed happy and excited. Excited to be out, excited to be alive. Enthusiastic in a city where almost everyone I met was surly, jaded, and uninterested in you unless they knew there was something you could do for them.

Patrick lived (and maybe still does) in the former hat-and-coat checkroom of a hotel that had long since been converted to residential apartments. I thought it unimaginably cool, living in a hat checkroom. But unlike most people who live in unusual or quirky circumstances, Patrick didn't act cool--he acted warm.

He acted warm to everybody. He didn't discriminate, whether a person was rich and famous, or poor and 'unimportant' by New York City standards.

He was always with his little camera, whenever I saw him, but--a bit like Andy Warhol, who I knew back then--he was never obnoxious or intrusive, at least not intrusive with a camera in the ordinary sense. He would just say, "Oh, you look, great, let me take your picture"--and then, realizing there was someone else in the room near you, he would say, "And why don't you get in the picture, too!"

The other person might be someone he knew or didn't know. He might place a drag queen next to a society lady-who-lunched--if they happened to be in the same room. If the two didn't know each other, he would introduce them--even if he didn't actually know either of them.

Because he was always so friendly, bubbly, and relaxed, he got the picture.

He wasn't concerned with lighting equipment, or taking fancy photographs. Because of this he was a recorder of the times, the place, the event, the city: and while he might be placing two, three or more people together, it was never more staged than, say, a parent at their little kid's birthday party. It was just what was around. It wasn't about angles, or an evocative pose or setting, or fashion of the time--it was about people.

For years now I've thought of Patrick as the 'unofficial Mayor of New York.' He knows everyone, wherever he goes, which is everywhere. People recognized, at last, not only his talent but his personality, which is unique. And because of that he has been everywhere, uptown and down, and always making each person feel they are his dearest friend. Which in a sense they are.

Tama Janowitz
2003

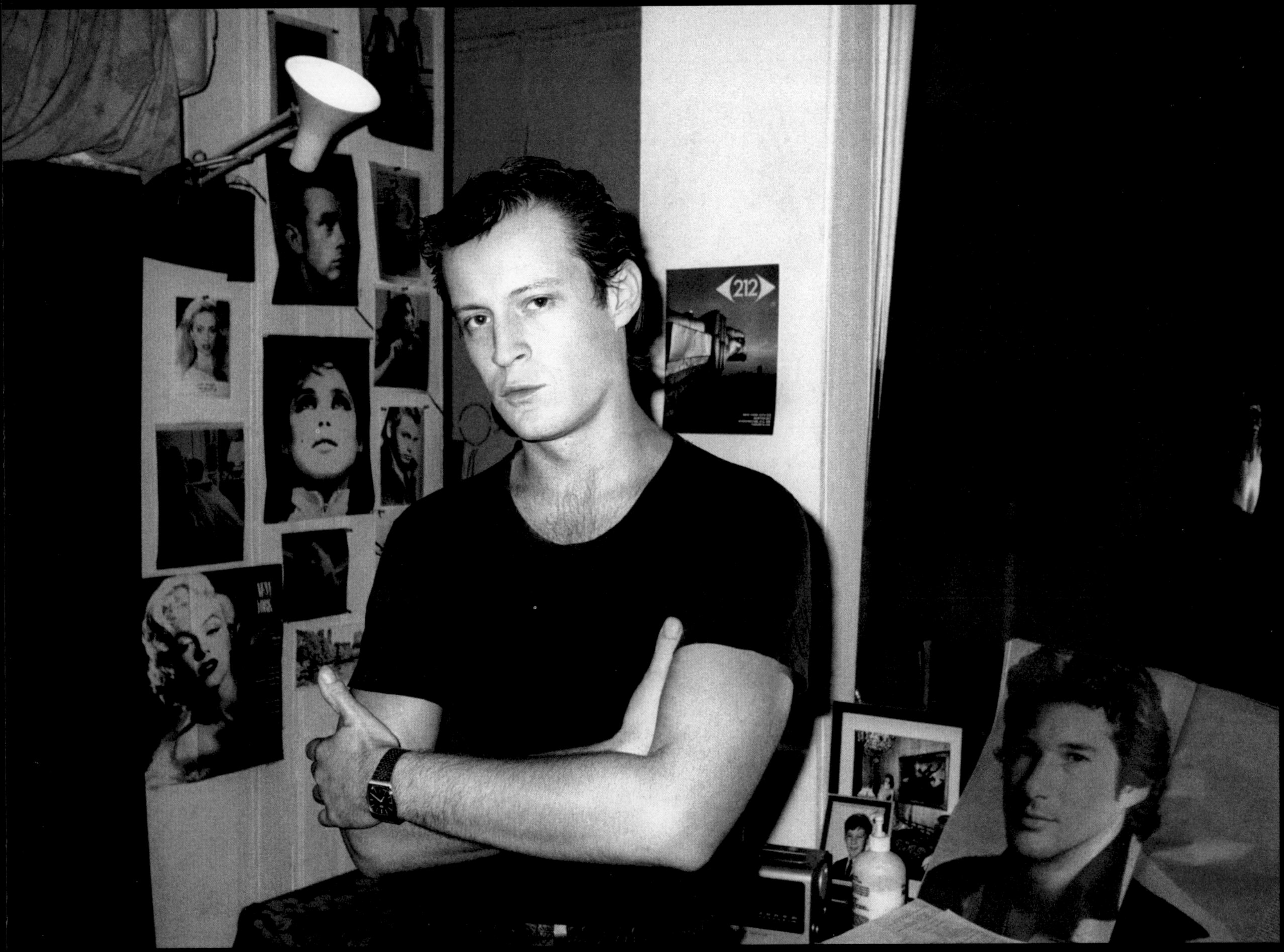

Patrick McMullan
at his 5th Avenue apartment.
(Portrait taken by Lori Scena)
December 1983

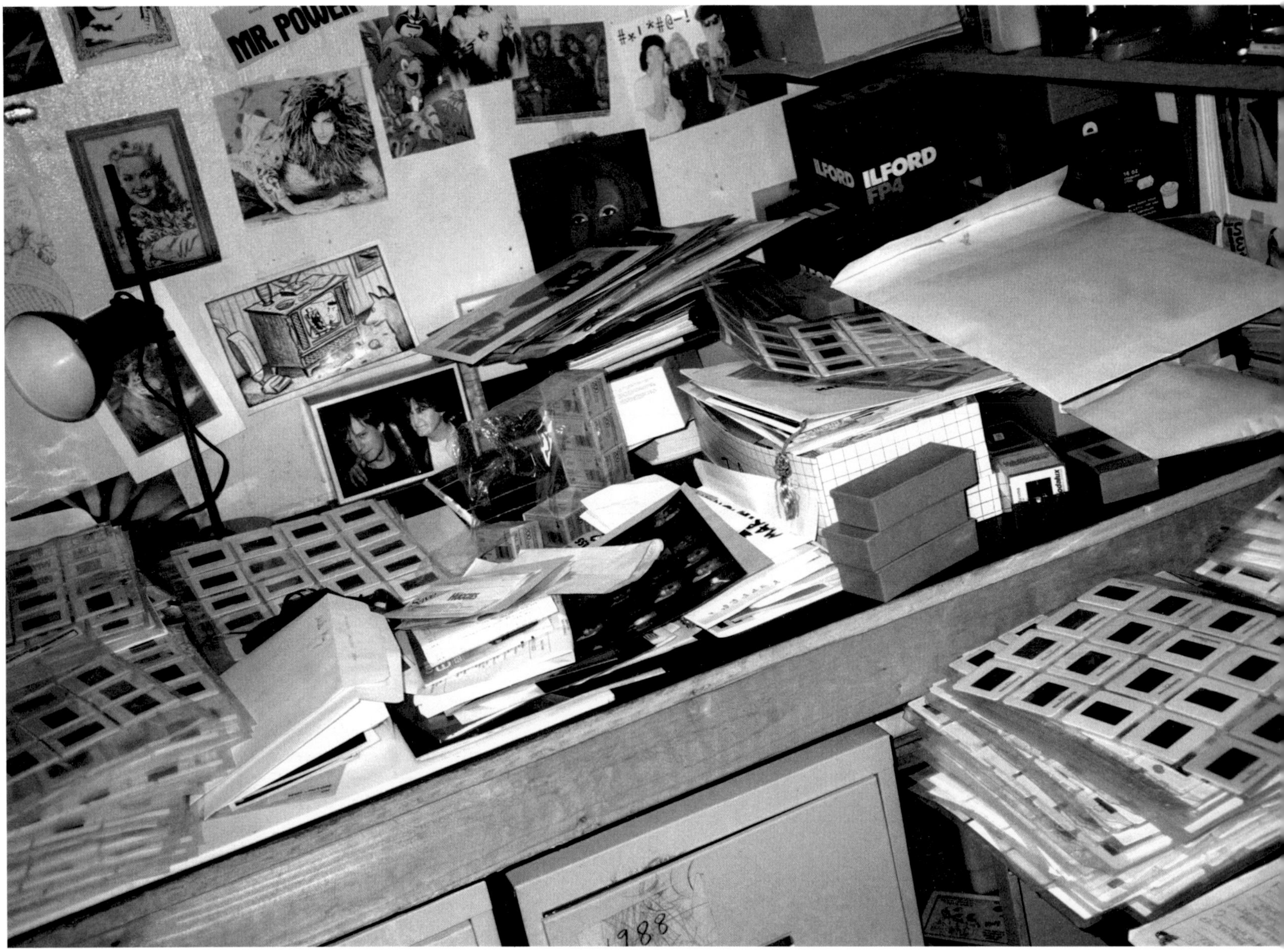

Patrick's desk
at his 5th Avenue apartment.
May 10, 1989

Dear Marie,

Well, what can I say about the 1980s. I started the decade with my mortality in question, having been diagnosed with cancer and told I had six months to live. I ended the 80s wondering about everyone else's mortality due to AIDS. In between I learned about love, drink tickets, sexuality, nightclubs, friendship, guest lists, drugs, depression, excitement, publicity, egos, deadlines, fame, being a father, being a son, brother, uncle, lover, and friend. I saw desperation, illness, glamour, vanity, beauty, wealth, poverty, kindness and anger, and people--so many people. But always there was my camera and the nightlife.

Having almost died, I took my second lease on life to go out as much as I could, to experience life in New York to its fullest. When I got a job taking pictures for Stephen Saban at Details magazine it was a dream come true (well, it certainly was a great excuse for being out every night anyway). I met so many wonderful people and had so much fun. I guess now comes the part to thank people. So many people became such good friends of mine so I should start with the photographers. I worked with Carl Paler, who taught me to work in a darkroom and taught me so many tricks and led me to Terry Stevenson, who hired me as an assistant, taught me so much about work and life, and always gave me plenty of Kodak Plus-X film (and made me develop it myself, along with his film). Christopher Scott, Danny fields, and John Reinhold who encouraged me to create my own darkroom at home. Ian Falconer, Tom Ford, Rob Robinson, Jill Kirby, Stephen Saban, Annie Flanders, and all the folks at Details magazine. Scott Feree, Jeffrey Sanker, and the 212 magazine gang who let me edit my own pictures. Tinkerbelle, the Interview magazine gang, Andy Warhol who influenced my perspective so much and was such a hero of mine, Paige Powell, Pat Hackett, Robert Hayes, Bob Colacello, Fred Hughes, Shelley Wanger, Glenn O'Brien, Leslie Russo, Ingrid Sichey, and Sandy Brant. The whole Spy magazine contingent especially Susan Morrison, Graydon Carter, and Kurt Andersen. The nightclub people like Rudolf and John Argento at Danceteria; Steve Mass at the Mudd Club; Peter Gatien, Fred Rothbell-Mista, and Claire O'Connor at Limelight; and everyone there then. The Area gang especially Eric Goode. Vito Bruno and Roman at Pizza a go go. Stacey Teele and Kirk Walsh at Kamikaze. Robert Shalom at Private Eyes. And especially Steve Rubell and Ian Schrager who invented nightlife for me at Studio 54 and the Palladium. The Glamour Girls like Susanne Bartsch, Anita Sarko, Cornelia Guest, Janis Savitt, Nikki Haskell, Chi Chi Valenti, Sylvia Miles, Dianne Brill, Lisa Edelstein, Sally Randall, Elizabeth Saltzman, Angela Janklow, Cookie Mueller, Janet Paist, Tama Janowitz, Hedy Klineman, Perri Lister, Jessica Blue, Ellen Kinnally, Larissa, Karen and Lyn Mandlebaum, and Karon Bihari. The Guys like Michael Musto, R. Couri Hay, Jay McInerney, Bret Easton Ellis, Richard Bernstein, Johnny Dynell, James St. James, Beauregard Houston-Montgomery, Michaelangelo Signorile, Michael Gross, Richard Johnson, Richard Turley, David Schlachet, Will Regan, Mitch Pearl, Haoui Montaug, Zach Galligan, and Billy Idol, to name a few.

Gee Marie, there are so many people I just can't remember, I hate to leave anyone out. Well, hey, I guess I should thank you Marie Havens, for art directing so80s and your truly tireless effort to make this into a book. Also, thanks to Anita Antonini, Sam Bolton, Joanna Um, Perrie Wardell, Alison Moore, Nick Papananias, Andrew Camp, Jonathan (Snoop) Grassi, and all the other leprechauns who cleaned up the images.

I want to thank my family, my mom Constance and Dad Patrick, Sr., my sister Sharon and brother-in-law Tony Shalinski, nieces Allana Shalinski and Candi McCarthy, my nephew Jamie McCarthy, my son Liam McMullan and his mom Laurie Ogle, and my dearest friend Margie Beck for their continued support, sense of humor, and love which kept me alive and real.

I also would like to thank all the people who have loved and lived in the 1980s and let me take their picture. I hope this is good.

Later, Patrick.

I N D E X

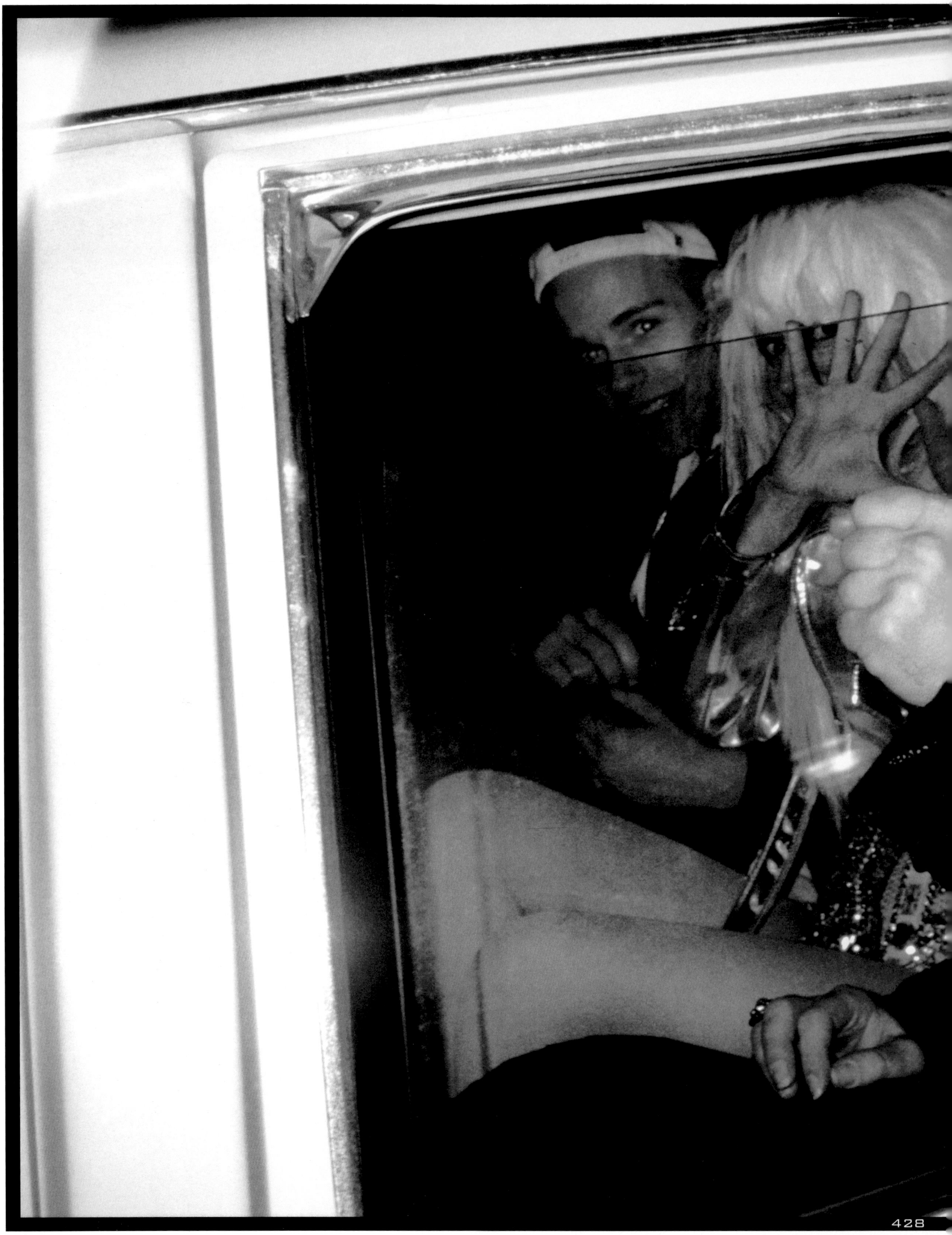

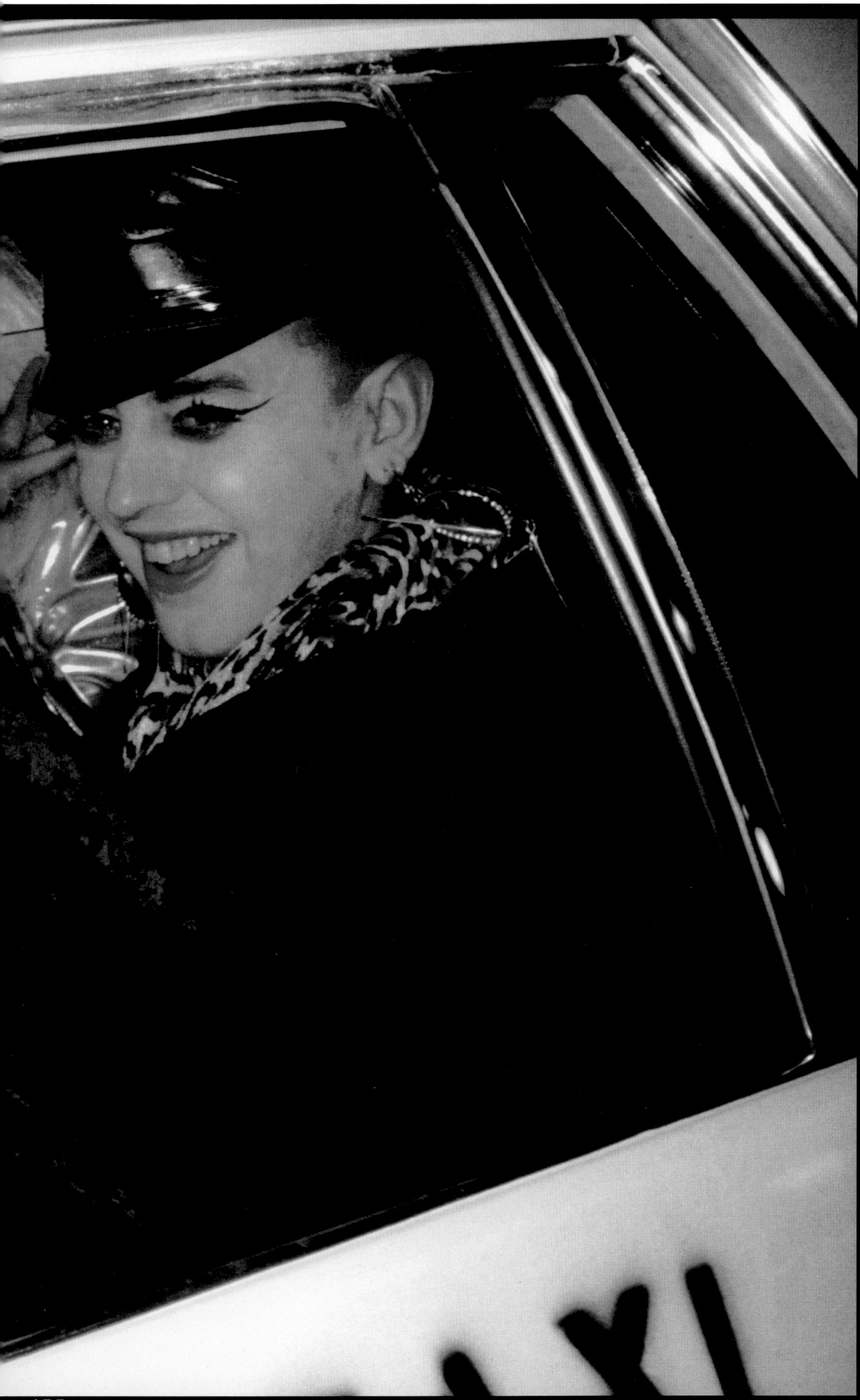

Ty Bassett, Susanne Bartsch, and Kenny Kenny in a NYC taxi leaving the World. November 1989

This book took 1 decade of relentless documenting,
3 decades of archiving, and 2 years to pull it all together.

We would like to thank the following people for their contributions:

Anita Antonini
Business & Creative Director, Curator

Marie Havens
Art & Creative Director, Archivist, Curator

Joanna Um- Assistant to Art Director, Text
Sam Bolton- Text, Contributor
Alison Moore- Book Advisor

Archival Re-touching:
Marie Havens and the following: Nikiya L. Carson, Jonathan Grassi, Emily Korsmo, Allison Murphy, Richard Orjis, Nick Papananias, Jill Pilotte, Eric Pitra, Joanna Um, and Perrie Wardell

powerHouse Books: Daniel Power, Craig Cohen, Sara Rosen, Kristian Orozco, Francesca Richer, Daniel Buckley, and staff

The Spike Gallery: Tina Brown, Donald Rosenfeld, Michael Chambers, Karyn Larkin, and staff
Workhouse Publicity: Adam Nelson and staff
The Gucci group: Tom Ford, Lisa Schiek, and Arabella Rufino

Thanks to the following for their words and memories:
Jay McInerney, Michael Musto, Tama Janowitz, Bob Colacello, Tom Ford, Cookie Mueller*, Glenn O'Brien, Paige Powell, Jeffrey Slonim, Richard Turley, and the following contributors: Susan Ainsworth, Tom Austin, Kevin Bacon, Marc Balet, David Barton, Susanne Bartsch, Karon Bihari, Phillip Bloch, Susan Blond, Sam Bolton, Mary Boone, Dianne Brill, Lady Bunny, Ronnie Cutrone, Kevin Downs, Johnny Dynell, Lisa Edelstein, Patricia Field, Danny Fields, Shelly Dunn Fremont, Vincent Fremont, Brad Gooch, Eric Goode, Cornelia Guest, Pat Hackett, Angela Janklow Harrington, Debbie Harry, Nikki Haskell, R. Couri Hay, Carolina Herrera, Jane Holzer, Beauregard Houston-Montgomery, Iman, Betsey Johnson, Nan Kempner, Hedy Klineman, Julie Lanke, Larissa, Fran Lebowitz, Perri Lister, Benjamin Liu, Roxanne Lowit, Robert Lund, Christopher Makos, Ann Magnuson, Sylvia Miles, Isaac Mizrahi, Claire O'Connor, Anka Radakovich, Sally Randall, John B. Reinhold, Alan Rish, Joan Rivers, Stephen Saban, Elizabeth Saltzman, Janis Savitt, Arnold Scassi, Kenny Scharf, Ian Schrager, Tony Shafrazi, Liz Smith, Stephen Sprouse, Ivana Trump, Chi Chi Valenti, Diane von Furstenberg, Ron Wanless, George Wayne, and Bobby Zarem

*=Published with the permission of the Estate of Cookie Mueller, and its executor, Richard Turley

Special thanks to the following Publications:
American Photo: Richard Rabinowitz, David Schonauer, Deborah Mauro, Beth Lusko, and Anthony Ruotolo
Details magazine: Leslie Russo and Andrew Kilbourn
Interview magazine: Sandy Brandt and Ingrid Sischy
New York Magazine: Caroline Miller and Alan Katz
Vanity Fair: Graydon Carter, David Friend, Elizabeth Saltzman, and Dana Brown

Additional thanks to the following:
Liz Dueland / Duggal: Jose Vargas / Bergdorf Goodman: Mallory Andrews / the Estate of Keith Haring: Julia Gruen / Kodak: Jeff Gunderman and Margo Robinson / LeSportsac: Tim Schifter / Lot 61: Amy Sacco / Man Ray: Thierry Klemeniuk / The Maritime Hotel: Eric Goode / Susan Morrison / The Estate of Cookie Mueller: Richard Turley / Porter Novelli: Jimmy Szczepanek / PMc staff / PMK: Allen Eichorn / Sally Randall / Peter Rogers / Charles Scheips / Christy M. Smith / Sony / The Estate of Zoë Tamerlis: Robert Lund / TBWA/Chiat/Day: Patrick O'Neill and Marilyn Kirk / Michel Witmer / The Estate of Andy Warhol